Transylvania

the Bradt Travel Guide

Lucy Mallows
Paul Brummell

With contributions from
Adriana Mitsue Ivama Brummell

Contributors to the first edition
Dr John Akeroyd, Danuţ Marin, Luminiţa Marin
& Nathaniel Page

edition
3

www.bradtguides.com

Bradt Travel Guides Ltd, UK
The Globe Pequot Press Inc, USA

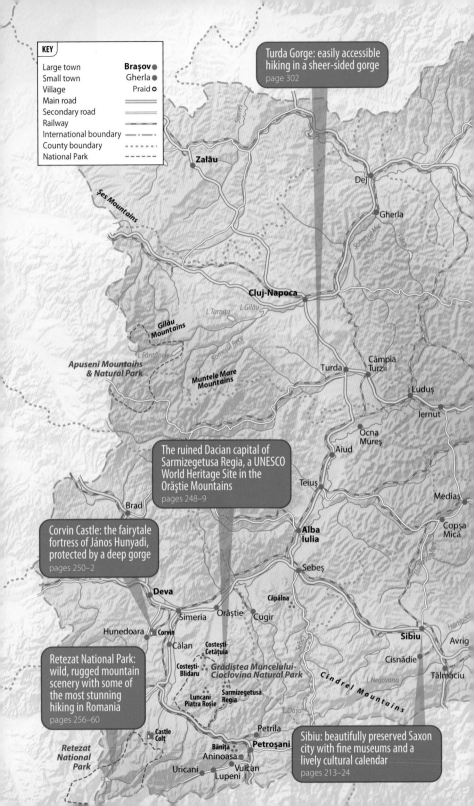

KEY

Large town	**Braşov** ●
Small town	Gherla ●
Village	Praid ○
Main road	
Secondary road	
Railway	
International boundary	
County boundary	
National Park	

Turda Gorge: easily accessible hiking in a sheer-sided gorge
page 302

The ruined Dacian capital of Sarmizegetusa Regia, a UNESCO World Heritage Site in the Orăştie Mountains
pages 248–9

Corvin Castle: the fairytale fortress of János Hunyadi, protected by a deep gorge
pages 250–2

Retezat National Park: wild, rugged mountain scenery with some of the most stunning hiking in Romania
pages 256–60

Sibiu: beautifully preserved Saxon city with fine museums and a lively cultural calendar
pages 213–24

Şes Mountains

Zalău

Dej

Gherla

Someşul Mic

Tisa

Cluj-Napoca

L Tarniţa

L Gilău

Gilău Mountains

L Fântânele

Someşul Rece

Apuseni Mountains & Natural Park

Muntele Mare Mountains

Turda

Câmpia Turzii

Luduş

Iernut

Ocna Mureş

Aiud

Teiuş

Mediaş

Copşa Mică

Brad

Alba Iulia

Sebeş

Căpâlna

Deva

Simeria

Orăştie

Cugir

Sibiu

Avrig

Hunedoara

Corvin

Călan

Costeşti-Cetăţuia

Cisnădie

Tălmaciu

Costeşti-Blidaru

Grădiştea Muncelului-Cioclovina Natural Park

Cindrel Mountains

L Negovanu

Hârtibaci

Luncani Piatra Roşie

Sarmizegetuşa Regia

L Oaşa

Castle Colţ

Petrila

Bănița

Petroşani

Retezat National Park

Aninoasa

Uricani

Vulcan

Lupeni

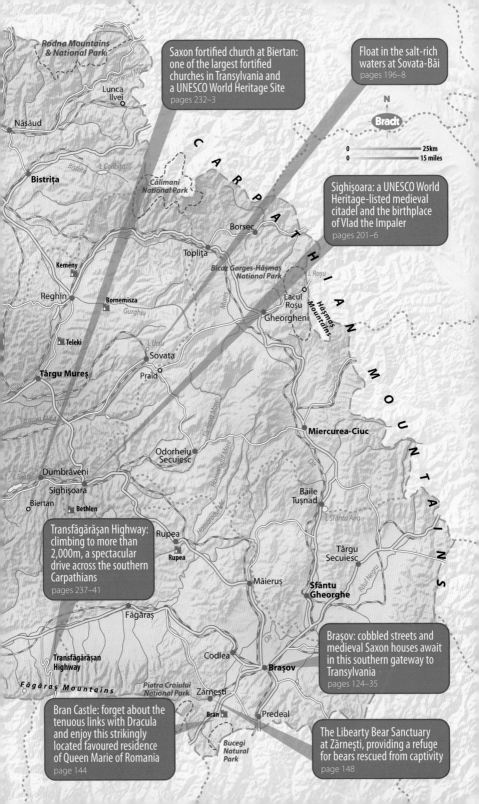

Saxon fortified church at Biertan: one of the largest fortified churches in Transylvania and a UNESCO World Heritage Site
pages 232–3

Float in the salt-rich waters at Sovata-Băi
pages 196–8

Sighișoara: a UNESCO World Heritage-listed medieval citadel and the birthplace of Vlad the Impaler
pages 201–6

Transfăgărășan Highway: climbing to more than 2,000m, a spectacular drive across the southern Carpathians
pages 237–41

Brașov: cobbled streets and medieval Saxon houses await in this southern gateway to Transylvania
pages 124–35

Bran Castle: forget about the tenuous links with Dracula and enjoy this strikingly located favoured residence of Queen Marie of Romania
page 144

The Libearty Bear Sanctuary at Zărnești, providing a refuge for bears rescued from captivity
page 148

Bradt

0 ——————— 25km
0 ——————— 15 miles

Transylvania
Don't miss...

Saxon fortified churches
One of the largest and most impressive fortified churches stands in Biertan, which is listed as a UNESCO World Heritage Site. A true fortress, the church is ringed by imposing walls (SS) page 232

Unspoiled landscapes
From flower-rich meadows to craggy peaks like the Ceahlău Massif, the Transylvanian countryside is ideal for exploring on foot or by car (CIP/S) page 111

Spectacular festivals

Offering dance, music and local delicacies, there are numerous festivals across the region. Braşov's Junii Pageant is one of the most colourful (RA) page 131

Majestic castles and palaces

Looking like everyone's fantasy of a medieval castle, Corvin Castle in Hunedoara is one of the many impressive historical sites in the region (GM-R/S) pages 250–2

Rural homestays

Experience traditional Transylvanian life in a beautifully restored guesthouse, such as those of Count Kálnoky in Micloşoara or the nearby guesthouse (pictured here) in Valea Zălanului owned by His Royal Highness The Prince of Wales

(KG/AWL) page 165

Transylvania in colour

above left   One of the distinctive Roma palaces, outside Hunedoara (PB) page 307

above right   Catherine's Gate guarding the medieval old town of Braşov (NN/S) page 134

below   The fortified Saxon town of Mediaş, dominated by the leaning Trumpeters' Tower
(ACL/D) pages 230–1

above left   No single image evokes the Dracula legend quite like the imposing Bran Castle – though its historical links to Vlad the Impaler are far more tenuous (W/D) page 144

above right   Built in the 13th century on a rocky crag, Poenari Castle was remodelled by Vlad the Impaler (CaP/S) page 241

below   Bust of *Dracula* author Bram Stoker in front of the Communist-era Hotel Castel Dracula, Bistriţa-Năsăud County (PB) page 309

AUTHORS

Born and educated in the UK, **Lucy Mallows** worked for 12 years in Budapest as a reporter and is the original author of this guide. She first visited Transylvania in 1997, but her links with Romania go back to the late 1980s when she worked as a volunteer for Operation Romanian Villages, and to an early childhood fairytale *The Lost Princess*, written in 1924 by Queen Marie of Romania.

Lucy Mallows is also the author of the Bradt guides to Bratislava and Slovakia. She now lives in Brighton from where she works as a freelance photojournalist and translator.

Paul Brummell, a career diplomat, is the British Ambassador to Romania. He has lived and worked in the country since August 2014, and speaks fluent Romanian. The third edition of this guide has been updated by Paul and his wife, Adriana. He is also an experienced travel writer, having written the first ever English-language travel guide to Turkmenistan (*Turkmenistan: The Bradt Travel Guide*, 2005) and the Bradt travel guide to Kazakhstan (2008).

Adriana Mitsue Ivama Brummell is an international public health expert who also speaks Romanian. She is a keen photographer and her work has been included in the 2016 and 2017 anthologies *Reflections of Romania*, albums of photographs produced by expatriate women in Romania.

PUBLISHER'S FOREWORD *Adrian Phillips, Managing Director*

Transylvania is a cauldron for the popular imagination; so blurred is the line between the real and the imagined that many people don't realise the region exists at all. I had wanted to visit ever since seeing statues of freedom-fighting Transylvanian princes in Budapest, and reading about their fierce struggles against the Habsburgs. These men were every bit as dashing and colourful as characters from a novel. When I did finally get to go there myself – on a short trip to Sighişoara – it lived up to expectations. This city was the birthplace of Vlad the Impaler, and I saw his shadow lurking behind the medieval walls and the impossibly quaint merchant houses. Transylvania is a place that cherishes its traditions, and where a past-century way of life is not just a cliché of the tourist postcard.

Third edition published November 2017
First published August 2008
Bradt Travel Guides Ltd
IDC House, The Vale, Chalfont St Peter, Bucks SL9 9RZ, England
www.bradtguides.com
Print edition published in the USA by The Globe Pequot Press Inc, PO Box 480, Guilford, Connecticut 06437-0480

Text copyright © 2017 Lucy Mallows and Paul Brummell
Maps copyright © 2017 Bradt Travel Guides Ltd; includes map data © OpenStreetMap contributors
Photographs copyright © 2017 Individual photographers (see below)
Project Managers: Claire Strange, Maisie Fitzpatrick and Guy Jackson
Cover research: Pepi Bluck, Perfect Picture

ISBN: 978 1 78477 053 2 (print)
e-ISBN: 978 1 78477 520 9 (e-pub)
e-ISBN: 978 1 78477 421 9 (mobi)

British Library Cataloguing in Publication Data
A catalogue record for this book is available from the British Library

Photographs
Alamy: Hemis (H/A), Paul Williams (PW/A); AWL Images: Danita Delimont Stock (DDS/AWL), Katie Garrod (KG/AWL); Rudolf Abraham (RA); Adriana Mitsue Ivana Brummell (AB); Paul Brummell (PB); Dreamstime: Adrian Catalin Lazar (ACL/D), Rechitan Sorin (RS/D), Warmcolours (W/D); FLPA: Jasper Doest/Minden Pictures (JD/MP/FLPA), Gianpiero Ferrari (GF/FLPA), Mike Lane (ML/FLPA), Michael Weber/Imagebroker (MW/I/FLPA), Liliac Winery (L); Shutterstock: alexcoman (A/S), Cartopphil (Ca/S), cge2010 (c/S), Emi Cristea (EC/S), Brandus Dan Lucian (BDL/S), Dejan Gospodarek (DG/S), Dragan Jovanovich (DJ/S), Martchan (M/S), Mikadun (Mi/S), Gaman Mihai-Radu (GM-R/S), Nataliya Nazarova (NN/S), Claudiu Paizan (CIP/S), Catalin Petolea (CaP/S), Photosebia (P/S), Sergej Razvodovskij (SR/S), Rechitan Sorin (RS/S), Razvan Stroie (RS/S) Dan Tautan (DT/S); Stephen Spinder/www.spinderartphoto.com (SSp); SuperStock (SS)
Front cover Village and citadel of Biertan (H/A)
Back cover Drummer in Sighişoara (SS), street in Sighişoara (SR/S)
Title page The Székely Stone from Rimetea village (AB), *tulnic* players in traditional costume (P/S), Batos vineyards (L)

Maps David McCutcheon FBCart.S. Regional base mapping, modified by Bradt Travel Guides, provided by ITMB Publishing Ltd (*www.itmb.com*) 2017. Dimap Bt, Budapest & Micromapper SRL, Cluj-Napoca
Colour map Relief base maps by Nick Rowland FRGS

Typeset by Ian Spick, Bradt Travel Guides Ltd
Production managed by Jellyfish Print Solutions; printed in India
Digital conversion by www.dataworks.co.in

Acknowledgements for the third edition

We would like to thank, among the many people to have shared their perspectives on this fascinating region, Lucy Abel Smith, Mariana Bocaneala and all at the Libearty Bear Sanctuary, Melinda Bolonyi, Cassandra Butu, Adela Cosma, Magor Csibi, Caroline Fernolend, Rodics Gergely, Bea Huszka, Tibor and Anna Kálnoky, Cora Moțoc, Charlie Ottley, Catalin Pana, Nat Page and all at ADEPT, Nicolae, Pamela and Indrei Rațiu, Shajjad and Katie Rizvi, Alexander and Gregor Roy Chowdhury and their families, Jonas and Ulrike Schäfer, Willy and Lavinia Schuster, Tony and the late Gerrit Timmerman, Iain Trewby and Aura Woodward. We would also like to thank Rachel Fielding, Anna Moores, Laura Pidgley, Claire Strange, Maisie Fitzpatrick and Guy Jackson at Bradt for their help and support.

Acknowledgements for the first edition

There are so many people to thank for their input, knowledge, experience and enthusiasm, I hope I haven't forgotten anybody. A massive *mulțumesc* goes out to Adeline Lörinczi in Mediaș; Alina Alexa, Andreea Bell and Georgiana Branescu in Brașov, Andrea Rost in Mălâncrav; Caroline Fernolend in Viscri; Erik László Szoboszlai in Sovata; Erika Stanciu, Ovidiu Bodean and Florin Emilian Tomuș in Retezat. Much support came from Anca Calugar in Saschiz, Andrea Fodor and Mike Wallace in Budapest, Dragoș Minea in Sibiu, Monica Cosma and Corina Vasiu in Biertan, Zorița Beisan in Bucium, Florin and Loredana Delinescu in Sarmizegetusa, Françoise Heidebroek in Roșia Montana, Ioana Alexandroaiei in Bucharest and Denisa Alexandroaiei in Brussels.

Danut and Luminița Marin in Zărnești, Tibor Kálnoky in Micloșoara and Gregor and Zsolna Roy Chowdhury in Zăbala all provided a valuable and real insight into the history and culture of their regions of Transylvania.

From Micloșoara, I am indebted to a host of knowledgeable Transylvania fans: Sabina & Robert ffrench Blake, Nathaniel and Katie Page, Barbara, Elfie and John Knowles, Ewen Cameron, Gill Graham Man, Richard Moon and Roy and Helen Pugh for their suggestions, advice and general enthusiasm. Dr John Akeroyd led a wonderful wild flower walk through the gorgeous countryside around the Olt River valley, and we even survived the bolting wild horse incident!

Many others have been generous with their knowledge and time: Alan Ogden, Jim Turnbull, Andy Hockley in Miercurea-Ciuc, Colin Shaw in Bod, Mike Morton,

Gavin Bell, Julian Ross at Lunca Ilvei, Isabela Tusa in Deva Town Hall, Istvan Vincze-Kecskes in Sâncraiu, Jenő Ujváry in Târgu Mureş and József Kuszálik in Cluj-Napoca. A special thank you to fellow Bradt authors Tim Burford and Neil Taylor who were generous with their knowledge and time. Thanks are also due to those who answered my endless questions; László Potozky, Sue Prince and Oliver Brind, Maria Iordache in London, Mária Portik in Sovata, Marina Cionca in Braşov and Simion Alb in New York. At Bradt, I'd like to thank Kelly Randell, Anna Moores, Adrian Phillips, Hilary Bradt and all the team for their help and enthusiasm. Big hugs and thanks to my mum for introducing me to the vivid imagination of Queen Marie of Romania.

CONTRIBUTORS Flora: Dr John Akeroyd; wildlife: Danuţ Marin; recipes: Luminiţa Marin; politics: Nathaniel Page.

AUTHOR'S STORY　　*Lucy Mallows*

Bradt is the only UK travel guide publisher to devote an entire guidebook to the Transylvania region and it is typical of their pioneering, ground-breaking attitude that they are the first to recognise that Transylvania has more than enough fascinating historical and cultural features, sporting hotspots and natural wonders to merit a book of its very own.

I wanted to write a travel guide that could lead travellers around a region that has an incredibly complicated history and blend of cultures and faiths, with Romanians, Hungarians, Saxons and Roma all struggling together and apart during the brutal Ceauşescu dictatorship. It is also quite a difficult region to visit; the infrastructure is not always in place and the roads are often diabolical. For an English-speaking visitor, there is a confusion of languages to wrestle with: Romanian, Hungarian, German, Romani and a complicated geographical demographic. However, Transylvania is an immensely rewarding country to visit, there is so much to discover and enjoy: romantic castles, Saxon fortress churches, secluded villages with ancient traditions and folk crafts, haystacks and hay-laden horse-drawn carts, gorgeous countryside, forests, rolling hills, more bears than anywhere else in Europe and welcoming, hospitable people offering delicious dishes and a wide range of lethal alcoholic drinks.

I haven't even mentioned Dracula yet! Although the Count's inspiration, Vlad III Ţepeş (the Impaler) was, in fact, a prince of Wallachia, a region to the south of Transylvania, Irish author Bram Stoker and later Hollywood placed him firmly in the more atmospheric setting of Transylvania and there are many places where his bloodthirsty name is evoked.

Bradt's unique brief gave me the chance to express personal feelings about the region (and Transylvania always elicits strong reactions). I hope this guidebook helps readers gain a deeper understanding of the region and a love for this unique, complicated and exciting part of Europe.

THE USE OF LANGUAGES IN THIS GUIDE Transylvania's diversity of languages is a fascinating aspect of its cultural heritage, but can pose challenges for the visitor. In this guide, place names are given in Romanian, which is the official language, but with the Hungarian and German names for each place in brackets thereafter, in the order (Hungarian/German). If only one other language name is given, the language is identified as either Hungarian (HU) or German (GE). All other references are in Romanian unless otherwise indicated.

Below are a few quick geographical references for maps (English–Romanian):

lac	lake	*vârf*	peak
râu	river	*platou*	plateau
munte	mountain		

See also *Hiking vocabulary* (see box, page 257) and *Appendix 1: Language* (pages 320–9).

Names of historical figures are given in their most common English-language form.

AUTHORS' FAVOURITES Finding genuinely characterful accommodation or that unmissable off-the-beaten-track café can be difficult, so the authors have chosen a few of their favourite places throughout the region to point you in the right direction. These 'authors' favourites' are marked with an ✳.

MAPS
Keys and symbols Maps include alphabetical keys covering the locations of those places to stay, eat or drink that are featured in the book. Note that regional maps may not show all hotels and restaurants in the area: other establishments may be located in towns shown on the map.

Grids and grid references Several maps use gridlines to allow easy location of sites. Map grid references are listed in square brackets after the name of the place or site of interest in the text, with page number followed by grid number, eg: [129 E4].

TELEPHONE NUMBERS When calling numbers in Romania from abroad, first dial Romania's country code (+40) then the local code (as set out in the relevant chapter of Part Two of this guide) minus the first zero, then the six-digit telephone number. We have given the +40 code for the numbers in Part One, as readers are more likely to be calling from abroad, but omitted them thereafter.

Contents

Introduction

Transylvania! The name is so evocative that it demands an exclamation mark, although perhaps it should be a question mark – Transylvania? What is it? Where is it?

In the popular imagination, Transylvania is filled with forest-covered mountains, sinister castles on rocky crags, counts with pallid skin and pointed teeth, wolves, bears, werewolves, eagles, haystacks and ancient farmsteads. But while some of this imagery has its roots in the real region of Transylvania, much of it emerges from the pen of Bram Stoker, the Irish novelist who never even visited the place. Forget about Dracula if you can, for the real Transylvania is a region much more interesting, and less dangerous.

'Transylvania had been a familiar name as long as I could remember. It was the very essence and symbol of remote, leafy, half-mythical strangeness; and, on the spot, it seemed remoter still, and more fraught with charms.' So wrote Patrick Leigh Fermor of his romantic walk across this strange and beautiful land in 1934. The real Transylvania, the land beyond the forest, is a place captured within the sheltering arc of the Carpathian Mountains. Its upland forests hold some of Europe's most important populations of bears, wolves and lynx, while further down the hillsides its meadows, still cut by scythe, play host to a late spring pageant of glorious wild flowers.

Its peoples and places reflect the shaping hands of its complex history. From the remote hill fortresses of its Dacian kings and the colonies established by the Romans emerge the roots which were to give birth to the Romanian people. Hungary was for centuries the dominant power, and ethnic Hungarians still form the majority of the population in the Székely lands, the ancestors of which people guarded the eastern frontiers of the Hungarian Kingdom. From beautifully carved wooden gates to a distinctive chimney-shaped cake, the Székely region is proud of its identity. In the south, the German-speaking Transylvanian Saxons were also brought to the region by the Hungarian kings to help guard its frontiers. While most have now departed for Germany they have left behind a legacy of beautiful villages centred on the remarkable fortified churches which are one of the most distinctive cultural features of the region.

Transylvania is an ideal escape from the hectic, stressed-out Western world. It's impossible to rush; the roads will see to that. You have to take your time, go with the flow and admire the scenery *en route*. And its tourist offering is developing impressively. While the region still has its share of clumsily renovated communist-era hotels, with surly reception staff and beige décor, there is a broadening range of hotels and guesthouses based around sensitively restored noble manors, village cottages and historic townhouses. Its largest cities, Cluj-Napoca, Sibiu and Braşov, combine historic centres with alluring cultural programmes, and Transylvania now boasts world-class theatre, film and music festivals. From birdwatching to mountain biking and skiing to botany, Transylvania is an attractive destination for seekers of many types of activity holidays, as well as for those looking for holiday inactivity and enjoying the slow pace of traditional village life. And with both hotel and restaurant costs much lower than in much of western Europe, it remains an affordable destination, too.

So come to Transylvania. There's no need to bring any garlic – you'll find plenty in the local food anyway.

Part One

GENERAL INFORMATION

Country name România (Romania)

Region name Transylvania (Ardeal/Erdély)

Location Romania is situated in central Europe, southeast of Hungary, north of Bulgaria, east of Serbia and west of the Republic of Moldova and the Black Sea. Transylvania is situated right in the heart of Romania.

Size/area (km) Romania has an area of 238,391km^2

Territory The territory of Transylvania broadly corresponds to that of ten modern Romanian counties (*judeţ*): Alba, Bistriţa-Năsăud, Braşov, Cluj, Covasna, Harghita, Hunedoara, Mureş, Sălaj and Sibiu

Population The 2011 census recorded Romania's population as 20,121,641, though it is believed to have declined to around 19.7 million in 2016 as a result of a low birth rate and out-migration. The population of the ten counties covered by this book was a little over 3.9 million in 2011.

President Klaus Iohannis (elected in November 2014)

Prime Minister Mihai Tudose (appointed in June 2017)

Capital Bucureşti (Bucharest), population 1.9 million

Languages Romanian is the only official language. According to the 2011 census it was the first language of 85% of the population; Hungarian is the first language of 6%.

Ethnic composition The main ethnic groups in Romania, as at the 2011 census, were Romanian 83%, Hungarian 6%, Roma 3%, German and Ukrainian each 0.2%. Within Transylvania the main ethnic groups (again as at 2011) were Romanian 71%, Hungarian 18%, German 0.4%. Eight Transylvanian counties have Romanian majorities, and two (Covasna and Harghita) are mostly Hungarian.

Religion The 2011 census figures recorded 81% of the population as Romanian Orthodox, 4.3% Roman Catholic, 3% reformed, 1.8% Pentecostal and 0.75% Greco-Catholic

Currency Leu (plural lei) (RON) 1 leu = 100 bani. Banknotes with a value of 1 leu and 5, 10, 50, 100, 200 and 500 lei; coins with a value of 1, 5, 10 and 50 bani.

Exchange rate £1 = 4.94RON, US$1 = 3.82RON, €1 = 4.60RON (August 2017)

International telephone code Romania +40, Bucharest +40 21

Time Romania falls into the East European Time Zone (EET), 2 hours ahead of GMT (Greenwich Mean Time), 7 hours ahead of New York (Eastern Standard Time) and 10 hours ahead of Los Angeles (Pacific Standard Time)

Electrical voltage 230V/50Hz; two round-pin plugs

Flag Three equal vertical bands of (from hoist side) blue, yellow and red

National anthem Deşteaptă-te, române ('Awaken, Romanian!'), lyrics by Andrei Mureşanu

Tourist board website w romaniatourism.com

Public holidays 1–2 January (New Year's Day celebrations), 24 January (Union of Romanian Principalities), April/May (Orthodox Easter), 1 May (Labour Day), May/June (Pentecost), 1 June (International Children's Day), 15 August (The Assumption), 30 November (St Andrew's Day), 1 December (National Day), 24–25 December (Christmas)

1

Background Information

GEOGRAPHY

Covering an area of 238,400km², Romania is the second-largest country in central Europe after Poland. Romania is situated in the southeastern Balkan region of central Europe and is bordered clockwise by Ukraine, the Republic of Moldova, the Black Sea, Bulgaria, Serbia and Hungary.

The historical region of Transylvania covers ten present-day counties (*judeţ* in Romanian, abbreviated in addresses as '*jud*'), right in the heart of Romania. The ten counties, surrounded on all sides by Romanian territory, are Alba, Bistriţa-Năsăud, Braşov, Cluj, Covasna, Harghita, Hunedoara, Mureş, Sălaj and Sibiu, covering a total area of around 57,000km². The major cities are Cluj-Napoca (with a population of 324,576 as at the 2011 census), Braşov (253,200), Sibiu (147,245) and Târgu Mureş (134,290).

Some authors and historians, usually Hungarian, include the western part of Romania – Banat, Crişana and even Maramureş – in their description of Transylvania. But these are geographically and culturally quite distinct regions. Transylvania in a strict sense, the 'land beyond the forest', begins at the Piatra Craiului mountain pass between Oradea and Cluj-Napoca, where the vast flat plains of eastern Hungary and Crişana give way to the forest-covered Apuseni Mountains.

Transylvania's borders are defined by **mountains**. The swooping crescent-shaped loop of the Carpathians encloses the eastern and southern edges of Transylvania. The Southern Carpathian range, marking the southern border of the region, is also sometimes known as the Transylvanian Alps. Forming the northwest border are the Apuseni Mountains, through which the Piatra Craiului breaks a passage. Access into this region was over mountain passes.

The arc of the Carpathian Mountains around Transylvania is just part of a 1,500km-long range which stretches from the Czech Republic in the north, runs across parts of Poland, Slovakia, Hungary, Ukraine and then Romania, before petering out in Serbia in the west. The Carpathians consist of several quite distinctive mountain ranges. Its very highest peaks lie in the High Tatras range in Slovakia, but these are followed by the Făgăraş Mountains on the southern border of Transylvania where Braşov and Argeş counties meet. The Făgăraş Mountains are home to Romania's highest peak, Moldoveanu, at 2,544m). The Pârang, Retezat and Bucegi mountain ranges, all within the Southern Carpathians, all have peaks higher than 2,500m.

The Apuseni Mountains are lower than the Carpathians, with their highest point at 1,849m, and again feature a series of ranges. They include impressive areas of limestone karst scenery, with many gorges and caves. They are also mineralogically rich, with the gold mines of the Apuseni an important source of wealth even in Roman times.

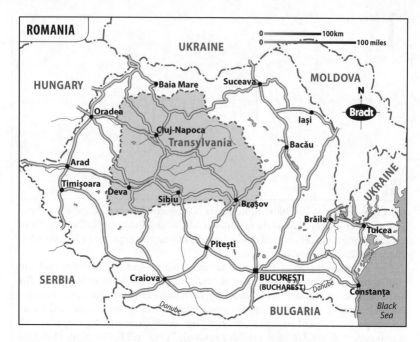

Within the sheltered Carpathian bowl, Transylvania is not all the forest-filled mountains, rocky crags and terrifying fortresses of Bram Stoker's imagination. The area between the mountain ranges marking the edges of Transylvania is known as the Transylvanian Plateau (Podişul Transilvaniei), though 'plateau' doesn't really give a good sense of the landscape, which is mostly characterised by river valleys separated by lines of hills reaching a couple of hundred metres above the height of the valleys. It incorporates a number of distinctive sub-regions, such as the Transylvanian Plain (Câmpia Transilvaniei), sitting between the Someş and Mureş rivers in the northern part of the region, rich in reserves of salt and natural gas, an area of lush rolling hills, fertile flower-filled meadows and numerous lakes and rivers.

Transylvania is criss-crossed by some significant **waterways**, which drain the Transylvanian Plateau. The Mureş River crosses right through the region, rising in the Eastern Carpathians and passing through Târgu Mureş, heading southwest through Alba Iulia to Deva before flowing into the Tisza River at Szeged in southern Hungary. The Olt River, known as Alutus in Roman times, also rises in the Eastern Carpathians, not far from the headwaters of the Mureş, and flows south through Miercurea-Ciuc and Sfântu Gheorghe before heading westwards through Făgăraş before a further southward push just beyond Avrig, cutting through the Southern Carpathians before joining the Danube. At 615km, the Olt has the distinction of being the longest river which flows solely through Romanian territory. The Târnava River flows through a beautiful part of southern Transylvania, characterised by the many fortified churches built by local Saxon communities, and for most of its length comprises two tributaries, the Greater (Târnava Mare) and Smaller (Târnava Mică). These come together at the town of Blaj, before flowing into the Mureş River near Teiuş.

Transylvania also offers some beautiful lakes. Some of these are the work of nature, such as the volcanic crater Lacul Sfânta Ana, and Lacul Roşu, formed as a

Sălaj

Bistriţa-Năsăud

Cluj

Mureş

Harghita

Alba

Covasna

Sibiu

Braşov

Hunedoara

1

result of a landslide, while others are the work of man, including Lacul Fântânele in Cluj County and Lacul Colibiţa in Bistriţa-Năsăud.

A third of Romania is covered by mountains, with forestland of beech, hornbeam, ash, lime, spruce, oak and fir below alpine meadows providing home to a rich wildlife including bears, wolves, deer, lynx and chamois. Another third is dominated by lower, rolling hills and plateaux where orchards and vineyards blossom in the long springs and summers. The final third is covered by fertile plains where cereals, particularly corn, and vegetables are grown. Traditional agricultural methods have maintained the high-nature value of many of the meadows and plains, offering an astonishing late-spring pageant of wild flowers. All of this can evoke a nostalgia for the similar landscapes that were once to be found in many parts of western Europe, but which have been lost to mechanisation and modernisation.

CLIMATE

Romania has a temperate-continental climate, with four distinct seasons. The spring is pleasant with cool mornings and nights and warm days. Summer is hot, especially in the south of the country, where Bucharest has an average high temperature in July of almost 30°C. Summer temperatures in Transylvania are usually a few degrees cooler than this, with the average high temperature in Cluj-Napoca around 25°C in July, but air conditioning in both city hotel rooms and transportation is particularly welcome. High mountain areas in Transylvania still feel fresh in the summer months. During the summer, you might encounter an intense and violent thunderstorm, with dramatic displays of lightning and sudden bursts of torrential rain. Autumns are cool, with meadows and trees producing beautifully coloured foliage, making the landscape look like a pastoral painting. Winters can be bitterly cold and snow-covered, especially in the mountains, where temperatures can drop to −20°C. The average high temperature in Cluj-Napoca in January is around 0°C. A bitter, icy wind called the *crivăț* sears through from Siberia, though its effects are more strongly felt in southeastern Romania. Transylvania is, however, often hit by winter fog, which can ground early morning flights to Cluj-Napoca and make driving difficult. Falls of heavy snow are likely at some point between December and mid-March, although the onset of winter snows can vary considerably from year to year. Nonetheless, your chances of a white Christmas are pretty high in Transylvania: around 85% in Cluj-Napoca. And, buoyed by the advantages of snow cannons, the main ski resorts around Brașov are usually able to offer snow from December until April. If you are hiring a car in the Transylvanian winter, make sure it is equipped with winter tyres.

Precipitation overall is relatively modest, averaging around 635mm a year in Transylvania, and peaks during the summer months, though there are on average a few precipitation days during each month of the year. In Cluj-Napoca this ranges from an average of five days of precipitation in February and March to 11 in May and June. Flooding can be a problem, its effects worsened by deforestation.

Weather forecasts are available at w accuweather.com.

NATURAL HISTORY AND CONSERVATION

For more on wildlife in Transylvania, check out Bradt's Central and Eastern European Wildlife. Get 10% off at w bradtguides.com/shop.

TRANSYLVANIAN FLORA (Dr John Akeroyd: botanist, conservationist and specialist on European flora; e jrakeroyd@gmail.com) Transylvania's botanical richness echoes its historical, cultural and ethnic diversity. The plateau (Podişul Transilvaniei), locally hilly and dissected by rivers, is bordered to the south by the Transylvanian Alps, with the high Făgăraş Mountains reaching 2,544m on Mt Moldoveanu, to the west by the lower Apuseni Mountains, and to the east by the Eastern Carpathians. Because of its location within the Carpathians and rich traditional farming culture, Transylvania retains high biodiversity and intact ecological systems. The cool dark forests and the colourful and often plentiful wild flowers are among the many pleasures for the visitor to this unspoiled region.

Much traditional agriculture survives, especially in hillier country – non-intensive crop cultivation, hay-meadows and pastures, interspersed with semi-natural woodland, scrub and grassland. Thus one sees vegetation ranging from moist and dry lowland grassland, oak-hornbeam woods, through extensive beech and conifer woods on the lower and middle mountain slopes, to high-altitude alpine grassland, heath, cliffs and rocks. The Carpathians possess some of Europe's largest undisturbed forests, and Transylvania not only has high geographical and ecological diversity but is also a transition zone between western and central Europe, the Eurasian steppes and Mediterranean vegetation and flora.

The forests of Transylvania are a mixture of oak, beech, hornbeam, spruce, fir and pine. They are particularly lovely in autumn. Romanian forests have the highest regeneration rate in Europe, although they are ever at threat from logging. Historically much of the region was wooded, with a mosaic of woodland, scrub and grassland on steeper, unstable or dry slopes. However, human clearance for farming has greatly reduced the woodland cover over large areas of central and

GIANT HAYSTACKS

Visitors to Transylvania will return home with abiding images of haystacks and horse and carts covered with enormous piles of precariously balanced hay. The traditional haystack (*căpiță de fân*) may vary quite markedly in shape from place to place, from chunky pear-shaped mounds to much thinner structures, but the basic construction technique is similar: there is a tall central wooden pole, supported by a wooden tripod structure, with a bed of branches, which will help to stop the hay from rotting. The hay is cut by scythe or small mechanical mower, and first placed on the ground to dry out. It is crucial that the hay is dry, or the stack will either rot or ferment, which in the latter case can even cause the haystack to catch fire. Traditionally, the building of the haystack involves the farmer passing hay up to his wife at the top. When the piling up has been completed, the haystack is combed with rakes so that rainwater runs down the sides of the haystack instead of soaking in. If the haystack has been properly raked there is no need for it to be covered, as the outer layer develops into a matted protective shell. The final touch is a wreath, placed on top of the haystack, which is less a piece of symbolism than a practical protection against the wind. Finally, the farmer's wife needs to slide down the haystack, which can reach a height of 4m, to safety below.

The traditional Romanian haystack is a remarkable feat of engineering when it comes to storing hay, and a well-prepared dry stack can survive for years, but it has some disadvantages when it comes to actually using the hay. As soon is the outer shell is broken, the rest of the haystack is vulnerable to wind and rain. This is why you will sometimes see horse-drawn carts transporting an entire haystack, taking it to a barn where it will be used as winter livestock fodder. In the Saxon villages hay is stored, by local tradition, loose in barns rather than in stacks. The great arched gates to the farmyards are large enough to admit a fully loaded haycart. And as you drive across the Transylvanian countryside you will notice that mechanisation is bringing competition to these traditional haystacks, in the form of plastic-covered rolls of hay. Let us hope that the traditional Romanian haystack, a signature feature of rural life in Transylvania, survives for generations to come.

northern Transylvania, and semi-natural grasslands too have retreated. Much of the landscape retains woods of hornbeam (*Carpinus betulus*) and oaks, mostly sessile oak (*Quercus petraea*) and pedunculate oak (*Quercus robor*), with downy oak (*Quercus pubescens*) on dry slopes. Beech (*Fagus sylvatica*) is often intermixed with hornbeam, especially on limestone and along ridges and on slopes, sometimes with small-leaved lime (*Tilia cordata*). The margins of these beech–oak–hornbeam forests, still widely present in southern Transylvania, often have a fringe of the striking yellow- and violet-flowered endemic cow-wheat (*Melampyrum bihariense*), more or less restricted to Romania. The woodland flora is sparse but includes spring-flowering plants such as wood anemone (*Anemone nemorosa*), coralroot (*Dentaria bulbifera*), purple hellebore (*Helleborus purpurascens*) and spring pea (*Lathyrus vernus*), and orchids in early summer. A few woods of downy oak (*Quercus pubescens*) occur on dry slopes.

Woodland along streams and rivers is dominated by alders, willows and black poplar (*Populus nigra*), sometimes festooned with wild hops. Wood margins often have scrub dominated by blackthorn (*Prunus spinosa*), with hawthorn, wild pear, privet, dogwood, spindle, elder and Cornelian cherry (*Cornus mas*). As farmers abandon some agricultural land, scrub spreads and develops into woodland. Wood-pasture too is widespread, for example in the Saxon villages and the adjacent Székely lands to the east and north, with great oaks or other trees growing as spaced individuals in grassland. A fine historic example lies just outside Sighişoara, on the plateau known as the Breite, where hundreds of veteran oaks grow in a clearing surrounded by dense woodland. The grassland is not wild flower-rich but locally has heath plants such as dwarf brooms, and taller species of marshy ground such as great burnet (*Sanguisorba officinalis*). Unfortunately the Breite, despite being a nature reserve, has been inadequately grazed and hornbeam scrub has invaded formerly open grassland between the trees. Some other wood-pastures have been felled or overgrazed, but large stands survive on the fringes of the Carpathians.

The spectacular wooded mountain scenery has many good plant habitats. In the foothills and lower slopes of the Eastern and Southern Carpathians up to 1,400m, the dominant trees are oak and beech. Along the margins of the lower woods grow endemic Transylvanian hepatica (*Hepatica transilvanica*), the candelabra-like martagon lily (*Lilium martagon*), sinister poisonous monkshood (*Aconitum lycoctonum*) and ancient relict species such as *Ligularia sibirica*, alongside the commoner oxslip (*Primula elatior*) and, in wet places, marsh marigold (*Caltha palustris*) and brook thistle (*Cirsium rivulare*). From 1,000m, beech grows in 'mountain forest' with sycamore (*Acer pseudoplatanus*), silver fir (*Abies alba*), and Norway spruce (*Picea abies*), which forms dense stands. Spruce in its native habitat is no spiky 'Christmas tree', but a tall, elegant spire of drooping branches.

From 1,600m to 1,800m, at and above the timberline, shrubby juniper (*Juniperus communis*), mountain pine (*Pinus mugo*) and Carpathian alpenrose (*Rhododendron myrtifolium*) gradually replaces the spruces. In the

OUR LADY'S BEDSTRAW

Lady's bedstraw, sometimes known rather more biblically as Our Lady's bedstraw, and in Latin as *Galium verum*, is an erect perennial with short branches covered by clusters of tiny golden-yellow flowers. Flowering in the summer, it can impart a scent of honey to meadowlands. In Romania it is called sânziene, and is particularly associated with the celebrations of midsummer on 24 June, a day also called Sânziene (page 102).

This species of bedstraw was formerly used in stuffing mattresses, for which purpose it was particularly valued both for its properties of discouraging fleas and for its scent. The more specific term Our Lady's bedstraw derives from the popular legend that the plant was one of the herbs in the hay of the manger at Bethlehem. The Latin name of the genus comes from the Greek noun 'gala', meaning 'milk', a reference to the role played by lady's bedstraw and other plants of the genus to helping milk coagulate during cheese-making. For this reason lady's bedstraw was also popularly known in some parts as cheese rennet or cheese renning. In Gloucestershire, England, it was used traditionally to give double Gloucester cheese its distinctive yellow colour. Another former popular name for the plant in England was maid's hair, as in the reign of Henry VIII the yellow flowers were stuffed into ladies' caps in order to dye their hair blonde.

Transylvanian Alps, heather-like *Brukenthalia spiculifolia*, named after Baron Samuel von Brukenthal (1721–1803), a distinguished 18th-century Governor of Transylvania, is locally abundant. These shrubs are interspersed with grassland, mostly managed as pasture. Above 2,200m is semi-natural alpine grassland with sedges and small rushes, and low alpenrose, bilberry (*Vaccinium myrtilus*) and dwarf willows. Late snow-patches have a flora of least willow (*Salix herbacea*), dwarf snowbell (*Soldanella pusilla*), white-flowered alpine buttercups and other alpine flowers. Grassland, rocks and screes are home to attractive flowers such as gentians, Carpathian bellflower (*Campanula carpatica*), edelweiss (*Leontopodium alpinum*), saxifrages and primulas.

Lime-rich rocks support special plants. The great ridge of Piatra Craiului National Park, southwest of Braşov, has woods, scrub and meadows, and an important gorge and rock flora. This includes narrowly distributed endemic plants such as two showy pinks, *Dianthus spiculifolius*, endemic to the Romanian Carpathians, and *Dianthus callizonus*, found only on Piatra Craiului. The mountain hay-meadows, a mixture of dry and damp grassland, around adjacent villages have beautiful wild flowers such as rosy vanilla orchid (*Nigritella rubra*) and globe orchid (*Traunsteinera globosa*), globeflower (*Trollius europaeus*), blue bellflowers and gentians, purple knapweeds and the famous medicinal herb arnica (*Arnica montana*). Many meadow plants are still used in herbal medicine and may well have inspired Samuel Hahnemann, for a while Bruckenthal's secretary and physician, to develop his alternative medicinal system, homoeopathy.

Retezat, Romania's first national park (1935), in far southeast Transylvania, has a similar range of habitats to Craiului and holds over 650 flowering plants, the richest flora on limestone. This is one of several Transylvanian sites for lady's slipper-orchid (*Cypripedium calceolus*), the over exploited medicinal herb yellow gentian (*Gentiana lutea*) and rare alpines.

Traditionally managed wild flower-rich **grassland** is the jewel in Transylvania's floral crown, a manifestation of the sheer richness of plant diversity – and perhaps the best hay-meadows in Europe. These meadows are a living link with the past, and show how plant and animal diversity can thrive alongside agriculture. Their conservation requires sensitive farming, employing modern techniques but maintaining the careful traditional husbandry that nurtured the landscape for centuries. The best areas of lowland and foothill 'meadow-steppe' grasslands are probably in the Saxon villages and Székely country, but there are plenty of examples along the Carpathians. The flora is a mix of western and central European plants, with a significant steppic element. Grasses share the sward with a wealth of wild flowers, including 20–30 or more clovers, vetches and other peaflowers, notably sainfoin (*Onobrychis viciifolia*) and stately Hungarian clover (*Trifolium pannonicum*), its scented sulphur-yellow flowers the shape and size of bantam eggs. The drier grasslands have an astonishing range of plants, including steppic gems such as yellow flax (*Linum flavum*) and Mediterranean plants such as tassel hyacinth (*Muscari comosa*).

The **meadow-steppe** species list runs into hundreds, among them the elegant lily-like *Anthericum ramosum* and *Ornithogalum pyramidale*, yellow- and white-flowered ox-eye daisy (*Leucanthemum vulgare*), frothy cream dropwort (*Filipendula vulgaris*), yellow Cerinthe minor and Our Lady's bedstraw (*Galium verum*), countless massed heads of the pale- and deep-yellow hay-rattle (*Rhinanthus rumelicus*), rich blue *Salvia pratensis*, pinkish-purple great milkwort (*Polygala major*) and crimson Charterhouse pink (*Dianthus carthusianorum*). In the Apuseni and Carpathian foothills, mountain grassland plants such as arnica, globeflower, sticky catchfly

Of the 14 national parks in Romania, a significant part of five lie within Transylvania. A tiny portion of a sixth, the Jiu Valley National Park, scrapes into Hunedoara County, but this park is much more strongly associated with Gorj County to the south. Two of these, the Rodna Mountains and Retezat national parks, are listed as UNESCO biosphere reserves. The five main Transylvanian national parks are the following.

NATIONAL PARKS
Călimani National Park (w *calimani.ro*) On the border of Mureş, Harghita, Bistriţa-Năsăud and Suceava counties in the far northeast of Transylvania, the park is focused around the volcanic complex of the Călimani Mountains. Area: 240km². See pages 200–1.

Bicaz Gorges-Hăşmaş National Park (w *cheilebicazului-hasmas.ro*) Straddling Harghita County and the neighbouring county of Neamţ in Moldavia, this is focused on the limestone and sandstone massifs of the Hăşmaş Mountains, characterised by striking gorges such as the Bicaz Gorge, as well as the picturesque Lacul Roşu. Area: 66km². See page 186.

Piatra Craiului National Park (w *pcrai.ro*) First declared a nature reserve in 1938, this is a popular park centred on a distinctive limestone ridge, some 25km long. Area: 148km². See pages 146–7.

Retezat National Park (w *retezat.ro*) Established in 1935, this is Romania's oldest national park. It is based around the Retezat Mountains, which have more peaks above 2,000m than any other range in Romania, and is known for a chain of glacial cirque lakes and for a particularly rich fauna. Area: 380km². See pages 256–60.

(*Lychnis viscaria*) and alpine forms of kidney-vetch (*Anthyllis vulneraria*) join the sward. South-facing grasslands in Transylvania are rich in Eurasian steppe species, adapted to habitats hot and dry in summer but cold and snowy in winter. From spring to early summer, before they turn greyish with drought, these grasslands reveal a burst of colour: spring pheasant's-eye (*Adonis vernalis*), Tartar cabbage (*Crambe tataria*), burning bush (*Dictamnus albus*), red viper's bugloss (*Echium maculatum*), purple-flowered *Iris aphylla*, pink steppe almond (*Prunus tenella*) and violet-blue nodding sage (*Salvia nutans*).

Reserves protect pockets of a vegetation and flora both attractive and increasingly diminished in eastern Europe: for example at Zau de Câmpie in Mureş County, the only place in Transylvania where the magnificent red-flowered *Paeonia tenuifolia* grows; and in Cluj County the species-rich Fânaţele Clujului ('Meadows of Cluj') and Suatu, which protects rare joint-pine *Ephedra distachya* and the only population of the endemic Transylvanian milk-vetch (*Astragalus peterfii*). The Saxon villages district in the south of Transylvania has south-facing slopes and hummocks covered with this type of flora, especially from around Saschiz and Mihai Viteazu to the south of Viscri, and to the west around Apold and Movile. These dry grasslands and scrub, set among dense oak–hornbeam woods, hold a representative selection of Transylvanian rarities and endemics, including the tall, branched yellow-flowered scabious (*Cephalaria radiata*) and the violet-flowered

Rodna Mountains National Park (w *parcrodna.ro*) The Rodna Mountains form one of the highest ranges of the Eastern Carpathians, with a continuous ridge stretching for more than 50km which marks the natural northern border of Transylvania with the neighbouring region of Maramureş. Area: 471km². See page 312.

NATURAL PARKS Romania also has a network of 18 natural parks, offering a somewhat lower degree of protection, the most recently established being the Văcăreşti Natural Park, an urban wetland in the heart of Bucharest. Seven are all or partly in Transylvania. Three of the best known of these are the following.

Apuseni Natural Park (w *parcapuseni.ro*) Covering part of the Apuseni Mountains in western Transylvania, this includes areas of impressive limestone karst scenery, with deep gorges and extensive cave systems. Area: 758km². See pages 269–71.

Bucegi Natural Park (w *bucegipark.ro*) The Bucegi range, towering above the mountain resorts of the Prahova Valley, is the most highly visited of all of Romania's mountain areas, with the Babele and Sfinxul rock formations among its best-known features. Area: 327km². See pages 138–9.

Grădiştea Muncelului-Cioclovina Natural Park (w *gradiste.ro*) UNESCO World Heritage-listed Dacian hill fortresses are hidden within the forested mountains of this park in Hunedoara County. Area: 381km². See page 248.

The other natural parks in Transylvania are the Cindrel and Dumbrava Sibiului parks in Sibiu County, the Haţeg County Dinosaurs Geopark in Hunedoara, and the Upper Mureş Defile in Mureş County.

Transylvanian sage (*Salvia transilvanica*). Adjacent, less dry slopes support plants of woodland margins or even of mountain slopes, such as the tussocky April-flowering grass *Sesleria heufleriana* – a remarkable mix of species.

A spectacular flower of the hills and lower mountains is pheasant's-eye narcissus (*Narcissus poeticus* ssp. *radiiflorus*), which in May gives massed displays, notably at Dumbrava Vadului southeast of Făgăraş, a site that attracts many visitors and is also commonly known as Poiana Narciselor ('Narcissus Glade'). Along woodland margins and streams in July and August blooms *Telekia speciosa*, a robust yellow daisy that commemorates after Sámuel Teleki (1739–1822), the Székely nobleman and Chancellor of Transylvania who presented his library to Târgu Mureş (page 195). This noble plant attracts a host of butterflies. A humbler wayside flower, chicory (*Cichorium intibus*), with pale blue dandelion flowers, tints roadsides and fields, and the cabbage family splashes the landscape with yellow from spring onwards, replaced in August by masses of white wild carrot (*Daucus carota*). Cornfield weeds too, almost lost from western Europe, persist in places – including deep-blue cornflower (*Centaurea cyanus*) and larkspur (*Consolida regalis*), and scarlet common poppy (*Papaver rhoeas*) and pheasant's-eye (*Adonis aestivalis*). Around villages, tall yellow-flowered elecampane (*Inula helenium*) and softly downy marsh-mallow (*Althaea pallida*) form patches, and even mauve burdocks and purple thistles have a stately air.

June and July are the best months for flowers, although plenty persist into autumn. September produces crowds of lilac-coloured autumn crocus or meadow saffron (*Colchicum autumnale*) in somewhat damper or overgrazed grasslands, and late gentians, especially fringed gentian (*Gentianopsis ciliata*) of dry pastures. On higher ground, lilac-mauve Banat Crocus (*Crocus banaticus*) colours woodland margins and sheltered meadows.

TRANSYLVANIAN FAUNA (Dan Marin: wildlife guide who runs Transylvanian Wolf in Zărneşti – pages 148–9) A combination of good forest management, traditional and wildlife-friendly farming activities makes Transylvania one of the best places in the whole of Europe for wildlife. Large numbers of wolf, bear and lynx still inhabit the forests that surround this place. Natural selection has ensured that there is a very good and healthy population of red and roe deer and wild boar. The variety of habitats – flood plains, river margins, hay-meadows, forested hills and high mountains – are good homes for an impressive number of species of butterflies, birds, mammals, reptiles and amphibians.

Wild plants and animals have always been very important in the traditional life of Transylvania. The folklore (traditions, stories, beliefs, superstitions) related to them is fascinating, with national festivities dedicated, for instance, to one flower, Our Lady's bedstraw. There are also folk tales that give the wolf a positive significance, which is something unique throughout Europe.

There is a good network of protected areas all across Transylvania. I will name a few of them, together with some of their highlights, in terms of the wildlife you might find there.

Piatra Craiului National Park (pages 146–7) is located in the southeastern part of Transylvania. The Piatra Craiului Mountains are considered by many to be the most beautiful and spectacular mountains in all Romania. The park includes a well-preserved forested area as well as two traditional Romanian mountain villages. An important wildlife research programme, the Carpathian Large Carnivore Project, has done some important work on human–wildlife interaction in the area.

The symbol of these mountains is an exquisite flower, the alpine pink (*Dianthus callizonus*), which grows near or right on the ridge. Wild flowers, especially orchids, are a delightful sight on walks in different parts of the park. If you don't see large mammals like wolf and bear, you will almost surely find their tracks or other signs on the trails that cross the forests here. Spending a few hours may be rewarded with good sightings of birds like the wallcreeper, alpine swift, crag martin, black stork, black and three-toed woodpecker as well as raptors. The small ponds or puddles in the horse-carts' wheel tracks are good places to find the yellow-bellied toad (*Bombina variegata*).

Southwestern Transylvania is home to **Retezat National Park** (pages 256–60). This was the first established national park in Romania (1935). Some 140 species of butterflies can be found here: the scarce swallowtail, clouded apollo and meadow fritillary as well as nine endemic species. A significant swathe of it has been declared an Important Bird Area (IBA), with birds like horned lark, golden eagle and white-backed woodpecker. A total of 15 species of bats have been recorded, among them the threatened species *Rhinolophus ferrumequinum*. The higher parts of the Retezat Mountains host an important population of chamois.

Bicaz Gorges-Hăşmaş National Park (page 186) is in northeastern Transylvania. The Bicaz Gorge (Cheile Bicazului) and Lacul Roşu are just two of the landscape highlights of this national park. Three species of newt live here: *Triturus alpestris*, *Triturus montandoni* and *Triturus cristatus*. There is often rain in this region, which

ANIMAL AND BIRD VOCABULARY

	Romanian	Hungarian
Animal	animal	állat
Cow	vacă	tehén
Pig	porc	disznó
Goat	capră	kecske
Sheep	oaie	birka/juh
Chicken/hen	pui/găină	csirke/tyúk
Bear	urs	medve
Wolf	lup	farkas
Dog	câine	kutya
Lynx	râs	hiúz
Cat/kitten	pisică/pisicuţă	macska/cica
Eagle	vultur	sas
Bird	pasăre	madár
Mammal	mamifer	emlős
Fish	peşte	hal
Butterfly	fluture	pillangó
Insect	insectă	rovar
Bee	albină	méh
Wasp	viespe	darázs
Reptile	reptilă	hüllő
Frog/toad	broască/	béka/varangy
	broască râioasă	

may not be great for walks, but it is wonderful for salamanders. Birdlife includes capercaillie, Ural and eagle owl, wallcreeper and rock bunting. Beech martens share the forests here with bear, wolf and lynx.

Apuseni Natural Park (pages 269–71) forms the western borders of historic Transylvania. The park has an impressive network of little-known caves, gorges, underground lakes and waterfalls as well as beautiful alpine meadows. A few endemic invertebrates are found in some of the caves here, as well as a good number of different bats. The clear streams have trout, Mediterranean barbel (*Barbus meridionalis petenyi*) and many others. The lesser-spotted, short-toed and golden eagle have been recorded in the region and the black woodpecker, dipper and ring ouzel are also found. Mammals are well represented and lucky visitors may spot wildcat, wild boar, wolf or otter.

Călimani National Park (pages 200–1) is in the northeast of Transylvania. A former volcano crater, 10km in diameter, huge expanses of different types of forest and a population of black grouse are the emblems for this important protected area. Sand lizards (*Lacerta agilis*) and smooth snakes (*Coronella austriaca*) are two of the reptiles that can be found here. Bear, wolf, red and roe deer and beech marten inhabit the forests of the park. Birds include the alpine accentor, black redstart and Tengmalm's owl.

What is really remarkable is that this rich and wild flora and fauna is equally and harmoniously distributed throughout the whole area. Interestingly, places that are not included in any protected areas are sometimes better than national or natural parks. For the forested areas, this is because there is less human activity. Most of the time there is almost no tourism at all, only seasonal sheep grazing and logging.

Background Information   NATURAL HISTORY AND CONSERVATION

1

13

THE BROWN BEAR

Extinct in the UK for centuries, the brown bear (*Ursus arctos*) exists only in tiny populations in western Europe. But Romania holds perhaps 6,000 brown bears, though population estimates are disputed, making it the largest community in Europe outside Russia. They live in the forests of the Carpathian and Apuseni Mountains, though they will seek out foraging opportunities in clearings and bogs. They are most active in the mornings and early evenings, resting during the remainder of the day, and cover large ranges.

Many of the local tour operators and accommodation providers in this guide offer bear watching or tracking excursions: Transylvanian Wolf at Zărneşti (pages 148–9) and the Mikes Estate at Zăbala (pages 168–9) are two with knowledgeable guides. Or you can get up close to bears at the Libearty Sanctuary, also in Zărneşti (page 148), a haven for bears that have been rescued from captivity.

But for others, bears have for hundreds of years meant an opportunity for hunting, and the trophy hunting of bears has been big business in Romania. There was much debate then when, in October 2016, the then Romanian Environment Minister announced that the trophy hunting of bears, wolves and lynx would not be allowed, criticising the methodology that had been used to establish the quotas. This relied on an exception to the protection for large carnivores afforded by the EU Habitats Directive in cases where the animals were a danger to humans or to private property. The problem was that the establishment of the populations of each carnivore in a specific area, and an assessment of how many were believed likely to cause damage, were carried out by hunting associations. Environmental groups argued that there was a clear conflict of interest here, fearing that the associations had every incentive to overstate the carnivore populations, and therefore secure a larger hunting quota. Even without any deliberate ill-intent, there was a risk of double counting, since brown bears roam widely, and so a single bear might be included in the tallies produced by several different associations.

The issue obviously pitches the hunting lobby against the environmental one, but also tends to pitch urban Romania against the villages. For while in Romania's cities the bears and wolves are seen as symbols of Romanian identity and pride, for many villagers they are a threat to livestock, crops and humans. This problem is becoming more acute as the natural habitats of brown bears are reduced, for example through deforestation, bringing hungry bears closer to human settlements. Bears have been known to raid the bins in the suburbs of cities like Braşov. In October 2016, a brown bear found wandering the streets of Sibiu in an agitated state was shot dead after attempts to tranquilise it reportedly failed. This is why environmental non-governmental organisations such as Fauna and Flora International are working hard to reduce the risks around human and bear interactions by trying to keep the two species as physically separate as possible. The focus of their activity is the Zarand landscape corridor in the northern part of Hunedoara County and neighbouring Arad County, which provides a habitat link between the brown bears of the Southern Carpathians and a smaller population in the Apuseni Mountains.

One example is the vast forests between the Piatra Craiului National Park and the Făgăraş Mountains, where there are no significant human settlements between the two mountain ranges, just the 'homes' of different wild animals and birds. Traditional farming methods result in lush hay-meadows and rich arable land.

Any stroll through the wonderful Transylvanian countryside can result in exciting sightings: impressive stork nests on top of chimneys; the unmistakable call of a corncrake from the grasses; and bear footprints right in the middle of a mountain village, especially in autumn when they come over for the ripe apples.

Also of note are the **47 IBAs** (Important Bird Areas) in Transylvania (there are 130 in Romania as a whole). They usually include a few different types of habitats, so although they are mainly interesting for their birdlife, sights of other interesting wildlife are almost guaranteed. For instance, the wetlands at Mândra or Rotbav in Braşov County offer potential sightings of beavers – a successful reintroduction programme was carried out in this area – besides the chance of spotting black stork, bee-eaters or little bittern.

The **Avrig-Scoreiu area** is a good place to find the corncrake, Syrian woodpecker or barred warbler. The Făgăraş Mountains (the Transylvanian Alps) are very close to this region and the fauna found here includes bear, wolf, chamois and marmot up or near the ridge.

The **Dealurile Homoroadelor** (Homorod Hills) cover different areas and habitats (wetlands, forests, meadows) in Mureş, Covasna, Harghita and Braşov counties. This area includes one of the best wetland areas in Transylvania and the birdlife found here includes bittern, lesser-spotted eagle and white-winged black tern.

Danuţ Marin has lived in Zărneşti (Braşov County) all his life. He left school when he was 14 to work in the local munitions factory. At the age of 30, he studied on a course to qualify as a wildlife guide and now works in the Piatra Craiului National Park. He and his wife Luminiţa run a guesthouse in Zărneşti (pages 147–9) where visitors can try traditional home cooking, stay in beautifully renovated rooms and explore the surrounding countryside under Dan's expert guidance. Since 2003, Dan has been heavily involved in the Rowan Romania Foundation (page 121) where he carries out cultural and social programmes for psychiatric hospital patients and Roma communities. As well as showing the country's mostly undiscovered wildlife gems and supporting ecotourism projects, he helps to open visitors' eyes to the realities of Romanian life.

ENVIRONMENTAL ISSUES The glorious natural environments of Transylvania, from its mountain forests to the high-value grasslands lower down, are the result of harmonious yet fragile interactions between humans and nature.

Illegal logging represents a major threat to the forests of the Carpathians. According to one environmental NGO, Agent Green, some 366,000ha of Romanian forest was lost to illegal logging between 1990 and 2011. A new forestry code was introduced in 2015, aiming to strengthen the hand of the authorities against illegal logging, but challenges persist.

The glorious meadows filled with wildflowers depend on traditional agricultural practices, such as scything the grass, and also depend on sufficient populations of grazing animals like sheep to keep back invasive species like ferns, which tend to reduce the biodiversity of the hillside. A major environmental challenge in this respect, counter-intuitive though it may sound, is **rural depopulation**. Traditional agriculture is labour-intensive, and for many young Romanians brought up in rural communities, the lure of the incomes that can be made by seeking work either in the cities or overseas is a powerful pull away from the hard life as a small farmer. Many

1

Romanian villages seem to be characterised these days mostly by the elderly and by their grandchildren, left with them while the children's parents are working overseas. Transylvania's natural environment suffered greatly under the communist regime, and particularly due to its dictator Ceaușescu's habit of foisting heavy industrial complexes on rural communities. Copșa Mică in Sibiu County (pages 229–30) is a particularly notorious example, and although the carbon black factory which covered everything in town with black powder has long closed, the town continues to grapple with the difficult legacy of **environmental pollution**. One of the most visually impressive castles in Romania, Corvin Castle, has as its neighbour a large steel plant. The exploitation of Transylvania's natural resources remains a controversial issue, best exemplified by the mobilisation of civil society groups following the announcement of plans to extract gold at Roșia Montană in Alba County with open-cast mining and the use of cyanide leach technology (see box, pages 272–3).

The built environment of Transylvania's traditional villages is also under threat. The programme of **'systematisation'** carried out by Communist leader Ceaușescu from 1974 was ostensibly aimed at bringing the advantages of urban living to the countryside. Larger villages were developed as industrial centres, with traditional buildings demolished and replaced by apartment blocks, and the inhabitants of smaller villages were encouraged to move to the larger ones. Following the Romanian Revolution, a different kind of challenge faced Transylvania's villages. The out-migration of ethnic Saxons, in particular to new homes in Germany, created problems of village abandonment and also of a changing rural social fabric, as in many cases poor Roma families moved into homes that had been abandoned. And **modernisation** presents an ongoing range of problems, as villagers are tempted to abandon traditional building techniques, opting for UPVC windows and metal-tiled roofs. Non-governmental organisations such as Monumentum, as well as HRH The Prince of Wales's Foundation Romania, are working to encourage the use of traditional techniques and materials, and to support the training of a new generation of craftsmen able to provide them.

Environmental contacts in Transylvania

Association of Ecotourism in Romania (AER) ☎+40 368 441 084; w eco-romania.ro. Organisation dedicated to developing & promoting ecotourism in Romania.

Centre for Mountain Ecology m +40 745 978 023; w cem.ro. Based in an attractive mountain area in Brașov County, close to the Bran Pass, the centre implements a range of environmental projects, including an attempt to develop the villages of Fundata & Moieciu de Sus as ecotourism destinations.

Fauna & Flora International ☎01223 571000; w fauna-flora.org. This UK-based environmental NGO is working in Romania to help preserve the Zarand landscape corridor through which large carnivores such as bears can move between the Apuseni & Carpathian mountains.

Focus Eco Center ☎+40 265 262 170; w focuseco.ro. Târgu Mureș-based environmental NGO promoting a range of environmental issues, including ecotourism.

Fundația ADEPT ☎+40 265 711 635; w fundatia-adept.org. Based in the historic village of Sasciz, this is a fine organisation promoting agricultural development & environmental protection in Transylvania (hence ADEPT). For more information on their work, see page 210.

Fundația Conservation Carpathia w carpathia.org. An initiative led by Christoph & Barbara Promberger, who run the Equus Silvania stables in Șinca Nouă, this aims to protect forested land around the Făgăraș Mountains by purchasing it, with the ultimate aim of developing a new national park in the area.

Kálnoky Foundation ☎+40 267 314 088; w kalnoky.org. Focuses on projects conserving the built environment & traditional landscapes in Covasna County.

Milvus Group ☎+40 265 264 726; w milvus.ro. A wildlife NGO based in Târgu Mureş, particularly focused on bird protection, including efforts to conserve the striking blue & orange European roller.

Pro Patrimonio Foundation m +40 731 862 541; w propatrimonio.org. Established in 2000 by the architect Şerban Cantacuzino, this aims to become Romania's equivalent to the UK's National Trust, helping to save & restore important buildings that form part of Romania's cultural heritage. Its projects include an effort to save 60 wooden churches that are at risk in the regions of northern Oltenia & southern Transylvania.

Romanian Environmental Partnership Foundation (REPF) ☎+40 266 310 678; w repf. ro. Based in Miercurea-Ciuc, the foundation supports community-based environmental improvement projects. It launched the **Transylvania Authentica** (w transylvania-authentica.ro) programme in 2007, focused on certification for businesses supporting the environment, heritage & culture of Transylvania.

The Mihai Eminescu Trust (MET) ☎+40 265 506 024; w www.mihaieminescutrust.org. Founded by Jessica Douglas-Home during the Communist era, initially to support dissident academics by smuggling in books & to oppose Ceauşescu's systematisation policies, the MET has helped to restore decaying traditional buildings across the Saxon areas of southern Transylvania, developing a 'whole village' concept which encourages the local villagers to engage with & support the work. Several of their restored properties are available as attractive tourist accommodation (page 233).

The Prince of Wales's Foundation Romania m +40 720 319 365; w printuldewales.org. Established by HRH The Prince of Wales to take forward his charitable work in Romania, including through the provision of training programmes in traditional skills at a centre in the village of Viscri (pages 157–8).

WWF Romania ☎+40 21 317 4996; w wwf. ro. Since its establishment in 2006, the Romanian branch of the major international wildlife NGO has focused on the Danube River & Carpathian Mountains, including tackling illegal logging & a project in conjunction with Rewilding Europe to reintroduce the European bison to Romania.

HISTORY

The name Transylvania derives from the Latin, meaning 'beyond the forest'. The earliest known documentary reference to this name comes from a medieval Latin document in 1075, which refers to the region as Ultra Silvam, 'ultra' being an alternative Latin prepositional prefix to 'trans'. The region has the distinction of being the only part of modern-day Romania referenced by Shakespeare: there is a passing reference to a recently deceased 'poor Transylvanian' in *Pericles*. The Hungarian name for the region, Erdély, also highlights the region's forested nature (*Erdő* is the Hungarian for 'forest').

The German name for the region, Siebenbürgen, meaning 'seven fortresses', has an entirely different root, and refers, it is usually argued, to seven Saxon-built cities in Transylvania. It is remarkably difficult to establish an agreed list of exactly which seven cities the term refers to. Pope Pius II set out the following list, which is the one most frequently quoted nowadays: Braşov (Kronstadt), Sighişoara (Schassburg), Mediaş (Mediasch), Sibiu (Hermannstadt), Sebeş (Mühlbach), Bistriţa (Bistritz) and Cluj-Napoca (Klausenburg). But many scholars argue that he was simply setting out the seven most important Saxon cities of the region at the time, not at the earlier point at which the term Siebenbürgen originated. And some even argue that the name may not originally have referred to seven cities at all, but was derived from an earlier name for Sibiu: Cibinium. Cibinium, the argument goes, was also sometimes referred to as Cibinburg, and from Cibinburg it is not so very far to Siebenbürgen.

In Romanian the region is known both as Transilvania and Ardeal, whose first known written mention is as 'Ardeliu' in a 1432 document.

THE ORIGINS OF THE ROMANIANS

There is much historical debate surrounding the origins of the Romanian people. The debate is highly politicised, with particularly strong arguments between Romanian and Hungarian historians because of the perceived political pertinence to the question of whether territories such as Transylvania were inhabited by ethnic Romanians from antiquity, or whether ethnic Romanians developed elsewhere, and migrated into the region.

The **immigration theory**, favoured by Hungarian historians, was developed amongst others by the Austrian historian Robert Roesler, writing in 1871. Historians supporting these theories tend to argue that the territories north of the Danube were depopulated following the Roman retreat in AD271. They argue that the Romans ruled Dacia for a period of only 165 years, from AD106 to AD271, and nowhere is it clear that the extent of Romanisation of the local people was particularly high during this period. It therefore seems strange, they argue, to conclude, as do the proponents of the continuity theory, that a Latin-speaking people, the successor of the Romans, survived north of the Danube but not south of it, where the duration of Roman colonisation was much longer. And they point in particular to the lack of very much in the way of evidence, written or archaeological, of a proto-Romanian people north of the Danube for a full millennium after the Romanian withdrawal. They argue instead that the Romanians were the descendants of Romanised peoples living south of the Danube, from areas which were under Roman rule for more than five centuries. And they point to a number of linguistic similarities between the Romanian and Albanian languages which suggest that the two peoples were once close neighbours. They argue that these proto-Romanians migrated north into the area of present-day Romania after the Hungarians had conquered the region, whether as shepherds or to serve as border guards on the southern frontier of the Hungarian Kingdom.

Romanian historians tend to favour the **Daco-Roman continuity theory**, that the Romanians are the descendants of Latin-speaking Dacian peasants who remained in Transylvania after the Roman exodus. Neagu Djuvara, in his *Brief Illustrated History of Romanians*, argues that the documentary silence about a proto-Romanian people north of the Danube might be explained by the abandonment of urban life following the Roman withdrawal and a regression to a more rural existence. The 'borrowed' words from Albanian amount to just a few dozen and might be explained, he concludes, from a common Indo-European origin of the languages. And he argues that Hungarian historians deliberately underplay the importance of a document which strengthens the continuity case: a chronicle written by a clerk of King Béla of Hungary which records that when the Hungarians first invaded Transylvania from the west they encountered three voievodships inhabited by Romanians and Slavs.

The Daco-Roman ancestry of the Romanian people is celebrated in the city of Deva by statues of Roman Emperor Trajan and Dacian leader Decebal in its central squares: the continuity theory worked into stone.

The history of Transylvania is a complex interplay of peoples, some settled, some migratory, some invading, of the territorial ambitions of large empires, whether Roman, Habsburg or Ottoman, as well as the rival scheming of local princes, and of the gradual development of political consciousness among the Romanian people, who were for several centuries excluded from major decisions affecting the region, which now forms a part of the state of Romania.

Transylvania was part of the Kingdom of Dacia in Antiquity, conquered by the Romans, crossed and settled by various migratory tribes, before being conquered by Hungary, and then a semi-independent state, the Principality of Transylvania, under the Ottoman Empire. In 1711, it fell under the control of the Habsburgs, and then in 1867 the Austro-Hungarian Empire. Following the peace settlement at the end of World War I it became part of Romania. Cluj-Napoca is considered by many to be the region's capital, although various other places have some claim to that title, with princely rulers, Habsburg governors and meetings of the Transylvanian Diet all having been associated with various cities. Alba Iulia is a city particularly close to the heart of ethnic Romanians, as the place where, in 1599, Michael the Brave became Voievode of Transylvania. Following his securing control of Moldavia the following year, he brought together the three principalities of Moldavia, Wallachia and Transylvania for a brief period. They would not be together again until the end of World War I, and it was again at Alba Iulia, on 1 December 1918, that the union of Transylvania with Romania was proclaimed.

ANCIENT HISTORY Man first appeared in the territory that we now call 'Transylvania' during the Pleistocene epoch. During the Neolithic period, the area was settled by migrating communities from the south and east, who brought with them the shift to a way of life focused on agriculture and the breeding of animals.

Around 2000BC, the Geto-Dacians appeared in Transylvania. The terms Getae and Dacians seem to have been largely interchangeable, although Getae was used more frequently in Ancient Greek writings, and Daci in Roman ones, and Romanian historian Neagu Djuvara argues that the term Dacians was used more widely for those living in Transylvania; Getae for those who settled further south and east, in Wallachia and Bessarabia. Ancient historians considered the Geto-Dacians to be Thracian tribes, but this is disputed by many Romanian historians, who view them as distinctive, and separate. Djuvara, for example, argues that the Geto-Dacians appear to have worshipped only one god, Zalmoxis, in contrast to the numerous deities favoured by the Thracians, and that their languages were different.

The Geto-Dacians were briefly united in the 1st century BC under **King Burebista**, a hero figure for many Romanians, who consider him the first to have united the ancestors of the Romanian people. Burebista moved the capital of the Dacian kingdom to Sarmizegetusa Regia, establishing a system of defensive citadels around it. He was assassinated in AD44, after which the united empire he had built was dissipated again into smaller kingdoms.

The other Dacian king whose name is known by every Romanian today is **Decebal**, who again led a united Dacian kingdom, from AD87, and was indeed to be the last king of Dacia. He was a shrewd military leader, and secured an annual tribute from Roman Emperor Domitian in return for maintaining peace with the Roman province of Moesia, south of the Danube. Domitian's successor, **Trajan**, resented the tribute and crossed the Danube into Dacia in AD101, defeating Decebal in the First Dacian War. Decebal immediately violated the peace treaty, and Trajan invaded again, in the Second Dacian War, conquering the fortress at Sarmizegetusa in AD106. Decebal escaped but, cornered by the Romans, he committed suicide by slashing his own throat. Trajan ensured that the memory of his great campaign in Dacia would be preserved by committing it to stone: the frieze around Trajan's Column in Rome is a detailed chronicle of the entire campaign, depicted of course firmly from the Roman perspective.

For Romanians today, Decebal and Trajan are often depicted as paired founding figures of national identity, as a fusion of the Dacian people and the Latin values brought from Rome.

THE ROMAN EMPIRE Following his conquest of the Kingdom of Dacia, Trajan established the imperial Roman province of Dacia, also sometimes referred to as Dacia Traiana or Dacia Felix. The Romans set about the colonisation of the province, establishing cities such as Apulum (present-day Alba Iulia) and Napoca (Cluj-Napoca). In Transylvania today, those cities which were established by the Romans are usually distinguished by the presence of a Rome-style statue of Romulus and Remus being suckled by the she-wolf. The capital of Roman Dacia was Colonia Ulpia Traiana Augusta Dacica Sarmizegetusa, taking part of its long name from the old Dacian capital, though confusingly located at a different place (pages 255–6). Dacia was particularly important for the Romanian economy because of its gold, mined in the Apuseni Mountains. The Roman galleries at Roșia Montană can still be visited (pages 272–3). Agriculture and cattle rearing were also important, and colonists arrived from other Roman provinces.

However, the province of Dacia was vulnerable to attack, including from various tribes of Goths, and from those Free Dacians who had remained outside the Roman Empire, and in AD271 Emperor Aurelian took the decision to abandon the province, evacuating the Roman population to the new province of Dacia Aureliana south of the Danube.

THE AGE OF THE GREAT MIGRATIONS Following the Roman withdrawal, a Gothic tribe known as the Thervingi settled in southern Transylvania. But the next few hundred years were characterised by waves of migrations: of Goths, Huns, Gepids, Avars, Slavs, Bulgars and Pechenegs, the new arrivals characteristically securing military success against the established populations before being defeated in turn by the next wave of migratory peoples. Much of the sophisticated economic activity of the Roman period, such as gold mining, simply ceased. It is likely that in the 9th century, following the demise of the Avars and before the arrival of the Magyars and Pechenegs, Transylvania formed part of the First Bulgarian Empire. Neagu Djuvara argues that it was from this period that the people of modern-day Romania first acquired the Cyrillic alphabet, which was in use in Romania until the 19th century. Modern-day traces of the occupation of the former Dacia by most of these tribes are few, but the same cannot be said of the next wave of migratory peoples to arrive in Transylvania: the Magyars.

THE ARRIVAL OF THE MAGYARS AND SAXONS The Magyars settled on the Pannonian Plain towards the end of the 9th century, and gradually conquered Transylvania from around AD900. **Stephen I**, who ruled as the first King of Hungary for the long period from 1000 until 1038, having outlived all of his children, encouraged the spread of Christianity and was later made a Catholic saint.

In Transylvania, the Hungarian Kingdom found that its newly conquered territory was under constant threat of attack from first Pecheneg and later Cuman tribes. The measure that successive kings of Hungary adopted to counter this threat was to have enormous significance for the ethnic composition and cultural history of Transylvania, and has done much to shape the character of the modern region of Transylvania. They encouraged the colonisation of Székely people (see box, page 180) to guard the frontier areas of the Eastern Carpathians, and in the southern part of Transylvania encouraged for the same purpose the colonisation of Germans, initially from the Rhine and Mosel regions, who came to be known, not entirely accurately, as 'Saxons'.

In the early 12th century, King Andrew II of Hungary invited the **Teutonic Knights** into the area known as the Burzenland, around the present-day city of Braşov, to protect the area from attacks by Cumans. But the Knights proved too independent-minded for the Hungarians' liking, and were expelled in 1225.

In what would be another recurring theme of Transylvanian history, the region suffered hugely during the Mongol invasion of 1241, provoking a population decline variously estimated as between 15% and 50%. The Mongols suddenly retreated the next year, on the news of the death of their Great Khan, Ögedei Khan. This allowed the Hungarian king, **Béla IV**, some breathing space in which he brought in more colonists, allowed trusted nobles to build fortresses and establish private armies, and introduced a range of other reforms, all with the aim of strengthening the kingdom before the Mongols returned. For this reason Hungarians often regard Béla IV as the 'second founder' of the state, after Stephen I.

The administration of Transylvania at that time was carried out by a *voievode* appointed by the Hungarian king. The Hungarian aristocracy was the most privileged class, but the Saxons also had a range of privileges that had been granted to them by a charter issued by King Andrew II in 1224. The privileges accorded to the Székely and Romanian communities were weaker.

THE OTTOMANS AND THEIR ADVERSARIES In the 14th century, the Ottoman Turks expanded their empire from Anatolia to the Balkans. They crossed into Europe around 1354 and crushed the Serbs on the Kosovo Field in 1389, effectively marking the end of Serbian power in the region. Constantinople was conquered in 1453, and the Ottomans continued to expand. This expansion would see the present-day Romanian regions of Wallachia and Moldavia falling under the sway of the Ottoman Empire and paying tribute to it for protracted periods.

Through this era the fortunes of Wallachia, Moldavia and Transylvania ebbed and flowed according to the complex interplay between the fortunes and ambitions of local leaders and the Ottoman Empire. The careers of four of the best-known leaders of these territories illustrate the point.

In Wallachia, **Mircea the Elder** (Mircea cel Bătrân) ushered in relative stability and brought Wallachia to its greatest geographical extent, defeated the Ottomans at the Battle of Rovine in 1394, but ended his reign by signing a treaty with the Ottomans, avoiding the incorporation of Wallachia into the Ottoman Empire in return for a tribute.

Moldavia's most celebrated ruler was **Stephen the Great**, who was *voievode* (prince) from 1457 until 1504, in a reign which saw him frequently at war against various adversaries. It is for his campaigns against the Ottomans, however, that he is most celebrated. He initially paid the yearly tribute to the Ottoman Empire, but abruptly stopped doing so in 1473, invading Wallachia, whose *voievode*, Radu the Fair, was close to the Ottomans. In the ensuing war with the Ottomans, Stephen secured a great victory at the Battle of Vaslui, but while he received praise among European leaders and Pope Sixtus IV as a great defender of Christianity, they gave him little practical support in his efforts to press home his advantage against the Ottomans. Further fighting with the Ottomans resulted in the loss of Moldavia's seaports of Chilia and Cetatea Albă, and Stephen the Great ended his rule, as had Mircea the Elder in Wallachia a century before, by paying tribute to the Ottomans in return for the relative autonomy and religious freedom that the Turks allowed them, and in recognition of the fact that real help from the Christian powers to the west was often slow to materialise.

Another Wallachian ruler whose name still resonates today is **Vlad the Impaler**, a grandson of Mircea the Elder, who was three times *voievode* in the 15th century, and whose campaigns against the Ottomans mean that his name continues to be regarded positively by many Romanians, notwithstanding the stories of his cruelty which were to lead the writer Bram Stoker to use him as an inspiration for the character of Count Dracula (see box, pages 208–9).

One of the most celebrated political figures in Transylvania in this period was **John Hunyadi** (see box, pages 250–1), a protégé of the Hungarian King Sigismund of Luxembourg, whose victory against the Ottomans in the defence of Belgrade in 1456 is still celebrated by the noonday ringing of the bells of Catholic churches. His son, **Matthias Corvinus**, became an admired king of Hungary, who embraced the Renaissance and brought it to the region.

PEASANT REVOLTS In parallel with the military conflicts between the Kingdom of Hungary and the Ottoman Empire, a series of peasant revolts in Transylvania were also significant in the course of the region's history. They had their roots in the social structure of Transylvania under the Hungarian kings, in which rights and privileges were largely held by the Hungarian nobility, the Saxons and the Székelys, but in which the condition of poor peasants, both Romanian and Hungarian, was increasingly difficult, and being made progressively worse by the numerous wars against the Ottomans.

The first of these rebellions was the **Bobâlna Revolt** of 1437. Led by a poor nobleman named Antal Nagy de Buda, the revolt was precipitated by tax arrears demanded of the peasantry by the Bishop of Transylvania, and involved both Hungarian and Romanian peasants who demanded rights through the creation of an Estate of Hungarians and Romanians. The rebels resisted for several months at a fortified encampment at Bobâlna, in present-day Cluj County, but were eventually defeated. Antal Nagy de Buda died on the battlefield, and the other leaders of the revolt were executed at Turda.

The main outcome of the revolt was to further worsen the political situation of the Romanian and Hungarian peasantry. In 1438, a formal alliance was established between the Hungarian nobles, the Saxons and the Székelys, known as the **Union of Three Nations** (*Unio Trio Nationum*), which treated these three groups as privileged social categories, who each pledged to defend their privileges against any power except that of Hungary's king. This was to form a central tenet of the political governance of Transylvania for centuries. The Romanians were excluded from it, and treated as politically insignificant, despite being the largest group of all in population terms.

There was a further peasant revolt in 1514, led by **György Dózsa** (known as Gheorghe Doja in Romanian), a Székely mercenary who had been initially appointed by Hungarian Cardinal Tamás Bakócz to help lead a crusade against the Ottomans, but ended up heading a peasant revolt. It was put down by an army led by the Voievode of Transylvania, John Zápolya, and Dósza put to death in a particularly brutal way by being seated on a red-hot throne, wearing a heated crown, in a show of mockery of his presumed ambitions to be king. There is more about the revolt in the box on page 167. Its two main consequences lay first in the elaboration of a new set of laws, the *Tripartitum*, by the Hungarian jurist Stephen Werbőczy, which greatly strengthened the status of the nobility and consolidated the subordination of the peasantry, and second, a weakening of Hungarian social unity which would greatly ease the task of the Ottomans when they prepared to invade in 1526.

TRANSYLVANIA UNDER OTTOMAN CONTROL The Ottomans under Suleiman the Magnificent stormed Belgrade in 1521 and thrashed a weak Hungarian army at Mohács in 1526, a battle in which the Hungarian king, Louis II, was killed. There

In many cities and towns in Transylvania, one of the major squares is dominated by a statue of Michael the Brave (1558–1601), known in Romanian as Mihai Viteazul, who is celebrated by Romanian historians and politicians as the first leader to have brought together the crowns of Transylvania, Wallachia and Moldavia, the three major regions that make up the modern-day state of Romania. As such, he is considered as a harbinger of Romanian unity. He may have been an illegitimate son of the Wallachian leader Pătrașcu the Good, but more important to his subsequent rapid rise was the influence in Constantinople of his mother's wealthy family, which helped him to secure Ottoman support for his accession to the throne of Wallachia in 1593. Michael almost immediately turned against the very people who had helped him to the throne, and started a campaign against the Turks. This continued until 1599, with many successes on Michael's side, but he lacked both the resources and external support to continue fighting the Ottomans indefinitely, and signed a peace treaty.

At this point a certain amount of chaos was ensuing in Transylvania, which had much to do with the fickle nature of the Transylvanian prince, Sigismund Báthory. In 1598, he decided to abdicate in favour of the Holy Roman Emperor, Rudolf II, who had agreed to reward him handsomely for stepping down. He then reneged on this decision, deciding to stand down instead in favour of his cousin, Cardinal Andrew Báthory. The latter was close to the Poles, who maintained friendly relations with the Ottomans, and Michael feared that he was being surrounded by hostile neighbours. He responded to the new threat by deciding to go straight on the offensive against Andrew Báthory's forces, with the assent of Rudolf II. He won a decisive victory at the Battle of Şelimbăr, close to Sibiu, in 1599, in the wake of which Andrew Báthory was beheaded by Michael's Székely allies. Michael then triumphantly entered the fortress of Alba Iulia, and was elected by the Transylvanian nobles as the Prince of Transylvania. He asked the Transylvanian estates to swear loyalty first to Emperor Rudolf, then to himself.

Michael then turned his attention to Moldavia, whose prince, Ieremia Movilă, was an old adversary, and whose brother Simion held out claims to Michael's Wallachian throne. He attacked Moldavia in April 1600, and for a few short months ruled all three provinces, minting coins that proclaimed him to be the Voievode of Wallachia, Transylvania and Moldavia. But he had overreached himself, and was quickly to lose all three crowns. In Transylvania the Hungarian nobility rebelled against Michael and, with the support of Austrian general Giorgio Basta, defeated him at the Battle of Mirăslău. A Polish army removed his forces from Moldavia, and in Wallachia the Poles helped install Simion Movilă as ruler.

With the assistance of Emperor Rudolf II, who was worried about the return of Sigismund Báthory to Transylvania, Michael managed something of a late comeback, defeating Báthory's army at the Battle of Guruslău, in alliance with Giorgio Basta. But Basta, who had his own ambitions, once again turned against Michael and organised his assassination in 1601. Historians are divided over whether Rudolf II may have had a hand in ordering the deed.

Background Information HISTORY

1

were two candidates to succeed him: John Zápolya, the Voievode of Transylvania, and the man who had put down the Dósza revolt so brutally, and Archduke Ferdinand of Austria, who claimed Hungary for the Habsburgs. The Habsburg case was that they could help the country stand up to the Ottomans, but the Hungarian elite sided with Zápolya, even at the cost of the country becoming virtually an Ottoman vassal. On Zápolya's death, Suleiman again invaded Hungary, taking its capital, Buda, in 1541. Hungary was divided, and would remain so for the next 150 years, with the west under Habsburg rule, the Banat and parts of central Hungary administered directly by the Ottomans, and Transylvania an autonomous principality, paying a tribute to the Ottomans, like the *voievodes* in Wallachia and Moldavia.

Although Transylvania was a vassal state of the Ottoman Porte, this period was one of relative autonomy for the region, and local *voivodes* governed Transylvania from 1540 to 1690. A parliament-like body, the Transylvanian Diet, made up of the three privileged nations of Hungarian nobility, Székelys and Saxons, decided on a range of legal and economic issues, with its sessions at Târgu Mureș and Turda at the start of 1542 establishing the basis for the administrative organisation of the principality.

While many of the *voievodes* of Transylvania were unexceptional, others left a stronger imprint on history. They include **Stephen Báthory**, who was Voievode of Transylvania from 1571 to 1586, and also for ten years the King of Poland, for which his claim had rested on his betrothal to the Polish Queen Anna Jagiellon. He is celebrated for a victorious campaign against Russia. Another such figure was **Michael the Brave**, known in Romanian as Mihai Viteazul, a figure revered in Romania as the first leader since ancient times to unite the principalities of Transylvania, Moldavia and Wallachia, albeit briefly (see box, page 23).

THE REFORMATION A further development of this period which would have a huge significance for the history of Transylvania was the Protestant Reformation, which spread rapidly in the area in the 16th century. It was greatly helped in this by the weakened position of the Catholic Church in Hungary, following the defeat at the Battle of Mohács. There was a strong ethnic dimension to the Reformation in Transylvania, in which Transylvania's Saxons adopted Lutheranism, and many Hungarians converted to Reformism. Many Székelys remained Catholic, though others also converted to Reformism. But the Romanians largely remained faithful to their Orthodox religion.

An interesting early attempt to guarantee a certain degree of religious freedom was the Edict of Turda of 1568, during a meeting of the Transylvanian Diet in that town. John Sigismund Zápolya, the Transylvanian ruler, had become perhaps the only monarch in history to adopt the Unitarian religion, through the influence of Ferenc Dávid, the founder of the Unitarian Church of Transylvania. Dávid was instrumental in encouraging Zápolya to issue a proclamation which allowed for a considerable degree of religious toleration, though largely encompassing only the Roman Catholic, Lutheran, Reformist and Unitarian faiths. Other groups, such as the Orthodox Romanians and the Jews, were given no specific legal guarantees.

The influence of the edict was considerable, and Transylvania was frequently regarded as a region of relatively high religious freedom, for example during the rule of Gabriel Bethlen as Prince of Transylvania from 1613 to 1629, himself a member of the Reformed Church. But in the shorter term there was a backlash against it. Dávid was accused of heresy and died in prison as the Catholic Church reasserted itself, and after the assassination of Michael the Brave in 1601 Giorgio Basta launched a reign of terror aimed at reclaiming Transylvania for Catholicism.

17TH-CENTURY STRUGGLES During much of the 17th century Transylvania was caught between the struggle for power between the Ottoman and the Habsburg empires, and by the end of the century its dominance by the Ottoman Empire was to be replaced by that of the Habsburgs. At the start of the century, the difficult years of Basta's control, in which he persecuted the Protestants and promoted the interests of Catholicism and Austria, were ended by the Reformist **Stephen Bocksai**, who rose up against Rudolf II and Basta with the help of the Turks, and who was elected Prince of Transylvania in 1605. Bocksai died the following year. Subsequent rulers were both good and bad. The latter category included **Gabriel Báthory**, whose tyrannical reign as Prince of Transylvania lasted from 1608 to 1613, but following his murder the Ottomans installed one of Transylvania's most impressive princes of all, **Gabriel Bethlen**, who ruled from 1613 to 1629. His rule was marked by the economic development of Transylvania, as well as the encouragement of education, including the founding in 1622 of the Bethlen Gábor College, now in Aiud, and promoting the teaching of the children of serfs. He sent troops to fight on the Protestant side in the Thirty Years' War, while supporting religious tolerance at home. The relative golden age in Transylvania initiated during the reign of Gabriel Bethlen continued under **George I Rákóczi**, who served as Prince of Transylvania from 1630 until 1648, during which period the principality secured its greatest degree of autonomy. Transylvania became a stronghold of Protestantism, but both Bethlen and Rákóczi also promoted a high degree of religious tolerance, at least between the four officially accepted religions of Roman Catholicism, Reformism, Lutheranism and Unitarianism. He was succeeded by his son, **George II Rákóczi**, whose rule was dominated by an ill-fated attack on Poland, which led to Turkish attempts to depose him for undertaking an unauthorised war, and finally to the Turkish invasion of Transylvania. Rákóczi died in 1660 from wounds received in battle.

TRANSYLVANIA UNDER THE HABSBURGS In 1683, John Sobieski's Polish army defeated an Ottoman army besieging Vienna, and Christian forces began to drive the Turks from Europe. The Austro-Ottoman War of 1683–97 culminated in the resounding defeat of the Ottomans at the Battle of Zenta, and at the subsequent Treaty of Karlowitz in 1699, Transylvania passed from Ottoman to Austrian control. The Transylvanian Diet had already voted to accept Habsburg protection 11 years earlier. The Habsburgs began to impose their rule on a Transylvania which under the Ottomans had enjoyed a high degree of autonomy. The staunchly Catholic Emperor Leopold I was particularly keen to re-establish a Catholic majority in the province, but the Austrians were unable to make a full-frontal attack on the beliefs of the privileged Saxons and Székelys. They focused instead on the Romanian Orthodox Church, whose Metropolitan archbishop in Transylvania, Atanasie Anghel, entered into full communion with the Holy See under the 1698 Act of Union. This created the new Greco-Catholic Church, also sometimes referred to as the Uniate church, which retained the Byzantine rite while accepting some key points of Catholic doctrine, notably the supreme authority of the Pope. Encouraged by Romanian Orthodox Wallachia and Moldavia, some Orthodox communities refused to remain with the Greco-Catholic Church, and suffered great persecution at the hands of the Austrians for their actions.

THE HABSBURGS ASSERT THEIR CONTROL Tensions quickly developed in Transylvania between the new Catholic overlords, the Habsburgs, and the mainly Protestant Hungarian nobility. These culminated in the uprising of 1703–11 of **Francis II Rákóczi** against the Habsburgs. Rákóczi was a wealthy Hungarian landowner who took up the cause of Hungarian independence in alliance with France, which was fighting Austria in the War of Spanish Succession. But Rákóczi's uprising secured only limited support from the Hungarian nobility, though it was backed by the Székelys. Facing defeat, Rákóczi fled for Poland in 1711 and the Hungarian nobility made peace with the Habsburgs. Rákóczi spent the last 18 years of his life in exile in the Turkish town of Tekirdağ.

The Treaty of Szatmár in 1711 formally ended the uprising, and while the Austrian Emperor undertook to preserve the Transylvanian estates, Habsburg control was strengthened over Transylvania. The Transylvanian princes were henceforth replaced by governors appointed by Vienna, and in 1765 the Grand Principality of Transylvania was established. From the 1730s Austrian Protestant groups known as Landler were settled in southern Transylvania, as exiles from the Catholic heartland of the Empire.

THE REIGN OF JOSEPH II (1780–90) Joseph II, the eldest son of Emperor Maria Theresa, was Holy Roman Emperor between 1765 and 1790, and ruler of the

Habsburg lands, including Transylvania, for the shorter period of 1780–90, having been made a co-regent by his mother from the time of his father's death in 1765 until her own demise in 1780. As a monarch he was associated with a Reformist policy of enlightened absolutism, enthusiastically developing the measures of emancipation of the peasantry started by his mother, promoting education and reducing the powers of the Church: all measures at the heart of the Enlightenment philosophy of the age. In 1781, he moved to abolish serfdom.

But as so often in history, measures of reform prompted discontent, both from those who opposed the reforms and those who felt that they did not go far or fast enough. In Transylvania, the continuing dreadful situation of the Romanian peasantry underlay the **Revolt of Horea, Cloşca and Crişan** in 1784, centred on the Apuseni Mountains (box, page 280). The revolt was put down by the Austrian army, and its leaders captured. Crişan hanged himself in his cell on the eve of his execution, sparing himself the execution by breaking wheel that was the fate of Horea and Cloşca.

Most of Joseph's actions in the wake of the revolt, including the dissolution of the Union of Three Nations, making German the official language, and the tax burdens which accompanied the emancipation of the serfs, ended up generating further discontent, and Joseph was to reverse many of his reforms.

In developments that were to prove defining for the political development of Transylvania over the decades to come, the Hungarians reacted to the germanising policies of the Habsburgs by appeals for the unification of Transylvania and Hungary, while the ethnic Romanians, alarmed at both germanisation and magyarisation, began to assert the rights of their hitherto marginalised community. Two petitions, known as the **Supplex Libellus Valachorum**, were sent in 1791 by the Greco-Catholic Bishop of Blaj and the Romanian Orthodox Bishop of Transylvania to Joseph's successor, Leopold II. They demanded for ethnic Romanians equal political rights with the other ethnic communities, including a fair share of the seats in the Transylvanian Diet. Their demands were rejected. Another petition sent a century later, the Transylvanian Memorandum of 1892, met with exactly the same response, and indeed its authors received prison sentences for incitement.

THE EARLY 19TH CENTURY Leopold ruled for less than two years before his death in 1792 at the age of 44. He was succeeded by his son Ferenc II, who as the last Holy Roman Emperor and first Emperor of Austria was later referred to as history's first and possibly only *Doppelkaiser*, or double emperor. The early part of his reign was dominated by war with Napoleon's France, and in his fear of liberal and nationalist movements came to be viewed as a reactionary monarch. He attempted to quash dissent through networks of spies and press censorship, and in both Hungary and Transylvania by simply failing to convene meetings of the Diet, which did not meet for 23 years. As soon as it did, the issue of language resurfaced, with resolutions of both the Hungarian and Transylvanian diets making Hungarian the official language.

THE 1848 REVOLUTION 1848 was a year of revolutions across Europe, and Transylvania would be no exception. In March of that year the Hungarian Diet introduced a collection of new laws, the April Laws, which aimed both to modernise the Kingdom of Hungary, including the abolition of serfdom, religious liberty and the right to public meeting, and to increase the degree of Hungarian control. The laws also proposed the reincorporation of Transylvania into Hungary. Ethnic Romanians in Transylvania, concerned that the liberal Hungarian revolutionaries were showing scant regard for the interests of the Romanian community, and concerned at the prospect of the incorporation of Transylvania with Hungary, which would leave them a minority group in the combined state, organised national assemblies in the town of Blaj in May and September of that year, and pushed an end to the discrimination against the Romanian community and its proportional representation in the Transylvanian Diet. As war broke out, the Romanians allied with the Austrians against the Hungarian revolutionaries, hoping that their loyalty to Austria would be rewarded with the granting of rights of equality. The Hungarians, under the command of Polish general Józef Bem, took the early victories, with the Romanians under Avram Iancu (see box, page 275) conducting guerrilla warfare from the fastnesses of the Apuseni Mountains, but after the Russians joined the war on the side of the Austrians the tide turned. An attempt by the Hungarians to come to a deal with the Romanians was too late, and too half-hearted. Following Bem's defeat at the Battle of Timişoara, the Hungarians surrendered. But victory did not secure for the Romanians anything like all that they had wished for: the Austrians were wary of bolstering the Romanian cause in a way that might fuel the risks of separatism.

UNIFICATION OF TRANSYLVANIA AND HUNGARY Following the defeat of the revolutionaries, Austria imposed a direct rule by military governor on Transylvania, used German as the official language, granted citizenship to Romanians and abolished the longstanding structure of the Union of the Three Nations. In an 1863 session of the Transylvanian Diet which was boycotted by the Hungarian deputies, because they argued that Emperor Franz Joseph I had not convened it in accordance with the rules, and in which Germans and Romanians made up the majority for the first time, laws were passed which allowed Transylvania's Romanians finally to take up their place as the fourth nation of the region, alongside the Hungarians, Székelys and Saxons. The Romanian Orthodox Church was also accorded increased rights. Among the Hungarians of Transylvania, anti-Habsburg feelings strengthened in response to policies which they perceived as targeted at them.

But problems elsewhere in the Empire were about to provoke a reversal of the Hungarians' fortunes. The Austrians had been on the losing side in the Second Italian War of Independence in 1859, and were again soundly defeated in the Austro-Prussian War of 1866, resulting in Prussian dominance over the German states at Austrian expense. The Austrian Empire was weakened and in debt. The Habsburgs realised that in order to save the Empire, they would have to come to a compromise with the Hungarians, where there were increasingly strong sentiments in favour of full independence. The **Austro-Hungarian Compromise** of 1867 was negotiated by Hungarian politician Ferenc Deák. It established the dual monarchy of Austria-Hungary, between the Austrian Empire and a Kingdom of Hungary that was no longer subject to it. There were separate parliaments, in Vienna and Budapest, and separate legal and judicial systems. The Austrian Emperor was separately crowned as King of Hungary. The Compromise meant an end to the special status of Transylvania, which simply became a province of Hungary. This was viewed as a disaster by the Romanians of Transylvania, who became a minority group in the wider Kingdom of Hungary, subject to the magyarising policies of Budapest.

ROMANIA UNDER CAROL I We now need to turn to events south and east of the Carpathians, where Romania had been created in 1859 as a personal union between Moldavia and Wallachia by virtue of both electing the same ruler: Alexandru Ioan Cuza. However, Cuza's rule soon ran into difficulties when his modernising reforms, especially in relation to land, faced opposition from major landowners, and a scandal around his extra-marital activities added to discontent. He was forced to abdicate in 1866, and the Romanian Liberal Party leader, Ion Brătianu, following a suggestion by Napoleon III of France, led the negotiations, which resulted in Prince Karl of Hohenzollern-Sigmaringen being invited to take the Romanian throne as **Carol I**. Carol did much to help modernise Romania, though he was no liberal reformer, and inequalities around access to land were at the root of a major revolt of the Romanian peasantry in 1907.

Carol was also extremely attached to his German roots, as a visit to his decidedly Germanic summer residence of Peleş Castle (pages 137–8) will quickly testify. As the alliances and alignments between Europe's great powers took shape in the years before World War I, Carol was keen to anchor Romania to Germany, and had concluded a secret treaty in 1883 with the Triple Alliance of Germany, Austria-Hungary and Italy, which also came in the wake of Russia's seizing of Bessarabia in 1878: the latest episode in a longstanding rankle between Romania and Russia. But during the same period in Transylvania, Romanian nationalist sentiment was building in the face of attempts at magyarisation by the Hungarians, and Romanian public opinion south of the Carpathians was hostile to Hungary.

WORLD WAR I On 28 June 1914, a Bosnian Serb called Gavrilo Princip assassinated **Archduke Franz Ferdinand**, the heir to the Austro-Hungarian throne, and his wife Sophie. The immediate reaction of the Romanians of Transylvania was to regard this event as a bitter blow, as they had held high hopes of Franz Ferdinand's apparent desire to grant greater autonomy to minority ethnic groups in the Empire. But the assassination had much wider consequences, as it set in motion a chain of events leading to the outbreak of war in Europe.

This put Romania in a difficult position. Carol favoured entering the war on the side of Germany and the central powers, but the Romanian public, hostile to Hungary, favoured the Entente powers of Britain, France and Russia. Romania initially remained neutral. The death of King Carol in October 1914 brought to the Romanian throne King Ferdinand whose wife, Queen Marie (see box, pages 146–7), was closely related to both the British and Russian royal families. Thanks to Marie's influence, Ferdinand was less implacably imposed to entering the war on the side of the Entente than Carol had been, and with designs on the Romanian-majority territories in Transylvania, Romania entered the war on the side of the Entente in 1916. The war was to prove a difficult one for Romania, with many casualties. Bucharest fell, and the government and court had to relocate to the main Moldavian city of Iaşi. They secured some notable victories in 1917 on the Eastern Carpathian front at Mărăşti and Mărăşeşti in the region of Moldavia, but the Russian Revolution left Romania isolated and forced it to agree an armistice with the central powers.

Romania re-entered the war on 10 November 1918, the day before it ended on the western front. On **1 December 1918,** the representatives of the Romanians in Transylvania gathered in Alba Iulia, and proclaimed the union of Transylvania with Romania. 1 December is now celebrated as Romania's national day. Romania wanted to ensure that its territorial claim on Transylvania would be successful at the coming peace conference, and decided to support its claim with an attack in April 1919 on a Hungary that had just fallen under the control of the Communist regime of Béla Kun. The Romanians occupied Budapest in August 1919, and Béla Kun fled to the Soviet Union.

Following intensive and often difficult peace negotiations at Versailles, during which the Romanians deployed the talents of Queen Marie to good effect, Romania secured a highly favourable peace settlement, enshrined within the **Treaty of**

Trianon of 4 June 1920, which defined the settlement in relation to the Kingdom of Hungary. Romania secured Transylvania, as well as the regions of Maramureş, Crişana and Banat. Under the separate Treaty of Versailles, Romania secured the eastern regions of Bucovina and Bessarabia, and it had earlier acquired Southern Dobruja from Bulgaria as a result of the Second Balkan War of 1913. The settlements brought Romania the greatest territorial extent it has ever known: referred to today as România Mare, or 'Great Romania'.

THE INTERWAR PERIOD In 1922, Romania's territorial expansion was celebrated by a grand coronation of King Ferdinand I and Queen Marie at Alba Iulia, marking their rule over Greater Romania. But in other respects the interwar period was a difficult one for Romania, a period of missed opportunity which ended in authoritarianism. Having acquired a large number of new territories, the Romanian administration found it a challenge to integrate them. The Romanians who had fought so hard during World War I had been promised land reform, and some was delivered, though at a cost in terms of agricultural productivity. The effects of this were exacerbated by the impact in Romania of the Great Depression, which provoked a fall in grain prices and plunged Romania into agricultural crisis. And there was much turmoil in the Romanian monarchy. Ferdinand died in 1927, but his son Crown Prince Carol had been disinherited after fleeing the country with his mistress, and the crown passed to Carol's six-year-old son Michael. In 1930, Carol returned to the country, instituted a coup against his own son, and was installed as King Carol II.

As far-right extremist movements took hold elsewhere in Europe, Romania developed its own version, the Legion of the Archangel Michael, also known as the **Iron Guard**. They combined fascist and anti-Semitic tendencies with a religious mysticism, and their support grew in the challenging economic times. When barred by Prime Minister Ion Duca from taking part in the 1933 parliamentary elections, they arranged for him to be assassinated on the platform at the railway station in Sinaia. During this period the rule of King Carol II was becoming increasingly authoritarian in nature. In December 1937, Carol nominated the anti-Semitic poet Octavian Goga, who had little popular support, as prime minister, and in February 1938 dispensed with even the fig leaf of democratic pretensions by installing a royal dictatorship. Carol was nonetheless opposed to the Iron Guard, whose leadership he could not control, and in November 1938 ordered the assassination of its leader, Corneliu Codreanu, an action which temporarily soured Carol's relationship with Nazi Germany.

WORLD WAR II King Carol proclaimed neutrality at the outbreak of World War II, but received a huge blow when in June 1940 the Soviet Union demanded that it hand over Bessarabia and northern Bukovina, and found that Romania lacked the strength to do anything other than comply. Worse was to follow, when Romania also had to cede southern Dobruja to Bulgaria and agree to a German-brokered settlement in respect of Hungarian demands on Transylvania, under which the northern part of the region went to Hungary while the southern part stayed with Romania. These humiliations discredited Carol in the eyes of the Romanian people, and he was forced to abdicate in September 1940 in favour of his son Michael. Power passed to the pro-German prime minister, **Ion Antonescu**, who immediately extended his dictatorial powers, confining Michael to an essentially ceremonial role. In June 1941, Romania declared war on the Soviet Union, aiming to recover Bessarabia and northern Bukovina. The Antonescu regime played a role in the Holocaust, and was responsible for the oppression of Jewish and Roma groups.

Romania was important for Nazi Germany both for the contribution of troops to the eastern front and for its strategic reserves of oil around Ploieşti, which were the target of Allied bombing raids in the later stages of the war.

As the course of the war turned against Germany and its allies, the Red Army entered Romania in August 1944. With defeat looming, King Michael moved against Antonescu, ordering his arrest and declaring war on Germany, an action which helped to shorten the war. Following the war, Romania secured back northern Transylvania from Hungary, which had also fought the war on the side of Germany, but the territories of northern Bukovina and Bessarabia were retained by the victor, the Soviet Union. Moreover, the Red Army had never left Romania after the war, and Moscow clearly had no intention of releasing Romania from its sphere of influence. Through Soviet-directed manipulations, Communist and allied parties were deemed to have swept to victory in the parliamentary elections of November 1946, which confirmed as prime minister Moscow's choice, **Petru Groza**. The latter forced King Michael to abdicate in 1947, and Romania was declared a republic.

ROMANIA UNDER GHEORGHIU-DEJ The Communists moved rapidly to consolidate their control, and Romania quickly became a one-party state. The Constitution of April 1948 was based on that of the Soviet Union. Fellow traveller Petru Groza had outlived his usefulness, and in 1952 was succeeded by **Gheorghe Gheorghiu-Dej**, who had been a Communist activist in the 1930s in the railway industry in the Transylvanian town of Dej. The double-barrelled surname was reportedly acquired via the secret police at the time, who had used it to distinguish him from other activists named Gheorghiu. He proved a hardline ruler, purging the party of real and perceived rivals, developing the repressive Securitate secret police agency, implementing forced collectivisation in the countryside, setting about the dismantling of previously privileged groups in society, and making extensive use of political prisons and forced labour camps in the process. He was, however, keen to develop Romania's foreign and economic policies in a way that maintained an independence from Moscow, for example by initiating a programme of heavy industrial development and securing the withdrawal of the last Red Army troops from Romania. But in a marked contrast to his successor Ceauşescu's reaction to the Soviet invasion of Czechoslovakia a decade later, Gheorghiu-Dej stayed firmly loyal to Moscow's tough line in responding to the 1956 Hungarian Revolution, though this was probably mainly down to concerns that the revolution might spread to ethnic Hungarians in Transylvania. Gheorghiu-Dej adopted a twin-pronged approach in respect of the latter, combining measures such as the merging of Hungarian and Romanian universities with ostensibly more permissive ones, such as the establishment of a Magyar Autonomous Region in the Székely lands.

THE CEAUŞESCU ERA Gheorghiu-Dej died of lung cancer in 1965, and was replaced by **Nicolae Ceauşescu**, who had also been involved in Communist Party activities in the interwar period. His rule was initially regarded with a degree of relative optimism in the West, due to his pursuit of a foreign policy line independent of Moscow, and in particular for his condemnation of the invasion of Czechoslovakia in 1968. Romania joined the International Monetary Fund and welcomed US President Nixon.

But it gradually became clear that there was much that was sinister about Ceauşescu's rule. Visits to China and North Korea fired his enthusiasm for the development of national transformation programmes and personality cults, and in his July Theses speech in 1971 he demanded ideological conformity and a stronger focus on the use of culture for ideological propaganda, reversing the relative cultural liberalisation which had accompanied the early years of his rule. He consolidated his powers by becoming an elected President of Romania from 1974, with all institutions of the state now subordinated to him. And he started to build a personality cult around himself and his wife Elena to accompany his increased powers, together with the use of an extraordinary degree of nepotism.

The relatively high oil prices through most of the 1970s benefited Romania, but Ceauşescu's heavy borrowing to finance his industrial development plans was storing up trouble, and Romania further had to grapple with an earthquake in 1977 which caused great loss of life and destruction in Bucharest. In a change of policy that was to prove disastrous, from 1981 Ceauşescu developed an **austerity plan** for Romania in which he single-mindedly focused on repaying all of Romania's foreign debt. By 1989 he had done so, but his failure to accompany this policy with appropriate reforms led to a focus on inefficient exports at the expense of all else, food shortages from a cutting of imports, wage reductions, price rises and an overall sharp decline in the standard of living. There was food rationing and regular power cuts; the television broadcast was reduced to just 2 hours per day.

Ceauşescu made use of the pervasive secret police organisation, the **Securitate**, to stamp out dissent. Romanians lived in fear of informers in their midst. In Transylvania, Ceauşescu intensified the policy of '**Romanianisation**' that had also been pursued by his predecessor, including bringing into the region ethnic Romanians from other parts of the country to work on new industrial projects. He even negotiated deals with the governments of West Germany and Israel, under which they would pay to allow the emigration to their countries of Saxons and Jews respectively. Some 300,000 Germans and 50,000 Jews emigrated on these terms, which both delivered Ceauşescu some welcome foreign exchange and further supported his goal of the Romanianisation of the country.

Ceauşescu's **systematisation programme** focused on resettling Romanian villagers in multi-storey apartment blocks. Following the 1977 earthquake, he set about rebuilding Bucharest in the style of Pyongyang, demolishing monasteries and city-centre buildings and starting the construction of an enormous Palace of the People. Abortion was criminalised in an attempt to combat the declining birth rate, and in his pursuit of large Romanian families Ceauşescu also criminalised homosexuality, restricted the conditions under which divorce could be obtained and consigned unmarried people to the poorest accommodation. As conditions for ordinary Romanians continued to decline through the 1980s, Ceauşescu insisted that the country was experiencing its Golden Age.

THE 1989 REVOLUTION The spark which was to ignite the Romanian Revolution of December 1989 was struck in the western city of Timişoara, when on the 16th of that month members of the local Hungarian minority protested at attempts to evict a Reformed Church pastor named **László Tőkés**, who had made comments to Hungarian television that were critical of the Romanian regime. The protests in that city turned into a more generalised attack on the regime, whereupon the army was called in and resorted to violence.

On 21 December, Ceauşescu addressed a large gathering in central Bucharest, many of whom had been bussed in for the occasion, to condemn the Timişoara uprising. But the response from the crowd was not the one Ceauşescu had been expecting, and they started to jeer the dictator. The rally had turned into a protest; Ceauşescu had lost control. More people took to the streets, some carrying the

Romanian flag with a hole in the middle, where the Communist insignia had been cut out. Protestors were confronted by military and Securitate forces, and there were many casualties.

The protestors regrouped the next morning, reinforced by large groups of workers from the main factories. As a huge crowd gathered in central Bucharest, Ceaușescu attempted to address them from the balcony of the Communist Party headquarters, today the Interior Ministry. But the crowd was in no mood to listen. Ceaușescu and his wife Elena headed for the roof of the building, protestors in pursuit, and left by helicopter. The pilot set them down in a field, and Ceaușescu's Securitate bodyguards resorted to flagging down cars, eventually getting them to the town of Târgoviște, where they were arrested by local police. In a hastily convened trial on 25 December, Nicolae and Elena Ceaușescu were convicted of 'crimes against the people' and summarily executed in the courtyard outside.

ROMANIA IN THE 1990S The political organisation which took control in the wake of the revolution was the **National Salvation Front** (FSN) headed by **Ion Iliescu**, a Communist Party figure who had been marginalised by Ceaușescu, who had seen him as a potential rival. But violence continued in Bucharest for several days, with a total of 1,104 people killed in the Romanian Revolution. A number of political parties emerged, with the National Liberal Party (PNL) and the Christian-Democratic National Peasants' Party (PNȚCD) claiming to be heirs of the parties suppressed during the Communist years and including political prisoners of the Communists amongst their leadership. The FSN announced that it would contest the upcoming elections as a political party, generating protests in Bucharest among those who felt its leadership was too packed with former Communist Party figures, like Iliescu, and who demanded that ex-communists be barred from holding official functions. This took the form of a sit-in known as the *Golaniad,* after the Romanian word for 'hooligan', *golan,* the term used by Iliescu to refer to the protestors. At the Romanian general election of May 1990, the first free election Romania had seen since before World War II, the National Salvation Front won most of the seats and Iliescu was separately elected president, securing more than 85% of the vote. Petre Roman was confirmed as prime minister.

After the FSN election victory only a relatively small group of opposition protestors remained camped out in Bucharest, but they showed no signs of giving up their protest. Iliescu decided to forcefully break it up, and brought in allied groups, especially the coal miners of the Jiu Valley, to help in this endeavour. They did so, but with much violence and at a cost of several lives, though the casualty figures remain disputed. Iliescu faces ongoing charges in relation to his role in the events, which are referred to in Romania as the *mineriad.*

There had been more violence in the Transylvanian city of Târgu Mureș in March 1990 during clashes between Romanian and Hungarian ethnic groups which led to the deaths of six people in the worst ethnic violence Romania has experienced since the revolution.

A new Constitution at the end of 1991 was followed by further general and presidential elections. Ahead of these the FSN had split into two separate parties: one led by Iliescu, the other by Roman. Iliescu's group maintained control, and he was re-elected as president in September 1992. After several changes of name, Iliescu's party would become the **Social Democratic Party (PSD)**. Iliescu suffered a reversal in the 1996 presidential elections, losing to a professor of geology named **Emil Constantinescu**, and the social democrats were also kept out of government by a centrist coalition, but these were economically difficult years for Romania, and the disparate coalition made limited progress towards economic modernisation and privatisation.

ROMANIA AFTER 2000 Iliescu returned as president in the elections in 2000, defeating Vadim Tudor of the far-right nationalistic Greater Romania Party, whose presence in the second round of the presidential elections marks the electoral high-water mark of the far right in post-revolution Romania, a sign perhaps of voter frustration by the modest progress made by the preceding centrist coalition. Since 2000 the share of the vote secured by Greater Romania and other extremist parties has dropped dramatically. Iliescu's Social Democratic Party was also successful in the accompanying parliamentary elections. **Adrian Năstase** became prime minister. These were years of economic growth and of success in what has been the centrepiece of Romania's post-revolution foreign policy: a desire to anchor itself firmly within the structures of Europe and the transatlantic alliance, and specifically membership of NATO and the EU. Romania joined NATO in 2004, and has been an active participant in NATO operations. But the government was also surrounded by accusations of corruption, which would eventually see Năstase given a two-year prison sentence in 2012 on corruption charges.

The 2004 presidential and parliamentary elections marked a political shift to the right. The new president was **Traian Băsescu**, a one-time merchant navy captain and former Mayor of Bucharest, who had replaced Petre Roman at the helm of the Democratic Party (PD). Under Prime Minister Călin Popescu-Tăriceanu, Romania joined the European Union, at the same time as Bulgaria, on 1 January 2007. The economy continued to grow, but political life was marked by feuding between government and president. A change of government in 2008 resulted in a broad-based coalition between the centre-left PSD and centre-right Democratic Liberal Party (PDL), the successor of the PD. In 2009, Traian Băsescu was voted back as president, in a close-fought election. Romania's **entry into the European Union** had been accompanied by the establishment of a co-operation and verification mechanism (CVM), recognising that it still required to make progress in judicial reform and combating corruption. Some impressive progress has been registered, especially through dedicated anti-corruption agencies. But from late 2009 Romania was hit heavily by the effects of the global economic crisis. When centre-right Prime Minister Mihai Răzvan Ungureanu lost a parliamentary vote of no confidence in May 2012 he was replaced by a centre-left-led coalition headed by PSD leader Victor Ponta, which almost immediately fell into conflict with Băsescu. This culminated in the holding of a referendum to impeach the president in July 2012, around claims that he had overstepped his powers. However, the referendum result was rendered invalid by the low turnout. The centre-left coalition won a majority in new elections in December 2012, continuing a period of uneasy cohabitation between centre-left government and centre-right president.

Ponta stood as the centre-left candidate for the presidency of Romania in November 2014, and was ahead in most opinion polls before the vote. But the election was won by his centre-right opponent, the ethnic German former Mayor of Sibiu, **Klaus Iohannis**, whose campaign was boosted by controversy over voting arrangements for members of the Romanian overseas diaspora, which resulted in long queues at many overseas polling stations.

Ponta remained prime minister, and the uneasy relationship he had enjoyed with Băsescu continued with Iohannis in the presidency. The Ponta government faced a series of corruption allegations, including the news that Ponta himself was under investigation for alleged corruption related to his earlier career as a lawyer.

On 30 October 2015, a fire broke out in the Club Colectiv nightclub in Bucharest, started by the pyrotechnic display accompanying a performance by heavy-metal band Goodbye to Gravity. Sixty-four people lost their lives. In the wake of street protests around the alleged widespread circumvention of fire safety and other certification, which was widely viewed as a factor behind this tragedy, the Ponta government fell. With the agreement of all major political parties, a technocratic government under former EU Agriculture Commissioner Dacian Cioloş took the helm for the remaining year until the next scheduled parliamentary elections in December 2016. These were won by the PSD, and Sorin Grindeanu became the new prime minister.

The new **PSD government** started controversially by voting to introduce emergency ordinance rules on 31 January 2017. These were widely viewed as shrinking the scope of corruption-related offences. The government explained that its motivation for this measure, and a related move to pardon some criminals convicted of relatively minor offences, was aimed at putting into practice a decision of Romania's Constitutional Court as well as addressing the problems of prison overcrowding in Romania. But the president, opposition and civil society groups were not convinced, accusing the government of seeking to reverse progress that Romania had made in its anti-corruption drive. A record 600,000 people took to the streets in the largest protests seen in Romania since the 1989 Revolution, and the emergency ordinance was withdrawn. Grindeanu was replaced in June 2017 by the former Economy Minister Mihai Tudose, after he had been ousted by a vote of no confidence initiated by his own governing coalition, following friction between Grindeanu and the leader of the PSD, Liviu Dragnea.

GOVERNMENT AND POLITICS

Romania is a parliamentary republic. There are two chambers of parliament. The lower chamber, with 330 seats, is called the Chamber of Deputies. The upper chamber, with 136 seats, is the Senate. Both deputies and senators are elected for four-year terms, on a proportional representation basis under party lists established in each of 43 constituencies, which are made up of Romania's 41 counties (*judeţ*), plus two additional constituencies representing Bucharest and the overseas diaspora. The most recent elections were in December 2016, and resulted in a parliamentary majority for a centre-left coalition headed by the Social Democratic Party (PSD).

The Head of State is the president, currently Klaus Iohannis. The post is directly elected: if no candidate secures an outright majority in the first round of voting, a second round is called. Presidents may serve a maximum of two terms. The president has significant powers, including chairing the National Defence Council, representing Romania at meetings of the European Council, and nominating the prime minister, although this must be someone able to secure the support of a majority of members of parliament. This has led to several periods of uneasy cohabitation between presidents and governments of different political colour.

At local government level, the counties each have county councils, whose members are elected for four-year terms. The president of the county council is now elected indirectly, by the councillors. Below this are the individual town or rural administrations (*comune*), whose mayors are directly elected.

ECONOMY

The economic strengths of Transylvania include a strong mineral resource base, including natural gas and salt, although controversy surrounds the exploitation of some of the region's mineral reserves, most clearly demonstrated by the bitter dispute around proposals to recommence gold mining at Roşia Montană (see box, pages 272–3). The fate of the coal-mining district of the Jiu Valley in the southern part of Hunedoara County is also an important political, social and environmental issue.

Agriculture is a major employer (indeed, in 2009, around 30% of the Romanian workforce was employed on the land), based around smallholdings and traditional methods of farming with low rates of mechanisation, although larger international food producers are an increasingly strong presence in Romania, with all the attendant consequences of this for the rural environment. Investments in Transylvanian agriculture have included the modernisation of wine production in the region, with a new focus on the production of higher quality wines, away from the emphasis on quantity that prevailed during the Communist period. Timber production is important, and combating illegal logging remains a major challenge.

Graduates in Computer Science and other IT disciplines from university cities, notably Cluj-Napoca, who have an excellent command of English and work at wage rates much lower than those in most EU countries, have proved a magnet for companies looking to base software design, website management and other **outsourced IT facilities** in Romania. The major Transylvanian cities have also developed strong bases in the automotive and electronics sectors. In part, these have built on established companies in the region, such as the Roman truck company in Braşov, but development has also been stimulated by the relative closeness of Transylvania to Germany and other central European markets, which has put the region at an advantage when compared with other parts of Romania. The production of ready-made clothing is concentrated in some parts of Transylvania, such as Covasna County. The region also has a number of heavy industrial complexes, many developed during the Communist period but which have struggled following the Romanian Revolution, such as the steel plant at Hunedoara and fertiliser factory in Târgu Mureş. Overall, Transylvania is one of the wealthier regions of Romania, with a GDP per capita above the national average, though behind that of the Romanian capital, Bucharest. In 2016, GDP per capita in Cluj County was some 10,655 euros, against 22,323 euros in Bucharest but just 4,093 euros in Romania's poorest county, Vaslui, in the eastern region of Moldavia.

At the time of writing, Romania was one of the fastest growing economies within the European Union. Most of the macro-economic indicators were pretty positive, including low inflation and public debt, and Romania fulfilled the majority of the convergence criteria required for euro adoption. Romania remains committed to the adoption of the euro, but not to a specific timetable, and many policymakers believe that the country must achieve much stronger real convergence with those of the Eurozone before euro membership becomes a realistic prospect.

Transylvania, and Romania more widely, face a number of important economic challenges looking forward. One is investment in **infrastructure**. While Transylvania is relatively better off than many parts of Romania, transport infrastructure is still relatively weaker than across much of Europe. There are only two relatively small stretches of motorway in the region; the rail network is extensive, but much has not been electrified and speeds are slow; while the closure of Târgu Mureş airport for runway repairs demonstrated the challenges in that sector. The development of large transport infrastructure projects is a priority for Romania in its disbursement of EU structural and investment funding.

Structural reform is another area of important challenges, including the further privatisation of state-owned enterprises and the professionalisation, and in some cases depoliticisation, of their management boards. There are challenges too around reform of public administration and removing some of the bureaucratic barriers to doing business in Romania. In the 2017 Ease of Doing Business rankings produced by the World Bank, overall Romania registered a relatively respectable 36th place globally. The ease of getting credit and of trading across borders were those in which it performed most strongly. But the ranking fell to 62nd when it came to actually starting a business, and 134th as regards the ease of obtaining electricity.

Across much of rural Transylvania, **population decline**, particularly in respect of the working age population, is an increasingly pressing problem, both because of the lure of better-paid jobs and better facilities in the cities and because of the opportunities to earn much higher incomes in wealthier member states of the EU. Many Transylvanian villages increasingly resemble settlements of pensioners, and of the children left behind with them while their parents work overseas, which generates its own range of social problems. There are specific shortages in rural areas of a number of key professionals, notably medical doctors.

Finally, a palpable challenge faced across Transylvania, the successful navigation of which will be centrally important to the future of the region, is the conflict between the demands of growth, modernisation, higher living standards and greater consumer choice against the preservation of the traditional crafts, lifestyles and environment, which are at the heart of why Transylvania is such a special region. As you travel around it, you will see many examples of where this conflict has led to jarring developments, but there are an increasing number of examples too of sympathetic ones, and good initiatives. Let us hope that the clatter is where the future lies.

PEOPLE

In the population of Transylvania there are four distinct nationalities: Saxons in the south, and mixed with them the Wallachs, who are the descendants of the Dacians; Magyars in the west; and Szekelys in the east and north. I am going among the latter, who claim to be descended from Attila and the Huns. This may be so, for when the Magyars conquered the country in the 11th century they found the Huns settled in it.

From Jonathan Harker's journal, Chapter 1, Dracula, *by Bram Stoker*

Transylvania has been shaped by the complex interconnected histories of its peoples, and in particular by that of six principal ethnic groups: the Romanians, Hungarians, Székelys, Saxons, Roma and Jews. By some margin, the largest group is that of the ethnic **Romanians**, comprising a little more than 70% of the Transylvanian population. The origins of the Romanian people are discussed in more detail in the box on page 18, and remain a subject of considerable academic debate, with most Romanian authorities arguing in favour of a Dacio-Roman continuity theory that sees the Romanians as the direct descendants of a Latin-speaking Dacian people, in which Dacian King Decebal and Roman Emperor Trajan are often depicted as joint ancestors of the Romanian people. The name Romania comes from the Latin word *Roman*, reflecting the self-identification of the Romanian people with the Romans. Other academics, predominantly those working with Hungarian sources, believe that the Romanians descended from a Latin-speaking people living south of the Danube, migrating later into the territory of present-day Romania. Another term that was often used historically, though not used by the Romanian people themselves, is Vlachs or Wallachs, which refers rather more widely to the speakers of all Romance languages in southeastern Europe, including Aromanians, an ethnic group distributed across several countries, including Greece, Albania, Bulgaria and Romania. The term 'Vlach' has a German origin, and was used by Germanic-speaking tribes of the region when referring to their neighbours. The name Wallachia was given to the principality of ethnic Romanians lying between the Southern Carpathians and the Danube, though again the term is not used by Romanians themselves, who refer to this area as Ţara Românească, the 'Romanian country'.

For centuries, while Transylvania was controlled by Hungary, the ethnic Romanians had few rights and were largely excluded from a power that was vested in the 'Three Nations' of Hungarian, Saxon and Székely. The growing Romanian cultural and political consciousness is one of the central themes of Transylvanian politics through the late 18th and 19th centuries, culminating in the Alba Iulia Declaration of 1 December 1918 in which the representatives of the Romanians of Transylvania, Banat, Crişana and Maramureş voted for their unification with Romania. One distinctive group among the ethnic Romanian population of the region is the **Moţi** (pronounced 'motz'), based in the high-altitude villages of the Apuseni Mountains. They were strongly associated with the struggles for the recognition of the rights of ethnic Romanians, from the 1784 revolt of Horea, Cloşca and Crişan (page 280) to their support for Avram Iancu in the revolutionary upheavals of 1848–49 (see box, page 275). See also page 280 for more about them.

Comprising around 18% of the population of Transylvania, the **Hungarians** are the second largest ethnic group. Indeed, Transylvania is, for historical reasons, home to the large majority of the ethnic Hungarians in Romania, Hungarians making up a little over 6% of the population of Romania nationally. They comprise two historically and culturally distinct Hungarian-speaking groups, of approximately equal size. The first is the **Magyars**, a tribe whose original homeland may have been in the Southern Urals, and who under their leader, Árpád, crossed into the Carpathian Basin at the end of the 9th century. Centred on the Pannonian Plain, they conquered Transylvania, which became part of Christendom after the ascension to the Hungarian throne of Stephen I in around AD1000. There is much historical debate about the ethnic composition of Transylvania and other parts of the Carpathian Basin during the Middle Ages, with some historians, mostly Hungarian, arguing that Hungarians at this stage formed a majority of the population, which would be reversed later through the in-migration of other peoples and the effects of Ottoman predations, while others, especially Romanian historians, believe that Hungarians always constituted a minority of the population of Transylvania.

The second major Hungarian-speaking ethnic group in Transylvania is the **Székelys**, known as Szeklers in German. These were guardians of the eastern frontier of the Kingdom of Hungary, and their origins are disputed. Some historians believe that they were Magyars who became culturally distinct because of their long isolation on the eastern borders of the kingdom. Others argue that they are the descendants of Turkic nomadic tribes who switched to Hungarian at an early stage. The Széklers themselves believe that they are the descendants of Prince Scaba, the youngest son of Attila the Hun. In Bram Stoker's *Dracula*, the count regards himself as a Székely: 'We Székelys have a right to be proud, for in our veins flows the blood of many brave races who fought as the lion fights, for lordship.' The Székelys are concentrated today in three counties of present-day Transylvania: Harghita, Covasna and Mureş. In the first two of these they form the large majority of the population, and in these parts of Transylvania you are more likely to hear Hungarian spoken than Romanian.

For centuries, the Székelys of Transylvania, as well as the Hungarian nobles (it was a different matter for the poor Hungarian peasantry) had a privileged position in the region as two of the Three Nations that controlled its structures of power. Following the incorporation of Transylvania into Romania after World War I, their position in respect of that of the ethnic Romanian majority changed, and this has led to tensions, from attempts during Ceaușescu's time to increase the Romanian populations of towns like Târgu Mureș by bringing ethnic Romanian workers into the region to staff new industrial complexes, to strikingly different perceptions of the important historical figures who shaped the region, as seen by the very different choices of statues chosen for the town squares of ethnic Romanian and ethnic Hungarian-majority communities in Transylvania.

The **Saxons** were German-speaking settlers who came to the southern parts of Transylvania from the middle of the 12th century, invited here by Hungarian kings, starting with Géza II, to help defend the southern borders of the kingdom. The first arrivals came to the area around present-day Sibiu, and although the German-speaking ethnic group of Transylvania is today known generically as 'Saxon', many of these early colonists were from the region around the Moselle River and from Luxembourg, a connection which was highlighted in 2007 when Luxembourg and Sibiu were chosen as the two European Capitals of Culture for that year. Later arrivals were drawn from other parts of Germany, destined for different parts of the Transylvanian borderland, including to an area known as Nösnerland centred on the modern city of Bistrița. In the early 13th century King Andrew II invited the Teutonic Knights to help defend the strategically important region of Burzenland, centred on the modern city of Brașov. The Knights proved to be too ambitious and independent-minded for the Hungarians' liking, and were soon expelled, but the settlers who accompanied them remained. There were further in-migrations of ethnic Germans in later centuries, notably the arrival into southern Transylvania in the 1730s of the Landler, Protestant Austrians who were despatched here in a form of internal exile by the Catholic imperial rulers.

The challenging frontier environment of southern Transylvania in the medieval period, subject to frequent Ottoman incursions, is demonstrated nowhere better than by the remarkable fortress churches of the Transylvanian Saxons, now listed as UNESCO World Heritage Sites. Along with the Hungarian nobility and the Székelys, the Saxons enjoyed a privileged status for many centuries in Transylvania. They were protective of the rights and privileges granted to them by Hungarian kings, and from 1438 were one of the recognised Three Nations to hold political power in the region.

Visitors to Transylvania will quickly observe that while the villages of southern Transylvania attest to the importance of the Transylvanian Saxon community to the history and development of the area, there are very few ethnic Germans to be found in most places. The position of wealthier Saxons was weakened following the land reforms which followed the unification of Transylvania with Romania. At the end of World War II, many Saxons were sent to labour camps in the Soviet Union, accused of having collaborated with Nazi Germany. With rights to German citizenship, and mistrusted by Ceaușescu, several thousand Transylvanian Saxons left for West Germany during the Communist period, particularly following an agreement signed with the West German authorities in 1978 under which the Romanian authorities were paid a fee for each migrant, which formally represented compensation to Romania for the costs of educating the emigrants, but which served as a useful source of foreign exchange for the Romanian regime. The flow of ethnic Germans to Germany became a flood before and immediately after the 1989

Revolution in Romania, and ethnic Germans now represent considerably less than 1% of the population of Transylvania. However, they continue to play an important role, and the current President of Romania, Klaus Iohannis, is an ethnic German from Sibiu.

Around 4% of the current population of Transylvania is ethnic **Roma**, although some researchers believe that this figure may underestimate the true size of the group because of the tendency of some wealthier Roma to identify as members of other groups. The Roma people originated in northern India, and have migrated progressively westwards. The use of the term 'gypsy' (or *Țigani* in Romanian) to describe the community is pejorative and should be avoided. The Roma have for centuries experienced varying degrees of social exclusion and marginalisation, and lived in conditions of slavery under the Kingdom of Hungary, this only being abolished with Habsburg rule in the 18th century. Roma slavery in Wallachia and Moldavia was abolished only in the 1850s.

Traditionally, the Roma in Romania are linked to particular tribes, distinguished by their specialising in particular occupations, although some Roma today do not feel a strong connection to any tribe. Some of the professions at the heart of these tribes are no longer practised, such as that of the *ursari*, or bear trainers, but others remain important, such as that of the *căldărari*, the metalworkers, who are known *inter alia* for the manufacture of the stills used by Romanian families for the production of *țuică*, plum brandy, and the *lăutari*, musicians. Some tribes, notably the *căldărari*, are particularly associated with the wearing of traditional dress, very much in evidence when travelling around Transylvania in a way which is only seen among other ethnic groups during festivals and holidays.

Many Roma families in Romania are caught in a vicious cycle of poverty, a lack of stable employment, low levels of educational attainment, poor quality healthcare, and poor housing. Very poor Roma communities are to be found on the outskirts of many Transylvanian towns, such as the Pata Rât settlement which developed around the municipal landfill on the edge of Cluj-Napoca. Other Roma communities are wealthier, with some characterised by elaborate, though often unfinished, spired 'palaces' (see box, page 307), often built with income remitted from Roma migrants in western Europe. There is a considerable degree of ongoing prejudice against Roma.

There have been **Jews** in Romania since the Roman conquest, though the Jewish communities in Transylvania and other parts of present-day Romania long suffered discrimination, leavened by periods of relative tolerance, such as the tenure of Gabriel Bethlen as Prince of Transylvania in the early 17th century, who awarded some privileges to Jews. With the Treaty of Berlin in 1878, the newly independent state of Romania was obliged by the great powers who were parties to it to grant full citizenship for Jews, but it deliberately made naturalisation procedures slow and cumbersome and discrimination continued. By 1900 Jews formed more than 3% of the Romanian population, with particularly high numbers in the cities of the eastern province of Moldavia. This would increase further following the incorporation of Transylvania, Bucovina and Bessarabia into Romania following World War I, and by the 1920s some 800,000 Jews lived in Romania. With the emergence of Nazism in Germany in the interwar period, and Romania's own far-right Iron Guard, anti-Semitism increased in intensity in Romania. In 1938, Prime Minister Octavian Goga introduced legislation to remove citizenship rights from Romanian Jews. In early 1941, the Iron Guard were responsible for a pogrom in Bucharest in which some 125 Jews were killed, and while this was ultimately crushed by the Romanian dictator Antonescu,

There was a major wave of Romanian migration to North America in the late 19th and early 20th centuries. During the Communist era there was further out-migration, including of ethnic Germans to Germany and Jews to Israel.

Researchers looking for information about their Romanian ancestors can access birth, marriage and death certificates and other documentation through the Romanian National Archives (w *arhivelenationale.ro*). Note that the information is mostly to be found at the local level, with pre-1890 documents available in the relevant county archive (Directia Judeţeana a Arhivelor Naţionale). The National Archives website gives the contact details and opening hours of each of these: they are typically open from Monday to Friday, in the mornings and early afternoons. More recent documents are generally to be found in the civil records section of the relevant town hall (Oficiul de Stare Civila al Primariei). Local travel agencies may be able to set up programmes to help visitors coming to research their Romanian ancestors in navigating the challenges around local bureaucracy and the language. The following two websites may be helpful if your ancestors were ethnic Hungarian or German, respectively.

w **familyhistory.ro** Contains a Transylvanian family history database in Hungarian, plus material about family history archives in English & Romanian.
w **compgen.de** A comprehensive source of online information for German genealogical searches, including the Transylvanian Germans, but in German only.

he would also be responsible for many anti-Semitic acts. A pogrom in the Moldavian city of Iaşi in June 1941 resulted in the deaths of more than 13,000 Jews. According to the 2004 report on the Holocaust in Romania produced by the Wiesel Commission, between 280,000 and 380,000 Romanian Jews perished in the Holocaust, as well as more than 11,000 Romanian Roma. Some 120,000 Jews living in northern Transylvania, that part of Transylvania which was administered by Hungary during World War II, were deported to Auschwitz and other concentration camps, where most perished.

The Wiesel Commission estimated that at least 290,000 Romanian Jews survived the predations of World War II. Immediately following the end of the war, many thousands of Romanian Jews left for Israel. The emigration of Jews to Israel was allowed to continue under the Communist regime, in return for economic assistance from Israel. Under Ceauşescu, a straight cash payment scheme was established, under which Israel made a payment in hard currency for each Jew allowed to leave Romania. Only 3,271 Jews were recorded in Romania in the 2011 census, but the legacy of the much larger historic Jewish populations is immediately visible, for example in the synagogues found in many Transylvanian towns.

Among the many smaller minority groups which helped to shape the identity of modern Transylvania, specific mention might be made of the **Armenians**, who played a historically significant role as traders. Armenians settled in Transylvania as early as the 10th century, but a notable development was the founding of the Armenian town of Armenopolis, present-day Gherla (pages 296–7), by Armenian immigrants who had arrived here from Bistriţa. The town of Dumbrăveni also historically had a large Armenian population: Armenian-Catholic places of worship are at the centre of both settlements. Armenians were increasingly assimilated into the Hungarian population from the 19th century, and mostly lost their fluency in the Armenian language. But many Armenians left Romania during the Communist period, either to the Armenian Soviet Socialist Republic or to the West, and the 2011 census recorded just 1,361 Armenians in Romania.

LANGUAGE

The official language of Romania is **Romanian** (*limba română*) and this is the language of the large majority of inhabitants of Transylvania. It is a Romance language that evolved from Vulgar Latin. More details about the language, together with the essentials of Romanian vocabulary, are set out in Appendix 1 of this guide – see pages 320–9.

The other language the traveller to Transylvania will hear frequently is **Hungarian**, the first language of the Hungarian minority, which makes up around 18% of the Transylvanian population. The Hungarian minority, and hence the Hungarian language, is very unevenly spread across the region. You will rarely hear any Hungarian spoken in counties such as Hunedoara, but in the counties of Harghita and Covasna, where Hungarian-speaking Székelys form the majority of the population, Hungarian is heard more frequently than Romanian. It is recognised as a minority language in those municipalities in Transylvania in which ethnic Hungarians exceed 20% of the overall population. It is a Finno-Ugric, not a Romance, language, and hence more challenging than Romanian to learn for speakers of other Romance languages. Some basic Hungarian phrases are listed on pages 328–9.

Although the ethnic **German** population in Transylvania is now tiny, a fraction of 1% of the overall population, a knowledge of German may occasionally prove useful in the areas of Transylvania settled by Saxons, particularly when trying to secure access to the fortified churches of the area, as the church key is frequently left in the charge of one of the few ethnic Germans to have stayed in the village.

The native language of the Roma of Transylvania is **Romani**, which, despite the similarities in the names, is not related to Romanian, but falls within the group of Indo-Aryan languages, the major language group of the Indian subcontinent. Some scholars regard Romani as a group of languages, as it contains several distinct dialects, which are sometimes regarded as independent languages. The main dialect of the Roma communities in Romania is Vlax Romani, the term 'Vlax' deriving from 'Vlachs', the word once frequently used to refer to the Romance-language-speaking peoples of the region. Roma will typically speak either Romanian or Hungarian in addition to Romani.

English is quite widely understood in Transylvania, though your attempts to speak any Romanian will be warmly applauded.

RELIGION

Transylvania is a region of many different faiths, which are linked strongly to ethnicity. The large majority of ethnic Romanians in the region are Romanian Orthodox, while ethnic Hungarians are most frequently Roman Catholic or members of the Reformed Church. Ethnic Germans tend to be Lutheran.

Transylvania was long characterised by relative freedom of religion, most clearly exemplified by the Edict of Turda in 1568, proclaimed by Hungarian King John Sigismund Zápolya at the urging of his Unitarian adviser Ferenc Dávid, which stated that 'no-one shall be reviled for his religion by anyone'. Periods of tolerance often alternated with more repressive times, and Dávid himself was convicted of heresy, dying in prison during a period in which the Roman Catholic Church asserted itself. But at its most liberal, such as during the rule of Gabriel Bethlen, a member of the Reformed Church, in the early 17th century, Transylvania was a much more tolerant place than most neighbouring lands. The **Romanian Orthodox Church** is by far the largest denomination in Romania, and according to the 2011 census is the faith of more than 86% of Romanians. A papal bull of 1234 provides evidence of an Orthodox Church structure among the Romanian communities north of the Danube. Under the Edict of Turda, Orthodox Christianity was not one of the four religions accorded a privileged status, being simply 'tolerated', and the wooden Orthodox churches characteristic of some parts of Transylvania, such as Sălaj County, are the result of a prohibition on the construction of Orthodox churches in stone. When Transylvania came under the control of the Habsburgs in the late 17th century they looked to re-establish a Catholic majority in a region in which the Reformation had exerted a strong influence. They focused in particular on the Romanian Orthodox Church, and in 1698 Atanasie Anghel, the Orthodox Metropolitan in Transylvania, entered into communion with the Holy See, creating the **Greco-Catholic** or **Uniate Church**, which combined a Byzantine rite with the acceptance of the supreme authority of the Pope. Greco-Catholic churches, such as the Holy Trinity Cathedral in Blaj (pages 277–8), often resemble Catholic churches externally, while their interiors look more like Orthodox churches, centred on an ornate iconostasis. The Greco-Catholic Church suffered greatly during the Communist period in Romania, when it was abolished by the authorities, and there are many ongoing restitution cases involving Greco-Catholic properties which were transferred during the Communist period to the Orthodox Church.

By no means all members of the Romanian Orthodox communities in Transylvania became members of the Greco-Catholic Church: those Orthodox communities that refused to do so faced persecution under the Habsburgs, but eventually, in 1761, an Orthodox diocese was permitted in Sibiu, albeit under the purview of the Serbian Metropolitan. The charismatic bishop of the Romanian Orthodox Church in Sibiu in the mid 19th century, Andrei Şaguna, eventually freed the local church from the control of the Serbian Metropolitan. Following the peace settlement at the end of World War I and the incorporation of Transylvania into an enlarged Romania, new Orthodox bishops were established, for example in Cluj-Napoca, and in 1925 the head of the Romanian Orthodox Church was given the elevated title of Patriarch. Many large Romanian Orthodox churches were built in this period in the main cities and towns of Transylvania, in several cases placed close to, and larger than, the main Roman Catholic church of the city. The 1923 Constitution included provisions on the freedom of religion but also established the Romanian Orthodox Church as the predominant denomination. During the Communist period the Orthodox Church was tolerated by the state, who came to see it as helpful in promoting Romanian nationalism, even though the regime formally subscribed to a doctrine of atheism. But many Orthodox priests who took more independent positions were arrested. Since the fall of Communism many new Orthodox churches and monasteries have been constructed, though the quality of the buildings has sometimes fallen victim to the pace of construction.

Romanian Orthodox churches typically involve first a narthex, the room which symbolises the point of access to the church from the outside world. From here a door leads into the nave. Unlike the churches of most Western denominations there are no pews here, as it is the custom to stand during services, though high-armed chairs do usually line the walls. An elaborate iconostasis, gold in colour

1

and covered with icons, separates the nave from the sanctuary, which may not be entered without the blessing of the priest. Note that the central door of the iconostasis may only be used by the clergy. The walls of the church are typically covered with frescoes, depicting biblical scenes and saints. Typically there will be a painting of the founder of the church on the rear wall of the nave, usually depicted holding a model of the building his funds have been used to erect. Orthodox church interiors tend to be dark. Candles are important, and usually for sale cheaply just inside the church. Romanians typically light two candles: one for the living (*vii*), the other for the dead (*morţi*). These are usually placed outside the church, in specially marked cupboards. The **Roman Catholic Church** makes up the second-largest religious group in Transylvania, and according to the 2011 census is the faith of some 4.3% of the Romanian population. Most Romanian Catholics are ethnic Hungarian, although there are around 300,000 ethnic Romanians who are Catholics. There is also a small Armenian Catholic community, adhering to the Armenian Rite. The history of the Roman Catholic Church in Transylvania is linked to the region's position as part of the Kingdom of Hungary under the rule of its first Christian king, Stephen I, from AD1000. The Catholic Church lost ground in the area following the Hungarian defeat at the Battle of Mohács in 1526, and then with the Reformation, when many Transylvanian Saxons embraced the Lutheran Church and significant numbers of ethnic Hungarians opted for the Reformed Church. Against this background, the Edict of Turda of 1568 appears essentially as an acceptance of the plurality of faiths which characterised the period. There were many local compromises. In Biertan in Sibiu County (pages 232–3) the main fortified church was used for services by the Lutheran community, which represented the majority of citizens, while the smaller number of local Catholics were allowed to hold their services in a specially designated 'Catholic tower'. By the time the Habsburgs took control over Transylvania in the late 17th century, and sought to promote a more aggressive policy of re-Catholicisation, Roman Catholics were already a minority. During the Communist period both the Roman Catholic and Greco-Catholic churches were subject to persecution, with many senior figures in the Roman Catholic Church imprisoned by the Communists, including bishops Áron Márton and Anton Durcovici. The latter died in Sighet Prison in 1951.

The **Lutheran Church** is particularly associated with the Transylvanian Saxons, who are mostly members of the Evangelical Church of Augustan Confession in Romania. The Braşov-born cartographer Johannes Honterus, who had been exposed to Protestant ideas while living in Basel, was particularly important in the introduction of Lutheranism to Transylvania in the mid 16th century, including through the establishment of a printing press and a school in Braşov. Many of the fortified churches of the Saxon villages of Transylvania moved at this stage from Roman Catholic to Lutheran congregations, a process often accompanied by the whitewashing over of the frescoes of the originally Catholic churches. Some of these have been uncovered during subsequent restorations. There is a separate Lutheran denomination, the Evangelical Lutheran Church of Romania, which is mainly associated with members of the ethnic Hungarian community rather than the ethnic German one.

The **Reformed Church**, also sometimes referred to as the **Calvinist Church**, is the religion of just over 3% of the Romanian population, almost all of whom are ethnic Hungarian. The Reformed Church was one of the faiths recognised as a free and accepted religion under the Edict of Turda in 1568, together with the Roman Catholic, Lutheran and Unitarian faiths, and it reached its political zenith in Transylvania in the first half of the 17th century, under the rule of princes

Gabriel Bethlen and George I Rákóczi, both of whom were members of the Reformed Church. The Reformed Church was persecuted during the Communist era and its properties nationalised. Indeed, it was the protests surrounding an attempt to evict the Reformed Church pastor László Tőkés from a church in the western city of Timişoara in 1989 that sparked the Romanian Revolution and the downfall of Communism.

CHURCHES WITH ATTRACTIVE INTERIORS

Here is a selection of ten fine interiors to be found in Transylvanian churches.

BRAŞOV (Braşov County) The Black Church (Biserică Neagra) is the largest Gothic church in Romania, whose interior is enlivened by a wonderful collection of Turkish carpets, brought here by Saxon merchants to adorn the place (pages 124–5).

CLUJ-NAPOCA (Cluj County) St Michael's Church is another fine Gothic church, its interior featuring some fine soaring arches (page 290).

CRASNA (Sălaj County) A 14th-century Reformed church with a ceiling installed in 1736 featuring painted wooden panels decorated with flowers and animals (pages 317–18).

DÂRJIU (Harghita County) A UNESCO World Heritage-listed 15th-century fortified church, now Unitarian, with wall paintings showing St Ladislaus pursuing a Cuman raider who has snatched a young maiden (pages 182–3).

DENSUŞ (Hunedoara County) A curious and ancient church incorporating material from an adjacent Roman site, with murals that include a portrayal of Jesus in traditional Romanian clothing (pages 254–5).

FILDU DE SUS (Sălaj County) An 18th-century Romanian wooden church with well-preserved frescoes dating from 1856 (page 319).

GHELINŢA (Covasna County) The 13th-century Catholic Church of St Emeric of Hungary, celebrated for its frescoes depicting the legend of St Ladislaus as well as a fine wooden-panelled ceiling, decorated with floral motifs (page 168).

MĂLÂNCRAV (Sibiu County) A 14th-century fortified church with some of the most important Gothic wall paintings in Romania in the choir (pages 234–5).

MUGENI (Harghita County) A relatively little-visited but fascinating Reformed church featuring 14th-century wall paintings that include some rather gruesome depictions of the tortures endured by St Margaret of Antioch (page 182).

SIBIU (Sibiu County) A Gothic Evangelical cathedral with a 15th-century fresco of the Crucifixion by Johannes of Rosenau (page 222).

The **Unitarian Church** is named for its central belief that God is one entity, in counterposition to notions of the Trinity, which sees God as Father, Son and Holy Spirit. In this framework, Jesus is seen as a saviour who was inspired by God, but a human one. The spread of Unitarianism in Transylvania is closely associated with Ferenc Dávid, an originally Calvinist bishop who was appointed preacher to the King of Hungary, John Sigismund Zápolya. Dávid was influenced by an Italian physician named Giorgio Biandrata, who served the Transylvanian court. Dávid was influential in the drafting of the Edict of Turda in 1568, which included Unitarianism as one of the accepted and recognised religions, and transferred his own episcopate to the anti-Trinitarian faith. Dávid was deemed a heretic under Zápolya's successor, the Catholic Stephen Báthory, and was to die in prison. The Unitarian Church of Transylvania has around 65,000 members, and is particularly strong among the Székely community. The UNESCO-listed fortified church at Dârjiu in Harghita County (pages 182–3) is a Unitarian church.

EDUCATION

Compulsory education in Romania starts at six years old. Before that, three optional years can be taken in the pre-school kindergarten system. An impressive non-governmental organisation, OvidiuRo, has been encouraging the take-up of places in kindergartens by children from poorer families through the Fiecare Copil în Grădiniță ('Every Child in the Kindergarten') programme, based on the provision of food coupons to the parents of children from low-income families who attend kindergarten. The programme (w *fiecarecopilingradinita.ro*) has now been rolled out nationally.

There is then a compulsory 'preparatory year' at the age of six, prior to entry into the first year of primary school. After spending years 1 to 4 at primary school (*școală primară*), the child then transfers to a middle school, or gymnasium (*gimnaziu*), for four further years of study (classes 5 to 8) and finally to a high school (*liceu*), where there are two compulsory years of study (classes 9 and 10), taking the child to 17 years of age, followed by two optional ones (classes 11 and 12). In some areas, because of the demand for places, two shifts are held at the primary school and gymnasium, with children attending either an early or late shift. At the end of the child's study at a gymnasium, thus at an age of 14 or 15, there is a national examination, the Evaluarea Națională, to determine access to high school. This is very competitive, as there is great demand to enter the most prestigious high schools, which have the title of 'National College' (Colegiu Național). A standard high school is known as a *liceu*. There are few high schools in rural areas, which exacerbates the challenges of school abandonment among poorer rural families.

At the end of their time at high school, students take the National Baccalaureate Exam, which comprises a mix of oral and written papers. Marked on a scale of 1 to 10, the Baccalaureate is competitive, though many Romanian universities also operate their own entrance exams.

Romania has a large number of **universities**, both state and private, and their quality is variable. The best known and most prestigious university in Transylvania is the **Babeș-Bolyai University** in Cluj-Napoca (w *ubbcluj.ro*), which with more than 40,000 students is the largest university in Romania. Named in honour of ethnic Romanian bacteriologist Victor Babeș and ethnic Hungarian mathematician János Bolyai, it offers courses of study in both Romanian and Hungarian, as well as German, and some programmes in English and French. The precise relationship between the Romanian- and Hungarian-speaking sections of the university has been the subject of periodic controversy. Cluj-Napoca also has a number of other state and private universities, making it feel more like a student town than any other Transylvanian city. It even has a considerable cohort of French medical students, attracted by the easier admission criteria and lower costs of study than in France. Other Cluj-based universities include the **Technical University of Cluj-Napoca** (w *utcluj.ro*), which specialises in Engineering and related disciplines.

Târgu Mureș is home to the **University of Medicine and Pharmacy** (w *umftgm.ro*), founded in 1945, which is one of the six so-called 'traditional' medical schools in Romania, established before the 1989 Revolution. It offers teaching in Romanian, Hungarian and English. The **Transilvania University of Brașov** (w *unitbv.ro*) was founded in 1971 as the University of Brașov, adding the 'Transilvania' to its name following the revolution. Other universities in the region are of an even more recent vintage, established after the revolution. These include the **Lucian Blaga University** (w *ulbsibiu.ro*) in Sibiu, founded in 1990 and named after one of the leading figures of Romanian interwar cultural life. There is also the **1 December 1918 University** in Alba Iulia (w *uab.ro*), founded in 1991, which sits within the city's star-shaped citadel. Increasing numbers of Romanian students, however, look to study abroad at the prestigious universities of western Europe.

A university degree is a *licență*; a Master's degree is a *masterat*. A *doctorat* is a PhD, though the Romanian media delights in scandals surrounding allegations in respect of the quality and originality of the PhD theses of various prominent people.

CULTURE

The complex history of Transylvania has produced a complex cultural life, in which the cultures of its ethnic Romanian, Hungarian and German communities are both highly distinctive and constituent elements of a Transylvanian regional culture. Many festivals across the region celebrate individual communities, whether the Saxon Kronenfest at Mălâncrav, the Székely Festival of 1,000 Székely Maidens just outside Miercurea-Ciuc, or the Romanian Junii Parade in Brașov. The 'town days' held in many communities also fall into this category of celebrations of local community: while visitors are welcome to join in, the events are not designed with outside visitors in mind. Other events in Transylvania are increasingly international in outlook, like the Transylvania International Film Festival and Untold music festival in Cluj-Napoca, or the International Theatre Festival in Sibiu. These are events of European renown, reflecting a Transylvania which is increasingly confident of its place on a wider stage.

CINEMA Romanian cinema has enjoyed considerable success on the international film festival circuit in recent years, with a series of impressive, often low-key productions, in some cases exploring the legacy of Romania's Communist past, and in others focusing on the challenges of post-revolution Romanian society. The following are three of the best known directors of this Romanian 'new wave'.

Cristian Mungiu is from Iași in the eastern region of Moldavia. His major breakthrough was his second feature film, *4 Months, 3 Weeks and 2 Days* (*4 luni, 3 săptămâni și 2 zile*), which focused on two students trying to arrange an illegal abortion in Ceaușescu's Romania, winning the Palme d'Or at the Cannes Film Festival, the first time a Romanian film had ever taken this award. Other notable Mungiu films have included the 2012 production *Beyond the Hills* (*După Dealuri*), about an exorcism, with tragic consequences, in a Romanian Orthodox convent, and *Graduation* (*Bacalaureat*) in 2016, a film which explores issues around corruption in the education system triggered by an assault on a girl as she is about to take her final school exam. Mungiu took the Best Director award at Cannes for the film. A 2009 Mungiu film, *Tales from the Golden Age* (*Amintiri din Epoca de Aur*) is also well worth tracking down, as a series of vignettes highlighting some of the absurd tales which circulated during the Ceaușescu era, demonstrating the excesses of the period. The tale about press photographers fretting about how best to doctor an image of Ceaușescu and visiting French President Giscard d'Estaing in order to flatter the Romanian dictator is particularly wonderful.

Cristi Puiu, from Bucharest, is the director whose work did most to initiate the Romanian new wave, first with a low-budget production in 2001 entitled *Stuff and Dough* (*Marfa și Banii*) and then to international acclaim with his second feature *The Death of Mr Lăzărescu* (*Moartea Domnului Lăzărescu*), which highlighted the poor state of the Romanian health system as an ailing man is taken by ambulance from hospital to hospital in a largely futile attempt to receive proper treatment. *Aurora* in 2010, which is similarly set in Bucharest, and with Puiu himself in the lead role, was a rather bleak 3-hour-long film about a divorced man who exacts a terrible revenge on those he associates with his divorce. His 2016 film *Sieranevada* is a lengthy conversation piece set during the 40-day commemoration following the death of the family patriarch.

Radu Jude, also from Bucharest, was assistant director on Puiu's *The Death of Mr Lăzărescu*, and his own films have included the 2009 *The Happiest Girl in the World* (*Cea mai fericită fată din lume*), about a girl who wins a car in an advertising campaign by a fruit juice company, and spends most of the film in a rather, er, fruitless attempt to record a TV advert explaining how happy she is at this fact. Jude's 2015 drama *Aferim!* (*Bravo!*) is highly recommended: filmed in black and white, and in the style of a western, it focuses on the neglected theme of Roma slavery in 19th-century Wallachia. It took the Silver Bear for Best Director at the Berlin International Film Festival. He followed this up in 2016 with *Scarred Hearts* (*Inimi Cicatrizate*), based on the semi-autobiographical work of Romanian writer Max Blecher, who spent most of his short adult life confined to sanatoria beds with spinal tuberculosis.

Transylvania, with its impressive landscapes, availability of skilled crews and relatively low costs, has also proved an important location for international productions. Many scenes from *Cold Mountain*, the late Anthony Minghella's

WILD CARPATHIA

An excellent pre-visit introduction to the glorious natural landscapes of Transylvania and some of the threats to them is provided by the four-part documentary series *Wild Carpathia*. Written and presented by Charlie Ottley and featuring interviews with many people who have worked to preserve the environment and rural livelihoods of Transylvania, including HRH The Prince of Wales, as well as others who have been working to promote sustainable tourism, a new appreciation for the traditional crafts and cultures of the region, and an awareness of the dangers to fragile ecosystems from, for example, illegal logging, it will help to enhance an understanding of this remarkable region. And there is some wonderful photography of the forested Carpathian Mountains and of the bears and other carnivores which inhabit them. The first three episodes can be viewed on their website w *wildcarpathia.tv*.

2003 American Civil War drama with Jude Law and Nicole Kidman, were shot in the Carpathians here. Bogdan Dreyer's 2013 drama *A Farewell to Fools*, with Gérard Depardieu and Harvey Keitel, a World War II film in which local villagers try to persuade the local madman to claim responsibility for the death of a German soldier in order to save their own skins, was partly shot in Sighişoara and Saschiz. And the 2012 US television mini series *Hatfields and McCoys*, with Kevin Costner and Bill Paxton, was shot outside Braşov with, as in *Cold Mountain*, the Carpathians impersonating the Appalachians.

A particular mention might be made of Tony Gatlif, a French director of Roma ethnicity, whose work has focused on the culture of the Roma peoples of central and eastern Europe. His 1993 documentary *Latcho Drom* uses Roma music to chronicle the journey of Roma people from India to western Europe. In 2006, he directed *Transylvania*, starring Asia Argento, in a story of love and loss among Roma music festivals in Transylvania. *Korkoro* from 2009, whose cast includes Roma recruited by Gatlif in Transylvania, is a drama based on the theme of the Roma Holocaust.

LITERATURE The first book to be printed in the Romanian language, in 1559, was a catechism, made by Deacon Coresi at his printing house in Braşov. Most early works in Romanian were religious texts, and a full Romanian translation of the Bible was first printed in 1688, the so-called 'Bucharest Bible'.

A flowering of Romanian literature came in the 19th century, and was strongly linked to nationalist movements in Wallachia, Moldavia and Transylvania, focused around the desire for a Romanian state and, in Transylvania, the granting of political rights for ethnic Romanians. A cultural movement in Transylvania known as the Şcoala Ardeleană, or **Transylvanian School**, focused on highlighting the Daco-Roman origins of the Romanians of Transylvania, seeing the ethnic Romanians as the direct descendants of the ancestral owners of the lands. Avowedly Western in orientation, the Transylvanian School encouraged the use of a Latin rather than Cyrillic alphabet for Romanian, as well as the importation of many words derived from Italian or French rather than those with a Slavic root. Leading figures in the movement included Samuil Micu-Klein, Gheorghe Şincai, Petru Maior and Ion Budai-Deleanu. The last was the author of a satirical poem, *Ţiganiada*, (*Gypsy Saga*) published at the dawn of the 19th century, which was the first major epic poem in the Romanian language.

In the second part of the 19th century, many of the leading figures of Romanian literature hailed from the region of Moldavia, among them Vasile Alecsandri, a poet, nationalist politician and collector of traditional folk songs who established the cultural magazine *România Literară* and promoted the union of Moldavia and Wallachia. The important *Junimea* **literary society** was founded in the principal Moldavian city of Iaşi in 1863, shortly after the union of the two principalities. The society encouraged some of the towering figures of Romanian literature, among them the playwright Ion Luca Caragiale, whose most popular works, such as *O Scrisoare Pierdută* (*A Lost Letter*) and *O Noapte Furtunoasă* (*A Stormy Night*), still regularly performed in Romania, highlight the political corruption and social climbing of the era. But the pre-eminent Romanian literary figure, also an active member of the *Junimea* society, was the poet Mihai Eminescu, who died in 1889 at the age of just 39, but whose bust is to be found today in almost every Romanian town. Many Romanians can quote his most famous poems by heart.

In the first part of the 20th century, major Romanian literary figures from Transylvania included the novelist Liviu Rebreanu, born in Bistriţa-Năsăud County, and the philosopher, poet and commanding cultural figure Lucian Blaga, born in

Alba County. In the latter part of the century, important Romanian figures included the philosopher and one-time Nazi sympathiser Emil Cioran, born in Rășinari in Sibiu County, though he spent much of his adult life in Paris, and much of his later work was written in French. And back in Romania there was the Wallachian novelist Marin Preda, whose last novel, published in 1980, *Cel Mai Iubit Dintre Pământeni* (*The Most Beloved Earthling*), was a thinly veiled critique of Communism. He died shortly afterwards in unclear circumstances.

Among the Hungarian literary figures in Transylvania, one name to look out for is that of the early 20th-century politician and historical novelist Count Miklós Bánffy, whose *Transylvanian Trilogy* is a fascinating study, with a presciently pessimistic tone, of the Hungarian aristocracy in Transylvania immediately before World War II. Of the many foreigners who have written about Transylvania, one notable figure is the great British travel writer Patrick Leigh Fermor, whose *Between The Woods and The Water* is an account of his pre-war wanderings in the area, where he had intended to sleep out rough under the stars but ended up mostly by being put up by the Hungarian aristocrats at the heart of Bánffy's tales.

ART AND CRAFT Religion formed a central driver for artistic development in Transylvania, from the frescoes enlivening church walls to the painted panelled ceilings and galleries found in many Reformed churches, often using simple floral decoration. The painting of icons on wood and glass is a notable artistic tradition of Transylvania, and at Sibiel in Sibiu County there is a whole museum dedicated to the painting of icons on glass (page 228), a technique that developed in the 18th century. The elaborately painted eggs found throughout Romania, though particularly associated with the Bucovina region in the northeast of the country, are another fine craft tradition with a clearly religious inspiration.

Among the centres of **pottery** production in Transylvania, the village of Corund in Harghita County (page 183) is the best known: the sale of pottery dominates the whole place. The **carving** of wood is another important rural tradition, seen at every scale from the impressive wooden gates, topped with a dovecote, characteristic of the Székely lands, to the carved wooden spoons on sale at markets and souvenir shops. In many Romanian villages, the rich carving of a distaff, used in spinning, by a young man for the object of his attractions was traditionally an important part of courtship. The **weaving and embroidery** of textiles was traditionally practised in every rural family, with patterns of clothing distinct for each community. The traditionally Saxon lands of southern Transylvania are, for example, associated with a rather more austere palette of clothing colours, with black and white dominating, than much of Wallachia to the south, where more colourful Ottoman influences were felt. Among the clothing items to look out for in souvenir and clothing stores today is the embroidered blouse known as the *ie,* which represents the very essence of Romanian fashion and remains highly fashionable in both traditional and reworked forms.

Secular Romanian **painting** received a great impetus in the 19th century through a group of Romanian artists who developed their skills overseas, particularly in France. The most important of them was Nicolae Grigorescu, who started his career painting frescoes in Romanian churches, but left for study in Paris in 1861. He became noted for his paintings of rural themes, in particular ox carts trundling slowly along country roads, as well as bucolic portraits of peasant girls. Other noted Romanian painters of the 19th century include Theodor Aman and Ștefan Luchian, both of whom also studied in Paris. Within Transylvania, Cluj-Napoca has established itself as a particularly important centre for modern art.

Among Romanian **sculptors**, the pre-eminent name is that of Constantin Brâncuşi, born in Gorj County to the south of Transylvania, who developed his career in Paris, becoming one of the most influential sculptors of the 20th century.

MUSIC Transylvania has a particularly rich folk music tradition. In most places, the musical performances at weddings and other social events are typically in the hands of bands of Roma musicians, members of the *lăutari*, or musicians', clan. The typical line-up of instruments in a folk band involves two violins or fiddles, two *contras* (a form of viola) and one double bass. Some more traditional bands, such as the Palatka Band, stick to this line-up, but others have added further instruments. These might include a cimbalom, a hammered dulcimer, an accordion, and various brass and wind instruments. Clarinets are quite popular in Transylvanian bands, and guitars, drums and keyboards are increasingly so. The bands usually take the name either of the village they hail from, or the name of the band leader, who is typically the lead fiddle player. A Roma band is usually called a *taraf*. The lead fiddle plays the melody, with the *contras* and double bass providing the rhythm.

Because Roma musicians would be hired to play at both ethnic Hungarian and ethnic Romanian events, their repertoires typically range across Romanian, Hungarian and Roma tunes. Newer musical styles are also increasingly entering the repertoires heard at weddings and other events, of which the most controversial is *manele*, which adds Turkish or Balkan influences, and frequently rather base and sexist lyrics.

Among the ethnic Hungarian communities, the revival of popularity from the 1970s of the *táncház*, literally 'dance house', movement, focused on community-based folk dancing, initially as a reaction against attempts by the Communist regime to suppress Hungarian culture, provided a further source of employment for the Roma bands, and are a good place to hear folk music. The Hungarian composers **Béla Bartók and Zoltán Kodály** travelled extensively in Transylvania to research Hungarian folk music in the early part of the 20th century, and incorporated elements of these melodies into their compositions. The contemporary Hungarian folk group Muzsikás has specialised in helping to preserve the legacy of Bartók's folk-music-collecting trips by holding concerts combining the classical compositions of Bartók and Kodály with traditional tunes.

Among Romanian classical composers, the most influential and best known is **George Enescu**, who hailed from the far northeast of the country and was strongly influenced by the folk music of Romania, seen to striking effect in his most famous compositions, the two *Romanian Rhapsodies*. The first rhapsody even starts out by referencing a folk song titled 'I Have a Coin and Want to Drink It'.

As regards pop music, the most successful Romanian-language pop song internationally, *Dragostea din Tei* in 2003, was actually the work of a band from the Republic of Moldova, O-Zone. A duo from Cluj-Napoca did reach number two in the UK singles charts in 2002: unfortunately the name of that duo was The Cheeky Girls, and their hit, *Cheeky Song* ('*Touch My Bum*') is a track regularly at risk of being voted the worst pop record of all time.

ARCHITECTURE Transylvania offers a broad range of architectural styles. Many of the fortified churches established by the Transylvanian Saxons began life as **Romanesque** buildings, although most were later reworked in a Gothic style, with their Romanesque roots seen in a few elements of the present-day buildings. **Gothic** architecture is well represented in the churches across the region. The Black Church in Braşov (pages 124–5), a three-nave basilica, is the largest Gothic church in Romania. St Michael's Church in Cluj-Napoca (page 290) and the Evangelical

Roma musicians, traditionally those of the *lăutari* clan, have played an important role in the musical life of Transylvania. Accustomed to performing at weddings and other social events of both ethnic Romanian and ethnic Hungarian communities, their repertoire typically mixes Hungarian, Romanian and Roma styles. Some Roma bands from Romania have received international recognition and fans, through a fast-paced style characterised by a large role for brass instruments alongside the violins and accordions, and mixing in a Balkan beat sound with more traditional arrangements. Here are the major names to look out for: the first three are the big-hitters, all hailing from outside Transylvania, while the remaining names are smaller-scale and traditional groups and artists from Transylvania, all of which have produced recordings that offer good introductions to the Roma music of the region.

FANFARE CIOCĂRLIA A Roma band in the Balkan brass tradition, from the village of Zece Prăjini in the Moldavia region of eastern Romania, they are known for their fast sound and eccentric renditions of songs such as 'Born to be Wild.'

MAHALA RAI BANDA A Bucharest-based band with links both to the *lăutari* of the village of Clejani south of the capital, and to Zece Prăjini in Moldavia, they combine traditional folk tunes with a Balkan-influenced beat.

TARAF DE HAÏDOUKS From the village of Clejani south of Bucharest, whose Roma *lăutari* have long been renowned as accomplished musicians, they were launched internationally soon after the Romanian Revolution, and appeared alongside Johnny Depp in Sally Potter's 2000 film *The Man Who Cried*.

cathedral in Sibiu (page 222) are both fine Gothic buildings. And a large number of the fortified churches in the Saxon areas of southern Transylvania were reworked as Gothic hall churches in the 14th century.

The **Renaissance** style is Represented in both religious and secular buildings. Thus the Gothic Evangelical church in Bistrița was reworked in a Renaissance style in 1560 by a Swiss architect named Petrus Italus da Lugano, who also provided a Renaissance makeover to the nearby Casa Argintarului. The Renaissance style is also seen in some of the aristocratic castles of the region, such as Kemény Castle in Brâncoveneşti (pages 199–200) and Bethlen Castle at Criş (page 207), both in Mureş County. In the late 17th century, an important architectural style was evolving in the Principality of Wallachia to the south of Transylvania, known as the **Brâncovenesc** style, sometimes also referred to as the Romanian Renaissance style. This was associated with the then ruler of Wallachia, Constantin Brâncoveanu, and synthesised the late Renaissance and emerging Baroque styles of the West with eastern Byzantine and Ottoman styles. The best example of this style to be found within Transylvania is at the Sâmbăta de Sus Monastery in Braşov County (pages 150–1).

The **Baroque** is well represented in Transylvania. With the rise of Habsburg power, aristocratic families across the region modelled their palaces on a Viennese Imperial Baroque style, seen for example at the Bánffy Castle at Bonţida in Cluj County (pages 295–6) and the Brukenthal Palace in Sibiu (page 220). And many of the Gothic fortified churches of southern Transylvania display a number of Baroque

PALATKA BAND From the village of Pălatca, Palatka in Hungarian, in Cluj County, an area within the Câmpia Transilvaniei, which is known for its strong musical tradition. Led by violinist Florin Codoba, the band comprises two violins, two violas and one double bass.

SÁNDOR 'NETI' FODOR A renowned fiddle player from the Kalotaszeg region, he died in 2004, but a CD of his energetic playing entitled *Hungarian Music from Transylvania,* accompanied by a group of dance house musicians from Budapest, is well worth seeking out (page 335).

THE MÁCSINGÓ FAMILY Like the Palatka Band, based around the traditional line-up of two fiddles, two violas and one double bass, this band is headed by György Mácsingó and hails from Bărăi (Báré in Hungarian) near Pălatca, and from Deva.

ÖKRÖS ENSEMBLE Led by fiddle player Csaba Ökrös, they are typically a six-piece band, adding a cimbalom to the traditional line-up of two fiddles, two violas and one double bass. Their CD entitled *Transylvanian Village Music* also features the fiddle playing of Sándor 'Neti' Fodor.

TARAFUL LUI ALESANDRU CIURCUI DIN SOPORU DE CÂMPIE Led by Alesandru Ciurcui, this is another good Roma band from the Câmpia Transilvaniei area of Cluj County.

SZÁSZCSÁVÁS BAND From the village of Szászcsávás (Ceuaş in Romanian), a majority ethnic Hungarian settlement in Mureş County, this band is led by fiddle player Jámbor István, nicknamed 'Dumnezu'. Szászcsávás is, incidentally, also known musically for the unusual polyphonic singing style of the village choir.

features in their interiors, frequently including the pulpit and altar. Another of the distinctive architectural features of the region derives from a prohibition by the Catholic Habsburg rulers of the building of Romanian Orthodox churches in stone. The result was the appearance of some fine **wooden churches**, with their distinctive tall and slender spires, for example that at Fildu de Sus in Sălaj County (page 319), which dates from 1727.

Towards the end of the 19th century, following the union of Wallachia and Moldavia and the establishment of modern Romania, a new **neo-Romanian** architectural style developed, associated with Ion Mincu, who is considered the founder of modern Romanian architecture. This combined neoclassical elements with a renewed focus on traditional Romanian styles, particularly Brâncovenesc architecture. There are many examples of this work to be seen today in Bucharest. Transylvania during this period was part of Hungary, and subject to very different architectural influences. The **Art Nouveau** Secession style is particularly well represented in Târgu Mureş, above all in its outstanding Palace of Culture, built between 1911 and 1913. But there are fine Art Nouveau buildings from this period elsewhere in Transylvania too, for example the Art Theatre in Deva. Also look out for the highly distinctive works of the architect Károly Kós, who was influenced by the Secession style, but combined this with a passion for traditional folk architecture, particularly of the Székely lands. His works include the Székely National Museum in Sfântu Gheorghe and the Cockerel Church in Cluj-Napoca.

The **Communist** period was characterised by an emphasis on industrialisation, and on a programme of urban planning based on the policy of systematisation which has resulted in urban landscapes of high-density apartment blocks, ugly and often crumbling administrative buildings and cultural centres and windswept concrete squares. While the historic centres of cities such as Braşov and Sibiu were fortunately spared, the effects of this Communist urban planning can be seen all too easily outside of these historic cores.

2

Practical Information

WHEN TO VISIT

Romanian winters are cold, especially in the mountains and on the high plateaux of Transylvania. This is the most challenging time to travel, with some high mountain passes closed, but Transylvania also offers a range of winter pursuits. Snow cannons help to ensure good skiing at the most important winter resort, Poiana Brașov, from December to April, and there is skiing at a range of other upland resorts too, though the season may be shorter. Winter is also the time to try out the Hotel of Ice at Lake Balea (pages 240–1).

April and, especially, May bring forth the best of the wild flowers carpeting the hay-meadows of the Carpathian lowlands and, avoiding the searing heat of the summer, are generally an excellent time to visit Transylvania, though spring rains are a risk. The summer months are considered the peak tourist season, including for domestic Romanian tourists, but can sizzle, and the larger cities of Brașov, Sibiu and Cluj-Napoca in particular can be stifling in summer, although Cluj-Napoca is a major student city and quieter during the summer break. This is a good time to visit more mountainous destinations.

While autumn offers less meteorological predictability than the height of summer, it is also a good time to visit, as the leaves paint the landscape in beautiful hues and there are many festivals connected with the harvest.

Spring and autumn are best for tackling strenuous hiking routes and give good opportunities for wildlife-watching. Note too that many accommodation providers offer discounted rates away from the summer season. In more touristy places such as Brașov and Sighișoara the difference between high- and off-season rates can be considerable. Conversely, many attractions open for longer periods in summer.

HIGHLIGHTS

Transylvania offers such an abundance of adventure, culture, history and natural interest that there really is something for everybody. Those wanting to ski will find slopes that suit all levels, from beginner to expert. Hikers, cyclists or simply those who wish to ramble through stunning countryside, track bear or wolf, watch birds or admire wild flowers can find some of the best environments in Europe in which to do all of these. There are now a number of UNESCO World Heritage-listed sights: the Dacian fortresses of the Orăștie Mountains, the medieval citadel of Sighișoara and remarkable Saxon fortified churches; not to mention delightful cities such as Sibiu and Brașov, offering a mix of medieval cityscapes and thoroughly modern festivals. And there are quirkier options to be had too, from following the trail of Dracula to joining the locals in health tourism options including taking the waters at numerous spas and spending time underground in a salt mine.

Getting around Transylvania still takes time: the motorway construction programme is years behind schedule and Romanian trains proceed at a gentle pace. But with horse-drawn carts still to be seen on many Transylvanian roads, and a range of truly spectacular drives to be had, travelling is part of the fun of a Transylvanian holiday. The following is a personal list of some of the highlights to aim for.

SIGHIŞOARA This gloriously preserved medieval citadel is a UNESCO World Heritage Site, and also the birthplace of Vlad the Impaler (pages 201–6).

BIERTAN A picturesque village offering one of the largest and most impressive of the Saxon fortified churches, set amid some great scenery (pages 232–3).

SIBIU A great mix of beautiful squares, fine museums and a cultural programme worthy of the 2007 European Capital of Culture (pages 213–24).

SOVATA-BĂI An enjoyable spa resort based around the saltwater Lake Ursu (pages 196–8).

ZĂRNEŞTI WOLF TOURS Visit the Marin family at their lovely guesthouse and spend the days walking and wildlife-watching in the Piatra Craiului National Park with *Wanderlust's* Guide of the Year 2007 (see pages 148–9).

TRADITIONAL ACCOMMODATION Transylvania has an increasingly wide offering of excellent accommodation options in thoughtfully preserved traditional buildings. Count Tibor Kálnoky's estate at Micloşoara (page 164), the Mikes Estate at Zăbala (pages 168–9) and the Raven's Nest resort high in the Apuseni Mountains (page 277) are among the best.

TURDA SALT MINE Ride a Ferris wheel in the depths of a salt mine (page 300).

TURDA GORGE A fine place to hike along the floor of a spectacular gorge (page 302).

LACUL ROŞU A mountain lake which is both beautiful and rather eerie, befitting its alternative name of Murderer's Lake (page 186).

BRAŞOV Combines a delightful historic city centre around the Gothic Black Church, with a great natural setting at the base of Mount Tâmpa (pages 124–5).

BRAN CASTLE While marketed inaccurately as 'Dracula's Castle', this is a worthy sight in its own right as a former favoured residence of Queen Marie (page 144).

RETEZAT NATIONAL PARK Transylvania contains some fine national parks; Retezat is particularly wild and spectacular (pages 256–60).

PREJMER Of all the Saxon fortified churches of Transylvania, this is the one which most closely resembles a fortress (pages 155–6).

THE APUSENI MOUNTAINS A great range of sites, from karst scenery to the Scarişoara Ice Cave and the amazing Roman gold-mine galleries at Roşia Montana (pages 269–77).

CORVIN CASTLE Somewhat incongruously located in the industrial town of Hunedoara, this is everyone's idea of a fairytale medieval castle, with a deep ravine, forbidding battlements and dark legends around its deep well (pages 250–2).

CLUJ-NAPOCA Transylvania's largest city has stacks to see and do and a relaxed studenty feel (pages 283–93).

MĂMĂLIGĂ, SARMALE* AND *ŢUICĂ Transylvania's culinary delights are an essential part of any holiday here (pages 92–6).

FOLK MUSIC Visit one of the many local music festivals across the region or hunt down Roma musicians in clubs and restaurants all over Transylvania (pages 51–53).

WILD FLOWERS The amazing late-spring carpet of wild flowers in hay-meadows across the region is one of its true treasures; the outcome of a complex interrelationship between humans and nature (pages 6–12).

SARMIZEGETUSA REGIA The most important and impressive of the UNESCO-listed Dacian hill fortresses, featuring the remains of mysterious circular temples (pages 248–9).

SUGGESTED ITINERARIES

A LONG WEEKEND Fly to Cluj-Napoca or Sibiu on one of the low-cost airlines. In Cluj, spend a leisurely morning exploring the town, admiring the view from the citadel hill, and talking in the fine Gothic interior of St Michael's Church and the controversial statue of Hungarian King Matthias Corvinus – his birthplace is also nearby. Enjoy a sustaining lunch in one of the many student pubs in this young, vibrant city and walk off the calories on a promenade around Cluj's lovely botanical garden. In the evening, tuck into a meal in a traditional restaurant or take in a performance at the brightly coloured Romanian National Theatre and Opera House.

The following day, take a trip to the nearby town of Turda and get a feel for the distinctively Romanian pursuit of therapeutic visits to the depths of a salt mine, complete with subterranean amusement park and boating lake. A walk through the scenic Turda Gorge is a great way to get some exercise and a taste of the Transylvanian countryside.

Alternatively, fly to Sibiu and spend the day wandering the streets of the beautifully restored historic centre. Take in the artistic treasures of the Brukenthal Museum before enjoying lunch alfresco at one of the many pavement café terraces. The following day could be spent either learning about Transylvanian rural architecture at the Astra open-air museum just outside the city, or for the more restless taking a day trip to Braşov, another fine Saxon city. Explore the medieval pedestrianised centre before taking a cable car up Tâmpa Hill to look down on the city.

ONE WEEK A week allows for a fine holiday exploring the fortified church villages of the former Saxon communities of southern Transylvania. Fly to Cluj-Napoca or Sibiu and stay locally in one of the traditional guesthouses in Biertan, Viscri, Saschiz, Mălâncrav or Micloşoara. Late spring or early summer is an ideal time to stay in this area, when the wild flowers in the meadows are at their finest.

Transylvania has something of a love-hate relationship with Dracula tourism. On the one hand, the inhabitants of a region so rich in treasures can find it rather galling that their home has been placed on the international tourist map less by virtue of any of these than by the fictional writings of a 19th-century Irish author who never actually set foot in the place. And these concerns are compounded for many Romanians by the fact that Count Dracula draws on a real historical figure, the 15th-century Vlad III Țepeș, Vlad the Impaler, who in contrast to his negative image abroad is viewed by many Romanians rather positively, in particular for his defence of Christendom against the Ottomans. On the other hand, there is an increasing recognition that Dracula draws in the tourists.

The use of Dracula by the tourist industry in Transylvania is often decidedly superficial, from the many hotels and restaurants across the region which have decided that simply adding 'Dracula' to their name, coupled with a bit of faux-medieval décor in the restaurant, is the way to pull in a few extra foreigners. Avoid dishes on menus with names like 'Dracula burger', which just indicates that you are likely to be served up something smothered in ketchup. There are many opportunities to buy Dracula-related merchandise, from the classical creepy masks to a Count Dracula snow globe, novelty T-shirt, or branded Dracula wine.

Those looking for more serious Dracula tourism have two broad options. The first is to visit places mentioned in or linked to Bram Stoker's novel. The key county in this respect is Bistrița-Năsăud, where the Transylvanian parts of the novel are set. One key place to aim for is the **Golden Krone Hotel in Bistrița**: in Bram Stoker's novel *Dracula*, Jonathan Harker stayed here in 'Bistritz' *en route* to the Count's castle (page 305). And then there's **Bran Castle**, marketed as 'Dracula's Castle' by tourist companies across Romania, though actually nowhere near the site of

TWO WEEKS Fly to Bucharest and hire a car. Drive up to Transylvania through the wine-growing Prahova Valley. Stay with Dan and Luminița Marin at their Zărnești guesthouse and visit the sights in the surrounding area, like Bran Castle and the Libearty Bear Sanctuary, as well as some invigorating and inspiring walks in the Piatra Craiului National Park. Make Brașov your next base and enjoy the sights of this beautiful Saxon city. Head leisurely northwards along the E60 highway, taking in the gorgeous medieval citadel of Sighișoara, as well as some of the fortified Saxon church villages, like Saschiz, Viscri and Biertan. You might want a breather by now, so visit Sovata-Băi and wallow in the warm, salty Lacul Ursu. Take in the unusual attraction of Praid's salt mine, complete with subterranean restaurant and cinema, and pick up some folk pottery in nearby Corund. Târgu Mureș is a good next stop, with some fine buildings. You shouldn't miss the stained-glass windows of its Art Nouveau Palace of Culture. The E60 continues to cosmopolitan Cluj-Napoca, but you might fancy a spot of hiking in the Apuseni Mountains or a lakeside rest at Lacul Fântânele in the Kalotaszeg region of gentle rolling hills and traditional ethnic Hungarian villages.

TOUR OPERATORS

INTERNATIONAL TOUR OPERATORS A wide variety of tour operators in the UK and North America offer holidays in Transylvania. They cover a wide range of specialist interests, as well as more general tours, reflecting the breadth of Transylvania's attractions: from Dracula to birdwatching; downhill skiing to bear tracking.

the Count's castle as suggested in the novel. Stoker had probably seen pictures of this strikingly located castle, at the top of a steep crag, when researching his novel (page 144). Before arriving in Bistriţa, Jonathan Harker stayed a night at the fictional **Hotel Royale in Cluj-Napoca**, referred to as 'Klausenburgh' in the novel (pages 283–93). The **Tihuţa Pass in Bistriţa-Năsăud County** is the 'Borgo Pass' from Bram Stoker's novel, and the setting for the Castel Dracula Hotel, built in the Communist period (pages 309–10).

The other option is to visit sites linked to the life of vlad the Impaler, the real historical figure who served as an inspiration for Stoker's count. This offers some rich touristic possibilities, but note that, although he was born in Transylvania, Vlad Ţepeş was prince not of Transylvania but of the more southerly region of Wallachia. Most of the main sites associated with his life therefore lie outside Transylvania. Vlad the Impaler built the Old Princely Court, the Curtea Veche, as his residence while he was protecting the southern boundary of Wallachia against the Turks. The Court lies in the attractive Old Town of present-day **Bucharest**, close to the Piaţa Unirii metro station. In an impressive spot on a high precipice, **Poenari Castle** was strengthened by Vlad the Impaler, for whom it was an important fortress. It is now a ruin, located on the DN7C, the Transfăgărăşan Highway (page 241). Vlad was born in 1431 in **Sighişoara**, where his father had settled a couple of years earlier (pages 201–6). Some claim that Vlad the Impaler is buried at **Snagov Monastery** (pages 136–7), attractively sited on a small island in a lake some 35km north of Bucharest off the main route DN1/E60. On the other hand, he is also said to be buried in the monastery at Comana, south of Bucharest. Basically, nobody knows. Lastly, **Târgovişte** was the capital of Wallachia at the time, and its royal court was extended by Vlad the Impaler, who added the Chindia Tower, the symbol of the town.

UK

Balkan Holidays ☎ 0207 543 5555;
w balkanholidays.co.uk. Specialists in beach & ski holidays in Bulgaria & other Balkan countries, they offer ski & snowboard trips in Poiana Braşov.
Beyond the Forest ☎ 01900 838570;
w beyondtheforest.com. Mike Morton runs one of the best specialist tour companies to all parts of Transylvania with tailor-made trips, including Count Tibor Kálnoky's estate (pages 163–4). Their website includes good background information on a range of Romania-related themes, from the legacy of Ceauşescu to Romanian trams.
Charity Challenge ☎ 020 8346 0500;
w charitychallenge.com. Adventure travel company specialising in charity fundraising expeditions. Offers a challenging 6-day Transylvania trek in Aug.
Exodus ☎ 0203 131 8320; w exodus.co.uk. The global adventure specialists have several Transylvania options, including an 8-day

Carpathian walking & wildlife-watching tour & a 9-day self-guided cycling trip.
Explore ☎ 01252 883702; w explore.co.uk. Transylvania tours including a winter adventure featuring a night at the Ice Hotel at Balea Lake & a long weekend trip combining castles & bear watching.
Regent Holidays ☎ 0207 666 1244; w regent-holidays.co.uk. Independent operator specialising in eastern European destinations. Several tours featuring Transylvania, including one focused on the life of Vlad the Impaler.
Responsible Travel ☎ 01273 823700;
w responsibletravel.com. Responsible Travel is an online travel directory for travellers who want authentic holidays that benefit the local people. They feature a wide range of Transylvania options, eg: a week volunteering at the Libearty Bear Sanctuary in Zărneşti. Their website includes an online Romania Travel Guide.
Riding Holidays w ridingholidays.com. Directory of riding holidays worldwide. Featured

2

Transylvanian providers include Equus Silvania in Şinca Nouă (page 149).

Transylvania Live UK ✆0808 101 6781, Romania ✆+40 364 411 666; w visit-transylvania. co.uk. Anglo-Romanian tour operator, with a responsible travel policy, based in the UK & Turda. Offers a wide range of tours, including walking, cycling & motorbike itineraries, Dracula-themed breaks & skiing.

Undiscovered Destinations ✆0191 296 2674; w undiscovered-destinations.com. Offers a 14-day Romania tour combining Transylvania, Bucovina & the Danube Delta.

Walks Worldwide ✆01962 737 565; w walksworldwide.com. Offers Transylvania hiking tours including a mountain trek involving a climb of Romania's highest peak.

Wild Frontiers Travel UK ✆020 8741 7390, US ✆+1 800 454 1080; w wildfrontierstravel.com. Adventure travel company offering an interesting 10-day walking tour in Maramureş & Transylvania inspired by William Blacker's book *Along the Enchanted Way* (page 331).

World Expeditions ✆020 8875 5060, freephone 0800 0744 135; w worldexpeditions.com. With offices also in Australia, Canada & New Zealand, these trekking & adventure travel specialists offer a range of guided & self-guided walking & cycling holidays.

Wildlife specialists in the UK
Naturetrek ✆01962 733051; w naturetrek.co.uk. Offers general wildlife tours of Transylvania, covering birds, bears & butterflies, as well as a combined Transylvania & Danube Delta tour.

Probirder w probirder.com. Specialising in birding & wildlife tours based in Budapest. British birding & wildlife tour leader Gerard Gorman & his team have been leading tours to the region for over 25 years. Birding tours to Romania & winter wildlife tracking in Transylvania.

The Travelling Naturalist ✆01305 267994; w naturalist.co.uk. Offers an 8-day birds & bears in Transylvania tour ranging from Zărneşti to Lacul Roşu.

USA & Canada

Adventure Transylvania ✆+1 360 851 4444, Romania m 0762 181 664; w adventuretransylvania.com. Tour company originally based in Romania, but which moved to the USA in 2015, focused on tailor-made private tours.

Adventures Abroad Canada ✆toll free +1 800 665 3998 or +1 604 303 1099, US ✆+1 360 755 9926; w adventures-abroad.com. Offers an 8-day Romania tour, including Transylvania, as well as several wider regional tours.

Quest Tours & Adventures ✆toll free +1 800 621 8687; w romtour.com. Specialising in Romania & Bulgaria, they offer a range of tours, from Dracula to Romanian UNESCO World Heritage Sites.

Wilderness Travel ✆toll free +1 800 368 2794 or +1 510 558 2488; w wildernesstravel.com. Tours include a 2-week hiking package with treks in 5 different Carpathian countries, including Romania.

LOCAL TRAVEL AGENTS Transylvania is a pretty accessible option for travellers looking to self-drive by hire car: there is an increasingly broad range of accommodation options available, prices are lower than in most of western Europe, and Romanians have a high level of knowledge of English. The quality of some of the driving you will encounter is the major challenge. Putting together your own itinerary using public transport can be more difficult if you intend to do more than visit the main cities, as public transport connections to some of the more out-of-the-way locations can be poor or non-existent. Here the use of a local travel agency to set up a tailor-made programme can be an option well worth considering. Of course, a good local guide is also a fount of information on local history, culture, flora and fauna, and can add considerably to your understanding.

A number of specialised accommodation providers offer all-inclusive packages, frequently including airport pickups, full board and a range of local excursions. While this is less flexible than do-it-yourself travel and more expensive than basic DIY itineraries, it can be a great hassle-free way to visit Transylvania. Detailed information on these is given in the relevant county chapters, with the best identified as author recommendations.

Absolute Carpathian ✆0368 413 524; m 0788 578 796; e book@absolute-nature.ro; w absolute-nature.ro. Formed by a team originally from the Carpathian Large Carnivore Project, they offer a range of wildlife-watching programmes, including bear, wolf & the elusive lynx, as well as tailor-made holidays.

Apuseni Experience ✆ 0359 410 556; m 0745 602 301; e contact@apuseniexperience.ro; w apuseniexperience.ro. Offers a wide range of trips in the Apuseni Mountains, covering trekking, cycling, caving, skiing & botany. Also happy to set up tailor-made trips.

Caliman Club Holidays ✆0363 401 510; e calimanclub@gmail.com; w calimanclub.com. Offers a wide range of energetic pursuits from white-water rafting to skiing, kayaking to mountain biking. With its own outdoor centre at Lacul Colibiţa (page 309).

Cycling Romania m 0746 110 033; e mircea@cyclingromania.ro; w cyclingromania.ro. Cycling specialists who offer a 7-day Saxon Transylvania bike tour.

DiscoveRomania m 0722 746 262; e office@discoveromania.ro; w discoveromania.ro. Braşov-based agency which offers a wide range of itineraries, including trekking, Saxon fortified churches & wildlife tours, as well as tailor-made programmes.

Johan's Green Mountain m 0744 637 227; e office@greenmountain.ro; w greenmountain.ro. Cluj-Napoca-based tour operator specialising in active holidays, offering self-guided hiking & cycling tours, & guided riding, hiking & caving itineraries.

MC Transylvania ✆0265 260 881; m 0751 254 117; e info@mctransylvania.com; w mctransylvania.com. Set up by Frenchman Jean Michel Corbet, they offer individual & group programmes, including Dracula-themed evenings.

Mihai Eminescu Trust (MET) ✆0265 506 024; e booking@experiencetransylvania.ro; w experiencetransylvania.ro. This organisation is dedicated to the conservation & regeneration of villages in Transylvania & offers accommodation in beautifully restored guesthouses in Mălâncrav, Alma Vii, Biertan, Criţ, Sighişoara & Viscri, ranging from simple village houses to the Apafi Manor in Mălâncrav.

MTB Tours m 0740 248 246; e contact@mtbtours.ro; w mtbtours.ro. Braşov-based mountain-bike specialists, associated with Iulian Cozma's Step by Step Agency.

Professional Team ✆0374 977 098; m 0730 653 747; e contact@professionalteam.ro;

w professionalteam.ro. Professional mountain guides, organising wildlife-tracking tours in the Carpathians, team-building events, ecological education camps for young people, & opportunities to volunteer on nature conservation projects in Piatra Craiului National Park.

Rina Tours & Travel ✆021 318 6184; e office@rinatours.ro; w rinatours.ro. Bucharest-based agency offering a 4-day Dracula tour as well as bespoke itineraries, including cycling, hiking & even snowmobile riding.

Roving România m 0724 348 272; e rovingrom@gmail.com; w roving-romania.co.uk. An Englishman in Braşov, Colin Shaw specialises in tailor-made Land Rover-based small group tours, with Colin acting as both driver & guide. They also offer tailor-made hiking, cycling & mountain-biking tours.

Step by Step Agency m 0744 327 686; e contact@mountainguide.ro; w mountainguide.ro. Iulian Cozma is a professional mountain guide based in Braşov & takes visitors hiking, trekking & ski touring in the Făgăraş, Retezat, Bucegi & Piatra Craiului ranges.

Tioc Naturund Studienreisen m 0743 025 154; e contact@tioc-reisen.ro; w tioc-reisen.ro. Ecologist Emil Tiberiu Tioc offers nature tours combining the Transylvanian mountains with the Danube Delta as well as ski touring & mountain biking in Transylvania.

Transylvanian Wolf Contact Dan Marin, Str Mitropolit Ioan Metianu nr 108, Zărneşti 505800, jud Braşov; m 0744 319 708; e transylvanian_wolf@yahoo.com; w transylvanianwolf.ro. Guided tours with *Wanderlust* award-winning guide exploring traditional rural areas, Roma music & dance evenings, birdwatching, wildlife tracking, guesthouse accommodation & delicious homecooked meals. For more information, see the Braşov County chapter, pages 148–9.

True Romania Tours m 0755 365 778; e info@true-romania.tours; w true-romania.tours. Offers private-guided & self-drive tours, with both suggested & tailor-made itineraries for small groups & families. Focus on cultural, nature, food & wine, genealogy & photo tours. See ad, page 54.

Visit Transylvania m 0744 693 232; e office@visittransilvania.ro; w visittransilvania.ro. Offers small-group tours (with up to 12 people) starting from Bucharest including a 4-day Transylvania tour covering Braşov, Sibiu & Sighişoara, a 3-day Dracula tour, & a 5-day discover Romania tour which combines Transylvania with the painted monasteries of Bucovina. Also offers tailored private tours.

TOURIST OFFICES

The Romanian governmental structure for the promotion of tourism has been undergoing considerable changes. The centre-left coalition government elected following the December 2016 parliamentary elections announced the establishment of a fully fledged Ministry of Tourism (w *turism.gov.ro*), absorbing the structures of the former National Tourism Authority (Autoritatea Naţională pentru Turism – ANT), which had hitherto been subordinated to the Ministry of the Economy. The Ministry of Tourism operates a small network of overseas offices, though it announced in May 2017 that these would all be closed, while the way in which Romania's tourism is represented abroad was revised.

At a local level, Transylvania has seen a mushrooming in recent years of tourist information centres, often supported by EU funding. Many of the new arrivals have been set up in gleaming pavilions, and are known as National Centres for Tourist Information and Promotion (Centrele Naţionale de Informare şi Promovare Turistică – CNIPT). They are co-ordinated by the local authorities but accredited by the national Ministry of Tourism. Their details are given under the relevant entries in Part Two of the guide. But some of those established in towns and villages with a relatively modest tourist flux seem unsure of their purpose, fail to maintain the advertised opening hours and, when they are open, are rather at a loss as to what to provide beyond a brochure or two. The lady at the tourist office in Sovata-Băi attempted to discourage me from entering her office at all by calling out 'We can't help you find accommodation!' The offices in the larger cities, especially Cluj-Napoca and Sibiu, tend to be better, and there is an excellent tourist information point in Saschiz (page 210), privately run by the ADEPT non-governmental organisation.

IN TRANSYLVANIA
Contact information for individual tourist information offices in Transylvania is given in the relevant city entries in Part Two of the guide.

ROMANIAN TOURISM ASSOCIATIONS
AER (Romanian Ecotourism Association) w asociatiaaer.ro
AGMR (Romanian Mountain Guides Association) w agmr.ro

ANAT (National Association of Travel Agencies in Romania) w anat.ro
ANTREC (National Association of Rural Ecological and Cultural Tourism) w antrec.ro
OPTBR (Organisation of Spa Owners in Romania) w romanian-spas.ro

RED TAPE

Romania became a member of the European Union on 1 January 2007, although at the time of writing it is not part of the Schengen Agreement, between whose member states internal border checks have largely been abolished, although has applied to join. However, for visitors coming for stays of less than 90 days, travel from all EU but also many other countries, including the USA and Canada, is visa-free and straightforward.

ENTRY REQUIREMENTS At the time of research, the citizens of some 58 countries do not need a visa to enter Romania as a tourist for stays of up to 90 days, including UK and all EU citizens and those of Canada, the USA, Australia, New Zealand, Israel and Japan (full list on the Ministry of Foreign Affairs website, w *mae.ro*). EU citizens may enter the country with their national identity card; all other visitors require a valid passport. It is recommended that passports are valid for at least six months from the date of travel, since some airlines refuse boarding if the passport is not valid for at least three months beyond the intended departure date.

Holders of passports not exempt from visa requirements must obtain a visa from a Romanian embassy outside Romania before travelling. For stays of up to 90 days, the visa requirement is exempted for holders of Schengen visas, even though Romania is not in the Schengen Agreement, but only if the Schengen visa allows for at least two entries in the Schengen space and both the number of entries and permitted length of stay have not been exhausted. The visa requirement may also be exempted for holders of national visas or residence permits issued by Schengen member states or permanent residence permits issued by the UK or the Republic of Ireland. There is an online application process at w evisa.mae.ro.

If you intend to stay longer than 90 days in Romania, whether for business, study or to carry out volunteer work, you will need a temporary residence permit. This must be applied for at the Immigration Office (Birou Imigrări) nearest to you, at least 30 days before the expiry of your current status. The contact details and opening hours of all of these are listed on the website of the General Inspectorate for Immigration (w *igi.mai.gov.ro*). This is a somewhat bureaucratic procedure, involving an application form, proof of employment, study or sufficient funds, and some additional requirements for non-EU citizens, including proof of accommodation. There are also some fees to pay: tiny but fiddly for EU citizens, rather more substantial for non-EU citizens.

Despite the red tape involved, please don't be tempted to ignore the requirement to obtain a temporary residence permit as overstays can incur both a fine and a temporary ban on returning to Romania.

CUSTOMS REGULATIONS Romanian customs regulations are in line with other EU countries. Visitors arriving from a non-EU country can bring into Romania goods of no commercial character up to a limit of 40 cigarettes, 50 cigars, four litres of wine and one litre of spirits and goods including perfume up to a value of €430 for air and sea travellers and €300 for other travellers. Travellers entering or leaving the EU with more than €10,000 in cash or travellers' cheques must declare this to the customs authorities. Full details on Romanian customs regulations is available at w www.customs.ro, but this is mostly in Romanian only. There is general guidance in English on the European Commission site w ec.europa.eu. If you are arriving into Romania from an EU country there are no limits on what you can bring with you provided that the items are for your personal use and not to be resold.

As in other EU countries, a sales tax (VAT) is in use in Romania. This is currently 20% in respect of most purchases, though is scheduled to reduce to 19%, and a lower rate of 9% for hotel stays. Visitors from countries outside the EU can claim a **VAT/tax refund** on departure, under certain conditions. This must be done at a VAT refund office (Birou de Restituire TVA), which are found at major border crossings. You will need to present both a receipt (*factura fiscală*) for your purchase, and a tax refund form (*formular de restituire TVA*); only high-end stores tend to be able to provide the necessary paperwork, which needs to be validated by the customs office. The purchases must have a total value of more than 250RON, and have been purchased 90 days or less before your departure from Romania.

EMBASSIES AND CONSULATES

OVERSEAS A comprehensive list of Romania's embassies overseas can be found on the website of the Romanian Ministry of Foreign Affairs (w *mae.ro*).

IN ROMANIA

🇦 Australia Level 6, Thon Bldg, Cnr Kifisias & Alexandras Av, Ambelokipi, 11523, Athens (Greece); +30 210 870 40 00; Honorary Consulate: The Group, Str Praga, 3, Bucharest; +40 21 062 200; e office@australianconsulate. ro; w greece.embassy.gov.au

🇧 Belgium B-dul Dacia 58, Sector 2, Bucharest; +40 21 210 2969; e ambabuc@gmail.com

🇨 Canada Str Tuberozelor 1–3, Sector 1, Bucharest; +40 21 307 5000; e bucst@ international.gc.ca; w canadainternational.gc.ca/ romania-roumanie

🇫 France Str Biserica Amzei 13–15, Sector 1, Bucharest; +40 21 303 1000; e chancellerie-bucaerest@diplomatie.gouv.fr; w ambafrance-ro.org

🇩 Germany Str Gheorghe Demetriade 6–8, Sector 1, Bucharest; +40 21 202 9830; e info@bukarest.diplo.de; w bukarest.diplo.de. Within Transylvania, Germany also maintains a consulate in Sibiu: Str Lucian Blaga 15–17; +40

269 206 211; e info@hermannstadt.diplo.de; w hermannstadt.diplo.de

🇭 Hungary Str Jean-Louis Calderon 63–65, Sector 2, Bucharest; +40 21 620 4300; e mission.buc@mfa.gov.hu; w bukarest.mfa. gov.hu. Hungary is the only country to maintain significant diplomatic missions in Transylvania itself, reflecting the sizeable ethnic Hungarian community, many members of whom have Hungarian as well as Romanian citizenship. Consulate-General in Miercurea-Ciuc: Str Petöfi Sándor 45; +40 266 207 335; e titkarsag.csk@ mfa.gov.hu. Consulate-General in Cluj-Napoca: Piaţa Unirii 23; +40 264 590 561.

🇬 UK Str Jules Michelet 24, Sector 1, Bucharest; +40 21 201 7200 (general enquiries), +40 21 201 7351 (consular enquiries); e BritishEmbassy. Bucharest@fco.gov.uk

🇺 USA B-dul Dr Liviu Librescu, 4–6, Sector 1, Bucharest; +40 21 200 3300; e visasbucharest@ state.gov; w ro.usembassy.gov

GETTING THERE AND AWAY

BY AIR Transylvania has three international airports (Cluj-Napoca, Sibiu and Târgu Mureş), although the airport at Târgu Mureş was closed for repairs at the time of research. But many visitors arrive at the international airport in Bucharest, which offers a much wider range of flight destinations and is straightforward to access by both road and rail, albeit at the cost of bringing you into Romania outside of Transylvania itself. There are also longstanding plans to construct a further international airport at Ghimbav, just outside Braşov, although these have long been stalled.

Airlines serving Bucharest are a mix of traditional or legacy carriers (including the Romanian national carrier, Tarom) and budget airlines. The former are more likely to offer more central airports at your city of departure (in London, Heathrow, rather than Luton or Stansted), better baggage allowances and some in-flight catering, but at a higher ticket cost. But the difference between the two types of airlines is gradually becoming less marked, particularly on the short European routes that make up the overwhelming majority of flights into Romania, as the legacy carriers trim all frills, including in-flight catering, and both types of airlines offer low prices for customers able to book their flights well in advance. Discount travel websites such as w cheapflights.co.uk, w expedia. com and w lastminute.co.uk can offer bargain flight prices. If you travel by plane and feel bad about climate change, w climatecare.org has a carbon calculator that allows travellers to offset their greenhouse gas emissions by contributing to energy-saving projects in the developing world. Or take the sedate way to Transylvania and travel by train.

Airlines flying to Romania and Transylvania
From the UK

✈ British Airways 0344 493 0787; w britishairways.com. British Airways fly twice daily from London Heathrow to Bucharest (return

tickets start from £136). Flight time is 3hrs 20mins.

✈ Blue Air UK 0903 760 130, Romania +40 374 281 841; w blueairweb.com. The low-cost

Romanian airline offers a rapidly growing range of connections between UK & Romanian airports. It has at least 4 flights daily from London Luton to Bucharest Otopeni with prices starting from £97 return including taxes. It also has 4 flights a week from London Luton to Cluj-Napoca, & serves Cluj-Napoca from Birmingham (3 flights a week) & Liverpool (2 per week). Blue Air also has flights from Birmingham, Glasgow & Liverpool to Bucharest.

✈ **Ryanair** 📞0871 246 0000; **w** ryanair.com. Ryanair flies twice daily from London Stansted to Bucharest (return from £56), 3 times a week to Oradea (return from £70) & daily to Timişoara (return from £20). It also has a weekly flight from Bristol to Bucharest.

✈ **Tarom** UK📞0208 745 5542; **e** lonoffice@ taromuk.co.uk, Romania📞+40 21 204 6464; **w** tarom.ro. The Romanian national carrier has daily flights from London Heathrow to Bucharest Otopeni, & from London Luton to Iaşi twice a week.

✈ **Wizz Air** **w** wizzair.com. Wizz Air flies from London Luton to Bucharest 2–3 times a day, & also serves the Romanian capital from London Gatwick (5 flights per week), Birmingham (3 flights per week), Doncaster/Sheffield (2–3 flights per week) & Glasgow (2 flights per week). It flies twice a week from Doncaster/Sheffield to Cluj-Napoca & 5 times a week from London Luton to Sibiu. The Wizz Air service from London Luton to Târgu Mureş was suspended at the time of research while repairs to the runway were carried out. Wizz Air also serves a host of other Romanian cities from London Luton: Constanţa, Craiova, Iaşi, Satu Mare, Suceava & Timişoara, & has a service from Liverpool to Craiova.

From the Irish Republic
There is a wide range of options from Dublin to Bucharest connecting through other European cities, but the following 2 airlines fly direct.

✈ **Blue Air** **w** blueairweb.com. Flies daily from Dublin to Bucharest & 3 times a week to Cluj-Napoca.

✈ **Ryanair** **w** ryanair.com. Flies 5 times a week from Dublin to Bucharest.

From Europe
There are numerous services to Bucharest from a wide range of cities across western Europe. Cluj-Napoca has direct connections to many European destinations, although flight frequencies to most

are no more than 2 or 3 flights per week, & there is a smaller selection of direct services to Sibiu, with the many connections to that city from Munich a reflection of southern Transylvania's close cultural links with southern Germany. Wizz Air services to Târgu Mureş were suspended at the time of research as that airport was closed for repair.

✈ **Air France** **w** airfrance.com. Flights from Paris to Bucharest.

✈ **Austrian Airlines** **w** austrian.com. Flights from Vienna to both Bucharest & Sibiu.

✈ **Blue Air** **w** blueairweb.com. Flights to Bucharest from a large range of European airports, plus Tel Aviv, & to Cluj-Napoca from Hamburg, Larnaca & Nice.

✈ **Eurowings** **w** eurowings.com. Flights to Bucharest from Düsseldorf.

✈ **KLM** **w** klm.com. Flights to Bucharest from Amsterdam.

✈ **LOT** **w** lot.com. Flights from Warsaw to both Bucharest & Cluj-Napoca.

✈ **Lufthansa** **w** lufthansa.com. Flights to Cluj-Napoca (3 times daily) & Sibiu (twice daily) from Munich, & from Bucharest to Frankfurt & Munich.

✈ **Ryanair** **w** ryanair.com. Flights to Bucharest from several European cities.

✈ **Scandinavian Airlines** **w** flysas.com. Flights to Bucharest from Copenhagen.

✈ **Swiss International Airlines** **w** swiss.com. Flights to Bucharest from Zürich.

✈ **Tarom** **w** tarom.ro. The Romanian national carrier flies to Bucharest from a range of cities, including Amsterdam, Athens, Barcelona, Budapest, Frankfurt, Hamburg, Istanbul, Madrid, Munich, Paris, Stockholm & Vienna, as well as Tel Aviv. It also serves Munich from Sibiu.

✈ **Turkish Airlines** **w** turkishairlines.com. Flights to both Bucharest & Cluj-Napoca from Istanbul.

✈ **Wizz Air** **w** wizzair.com. Wizz Air flies from both Bucharest & Cluj-Napoca to a large range of European destinations & from Sibiu to Madrid, Milan & several destinations in Germany.

Long-haul flights to Romania
At the time of research there weren't any direct long-haul flights to Romania. Travellers from the USA, Canada, Australia or New Zealand will have to change at one of a range of European airports. Flight websites such as **w** expedia.com will help you find the best deals.

Main airport

Bucharest Otopeni-Henri Coandă International Airport (OTP)

(w *bucharestairports.ro*) The airport is 16km north of central Bucharest (*25mins*) on the main DN1/E60 highway from Bucharest to Ploiesti and on to Braşov. It is by some margin the busiest airport in Romania, and is generally known as Otopeni, after the Bucharest suburb in which it is located. It is also officially named after Henri Coandă, honouring a distinguished Romanian aircraft builder and pioneer of aerodynamics. Note that Bucharest has a second airport, much closer to the city centre, formally known as Aurel Vlaicu Airport, honouring another great name in Romanian aviation, the flight pioneer Aurel Vlaicu, but much more commonly known as Băneasa airport after the local district of the city. But in 2012 all scheduled flights were moved to Otopeni airport, and Băneasa is reserved for private jets and charter flights.

Otopeni airport is modern and broadly efficient, though the recent expansion in the volume of traffic at the airport is starting to put a strain on the capacity of the existing terminal. A second terminal is planned, and there are also plans for improvements to the public transport options between Otopeni airport and central Bucharest.

Transfer to and from the airport There is an express **bus service** from the airport into the centre of Bucharest, with stops at both the Arrivals and Departures terminals. Bus 780 runs to the main railway station of Bucharest, Gara de Nord. Departures are roughly every 30 minutes, with the first bus at 05.35 and the last one at 23.10. A second express bus, 783, runs to the city centre, serving the main central squares of Piaţa Victoriei, Piaţa Romană and Piaţa Unirii, all of which link to the Bucharest metro network. This service helpfully runs 24 hours a day, with frequencies ranging from every 15 minutes at peak times during weekdays, to every 40 minutes in the small hours of the night. A return journey costs 7RON. You need to purchase an Activ card from the booth in Arrivals, which will cost you an additional 3.7RON. Keep the card, as you can use it to purchase further bus journeys in Bucharest. Further information on bus services in Bucharest is given on the website of the municipal bus company, the Regia Autonomă de Transport Bucureşti (w *ratb.ro*).

There is also, in theory, a **train** connection with the airport, but its name, Henri Coandă Express, is the only express feature about it. This involves taking a shuttle bus to the airport train stop, and thence to Gara de Nord. Tickets can be purchased in the arrivals hall, and cost 6.8RON. But the service is both less frequent and longer than the bus.

The other main option to get into Bucharest from the airport is to take a **taxi**. These are much cheaper in Romania than in many European countries, though like many international airports, Otopeni has its share of sharks, and you should avoid any driver who approaches you. You can either use the taxi rank or order taxis from specific companies using the touch-screen terminals in Arrivals. In either case, look carefully at the rate being charged per kilometre. Most Bucharest taxis charge 1.39RON/km, but some will cost you 3.50RON. The rate charged is clearly written on the doors of the taxi.

Car-hire companies at Otopeni-Henri Coandă International Airport Alternatively, you could try just turning up at the airport during office hours, and calling in at one of these offices, situated all in a cluster on the first floor between Departures and Arrivals. See *Getting around*, pages 81–9, for average rental prices.

Autonom m +40 742 215 361; e otopeni@autonom.ro; w autonom.ro; ⊕ 24hrs daily
Avis ☏+40 21 204 1957; m +40 722 636 595; e otopeni.airport@avis.ro; w avis.ro; ⊕ 07.00–01.00 daily
Budget ☏+40 21 204 1667; e bucharestairport@budgetro.ro; w budget.ro; ⊕ 07.00–01.00 daily
Enterprise m +40 722 397 855; w enterprise.com; ⊕ 24hrs daily

Europcar m +40 740 044 964; e office@europcar.com.ro; w europcar.ro; ⊕ 08.00–22.00 Mon–Fri, 10.00–22.00 Sat/Sun
Hertz ☏+40 21 204 1278; m +40 732 222 325; e bucharestAP@hertz.ro; w hertz.ro; ⊕ 08.00–22.00 daily
Sixt ☏+40 21 9400; m +40 729 209 997; w sixt.com; ⊕ 24hrs daily

🏠 **Where to stay near Otopeni Airport** For early flights, possible flight delays, or late arrivals, there are some reasonable hotels close to the airport.

🏠 **Angelo by Vienna House Bucharest** (177 rooms) Calea Bucureştilor 283, Otopeni; ☏+40 21 203 6500; e info.angelo-bucharest@viennahouse.com; w viennahouse.com. This 4-star hotel is part of an Austrian chain. Just 300m from the airport, it has a gym, sauna, smart rooms & a free airport shuttle. 'Angelo' is helpfully written in enormous letters on the side of the building in case you forget where you are staying. **$$$$**

🏠 **Rin Airport Hotel** (258 rooms) Calea Bucureştilor 255A, Otopeni; ☏+40 21 350 4110; e reservations.rinairport@rinhotels.ro; w airport.rinhotels.ro. The 4-star Rin Airport Hotel offers smart rooms & a large spa with pool, sauna, jacuzzi & fitness centre, & (summer only) a water park. Also operates a free airport shuttle. **$$$$**

Airports in Transylvania
Avram Iancu International Airport Cluj
(CLJ) Str Traian Vuia 149; ☏+40 264 307 500; e office@airportcluj.ro; w airportcluj.ro. See also page 284 for more information on the airport, transfers & car hire.
Sibiu Airport (SBZ) Sos Alba Iulia 73; ☏+40 269 253 135; w sibiuairport.ro. Sibiu International Airport is situated 5km west of Sibiu city centre on highway 1/7/E68/E81. See also pages 214–15 for more information on the airport, transfers & car hire.

Târgu Mureş Transylvania Airport
(TGM) Târgu Mureş–Ludus road Km 14.5, Vidrasău, 547612 Mureş County; ☏+40 265 328 259; e office@aeroportultransilvania.ro; w aeroportultransilvania.ro. See also pages 190–1 for more information on the airport, transfers & car hire. The airport was, however, closed at the time of research for repairs to the runway.

BY TRAIN It's more expensive to travel to Transylvania by train (*tren*), but you can take your time, admire the view and feel good about decreasing your carbon footprint. Train tickets often allow stopovers *en route*, so train travel can be an affordable and relaxing way to include Romania in a European trip.

The shortest London–Bucharest train journey takes about 36 hours, but you can choose from a variety of routes. If you are travelling from the UK, note that British railway stations generally do not sell international tickets, with the exception of the Eurostar office at London's St Pancras station (w *eurostar.com*), which just sells tickets on that service to Paris and Brussels. The following agencies are specialised in international rail bookings.

Traineurope 4 Station Approach, March, Cambs PE15 8SJ; ☏0871 700 7722; e enquiries@traineurope.co.uk; w traineurope.co.uk. They offer an online & phone service as well as in person at either their Cambridgeshire office or at the 'We Know London' desk at St Pancras station, close to the Eurostar check-in.
International Rail ☏0871 231 0790; e sales@internationalrail.com; w internationalrail.com. Rail specialists offering an online & phone service.

A possible journey from London to Transylvania could be to take the Eurostar to Paris Gare du Nord, then walk across to the Gare de l'Est. From there take a train to Munich, and the onward overnight sleeper to Budapest. Take a day to explore Budapest, before another night on an overnight sleeper, this time taking you to Braşov. Remember to always make reservations for sleepers. For trains **from Hungary** to Romania, see the website w elvira.hu. For trains **from Germany**, consult either the Deutsche Bahn website (w *bahn.com*) or their UK contact centre (☏ *+44 871 880 8066*; e *sales@bahn.co.uk*). The website of the Romanian state railway company CFR is w cfr.ro. It operates services to many European cities, with sleepers available for longer journeys, though tickets for international destinations must currently be purchased at their ticket offices, as the website only allows for domestic bookings. The website **The Man in Seat 61** (w *seat61.com*) is a mine of useful information on European rail travel.

Rail passes Two types of ticket are offered by **InterRail** (w *interrail.eu*): a global pass (valid in all participating countries, currently 30) and a one-country pass. These are only available to citizens and official residents of a European country, including those not in the EU. Tickets are priced according to three sets of criteria. First, age, with a youth ticket (for those aged 27 and under) the cheapest, followed by seniors (60 and over) and then adults (28–59). Second, planned frequency of travel, with the cheapest global pass option allowing for five travel days in a 15-day period; the most expensive option being daily travel for a month. And third, class of travel.

Prices in 2017 for the Romania one-country pass ranged from €59 for a youth (aged 12–27) travelling second class on three days within a month, to €198 for an adult (aged 28–59) travelling first class on eight days within a month.

If you are not a European citizen or resident you are restricted to a Eurail pass (w *eurail.com*), which works out slightly more expensive. It is available in three options: a global pass for those looking to visit five countries or more, a select pass, which covers between two and four neighbouring countries, and a one-country pass. 2017 prices for the Romania pass ranged from €60 for a youth travelling second class for three days a month, to €199 for an adult travelling first class on eight days in a month.

Both types of passes can be purchased online on their respective websites.

Bucharest Gara de Nord (*Piaţa Gării de Nord 1–3*; ☏ *+40 21 9521*) is the capital city's main railway station, and the starting point for rail routes into Transylvania via Braşov for those who have arrived into Romania at Bucharest Otopeni airport. It does not have the most glowing of reputations, though in this it is little different from the main railway stations in many European capitals. In truth, the scare stories about scammers and pickpocketing here are overstated, though you should be on your guard, particularly if newly arrived in the country and jockeying with luggage. Around the main hall as you enter the station are the Regiotrans ticket office, a 24-hour left-luggage office (*10RON/suitcase/day, 5RON/small bag*), pharmacy (☏ *021 317 0358*; ◷ *06.30–22.00 daily*) and post office (◷ *08.00–21.30 Mon–Fri, 09.00–13.00 Sat/Sun*). The ticket office for the Romanian state railway company CFR is in a hall to the right of this: counters 1 and 2 are for international travel, 8 and 9 for sleeping cars, and 3 to 7 for everything else. There are also automatic ticket machines, though these usually seem to be out of order.

To get to Gara de Nord from Otopeni airport, take a taxi or bus 780 direct, or bus 783 to Piaţa Victoriei and then take the red metro 1 for one stop westwards to Gara de Nord. Remember that a seat reservation is compulsory when travelling with an Interrail or Eurail pass, and advisable on main routes anyway. See pages

82–3 for further information on domestic rail tickets and trains, and the relevant city sections for information on their railway stations.

BY COACH OR BUS

International services There is quite a number of long-distance coach connections between Romania and western European cities, including the UK. Prices are considerably cheaper than train travel, though will not necessarily work out less expensive than flying on a low-cost airline if you book your plane ticket well in advance. And you do spend a lot of time in a coach seat. Thus the Eurolines coach departing London Victoria at 23.00 on a Sunday evening does not arrive in Braşov until 19.00 on Tuesday. The services tend mostly to be used by Romanian migrant workers attracted by the more generous baggage allowance of coach services as against flying.

If you are opting to travel to Romania by coach, **Eurolines** is a good choice. This is a network of European coach companies that offer partially integrated ticketing. The UK partner is National Express. Eurolines also offers a Eurolines pass, which allows for unlimited travel between 53 European cities, including Bucharest, over either a 15- or 30-day period. A cheaper youth pass is available for travellers aged 26 and under. The price varies considerably according to season, with the highest rates in a high season running (at the time of writing) from 14 June to 6 September. Low season runs from 1 October to 31 March, with a mid-priced mid season in between. When we were researching the new edition, prices ranged from €195 for a 15-day youth pass in low season, to €425 for a 30-day adult pass in high season.

Eurolines UK Victoria Coach station, 164 Buckingham Palace Rd, SW1 9TP; ☎08717 818 177; w eurolines.com

Eurolines Romania ☎+40 21 316 7782; w eurolines.ro. The main Eurolines station in Bucharest is Eurolines Bucharest Buzeşti (*Str Buzeşti 44, Sector 1;* ☎+40 21 316 3661; e buzesti@eurolines.ro).

The Sibiu-based Romanian company **AtlasSib** (*Str Tractorului 14, Sibiu;* ☎+40 269 229 224; e informatii@atlassib.ro; w atlassib.ro) has routes to many European countries, eg: a service departing Iaşi in Moldavia at 06.30, via Bistriţa and Cluj-Napoca, which reaches London at 03.45 two days later before travelling on to Liverpool and Glasgow. With many stops through the night, this is not a restful option. Another operator which may be worth considering is the German company **FlixBus** (*+49 30 300 137 300;* w flixbus.com). It has a route from Bucharest to Vienna, Linz and Salzburg via Braşov, Făgăraş and Sebeş. In Bucharest, both these companies use the bus station run by AtlasSib, **Autogara Rahova** (*Şoseaua Alexandriei 164*).

Domestic services For travellers who have arrived into Romania through the airport in Bucharest, the options for onward travel to Transylvania by bus are surprisingly poor, and not helped by the fact that Bucharest doesn't have a single central bus station. Most visitors therefore opt either to hire a car or to take the train. There are some potentially attractive bus options, though. One is **CDI** (☎+40 21 9456; w cditransport.ro), which operates a minibus service hourly or less, departing from 05.30 until 22.30, between Bucharest and Braşov, stopping at the mountain resorts Sinaia, Buşteni, Azuga and Predeal on the way. A particular attraction for those arriving in Romania at Bucharest airport is that the minibuses also stop at Otopeni airport on the way, avoiding the additional effort of getting into central

2

Bucharest. They also have a coach service from Bucharest to Târgu Mureș, with departures every 2 hours between 05.30 and 19.30, which again stop at Otopeni Airport on the way, as well as Brașov, Rupea and Sighișoara.

Another interesting bus option is **MementoBUS** (📞 *+40 317 105 518;* e *rezervari@ mementobus.com;* w *mementobus.com*), which is linked with the Romanian travel agency Christian Tour (started by someone named Cristian Pandel, rather than being a specifically religion-focused agency, though coincidentally they do organise pilgrimage tours). This has a daily service from Bucharest to Cluj-Napoca, stopping *inter alia* in Brașov, Sighișoara, Târgu Mureș and Turda. Prices rise close to the date of departure, but start out very low, eg: €5 for the 3-hour journey to Brașov. They also operate a range of international bus routes, but these are mostly focused on Romanian tourists heading for the Mediterranean sun. Departures from Bucharest are from the MementoBUS terminal, located immediately behind the Autogara IDM Basarab.

Main bus stations in Bucharest

Autogara Filaret Piața Gării Filaret 1, Sector 4; 📞 +40 21 336 0692; e office@acfilaret. ro; w acfilaret.ro. Located 3km south of Piața Universității near Carol Park. Bus 232 from Piața Unirii will get you here. The closest that Bucharest gets to a central bus station, but departures to Transylvania are few & far between, & scattered across a range of companies.

Autogara IDM Basarab Șoseaua Orhideelor 31; 📞 +40 21 310 7571. Located next to the Basarab railway station, & a short walk from the Basarab metro stop. The MementoBUS departs from around the back of here, though otherwise this station mostly serves destinations in Moldavia, as well as Târgoviște.

Autogara Militari Str Valea Cascadelor 1, Sector 6; m 0725 939 939; e office@autogaramilitari. ro; w autogaramilitari.ro. Has a few buses to Transylvanian destinations including Sibiu, Alba Iulia & Cluj-Napoca. It's a long way west of the centre, though easily accessible from the city centre by metro (the stop closest to the bus station is Păcii).

BY CAR It is possible to drive from the UK or continental Europe to Transylvania and do some sightseeing on the way. The shortest driving distance between London and Bucharest is around 2,500km, or 1,500 miles. That between London and Târgu Mureș is around 2,280km.

EU citizens can drive in Romania with the **driving licence** from their home country. Citizens of a range of other countries, including the USA, Canada, Australia and New Zealand, are also able to drive using their home-country driving licence for a period of 90 days from their arrival in Romania. The other documents you will be asked to produce by Romanian border police are the vehicle's registration and proof of insurance. If you are planning to rent a car outside Romania, do check with the company as to whether it permits taking the car across national borders.

The other key piece of bureaucracy is that, whether you are driving your own car or a rental, you will need to obtain a vignette called a **rovinieta** (m *+40 732 773 773*; w *roviniete.com*), which is essentially a form of road toll. These can be purchased online, as well as at the border crossings, post offices and many petrol stations, and have a validity period of one, seven, 30 or 90 days, or one year. If you are travelling from the UK, note that some of the other countries you will pass through *en route* have their own form of vignette requirements, though in most of these, unlike Romania, vignettes are only required for travel on motorways. They are usually obtainable at border crossings and petrol stations. Austria, the Czech Republic, Hungary and Switzerland are among the countries operating a vignette system. Hungarian vignettes, like those in Romania, are electronic, while those in Austria, the Czech Republic and Switzerland involve a sticker physically attached to the windscreen. The website w viamichelin.co.uk is a helpful resource for European route planning.

From western Europe, the major road routes into Transylvania are through Hungary. From Budapest, the main E60 runs eastwards into Romania near Oradea, and thence to Cluj-Napoca, Târgu Mureş, Sighişoara and Braşov. For southern Transylvania, the border crossing with Hungary near the Romanian town of Nădlac will in due course put you straight onto the A1 motorway, currently under construction, for a fast connection with Sibiu.

Information on **car hire** in Romania can be found on page 86 and the relevant city sections in Part Two of the guide.

HEALTH   *with Dr Felicity Nicholson*

If you are living in one of the member states of the European Economic Area (EEA) plus Switzerland you should obtain a **European Health Insurance Card (EHIC)** before travelling to Romania, in order to allow free or reduced-cost access to healthcare provided by the statutory healthcare system. If you are resident in the UK you can apply for an EHIC on the website w nhs.uk, free of charge. Note that the EHIC is not an alternative to taking out **travel insurance**, as it does not cover the costs of private medical treatment, or the considerable costs of being flown back home in the case of serious accidents like a skiing injury, or any of the non-medical features of travel insurance, such as loss of luggage.

No **vaccinations** are legally required, but it is wise to be up to date with routine vaccinations such as the **diphtheria, tetanus and polio** and **measles, mumps and rubella** vaccines. **Hepatitis A** should also be considered – a viral infection which is spread by infected food and water. For those who are going to be working in hospitals or in close contact with children, or for those whose activities otherwise put them at increased risk, **hepatitis B** vaccination may be recommended. **Typhoid** vaccine may also be considered for longer-stay travellers.

General standards of healthcare in the towns are satisfactory but in the countryside it can be a long journey before you reach a qualified medical worker. The standard of medical training in Romania is high, but wages for doctors and other medical personnel are considerably lower than those in western European countries, which has fuelled a brain drain that has left many positions vacant. Coupled with underfunding and persistent problems of corruption, this means that the health sector in Romania faces considerable challenges. Emergency medical treatment is free, but you may have to pay for some medicines.

A 2010 report by the Health Protection Agency in the UK categorised Romania as a country of intermediate-level risk for **travellers' diarrhoea**, so you should exercise usual good practice around frequent hand-washing, choosing freshly prepared, well-cooked food served hot, and avoiding tap water if in doubt about the quality of the local water (although it is fine to drink in many places), but there is no need to get obsessive.

Rabies has been reported in both domestic and wild animals in Romania. Visitors should be wary of, and try to avoid, contact with stray dogs and sheepdogs guarding flocks in the mountains. But remember rabies can be carried by any warm-blooded mammal and not just dogs! If bitten, scratched or simply licked visitors should thoroughly clean the wound immediately with soap and water, and seek an urgent local medical assessment, even if the wound appears a minor one. The assessment will establish the appropriate post-exposure treatment: if no pre-exposure rabies vaccine has been taken this might involve five doses of vaccine over a month, typically coupled with human rabies immunoglobulin (HRIG) if you have been bitten or scratched. HRIG is hard to come by and may not be available in Romania. Pre-exposure rabies vaccinations, which involve a course of three inoculations, may be advisable for travellers planning sustained trekking or mountain-biking holidays, as well as those coming to Romania to work with or near animals. Having the pre-exposure vaccinations means that you no longer need the HRIG and in most cases will reduce the number of post-exposure vaccinations from five doses to two doses given three days apart.

Another risk to be aware of is posed by the humble **tick**, again a particular concern for trekkers, mountain-bikers and anyone whose Romanian holiday plans are more focused on the countryside than the cities. Ticks are most active between spring and autumn, and typically at altitudes below 1,500m. Infected ticks can carry a viral infection called **tick-borne encephalitis (TBE)**. The foothills of the Carpathians in Transylvania are among the areas presumed to be infected. You may wish to ask about vaccination, particularly if planning to camp or hike in Transylvania. The schedule involves three doses, with the first two being given a month apart and the third taken between five and 12 months after the first. If time is short then the first two doses can be given two weeks apart. There is also a paediatric version of the vaccine which can be given over the same schedule. **The website Tick Alert** (w *tickalert.org*) has more information about TBE.

Lyme disease is another infection spread to humans by ticks, and in this case there is currently no vaccine available to prevent it. The most distinctive symptom, though not everyone with Lyme disease experiences it, is a circular rash at the site of the bite, usually between three and 30 days after being bitten, often described as similar in appearance to the bull's-eye on a dartboard. Fever, chills, fatigue, muscle aches and a headache may accompany the rash. Early treatment, usually by means of antibiotics, should prevent the emergence of more serious later symptoms.

Whether you are immunised against TBE or not, you should of course do all you can to avoid tick bites, including wearing suitable clothing, such as long trousers tucked into boots and a long-sleeved shirt, keeping to footpaths where possible when walking, avoiding areas of long grass and using tick repellents. You should check your skin regularly for ticks, and if you find one remove it promptly. There is something of a knack to doing this, but the most effective method is to use fine-tipped tweezers, available in larger travel shops as tick tweezers. Grasp the tick as close to your body as possible and pull steadily and firmly away at right angles to your skin. The tick will then come away complete as long as you do not jerk or twist. If possible, douse the wound and your hands with rubbing alcohol (though any spirit will do) or iodine, or if these are not available simply with soap and water. Suggested methods of tick removal such as painting it with nail polish or using a lit cigarette are to be avoided. If you are travelling with small children remember to check their heads, and particularly behind the ears. If you think you have been bitten by a tick then seek medical advice locally and tell the doctor whether or not you have been immunised.

Mosquitoes can be irritating, but fortunately not more than that, as Romania does not fall within a malarial area. Take a good supply of insect repellent and cream. Other health risks to be aware of are those connected with the **sun** and **altitude**.

The best recent health news from Romania was the introduction in 2016 of a ban on **smoking** in enclosed areas in bars, nightclubs and restaurants. Romania is a country of heavy smokers, and it had been difficult to find a place for a smoke-free drink or meal. Implementation of the ban has not been without its challenges, and there are some voices lobbying to reverse it, or water it down, but its effect was immediate and positive. The traditional Romanian **diet**, with restaurants offering large portions of meat-laden fare, served with *mămăligă* (polenta) and plenty of cheese and cream, is not the healthiest in the world, although obesity is nowhere near western European levels, and it is of course sensible to watch your **alcohol** intake, given both the cheapness of local drinks in comparison with western European prices and the potency of some of the spirits on offer, especially *palincă*.

UK Government travel advice for Romania, including health information, is available at w gov.uk. Good country-specific health advice, including up-to-date recommendations on vaccinations and information on current outbreaks of diseases, is on the Travel Health Pro website (w *travelhealthpro.org.uk*). Another site offering country-specific health information is w tripprep.com. There is a comprehensive global directory of travel clinics on the website of the International Society of Travel Medicine (w *istm.org*).

PHARMACIES For minor ailments, a visit to the nearest pharmacy (*farmacie*) may suffice. Romanian towns offer a huge number of them. Some open until late, and in some cases offer a 24-hour emergency service; the staff are well trained and often multi-lingual, especially if you know the Latin name for the problem.

International brands of many over-the-counter products are available and can be requested by name.

SPAS Romanians are hugely enthusiastic about the curative properties of treatments in spa resorts, whether these are based around the chemical composition of the waters, the gases in mofettes, the quality of the atmosphere at high altitude or even the distinctive environment within a salt mine. Transylvania is full of spa resorts, the best of which are described on page 108 and the relevant chapters in Part Two of this guide.

SAFETY

The vast majority of visits to Romania are trouble-free, and Transylvanian cities and villages alike are welcoming and feel safe. Violent street crime is very rare in Romania. In many villages, where everyone knows everyone else, doors are left open and children run around until late at night. As anywhere though, you should maintain a good level of personal security awareness. Petty theft does occur, with pickpockets operating in crowded places frequented by tourists, including airport terminals and railway stations, and on public transport, especially busy buses. Thefts of valuables from hotel rooms are also a risk, as worldwide, and you should use hotel safes if available. There are occasional reports of scams, sometimes involving thieves impersonating plain-clothes policemen and asking to check documents as a way of trying to syphon away some cash, or involving demands for on-the-spot payments of fines for fictitious offences. The incidence of this type of activity seems to be declining, and you are highly unlikely to encounter anything like this.

The tragic fire at the Club Colectiv nightclub in Bucharest on 31 October 2015, which resulted in the deaths of 64 people, highlighted the risks of some venues circumventing fire safety and other rules. If you do not feel safe in a club or restaurant, you might wish to choose somewhere else.

Stories of the threats posed by stray dogs are largely outdated. Those which formerly roamed central Bucharest have largely gone, and while there are stray dogs in other parts of Romania, they are more to be pitied as victims of ill-treatment than regarded as a major safety risk. A much bigger problem is presented by the sheepdogs trained to guard flocks. They can be very aggressive if chanced upon during a country hike, and if their shepherd is nowhere in sight can give rise to a nervous encounter.

Road safety is an issue in Romania, and the statistics are not at all encouraging. Road deaths in Romania in 2015, for example, equated to 9.5 per 100,000 people, against 2.8 in the UK over the same period. Aggressive and poor driving seem to go hand in hand in Romania, and the risks are compounded by the sheer variety of vehicles on many Romanian roads, all travelling at different speeds, from horse-drawn carts to BMWs. Constant vigilance is required when driving a hire car. If you are unlucky enough to have an accident, do not leave the site or attempt to move the car. You should call the police (on the ☎112 emergency number) and make sure that you obtain a copy of the police report, as you will need it for your insurers.

IN AN EMERGENCY The common phone number for all emergency services in Romania is ☎ 112. It covers the police, ambulance, General Inspectorate for Emergency Situations, gendarmerie (an agency with military status responsible for defending public order) and SMURD, a mobile emergency service for resuscitation and extrication. Call centres are usually able to respond in English. The only additional emergency number you might need, and should have ready if you are planning any climbing or remote trekking in Romania, is that of the mountain rescue service **Salvamont**: m 0725 826 668, or m 0Salvamont for phone keypads featuring letters as well as numbers.

WOMEN TRAVELLERS

Conservative attitudes are still pretty common in Transylvania, and women travelling on their own are likely to encounter some surprise from the locals at the idea, particularly if the women in question should enter such traditionally male preserves as the village bar. But with the right precautions and security awareness it is unlikely to be a dangerous experience, and Transylvanian friendliness and hospitality usually win out. While you will see women of all ages hitchhiking, particularly in rural areas with little or no public transport, it would, however, be particularly risky for a single woman traveller to attempt to do so.

TRAVELLING WITH CHILDREN

Transylvania can be a great place to travel with children, given the diversity of its attractions and links to all sorts of themes that fascinate young ones, from vampires to dinosaurs, medieval knights to bears. The updating of this guide was done in the company of three-year-old George: his personal Transylvanian top ten is listed in the box opposite. Entrance tickets for children to most attractions are considerably reduced. Many hotels offer cots for babies and small children; you are more likely to have to pay a charge for these (usually around €10–15) at more expensive hotels, while they are often given free of charge where available at pensions. And if cots were not available hosts often used considerable ingenuity to provide a safe bed for George, like the lady at the guesthouse in Bran who virtually remodelled the entire room in the process. Highchairs for children are available in many restaurants.

A rather less positive approach to children is, however, sometimes characteristic of the staff at museums. While there are a few happy examples of Transylvanian museums that have adopted an enthusiastically child-friendly approach (the Székely

A TRANSYLVANIAN TOP TEN FOR TODDLERS

1. Looking for lizards at Sarmizegetusa Regia (pages 248–9)
2. The DinoParc at Râşnov (page 142)
3. Playgrounds, like the fortress-themed one at Făgăraş, in the shadow of the real fortress (page 150)
4. The playful fountains in Piaţa Victoriei, Deva (page 247)
5. Riding the *mocăniţă* on the Sibiu–Agnita Railway (page 235)
6. Horse-drawn travel in Cund (pages 207–10)
7. Pretending to be a medieval knight at Corvinus Castle (pages 250–2)
8. The water slide in the children's pool at the Danubius Hotel Sovata-Băi (pages 197–8)
9. The Libearty Bear Sanctuary in Zărneşti (page 148)
10. Spotting the painted ostriches around Bistriţa (pages 303–8)

National Museum in Sfântu Gheorghe being one), there are many more examples of museum staff whose sole objective is to ensure that no sticky fingerprints get anywhere near a display case, and for whom children are a danger to be managed rather than a future generation to be encouraged.

TRAVELLING WITH A DISABILITY

Disabled travellers will find Transylvania a challenge. Its towns, with their winding, cobbled streets, frequently with cars parked astride pavements, are not wheelchair-friendly. Buses in some cities offer wheelchair access, but these are still far from the standard. And a surprisingly large number of hotels and guesthouses lack lifts. Awareness in Romania of the needs of disabled people is patchy too. A Bucharest-based charity providing training for guide dogs for the blind found during trials in local stores and supermarkets that many outlets were unwilling to grant an exception to their policies of no dogs in the store to guide dogs.

There are signs of positive changes being made, including the provision of ramps to allow wheelchair access to banks and hotel receptions. But it still seems in all too many towns that, for every accessible restaurant, there are half a dozen more for which the only access is down a steep flight of stairs. One relative exception to the overall somewhat gloomy picture is in the more modern of the spa resorts, where hotels are more likely to offer spacious lifts and rooms fitted out to meet the needs of guests with disabilities. Romanians are, however, very willing to help where they can.

Useful sources of general information for travellers with disabilities include the website of Tourism for All UK (w *tourismforall.org.uk*), the Rolling Rains Report (w *rollingrains.com*) and the UK Government's site (w *gov.uk/guidance/foreign-travel-for-disabled-people*).

GAY AND LESBIAN TRAVELLERS

The lesbian and gay community in Romania faced persecution during the Communist period. Article 200 of the Penal Code, introduced by Ceauşescu in 1968, criminalised homosexual relationships. The repeal of the last vestiges of Article 200, and thus the final decriminalisation of all same-sex sexual activity, only took effect in 2002. Attitudes towards gays, lesbians, bisexual and trans-gender people are often unsympathetic, and at the time of writing a campaign was underway promoted by a group of organisations calling themselves the Coalition for Family for a referendum aiming to revise the Constitution in such a way as to prevent any possibility of the introduction of gay marriage in Romania.

The major non-governmental organisation in Romania campaigning for the rights of lesbian, gay, bisexual and trans-gender people is Asociaţia ACCEPT (*Str Lirei 2, Bucureşti;* \ *+40 21 252 5620;* w *acceptromania.ro*), which organises the annual Bucharest Pride parade in May (more details at w *bucharestpride.ro*). The university city of Cluj-Napoca has a reputation as the most gay-friendly city in Transylvania, and has a number of gay and gay-friendly bars and clubs. Elsewhere, conservatism tends to increase with decreasing settlement size. You are less likely to face prejudice when booking into larger hotels than family-owned guesthouses, but of course there are many exceptions. And it would be wise to be cautious about public displays of affection, especially in smaller communities.

WHAT TO TAKE

A trip to rural Transylvania may seem like a journey back in time, but with few additions to your suitcase or the occasional trip to a larger city, should provide all the comforts of (a 21st-century) home.

The summer months are hot and few hotels are air conditioned. This is less of a problem in mountain villages, but cities like Bucharest can be stifling. Bring along some **mosquito repellent**, especially if staying in the south and in Bucharest.

You may also want to bring along some **earplugs** if you are a light sleeper. A key source of income for many Transylvanian hotels is the hosting of wedding receptions, and these can be noisy affairs which go on all night. 'If you can't beat them, join them' can be another way of responding to these and, particularly in the case of parties and receptions in smaller settlements, you might find yourself invited in to join the dancing. **Eye masks** can be worthwhile too, as curtains can often be flimsy or non-existent.

Many of the historic towns are best explored on foot, so pack some **comfortable shoes** and perhaps an **anorak** for the occasional summer shower. Winters can be chilly and summers baking, so choose clothes accordingly. The mountains are significant skiing and hiking venues, so take sturdy **walking boots**, water and a whistle.

Take out comprehensive **travel insurance** before your trip to cover lost baggage, theft and medical emergencies, and bring photocopies of the documentation with you. A **credit or debit card** will enable you to withdraw money as you need it from the many ATMs found in all large settlements. Extra **passport photos** are always a good idea, as is taking a **photocopy** of your passport, driving licence and insurance documents. If you plan to stay in hostels or take overnight trains or buses, a **money belt** is invaluable for the storage of your key valuables. A **sink plug** is another recommendation for those planning to stay at cheaper accommodation, and if you intend to camp don't forget to pack a **torch**. Pack a **penknife** with a corkscrew and bottle opener, but remember not to take such an implement in hand luggage on planes but in checked-in luggage only.

ELECTRICITY

Romania's electrical current is 230V/50Hz, and uses the two round-pin plugs typical of continental Europe, so if you're coming from the UK or North America you'll need a plug adaptor. Additionally, if your appliance is set for use with a standard voltage of 110V, you will need a voltage converter.

MONEY

The Romanian currency is the leu (plural: lei), often written out in full after the figure or shown as RON (Romanian new leu).

The leu (which means 'lion') comes in the following denomination banknotes: 1 leu and 5, 10, 50, 100, 200 and 500 lei. The 500 lei notes are rarely seen in circulation, since they are not distributed through ATM machines, and you might experience problems in trying to use them, particularly in smaller communities. Even the 200 lei notes are seen relatively rarely. Each leu is divided into 100 bani, available as coins of 1, 2, 5, 10 and 50 bani. Although these have a very low value, 50 bani coins in particular can be remarkably useful if you are driving, because the parking meters in use in some cities don't take notes, and so require large quantities of these if you are planning a lengthy stay.

These notes were issued in 2005 and follow a revaluation of the leu at the rate of 10,000 'old' lei (ROL) for one new leu (RON), thus psychologically bringing the purchasing power of the leu back in line with those of other major Western currencies. Although the change took place well over a decade ago you will still hear some shopkeepers, particularly in rural communities, speaking in 'old lei' terms, and you may be somewhat taken aback when you are charged 10,000 lei for a bottle of mineral water.

1 new leu (RON) = 10,000 old lei (ROL)
100 new lei (RON) = 1,000,000 old lei (ROL)

The banknotes are printed on plastic polymer, with a transparent window whose shape alludes to the profession of the particular Romanian personality depicted on the note (see box, pages 78–9).

GETTING AND USING MONEY The most straightforward way to obtain Romanian currency is by using your debit or credit card at one of the numerous **ATM** machines to be found in all Romanian towns. Look for ATMs with symbols for international networks such as STAR and PLUS, or displaying the logo of your credit or debit card. The downside is that you will lose some of your money to transaction charges: the upside is the convenience, and the security benefit in not having to carry large amounts of cash with you. Bear in mind that ATMs are few and far between in rural areas, so if you are spending a few days off the beaten track you'll need to make sure that you bring enough money in advance to cover that portion of your trip. You will also want to change some money back home into Romanian lei, to cover your immediate needs on arrival until you can find a working ATM, and also as a contingency in case you experience any problems with your card. You might need to allow time to order this, as currency exchange providers overseas do not always keep a ready stock of Romanian lei.

Walking into a Romanian hotel or large department store, you may be forgiven for wondering whether Romania has adopted **the euro** as its currency, as you will see prices quoted in euros. But if you pay cash, you will need to pay in Romanian lei, irrespective of whether the price you have been given is in lei or euros. This has given rise to a scam you might occasionally encounter in Transylvanian hotels, where the guest is quoted a price in euros, but is presented on departure with a bill in lei which corresponds to a different (higher) euro rate, relying on a lack of familiarity of the foreign guest with the correct exchange rate. The hotel staff will quickly correct the 'mistake' on being challenged. This is easily countered by establishing from the outset the rate in lei.

Some sources recommend that visitors from the UK or USA exchange some of their sterling or dollars into euros in addition to Romanian lei, but I would counsel against this: since you have to pay in lei, this practice would have the effect of requiring you to pay two sets of currency exchange charges rather than one.

Credit cards, including American Express, MasterCard and Visa, are accepted at large hotels, many guesthouses, car-hire companies and restaurants, but you should not rely on them completely, as rates of acceptance are patchy at best in rural areas, and you will quite frequently encounter places which normally accept credit cards presenting your bill with a shrugged apology that the card machine isn't currently working due to poor reception and asking for cash. Note that, when asking for your restaurant bill in Romania, the waiter will ask you in return whether you intend to pay by card or with cash.

There are numerous places to **exchange money**, including banks, exchange offices (*birou de schimb valutar*) and larger hotels. A bank is usually the best option. Raiffeisen, Banca Transilvania and BRD are among the reliable choices. Note that banks in Romania generally do not open at weekends. Be wary of currency exchange offices at airports and other border crossings, as these generally offer particularly poor rates.

his plane *Vlaicu II*. The see-through part depicts an eagle's head. Born near Orăştie, Transylvania, in the village of Binţinţi, which now bears his name, Vlaicu began the construction of his first powered plane in 1909 and became a distinguished early flight pioneer in a career which was cut tragically short when his *Vlaicu II* plane crashed in 1913.

100 LEI (*o sută de lei*) Playwright Ion Luca Caragiale (1852–1912). The main colour of the note is blue, with a violet flower and theatrical mask next to the portrait. The reverse shows the old building of Bucharest's National Theatre. The see-through part depicts a theatrical mask. Caragiale's plays were wry social commentaries with acute observations of Romania's modernising process at the end of the 19th century. He is usually considered Romania's greatest playwright.

200 LEI (*două sute de lei*) Philosopher, poet and dramatist Lucian Blaga (1895–1961). This note is legal tender but rarely used. The main colour of the note is orange with three red poppies and a book of poetry next to the portrait. The reverse shows a rainbow behind a watermill and the *Hamangia Thinker* sculpture, a figurine discovered in Romania's Dobruja region which is considered a masterpiece of Neolithic art. The see-through part shows an oil lamp and a sheet of paper. Born in Lancrăm near Sebeş in Alba County, Blaga was a major Romanian cultural figure of the interwar period.

500 LEI (*cinci sute de lei*) National poet Mihai Eminescu (1850–89). The main colours of the note are green and purple with lime tree blossoms next to a quill and an ink pot. The reverse shows the *Timpul* newspaper and the façade of the university library in Iaşi. The see-through part depicts an egg-timer. Eminescu's poems are known by all Romanians, if not always by heart, and his birthday on 15 January is celebrated today as the Day of National Culture. The banknote celebrating him is, however, hardly ever seen.

Travellers' cheques are not particularly useful in Romania: you may find it a challenge to find a bank, hotel or exchange office wiling to cash them, and expect to be charged a hefty commission if they do. An alternative that preserves similar security advantages to traditional travellers' cheques but which is more flexible to use in Romania is the **Cash Passport** (w *cashpassport.com*) system, based around a pre-paid travel card, with its own PIN number, which you use in ATM machines but which is entirely separate from your own bank account. Note though that these are not currently available in Romanian lei, so ATM transactions will still be subject to currency exchange fees, and there is also a fee payable to purchase and reload the cards.

DISCOUNT CARDS The International Student Identity Card (ISIC; w *isic.org*) for full-time students aged 12 or over can be useful in proving your student status in order to qualify for the relevant discounts at museums, galleries and other attractions, although your own university card often works well. There are a range of other discounts available to ISIC holders, detailed on their website, and for those who are 30 years old or younger but no longer a student, the International Youth Travel Card, also available from ISIC, may be worth considering, but the benefits are less extensive, and some are not available to those aged over 26. If you

Romanians are generally quite modest tippers. If a service charge has been included in your restaurant bill no further tip is expected, although many locals will additionally leave a small note. If a service charge has not been included, a tip of around 10% is appropriate. Note that, if you are paying by credit card, some restaurants will not allow you to add a tip to the credit card bill, and may ask you instead either to pay the tip in cash or as a separate charge to your credit card. A 10% tip would also usually be given to a hairdresser. A hotel porter might be given 5–10RON depending on how much luggage you have. Romanians do not usually tip taxi drivers.

are an EU citizen of pensionable age you should in theory also be eligible for the concessionary rates available at museums and galleries for that age group.

BANKS Cities and larger towns in Transylvania all seem to have quite a range of banks clustered in their centres, although banks are few and far between in rural areas. Opening hours vary a little between banks, but are most usually from 09.00 or 09.30 until 17.00 or 17.30 between Monday and Friday. There is usually an ATM in the wall outside the bank, which you can use if it is shut. The list below covers the banks you will see most frequently on high streets in Transylvania, though there are many others.

$ Banca Comercială Română (BCR) \+40 21 407 4200; w bcr.ro. The largest Romanian bank by asset value, with the largest network of ATMs in the country.

$ Banca Transilvania \+40 264 308 028; w bancatransilvania.ro. Founded in Cluj-Napoca in 1993, this has a good network of branches throughout Transylvania & more widely across Romania.

$ BRD \+40 21 302 6161; w brd.ro. A Romanian bank with a majority shareholding held by the French group Société Générale, with more than 900 branches.

$ Patria Bank w patriabank.ro. With its headquarters in Târgu Mureș, Patria Bank had at the time of research announced a fusion with the Sibiu-based Banca Comercială Carpatica, which when completed will constitute a network of more than 70 towns, many in Transylvania.

$ Raiffeisen Bank \+40 21 323 9542; w raiffeisen.ro. With its distinctive yellow & black livery, this is the Romanian subsidiary of an Austrian banking group. It has more than 350 branches in Romania and is present in most large towns in Transylvania.

$ UniCredit Bank w unicredit.ro. A member of the Italian UniCredit group, with more than 200 branches in Romania.

BUDGETING

Transylvania is a much lower-cost destination than western Europe. That said, there are considerable differences within the region, with high-season accommodation prices in the major cities of Brașov, Sibiu and Cluj-Napoca, as well as the popular tourist town of Sighișoara, gradually pushing up towards rates characteristic of more expensive central European destinations. At the other end of the scale, if you stay in the heart of the Transylvanian countryside, hike or cycle everywhere and eat at local restaurants, your lei will go a long way.

Relatively speaking, car hire is quite pricey, while public transport, including taxis, remains cheap. Even the more expensive restaurants generally have good-value options, typically based around traditional Romanian dishes or pizza, and portions tend to be huge, so one or two courses will suffice rather than three. And while the network of hostels is not well developed in Transylvania, though there are a few distinguished exceptions, room rates in the cheaper guesthouses in Transylvania come close to those of a hostel bed in more expensive places, and you get a good deal more privacy for your money.

The following guide lists daily budgets for one person, based on two people sharing accommodation and in the luxury category a hire car (and therefore paying less on the room bill and motoring costs). Note though that they don't include the costs of actually getting to Transylvania or souvenirs.

PENNY-PINCHING You can probably get by on a budget of around 120RON for a hostel dorm, travelling on the cheapest public transport available, eating in one of the local cafés, entry to a few museums and rounded off by a meal with drinks in a modest pub.

MODEST You'll spend about 180RON a day if you travel by public transport and aim for basic accommodation in a two-star hotel, cheered on by occasional treats, a ticket to a performance at one of the concert halls or a decent meal in a good restaurant. However, renting a car will push your daily budget higher than this.

LUXURY A daily allowance of 500RON will allow a stay in a swanky boutique hotel in Braşov, Sibiu or Cluj-Napoca, car rental, some sightseeing, stops for coffee, cake and beer, a meal in a decent restaurant, late-night drinks in a club and a taxi back to base.

GETTING AROUND

Public transport in Transylvania is cheap but decidedly patchy. There is usually a good bus service between two reasonably large adjacent towns, but it can be

SOME SAMPLE PRICES

1RON = £0.20/US$0.26/€0.22 (August 2017)

Loaf of white bread (500g)	3.6RON
One litre of milk	5.2RON
Bowl of soup in restaurant	12.5RON
Bottle of Ciuc lager (0.33l)	2.7RON
Bottle of Romanian wine	20–45RON
Bottle of mineral water (2l)	2.2RON
Cup of coffee in café	5–7RON
Train ticket Bucharest–Cluj (first class on InterRegio)	140RON
One litre of petrol (benzină)	4.93RON
One litre of diesel fuel (motorină)	4.89RON
Museum/gallery entrance ticket	7–20RON
Smart restaurant meal for two with main, salad, water and wine	100–150RON
Pizza in café	20–30RON
New Dacia Logan car	from €6,950
Average Romanian monthly wage	€463

limited or non-existent in more isolated areas. And although Romania has one of the densest train networks in Europe, the speed of travel is slow, frequencies can be limited and train times inconvenient. In rural areas with little public transport, the locals resort to hitchhiking. While most, though not all, of the places listed in Part Two of this guide can be accessed by public transport one way or another, if your Transylvanian itinerary will take you away from the larger towns and cities for sustained periods then you are likely to be best off either hiring a car or arranging an organised or tailor-made tour.

BY AIR Until recently, the domestic flight network in Romania was the preserve of the Romanian state carrier Tarom, but routes are also now being served by the low-cost carriers Wizz Air and Blue Air, which has brought down prices.

✈ **Blue Air** w blueairweb.com. Operates the core Bucharest–Cluj-Napoca route, & is also the only carrier offering flights to Cluj-Napoca from Romanian airports other than the capital, linking Transylvania's largest city with Constanța twice a week, & Iași daily, with the latter service sometimes via Timișoara.
✈ **Tarom** w tarom.ro. The Romanian state carrier flies from Bucharest Otopeni to Cluj-Napoca several times daily. While not the cheapest option on this route, it is the most frequent, & may therefore be a good option if you are flying to Cluj-Napoca from outside Romania & need a transfer in Bucharest.
✈ **Wizz Air** w wizzair.com. Operates at least 1 flight on most dates between Bucharest & Cluj-Napoca.

BY TRAIN Romania has a dense railway network, with more than 10,000km of track, although less than half of this is electrified. The state railway company is Căile Ferate Române, universally known as **CFR** (w *cfr.ro*). The good news is that railways will take you between most cities and towns in Transylvania, and many small settlements, too; the bad news is that they will rarely do so quickly.

There are several different types of train in Romania. **InterCity** (IC) trains are the fastest, most modern and comfortable. Unfortunately, they are few and far between, and only used on a few main routes. **InterRegio** (IR) trains will prove the mainstay of a train-based Transylvania tour. Until 2011 they were known as Accelerat or slightly faster Rapid trains, and you may still hear these terms used colloquially. Reservations are required on some, though not all, IR routes. They stop at most towns *en route*, but not the smaller village halts. **Regio** trains are to be avoided, except where your destination is a small station not served by the IR trains. Known as Personal trains until 2011, they are grindingly slow, with an average speed not much more than 30km/h, stop everywhere, tend to use old and frayed rolling stock, and can get very crowded. Reservations are only possible on a few Regio routes. Fares are cheaper than on any of the other trains: with a Regio train you simply pay the base fare for the route concerned, with no supplement applied, as is the case with the other train types.

Tickets can be purchased at railway stations, at either the ticket office or, in a few stations, at automatic vending machines, although the latter rarely seem to work. They can also be bought at a CFR agency. Finally, tickets for trains for which reservations are possible can be purchased through the website w cfrcalatori.ro, though it is not the most user-friendly site and requires pre-registration. A *bilet* is a basic second-class fare for a Regio train. The *supliment* is the supplementary fare to upgrade to a faster train, to first class or to sleeping accommodation (*cușetă*). The *loc rezervat* is the seat reservation.

CFR no longer has a monopoly on the provision of passenger services in Romania, and, though it accounts for the large majority of passenger traffic,

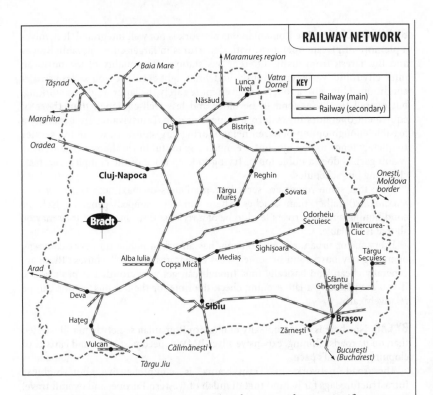

KEY
Railway (main)
Railway (secondary)

Maramureş region
Baia Mare
Tăşnad
Lunca Ilvei
Vatra Dornei
Năsăud
Marghita
Dej
Bistrița
Oradea
Cluj-Napoca
Reghin
Onești, Moldova border
Târgu Mureş
Sovata
N
Bradt
Odorheiu Secuiesc
Miercurea-Ciuc
Sighişoara
Alba Iulia
Copşa Mică
Mediaş
Târgu Secuiesc
Arad
Sfântu Gheorghe
Deva
Sibiu
Braşov
Haţeg
Zărneşti
Vulcan
Călimăneşti
București (Bucharest)
Târgu Jiu

there are two private operators you may wish to consider on specific routes to and within Transylvania. **Regiotrans** (☏ *0310 800 900;* w *regiotrans.ro*), which was founded in 2005, has its headquarters in Braşov. It runs four trains a day on the Braşov–Bucharest route, and a number of local train services out of Braşov, notably the routes to Zărneşti, to Întorsura Buzăului and to Breţcu via Sfântu Gheorghe. Tickets can be purchased online or at Regiotrans offices in train stations. Where there is no such Regiotrans office they can be purchased on board at the standard price; but if there is an office at the station at which you boarded, a supplement is payable for on-board purchase. **Softrans** (☏ *0351 409 153;* w *softrans.ro*), based in the southern Romanian city of Craiova, operates only two routes, and the only one of these involving Transylvania is a route from Craiova to Braşov via Bucharest. But this latter route is well worth considering for arrivals into Transylvania from the Romanian capital. In 2017, the single train a day run by Softrans on this route departed Bucharest Gara de Nord at 09.23, arriving in Braşov at 11.55. It used the comfortable new electric *Hyperion* train, with tickets costing just 30RON, making them much cheaper than CFR. Tickets can be purchased online or on board.

Sample 2017 train ticket prices

- Bucharest to Cluj-Napoca first class on an InterRegio (IR) train costs 140RON
- Bucharest to Cluj-Napoca second class on an InterRegio (IR) train costs 90RON
- Cluj-Napoca to Mediaş second class on an InterRegio train costs 48RON
- Sibiu to Braşov second class on an InterRegio train costs 44RON
- Braşov to Sighişoara second class on an InterRegio train costs 39RON

BY BUS OR COACH The Romanian bus network is not well integrated. It involves a plethora of private operators, with departures in larger cities, notably Braşov and Bucharest, from many different bus stations. The quality of the buses on inter-city routes varies enormously, and you might even find yourself on an air-conditioned bus with a toilet, and even more rarely the latter might be working, but overall the buses tend to be older and less well-equipped than those of equivalent operators in western Europe. Buses in Transylvania are generally a feasible enough option between neighbouring largish towns, where the service frequency tends to be high, but are much less useful in rural areas. The website w autogari.ro does a noble job of trying to keep track of the complex and fast-changing bus schedules.

Note that some routes are served by minibuses or maxi-taxis (*microbuze* or *maxitaxiuri*) rather than coaches. These can get cramped, generally lack air conditioning and the drivers tend to be of a reckless disposition, but they may be all that is available.

Every major urban area in Romania has an urban public transport company operating city buses, and in some places also trams and trolleybuses. These are generally cheap, and basically fine, though can get very crowded at peak hours. If you are planning a late evening check the time for the last bus, as this can be relatively early.

BY CAR Nowhere is the complexity of modern Romanian society better illustrated than on its roads. Shining, expensive silver BMWs speed past horse and carts clip-clopping at a snail's pace.

The road network in Transylvania is comprehensive, but highway infrastructure lags far behind that of much of western Europe, and overall travel speeds can be slow. Expect an average driving time of around 50km/h, although this masks sharp variations. There are two **motorways** (*autostrăzi*) currently under construction in Transylvania. The A1 motorway will eventually run from Bucharest to Piteşti, then up the valley of the Olt River into Transylvania, then past Sibiu and Deva to the Hungarian border at Nădlac. The section between Bucharest and Piteşti has long been complete, but the rest is years late. The section between Sibiu and Deva is now operational, and has had the effect of considerably speeding up travel westwards into Hunedoara County, although the completion of this segment of the road has been subject to ongoing feuding over quality and performance issues between the Romanian roads agency CNADNR and the Italian construction company.

The A3 motorway is planned to run from Bucharest up the Prahova Valley to Braşov, and thence to Făgăraş, Târgu Mureş, Cluj-Napoca and Oradea, before connecting with the Hungarian M4 motorway. Only two segments of this motorway have been completed: that from Bucharest to Ploieşti and a short section near Cluj between Câmpia Turzii and Gilău. The completion of the A3 has been subject to ongoing controversies too, especially in respect of the difficult mountain section along the Prahova Valley between Comarnic and Braşov, where the concession has twice been retendered.

After the motorways, the next most important roads, and ones that will form a mainstay of any road trip around Transylvania, are the **national roads** (*drumuri naţionale*). These are designated by the letters DN, followed by a number. Many of these are also part of the European route network, denoted by the letter E followed by another number. Confusingly, the numbers are different. Thus the DN13 between Braşov and Sighişoara is also known as the E60.

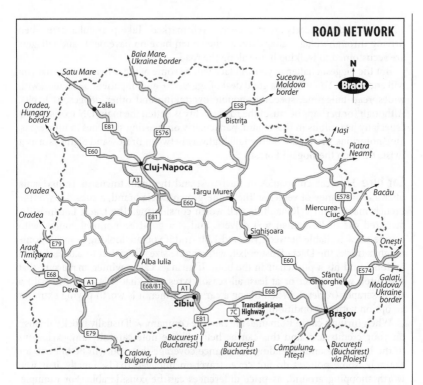

Below these are the **county roads** (*drumuri judeţene*). These are denoted by the letters DJ followed by a number. Upkeep of these falls to the county, and it is not unusual to find, when these roads cross a county boundary, a sudden sharp change in the quality of the maintenance of the road, according to the relative degree of prioritisation placed on the road by the different county administrations.

The **local roads** (*drumuri comunale*) below these are denoted by the letters DC followed by a number. **Forest roads** (*drumuri forestiere*) are basically tracks, which can get impassably muddy after rain.

Overall, and in part through the injection of EU structural funding, the quality of the roads in Transylvania has improved markedly in recent years, and many of the roads described in earlier editions of this guide as rough tracks now offer good-quality paved surfaces. But on a driving holiday in Transylvania, particularly one that involves any length of time in rural areas, you will encounter your fair share of rough tracks and pot-holed roads too. A 4x4 hire car is well worth considering. On particularly pot-holed stretches, following behind a local can be helpful, as they usually have a good idea of the best course to chart.

With road fatalities per kilometre several times that of most western European countries, you need to take great care while driving in Romania. In part this is due to the physical environment, with many steep mountain roads involving numerous hairpin bends. It is also a function of the wide variety of road users, from the fastest modern cars to horses and carts, overladen tractors, and in many places farm animals. You need to take particular care at dusk, when cows are a common sight on country lanes as they return home from the fields, and at night, when horse-drawn carts are not always well marked. Take particular care when driving through villages after dark, as they often have no pavements and villagers are accustomed to walking home along the road.

But the biggest challenge you will face will be some of the other driving that you will encounter. You will see a good deal of aggressive and impatient behaviour, with widespread tailgating, speeding, double overtaking and other dangerous habits. Although (or perhaps because) the road quality is better, the main DN roads can be especially hazardous in this regard, particularly on twisting stretches in hilly areas. One notorious stretch lies on the E60 highway between Braşov and Sighişoara as it twists through the Bogăţii Forest.

Car hire Hire-car companies in Bucharest and the main towns in Transylvania offer a broad range of vehicles. The home-grown Dacia brand, a subsidiary of the French manufacturer Renault, is well worth considering. The Dacia Logan is the favoured car of Romanian taxi drivers, and is a good economical choice, with engine sizes available between 1.0l and 1.5l. And if you are looking to tackle some tougher tracks the Dacia Duster 4x4, with engine sizes from 1.2l to 2.0l, is a good option – and fits a pushchair in the boot. If hiring a car in winter, make sure that it is fitted with winter or at least all-season tyres, and that it is equipped with a snow-scraper (*racletă*). When hiring a car in summer, it is worth paying extra for an option with air conditioning.

When hiring a car in Romania, the car-hire company will usually block a deposit on your credit card, and this can be hefty. Please note carefully any exclusions to the insurance and breakdown assistance coverage that you will be offered: for example, some policies do not cover travel on unpaved roads. Finally, it is well worth shopping around, as price differences can be considerable. For example, the daily rate offered for a Dacia Duster by three different companies at Bucharest airport approached on the same day ranged from €45 to €85, although variations in the price of (additional) comprehensive insurance and breakdown assistance cover tended to reduce the differentials.

Sample prices for a two-week period
- Ford Focus €25 a day
- VW Passat €47 a day
- Dacia Duster €60 a day
- Opel Insignia €65 a day
- Mitsubishi Outlander €79 a day

Petrol stations (*benzinării*) in Transylvania The main stations you will come across in Transylvania are Lukoil, MOL, OMV, Petrom and Rompetrol. You will also come across deserted-looking petrol stations, advertising an unknown name. These should be avoided except in a real emergency, as the fuel quality may be doubtful. At the time of research, the price of diesel (*motorină*) was 5.28RON a litre for premium and 4.89RON a litre for standard, while petrol (*benzină*) was 5.60RON a litre for premium and 4.93RON a litre for standard.

The website w gazonline.ro gives updated fuel prices in every Romanian county.

Parking In some Transylvanian towns there is ample, free car parking available. But in larger cities and more tourist-oriented places you will often have to pay to park your car, and in a few actually finding an unoccupied parking place can be a challenge. The system tends to vary from place to place, but the words '*cu plată*' next to the car park sign are an indication that you have to pay. In tourist hotspots like Bran, Corvin Castle and Sighişoara this means paying an attendant. In larger cities like Cluj-Napoca it means either, or a combination of, parking meters and purchasing parking tickets from whichever local shops stock them. Not all parking meters take banknotes: those in Cluj-Napoca, for example, worked at the time of research only with coins or credit cards and, since the credit card facility rarely seemed to be functional, this in practice meant a lot of fiddling with 50 bani coins. Carefully check the rules set out on parking meters or the car park signs as to when payment is necessary: car parks in some places in Transylvania only incur a charge on weekdays, and offer free parking at weekends.

Parking is a particular challenge in cities with historic pedestrian-only centres, especially Sibiu where, if you have chosen a characterful guesthouse in the heart of the historic centre, you might find that you have a long walk with your luggage between car and bed. In Sighişoara, if you have booked a guesthouse in the historic citadel you are allowed to drive up to it and park your car there, if you can find a space.

Driving regulations Speed limits in Romania for motorcars and motorcycles are usually 50 km/h (31mph) in built-up areas, 130km/h (80mph) on motorways, 100km/h (62mph) on European roads (those marked with an E designation), and 90km/h (56mph) on other roads. Speed limits for lorries and buses with more than nine seats are lower. However, there are some variations to the allowable speeds, particularly in built-up areas, so you should keep a close eye on the road signs. Police cars waiting by the side of the road with speed cameras are encountered frequently in Transylvania. If the driver in the oncoming traffic heading towards you is flashing furiously at you with his headlamps, this is intended to warn you of police ahead.

Note that driving in Romania is on the right side of the road. Unless otherwise indicated, by stop or yield sign, or at roundabouts (where vehicles already on the roundabout have priority, except where otherwise indicated), traffic coming from the right has the right of way. Overtake on the left, except in the case of trams, which should be overtaken on the right. The wearing of seatbelts is compulsory, and children aged under 12 must sit in the back.

Driving under the influence of alcohol is a criminal offence; the police have the right to carry out breathalyser tests, and the allowable threshold is very low, so don't drink and drive. The use of mobile phones (other than hands-free devices) is also banned while driving, not that you would realise this from the number of times you will see Romanian drivers happily chatting away on their mobiles. All drivers are required to have a warning triangle in their vehicle (check when you hire a car that it contains this). Drivers should ensure that they have with them their driving licence, another form of ID (such as a passport), proof of insurance and proof of ownership of the vehicle. And finally, note that the minimum driving age in Romania is 18. The Romanian Automobile Club (*Automobil Clubul Român; ACR;* \ *+40 21 317 8249*; e *acr@acr.ro;* w *acr.ro*) is a source of advice about all motoring matters in Romania. Good road maps are widely available, including from the shops at the larger petrol stations.

Accidents and breakdowns If you have a road accident, don't try to move your car or leave the site. You should call the police and ensure that you get a copy of the police report. In the event of a breakdown, the car-hire firm should have given you an emergency contact number to use.

If you are driving your own car to Romania, the following UK organisations offer European breakdown cover schemes.

THE BEST DRIVES IN TRANSYLVANIA

For all the challenges of driving in Transylvania, there are also drives that are likely to be a highlight of your holiday. Transylvania offers some stunning drives, whether over high mountain passes, winding through coniferous forests, or between meadows resplendent with a multi-coloured carpet of wild flowers. You will find your own favourites, but here are a few recommended drives.

- The Transfăgărășan Highway (DN7C) (pages 237–41)
- Miercurea-Ciuc to Odorheiu Secuiesc (DN13A) (page 179)
- The Transursoaia Highway from Albac to Huedin (DN1R) (page 276)
- Gheorgheni to Bicazul Ardelean (DN12C) (pages 185–6)
- Reghin to Lăpușna (minor road 153C) (page 200)
- Predeal to Șinca Veche via Râșnov (DN73A) (page 142)

AA UK ℡0800 072 3279; w theaa.com. Offers both single-trip & annual European breakdown cover, with a 24hr helpline on ℡00 800 8877 6655.

RAC UK ℡0330 332 8302; w rac.co.uk. Offers European breakdown cover, with a helpline on ℡+33 472 43 52 44.

BY TAXI Taxis in Romania are much cheaper than those in most western European countries, and are plentiful in large cities and towns (except when it rains). With the bus and railway stations in many Transylvanian towns located a long way from the centre, they can be a convenient means of getting to your accommodation. The relevant city entries in Part Two of this guide lists the phone numbers of the main local taxi companies.

As regards Bucharest, where you might wish to use a taxi to transfer from airport to public transport on your way to Transylvania, or if you have booked overnight accommodation, the taxis mostly seem to be yellow Dacia Logans. The most important advice is to check carefully the price charged per kilometre, either by phone when you book a taxi or, at a taxi rank, by checking the price written on the door. The typical rate at the time of research was 1.39RON/km, but some taxis charge 3.50RON/km, or even more. The other prices you will see displayed are *pornire*, the starting price you will pay having taken the taxi, and *stationare*, expressed as a rate per hour, which comes into play if you get stuck in traffic. Do check that the driver has the meter switched on.

Trustworthy **taxi companies in Bucharest** include Apolodor (℡021 9499), Cristaxi (℡021 9461), Mondial (℡021 9423) and Pelicanul (℡021 9665).

HITCHHIKING Hitchhiking is called *autostop* in Romania. You will see it in use frequently in isolated rural areas where there is little or no public transport, and it is not an uncommon sight to spot hitchhiking grannies or even nuns. Longer-distance hitchhikers, waiting on the roads out of major towns, will hold up pieces of cardboard indicating their desired destination: thus BV for Brașov. Hitchhikers in Romania tend to wave their arm furiously, rather than relying just on a discreetly raised thumb, which is liable to be quite disconcerting for car drivers who may think that an accident has happened.

But despite the bucolic connotations of rural hitchhiking in Romania, you should exercise all the usual precautions if planning to hitch and, as in all European countries, women travellers should avoid hitching alone.

THE HORSE AND CART

The horse and cart is an intrinsic part of rural life in Romania. A ride in a horse and cart is offered to tourists by enterprising providers of rural accommodation, as at the Kálnoky guesthouse in Micloşoara and the Valea Verde resort in Cund. But there have been challenges around reconciling this traditional mode of transport with the speed of 21st-century life. The presence of horses and carts on the main national roads in Transylvania was blamed by traffic planners on slowing the speed of circulation and by police on causing accidents as impatient drivers pressed to overtake the often heavily laden carts. In 2015, four passengers of a horse-drawn cart died after a collision with a vehicle being driven by Diana Dinu, a former Miss Globe Romania.

Horse-drawn carts have been banned from Romania's main roads since 2007. In Transylvania, however, main roads don't usually bypass villages, but run right through the centre of them, so avoiding main roads was easier said than done for many owners. In some cases, farmers were left without any legal way of taking their carts to their own fields. And, against a backdrop of rising costs for fodder, for an increasing number of owners the new law was the final nail in the coffin for their traditional method of transport. Following the introduction of the ban there were press reports of increasing numbers of horses simply let loose to starve, or sent to the slaughterhouses. Horsemeat exports from Romania boomed.

There have been many worthwhile initiatives to resolve the conflicts between horses and motor vehicles, including the construction of alternative side routes for horse-drawn carts to use. Let us hope that the traditional horse-drawn cart will remain a feature of Romanian rural life for generations to come.

ON FOOT Pedestrians should approach busy roads with care. Car drivers are unwilling to stop at zebra crossings, so avoid stepping off the pavement in front of an approaching car.

BY BICYCLE Cycling on a main highway in Romania is a challenge, both because of the wide variety of other vehicles using the road, and the patchy overall standard of driving. Designated cycle paths have not yet caught on in Romanian cities. But cycling can be an enjoyable way of exploring the Romanian countryside, and some of the travel companies listed on pages 58–61 offer mountain-bike tours. A good mountain bike with tough suspension will be important to your enjoyment of the experience. And there will be challenges on the way, notably being chased by dogs, whether strays or sheepdogs.

ACCOMMODATION

The range and quality of accommodation options across Transylvania has improved markedly in recent years. There is a good choice of hotels and guesthouses available in most places, suiting most budgets, and a pleasing increase in the number of more imaginative offerings, from village houses refurbished sensitively in traditional styles as guesthouses to opportunities to stay in restored aristocratic manors. In some places there are relatively few options at the very top and bottom of the scale: high-end hotels and hostels. And you should book early if your visit is likely to coincide with everyone else's: for example to Sibiu during the theatre festival, Cluj-

Napoca when the Untold Festival is on, or Sovata-Băi at the height of summer. That said, you can usually find somewhere with available rooms at your chosen destination, even if not your first choice.

Prices have risen in recent years but Transylvania is still cheaper than almost anywhere in western Europe. Many hotels post their tariffs in euros, with prices ranging from €18 (80RON) for a room in a basic guesthouse off the beaten track to €120 or more (535RON+) for a night in a top-range hotel in one of the main cities.

HOTELS The hotel scene in Transylvania has been transformed in recent years. Yes, you will still find unrestored examples of the former Communist-era hotels, which have a certain charm for those in search of Communist retro architecture and design, but at the cost of creaking smoke-filled lifts, dodgy plumbing and erratic hot water. These are now mostly to be found in those spa resorts, like Sângeorz-Băi, where investment hasn't really taken off in a big way since the revolution, or in those mid-sized towns bypassed by business and tourists. But in most other places, the former Communist hotels have been refurbished out of recognition, and joined by newcomers. Both Târgu Mureş and Cluj-Napoca offer a good range of modern offerings, with the latter sporting some funkier boutique hotels of a type found only occasionally elsewhere in the region. Sibiu, Braşov and Sighişoara all have a great selection of atmospheric places in refurbished historic buildings right in their medieval cores.

Wi-Fi is a particular strength of Romanian hotels: it is available free of charge almost everywhere. Wheelchair and pushchair accessibility is less good: one of the downsides of the fact that so many of the more interesting options are in characterful historic buildings is that many of them lack lifts. Breakfast is generally, though not always, included in the room rate, and is usually buffet-style, especially in larger hotels. There is a rating system in operation, from the basic one-star to luxury five-star accommodation, but it tends to offer only a rather general indication of the quality you will experience, and the four- or five-star ratings of some Transylvanian hotels seem rather generous. Service quality ranges from delightful warm hospitality to the dourest of dour.

MOTELS Roadside motels are a common sight along Transylvania's highways. Some of these are mainly geared to long-distance truck drivers (the presence of adjacent truck parks is the giveaway), but others have more of an eye on passing tourists. You will sometimes see roadside places describing themselves with the Romanian word *popas*, which means resting place, but with a distinctly rustic connotation. These cluster around the more scenic parts of the main European highways through Transylvania, for example the Bogăţii Forest stretch of the E60 between Braşov and Sighişoara, and are usually a good bet for traditional Romanian cooking served up in a rural life-themed dining room. Some, though not all, also offer accommodation.

PENSIONS AND GUESTHOUSES Since the fall of Ceauşescu in 1989 and the arrival of private enterprise there has been a boom in the family-run accommodation known here as pensions (*pensiuni*). The term covers a large range of establishments, from small guesthouses to places with several floors of rooms and capacious restaurants which are hotels in all but name. Pensions in rural areas have their own classification system, based on daisies (*margarete*), running from the basic one daisy to the luxury five daisies. These are awarded on the basis of the fulfilment of quite technical criteria, so only give a general sense of how nice the place is. Many pensions have been set up by former Romanian migrants to western Europe who have invested their savings from that work into setting up a business back home. All too often they have gone for purpose-built modern-looking constructions which, while comfortable enough, are out of tune with the surrounding rural environment. But this is starting to change, and there are an increasing number of pensions and guesthouses more focused on celebrating the best of Romanian rural traditions.

A particularly important role in the development of foreign tourism in Transylvania is being played by those families who have sympathetically restored traditional properties, whether grand manor houses or humble village homes, and converted these to relatively high-end tourist accommodation. Some of the most notable examples are the work of aristocratic ethnic Hungarian families, seeking to breathe new life into properties once seized by the Communists, but now restored to them. The Mikes Estate at Zăbala (pages 168–9) and Tibor Kálnoky's guesthouses at Micloşoara (page 164) are good examples. Another significant group comprises foreign citizens who have made Transylvania their home and invested in the restoration of village homes for holiday lets or as guesthouses. Examples include the Schäfers at Cund (pages 209–10) and the Bassettis at Copşa Mare (page 233). And there are growing numbers of home-grown Romanian investors following suit, such as the developers of the Raven's Nest complex in the Apuseni Mountains (page 277). Non-governmental organisations, notably the Mihai Eminescu Trust (page 61) have also played an important role in restoring village houses and developing them as guesthouses. The providers of this kind of high-end guesthouse accommodation generally offer an interesting range of excursions, which might include bear-watching or truffle hunting, home-cooked meals based around traditional ingredients and recipes, and airport pickups. This is not a cheap way to see Transylvania, with prices at most of these options working out on a par with those of higher-end hotel accommodation in the cities, but it is a highly rewarding one, and a stay at one or more of the traditionally restored village accommodation options forms a highlight of many visitors' Transylvanian holidays.

The other end of the rural guesthouse scale is made up of families who rent out a room or two to tourists (look for signs saying *camere de închiriat*). The availability of this kind of accommodation varies markedly. In some Transylvanian villages, for example Rimetea in Alba County, it can seem that almost every house has holiday rooms available, whereas in many other picturesque villages you will see none.

The **Romanian Ecotourism Association** (*Asociaţia de Ecotourism din România;* \0368 441 084; e info@eco-romania.ro; w asociatiaaer.ro) provides an ecotourism certification, and is a good source of further information about the sector. There is also a National Association of Rural, Eco and Cultural Tourism in Romania (*ANTREC;* \021 222 8001; e office@antrec.ro; w antrec.ro), but its website is pretty unhelpful.

MOUNTAIN REFUGES In and around the national and natural parks in mountain areas in Romania are hikers' huts (*cabane*). These vary enormously in size and standard, from some which are essentially decent if unfancy high-altitude hotel accommodation, with private bedrooms, to very basic huts where you need to use your own sleeping bag on a dormitory bed or even the floor. The prices vary accordingly. There is an equally wide variation in their degree of accessibility. The Cabana Bâlea Cascadă (pages 240–1) in the Făgăraș Mountains is right by the side of the main road, and Cabana Babele (page 139) in the Bucegi range just a few metres from the cable-car station, while others require a considerable hike. They are not supposed to turn anyone away, which is where the floors come in to play. They are marked on all good hiking maps. Note that these are different from the emergency shelters found in some high mountain areas popular with climbers and trekkers, which are not charged accommodation but places for emergency use only if you are stranded by a sudden change in the weather.

Some ordinary pensions and guesthouses in upland areas have 'cabana' in their name, but this is just marketing to convey a sense of mountain wildness.

HOSTELS The hostel network is not well developed in Transylvania, although there is at least one reasonable and central hostel in the major cities, plus tourist hotspots such as Sighișoara. A dormitory bed price should be around 50RON, possibly with a basic breakfast thrown in. **Hostelling International Romania** (\+40 264 450 452; e office@hihostels-romania.ro; w hihostels-romania.ro) has only 11 accredited hostels in Romania, only three of which are in Transylvania: one each in Brașov, Cluj-Napoca and Sibiu.

CAMPSITES Campsites (locuri de campare) are not particularly developed in Transylvania, and vary considerably in quality. Many also offer little wooden huts (căsuțe) for rental, though the outwardly bucolic charms of these hide the fact that they are decidedly spartan. The website of campsite specialists ACSI (w eurocampings.co.uk) has a digest of more than 40 campsites in Romania. 'Wild camping' is not allowed and, given the range of Romanian carnivores, as well as the challenges that can be posed by stray dogs and sheepdogs, would not in any case be advisable without an expert guide. National parks have strict regulations on where camping is possible: usually in areas immediately adjacent to the cabane.

EATING AND DRINKING

I had for breakfast more paprika, and a sort of porridge of maize flour which they said was mamaliga, and eggplant stuffed with forcemeat, a very excellent dish, which they call impletata.

From Jonathan Harker's journal, Chapter 1, Dracula, by Bram Stoker

The cuisine of Romania is a reflection of the country's history and geographical location. It is strongly influenced by the cuisines of the various countries which ruled over or otherwise influenced its territories at different times, with the particularly strong influence of Ottoman cuisine, via Wallachia and Moldavia, and of a more typically central European cuisine introduced through the Hungarian and Saxon communities in Transylvania. It has emerged as a distinctive Romanian cuisine, found in restaurants across the country, expressed in no dish more clearly than the humble mămăligă, the polenta to which Jonathan Harker was introduced on his first morning in Transylvania. Transylvanian cuisine (you will also hear it expressed as ardelean) reflects the wider array of Romanian dishes, but with a stronger influence from Hungarian and German ideas and flavours, with Hungarian dishes such as chicken paprikash featuring on menus.

BREAKFAST Jonathan Harker may have been served *mămăligă* for breakfast (*micul dejun*), but you are unlikely to encounter it very often on breakfast menus nowadays; breakfast is often quite a simple affair enhanced with natural local produce. Crusty bread (*pâine*) is accompanied by homemade jam (*gem*). If you stay with the Marins in Zărneşti, be sure to try Luminiţa's superb jams made from wild cherry, rose hip and divine elderberry, for which a recipe is given overleaf (see box, pages 94–5). Many small guesthouses offer their own yoghurt and the honey may have come from local beehives. Lorries with many-coloured hives installed in the side tour the countryside pursuing the best blossoms. Acacia honey (*salcâm*) is particularly good. *Poliflora* means that the bees have been feasting on a variety of different flowers. There may also be cheese (*brânză*), perhaps a Cheddar-like *caşcaval* or the unsalted semi-soft ewe's milk *caş*, a feta-like cheese, sometimes mixed with fresh dill and stuffed into fresh peppers. You may also be offered peppers, cucumber and tomatoes, served with a selection of salami and cold cuts. Two great spreads, often found at breakfast buffets in hotels, are the green *salată de vinete*, made from aubergines, and the reddish *zacuscă*, which may contain various vegetables but usually includes peppers, tomato, onion and carrot. Recipes for both are given in the box on pages 94–5. More elaborate additions may be omelette or frankfurter sausage (*crenvurşt*), which is very popular in Romania and usually served with mustard. This is washed down with orange juice, coffee or tea. Romanians opt for a variety of fruit teas, but something approaching English breakfast tea, and the milk to drink it with, is usually available, especially at larger hotels.

SNACKS One of the delights of Romanian towns is the hole-in-the-wall places that specialise in freshly made snacks (*gustări*) and pastries, notably *covrigi,* spirals of salted bread shaped like pretzels. These come in various flavours, from simple affairs with a topping of sesame seeds to more complex concoctions filled with cherry jam or chocolate. They are cheap, with the basic version typically 1RON, and very good. More elaborate and sweeter Romanian snacks include *gogoşi,* sweet doughnuts and *papanaşi,* cheese-filled pastries slathered with cream and jam.

In areas with a large ethnic Hungarian population, notably Mureş, Harghita and Covasna counties, and at fairs and markets everywhere in Transylvania, you will also come across typically Hungarian snacks, notably *lángos,* giant frisbees of deep-fried dough, served with an imaginative selection of toppings: sour cream, grated cheese, ketchup or even cabbage. A distinctive Székely culinary contribution is the chimney-shaped *kürtös kalács,* a hollow cylinder of sweet bread rolled in sugar, cinnamon, coconut or walnuts and cooked by wrapping it around metal poles on a kind of barbecue. It is fascinating to watch these being made on the spot. They usually sell for 10RON at fairs.

LUNCH AND DINNER Lunch (*dejunul/masa de prânz*) is usually the main meal of the day for most Romanians. Dinner (*cina*) is more modest. But restaurants generally offer the same menu at lunch and dinner, and so I will treat them together.

Romanian cuisine, when served in restaurants, is pretty heavy and filling, with portions typically large. One curious affectation of Romanian menus is frequently to use the diminutive – *uţă* or -*iţă*; eg: *mămăligă* becomes *mămăliguţă*. The suggestion that you are about to be offered a small portion is immediately belied by the huge pile of polenta that will arrive at your table. The diminutive here serves simply to offer a sense of charm or cuteness, rather than a statement of the quantity of food.

Restaurant meals can be a hit-and-miss affair, although they are improving both in quality and range of food, and there is an excellent choice of restaurants in the major cities. Small-town dining in Transylvania can, however, quickly induce a sense of sameness.

There is still an emphasis on **meat** in many restaurant menus and guesthouse offerings. Pork has a central place in the Romanian culinary consciousness, and the slaughter of a pig in the run-up to Christmas remains an important event in the calendar of many Romanian families. Vegetarians can ask for something *fără carne*, meaning 'without meat', or for *mâncare de post*, traditionally the dishes served during periods of fasting, observed by many Orthodox Romanians, when meat is avoided.

A typical large lunch might begin with *hors d'oeuvres* (*gustări*) with a range of salamis and cold cuts, home-pickled *gogoşari* (peppers) and *castraveţi* (baby cucumbers). They may be accompanied by *vinete* and *zacuscă*, or by a paste of carp roe (*salata de icre de crap*).

Soups are a very popular element of the Transylvanian diet. Romanians draw a fundamental distinction between an ordinary soup, or *supă*, and a sour soup, known as *ciorbă* or *borş*. Sour soups are prepared with the addition of a liquid, also called *borş*, made of wheat or barley bran fermented in water. You can buy this liquid in

TRANSYLVANIAN RECIPES

LUMINIŢA'S SECRET ELDERBERRY JAM RECIPE Elderberries are an excellent natural remedy, easing the symptoms of rheumatism and arthritis. Luminiţa's recipe makes a delicious jam which goes well with yoghurt as it is slightly crunchy. It's also great on fresh, crusty homemade bread.

Ingredients: 1kg elderberries, 1kg sugar, 50ml fresh lemon juice.

Remove the stalks from fresh and ripe berries, put the berries in a sieve and wash them under a strong water flow. Put the washed berries in a three- to four-litre pan (preferably a cast-iron one), in alternative layers with the sugar and lemon juice. Leave it covered until the next day to allow the fruit to let their juice. Boil it over a high flame to let the syrup thicken quickly.

Remove the pan from the heat and cover it with a moist dishcloth. When the jam has cooled, put it in jars, fasten the lids and keep them in a cool and dry place.

Tips: Sugar is boiled together with lemon juice so that it is transformed into more simple sugars (glucose and fructose).

Moisten the inner part of the lid and edge of the jar with rum.

Traditional medicinal use: rheumatic pains and gout, cleaning the kidneys, easing neuralgia.

MĂMĂLIGĂ RECIPE

Ingredients: 0.5l of water, salt, 1kg of cornmeal (*polenta, puliszka*), sour cream, sheep's cheese.

Boil half a litre of salted water. Add 1kg of cornmeal, pouring it gradually into the boiling water, stirring all the time. As you stir vigorously, the mixture will get stiffer. Stop adding the cornmeal once you get a firm consistency that will still pour, and continue on the lowest heat possible for about ten minutes with a lid half on as it will bubble and spit. Pour into small bowls or one large flattish dish and leave to set. Turn out the bowls onto a plate as individual portions. Serve with sour cream and a soft, salty curd cheese.

bottles in Romanian supermarkets. Note that the Romanian *borş* is less specific in meaning than the Russian *borscht*, which refers to a beetroot soup; here it does not necessarily involve beetroot at all. *Borş/ciorbă de perişoare*, a sour meatball soup, is one common variety. Another is the creamy *ciorbă de burtă* (tripe soup). Soups tend to be served with a dish of sour cream (*smântană*) and a small plate of hot green peppers. Romanians bite their way through these as they eat the soup.

Mămăligă, made from stone-ground cornmeal (polenta) is the unofficial national dish and is as essential to Romanian cuisine as pasta is to Italian. It forms the basis of a large number of heavy but hearty dishes, such as *bulz*, an oven-roasted mix of *mămăligă* and cheese. You may also come across *balmoş*, a smooth and rich puree of corn flour and whey cream. *Mămăligă* also forms the chief accompaniment to many signature Romanian dishes. Pride of place here goes to *sarmale* (cabbage or sometimes vine leaves stuffed with minced pork). Another important dish is *tochitură*, a meat stew that might also contain pork

SALATĂ DE VINETE (AUBERGINE CREME) *Delicious on homemade bread or toast*
Ingredients: Two big aubergines, one onion, four tablespoons of sunflower oil, a pinch of pepper, salt.

Roast the aubergines, peel while still hot and then leave on a slanted cutting board to drain. Chop into small pieces, place in a bowl and then mix using a wooden spoon, with a little oil at a time, until it whitens and becomes foamy. Add finely chopped onions to taste, also pepper and salt. Serve in a shallow bowl and garnish with tomato slices and rounds of green pepper.

ZACUSCĂ *Great for a quick snack when spread on bread*
In Slavic languages, *zakuska* means 'snack' from the word *kus* or 'taste'.
Ingredients: 750g carrots, 0.5kg onions, 12 long red peppers, 1kg tomatoes, 25dl sunflower oil.

Finely shred the carrots, onions and red peppers. Crush up the tomatoes. Put the onions, carrots and peppers in a pan to simmer slowly in the sunflower oil. Then add the crushed tomato and simmer until the oil rises to the top. Skim off the oil. Add salt and pepper to taste.

CIORBĂ RUSEASCĂ FĂRĂ CARNE (Russian soup without meat)
Ingredients: 3l water, one carrot, one parsley root, one big onion, one handful green beans, one small beetroot, a quarter of a small cabbage, two green peppers, one tablespoon butter, one tablespoon chopped parsley and dill, half a teaspoon flour, salt, 1 cup sour cream.

Finely chop the carrot, parsley root and onion. Add to the three litres of water and bring to the boil, adding the beans and the beetroot cut into julienne strips. Let it boil for half an hour, then add the cabbage and strips of peppers, salt and peeled, seeded and diced tomatoes. Make a roux with the flour and oil on a gentle heat, add some of the vegetable liquid then mix the roux back into the soup. When the vegetables are tender, add chopped parsley and dill. When serving, add a tablespoon of sour cream to each bowl.

fat, sausage and various internal organs, which is generally served with *mămăligă* and a salty sheep's cheese. *Tochitură ardelenească* is the name for the specifically Transylvanian version of this stew. A less heavy alternative, particularly popular in Romania during periods of religious fasting, is *ghiveci*, a ratatouille-like vegetable stew. Romanians also frequently eat *mămăligă* simply with sour cream and cheese.

Romanians are also highly attached to the **barbecue** (*grătar*). The distinctively Romanian contribution here are the little skinless sausages known as *mititei* or *mici* (literally 'small ones'). You will see these being cooked up on roadside barbecues all over the region; they are typically served with bread, mustard and perhaps a pickled cucumber, and cost very little, so are a great, if not particularly healthy, choice for travellers on a budget.

It's also common to find **fish** on the menu. *Saramură de crap* is is a particularly well-known dish, involving grilled carp which is then soaked in brine. *Păstrăv afumat* is also well-worth seeking out: trout wrapped in fir twigs and smoked.

Local fruit and vegetables are one of the joys of Transylvania, and a trip to the local **fruit and vegetable market** is a pleasure in every town. Just-picked apples, plums, walnuts and tomatoes are full of an intense flavour long forgotten in modern supermarkets in western Europe. Many villages in Transylvania have developed a particularly strong reputation for one specific product, and if you find yourself driving through one such village in season don't be surprised to be confronted with, say, trellises groaning with onions outside almost every house. Herbs such as basil, caraway, dill, juniper, lovage, marjoram, rosemary, tarragon and thyme are all popular in Transylvanian cooking. Homemade jams and herbal teas are great, and can make good souvenirs.

Look out for **local specialities**, such as the meat and cabbage dish from Cluj-Napoca known as *varză a la Cluj*. In the Hațeg area of Hunedoara County you might find *pup de crump*, a plate-sized dish of fried, grated potato and *brânză* patty served with a mug of thick drinking yoghurt. Some dishes are also associated with particular seasons. Autumn is the best time to find *pastramă*, a dish made from lamb treated in a way that allowed it to be better preserved in the days before modern refrigeration. The lamb dish *drob de miel,* which bears some similarities to haggis, is served at Easter and rarely encountered at other times.

Most restaurant menus feature some international standards as well as Romanian dishes. As regards specific foreign cuisines, Italian is by far the most popular, and almost every Transylvanian town of any size boasts at least one pizzeria.

If you have any room for **desserts** (*deserturi*), you'll find that ice cream (*înghețată*) is available everywhere, along with fresh fruit in summer and autumn. The other desserts commonly found on restaurant menus include *clătite* (pancakes), *plăcinte* (various sorts of pies) and *găluști* (plum dumplings). If you are coming to Transylvania close to Christmas, be sure to try the fruit loaf known as *cozonac*, which has a flavour not unlike panettone. In Zărnești, Luminița Marin makes a delicious *budincă*. She calls it a cake but it's almost more of a soufflé with apples, which is a treat for those on a gluten-free diet.

Să vă fie de bine! (I hope you enjoyed it!)

OPENING HOURS Bars and pubs open around lunchtime and stay open until at least 02.00 at weekends. Most restaurants open for lunch at noon and take their last orders around 22.30, though some open earlier and offer breakfast. Restaurants don't usually close during the afternoon.

DRINKS Mineral water is widely available: the major names include Dorna, Borsec, Harghita and Perla. Alongside the usual range of international fizzy drinks, Romanian restaurants often offer good homemade **lemonade**, which may be flavoured with ginger or other products. This is usually served up not in a glass, but in a jar with a straw, and sweetened

with honey to taste. More rarely, you might come across an elderflower cordial known as *socată*. In the case of both lemonade and *socată* you may be asked whether you would like it made with still or sparkling water. Another great non-alcoholic drink is *must*, freshly pressed grape juice which appears at the time of the autumn grape harvest. It is a mainstay of Romanian harvest festivals but is not found at other times of the year. Fruit juices on restaurant menus are more often packaged brands than homemade, but there are a few places offering great fresh juices and smoothies, like the Fresh Healthy Drink Bar (page 288) in Cluj-Napoca.

Romania produces some good **beers**. For more on the Ciuc and Igazí Csíki Sör brands produced in Harghita County, see the box on page 177. Other popular Romanian brands include Ursus, Timişoreana and Bergenbier. Beer is usually served in a half-litre mug known as a *halbă*. Romania produces a great range of wines (see below). Restaurants usually, but not always, serve at least one wine by the glass, although for better-quality wines you will generally have to buy a bottle. A *spriţ* (spritzer) of white wine mixed with sparkling mineral water is a popular summer drink. Mulled wine (*vin fiert*) with sugar and cinnamon is great on cold winter days. For something stronger, try *ţuică fiartă* (hot plum brandy with sugar and peppercorns).

Coffee (*cafea*) is the favoured hot drink, and urban Romanians have embraced speciality coffee shops offering a choice of beans for their cappuccinos. Thick Turkish coffee is also found in a few places. The drinking of **tea** (*ceai*) has been turned into an art in places like Demmers Teehaus in Cluj-Napoca (page 288), but in other places is more hit-and-miss. Herbal teas are a real strength, and you may well be treated to some wonderful home-grown preparations in rural guesthouses.

Transylvanian wine

Music and wine are the most direct and sincere manifestation of the feelings.

George Enescu, Romania's greatest composer

Transylvania has been a wine-producing region since before Roman times. The climate, relief and soils in several parts of the region all favour wine production, though it is particularly known for the production of white wines rather than the reds characteristic of more southerly regions of Romania. The country has its own grape varieties, in addition to internationally known varieties like merlot. These include *fetească neagră* for red wines, *fetească albă* and *fetească regală* for white wines, and the aromatic variety *tămâioasă românească*. The quality of wine produced here, as elsewhere in Romania, fell during the Communist period, when the authorities valued quantity over quality, and pushed growers together into collective farms. But since the revolution entrepreneurs from both Romania and overseas have been investing in the rehabilitation of vineyards and the development of higher-quality wines, often in much smaller quantities.

Restaurants in Transylvania usually offer a good range of Romanian wines on their menus, typically including wines produced outside Transylvania, such as Halewood's Prahova Valley range or the excellent wines of the Recaş winery outside Timişoara. But there will generally be some Transylvanian wines on the menu too. The price of a bottle of wine in a restaurant can range anywhere from €6 for the cheapest house wine to several times that for top-range Romanian or foreign offerings. *Vin roşu* is red wine, *vin alb* is white and *roze* is rosé, while *sec* is dry, *demi-sec* is medium dry, *dulce* is sweet, *spumant* is naturally sparking and *spumos* is artificially sparkling. Romanians traditionally prefer sweeter wines than those favoured by western European palates, although this is changing.

Here are some of the Transylvanian producers to look out for. Winery tours and tastings can be booked with the Jidvei, Liliac and Villa Vinèa wineries. See below for details.

Domeniile Boieru Ciumbrud, Aiud, Alba County; \0258 866 216; w vindeciumbrud.ro. Established in 2005, they produce low-cost white wines from the Ciumbrud area of Alba County.
Jidvei Str Gării 45, Jidvei, Alba County; m 0745 109 458; w jidvei.ro. Originally established in 1949 during the Communist period, this is now Romania's largest family-owned winery, & specialises in white wines from grapes grown along the Târnava Mare & Târnava Mică rivers.

Liliac Str Principală 41, Batoş, Mureş County; m 0732 153 189; w liliac.com. A relative newcomer on the scene, Liliac was set up in 2010 by entrepreneur Alfred Michael Beck & produces mid-range white & rosé wines, & smaller quantities of more expensive reds.
Villa Vinèa Sat Mica no 243, Mureş County; \0365 505 107; w villavinea.com. Established in 2004 by Heiner Oberrauch, they specialise in top-range red & white wines.

Ţuică and pălincă *Ţuică* (pronounced 'tsui-kuh') is a traditional Romanian spirit, usually presented to house guests on arrival or served with appetisers. It is generally accompanied by a toast of health or welcome. It is prepared in a brass still and made from plums which have been left to ferment for six to eight weeks. It generally has a strength of around 20–30%. A much stronger double-distilled plum brandy, with a strength above 40%, is known as *pălincă*. *Ţuică* is also used more loosely as a generic term that encompasses *pălincă* and spirits made from other fruits, which can give rise to some confusion about what it is that you are actually being served. In general terms, *ţuică* tends to predominate in southern Romania, with *pălincă* encountered more frequently in Transylvania and the northern region of Maramureş, where it is known as *horincă*. At a Romanian home or family-run guesthouse, you may well be served *ţuică* in a recycled fizzy drink or mineral water bottle, since in rural communities the home production of plum brandy is considered a right. If you head to the fridge in the middle of the night in search of a drink of water, make sure you gulp from the right bottle. It is said that most of the plums grown in Romania are used to make *ţuică*.

If this kind of fierce firewater is not your passion, you might be more tempted by the locally produced liqueurs made from a range of different fruits, like the blueberry liqueur known as *afinată*. These are made by allowing the fruit to ferment with sugar, and then blending this with *ţuică*.

PUBLIC HOLIDAYS AND FESTIVALS

PUBLIC HOLIDAYS (*SĂRBĂTORI LEGALE*) Businesses and shops close for the following public holidays.

1 and 2 January	New Year's Day (*Anul Nou*)
24 January	Union of Romanian Principalities (*Ziua Unirii Principatelor Române*)
April/May	Orthodox Easter (*Paşte*) Sunday and Monday, usually celebrated later than in western Europe. Easter Sunday/Monday dates: 8/9 April 2018, 28/29 April 2019, 19/20 April 2020.
1 May	International Labour Day (*Ziua Internaţională a Muncii*)
May/June	Descent of the Holy Spirit/Orthodox Pentecost (*Rusalii*) – falls on the Sunday/Monday 50 days after Orthodox Easter. Dates: 28/29 May 2018, 16/17 June 2019, 7/8 June 2020.
1 June	International Children's Day (*Ziua Internaţională a copilului*)
15 August	The Assumption (*Adormirea Maicii Domnului*)
30 November	St Andrew's Day (*Sfântul Andrei*), Patron Saint of Romania
1 December	Romanian National Day (*Ziua Naţională a României*) or Great Union Day (*Ziua Marii Uniri*), celebrating the union of Transylvania, Wallachia and Moldavia in 1918
25 and 26 December	Christmas (*Crăciun*)

THE TRANSYLVANIAN YEAR: FEASTS AND FESTIVALS Many of the feasts and festivals celebrated throughout Transylvania are linked with major religious celebrations, or those connected with the changing seasons. Some traditional events are dying out, others have been reborn, though often in changed formats, while many of the Romanian traditions around the great feasts of Christmas and Easter have proved remarkably durable, and in many cases happily coexist with foreign imports. Thus at Easter the Romanian tradition of knocking together painted hard-boiled eggs is alive and well, though Romanians happily give and receive chocolate eggs too.

New Year (*Anul Nou*) In Transylvanian villages you will still come across folk traditions associated with New Year. On New Year's Eve, these include a performance called *pluguşorul* (the little plough) by groups of children moving from house to house. The performance, which is usually accompanied by a good deal of energetic whip-cracking, is centred around wishes of good health for the coming season. In some villages the New Year's Eve celebrations are more elaborate, and involve mask dances, with villagers taking on various roles, including bears, goats, brides and even the devil. The 'dance of the goat' is one of the best known. On New Year's Day children brandish a decorated stick known as a *sorcova*, with which they lightly touch their parents or friends, wishing them good luck and good health through special set verses. In some communities children go from house to house with the *sorcova*, pronouncing their good wishes in return for some small treat.

Epiphany (*Bobotează*) Although not a public holiday, this is an important event in the religious calendar in Romania, and marks the day on which Jesus was baptised by John the Baptist. After the mass on Epiphany Day, 6 January, Romanian priests give out a holy water known as *agheasmă mare*, or 'big holy water', which is considered by the faithful as more potent than water blessed on other days of the year, which is known as 'little holy water' or *agheasmă mica*. There are numerous water-related superstitions associated with Epiphany. It is said, for example, that if a young unmarried woman puts a sprig of basil which has been blessed with holy water under her pillow, she will dream of her future husband. And laundry should

2

not be done on Epiphany, since all waters are considered to be blessed on this day. Religious ceremonies are also often held near large bodies of water on this day, and culminate with the priest throwing a wooden cross into the icy waters. Whoever retrieves the cross will have luck the entire year, unless hypothermia sets in.

Carnival An important event among the ethnic Hungarian communities in Transylvania is *Farsang*, Hungarian Carnival season, which runs between Epiphany and Ash Wednesday. The final three days of this period are traditionally the main focus of merriment. In Rimetea, in Alba County, for example, the main event is known as the Burial of Carnival (*Înmormântarea Fărşangului*), in which young men of the village dressed up in all manner of outfits, from clowns to soldiers to priests, process alongside a donkey pulling a cart carrying a coffin, which is destroyed at the end of the proceedings. Among ethnic Romanian communities, the equivalent period of pre-Lent merriment is known as *Săptămână Nebunlior* ('mad week').

Dragobete Celebrated on 24 February, this is the Romanian equivalent of St Valentine's Day. Dragobete was by legend the kind son of Baba Dochia, the old woman who in Romanian mythology is associated with the coming of spring. Girls and boys traditionally pick the first flowers of spring on this day for their loved ones. A separate and rather curious Romanian superstition associated with Baba Dochia involves choosing a day between 1 and 9 March: if the day turns out to be fair, good luck ensues, but woe betide you if it turns out to be a miserable day.

Mărţişor (1 March) Literally meaning 'little March', this is an important spring celebration throughout Romania, and centres on a small talisman with a length of red and white string attached to it, also known as a *mărţişor*. They are sold at shops and stalls everywhere from Dragobete until International Women's day on 8 March, and usually display symbols associated with either good luck or springtime: a four-leaf clover, chimney sweep, a horseshoe, a ladybird or snowdrop. In Romania, they are generally only given by men to women. By tradition girls and women wear these talismans through the month of March, then hang them up in fruit trees. If you stroll through a Romanian park in April, you will find lengths of red and white string dangling picturesquely from the branches of cherry trees. On 8 March, for International Women's Day, it is customary for Romanian men to buy flowers for close female friends and work colleagues.

Easter (Paşte) Easter is a huge event in Romania. Note that the Romanian Orthodox Church calculates the date of Easter using the Julian rather than the Gregorian calendar, so it generally falls on a different day from that observed by Catholics or Protestants. One curiosity here is that unlike most other Orthodox communities, the Romanian Orthodox Church calculates Christmas and most other religious festivals using the Gregorian calendar – thus Christmas in Romania falls on 25 December. The enthusiasm with which Easter is celebrated is associated with the strictness of Lent, during which Orthodox Romanians adopt a very restricted diet (known as a 'fasting diet' or *post*) and celebrations such as weddings or baptisms are not held.

Palm Sunday (*Floriile*), held on the last Sunday before Easter, heralds the Holy Week preparations. The major tradition on this day is the blessing of willow branches at church, which are then used to decorate fruit trees or beehives so that the trees are fruitful; the hives produce abundant honey. Good Friday (*Vinerea mare*) is not a public holiday in Romania, and the strictures of Lent continue until midnight on the eve of Easter Sunday. The Orthodox church service on the Saturday evening is a major one, and after midnight the priest will declare that Christ has risen: 'Hristos a înviat'. The congregation responds, 'Adevărat a înviat' ('Christ is risen indeed'). Everybody lights a candle from the priest's candle, and after the service walk gingerly home trying to keep their candles alight. On returning home from this midnight mass, in the small hours of the morning, an enormous Easter meal is then eaten.

The main Easter dish is lamb, a meat which is little consumed by Romanians at other times of the year. Among several lamb-based dishes to look out for at this time of year is *drob*, made from the lamb's internal organs, which is somewhere between haggis and pâté. A special dessert eaten only at Easter is *pască*, somewhat like cheesecake. As at Christmas, Romanians also consume large quantities of the panettone-like cake called *cozonac*. The first washing of the face on Easter morning is traditionally done from a bowl in which a red-painted egg and a coin have been placed, as a guarantor of health and good fortune.

The cracking of red-painted hard-boiled eggs between two friends or family members, accompanied by a conversation of 'Hristos a înviat', 'Adevărat a înviat', is a widely practised Easter tradition, and can get somewhat competitive, like an egg-based version of conkers. For days after Easter Romanians greet each other in the street with this exchange. While the eggs used for cracking within Romanian families are generally simply painted affairs in a monochrome red, in parts of Romania, especially the Bucovina region, there is a tradition of elaborately painted eggs, using melted beeswax to create intricate patterns. These make great, if rather fragile, souvenirs.

St George's Day (*Sângeorz*) Falling on 23 April, this is celebrated in many parts of Transylvania with festivals linked to springtime and fertility. One variant of the theme involves a young man covered in green branches and twigs being taken from house to house in the village, where he is liberally doused with water for his pains. And at the end of the procession he is thrown into the village fountain. St George's Day is also by tradition the day on which shepherds take their flocks up to their summer pastures in the mountains, coming back down on St Demetrios's Day, 26 October.

Armindeni In rural areas the coming of spring on 1 May is marked by customs of pagan origin aimed at ensuring a good crop to come and avoiding natural disasters like drought or hailstorms. A green branch is traditionally placed by the gate or door of the house. The tradition of planting a 'tree of life' on this day in the courtyard of a house, which is then richly decorated, is rarely seen nowadays. The day is also known in many parts of Romania as *Ziua Bețivului* ('drunkards' day').

The Measurement of the Milk Festival (*Măsurişul Laptelui*) Also known as *Sâmbra* in some areas, this feast is traditionally held in shepherding areas across the region in spring, usually in or around early May, when the sheep are taken up to the sheepfold (*stâna*) where they will spend the summer. The sheep and their new pastures are blessed by a priest, and then the ewes are milked by each family, and the results measured. There is a practical reason for this: the milk tally determines the share of the cheese produced by the shepherd while up in the summer pastures that will go to each family. The milk-measuring part of proceedings is followed by music, dancing and food. Where these festivals have been preserved, they have largely remained local community events. The hills around Ciucea near Huedin in Cluj County are one of the best places to see these festivals, but they are found in many areas.

Midsummer (*Sânziene*) The pagan midsummer festival of *Sânziene* is celebrated on 24 June. As a celebration of the powers of the sun, it is associated with the lighting of campfires, and in some places a test of bravery in attempting to jump over them. Romanians traditionally believe that good fairies known as *Sânzienele* fly around the countryside on the night before 24 June, and that every herb they touch during their flight will be given an additional healing potency. One particular flower, also known in Romanian as *sânziene*, is specifically associated with the day: this is the yellow-flowered plant known in English as lady's bedstraw, and in Latin as *Galium verum* (see box, page 8). This is collected by unmarried girls and in some places placed under the girl's pillow at night, so that she may dream about her future partner. In others, the tradition is to create wreaths from these flowers. The wreaths are thrown onto the roof of the house: if they stay there, the girl will get married soon; if they fall down, she'll have to wait a while yet. Village celebrations of *Sânziene* also tend to involve the local girls dressing up as fairies, with floral garlands on their heads.

The Girls' Fair (*Târgul Fetelor*) This is another festival which developed to meet the exigencies of Romanian rural life. With families living in often isolated villages, the pool of potential spouses was decidedly limited, with all the attendant risks around in-breeding in rural communities. The Girls' Fair was a way of combating this, in providing a setting in which girls and boys looking to wed could get a chance to meet potential partners hailing from a much wider area. It is said that girls would even bring their dowries along in a cart, to help to seal a deal. These fairs today have lost their original purpose, and become more general celebrations of rural traditions, with plenty of folk music and dance. One popular example is held at the end of June near the village of Gurghiu in Mureş County (page 200). But by far the most famous example of the genre is the **Mount Găina Girls' Fair**, held in July above the village of Avram Iancu in the Apuseni Mountains (page 274). This is one of the most popular rural festivals in Transylvania, attracting thousands of visitors each year, but note that its purpose has changed entirely. It is now basically a folk-music festival focused around a stage high up on a mountain plateau, with the festival-goers camping out in tents.

St Andrew's Night (*Noaptea Sfântului Andrei*) This falls on 29 November, the eve of St Andrew's Day, commemorating Romania's patron saint. While Romania has imported Halloween traditions from elsewhere, via Hollywood, St Andrew's Night is the home-grown version, the 'night of the vampires' at which it is said that vampires and undead souls (*strigoi*) come out. This is traditionally the time for vampire-related partying, though party-goers ensure that doors and window frames are liberally rubbed with garlic.

Christmas (*Crăciun*) The Christmas season in Romania is celebrated with enthusiasm, and kicks off around the time of Romania's national day, 1 December, with the opening of Christmas markets in the larger towns. These are well worth catching if you are in Romania over this period: little wooden huts dispense mulled wine (*vin fiert*) and an array of sweet Christmas goodies, there will usually be concerts programmed in the evenings, and children get to visit Santa's grotto. He's known as *Moş Crăciun* in Romania. On the evening of 5 December, the eve of St Nicholas's Day, Romanian children leave their shoes by the door, which are supposed to be freshly cleaned, in the hope that St Nicholas will put some sweets or other presents inside them overnight. If the child has been particularly naughty, they might find that a whip has been placed in their shoe instead. The next key date in the pre-Christmas calendar is St Ignatius's Day, 20 December, upon which under Romanian tradition each family slaughters a pig. The meat from every part of the pig goes to make the various pork-related dishes that form the centrepiece of the Romanian Christmas feast. A meal of pork served immediately upon the slaughter of the pig is known as *pomana porcului,* literally 'the pig's alms', although, since the Romanian Orthodox church has a pre-Christmas Lent tradition, this is not observed by all families. The Christmas tree is traditionally decorated on 24 December, and Christmas Eve also represents the peak of the singing of Christmas carols (*colinde*), which started in early December. Groups of carol singers go from house to house offering a carol or two, for which children expect sweets, adults a glass of wine, or everyone ideally some money. The quality of singing varies enormously, from beautiful verses sung by trainee priests to the inebriated mutterings of those singers who have already been overcome by the wine. The singing of the *Carol of the Star* is usually accompanied by the prop of a stick with a cardboard star stuck on top, and the other carols sometimes come with more elaborate traditions involving complex performances by different masked characters, although these tend to be more associated with the run-up to New Year's Day (page 99). The main Christmas meal is both heavy and pork-oriented, typically featuring a *ciorbă* (sour soup), pork sausages, *sarmale* (cabbage leaves stuffed with pork), and plenty of roast pork. As at Easter, panettone-like *cozonac* is eaten as a traditional dessert.

TRANSYLVANIA'S BEST FESTIVALS There is a huge range of festivals on offer in Transylvania. Almost every town has its **Town Days** (*Zilele Orașului*), made up of a whole series of concerts, dance, sports events and competitions, when the people of the town let their collective hair down. These events tend to be homespun and are targeted at locals rather than tourists, but all are welcome to join in. Most ethnic communities in Transylvania hold a wide range of festivals aimed at celebrating and helping to preserve the traditions of that community. Hungarian community events often feature big-name performers brought from Budapest, while community events in the Saxon community are often held in the summer period, aiming to coincide with the holidays of locals who left for Germany at the time of the revolution. Rural communities have retained festivals linked to traditions such as the measurement of the milk, or the matchmaking events known as girls fairs, although in many cases the festivals have lost much of their original purpose, and have become generalised celebrations of folk music and traditional ways of life. Cities such as Sibiu and Cluj-Napoca have increasingly focused on the development of active cultural programmes as a major component of their touristic and wider economic development, seen to strongest effect with events like the International Theatre Festival in Sibiu and the Untold music festival in Cluj-Napoca.

Details of the most important and interesting festivals in Transylvania are set out in Part Two of this guide under the relevant city or village entry, but here is a personal selection of the ten best festivals in Transylvania, from the highly traditional to the ultramodern.

- Electric Castle music festival, Bonțida, Cluj County, June/July (page 296)
- Junii Parade, Brașov, spring (page 131)
- Mount Găina Girls' Fair, Avram Iancu, Alba County, July (page 274)
- Nedeia Munților, Fundata, Brașov County, summer (page 145)
- Răvășitul Oilor, Bran, Brașov County, September/October (page 145)

- Sibiu International Theatre Festival, June (page 219)
- Sibiu Jazz Festival, May (page 219)
- Transylvania International Film Festival, Cluj-Napoca, June (pages 288–9)
- Untold Festival, Cluj-Napoca, August (page 289)
- Whitsun pilgrimage to Şumuleu, Miercurea-Ciuc (page 176)

SHOPPING

Urban Romanians increasingly shop in large malls. These are typically open every day, often 10.00–22.00, and generally contain a large supermarket, part of a major international chain such as Auchan or Carrefour. The downside for tourists is that the malls are often located on the edge of town, miles from the sights, and can be difficult to reach without a car. But city centres still retain a good enough range of shops to suit most needs, although they typically close around 18.00 and may not open on Sundays. The main cities in Transylvania all have central bookshops, with maps and at least some English-language books. Some kiosks selling cigarettes, alcohol, soft drinks and snacks stay open until late in the evening. Every town has a

---

NAME DAYS

There is a strong tradition in Romania of celebrating one's name day (*zi onomastică*), on which people named after Orthodox saints celebrate the day associated with 'their' saint, almost in the fashion of a second birthday – except without a candle-bedecked cake. Flowers are given to work colleagues celebrating their name day, and those who are celebrating one may organise a party or dinner to mark the occasion. Palm Sunday (*Floriile*), the last Sunday before Easter, scoops up all ladies named after flowers rather than saints. Romanians whose name does not quite match those of any established saints may have a choice at to which date to choose. Thus some girls named Oana go with Saint Ann, while others, considering that their name derives from a feminised version of John, plump for Saint John. The following are among the most popular:

1 January	Sf Vasile (St Basil)
7 January	Sf Ioan (St John)
23 April	Sf Gheorghe (St George)
21 May	Sf Constantin şi Elena (a big one this, as it covers all Constantines and Helens)
29 June	Sf Petru şi Pavel (another important day, celebrating all Peters and Pauls)
20 July	Sf Ilie (St Elias)
15 August	Sf Maria (St Mary, though many Romanians celebrate 8 September, the date of the birth of the Virgin Mary instead, because of the connotations of death associated with 15 August, the Assumption of Mary into Heaven)
9 September	Sf Ana (St Ann)
8 November	Sf Mihail şi Gavril (SS Michael and Gabriel)
30 November	Sf Andrei (St Andrew, the Patron Saint of Romania)
6 December	Sf Nicolae (St Nicholas)
27 December	Sf Stefan (St Stephen)

large **central market** (*piaţa centrală*), often open air, which can be fascinating places to wander around and good spots to purchase fruit and vegetables.

In rural areas the picture is very different, but large villages will have a ***magazin mixt***, a small general store that offers all the essentials. The opening hours of village stores can be erratic.

If you are driving around Transylvania you will quickly notice the large number of goods offered by roadside vendors. **Honey** can be a particularly good choice, though does come with an attendant risk of leakage into your baggage on the journey home. It is sold close to parked lorries that carry hives, offering a mobile service for the bees in order to track the tastiest blossoms around the countryside. As you pass in season through villages known for the production of particular fruits or vegetables, local householders will be ready with the product in question laden in buckets, set out on trestle tables or hanging from wooden frames by the side of the road. Last and very definitely least in the category of roadside offerings are the little wooden huts in tourist areas, whose vendors sell all manner of tat, from wooden shields to plastic sunglasses, and a curious preponderance of garden gnomes.

As regards souvenirs, **folk arts and crafts** are probably the most popular choice. The Galeriile de Artă Populară in Sibiu (page 220) is particularly good. Alternatively, you can buy direct from the craftsman, for example at the pottery town of Corund in Harghita County (page 183), or the cobalt-blue pottery from the ADEPT workshop at Saschiz (page 210). As well as pottery, good small souvenir options include beautiful painted eggs and hand-carved wooden spoons. Hand-painted icons on wood or glass make for a more expensive souvenir, as do the magnificent embroidered women's blouses. These are called *ie* ('ee-ay'), which in the plural is the even more curious-looking *ii*. *Ţuică*, *palincă* or a good bottle of **Romanian wine** can also make for welcome presents, though again presenting a challenge for your homeward packing, as can locally produced jams and preserves. Pivniţa Bunici in Saschiz (page 210) offers a good range of jams, chutneys and cordials, and if you really must buy some Dracula tat for the folks back home, the stalls clustering beneath Bran Castle (page 144) are your place.

ARTS AND ENTERTAINMENT

MUSIC AND DANCE The main Transylvanian cities have good opera houses and philharmonics where you can watch high-quality classical performances much more cheaply than in western Europe. The cultural programmes of cities such as Cluj-Napoca, Sibiu, Braşov and Sighişoara include festivals and concerts covering a variety of genres, including jazz, blues, rock and folk. Music is indeed central to almost every festival programme in Transylvania: even gatherings with no obvious musical base, such as the International Theatre Festival in Sibiu or the literary Dilema Veche Festival in Alba Iulia, tend to feature evening concerts. The number of evening concerts held in cities such as Sibiu at the height of summer is such that it sometimes seems that a stage is an almost permanent feature of the central square. These open-air concerts are generally free of charge.

Other musical events to watch out for are organ and other classical music concerts performed in a number of churches in Transylvania, mainly during the early evening in summer. Those at the Black Church in Braşov are particularly popular. They rarely cost more than a few lei. The music of Roma musicians (*lăutari*), often based around violin and accordion and sometimes the hammered dulcimer known as a cimbalom, is a highlight of an evening at one of the many Transylvanian restaurants that feature their performances.

Details of upcoming performances in all genres in the larger cities can be found in free listings magazines like *Şapte Seri* (w *sapteseri.ro*), *Zile şi Nopţi* (w *zilesinopti.ro*) or *24-Fun* (w *24fun.ro*), to be found in hotels, bars and restaurants.

Dance is a major feature of most of the traditional folk festivals listed in Part Two of the guide, and many of Transylvania's ethnic communities, large and small, are focusing on the teaching of traditional dance as an important element of community identity. This is true of the Hungarian community, where a '**dance house**' (HU: *táncház*) is a combination of folk-dance lesson and performance. The website w tanchaz.hu has information in English on summer dance camps in both Hungary and Romania.

CINEMA Given the success of Romanian films in recent years at international festivals, it is disappointing to find that they are difficult to see in Romania itself. Mainstream cinemas focus instead on the major international blockbusters of the moment, and your best opportunity to see Romanian productions lies with film festivals such as the Transylvania International Film Festival (w *tiff.ro*).

The free listings magazines available in the main cities (see above) have details of the cinema programmes. Most of the modern cinemas are now in malls outside the city centres, with the old central cinemas either closed completely or having a rather decrepit air, although the latter are in many cases a better bet for an interesting non-mainstream offering.

A major advantage of Romanian cinemas for foreign visitors is that a high percentage of films are shown in their original language, with Romanian subtitles, rather than dubbed. This should be made clear from the film poster: *dublat* is what you are trying to avoid. Cartoon films for children are likely to be dubbed into Romanian. Prices are cheaper than in western Europe, with the average at a modern multiplex around 20–25RON.

CULTURAL ATTRACTIONS

CHURCHES AND MONASTERIES Churches are among the major sights of Transylvania, from the UNESCO-listed Saxon fortified churches of the south to remote Romanian Orthodox monasteries. The many different denominations are a reflection of the complex history and ethnic mix of the region. The Orthodox **monasteries** tend always to be open, at least during daylight hours, and some offer basic accommodation. But at the other end of the scale, particularly in respect of those of the Lutheran **fortified churches** where, because of the out-migration of Saxons to Germany, there are no longer many services, you will find that one of the recurring challenges of ecclesiastical sightseeing in the region is getting someone to open the church up for you. In most villages there is usually an officially designated keyholder, normally the priest where one exists or otherwise a senior member of the Saxon community. Contact telephone numbers effective at the time of research are given in Part Two of the guide, but otherwise it is a matter of asking around in the village. '*Cine are cheia?*/*Kinél van a kulcs?*' ('Who keeps the keys?') is a phrase you might find yourself using quite often.

MUSEUMS AND GALLERIES There is quite a range of museums in Transylvania, from the county museums in each county capital to art galleries in the major cities to 'memorial houses' (*casă memorială*) at the birthplaces of noted writers and political figures, typically combining restored interiors with a small museum chronicling his (or, rarely, her) worthy deeds. There have been recent improvements to the quality of a number of museums in the region, in many cases fuelled by an injection of grant funding, but there are still too many examples of museum displays that have remained unchanged since the revolution, with natural history sections dominated by rows of stuffed animals looking out from behind glass cases, and history sections which peter out in the interwar years because museum curators have thrown out the hagiographic displays of the Communist era, but are unsure how to replace them. While increasing numbers of museums have material available in English, many, particularly the memorial houses, offer descriptions in Romanian only. And while there are some good, knowledgeable museum staff, you will more often encounter those who see their sole role as preventing visitors from touching anything, and certainly not to provide any information on what is on offer.

Most museums are closed on Mondays, and they rarely stay open beyond 17.00 on other days. Note too that the closing time of Romanian museums means the time at which the staff lock up the door and leave. They generally stop allowing admissions half an hour before this closing time, and in larger museums will start to close off individual rooms during this final half hour.

One interesting type of Romanian museum worthy of specific mention is the **open-air** museum, usually focused around traditional rural dwellings and structures such as windmills, which have been brought to the museums and painstakingly reassembled in order to preserve them. There are good examples of the genre in both Bran and Cluj-Napoca, but by far the most impressive in Transylvania is the wonderful ASTRA Museum of Traditional Folk Civilisation outside Sibiu (page 224).

Excluding places like Bran and Corvinus castles, which are more castle than museum, here is a personal choice of the **ten top museums in Transylvania.**

- Art Museum, Cluj-Napoca (pages 290–1)
- ASTRA Museum of Traditional Folk Civilisation, Sibiu (page 224)
- Brukenthal National Museum, Sibiu (pages 220–1)
- Ethnographic Museum of Transylvania, Cluj-Napoca (page 292)
- History Museum, Sibiu (page 223)
- Museum of Braşov Urban Civilisation, Braşov (page 132)
- Pamfil Albu Ethnography Museum, Lupşa, Alba County (pages 276–7)
- Pharmacy Museum, Cluj-Napoca (page 291)
- Roşia Montană Gold Mining Museum, Alba County (pages 272–4)
- Székely National Museum, Sfântu Gheorghe, Covasna County (page 163)

CASTLES, FORTRESSES AND PALACES The castles and fortifications of Transylvania are a testament of the difficulty of life here for many centuries, buffeted by frequent attacks from Turks and Tatars as well as the scheming of rival forces closer to home. In southern Transylvania, even the churches were fortified. With the passing of the centuries and stronger feelings of security, hilltop castles were gradually abandoned by the rulers of the region in favour of grand palaces. Many of the latter endured astonishing changes of fortune during the 20th century; from the seats of Hungarian aristocratic families through seizure by the Communists and conversion into sanatoria or orphanages to restoration to the heirs of their former owners, but in a deeply degraded state.

Transylvania's fortresses and palaces include a huge range of types of building, from UNESCO World Heritage-listed Dacian hilltop fortresses to the headquarters of Roman legions, from formidable medieval hilltop castles to genteel Renaissance and Baroque palaces. Here is a personal choice of the **top ten castles, fortresses and palaces of Transylvania.**

- Alba Iulia Citadel, Alba County (page 265)
- Bran Castle, Brașov County (page 144)
- Brukenthal Palace, Sibiu (pages 220–1)
- Corvin Castle, Hunedoara County (pages 250–2)
- Făgăraș Fortress, Brașov County (page 150)
- Mikó Castle, Miercurea-Ciuc, Harghita County (page 176)
- Porolissum, Sălaj County (page 317)
- Sarmizegetusa Regia, Hunedoara County (pages 248–9)
- Sighișoara Citadel, Mureș County (page 204)
- Teleki Castle, Gornești, Mureș County (page 199)

SPAS Spas have been important in Romania since Roman times and have traditionally been a highly significant feature of domestic tourism. They include spas specialised in the taking of therapeutic waters, in bathing in salt-rich water, dry bathing in gaseous mofettes, spending time taking in the airs of the high mountains, or deep below ground in a salt mine. But a number of previously important spa resorts have struggled following the Romanian Revolution in 1989, the victim of changing tastes as a younger generation able to take their holidays abroad spurned the more sedate attractions of domestic spas, and facing huge challenges to secure the investment necessary to upgrade their ageing Communist-era infrastructure. Some spa resorts, like Sângeorz-Băi in Bistrița-Năsăud County, still seem stuck in an earlier era. But others have modernised successfully, like Sovata-Băi in Mureș County, fuelled by tourists from Hungary as well as Romania, and Turda in Cluj County, whose salt mines now constitute one of the most popular paying attractions in the country.

Here is a personal list of the **five top spas of Transylvania.**

- Turda Salt Mine, Cluj County (page 300)
- Băile Balvanyos, Covasna County (page 165)
- Covasna, Covasna County (pages 169–70)
- Praid Salt Mine, Harghita County (pages 183–4)
- Sovata-Băi, Mureș County (pages 196–8)

SPORTS AND ACTIVITIES

Romanians are proud of their sporting heroes. The very greatest include footballer **Gheorghe Hagi**, an attacking midfielder who was known as the 'Maradona of the Carpathians' and currently both owns and chairs the Viitorul Constanța side in Romania's largest port city. Then there's gymnast **Nadia Comăneci**, who won hearts the world over with her impish smile and the first perfect 10 score in Olympic history when aged just 14, at the 1976 Montreal Olympics. Another sporting star is **Ilie Năstase**, one of the top tennis players of the 1970s. The current leading light in Romanian sport is another tennis player, **Simona Halep**.

None of these Romanian legends is from Transylvania, but the region has produced its sports stars too. They include **Ion Țiriac**, a tennis player born in Brașov, best known as Ilie Năstase's doubles partner, as a former manager of Boris Becker, and for his magnificent moustache. Following his retirement from tennis he became a successful businessman and the founder of the Țiriac Bank, later sold to the Italian group UniCredit, emerging as one of Romania's richest men. At 7 feet 7 inches basketball player **Gheorghe Mureşan** was one of the tallest players in the history of the NBA. **Gabriela Szabo**, a runner who took Olympic gold at the 5,000m in Sydney in 2000, later became a Minister of Youth and Sport in the Romanian Government. **Béla and Márta Károlyi**, a husband-and-wife gymnastics coaching team, developed a centralised training programme that helped to build the golden age of Romanian female gymnastics through stars like Comăneci. They defected to the USA in 1981.

Football is the most popular sport. Many Romanians are passionate supporters of a top-flight English Premiership or Spanish club, though have more of an ambivalent relationship with their own national league, which has been riven by problems of corruption and funding challenges. The top division in Romanian football is Liga I, its most famous teams the two rival Bucharest sides of Steaua Bucureşti and Dinamo Bucureşti. Of the 14 sides contesting the 2016–17 season in Liga I (w *lpf.ro*), only three were from Transylvania. **CFR Cluj**, based in Cluj-Napoca, is historically linked with the Romanian national railway organisation (hence the 'CFR' in its name) and has one of the largest supporter bases of any Romanian team outside Bucharest. They have a longstanding rivalry with the other local team, Universitatea Cluj, though the latter are currently languishing in a lower division. **ASA Târgu Mureş** is a relative new arrival, having been founded only in 2008, its name coming from that of a previous team in the city that had been dissolved three years earlier. And the gloriously named **Gaz Metan Mediaş** ('Methane Gas Mediaş') are historically linked to the natural gas production company based in the town.

Prices to attend Liga I football matches are much lower than those for the top leagues in western Europe, but other than local derbies, which are hotly contested, attendance can be quite poor, and matches lacking in atmosphere. Derbies and other major matches apart, tickets are easily obtainable, and can in most cases simply be purchased as you go in on the day.

ACTIVITY HOLIDAYS

Birdwatching While the Danube Delta is the best-known destination for birdwatching holidays in Romania, Transylvania is also a popular choice. The bird migration season in spring runs from March to May; in autumn from August to October. There are many birdwatching tours that twitchers can arrange, either from home or in Transylvania. Gerard Gorman, author of Bradt's *Central and Eastern European Wildlife* guide, runs birdwatching trips throughout the region (see page 60). Tibor Kálnoky (see page 164) is an enthusiastic and knowledgeable birdwatcher and a stay at his estate includes several birding trails.

In Zărneşti, Dan Marin (see page 61), joint winner of the *Wanderlust* Paul Morrison Guide of the Year 2007 award, also takes visitors around the Piatra Craiului National Park on well-informed rambles (see pages 12–14 for Dan's section on wildlife), while the Retezat National Park reception centres have a lot of information on the local flora and fauna. For further information, see *Tour operators*, pages 58–61.

Caving The karst landscapes found in several parts of the region, notably in the Apuseni Mountains, are associated with impressive networks of caves, and caving opportunities range from guided tourist visits to the Scărişoara Ice Cave (pages 274–6) to much more specialised and adventurous affairs. Some of the local tour companies operating in the Apuseni region offer caving packages, notably Apuseni Experience (w *apuseniexperience.ro*) and Johan's Green Mountain (w *greenmountain.ro*). For further details, see pages 60–1.

Cycling and mountain biking Transylvania is developing as a destination for cycling and mountain-biking tours, and several of the local tour operators listed on pages 60–1 offer packages. Cycling Romania (w *cyclingromania.ro*) and MTB Tours (w *mtbtours.ro*) offer nothing other than cycling and mountain-biking tours, respectively. Bicycles and mountain bikes are available to rent from a small but growing number of hotels and other accommodation providers in the region.

Fishing There are attractive fishing opportunities, including for trout, grayling, carp and pike-perch, in the mountain rivers and lakes of Transylvania, with the Apuseni Mountains particularly known for good fishing, including along the Someşul Cald River, though the practicalities are somewhat complicated by the wide range of jurisdictions responsible for administering Romania's waters. You will need both an overall fly-fishing permit and a licence to fish specific waters. Specialist agencies such as Fly Fishing Romania (*Fegernic no 80, Bihor County*; m +40 724 938 557; e *info@flyfishingromania.com*; w *flyfishingromania.com*) should be able to help navigate the bureaucracy. The trout season typically runs from the beginning of May to mid-September.

Golf If you have come to Transylvania on a golfing holiday, then you are pretty unusual. The sport is not well developed in Romania and courses are few and far between. There is, however, a private 18-hole course at Pianu de Jos, west of Sebeş in Alba County. The **Golf Club Paul Tomiţă** (*Pianu de Jos, jud Alba*; m +40 750 990 200; e *office@golfclubpaultomita.ro*; w *golfclubpaultomita.ro*) was the project of Romania's most famous golfer, the late Paul Tomiţă, who was golf teacher to King Mihai, among others. They accept visitors, with green fees of 200RON. Accommodation is available at the course at the 27-room **Golf Hotel Pianu** (m +40 750 990 200; e *office@ golfhotelpianu.ro*; w *golfhotelpianu.ro*; **$$$**), which has a restaurant and pool.

There is also a nine-hole course at the **SunGarden Golf Club** (*Baciu, jud Cluj*; m +40 730 091 784; e *office@sungardenresort.ro*; w *sungardenresort.ro*; **$$$$$**), in a forested area 10km northwest of Cluj-Napoca. Green fees in 2017 were 135RON for nine holes, or 200RON to do them twice. It is part of the SunGarden Resort, a swanky five-star rural retreat with spa, indoor and outdoor pools, and a wide range of other sports available, including tennis and fishing.

Hiking The Carpathian and Apuseni mountains offer great hiking opportunities, with everything from climbing 2,500m peaks to more gentle walking across flower-filled lowland meadows. The most popular ranges for hiking include the Bucegi, Făgăraş, Retezat and Apuseni mountains, and the Piatra Craiului range, and feature well-marked hiking routes of different levels of difficulty and networks of *cabană* mountain huts (pages 91–2) to spend the night in. There is a full list of the *cabană* huts and mountain refuges in Romania on the website w alpinet.org. The hiking season begins in earnest in June, as before that unpredictable weather conditions make heading for the hills a risky business.

Horseriding Transylvania offers good opportunities for fine horseriding holidays amongst stunning countryside. Among the better centres highlighted in Part Two of this guide are Equus Silvania (page 149) at Şinca Nouă in Braşov County, Kálnoky's Equestrian Centre Transylvania (page 164) in Covasna County, and the Dracula Daneş Equestrian Centre (page 207) in Mureş County. Another good option is the **Merlelor Stables** (*Str Principală 143; Hălmeag, jud Braşov;* m *+40 746 690 098;* e *bertina@merlelor.com;* w *merlelor.com*) run by a Dutch couple, specialising in eight-day trail-riding tours, which are run between April and October, though with camping trails only from May to September. The stables are located in the village of Hălmeag, east of Făgăraş.

Hunting Hunting is a controversial matter in Romania. On the one hand, it is considered almost as a part of the Romanian national identity, the sport of rulers over centuries past, its products celebrated in the numerous restaurants around the country with 'hunting' or 'hunter' in their title, like the Vânatorul in Poiana Braşov. The organisation which represents the hunting and fishing community in Romania, the Asociaţia Generală a Vânatorilor şi Pescarilor Sportivi din România (*AGVPS;* w *agvps.ro*), is highly influential. On the other, environmental groups criticise alleged attempts by the hunting lobby to overstate the populations of top carnivores in Romania in order to boost the allowable hunting quotas. If you do want to hunt in Romania, you will probably need to go through a specialist operator to navigate the rules and regulations, which should include obtaining a Romanian hunting licence and appropriate insurance. Companies offering such services include **Hunt Romania** (m *+40 745 280 573;* e *contact@huntromania.com;* w *huntromania. com*) and the **Hunter Company** (m *+40 722 604 691;* e *info@huntercompany.net;* w *huntercompany.net*), although I can't attest to their quality. Hunts can be arranged for animals from duck and quail to wild boar, red stag, wolf and bear. Note that the trophy fees for bear, in particular, are several thousand euros and that, following a welcome recent tightening of the rules regarding permits to hunt species such as bear, they may not be available at all.

Paragliding This has become quite a popular pursuit in Romania. One of the major sites is in the hills around Săcele, southeast of Braşov, and this is the base of the **Paramania Paragliding Centre** (*Bunloc chair lift, Str Bunloc 185;* m *+40 723 920 453;* e *office@paramania.ro;* w *paramania.ro*), who offer paragliding training and tandem flights.

Rafting Generalist local adventure holiday operators offering rafting packages include **Caliman Club Holidays** (**w** *calimanclub.com*) (page 61). **Outdoor Experience** (**m** *+40 747 835 624;* **e** *office@whitewater.ro;* **w** *whitewater.ro*) are rafting specialists, and offer both tuition and trips. Among the rivers they favour is the Crişul Repede, which flows north from the Apuseni Mountains, through Huedin and Oradea, and into the Tisza River. The peak rafting season in Romania is between April and June, coinciding with the melting snows.

Rock climbing The Bucegi Mountains, Piatra Craiului and Postăvaru Massifs offer a reasonably compact group of rock-climbing sites around the Braşov area. **Climb Europe** (**** *01676 292003;* **w** *climb-europe.com*) sell a climbing guide to the Braşov Crags, which covers these areas. Other popular rock-climbing sites in Romania include the Turda Gorge (page 302) and Bicaz Gorge (page 186).

Skiing and snowboarding These are hugely and increasingly popular winter pursuits for many Romanians, and account for the long traffic jams on winter weekends on the E60 highway through the Prahova Valley. There are many places across Transylvania with ski slopes, although most such ski resorts are very small. The largest resorts, described in more detail in Part Two of this guide, include Poiana Braşov (pages 152–4), Predeal (page 141) in Braşov County and Păltiniş (pages 226–7) in Sibiu County. Tuition and equipment hire are available. At those major resorts where snow cannons are in use, the season typically runs from December to April.

MEDIA AND COMMUNICATIONS

PRINT There are a large number of **newspapers** in Romania. Tabloids like *Click* are far more widely read than more serious dailies, whose circulation is relatively low. The latter include ***Adevărul*** (**w** *adevarul.ro*), 'The Truth', which originated in 1871 as a left-leaning paper, and was closed down in the Communist period, though set up again immediately after the Romanian Revolution in 1989. ***România Liberă*** (**w** *romanialibera.ro*), 'Free Romania', another newspaper that traces its origins to the 1870s, survived the Communist period, and was owned by Dan Adamescu, a businessman who died in detention in January 2017, having been sentenced on corruption charges. ***Ziarul Financiar*** (**w** *zf.ro*) is the main business daily, and ***Gazeta Sporturilor*** (**w** *gsp.ro*) is the most widely read sports newspaper.

Freedom of the press is anchored in the Romanian Constitution and in specific legislation, though Reporters Without Borders (**w** *rsf.org*), in placing Romania 49th in the World Press Freedom Index in 2016, warned at the 'media's transformation into political propaganda tools', with the editorial lines of some newspapers seemingly linked to the interests of their owners.

For **entertainment listings**, there are several competing A5-sized free magazines. *Şapte Seri* (**w** *sapteseri.ro*), 'Seven Evenings', has different issues for each of the main cities in Transylvania, offering details of sporting and other events, concerts, films, bars and restaurants. It is in Romanian, but relatively easy to work out from the context if you're looking for a particular event. ***Zile şi Nopţi*** (**w** *zilesinopti.ro*), 'Days and Nights', and *24-Fun* (**w** *24fun.ro*) are similar in concept. They are distributed in hotels, bars and restaurants, and also have a good deal of listings information on their websites.

English-language press The Bucharest-based ***Nine O'Clock*** (**w** *nineoclock. ro*) is the main English-language newspaper, and offers a reasonable overview in

Salvamont (*Str Ecaterina Varga 23, Braşov;* \ *+40 268 471 517;* e *contact@0salvamont.org;* w *0salvamont.org*) is an emergency mountain rescue service, headquartered in Braşov, which also maintains emergency refuges in high mountain areas. If you are planning to trek or climb in the Romanian mountains, ensure that you save their emergency number in your phone.

Dial \ 0-SALVAMONT (the equivalent numbers on the dialling pad: 0-725826668) for help.

English of what is happening in Romanian politics both in its print edition and on its website. *Business Review* (w *business-review.eu*) is a business weekly.

TELEVISION In the late 1980s, during the Ceauşescu era, Romania famously had too little television, with just a 2-hour daily state television broadcast the only choice, an hour of which was devoted to propaganda. It can seem that in many ways Romania now has too much television, when confronted with the option of numerous channels, every one of which seems to be broadcasting a heated and interminable political debate, a Turkish soap opera or non-stop folk music.

The state broadcaster **Televiziunea Română** (TVR) offers two channels of national programming, and a third of regional programmes. It has been subject to political influence, faces continued funding challenges, and has a lower audience than some of the private channels. Private networks include the **Antena** group, whose owner, Dan Voiculescu, received a ten-year sentence for money laundering in 2014. The Antena 1 channel is one of the most popular in Romania, with a diet of reality shows and talent contests. **Pro TV** is another of the most highly watched TV channels, and home to the inordinately popular series *Românii au Talent* ('Romania's Got Talent').

Many hotels and guesthouses in Transylvania offer cable television, typically offering between 50 and 60 channels. The more expensive packages, which you will find in some hotels but not all, include a few premium channels with mainly English-language programming, notably HBO.

RADIO There is a huge range of national and local radio stations in Romania. The state radio service is **Radio România** (w *srr.ro*), which has several channels: Radio România Actualităţi mixes news and contemporary music, Radio România Cultural has classical music, while Radio Antena Satelor couples countryside news with folk music. Its international service, **Radio România Internaţional** (w *rri.ro*) has some English-language news programming. Among the huge range of private channels, **Europa FM** (w *europafm.ro*) and **Magic FM** (w *magicfm.ro*) are among those offering mainstream blends of music and chat.

TELEPHONE To dial a phone number abroad, dial 00 then the country code, shown below.

Australia	\61	Germany	\49	Poland	\48
Austria	\43	Greece	\30	Spain	\34
Belgium	\32	Hungary	\36	UK	\44
Canada	\1	Ireland	\53	USA	\1
France	\33	Italy	\9		

When calling numbers in Romania from abroad, first dial Romania's country code (+40) then the local code (as set out in the relevant chapter of Part Two of this guide) minus the first zero, then the six-digit telephone number.

Emergency telephone numbers The single combined emergency number is ⟍112. The only additional emergency number to be aware of is that of the mountain rescue service Salvamont (w 0salvamont.org), which is 0-SALVAMONT, corresponding to the numbers on the phone dialling pad, ie: 0-725826668 (see box, page 113).

Mobile phones Romanians have embraced mobile phones with enthusiasm. The relevant supervisory authority announced that there were 23.1 million active mobile phone users in Romania at the end of 2015, which is bigger than the total population of the country. The main mobile phone providers include **Vodafone** (w vodafone.ro), **Orange** (w orange.ro) and **Telekom** (w telekom.ro), and their shops are in all main towns. Particularly if you have come from outside the EU, note that roaming fees if you use your own phone and SIM card can be high. Additionally, mobile phone owners from the USA and Canada may find that their phones don't work on the GSM 900/1800 network in use in Romania. This is easily rectified if you have an 'unlocked' phone, by buying a pre-paid Romanian SIM card at any of the above providers, but it is unlikely to work with smartphones, which generally cannot easily be unlocked. In this case, your best bet is to discuss with your home provider what plan is likely to be most appropriate to your travel needs, switch off 'data roaming' in order to avoid roaming fees when using the internet on your smartphone.

To call a mobile number from within Transylvania dial all the numbers including the first zero; from outside the country dial +40 and omit the first zero.

POST OFFICES The national postal operator in Romania is Poşta Română. It is majority state-owned. Post offices in all main towns are identified by a distinctive red sign with a yellow RO bugle symbol. Opening hours for larger post offices are typically 08.00–19.00 Monday–Friday, 09.00–13.00 Saturday. You can send letters poste restante to major post offices. Make sure the letter clearly identifies the post office concerned, as well as the words poste restante, with the recipient's surname underlined. To collect the letter you'll need to show your passport and pay a fee.

INTERNET Internet access for travellers to Romania is excellent. The country prides itself on having some of the fastest download speeds in the world, and most hotels in Transylvania, as well as many pensions and guesthouses, offer free Wi-Fi. There is also free Wi-Fi available in many bars and restaurants.

MAPS

Some of the most useful general maps of Transylvania are produced by Hungarian cartographers. **Cartographia** (w cartographiaonline.com) produces a 1:500 000 map of Transylvania (Erdély in Hungarian) which gives all place names in both Romanian and Hungarian. They also offer city maps of several Transylvanian towns, and a really good spiral-bound Romania road atlas (1:300 000), which is about the most detailed readily available. **Dimap** (w dimap.hu) offers a 1:400 000 Transylvania map as well as some good hiking maps.

Romanian cartographers **Schubert and Franzke** (w schubert-franzke.com) produce useful hiking maps of most of the more popular Transylvanian destinations, including the Făgăraş, Retezat and Piatra Craiului ranges. They also offer a range of helpful specialist maps, including of cycling trails around Braşov and Cluj-Napoca.

Canadian cartographers **ITMB** (w *itmb.ca*) publish a full-country Romania map (1:850 000), available online.

The shops at major petrol stations generally stock decent, up-to-date road maps of Romania.

LOCAL TOURIST OFFICES Around Transylvania, local tourist offices (ANT) often have free town maps and sometimes maps of neighbouring natural parks. Schubert and Franzke produce very useful detailed tourist maps of many Transylvanian cities and towns. These are often available for free from local tourist information offices, although you may have to ask specifically for them; they are often hidden under the counter, and staff will first try to offer the visitor a much more basic town plan.

For bookshops in Transylvania, see the relevant town sections in Part Two of the guide.

MAP SHOPS

Cărtureşti Str Pictor Arthur Verona 13–15, Bucharest; \+40 728 828 916; e librarie.verona@ carturesti.net; w carturesti.ro; ⊕ 10.00–22.00 daily. Bucharest's best bookstore has a fair selection of maps in the basement, including Schubert & Franzke trekking maps. There is another branch in a gloriously restored building at Str Lipscani 55, in the heart of Bucharest Old Town.

Dimap Báthory utca 104, 1196 Budapest; \+36 1 377 7908; e info@dimap.hu; w dimap.hu. Hungarian mapmaker, whose very first map, in 1990, was of Transylvania (Erdély), with settlement names usefully in Romanian, Hungarian & German. They offer hiking & tourist maps of various Transylvanian destinations. Shop online only.

Stanfords 12–14 Long Acre, London WC2E 9LP; \0207 836 1321; e sales@stanfords.co.uk; w stanfords.co.uk; ⊕ 09.00–20.00 Mon–Sat, noon–18.00 Sun. Good range of books & maps on Transylvanian themes, as one would expect of this legendary travel bookstore. Also has a branch in Bristol (*29 Corn St, BS1 1HT;* *0117 929 9966; e Bristol@stanfords.co.uk;* ⊕ *09.00–18.00 Mon–Sat, 11.00–17.00 Sun*).

The Map Shop 15 High St, Upton-upon-Severn, Worcs WR8 0HJ; \01684 593146; e themapshop@ btinternet.com; w themapshop.co.uk; ⊕ 09.00–17.30 Mon–Sat. Transylvania maps include a good selection of the Hungarian-produced Szarvas Andras hiking maps.

BUSINESS

When doing business in Romania, note that age and position are respected. Initial greetings tend to be rather more reserved than in most western European countries, and Romanians will be careful to use professional or academic titles. If your meeting is with several people from the Romanian organisation, it is not unusual that only the most senior will speak, unless he or she asks questions of the others. You should be punctual even if, particularly in meetings with government agencies or state-owned enterprises, you are kept waiting. English is quite widely understood, but this is by no means universal, and you should establish ahead of the meeting whether you will need to bring an interpreter.

The legal and tax environment can be challenging and you should ensure that you consult qualified local independent advisors at an early stage. The local chamber of commerce or the trade and investment team at your embassy can offer helpful advice. British companies looking to do business in Romania should consult their local International Trade Team (w *gov.uk/dit*) for details about the range of services available. The Institute of Export has produced a useful online guide to doing business in Romania (w *Romania.DoingBusinessGuide.co.uk*).

USEFUL CONTACTS/WEBSITES

American Chamber of Commerce Floor 4, Union International Centre, Str Ion Câmpineanu 11, Bucharest; ☎+40 21 312 4834; e amcham@ amcham.ro; w amcham.ro

British Romanian Chamber of Commerce Apt 4, Floor 2, Str Praporgescu 1–5; Bucharest; ☎+40 372 032 515; e info@brcconline.eu; w brcconline.eu

European Commission Representation in Bucharest Str Vasile Lascăr 31, Bucharest; ☎+40 21 203 5400; e comm-rep-ro@ec.europa.eu; w ec.europa.eu

Romanian Chamber of Commerce and Industry B-dul Octavian Goga 2, Bucharest; ☎+40 21 319 0114; w ccir.ro

Cluj Chamber of Commerce and Industry Str Horea 3, Cluj-Napoca; ☎+40 364 730 980; e office@ccicj.ro; w ccicj.ro

Romanian Government website w gov.ro

Romanian Ministry of Economy w www.minind.ro

Romanian Ministry of Public Finance w mfinante.gov.ro

Romanian Ministry of Foreign Affairs w mae.ro

Bucharest Stock Exchange (Bursa de Valori București) w bvb.ro

BUYING PROPERTY

Transylvania remains extraordinarily good value compared with most parts of western Europe, whether you are looking to renovate a characterful rural farmhouse or buy a flat in central Braşov or Sibiu. In the main cities and towns, property prices rose from very low levels in the years following the revolution to an unsustainable peak in 2009. They are now starting to recover again following a sharp decline. The situation has been different in many Transylvanian villages, which face problems of continued out-migration and where house prices have remained low, though in those discovered by foreigners looking for a rural idyll there are local pockets of much higher prices. Thus a farmhouse in Viscri will cost far more than an equivalent property in one of the less known villages in the area. Following Romania's accession to the EU, a number of previous obstacles have been ironed out, including the removal of an earlier prohibition on foreigners purchasing land in Romania.

But there are some issues to be aware of. First, although estate agents are subject to various government regulations, they do not need to be licensed and are not subject to audit controls. You need to be careful in checking out any estate agents that you plan to use. Second, establishing title can be a complex business: a legacy of Romania's difficult 20th-century history in which many properties were seized by the Communists, and are slowly being restored to the heirs of their former owners. In some cases, this challenging process may be subject to various claims and counter-claims. A good lawyer is essential.

A range of fees is involved in purchasing a property in Romania, including a tax set by the local authority, typically 2–4% of the purchase price. There are also fees to pay to the notary, translators (foreigners are required to have all Romanian legal documents translated into their native language), surveyors, lawyer and estate agent. At present, residential property sales are normally exempt from VAT, but you should check the rules carefully, including if you are purchasing a property from a company (which might include the developer), as this might not be VAT-exempt.

Buying that run-down farmhouse in the wilds brings additional charges. Sellers in remote villages rely on word of mouth rather than estate agents. Documentation can be vague. The cost of restoring the property can far outstrip the purchase price. Water and sewerage may well be an issue. And if you are planning to make it your holiday home rather than your permanent residence you will want to consider a housekeeper, to help deter squatters.

The Mihai Eminescu Trust (page 17) can provide helpful advice on buying and restoring traditional properties in Transylvanian villages, as can those expatriates in villages like Richiş and Copşa Mare who are currently doing just that. The following is a list of estate agents offering Transylvanian properties with an eye on overseas buyers.

Homes in Romania m +40 720 161 616; e info@homesinromania.co.uk; w homesinromania.co.uk. A British-run company based in Romania.
Romanian Properties Ltd w romanianpropertiesltd.co.uk

Transylvanian Properties Str Brazilor 9; Târgu Secuiesc, jud Covasna; m +40 744 343 545; e office@transylvanianproperties.com; w transylvanianproperties.com
White Mountain Property Str Bariţiu 1a, Piaţa Sfatului, Braşov; ✆ +40 268 416 522; e damian. galvin@whitemountain.ro; w whitemountain.ro. British-run Braşov-based estate agency.

CULTURAL ETIQUETTE

In Chapter 2 of Bram Stoker's 1897 novel *Dracula*, the eponymous count says: 'We are in Transylvania; and Transylvania is not England. Our ways are not your ways, and there shall be to you many strange things.'

GREETINGS In Romanian, people are addressed using various different forms, depending on the degree of formality required. The informal for 'you' is *tu*, which Romanians will use to address a relative, close friend or a child, but visitors will generally be greeted by the more formal, and sadly less straightforward, *dumneavoastră*, which takes the second-person plural verb conjugation.

There is also the form *dumneata*, less polite than *dumneavoastră* but more formal than *tu*, which would generally be used to address a colleague or a subordinate, and *voi*, used to address two or more persons.

There are also a number of commonly used set phrases of greetings. Men can address ladies with *sărut mâna*, which means 'I kiss your hand'. The same phrase in Hungarian is *kezét csókolom* (pronounced 'kez-ate cho-ko-lom'). But this is considered somewhat old-fashioned by young Romanians, and is now mainly confined to the older generation.

When entering a shop, lift or intimate café, it is good manners to say (in Romanian/Hungarian) *Buna ziua/Jó napot* (Good day!) and *La revedere/Viszontlátásra* (Goodbye).

SPELLING One orthographic curiosity you will come across, for example in comparing different renditions of the same geographical name on maps and guides of different vintages, is the historical migration between 'â' and 'î'. These two letters are identical phonetically. In the first half of the 20th century, the practice was to use î at the beginning and end of the word, and â everywhere else. In the Communist era, î was favoured throughout, rather than â, in a bid to give the language a more eastern, Slavonic feel. Following the revolution, the Romanian Academy introduced a language reform in 1993 which essentially put the rules back to the pre-war situation. Thus it is Târgu Mureş, not Tîrgu Mureş. Nonetheless, some publications continue to be printed using the old forms.

DRINK AND DRUGS There are severe penalties in force for the possession of narcotic drugs. Alcohol is a different matter, and do be wary of the potency of that

Public toilets are relatively few and far between. Where you find them, there will usually be an attendant, and a small fee to use them. The portable plastic toilets typically found at concerts and events in other places are in common use in Romania, not just for temporary events but also as permanent public toilets, especially in city parks. They tend to be dirty, there is rarely water in the wash basin, and they are best left for emergency use only. Driving between towns, petrol stations, which should always have a toilet, are the best places to look out for, with OMV and MOL petrol stations generally offering the best facilities. But everywhere staff at bars and restaurants are usually happy to let non-clients come in to use their toilets, so finding one in towns is rarely a problem.

As regards public transport, toilets on trains tend to be functional but often dirty, while you might find that the toilet on your inter-city bus, if it exists at all, is not in use. You will get quite used to seeing signs marked with the word *defect* on the front of Romanian toilet cubicles, which basically means either 'this toilet is not working' or 'there is nothing wrong with this toilet, but I can't be bothered to keep cleaning it, so it's more straightforward to pretend that it is broken'.

Doors are marked in Romanian/Hungarian *femei/női* (ladies) and *bărbați/férfi* (gents). Though more often than not these days, especially in trendy bars and restaurants, the wording has been replaced by pictures or objects on the doors intended to convey a respective sense of masculinity and femininity. Try asking *Unde este toaleta?/Hol van a WC?* ('Where is the toilet?'). WC is pronounced 'vay-tsay'.

palincă you are being served. By tradition glasses are not topped up until they have been finished.

HOSPITALITY Romanians are hospitable and make foreigners welcome. They appreciate visitors who show an interest in their customs and traditions, and particularly in Romanian music and literature. Don't be surprised to be asked more personal questions about your family, job or religion than you might be used to from strangers back home. Older people expect to be treated in a respectful manner, with old-fashioned courtesies, such as a light kiss by a man on the hand of an older woman, still appreciated, although a simple handshake is fine.

If you are invited for a meal by a Romanian host, or invited to a gathering at a restaurant to celebrate their birthday or name day, it is customary to bring a gift. Flowers are the most common gift for women, though one important piece of etiquette is that you should always give an odd number of these, as even numbers of flowers are associated with funerals. You can readily buy bouquets from the flower stalls that dot every Romanian town: flower sellers are skilled at making up bouquets appropriate to every occasion, so tell them what it is for. The presentation of the gift is considered just as important as the actual contents, so do take the trouble to wrap up your gift, but don't be surprised if your host doesn't actually unwrap it in your presence.

When entering a Romanian house, offer to take your shoes off. Your host will sometimes simply urge you to keep your outdoor shoes on, but is more likely to offer you some slippers or beach sandals, as walking around in stockinged feet is to be avoided. Avoid kissing or shaking hands across the threshold on arrival, as it is considered bad luck. You will then be plied with more food and drink than you could possibly manage. Do your best to consume a polite share of the dishes your host has prepared (where 'polite' in this context means until you feel stuffed), and bear in mind that there are likely to be several courses coming, so don't overdo the (delicious) salads, cold meats and cheese which will probably be laid out on the table as a starter. And note that toasts must be made with alcoholic drinks, so if you are the designated driver and just sipping mineral water you shouldn't take part in the clinking of glasses (or do so using a glass of wine which you otherwise leave untouched).

DRAUGHTS Many Romanians are obsessed about avoiding draughts (*curent*), which are held responsible for all manner of illnesses and diseases. If you attempt to open the window on any form of Romanian public transport, be prepared for a combination of protests and withering looks from your fellow passengers.

PHOTOGRAPHY People's attitudes to having their photograph taken will always vary from person to person. While many people are perfectly happy to be photographed – and may even ask you specifically to take their photo – Transylvania remains a fairly conservative region, and some will object. It is always polite to ask someone before pointing a camera in their face. Military, police and other 'sensitive' buildings and vehicles should not be photographed.

BELIEFS AND SUPERSTITIONS Spending time during your holiday in a Romanian village will quickly make you very aware of the complex beliefs, customs and superstitions which mark both day-to-day village life and the passing of the seasons. Some of these derive from the Romanian Orthodox Church and its saints, others from pagan traditions, while still more have their roots in a practical response to the challenges of rural life. See pages 99–104 for more about the main events of the year, and the traditions which surround them.

'I read that every known superstition in the world is gathered into the horseshoe of the Carpathians, as if it were the centre of some sort of imaginative whirlpool.' So wrote Jonathan Harker in his journal, in Chapter 1 of Bram Stoker's *Dracula*. He had a point. Romanians are hugely superstitious. If a black cat walks in front of you, it is bad luck. The number seven is good luck, and to be the seventh child is particularly propitious, though presumably somewhat challenging for the parents. It is good luck if you meet someone carrying a full bucket of water, but woe betide you if that bucket is empty. It is bad luck to leave a house through a different door from the one you came in. Rain on your wedding day is good luck. Tuesdays are altogether considered rather dangerous, and it is particularly bad luck to wash your hair on that day. Unmarried people who eat at the corner of a table risk never getting wed. Whistling or opening an umbrella while indoors are bad luck, as is taking out the garbage after dark. Don't look back towards the house you have just left. And don't leave your handbag on the floor, as your money will walk away from it.

The colour **red** is considered most effective in protecting against the evil eye. Horses pulling carts in Romania are traditionally decorated with red tassels for this reason, and children often wear at least one red item of clothing. The plant **basil** is a symbol of love and happiness, with a particularly strong connection to the festival of the Epiphany (pages 99–100), when priests use a bouquet of basil to sprinkle holy water, and girls put a sprig of the basil from the priest's bouquet under their pillows at night. More generally, basil is traditionally considered to increase attractiveness, and may be worn by girls at village dances. And while Bram Stoker's *Dracula* is a work of fiction, it draws on a rich Romanian folklore full of tales of the undead, *strigoi*, and giant wolf-like monsters, not to mention wandering souls called *pricolici*. And, yes, **garlic** is traditionally believed to offer effective protection against them.

TRAVELLING POSITIVELY

Following the Romanian Revolution in 1989, a number of television programmes in western Europe highlighted to a shocked audience the excesses of the regime of Nicolae Ceauşescu, most harrowingly scenes of children who had been subjected to appalling treatment in Romania's orphanages. In the United Kingdom, two episodes of the reality TV show *Challenge Anneka* were set in Romania: one involved aid to the children of the Siret orphanage in Moldavia; the other, set in Transylvania, involved the construction of an emergency facility at the hospital in Târgu Mureş.

Many charities were set up by people who had been shocked at what they had seen, and who wanted to help. These often started out as simple donations of toys and clothes, sent to Romania by the lorryload. But a number of charities offered specialised support in a range of fields, from supporting the deinstitutionalisation of children from orphanages into smaller family-like homes to helping to establish a system of palliative care in Romania.

Other organisations developed in response to Ceauşescu's destructive environmental and rural policies, including the 'systematisation' of rural villages into modern apartment blocks, and have continued to support the preservation of traditional architecture and rural livelihoods. There are some great organisations working across Transylvania which welcome support, from donations of various kinds to volunteering. The work of some of these is described elsewhere in this guide, including Asociaţia ACCEPT (page 76), ADEPT (page 210), the Mihai Eminescu Trust (page 17), and Pro Patrimonio (page 17). Here are some of the best of the rest.

Asociaţia SCUT Str Ţebea 16, Braşov; m +40 751 093 622; e contact@scutbv.ro; w scutbv.ro. *Scut* means 'shield' in Romanian, & this Braşov-based organisation aims to provide a shield for disadvantaged groups in the community.

Asociaţia Un Pas Spre Viitor (A Step to the Future) Str Turnului 3, Braşov; m +40 751 219 999; w upsv.org. Braşov-based association run by Florin Cătănescu, who himself grew up in a Romanian orphanage, aiming to support the social integration of former orphanage residents into adulthood.

Blythswood Care \ 0845 456 9460; e info@ blythswood.org; w blythswood.org. Impressive Scottish Christian charity which runs the Daniel Centre outside Cluj-Napoca, providing a home to young men who have spent their lives in state care. Also run a Christmas shoebox appeal.

Bonus Pastor B-dul Pandurilor 73/2, Târgu Mureş; \ +40 265 254 460; e office@ bonuspastor.com; w bonuspastor.ro. Working mainly in parts of Transylvania with a large ethnic Hungarian population, & with links to the Reformed Church, the 'Good Shepherd' Foundation supports those suffering from drug or alcohol addiction.

Casa Mea Str Broaştei 354, Prejmer, jud Braşov; \ +40 268 362 740; w casamea.org. Founded by Janis Calos, an American who initially volunteered at a Braşov orphanage in 2001, this runs a small orphanage in Prejmer, aiming to provide a family-type environment for the children. They have another centre in Guatemala.

Community Aid Network Braşov Str George Moroianu 17, Săcele, jud Braşov; \ +40 268 275 011; e contact@canbv.ro; w canbv.ro. With the aim of supporting the development of civil society groups in the Braşov area, their website offers links to a wide range of organisations. Run by the people behind the FAST charity (see below).

Crucea Albastră România (Blue Cross Romania) Str Unirii 2, Şelimbăr, jud Sibiu; ☎+40 269 577 316; e office@dependenta.org; w dependenta. org. Part of the International Blue Cross federation of non-denominational Christian organisations, this organisation based in the Sibiu area offers treatment & counselling for people dependent on drugs & alcohol, with treatment centres for both men & women.

FAST (Fundaţia Pentru Asistenţă Socială şi Tineret) Str George Moroianu 17, Săcele, jud Braşov; ☎+40 268 274 365; e fastromania@gmail. com; w fastromania.eu. Set up by the inspirational Daniel & Ema Hristea, this group works with poor communities, especially among the Roma, in Săcele outside Braşov. They welcome volunteer groups from overseas to work on housing or educational projects, & offer accommodation for the volunteers.

Habitat for Humanity Romania Str Naum Râmniceanu 45A, Floor 1, Ap 3, Bucharest; ☎+40 21 311 3025; e info@habitat.ro; w habitat.ro. Part of the international Christian organisation Habitat for Humanity, whose mission is to build simple, decent and affordable housing. Organises 'Big Builds' in Romania, in which volunteers help to build houses for those in need.

Hope & Homes for Children ☎01722 790111; w hopeandhomes.org. Founded by Mark & Caroline Cook in 1994, after they were appalled by the plight of the children in an orphanage in Sarajevo, this charity is working to close old-style orphanages in Romania & elsewhere & to provide family-type accommodation instead.

Hospices of Hope ☎01959 525110; e office@ hospicesofhope.co.uk; w hospicesofhope.co.uk. Established by the inspiring Graham Perolls, this charity has helped to develop palliative care in Romania & other parts of southeast Europe, & has established hospices in Braşov & Bucharest.

Libra Foundation ☎01590 642185; w librafoundation.org.uk. Great organisation

taking UK students to Romania for summer volunteering in children's centres & with underprivileged children.

Little People m +40 743 773 843; e contact@ thelittlepeople.ro; w thelittlepeople.ro. Cluj-based organisation providing support for children suffering from cancer, including through the provision of playrooms in hospitals.

Noi Orizonturi (New Horizons) B-dul Păcii Bloc 5, Ap 9, Lupeni, jud Hunedoara; ☎+40 254 564 471; e comunicare@noi-orizonturi.ro; w noi-orizonturi.ro. A US-led organisation based in Hunedoara County aiming to develop children's capabilities through education.

Romanian Angel Appeal Str Rodiei 52, Bucharest; ☎+40 21 323 6868; e office@ raa.ro; w raa.ro. Founded in 1990 by Olivia Harrison, the widow of *Beatle* George Harrison, this initially focused on the refurbishment of orphanages & foster homes, but later moved its emphasis to supporting children & families affected by HIV/AIDS.

Romani Criss (Roma Centre for Social Intervention & Studies) Str Răspântiilor 11, Bucharest; ☎+40 21 310 7070; e office@ romanicriss.org; w romanicriss.org. Romani Criss was set up in 1993 to defend the rights of the Roma community in Romania, including supporting Roma access to education & health care, & providing legal assistance where rights have been violated.

Rowan Romania ☎01458 851167; w rowanromania.moonfruit.com. Somerset-based charity supporting adults with special needs at the psychiatric hospital in Zărneşti (Braşov County).

SOS Satele Copiilor Calea Floreasca 165, Bucharest; ☎+40 21 668 0077; w sos-satelecopiilor.ro. The Romanian unit of the SOS Children's Villages organisation, supporting children & their families in 3 locations in Romania, including Cisnădie in Transylvania.

STEPS Romania w stepscharityonline.co.uk. UK-based charity supporting underprivileged children in Romania & the Republic of Moldova.

Part Two

THE GUIDE

3

Braşov County

Braşov County, in the southeast corner of Transylvania, is one of the most tourist-oriented parts of Transylvania and contains some of the region's best-known sights. It was an area colonised by the ethnic German community known as Transylvanian Saxons, and while most of the members of this community left for Germany when the Romanian Revolution made this a straightforward possibility, the stamp of this community runs through the cities and villages of the region.

The county town, Braşov, is a major lure, with a well-preserved medieval core around the large Gothic Black Church, and a great range of places to stay and to eat. The small towns and villages around Braşov, in an area of Saxon settlement known in German as the Burzenland or in Romanian as Ţara Bârsei, contain some fine examples of the Saxon fortified churches which have earned a place on the UNESCO World Heritage list. The churches at Prejmer and Harman, which fall at the more fortified end of the spectrum, are particularly fine. There is another cluster of fortified churches in the northern part of the county, around Rupea. The church in the picture-postcard village of Viscri is a particular focus for visitors.

Braşov County also offers some fine upland environments. At Mount Tâmpa, the mountains reach almost into the heart of urban Braşov. The distinctive long limestone ridge at the heart of the Piatra Craiului National Park is one of the most popular hiking destinations in the country, and Poiana Braşov is Romania's best-known ski resort.

Bran Castle is marketed, with little real justification, as Dracula's Castle, but it is impressively sited, with an interesting history in its own right as a favoured residence of Queen Marie of Romania. Braşov Castle is home to two striking medieval castles perched on hills, at Râşnov and Rupea. There is a sanctuary for bears rescued from captivity at Zărneşti and a park filled with life-size model dinosaurs at Râşnov. The area is a riot of colour in late spring, when the meadows are filled with wild flowers, and in summer storks survey the villages below from their impressively constructed nests.

Altogether, Braşov County provides a compelling mix of some of Transylvania's very best features.

BRAŞOV *Telephone code 0268, sometimes 0368*

Braşov (Brassó/Kronstadt) is the seventh city of Romania and both one of the most important cities of Transylvania and one of the major tourist attractions of the region. It has a picture-postcard setting, in a basin guarded on three sides by Mount Tâmpa Hill, Dealul Cetăţii (Citadel Hill) and Warthe Hill, and is at the heart of the Bârsa Land region, named after a local river, settled by Germans in the 13th century. While the effects of 20th-century industrial development and urban sprawl mean some pretty ugly outer districts, the medieval core of the city is delightfully preserved. Piaţa Sfatului at its heart is one of the finest squares in Romania; the Black

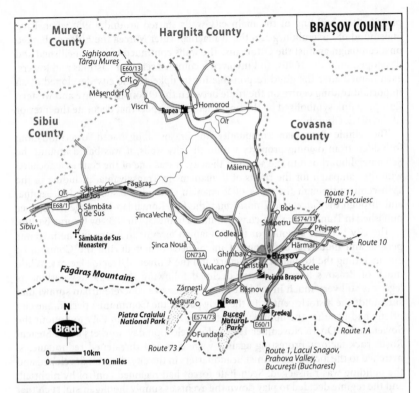

Church just off this is the largest Gothic church in the country. Other highlights of the city include exploring the towers and bastions of the medieval walls, the terrific views from the top of Mount Tâmpa, and some great bars and restaurants in picturesque settings along pedestrianised cobbled streets in the Old Town. Given the wealth of touristic attractions in the surrounding area, from UNESCO-listed fortified churches to the ski resort of Poiana Braşov to the fairytale Bran Castle, this is a city which rewards an extended stay.

HISTORY Braşov was founded in the 13th century by the **Teutonic Knights**, brought here by invitation of the Hungarian king to defend this vulnerable part of the borderlands of the kingdom. The Teutonic Knights were evicted soon afterwards, but the German colonists who had accompanied them remained. The settlement established here was known as Corona and Kronstadt, both names meaning the city of the crown, and a crown indeed features on the distinctive coat of arms of the city, which appears to feature a crown taking root. It is said that the trunk symbolises the city of Braşov, and the roots the Saxon communities of the Bârsa Land, the whole suggesting that the king can rely on the support of the inhabitants of the area. Another more literal explanation for the coat of arms has it that the Hungarian king, in battle with the Cumans, was attempting to retreat from a losing situation, but found that his crown readily identified him to the attackers. He accordingly threw his crown away: it landed on a tree. The Saxons recovered it for him many years later from the spot where it had lain.

From the time of initial settlement, the city was subject to repeated attacks from the east, which made the construction of fortified city walls an important priority. The building of the main city walls started around 1395, when King Sigismund of Luxembourg and the Wallachian ruler Mircea the Elder embarked on a campaign against the Ottomans. The walls continued to be embellished and developed until the 1640s, and involved a complex series of bastions and towers, each named after the guild responsible for its upkeep. The city developed as an important trading centre on the route between the Ottoman Empire and western Europe, a link symbolised by the fine Anatolian carpets that decorate the interior of the Black Church.

The **ethnic Romanian community** in Braşov long faced discrimination: forbidden from owning property within the city walls, it was based around the Şchei neighbourhood to the south of the city. It was one of the centres associated with the campaign for the rights of Romanians in Transylvania, including in the 19th century through the work of Romanian Orthodox bishop Andrei Şaguna, and through the *Gazeta de Transilvania*, the first Romanian-language newspaper published in Transylvania, which was founded in the city in 1838 by George Bariţiu.

The city became a centre of the Romanian aircraft industry in the interwar period, and **industrial development** intensified further during the Communist era, including the Roman truck factory and the Universal Tractor factory. While much of Braşov's heavy industry declined following the 1989 Revolution, its legacy is still very much in evidence in the extensive concrete urban sprawl that surrounds the historic centre. In the early part of the Communist period, the city briefly had to suffer the humiliation of being renamed Stalin City to honour the Soviet leader. On 15 November 1987, a local election day, workers at the Steagul Roşu truck factory, protesting against wage cuts and threatened redundancies, marched to the local Communist headquarters in the city. A revolt developed and the building was ransacked. Securitate forces had regained control by nightfall, and the regime decided to play down the events as simply 'hooliganism', such that prison sentences meted out were relatively minor. But the events of the rebellion were an advance warning of the discontent that was to fuel the Romanian Revolution two years later. The name of Bulevardul 15 Noiembrie, which runs northeastwards from the edge of the historic centre towards the modern centre, commemorates the events.

GETTING THERE, AWAY AND AROUND

By air There is a longstanding discussion around the opening of a passenger airport at Braşov. A runway has been constructed at Ghimbav, 5km west of Braşov, but the project has long stalled, and for the time being most visitors to Braşov use **Bucharest** (OTP) airport, 173km to the south. **Sibiu** (SBZ), to the west, is slightly closer, but has a much smaller range of flight destinations. **Cluj-Napoca (CLJ)**, some 200km to the northwest, is another possibility.

By rail Brasov Railway Station (Gară Braşov) (*B-dul Gării 5*; ☎ *0268 410 233*) is located 3km northeast of the historic centre. Buses 4 and 51 connect the station with the city centre. It is one of the busiest railway stations in the country, with a frequent service to Bucharest (*from 2hrs 40mins*), as well as services to a wide range of cities across Romania, including Sibiu (*from 2hrs 40mins*), Sighişoara (*from 2½hrs*), Târgu Mureş (*6hrs 20mins*) and Cluj-Napoca (*7hrs*). There is also an international service to Budapest (*13hrs*), departing three times daily. Updated timetable information for domestic routes is available at w cfrcalatori.ro.

By bus Braşov has several different inter-city bus stations, scattered across the city.

Autogara 1 [129 H2] B-dul Gării 5; 0268 427 267. Brașov's main bus station, this sits right next to the railway station, & is the most important station for larger and more distant cities, although it is also the terminus for some more local routes. Destinations include Bucharest (*3½hrs*), Cluj-Napoca (*5hrs*), Târgu Mureş (*3hrs*), Sighişoara (*2hrs*) & Predeal (*from 30mins*).

Autogara 2 [128 D1] Str Avram Iancu 114; 0268 426 332. Northwest of the centre, this offers frequent buses to Bran (*45mins*) & Râsnov (*25mins*).

Autogara 3 [129 H2] Str Hărmanului 47A; 0268 332 002. East of the centre on the Hărman road. It serves some villages east of Brașov, of

which the most likely to be useful from a tourist perspective is Hărman itself (*10–20mins*).

Autogara 4 [128 D1] Sos Cristianului; 0368 007 122. Also known as Autogara Internaţională Bartolomeu, this lies to the west of Autogara 2, & is mostly focused on international destinations, serving Romanian migrant communities across Europe.

Autogara Vest [128 D1] Str Pictor Andreescu 1A; 0268 510 668. It lies just off the E68 heading westwards out of Brașov, close to the Church of St Bartholomew, & to the west of Autogara 2 & 4. Minibuses depart from here to several local destinations, including Bod (*25mins*) & Ghimbav (*15mins*).

Public transport There is a well-developed local bus and trolleybus network run by the Braşov Regia Autonomă de Transport (*RATBV*; w *ratbv.ro*). Tickets cost 2RON and must be purchased from an RATBV kiosk or vending machine before you travel and then stamped once you are aboard the bus. Among the potentially most useful routes are 4 and 51, which link the historic centre with the railway station, and 20, which runs to the Poiana Braşov ski resort, starting at the major Livada Poştei bus stop close to the southwestern corner of the Parcul Central [129 E2].

Taxi companies
Bratax 0268 948, 0268 315 555
Martax 0268 944, 0268 313 040

Rey 0268 411 111
TOD Taxi 0268 321 111

Car hire
Autonom Rent-a-Car Str Bisericii Române 88; 0268 415 250; m 0742 800 700; e brasov@ autonom.ro; w autonom.ro

Ecoline Str Alexandru Vlahuta 10; 0268 546 137; m 0743 839 859; e office@ecoline.ro; w ecoline.ro

TOURIST INFORMATION The main tourist information centre [128 D6] (Centrul de Informare Turistică Braşov) (*Strada Prundului 1*; 0268 410 644; w *turism.brasovcity. ro*; ⊕ *09.30–17.30 Mon–Fri*) is close to the Şchei Gate at the southern edge of the city centre. There is a helpful website at w *brasovtravelguide.ro*.

WHERE TO STAY *Map, pages 128–9*
Aro Palace [129 E2] (195 rooms) B-dul Eroilor 27; 0268 478 800; e hotelaro@aro-palace. ro; w complexaropalace.ro. Large hotel dating from 1939, with a spa including swimming pool, several restaurants & a huge lobby. The claimed 5 stars seems generous, but the rooms are comfortable & many offer great views over the old city. **$$$$$**

Casa Albert [129 F3] (5 dbl, 2 apt) Str Republicii 38; m 0722 886 054; e rezervari@ casa-albert.ro; w casa-albert.ro. Small hotel down a vaulted brick passageway off Strada Republicii;

each of its rooms is decorated in a different colour scheme. The Albert Bistro in the cellar (⊕ *08.00– 22.30 daily; $$$*) has a good international menu & rather kitsch décor. **$$$$**

Casa Rozelor [129 E4] (4 apt, 1 studio) Str Michael Weiss 20; 0268 475 212; e casarozelor@ yahoo.com; w casarozelor.ro. In a 15th-century building off a tranquil courtyard behind Strada Weiss in the historic entre, this place offers apartments with kitchen facilities & interior design by artist Mihai Alexandru. **$$$$**

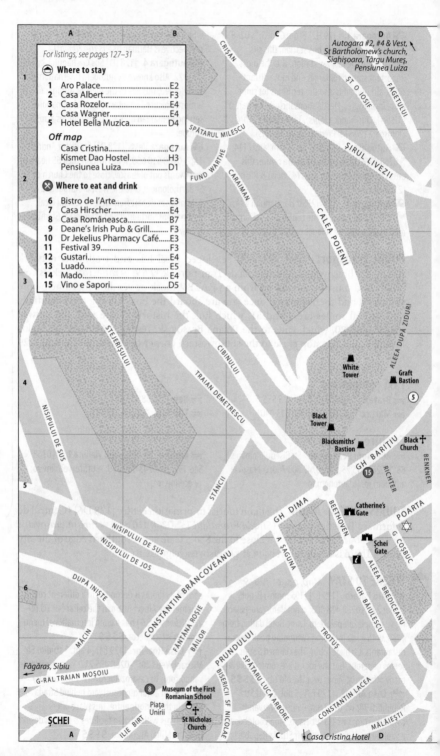

For listings, see pages 127–31

🏠 Where to stay

❌ Where to eat and drink

*Autogara #2, #4 & Vest,
St Bartholomew's church,
Sighișoara, Târgu Mureș,
Pensiunea Luiza*

CRISAN

ST O IOSIF

FAGETULUI

SPĂTARUL MILESCU

ȘIRUL LIVEZII

FUND WARTHE

CARAIMAN

CALEA POIENII

STEIERȘULUI

CIBINULUI

ALEEA DUPA ZIDURI

TRAIAN DEMETRESCU

White
Tower

Graft
Bastion

5

NISIPULUI DE SUS

Black
Tower

Blacksmiths'
Bastion

Black
Church

STANCII

GH BARITIU

RICHTER

BENKNER

15

GH DIMA

BEETHOVEN

Catherine's
Gate

POARTA

NISIPULUI DE SUS

A SAGUNA

Schei
Gate

G COSBUC

NISIPULUI DE JOS

ℹ

ALEEA T BREDICEANU

DUPA INIȘTE

CONSTANTIN BRÂNCOVEANU

FANTANA ROSIE

BAILOR

GH BAIULESCU

TROTUS

MACIN

PRUNDULUI

BISERICII SF NICOLAE

SPĂTARU LUCA ARBORE

CONSTANTIN LACEA

MĂLĂIEȘTI

Făgăras, Sibiu
G-RAL TRAIAN MOȘOIU

8

Museum of the First
Romanian School

Piața
Unirii

St Nicholas
Church

ILIE BIRT

ȘCHEI

Casa Cristina Hotel

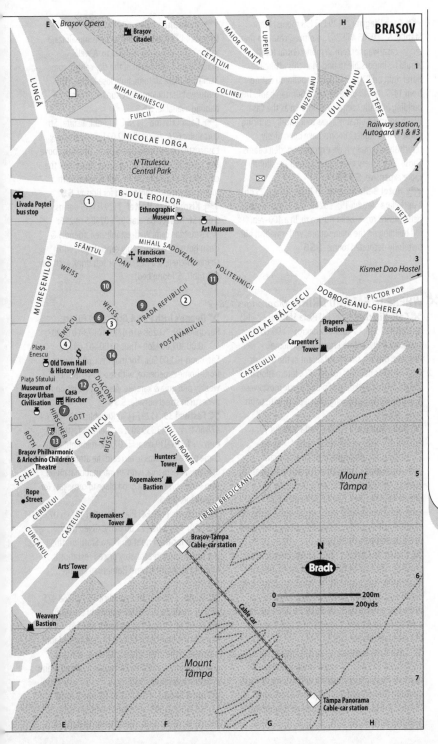

BRAȘOV

E Brașov Opera

Brașov Citadel

MAIOR CRANȚA

LUPENI

H BRAȘOV

1

CETĂTUIA

COLINEI

MIHAI EMINESCU

COL BUZOIANU

IULIU MANIU

VLAD TEPEȘ

FURCII

LUNGĂ

NICOLAE IORGA

Railway station,
Autogara #1 & #3

N Titulescu
Central Park

2

PIETII

Livada Poștei
bus stop

① B-DUL EROILOR

Ethnographic
Museum

Art Museum

SFÂNTUL

MIHAIL SADOVEANU

Franciscan
Monastery

POLITEHNICII

3

Kismet Dao Hostel

WEISS

IOAN

⑩

⑪

DOBROGEANU-GHEREA

PICTOR POP

MUREȘENILOR

WEISS

⑨

STRADA REPUBLICII

②

NICOLAE BĂLCESCU

Drapers'
Bastion

ENESCU

⑥

③

POSTĂVARULUI

Carpenter's
Tower

④

Piața
Enescu

$

⑭

CASTELULUI

4

Old Town Hall
& History Museum

⑫

Piața Sfatului

Museum of
Brașov Urban
Civilisation

Casa
Hirscher

DIACONU CORESI

⑦

GÖTT

HIRSCHER

ROTH

⑬

G DINICU

AL RUSSO

JULIUS ROMER

Hunters'
Tower

Mount
Tâmpa

5

Brașov Philharmonic
& Arlechino Children's
Theatre

SCHEI

Rope
Street

Ropemakers'
Bastion

CERBULUI

TIBERIU BREDICEANU

N

CURCANUL

CASTELULUI

Ropemakers'
Tower

Bradt

Brașov-Tâmpa
Cable-car station

0   200m
0   200yds

6

Arts' Tower

Cable car

Weavers'
Bastion

Mount
Tâmpa

7

Tâmpa Panorama
Cable-car station

E   F   G   H

Brașov County   BRAȘOV

3

⌂ Casa Wagner [129 E4] (33 rooms) Piaţa Sfatului 5; ☎0268 411 253; e office@casa-wagner.eu; w casa-wagner.com. A more central location would be impossible to find than this attractive hotel right on Piaţa Sfatului in a building dating from 1477, which once hosted a German bank. The building actually seems to be known as the Casa Wallbaum; presumably a less touristically enticing name than Wagner? Rooms have been nicely refurbished & many have exposed wooden beams. Those with a view over Piaţa Sfatului are slightly more expensive. **$$$$**

⌂ Hotel Bella Muzica [128 D4] (8 sgl, 25 dbl, 1 apt) Piaţa Sfatului 19; ☎0268 477 956; e hotel@bellamuzica.ro; w bellamuzica.ro. In a 400-year-old building on the main square, with smallish but tastefully decorated rooms. **$$$**

⌂ Pensiunea Luiza [128 D1] (15 rooms) Str Lunga 244; ☎0268 546 910; e pensiunealuiza@yahoo.com; w pensiunealuiza.ro. A well-maintained 3-star north of the city centre, some 3km from Piaţa Sfatului, but close to the 13th-century St Bartholomew's Church. Off-street parking available. **$$$**

⌂ Casa Cristina [128 C7] (7 dbl, 1 suite) Str Curcanilor 62A; m 0722 322 021; e rezervare@casacristina.ro; w casacristina.org. Situated above the Şchei District, & offering great views over the city, this is a friendly family-run pension with rooms very reasonably priced for Braşov. **$$**

⌂ Kismet Dao Hostel [129 H3] (5 dorms, 3 dbl) Str Neagoe Basarab 8; ☎0268 514 296; w kismetdao.com. Well-established, friendly & clean hostel in a reasonably central spot, with shared kitchen, & a free beer or soft drink each day. **$$** (dbl), **$** (dorm bed)

✗ WHERE TO EAT AND DRINK   *Map, pages 128–9*

✗ Casa Hirscher [129 E4] Piaţa Sfatului 12–14; ☎0268 410 533; w casahirscher.ro; ⏱ 09.00–last customer daily. Entered from Str Apollonia Hirscher, this is a smart restaurant in the historic Casa Hirscher building (page 132). International dishes, with a backdrop of piano music most eves & a glass-ceilinged dining area replete with palm trees. **$$$$**

✗ Bella Muzica [128 D4] Piaţa Sfatului 19; ☎0268 477 946; w bellamuzica.ro; ⏱ noon–23.30 daily. An atmospheric cellar restaurant, with smart white tablecloths & black-waistcoated waiters, though there are some decidedly unexpected touches, notably a menu which combines Hungarian & Mexican cuisine, & a choice of music which ranges in odd directions, from disco to 80s power ballads. **$$$**

✗ Bistro de l'Arte [129 E3] Piaţa Enescu 11 bis; m 0720 535 566; w bistrodelarte.ro; ⏱ 09.00–01.00 Mon–Sat, noon–01.00 Sun. Artsy bistro with live music, generally Wed–Sat eves, artworks on the walls, good b/fasts, smoothies & a tea list, but a pretty limited menu focused on salads & dishes like *croque monsieur*. **$$$**

✗ Casa Româneasca [128 B7] Piaţa Unirii 15; ☎0268 513 877; ⏱ noon–midnight daily. A spacious Romanian restaurant with a large terrace abutting the cobbled Unirii Square in the Şchei District. The place is quite focused on tour groups & wedding parties. **$$$**

✗ Deane's Irish Pub & Grill [129 F3] Str Republicii 19; ☎0268 416 478; m 0734 010 203; ⏱ 10.00–01.00 Mon–Thu, 10.00–03.00 Fri/Sat, noon–01.00 Sun. For that Irish-pub-away-from-home experience, with food, live music, a weekly pub quiz & karaoke. Also has tables on the pedestrian street outside. **$$$**

✗ Festival 39 [129 F3] Str Republicii 62; ☎0268 478 664; m 0743 339 909; e cafenea@festival39.com; w festival39.com; ⏱ 07.00–midnight daily. Large place that aims to recreate the atmosphere of interwar Romania, with an international menu. Also serves b/fast & is a good place to come just for a drink too. **$$$**

✗ Gustari [129 E4] Piaţa Sfatului 14; m 0773 948 110; ⏱ 08.00–22.00 daily. Given its premium location right on Piaţa Sfatului, this is a surprisingly reasonably priced restaurant offering straightforward Romanian cuisine. **$$$**

✗ Mado [129 E4] Str Republicii 10; ☎0268 475 385; w mado.ro; ⏱ 10.00–midnight Sun–Thu, 10.00–02.00 Fri/Sat. The pedestrianised Str Republicii is lined with cafés & restaurants. Mado is typical of the area: while unlikely to win any awards, it offers a Middle Eastern-influenced menu in a central location. **$$$**

♀ Vino e Sapori [128 D5] Str George Bariţiu 13; ☎0368 468 593; ⏱ noon–midnight daily. A homely wine bar with a good range of Italian &

Romanian wines available by the glass, & an Italian menu featuring homemade pasta. $$$

□ **Dr Jekelius Pharmacy Café** [129 E3] Str Michael Weiss 13; 0268 478 664; m 0758 624 781; ④ 08.00–midnight daily. Is it a café? Is it a pharmacy? Actually, it's a café. But decked out to look like a pharmacy, with waitresses in white aprons, shots served in test tubes & a fittingly large range of herbal teas. Under the same ownership as Festival 39. $

□ **Luadó** [129 E5] Str Apollonia Hirscher 10; m 0737 390 000; w luado.ro; ④ summer 10.00–21.00 Tue–Sun, 16.00–21.00 Mon, winter 10.00–19.00 Tue–Sun, noon–19.00 Mon. A great little shop offering Belgian-style chocolate & some of the best ice cream around to accompany an afternoon stroll. Try the cardamom & white Belgian chocolate flavour. $

ENTERTAINMENT

Festivals The most distinctive of Braşov's festivals is the **Junii parade**, held on the first Sunday after Easter, and following a range of festivities on the preceding days, involving seven groups of young men known as *Junii* from the Şchei neighbourhood of the city, each group wearing different costumes and carrying different banners. Romanian flags and colours are also much in evidence. The horseback procession on the Sunday starts at the St Nicholas Church in the Şchei, and eventually concludes at Solomon's Rocks (Pietrele lui Solomon), an impressive natural feature in the hills close to the Şchei District, where a large party concludes the event. The Mediateca Norbert Detaeye within the Braşov University of Transylvania is the main organiser of a three-day programme of events in November, under the overall heading of **Etnovember** (0268 412 921; w unitbv.ro), an eclectic mixture of medieval fair, art exhibitions and concerts. The **Braşov Jazz and Blues Festival** (m 0752 241 620; w brasovjazz.ro) is held later in the same month and attracts international acts. Other worthwhile festivals in the city include an **Oktoberfest**, curiously usually held in early September, and an enjoyable **Christmas market** around Piaţa Sfatului.

Theatres and concert halls

🎭 **Arlechino Children's Theatre** (Teatrul Pentru Copii Arlechino) [129 E5] Str Apollonia Hirscher 10; 0268 475 243; w teatrularlechino.ro. Centrally located, close to Piaţa Sfatului, with a programme oriented towards puppetry.

🎭 **Braşov Opera** [129 E1] Str Bisericii Române 51; 0268 415 990; e operabrasov@yahoo. com; w opera-brasov.ro. Established in 1953, it is

located to the north of the historic centre, beyond the citadel.

🎭 **Braşov Philharmonic** (Filarmonica Braşov) [129 E5] Str Apollonia Hirscher 10; 0268 473 058; e filarmonicabrasov@yahoo.com; w filarmonicabrasov.ro. At the same address as the Arlechino Children's Theatre, this offers a good programme of classical music.

OTHER PRACTICALITIES

$ **CEC Bank** [129 E4] Piaţa Sfatului 9; ④ 09.00–16.30 Mon–Fri

➕ **Sensiblu** [129 E4] Str Republicii 15; 0268 411 248; ④ 08.00–21.00 Mon–Fri, 10.00–21.00 Sat/Sun

✉ **Post office** [129 G2] Str Nicolae Iorga 1; 0268 471 260; w posta-romana.ro; ④ 08.00–19.00 Mon–Fri, 09.00–13.00 Sat

WHAT TO SEE AND DO

Around Piaţa Sfatului Located at the heart of old medieval Braşov and lined with beautiful red-roofed merchant houses, **Council Square** (Piaţa Sfatului) [129 E4], known to the Saxons as the Marktplatz, is one of the finest central squares in the country. It is an irregular quadrilateral in form, with the curving northeastern side much longer than the southwestern one, and strangely, though perhaps in a sign of the times, there is a bank on each of its corners.

In the centre of the square stands the **Old Town Hall** (Casa Sfatului) [129 E4], which dates from the 15th century, its tower built a century later. That tower later became known as the Trumpeter's Tower, after the watchman of the tower, who blew on a trumpet to mark the hours. It served as the town hall until 1876, and then housed the municipal archives until 1923, when these were moved to the Blacksmiths' Bastion (see opposite). It became a museum in 1950 and remains the principal home of the **Brașov County History Museum** (Muzeul Județean de Istorie) [129 E4] (*Piața Sfatului 30;* ❧ *0268 472 363;* e *office@istoriebv.ro;* w *brasovistorie. ro;* ☉ *Mar–Nov 10.00–18.00 Tue–Sun, Dec–Apr 09.00–17.00 Tue–Sun; adult/child 7/1.5RON*).

At the southern side of the Piața Sfatului, where Strada Apollonia Hirscher joins the square, is the four-storey **Museum of Brașov Urban Civilisation** (Muzeul Civilizației Urbane a Brașovului) [129 E4] (*Piața Sfatului 15;* ❧ *0268 475 565;* w *mcubrasov.ro;* ☉ *summer 10.00–18.00 Tue–Sun, winter 09.00–17.00 Tue–Sun; adult/child 7/2RON*), centred around recreations of bygone stores and domestic interiors. Immediately opposite this, across Strada Apollonia Hirscher, is the **Casa Hirscher** [129 E4], built around 1545 as a merchants' trading house by Apollonia Hirscher, who was the wealthy widow of a Brașov mayor named Lukas Hirscher. One of the legends surrounding this place is that Apollonia had a daughter who fell ill, was pronounced dead, and was buried with all of her precious jewellery. Some graverobbers tried to steal the jewellery, but while they were attempting to prise a particularly luxuriant ring from her finger, the daughter awoke from her coma. Apollonia built the house as a celebration of her daughter's return from the dead.

Just south of the main square is Brașov's major landmark, the **Black Church** (Biserica Neagră) [128 D5] (*Curtea Johannes Honterus 2;* ❧ *0268 511 824;* e *guide@ biserica-neagra.ro;* w *bisericaneagra.ro;* ☉ *5 Apr–9 Oct 10.00–19.00 Tue–Sat, noon–19.00 Sun, 10 Oct–4 Apr 10.00–15.00 Tue–Sat, noon–15.00 Sun; adult/child 9/3RON; organ concerts Jun & Sep at 18.00 on Tue, Jul/Aug at 18.00 on Tue, Thu, Sat 12RON*), the largest Gothic church in Romania. It also apparently possesses the largest church bell in the country, weighing in at six tonnes. Building began in the late 14th century, but it was interrupted by Turkish predations in 1421, and was not completed until the late 15th century, as a Gothic three-nave basilica. It moved from a Catholic congregation to a Lutheran one in 1542. Its name derives from damage caused by a fire started in 1689 by invading Habsburg troops. The restoration of the church after the fire gave the interior a Baroque aspect. Its interior is enlivened by a rich collection of Anatolian rugs, dating from the 15th to the 17th centuries; these were donations by Transylvanian Saxon merchants, and were one of the few forms of church ornamentation seen in the relatively austere Lutheran church interiors. Its organ has some 4,000 pipes and dates from 1839.

The statue outside the church is of **Johannes Honterus**, depicted pointing towards the school that bears his name. He was a leading figure in the introduction of Lutheranism to the area as well as a renowned cartographer, whose 16th-century map of Transylvania was the first printed map of this region.

The vibrant pedestrian street **Strada Republicii** [129 F3] leads north from Piața Sfatului and is lined with terrace cafés and restaurants. These are mostly quite touristy: a more local, funkier crowd gathers in the bars and restaurants around **Piața George Enescu** [129 E4], one block to the west. A couple of blocks further to the north of here, on the quiet cobbled Strada Sfântul Ioan, is the **Franciscan Monastery of St John** (Mănăstirea Franciscană Sfântul Ioan) [129 F3] (*Str Sfântul Ioan 7;* w *bisericasfioan-brasov.ro*), its church built in a Gothic style but much modified. Franciscan monks were expelled from Braşov in 1530, accused of pro-Habsburg sympathies, but were allowed back in 1724, and the church today offers Catholic services in both Romanian and Hungarian.

Along the city walls Two main stretches of Braşov's once imposing city walls have been preserved, one lying along the southeastern side of the historic centre, the other on the west. The stretches along the northern and southern sides of the centre were destroyed to make room for urban expansion from the 18th century onward.

The restored **southeastern stretch** of the walls runs along the base of the natural feature which is at the heart of the city's identity, the limestone **Mount Tâmpa** (Muntele Tâmpa) [129 F7]. This rises to an elevation of 960m, and provides a platform for the Hollywood-style 'Braşov' sign in large white capital letters which is visible from many points in the town below. It was the site of a citadel, probably raised by Teutonic Knights in the 13th century, but demolished in the 15th in favour of a new citadel at a lower elevation. It is part of a Natura 2000 site, and despite its proximity to the city, bear, lynx and wild boar are all to be found here. There are several marked paths up to the summit, those from the city-centre side of the mountain taking around an hour. Alternatively, there is a **cable car** (Telecabina Tâmpa) [129 F6] (*Aleea Tiberiu Brediceanu;* ⊕ *09.30–18.00 Tue–Sun, noon–18.00 Mon; return adult/child 16/9RON, one-way adult/child 10/6RON*), which does the journey in less than 3 minutes. The view from the top looking back down over the town is superb.

There is a pleasant leafy walk to be had along the base of Tâmpa Mountain, which closely follows the line of the restored walls, punctuated by a series of square-based towers and more elaborate bastions. From northeast to southwest these are the **Drapers' Bastion** (Bastionul Postăvarilor) [129 H4], **Carpenter's Tower** (Turnul Lemnarului) [129 H4], **Hunters' Tower** (Turnul Vânătorilor) [129 F5], the hexagonal **Ropemakers' Bastion** (Bastionul Funarilor) [129 F5], **Ropemakers' Tower** (Turnul Funarilor) [129 F5], and the **Arts' Tower** (Turnul Artelor) [129 E6]. It is possible to clamber around inside some of these; the views from the Hunters' Tower are particularly good.

Continuing southeastwards, the final bastion on this stretch of the wall is worthy of a more in-depth visit. The **Weavers' Bastion** (Bastionul Ţesătorilor) [129 E6] (*Str George Coşbuc 9;* ☎ *0268 472 368;* ⊕ *10.00–18.00 Tue–Sun; adult/child 7/1.50RON*) was built in two stages, the first in the early 15th century, when the lower two fortified levels were constructed. More than a century later, the bastion was heightened, with the addition of upper galleries. The internal wooden walkways make for an impressive sight. The bastion currently hosts an exhibition dedicated to Braşov Citadel and the fortifications of the surrounding Ţara Bârsei area. There is also a model of Braşov Fortress in its medieval heyday, dating from 1896.

From here, turn left onto Strada Castelului, and then take the first right onto Aleea Tiberiu Brediceanu, crossing over the Strada Poarta Şchei at the Şchei Gate (page 134), maintaining the same direction along Şirul Ludwig van Beethoven. This brings you on your right to another bastion of the medieval city walls, the 16th-century **Blacksmiths' Bastion** (Bastionul Fierarilor) [128 D5], which has been the home of the city archives since the 1920s. The road descending to the left of here, the Aleea După Ziduri, 'alley behind the walls', is mostly pedestrianised, and makes for a delightful walk, with the **western stretch** of the city walls on the right-hand side of the path, and a small canal and wooded hillside to the left.

Four towers were constructed just outside the city walls and, a short distance down the Strada După Ziduri, a steep signposted path to the left takes you to one of these, the **Black Tower** (Turnul Negru) [128 D4] (⊕ *10.00–18.00 Tue–Sun; adult/*

child 7/2RON), an 11m-high square-based tower on a large rock. Built in the 15th century, it received its current name following blackening by a lightning-induced fire in 1559, though is today black in name only.

Continuing along the Aleea După Ziduri, you reach the **Graft Bastion** (Bastionul Graft) [128 D4] (*Aleea După Ziduri;* ⊕ *10.00–18.00 Tue–Sun; adult/ child 5/1RON*), extending over both path and canal, which are contained by a large semicircular arch. It was built in the early 16th century, with the aim of supporting troops based in the White Tower outside the walls. It serves as part of the Braşov County Museum, with some missable historical displays. A steep flight of steps up the hill here takes you to the 15th-century **White Tower** (Turnul Alb) [128 D4] (*Aleea După Ziduri;* ⊕ *10.00–18.00 Tue–Sun; adult/child 7/2RON*), which is larger than the Black Tower though likewise offers some great views of the city.

The Şchei District From Piaţa Sfatului head south along Strada Apollonia Hirscher and then turn right onto Strada Poarta Şchei, which takes you out of the centre in a southwestwards direction. On your left you pass one of the curiosities of the city, **Rope Street** (Strada Sforii) [129 E5], one of the narrowest streets in Europe, some 83m long and only 1.3m wide. A sign points the way in from each end, which is helpful as otherwise it's all too easy to walk right past it. A little further on, again on the left, is the **Neolog Synagogue** (Sinagoga Neologă) [128 D5] (*Str Poarta Şchei 29;* \0268 511 867; ⊕ *09.00–16.00 Mon–Fri; 5RON*), constructed between 1899 and 1901 in a neo-Gothic style with distinct Moorish influences. Jews were first granted permission by the Saxon municipal authorities to live in Braşov in 1807, and the Jewish community was officially founded 19 years later. Jews were only allowed to take up jobs which no Saxon would do, and many became merchants. By 1940 there were around 6,000 Jews in Braşov, but the predations of World War II, and then post-war emigration to Israel, has brought this figure down to a few hundred.

Strada Poarta Şchei exits the old city, logically enough, at the **Şchei Gate** (Poarta Şchei) [128 D6], a classical-style gate with three semicircular arches, a larger central one for traffic, and two smaller side ones for pedestrians. It was built in the 1820s, following a visit to Braşov by Austrian Emperor Francis I, when the level of traffic became too much for the neighbouring **Catherine's Gate** (Poarta Ecaterinei) [128 D5] to the right, which was bricked up. Catherine's gate is the older and more impressive of the two, a spired fairytale of a gateway which was built in 1559 by the Tailors' Guild. The only one of the medieval city gates to have survived, it was also for centuries the only gate into the city that the ethnic Romanians of the Şchei District could use. They had to pay a toll for the privilege of selling their produce within the city walls. Although the four corner turrets around the central spire of the gate look charming, their purpose was to inform visitors that the city of Braşov had the right to administer the death penalty.

Beyond the Şchei Gate, Strada Poarta Şchei renames itself Strada Prundului, which brings you to the quiet, cobbled Piaţa Unirii. This is the heart of the **Şchei District**, originally the home of an ethnic Bulgarian community, which arrived here at the end of the 14th century to work on the reconstruction of the Black Church, following its destruction by Tatars. Şchei is an old Romanian word used particularly in Transylvania to refer to Bulgarians. The community gradually developed into a Romanian one, its inhabitants for centuries forbidden from owning property within the city walls, and it became a centre for Romanian ecclesiastical and educational life.

Off Piaţa Unirii is a peaceful compound housing the **Romanian Orthodox St Nicholas Church** (Biserica Sfântul Nicolae) [128 B7] (*Piaţa Unirii 1;*

⊕ 08.00–18.00 daily), with its tall slender tower topped by a spire, giving it an appearance very different from those of most Romanian Orthodox churches. It was first established as a wooden church in the late 13th century, though rebuilt in stone in a Gothic style in 1495, its construction supported by the *voivodes* of Wallachia. Its interior was redecorated in a Baroque style in the 18th century, and also has murals from local 19th-century artist Mişu Popp. Celebrated Romanian diplomat Nicolae Titulescu, who served in the interwar period as a President of the General Assembly of the League of Nations, is among those buried in the churchyard. Titulescu died in Cannes in 1941; he was reburied in Braşov, following a request in his will, in 1992.

In the same compound is the **Museum of the First Romanian School** (Muzeul Prima Şcoală Românească) [128 B7] (✆0268 511 411; w primascoalaromaneasca.ro; ⊕ 09.00–17.00 daily, except during religious services on Sun; adult/child 10/5RON), housed in a two-storey 18th-century building, on the site of the place where the first lessons in the Romanian language were conducted in the 16th century. The director of the museum, a theologian and polymath named Vasile Oltean, makes for an enthusiastic guide to the museum's treasures. The museum includes a mock-up of an early classroom, and numerous historic books in the Romanian language, including the 1688 Bucharest Bible, the first printed complete translation of the Bible in Romanian. There is also a display about the printing press established here in the 16th century by Diaconul Coresi, used to print some of the earliest works in the Romanian language. His statue is in the grounds outside.

Around Bulevardul Eroilor
The busy Bulevardul Eroilor running along the northern edge of the historic centre brings you rather starkly into modern Braşov and a world of 21st-century traffic. The city's pleasant **Central Park** (Parcul Central) [129 F2], more formally known as Parcul Nicolae Titulescu, runs along the northern side of the boulevard. This is the administrative centre of Braşov, with the town hall, prefecture and main post office all close by. There are a couple of worthwhile museums close to each other on the southern side of the street.

The **Ethnographic Museum** (Muzeul de Etnografie) [129 F2] (*B-dul Eroilor 21A*; ✆0268 476 243; e muzeu@etnobrasov.ro; w etnobrasov.ro; ⊕ Mar–Nov 10.00–18.00 Tue–Sun, Dec–Apr 09.00–17.00 Tue–Sun; adult/child 5/2RON) features an interesting permanent exhibition on textile-making in southern Transylvania, covering techniques of spinning, weaving, a mock-up of a tailor's workshop and the role of the introduction of mechanical weaving looms in local industrialisation. A second room focuses on customs linked to feast days.

The **Art Museum** (Muzeul de Artă) [129 F3] (*B-dul Eroilor 21*; ✆0268 477 286; e contact@muzeulartabv.ro; w muzeulartabv.ro; ⊕ Apr–Sep 10.00–18.00 Tue–Sun, Oct–Mar 09.00–17.00 Tue–Sun; adult/child 5/1RON) offers a good selection of works by most of the best-known Romanian painters, including Theodor Aman, Stefan Luchian, Theodor Pallady and Nicolae Grigorescu. Also represented is the Braşov avant-garde artist János Máttis-Teutsch.

Strategically located on the hill to the north of Central Park is **Braşov Citadel** (Cetăţuia de pe Strajă) [129 F1] (*Str Dealul Cetăţii 5*). There was a watchtower here at the start of the 15th century, and in 1524 a wooden fortress was built on the hill, only to be destroyed five years later by the army of Moldavian ruler Petru Rareş. The walls were rebuilt in stone, and then reconstructed in 1625, with the building of four imposing corner bastions. Gradually losing its importance, it served as a barracks and later a prison, has been the subject of various tourism initiatives, but currently lies closed.

PLACES TO VISIT *EN ROUTE* FROM BUCHAREST TO BRAŞOV

If you are arriving into Romania at Bucharest Otopeni airport, and plan to drive to Transylvania by **hire car**, the good news is that the airport is nicely sited beyond the northern edge of the city, right on the main E60/DN1 road, which is the principal route up into Braşov County from this part of Romania. While Bucharest is a fascinating city, driving into the centre from Otopeni, particularly as a first experience of negotiating Romanian roads, is challenging as well as time-consuming. If you are taking the **train**, you will have to go into Bucharest by taxi or bus to get to the Gara de Nord railway station (pages 68–9).

From Otopeni airport, the E60/DN1 to Braşov is a drive of 158km. Its popularity as the main route to the attractions of Transylvania for the citizens of Bucharest mean that it can get crowded, particularly on Friday afternoons and Saturday mornings at the height of both the summer holiday season and winter ski season. The sector climbing up into the mountains between Comarnic and Predeal, where the road is narrower, is particularly notorious for traffic jams. On a good day you could be in Braşov in 2½ hours, but pick a bad one and it could be more like 4 hours.

If you want to make the drive from Bucharest part of your holiday, there are some really worthwhile sites *en route* to Braşov. Here are some suggestions.

LACUL SNAGOV Some 26km north of Otopeni airport on route E60/DN1 towards Ploieşti, turn right at the village of Ciolpani (signposted for Mănăstirea Snagov). This brings you to the small island at the northeastern end of Lake Snagov, which is the peaceful home of **Snagov Monastery** (Mănăstirea Snagov) (\ 021 491 0394; m 0724 768 949; ⊕ summer 08.00–18.00 Mon–Sat, 13.00–18.00 Sun, winter 09.00–16.00 Mon–Sat, 13.00–16.00 Sun; 15RON). Believed to have been founded by Wallachian

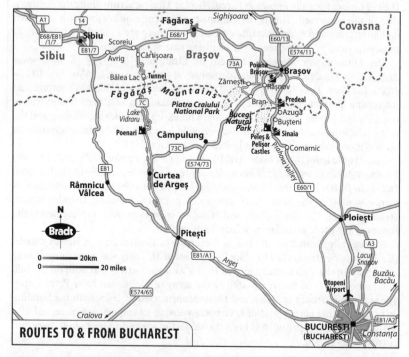

ROUTES TO & FROM BUCHAREST

ruler Mircea the Elder in the late 14th century, the monastery is best known today as the rumoured burial place of Vlad the Impaler, the real historical figure who inspired Bram Stoker's Dracula. This is debateable, and other places in Romania also claim to be Vlad the Impaler's place of rest, notably Comana Monastery south of Bucharest, but there is no doubting that Snagov Monastery, which is accessed by a small footbridge from the mainland, is an attractive and tranquil spot.

Snagov Lake itself, long and narrow in shape, stretching for some 12km, was a favoured place of relaxation for the Communist elite in the Ceauşescu era, and its shores today are dotted with swanky clubs and the villas of wealthy Romanians.

PRAHOVA VALLEY The E60/DN1 skirts the oil-refining city of Ploieşti, heading northwards via Câmpina as the mountains ahead come into view. The road then takes a historically important pass along the Prahova Valley (Valea Prahovei), following the Prahova River. This separates the Bucegi Mountains to the west, considered the easternmost part of the Southern Carpathians, with the Baiu Mountains to the east, at the southwestern tip of the Eastern Carpathians. The Prahova Valley was long an important conduit between the principalities of Wallachia and Transylvania.

North of the rather scruffy village of Comarnic the road begins to climb, and the increasingly attractive scenery quickly dispels all memories of the dull flat Wallachian plains behind you. This is one of the most important tourist areas in Romania in both summer and winter, and if you would like to break your journey in this area before entering Transylvania, the three major mountain resorts, reached in quick succession along the E60, are Sinaia, Buşteni and Azuga. The next resort above Azuga, Predeal, is already in Braşov County and hence Transylvania.

Sinaia With its Romanian royal connections, the town of Sinaia is the most important and historically interesting of the resorts of the Prahova Valley. The name of the town derives from the Sinaia Monastery, founded here in 1695 by Prince Mihail Cantacuzino and named in turn after St Catherine's Monastery on Mount Sinai, to which the prince had made a pilgrimage. With courtyards surrounding two churches, the newer of which dates from the mid 19th century, and the grave of former Romanian Prime Minister Take Ionescu, the monastery, which is located just above the town, is an interesting place to visit.

But the top attraction here is Peleş Castle (see below), the summer palace of King Carol I, and it was Romanian royal patronage from the late 19th century that really bolstered the development of the town as a well-heeled resort, with a casino, large villas and tree-lined promenades. Romania's most famous composer, George Enescu, who had long enjoyed the support of the Romanian royal family, built an elegant house here which now holds a **museum** (Casa Memorială George Enescu); (*Str Yehudi Menuhin 2;* ☏ *0244 311 753;* ⊕ *10.00–17.00 Tue–Sun*) in his honour. Here Enescu tutored the young American violin prodigy Yehudi Menuhin, and the street on which the house sits has now been named Strada Yehudi Menuhin.

Sinaia is today a significant ski resort, with 16 pistes served by eight lifts, including three cable cars. It offers the longest vertical drop, more than 1,000m, of any ski resort in Romania. A stay here is also a straightforward option for those travelling between Bucharest and Transylvania by **train** (*fast trains 1hr 40mins*).

Peleş Castle (Castelul Peleş) (ⓦ *peles.ro;* ⊕ *15 May–15 Sep 09.15–16.15 Tue & Thu–Sun, 11.00–16.15 Wed, 16 Sep–14 May 09.15–16.15 Thu–Sun, 11.00–16.15 Wed; adult/child 30/7.5RON ground-floor tour, 60/15RON ground- & 1st-floor tour*) Located in an idyllic position in a glade amid woodland above Sinaia, Peleş

Castle was built from 1875 by King Carol I as his royal summer palace. It offers a decidedly romantic blend of Gothic Revival and neo-Renaissance architecture, somewhat reminiscent of Neuschwanstein Castle in Bavaria. The king first occupied the castle in 1883 and continued to modify it for the rest of his life. It was a modern castle in many ways, having both electricity and central heating right from its inauguration, and other novelties for the time such as bathtubs with hot-and cold-water taps. Given the presence of central heating, the attractive tiled traditional wood-fired heaters known as *sobas* found in many of the rooms had a purely decorative function.

The castle centres around the 16m-high Hall of Honour, which has a retractable glass ceiling installed in 1911, and panels of walnut wood including marquetry scenes of German and Swiss castles on the walls. There are many reminders of King Carol's German origins, including the German-style decoration of his apartments, but the overwhelming impression is of the eclecticism of the various rooms, which range from a French Rococo guest bedroom to a Florentine-style mirrored reception room, to a Turkish parlour used as a gentlemen's smoking room. Other highlights include a 60-seat theatre with a frieze by Gustav Klimt, and an armoury displaying Carol's extensive weapon collection. It hasn't been regularly lived in since King Carol's death. Restored to the Romanian royal family in 2007, it has been rented back to the Romanian Government since then as a museum. Visits are by guided tour only, with tours offered in Romanian, English, French, Spanish and Italian. Since the castle is one of the most popular attractions in Romania, and welcomes numerous day coach parties from Bucharest, this can mean a lengthy wait at peak times to get onto a tour, as well as a larger-than-ideal group size.

Pelişor Castle (Castelul Pelişor) (w *peles.ro*; ⊕ *09.15–16.15 Thu–Sun, 11.00– 16.15 Wed; adult/child 20/5RON*) Pelişor Castle is just a short walk away from Peleş Castle, and is the much smaller and more intimate of the two. This was built by King Carol I between 1899 and 1902 as a residence for his heir, Ferdinand, and the latter's consort, the British-born future Queen Marie (see box, pages 146–7). It is much lighter in feel than Peleş Castle, in part because of the use of paler woods, notably sycamore and pine. The imprint of Marie's taste is felt very strongly in the decoration, which has an overall Art Nouveau theme, though with influences ranging from Brancovean to Celtic.

Both King Ferdinand and Queen Marie died in Pelişor Castle, and the queen's heart is still there, inside a box of gilded linden wood in the middle of the overpoweringly decorated Gold Room. Both Ferdinand and Marie were buried in Curtea de Argeş, in accordance with Romanian royal tradition, but Marie's heart was removed before her burial, as her will stipulated, and placed in the chapel in her beloved seaside residence in Balchik. However, this is now part of Bulgaria, so her heart embarked on a complex journey, ending up in storage in the History Museum in Bucharest, before being brought to its current home in Pelişor in a solemn ceremony in 2015. A further walk up the hill, the **Foişor Castle** (Castelul Foişor), a hunting lodge of Carol I and briefly a royal residence while Peleş Castle was being finished, is run by Romanian State Protocol and is not open to visitors.

Bucegi Natural Park (*Str Principală 71, Moroeni, jud Dâmboviţa;* ✆ *0372 758 550;* e *bucegipark@gmail.com;* w *bucegipark.ro*) The Bucegi Mountains loom over the resorts of the Prahova Valley as imposing rocky peaks. Part of the Southern Carpathian range, the Bucegi are among the most popular mountain ranges in

Romania with both hikers in summer and skiers in winter, a function both of their beauty and of the well-developed resorts serving them, which in turn has much to do with their relative proximity to Bucharest. The Bucegi are much more straightforwardly accessible for the casual visitor than most of Romania's other major ranges. The cable car from Buşteni brings you straight up the steep western slope of the range and onto the plateau above, a short strolling distance from the two best-known natural features of the Bucegi. Taking the path north from the cable car, you come almost immediately to the Cabana Babele mountain lodge, next to which is an assemblage of eroded rocks, looking somewhat like stone mushrooms, which goes by the name of **Babele** and is said to resemble a group of old ladies. You would need a certain amount of imagination to see anything very old-ladylike in them, but the next outcrop, **Sfinxul**, a few hundred metres further along the path, is much more satisfyingly Sphinx-like.

While you will be in plenty of company visiting Babele and Sfinxul, the trails get much quieter away from the cable-car stations. There are trails up to the highest peak in the range, **Omu**, at a height of 2,505m. For the experienced there are also marked trails from this peak northwestwards right down into Bran in Braşov County. From the cable-car station near Cabana Babele, another cable car takes you down to the **Peştera Ialomiţei Monastery** (Mănăstirea Peştera Ialomiţei), dating from the 16th century and strikingly situated at the mouth of a cave. The range is now protected as the Bucegi Natural Park.

Buşteni Continuing northwards along the Prahova Valley, the next resort above Sinaia on the E60/DN1 is Buşteni, 6km on, a busy place in both winter and summer, and set at an altitude of 900m. It is home to the **Cantacuzino Castle** (Castelul Cantacuzino) (*Str Zamorei 1;* m *0722 960 606;* e *office@cantacuzinocastle.ro;* w *cantacuzinocastle.com;* ◐ *10.00–18.00 Mon–Thu, 10.00–19.00 Fri–Sun; adult/child 20/10RON tour & grounds only, 30/16RON with art gallery admission as well as tour*), across the Prahova River from the town centre. This is much more modern than it looks from afar, and was built by Romanian politician Prince Gheorghe Cantacuzino in 1911 in a neo-Romanian style. Cantacuzino was known as the '*nabob*' because of his immense wealth, and this was just one of three grand palaces he built in Romania. The place has been developed as an upmarket restaurant and conference centre, but they also offer guided tours, starting at 5 minutes past the hour, and there is an art gallery housing temporary exhibitions. The park around the castle is pleasant too.

Buşteni, while a more formless resort than Sinaia, is an excellent base for explorations of the Bucegi Mountains, since the cable car here takes you straight up onto the Bucegi Plateau, close to the Babele outcrop. Its physical location is impressive too, with the peaks of Caraiman and Costila towering above the town. Caraiman forms a particularly notable landmark by virtue of the 28m-high cross, the **Heroes' Cross** (Crucea Eroilor Neamului), built on a pedestal itself more than 7m high, overlooking the valley below. The cross is a little below the peak of Caraiman, at an altitude of 2,291m. It was constructed in the 1920s to commemorate employees of the Romanian railways killed in World War I.

Azuga The last of the Prahova Valley resorts within Prahova County, before you enter Transylvania, is Azuga, 4km on from Buşteni. It is particularly known as a developing ski resort, with its Sorica piste, accessible by gondola lift, offering a run of some 2,100m. There is a large collection of stalls along the E60 road here selling a particularly depressing range of tatty souvenirs, giving the place a slightly scruffy appearance. Azuga is also known for the manufacture of beer and wine.

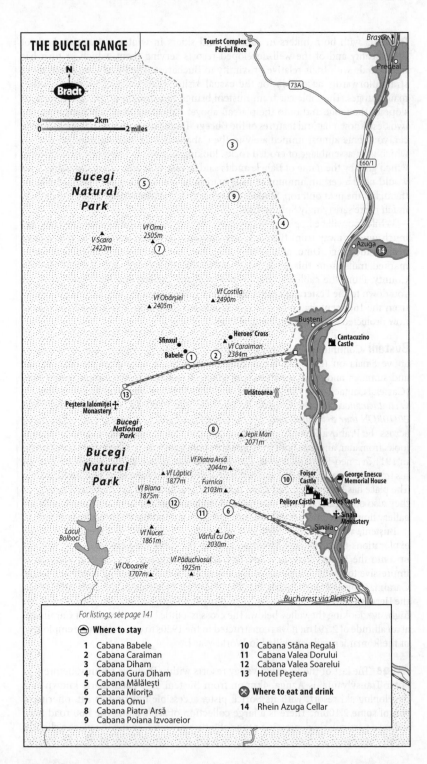

THE BUCEGI RANGE

Brasov

Predeal

73A

E60/1

Bucegi Natural Park

③

⑤

⑨

④

Azuga ⊗⑭

V. Scara 2422m ▲

Vf Omu 2505m ▲ ⑦

Vf Obârşiei 2405m ▲

Vf Costila 2490m ▲

Buşteni

Cantacuzino Castle

Sfinxul ●

Heroes' Cross ✚

Babele ● ①

② Vf Caraiman 2384m ▲

Urlătoarea ⧼⧼

Peştera Ialomiţei ✚ Monastery

⑬

Bucegi National Park

⑧

Jepii Mari 2071m ▲

Bucegi Natural Park

Vf Piatra Arsă 2044m ▲▲

Vf Lăptici 1877m ▲

Furnica 2103m ▲

Foişor Castle

George Enescu Memorial House

⑩

Pelişor Castle

Peleş Castle

Vf Blana 1875m ▲

⑫

⑪ ⑥

Sinaia Monastery ✚

Lacul Bolboci

Vf Nucet 1861m ▲

Vârful cu Dor 2030m ▲

Sinaia

Vf Oboarele 1707m ▲

Vf Păduchiosul 1925m ▲

Bucharest via Ploieşti

N

Bradt

0 ——— 2km
0 ——— 2 miles

For listings, see page 141

🏠 **Where to stay**

1 Cabana Babele
2 Cabana Caraiman
3 Cabana Diham
4 Cabana Gura Diham
5 Cabana Mălăeşti
6 Cabana Mioriţa
7 Cabana Omu
8 Cabana Piatra Arsă
9 Cabana Poiana Izvoareior

10 Cabana Stâna Regală
11 Cabana Valea Dorului
12 Cabana Valea Soarelui
13 Hotel Peştera

✖ **Where to eat and drink**

14 Rhein Azuga Cellar

140

The Azuga brewery has now closed, though the brand name lives on, produced by Ursus Breweries and now manufactured in Braşov. But still to be found in the town is the **Rhein Azuga Cellar** (*Str Independenţei 24;* \0244 326 560; e *azuga@halewood.co.ro;* w *halewood.co.ro*), built in 1892 and producing sparkling wine using the traditional method of hand-turning the bottles. Tours of the cellar and wine tasting are offered by appointment, though only for a minimum group size of eight, and drivers will be pleased to note there is also a 16-room guesthouse here (**$$**) as well as a restaurant.

ENTERING BRAŞOV COUNTY AND TRANSYLVANIA

PREDEAL Continuing along the E60 from Sinaia, Buşteni and Azuga, we enter Braşov County and the beginning of Transylvania at Predeal, the northernmost resort in the Prahova Valley, 25km south of Braşov and 16km north of Sinaia. Predeal (Predeál/Schanzpass) is the highest town in Romania at an elevation of just over 1,000m, and is best known as a winter-sports destination, with five ski runs. It has been the subject of something of a construction boom in recent years: like the other resort towns of the Prahova Valley it is a favoured spot for weekend second homes of wealthy families from Bucharest. The outcome is a somewhat formless, sprawling feel to the place. It is surrounded by five massifs – Postăvarul, Piatra Mare, Bucegi, Baiului and Fitifoi – and is a good base for mountain hikes.

The **tourist information centre** (*Bd Mihail Săulescu;* \0268 455 330; e *info@predeal.ro;* w *predeal.ro;* ⊕ *10.00–18.00 daily*) sits in the circular pavilion on the main road opposite the railway station.

The **train station** (\0268 410 233) is central: Predeal is well served on the main line between Bucharest (*from 2hrs*) and Braşov (*40mins*). There are several buses a day to Braşov (Autogara 1).

🏠 Where to stay and eat

🏠 **Predeal Comfort Suites** (16 dbl, 16 apt) Str Trei Brazi 33; \0268 455 795; e office@predealcomfortsuites.ro; w predealcomfortsuites.ro. Promising a luxury experience throughout, it does offer rooms with four-poster beds, spa & sauna, but at root it's a pleasant enough place that doesn't live up to its 5-star billing. Its restaurant (**$$$$**) is Lebanese & pretty good. **$$$$**

🏠 **Hotel Carmen** (58 rooms) Bd Mihail Săulescu 121; \0268 456 517; e office@hotelcarmenpredeal.ro; w hotelcarmenpredeal.ro. New, central 4-star hotel in the form of a huge beige brick chalet, with spa & pool. They also have smaller 3-star-rated rooms. **$$$$** (4-star rooms), **$$$** (3-star)

🏠 **Red & Black Hotel** (58 dbl, 6 apt) Bd Mihail Săulescu 119; \0268 457 060; e receptie.CPP_Predeal@brd.ro. Central hotel in an ugly modern-looking building whose metallic lines jar with the setting. The place mainly serves as a training centre for staff of the BRD bank, but when

not booked out for a bank event offers good value if uninspiring rooms. **$$$**

🏠 **Vila Vitalis** (12 dbl) Sos Nationala 70; m 0736 640 450; e vitalis.ro@gmail.com. Located on the main road just to the south of town, this is a friendly Israeli-run place offering enthusiastic advice on local hiking options. Mountain-bike rentals available. 2 rooms have balconies. **$$$**

🏠 **Vila Andra 1 & 2** (Andra 1,12 dbl; Andra 2, 15 dbl) Str Libertăţii 38 & 39; m 0722 425 330; e rezervare@vilele-andra-predeal.ro; w vilele-andra-predeal.ro. Pleasant rooms with terraces in 2 adjacent buildings. **$$**

🗙 **Vatra Regală** Bd Mihail Săulescu 117; m 0742 144 189; e vatraregala@gmail.com; w vatraregala.ro; ⊕ 09.00–23.00 daily. Hearty Romanian dishes in a mock-medieval setting. The interior majors on replica weaponry with a copy of Stefan the Great's sword guarding the toilets. Central location on the main road opposite the Petrom service station. **$$$**

RÂŞNOV Râşnov (Barcarozsnyó/Rosenau) is a small town of some 14,000 inhabitants, 15km southwest of Braşov. It is dominated by the medieval hilltop fortress which sits on an outcrop overlooking the town, marked for good effect by a Hollywood-style 'Râşnov' sign similar to those in Braşov and Deva. It was one of the towns of the historic region of Burzenland (known in Romanian as Ţara Bârsei), which was centred on Braşov and colonised by Germans from the mid 12th century.

There are plentiful **bus** connections to Braşov (*Autogara 2; 25mins*), and it is also a stop on the **railway** line between Braşov and Zărneşti, with nine daily trains in each direction. If you have your own transport, and are arriving into Transylvania on the busy E60 road from Bucharest, there is a pleasant alternative from Predeal to continuing on the E60 all the way to Braşov. Instead, turn left onto the 73A road, which offers a lovely winding drive ascending an aromatic pine-and-birch-covered mountain before descending to the flat plains close to Râşnov.

 Where to stay A tastefully furnished small hotel in a nice quiet location is **Edel House** (*16 dbl, 6 apt; Str Florilor 69;* ✆ *0268 230 430;* e *office@edelhouse.ro;* w *edelhouse. ro;* **$$$**).

What to see and do
Râşnov Citadel (Cetatea Râşnov) (🕘 *May–Sep 09.00–19.00 daily, Oct–Apr 09.00–17.00 daily; adult/child 12/3RON*) The citadel dates from the early 13th century, in the period in which the Burzenland region was given by the King of Hungary to the Teutonic Knights, in exchange for their guarding the borders of the kingdom against the predations of the Cumans. In 1335, the fortress proved its mettle during a Tatar invasion: the surrounding areas were devastated but the invaders could not conquer the citadel, and the inhabitants of Râşnov were thereby saved. The fortress was conquered only once, by Gábor Báthory at the beginning of the 17th century, when lack of water proved its undoing. The locals took the lesson from this that a water source was needed within the citadel itself, resulting in the construction of a 146m-deep well, one of the sights of the fortress today, between 1625 and 1640.

The fortress served as a place of refuge for the inhabitants of Râşnov as recently as the revolutionary period of 1848–49, but it was abandoned soon after. Its form today gives a strong sense of a fortress which served as an urban community, with numerous houses preserved within the walls in various states of repair. Many of these are now given over to souvenir shops, and overall the fortress, while well worth a visit, is one of those places which looks more impressive from afar than up close. The views from the top are great, though.

A **funicular** (🕘 *Nov–Feb 09.00–17.00 daily, Oct & Mar 09.00–18.00 daily, Apr–Sep 09.00–19.00 daily; return adult/child 12/6RON, one-way 8/4RON*) runs up the steep hillside from the town: it is accessed through an archway off Piaţa Unirii. Or head out of town along Strada Cetăţii: after a few hundred metres you reach on your left a large car park fringed by souvenir and snack stalls. You can either walk up to the citadel from here or take a carriage pulled by a tractor.

The path reaches the citadel via another, much newer, attraction: **DinoParc Râşnov** (*Str Cetăţii;* ✆ *0368 808 805;* e *info@dinoparc.ro;* w *dinoparc.ro;* 🕘 *10.00–18.00 Mon–Thu, 10.00–20.00 Fri/Sat, 10.00–19.00 Sun; adult/child 28/22RON*). A path heads through the forest, punctuated by life-size models of the dinosaurs of the Triassic, Jurassic and Cretaceous eras, plus a bonus smouldering volcano.

The town Modern-day Râşnov is a sleepy sort of place lying under the citadel hill. Many of the houses bear the names of their former Saxon owners and the date of their construction. Activity centres on the cobbled Piaţa Unirii, the main square, which has recently been remodelled to accommodate an underground car park, which seems an unnecessary and jarring feature in such a small, quiet town. At its northern end is a 14th-century **Evangelical Church** (Biserica Evanghelică) (*Str Republicii 1; ⊕ 10.00–17.00 Tue–Sat, 13.00–16.00 Sun*).

A couple of streets to the south, the **Cinema Amza Pellea** takes his name from a Romanian actor noted for his portrayals of Romanian heroes in Communist-era historical productions, for which the Râşnov Citadel was a frequent shooting location. It is the focus of the **Râşnov Historic Film Festival** (Festivalul de Film Istoric) (*w ffir.ro*), a low-key but pleasant festival held at the start of August.

BRAN Bran (Törcsvár/Törzburg) is one of the most touristy villages in Transylvania, and can at times feel swamped by the tour buses which disgorge their loads of sightseers at the base of its central attraction, Bran Castle. But the castle is both visually impressive and historically fascinating, and makes for a worthy stop on any itinerary exploring the highlights of Transylvania. And Bran has some interesting further attractions which lie well off the radars of the tour groups, and reward a more in-depth visit here.

Bran is 30km southwest of Braşov on the busy main road E574/DN73. This runs straight through the heart of the village: be careful when crossing it, as much of the traffic is speeding too fast. If you are not overnighting here, be prepared for some expensive car parking. The car parks closest to the castle charge 5RON an hour, though cheaper rates can easily be had if you are prepared to walk a little further: the car parking area down Strada Sextil Puşcariu a few hundred metres to the north of the castle charges 9RON a day. There are many buses (*45mins*) daily from Braşov Autogara 2. Note that recent street renaming has made navigation in Bran somewhat challenging of late, as both locals and car GPS systems have struggled to keep up with the new names.

🏠 Where to stay and eat

🏠 **Club Vila Bran** (107 rooms, 19 apt) Str Alunis 13; ☎ 0268 236 866; e rezervari@vilabran.ro; w vilabran.ro. Some 1km north of the village centre, just off the road from Braşov, this is a huge complex with rooms spread across 11 blocks, plus the separate Micul Castel Vila Bran (2 dbl, 2 apt), an extravagantly designed building located 700m down the road, closer to Bran Castle. They also offer the chance to stay in 1 of 2 fairytale cottages, Red Riding Hood's house (minus wolf) & Bambi's cottage (though book well ahead for these). With outdoor pools, playgrounds, tennis courts, concerts of big-name Romanian singers & even a statue park of Romanian heroes, the place has something of a holiday-camp feel, but is child-friendly & reasonably priced. The barn-like main restaurant (⊕ 08.00–22.00 daily; $$$) has a good Romanian menu & a large model toucan $$$– $$; Red Riding Hood's & Bambi's cottages $$$$$

🏠 **Hanul Bran** (40 rooms) Str Gen Moşoiu 4; ☎ 0268 236 556; e hanulbran@yahoo.com;

w hanulbran.ro. A 3-star renovated Communist-era hotel on the main road in the centre of the village, this is comfortable enough but would benefit from further modernising. The restaurant ($$$) is rather bleak-looking, but offers a good range of classic Romanian dishes. $$$

🏠 **Pensiunea Ana** (6 dbl, 1 trpl) Str Gen Moşoiu 25; ☎ 0268 236 463; w anabran.ro. Just across the main road from the entrance to the castle, this small, friendly pension, with off-street parking, is one of the most central options in Bran. $$

🏠 **Vila Alisa** (15 dbl, 2 apt) Str Sextil Puşcariu 53; ☎ 0268 236 704; e office@alisaturism.ro; w alisaturism.ro. Large detached 4-storey villa, offering comfortable rooms a few hundred metres to the north of the castle. $$

✳ 🏠 **The Guest House** (6 dbl) Str Gen Moşoiu 7; m 0745 179 475, 0744 306 062; e office@ guesthouse.ro; w guesthouse.ro. Central, simply but nicely furnished & friendly British–Romanian family-run guesthouse with views of Bran Castle, with shared kitchen & large living area downstairs & children's play area in the garden. **$$**

✗ Trattoria Al Gallo Str Sextil Pușcariu 31; ☎0368 453 671; w trattoriaalgallo.ro; ⏰ 08.30–22.00 Mon–Sat, 08.30–20.00 Sun. Good, central Italian restaurant which, like most places to eat in Bran, is also a guesthouse (**$$$**). **$$$**

What to see and do

Bran Castle (Castelul Bran) The heart of the village of Bran seems to be buckling under the pressure of mass tourism. The central Piața Ioan Stoian houses the town hall and a huge number of stalls selling Dracula-related tat in a heady ambience of candyfloss and burgers.

The chief attraction of the village, and the reason all those souvenir stalls are here, Bran Castle (*Str Gen Moșoiu 24;* ☎*0268 237 700;* e *office@bran-castle.com;* w *bran-castle.com;* ⏰ *Apr–Sep noon–18.00 Mon, 09.00–18.00 Tue–Sun, Oct–Mar noon–16.00 Mon, 09.00–16.00 Tue–Sun; adult/child 35/7RON, audio guide 10RON*) does not disappoint. With its turrets, steep walls and imposing location atop a rocky crag, Bran Castle looks every inch the Transylvanian castle, and this is the place visitors to Romania come in order to see the real Dracula's home. Except that it isn't. Author Bram Stoker located the castle of his fictional Count Dracula far to the north, near Bistrița, although he probably saw drawings of Bran in the course of his research for the book, and its striking features may have been one source of inspiration for his fictional castle. And the castle had precious little connection either with Vlad the Impaler, the historical figure most linked to Count Dracula, beyond the possibility that he was briefly imprisoned here and the fact that he passed through the area in 1459 on his way to attack Brașov. While there are displays about Count Dracula and vampires in the castle, it is best appreciated by putting Dracula to one side and focusing instead on the real history of the place, which is of great interest.

Bran Castle lies at a point of considerable strategic importance, guarding a mountain pass which served as a trading route between Transylvania and Wallachia. In 1377, King Louis I of Hungary gave the Saxons of Brașov permission to build a castle here at their own expense. The castle had the dual role of defending the pass against Ottoman incursions, and as a customs post. It was an important component of the defence of Transylvania, and by the late 15th century the commander of the castle also bore the title of Vice-Voivode of Transylvania. It lost most of its remaining military and customs role during the 19th century, and in 1888 responsibility for the place was transferred to the regional forestry administration. Following the absorption of Transylvania into Greater Romania the city council of Brașov, who had no clear use for the place, decided to offer it in 1920 to the popular Queen Marie of Romania (see box, pages 146–7), for whom Bran Castle became a favoured summer residence.

It is a hugely atmospheric place, centred around a cobbled courtyard focused on an impossibly romantic 57m-deep well. It offers a mix of the medieval, with spiral staircases, loggias and turrets, and the rather comfortable-looking rooms of a 20th-century royal family, decorated in Queen Marie's trademark confident mix of Art Nouveau, Celtic and Byzantine styles. You can even see the machinery of the lift that was installed to ease her access to the place.

On Queen Marie's death in 1938 she left the castle to Princess Ileana, reputedly the favourite of her daughters. She was forced into exile in 1948, along with the rest of her family, by the Communist regime, who turned the castle into a museum. Ileana moved to the US where she became a nun, dying in 1991. After protracted legal proceedings, the castle was returned to Princess Ileana's heirs, and now operates as a private museum.

Other attractions in Bran At the foot of the castle, close to the ticket office, is the separate **Village Museum** (Muzeul Satului) (⊕ *May–Oct noon–16.00 Mon, 09.00–16.00 Tue–Sun, Nov–Apr 09.00–16.00 Tue–Sun; adult/child 8/2RON*), a collection of 16 traditional rural buildings, which were moved to the site from neighbouring villages.

While most visitors to Bran see the castle, dodge or embrace the souvenir shops beneath it according to taste and then leave, there is a very interesting short walk to be had to some further places of interest right off the tourist trail. On exiting the castle and passing through the forest of souvenir stalls, turn left on the main E574/DN73 road. Walk around the edge of the Royal Park below the castle, entering into a wooded valley with a stream on the right hand side of the road. On your left you will come to the **Medieval Custom House Museum** (Muzeul Vama Medievală Bran) (*Str Gen Moşoiu 28;* ☏*0268 283 332;* ⊕ *May–Oct noon–16.00 Mon, 09.00–16.00 Tue–Sun, Nov–Apr 09.00–16.00 Tue–Sun; adult/child 8/2RON*). Cross the road here and go over the stream on a wooden footbridge, marked for a red stripe trail. You should be able to make out a niche in the rock on the side of the wooded hill just beyond. Some steps lead up to the niche, which contains a stone sarcophagus. This served as the decidedly unusual resting place for the **Heart of Queen Marie**, which had initially been placed, in accordance with her will, in the Stella Maris Chapel of her seaside residence at Balchik, but was brought here in 1940 in order to remain on Romanian territory when Balchik was ceded to Bulgaria. However, it wasn't allowed to rest here peacefully for long: the site was desecrated by the Communists and the queen's heart moved to the National History Museum in Bucharest, where it languished in storage before being moved to its current resting place in Pelişor Castle (page 138) in 2015.

Keep walking along the riverside away from Bran village, and after a few metres you reach the attractive stone-walled church that was built as a replica of Queen Marie's beloved **Stella Maris Chapel** (Capela Stella Maris) in Balchik and now lies sadly abandoned.

Bran is also host to the picturesque festival of **Răvăşitul Oilor** at the end of September or beginning of October. A kind of coming-home party for the sheep returning from their mountain pastures, it features plenty of sheep-related activity, such as cheese tasting and even a most beautiful sheep competition.

FUNDATA Accessed via the DN73/E574 running south from Bran towards Câmpulung, but then turning left after 13km, Fundata (Fundáta/Fundatten) claims the distinction of being the highest commune capital in Romania, at an altitude of 1,360m. It is almost on the border between Transylvania and Argeş County to the south, the location of the **Bran Pass** and offering great views towards both the Bucegi and the Piatra Craiului mountains. The village of **Şirnea** within the commune was a pioneer in the Communist-era concept of a 'tourist village', developed in the late 1960s. Following the Romanian Revolution, the idea of organised group visits to specially designated tourist villages, where visitors would be given programmes presenting idealised visions of rural lifestyles, was rendered immediately redundant, but the area is still a focus for visitors wishing to spend time among these mountain village communities.

Fundata is also known for the **Nedeia Munţilor** festival, held over a couple of days in summer, based on the concept of a fair linking the two regions of Wallachia and Transylvania, and involving traditional food and costumes and plenty of folk music.

🏠 **Where to stay** In the small village of Ciocanu within Fundata commune is the **Pensiunea Pui de Urs Şirnea** (*10 rooms; Sat Ciocanu;* m *0744 607 414;* e *pui.deurs@*

yahoo.com; w *pensiuneapuideurs.ro;* $), offering great views, a terrace, shared lounge and good local cooking.

PIATRA CRAIULUI NATIONAL PARK Piatra Craiului (King's Stone) is one of the most impressive mountain ranges in Transylvania, popular with hikers and climbers, comprising a distinctive narrow limestone ridge, about 25km long, and reaching a maximum elevation of 2,238m. The views both towards and from the mountains are superb. The wildlife is diverse, with chamois on the high cliffs and brown bear, wild boar, red and roe deer, foxes, wolves, pine martens, red squirrels and even lynx in the mixed forests. There is an abundance and variety of wild flowers, including orchids. The gorges are a good place to see wallcreepers and alpine swifts, as well as three-toed and white-backed woodpeckers and Ural owls in the forested parts.

Piatra Craiului was first established as a nature reserve in 1938, initially covering an area of just 440ha. This has been progressively extended, and in 1990 it became a national park, covering a total area of 9,894ha. The **National Park Visitor Centre** (Centrul de Vizitare al Parcului Naţional Piatra Craiului) (*Str Topliţa 150, Zărneşti;* ⟍*0268 223 165;* e *office@pcrai.ro;* w *pcrai.ro;* ⏱ *10.00–16.00 Tue–Thu & Sat, 10.00– 14.00 Fri & Sun*) lies on the small road into the park heading west out of the town of Zărneşti, which serves as the main gateway into the park. All visitors to the park aged 14 or over entering the park between the months of May and October need to purchase a park ticket, costing 5RON and valid for seven days. This can be obtained online, as well as at the visitor centre, at the Zărneşti Post Office

QUEEN MARIE OF ROMANIA

Queen Marie of Romania was probably the British citizen to have had the greatest influence on the history of Romania. Born in 1875, she was the daughter of Prince Alfred, second son of Queen Victoria. Her mother was Grand Duchess Maria Alexandrovna, the only surviving daughter of Tsar Alexander II of Russia. King Carol I of Romania had only one child, a daughter, who died in infancy. Carol's nephew Ferdinand was the designated heir, but was in need of a suitable bride. He duly proposed to the 16-year-old Marie, who with her close connections to the great royal families of both the United Kingdom and Russia, seemed an ideal choice for the new state of Romania. In other respects, however, the match was less obvious: there was a ten-year age difference, and she was beautiful and sporty while he was intellectual and shy.

They married in 1893, and Marie initially found her life in Bucharest highly isolated, as King Carol tried to prevent the couple from developing outside friendships, fearing they would come under the influence of one Romanian political group or another. But Marie worked on getting to know the country and its people. She performed her royal duties efficiently, too, falling pregnant within two weeks of her marriage and giving birth to a son, Carol.

Marie was to become hugely popular in Romania, in part through her care for wounded soldiers, which earnt her the nickname 'mother of the wounded'. This work had its origins in the Second Balkan War of 1913, when Romanian troops, though victorious, had to contend with an epidemic of cholera. And Marie continued with this work in World War I, dressing as a nurse and spending much time in military hospitals. The importance of her role during and after World War I was not, however, confined to looking after the sick. Romania remained neutral at the outbreak of war, but while the German-born King Carol, who died in October 1914, favoured alliance with Germany, Marie, with her British and

(*Str Tiberiu Spârchez 12A, Zărneşti*) or at the Cabana Plaiul Foii lodge (see below). The park has six mountain shelters to be used in case of bad weather or ill health.

🏠 **Where to stay** Zărneşti (see below) offers a good base for exploring the park, but there are some other worthwhile options elsewhere.

🏠 **Vila Hermani** (17 rooms) Sat Măgura 130; **m** 0740 022 384; **e** office@cntours.ro; **w** cntours.ro. In a truly picturesque setting in the mountain village of Măgura within the national park itself, this is a comfortable guesthouse run by Hermann Kurmes, a Transylvanian Saxon who emigrated to Germany but then returned with his wife Katharina to set up Carpathian Nature Tours. All rooms have a balcony & great views. HB & FB options can be arranged, which is helpful, as Măgura doesn't do restaurants. They can arrange transfers from Bucharest or Sibiu airports &

Braşov railway station, & offer bicycle hire (*€15/ day*) & English-speaking guides (*€70/day*). If you're driving note that Măgura is somewhat challenging to reach, though the road from Zărneşti, although unpaved, is better than the poor track from Moieciu de Jos. **$$$**

🏠 **Cabana Plaiul Foii** (15 rooms) **m** 0726 380 323; **w** cabanaplaiulfoii.ro. A rustic lodge close to the Bârsa River at the foot of the massif, & well placed for hiking trails into the national park, along a poor but scenic road to the west of Zărneşti, with a restaurant (**$$$**) serving traditional Romanian dishes. **$$**

ZĂRNEŞTI The rather sprawling small town of Zărneşti (Zernest/Molkendorf), with a population of some 21,000, is not the most immediately visually appealing settlement in Transylvania, but has developed a quite significant tourist profile

Russian background, supported an alliance with the Triple Entente, on whose side Romania ultimately joined the war in August 1916.

At the Paris Peace Conference at the end of the war, Romania was one of the victorious powers, but Prime Minister Brătianu was making little headway in the negotiations. Queen Marie was sent to Paris to support the Romanian cause. It was her finest hour, as she charmed Clemenceau and the other leaders, helping to secure a highly favourable settlement for Romania.

Another name by which Marie was known was 'mother-in-law of the Balkans', because of her efforts to secure politically advantageous matches for her children, who she saw married into the royal families of Greece and Serbia. She pioneered interior fashions in Romania, seen in her confident mixing of Romanian, Celtic and Art Deco styles in various royal palaces. She was a prolific author, publishing some 34 books, from autobiography to fairy tales. And she was a modern queen in her relations with the media, seen particularly in her tour of the US in 1926, when she was greeted enthusiastically in every city.

Following King Ferdinand's death in 1927, the last 11 years of her life were difficult, marked by an estranged relationship with her son Carol, who had renounced his rights to succeed Ferdinand in 1926 and went to live abroad with his mistress, an act which put his five-year-old son Michael on the throne on Ferdinand's death. But by 1930 Carol had changed his mind, returned to Bucharest and usurped the throne from his own son. King Carol II marginalised Queen Marie, jealous of her popularity with the Romanian people, and she spent much time travelling abroad and at her retreats in Balchik and Bran. She died at Pelişor Castle in Sinaia in 1938. Thousands of people filed by during her lying-in-state at Cotroceni Palace in Bucharest.

3

thanks to its position as the gateway to the neighbouring Piatra Craiului National Park, some good accommodation and local guide options, and the presence of a remarkable bear sanctuary which offers perhaps the best and certainly the safest way to get to know these magnificent creatures. There is a **tourist office** (*Str Tiberiu Spârchez 12;* \0368 003 376; ⊕ *10.00–16.00 daily*) in a circular pavilion in the town centre. Zărneşti hosts the colourful **Edelweiss Festival** (*Festivalul Floare de Colţ*) in August, usually on the first Sunday after Assumption Day. Expect a horse parade, traditional costumes, folk music and fireworks.

The town is just 11km from Râşnov along a side road off the main DN73/E574. Buses depart Braşov Autogara 2 roughly every 30 minutes for Zărneşti (*1hr*) on weekdays, though they are much less frequent at the weekend.

The **Libearty Bear Sanctuary** (✳ \0268 471 202; e *milioanedeprieteni@gmail. com;* w *ampbears.ro;* ⊕ *May–Oct entry at 09.00, 10.00 & 11.00 Tue–Sun, Nov–Apr entry at 10.00 if there are at least 10 visitors, 11.00 & noon Tue–Sun; adult/child 40/10 RON Tue–Fri, 50/15RON Sat/Sun, train tour adult/child 20/10RON; children under 5 are not allowed in the sanctuary*) lies on a hill just outside the town. Run by local NGO Milioane de Prieteni, with support from the UK-based charity World Animal Protection, it is a remarkable place, with some 88 bears, mostly living in three large enclosures in 69ha of oak forest. Another five smaller enclosures cater for bears with specific problems. All of the bears in the sanctuary were rescued from captivity, and many of their tales are truly harrowing, such as that of Max, the blind bear from Sinaia who for years was chained up near Peleş Castle, where visiting tourists would pay to have their photo taken with him. They are also setting up a Teddy Bear Museum here centred around two huge bears donated by British bookmakers William Hill, which were originally used in a promotional campaign to encourage punters to take a flutter on the sex of a royal baby. Other bears have been donated by celebrities ranging from Brigitte Bardot to Luna Lovegood. There are also enclosures for wolves and deer. The reason that the place can only be visited at specific points in the morning is that the bears come out from the depths of the wood only during feeding times, which are set to coincide with the tours. And yes, there are bears here named both Baloo and Yogi. To get to the sanctuary take road 73A eastwards from Zărneşti towards Râşnov, turning left onto an unpaved road at a turning signposted for the sanctuary. This lies up the hill and around 3km further on, along a road which is not easy to navigate in muddy weather.

The dedication of one man established Zărneşti as an important and popular stop on any ecotourist's agenda. Danuţ 'Dan' Marin was the joint winner of *Wanderlust's* Paul Morrison Guide of the Year 2007, a richly deserved award for his efforts, together with his wife Luminiţa, to promote the local natural attributes as well as working for the community. Together, Dan and Luminiţa run a guesthouse called Transylvanian Wolf (see opposite for contact details), which they bought in 2003. The spacious rooms have log-burning ceramic stoves and modern bathrooms. A visit to their Zărneşti home gives a thoroughly satisfying glimpse into the society, nature, culture, history and legends of the region. Dan is an extremely knowledgeable host and guide, and, after a fantastic breakfast, leads walking tours of the surrounding region, including the Piatra Craiului National Park, the village of Vulcan and the difficult-to-reach village of Măgura. He is informative on the flora and fauna and reads animal footprints, follows shepherds' trails, spots distant soaring birds and recounts myths and legends for the guests. Dan can also arrange bear-watching trips to one of the hides in the area. He also speaks impeccable accent-free English, which is amazing considering he is entirely self-taught from a book, as well as French. Dan's charming and hospitable wife, Luminiţa, prepares delicious Romanian, Transylvanian and Roma dishes, lighter Western-style dishes and caters for special dietary needs.

She also gives classes in the art of local cuisine and brews all manner of healing herbal teas. A recipe for her delicious elderberry jam is on page 94. On a walk with Dan, visitors can meet a shepherd in his isolated mountain hut and assist with the cheese making. This is very much a family business, and Dan and Luminita have now been joined by their daughter Dana, who has a degree in tourism and is, literally, following in her father's footprints as a guide. This is a genuine highlight of any visit to Transylvania, whether in search of culture, food or wildlife. Read Dan's account of Transylvanian wildlife on pages 12–15.

Where to stay, eat and drink

Pensiunea Hora cu Brazi (19 rooms) Str Râului 34–36; **m** 0752 136 653; **e** contact@ horacubrazi.ro; **w** horacubrazi.ro. Nicely furnished pension on the edge of town, with traditional Romanian décor & a restaurant (**$$$**) serving local dishes. They organise the Zărneşti Folk Day each Oct in their extensive gardens, with fine views of the surrounding hills. **$$**

Transylvanian Wolf (4 dbl) Str Mitropolit Ioan Metianu 108; **m** 0744 319 708; **e** transylvanian_wolf@yahoo.com; **w** transylvanianwolf.ro. Guesthouse furnished in traditional style run by Dan & Luminiţa Marin, who offer a range of walks guided by the knowledgeable & informative Dan, focusing on the fauna of the Piatra Craiului National Park. Good local meals are prepared by Luminiţa, who also offers cooking lessons & tastes of a whole cheese encased in pine tree bark, which gave the chunky cheesy tube a wonderful pine flavour. **$$**

ŞINCA NOUĂ The road from Zărneşti heading northwest towards Făgăraş follows the glorious 73A route, one of the nicest drives in Transylvania. In the picturesque valley, some 20km north of Zărneşti, is the village of Şinca Nouă, where the Equus Silvania stables run by Christoph Promberger offer fine riding holidays. In mid-September the village of Poiana Mărului, between Zărneşti and Şinca Nouă (Újsinka/Neu-Schenk), hosts **Autumn Festival** (Târg de Toamnă), offering a mix of rural activities and produce and plenty of folk music.

Where to stay
With their own stables in idyllic, pastoral surroundings, 27 horses and three ponies, **Equus Silvania** (9 dbl; Şinca Nouă 507210; **m** 0740 185 583; **e** bookings@equus-silvania.com; **w** equus-silvania.com; **$$$$**) offers both centre-based and six-day trail-riding programmes, as well as bear watching (€30). Note that a €10 per person supplement is payable for guests staying just one night.

FĂGĂRAŞ Făgăraş (Fogaras/Fogarasch) is a town of some 30,000 people on the main E68 route between Braşov and Sibiu. Among the numerous theories around the origin of the town's name is the assumption that it refers to beech forests, deriving from the Romanian word for beech (fag). Another local version is that the name derives from Hungarian words meaning 'wooden money', surmising that the builders of Făgăraş Fortress were paid in such a currency. With a townscape dominated by Communist-era concrete apartment blocks, it is not the most attractive place in the region.

Getting there and away There are frequent **buses** to Braşov (1hr 40mins) and a few a day to Sibiu (1hr 30mins), confusingly departing from several different locations in town depending on the bus company, though the most convenient is from the Casa de Cultura just outside the fortress. The **railway station** (\0268 211 125) is south of the centre. Făgăraş lies on the line between Braşov (1–1½hrs) and Sibiu (1hr 40mins), with several trains daily to both. For the Transfăgărăşan Highway and Făgăraş Mountains, see pages 237–8.

What to see and do

Făgăraş Fortress (Cetatea Făgăraş) (\ *0268 211 862;* e *muzeufagaras@ yahoo.com;* w *muzeufagaras.ro;* ⊕ *Jun–Sep 08.00–19.00 Tue–Fri, 10.00–18.00 Sat/ Sun, Oct–May 08.00–17.00 Tue–Fri, 09.00–17.00 Sat/Sun; adult/child 15/7RON*) is at the heart of the town, and is the main reason to visit. It is an impressive moated citadel, with an imposing outer wall with four corner bastions, and a castle within. Construction began in the late 14th century, but the castle continued to be developed until the 17th. Starting out life as a military fortification, it evolved into a royal court in the 17th century, having been rebuilt in the early part of that century, during the reign of Prince Gabriel Bethlen. It became a residence of the princes of Transylvania, and more frequently of their wives. Attacked many times over the centuries, it was never conquered. At its height, under Transylvanian princes such as Michael Apafi, envoys from neighbouring Wallachia and Moldavia were received here. It hosted the Transylvanian Diet on several occasions, and the Diploma Leopoldină, which served as the Transylvanian Constitution until the 19th century, was accepted here. From the end of the 17th century it was used successively as a garrison of the Austrian, Austro-Hungarian and Romanian armies.

The moat surrounding the fortress is today a rather calming feature, with willow trees on its banks and photogenic swans. Some segments of the external walls and bastions have been lost, but the castle within is well preserved. Within the grounds, a wooden gibbet has been set up, where visitors seem to delight in taking photos of their loved ones pretending to die by hanging. The inner castle itself has corner towers. One of these, the 16th-century Prison Tower, served as a political prison in the Communist era from 1948 to 1960. More than 4,000 people were incarcerated here in total, including former magistrates, officials, police officers and diplomats. It houses a moving exhibition chronicling Communist repression in the Ţara Făgăraşului region. Another of the towers is named the Thomory Tower, named after an early captain of the fortress, Paul Thomory, who had an interesting career. He later became a monk and then Archbishop of Kalocsa in present-day Hungary, ending up as the joint commander of the Hungarian army at the Battle of Mohács, where he met his end in 1526.

The interior castle centres on a courtyard, above which lies the **Valer Literat Museum** (Muzeul Valer Literat), named after its founder in 1923, offering a mix of history and ethnography, and displays of decorative objects from clocks to glassware. A further flight of stairs up, you can visit the Throne Hall, built in the late 16th century in a Renaissance style.

SÂMBĂTA DE SUS The village of Sâmbăta de Sus (Felsőszombatfalva/Obermühlendorf), southwest of Făgăraş, is on tourist itineraries by virtue of the **Sâmbăta de Sus Monastery** (Mănăstirea Sâmbăta de Sus) (m *0730 556 342;* e *manastireabrancoveanu@yahoo.com;* w *manastireabrancoveanu.ro*), also sometimes known as the Brâncoveanu Monastery (Mănăstirea Brâncoveanu). This is a rare Transylvanian building associated with Constantin Brâncoveanu, who was Prince of Wallachia between 1688 and 1714, and who is associated with the development of the Brâncovenesc architectural style, combining local, Byzantine and Italian Renaissance features. Brâncoveanu is also remembered now for the circumstances of his death. Having fallen foul of the Ottomans, under whose suzerainty he was chafing, Brâncoveanu was brought to Constantinople under arrest, where having refused to convert to Islam, his four sons were each decapitated in front of him before Brâncoveanu was himself beheaded. He has been made a saint of the Romanian Orthodox Church.

The village and surrounding land had come into the possession of Brâncoveanu's family in the mid 17th century, and he built a stone church here around 1696, with

above   A horse-drawn cart, an intrinsic part of rural life in Transylvania (PB) page 89

right   Traditional haystacks are a signature image of the Transylvanian countryside (DDS/AWL) page 7

below   Sheep farming in the Transylvanian winter (A/S)

bottom   Cattle returning home after a hard day's grazing make a fine sight in villages such as Micloşoara (M/S) page 164

above left **A traditional Saxon house in the lovely village of Biertan** (Ca/S) pages 232–3

above right **The sale of woollen socks is part of the developing rural tourist industry in the village of Viscri** (P/S) page 157

left **The *tulnic*, a mountain instrument akin to an alpenhorn** (P/S) page 280

below **A group of dancers in traditional dress practise in Cluj-Napoca** (SSp) page 105

above   Bringing milk to be measured at a village co-operative in **Viscri** (KG/AWL) page 101

right   Baking *kürtőskalács* – this chimney-shaped cake is a symbol of the Székely areas (PB) page 180

below   Musicians playing outside a restaurant in Poiana Braşov (SS) pages 152–4

above The Coronation Cathedral in Alba Iulia, built for the 1922 coronation of Ferdinand and Marie (PB) page 267

below Designed to resemble a grand hunting lodge, Peleş Castle was built as a royal summer residence of King Carol I (EC/S) pages 137–8

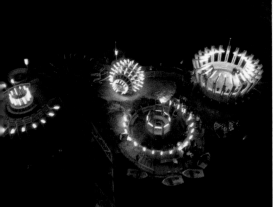

above Cabana Caraiman in the Bucegi Mountains — one of the many *cabanas* that cater to hikers and trekkers (SS) page 139

left The Turda salt mine houses a subterranean funfair (AB) page 300

below The Retezat National Park is the oldest in Romania and a UNESCO biosphere reserve (Mi/S) pages 256–60

right Romania is home to the largest community of brown bears (*Ursus arctos*) in Europe outside Russia (MW/I/FLPA) page 14

below left There is excellent birdwatching in Transylvania — spot golden eagles (*Aquila chrysaetos*) catching updraughts in Apuseni Nature Park (ML/FLPA) page 13

below right The distinctive colouring of the scarce swallowtail butterfly (*Iphiclides podalirius*) (GF/FLPA) page 12

bottom The wolf (*Canis lupus*), traditionally regarded in Romania as a protector against evil, but also inspiring (mostly unjustified) fear (JD/MP/FLPA) pages 12–13

above You don't have to go far to find incredible hiking and trekking in the Carpathian Mountains (DT/S) page 111

left The Transfăgărăşan Highway is the most exciting road in Europe for those on two wheels or four (RS/S) page 237

below Skiers take advantage of the soft powder in Poiana Braşov — Transylvania is a great skiing destination for all levels and styles (BDL/S) pages 152–4 a monastery established soon afterwards. In this period, immediately following the establishment of Habsburg control in Transylvania, there was strong pressure on Orthodox communities to convert to the new Greco-Catholic Church. The monks at Sâmbăta de Sus resolutely refused to convert, but under increasing pressure from Vienna the monastery was eventually disbanded in 1785. Following the absorption of Transylvania into Romania after World War I, the religious authorities in Romania decided to restore the monastery. The charismatic Romanian priest Arsenie Boca was abbot here in the 1940s, before being moved to Prislop Monastery in Hunedoara County (page 254). The monastery provides a good example of the Brâncovenesc style. There is also a museum here with religious books and vestments and icons painted on both glass and wood, and the place is calming and tranquil.

Some 8km north of Sâmbăta de Sus, 'Upper Sâmbăta' is, logically enough, the sister village of **Sâmbăta de Jos**, 'Lower Sâmbăta'. This is home to the **Sâmbăta de Jos Stud Farm** (Herghelia Sâmbăta de Jos) (*Str Principală 45;* \ *0268 517 686;* e *herghelie@brasov.rosilva.ro;* w *sambata-de-jos.ro;* ◯ *10.00–16.00 Mon–Fri; 10RON*), which dates back to 1874, is now administered by the Romsilva state forestry agency, and is specialised in the breeding of Lippizaners. Horseriding and carriage-riding are available by appointment, and riding displays can also be set up for groups. The run-down Brukenthal Castle close by was built in the 18th century by the brother of Samuel von Brukenthal, Governor of Transylvania.

To get here, take the E68/DN1 west from Făgăraş, turning left onto a more minor road at Sâmbăta de Jos. The monastery is located several kilometres south of the Sâmbăta de Sus village at the Staţiunea Climaterică Sâmbăta.

CRISTIAN The village of Cristian (Keresztényfalva/Neustadt) is approached from Braşov by a rather unpromising drive through an industrial estate, but has an attractive centre around its **fortified church** (m *0763 281 128;* ◯ *09.00–11.00 & noon–16.00 daily, though call if it is locked during these times*). It is based around an early Gothic basilica built around 1270, evidence of which is focused on the lower level of the bell tower. But the medieval church was demolished in 1839, to make way for a new hall church in Neoclassical style. The yellow-painted tower was extended in 1903 and given its present form, with four small corner spires around the central one. An oval-shaped double defensive wall surrounds the church, the inner wall much higher than the outer, with eight of the original nine towers still preserved.

There is a **tourist information office** (*Str Morii 2A;* m *0740 176 156;* ◯ *08.00– 16.00 Mon–Fri*) a block away from the church.

Cristian is 13km southwest of Braşov, on the E574 towards Râşnov. There are frequent **buses** from Braşov Autogara 2, taking around 20 minutes. Confusingly, there is another village called Cristian with a fortified church in Sibiu County (page 227).

Cristian also makes for a good base for exploring a group of three more Saxon fortified churches lying in close proximity to the west of Braşov, part of the wider region known as Burzenland, or Ţara Bârsei. These can be visited as a circuit from Cristian. Taking this in a clockwise direction, the first stop is **Vulcan** (Szászvolkány/Wolkendorf), 6km to the west. The fortified church (\ *0268 256 477;* m *0745 108 974;* ◯ *summer 09.00–18.00 Mon–Sat, 11.00–18.00 Sun, winter 09.00–16.00 Mon–Sat, 11.00–16.00 Sun, but call in advance; donation expected*) here dates from the 14th century, with a chancel arch dating from the original Romanesque church, and a Gothic choir added in the 15th century. The church was heavily damaged by the forces of Gabriel Báthory in 1611, but rebuilt later in the century. The current bell tower is more modern, dating from the late 18th century. The church is surrounded by a relatively large defensive enclosure.

Some 6km north of here is **Codlea** (Feketehalom/Zeiden), a larger town of some 20,000 people. The fortified church (✆ *0268 251 853;* e *zeiden@evang.ro;* ⊕ *Jun–Sep 10.00–18.00 daily, Oct–May, call in advance; donation expected*) was originally built in the Romanesque style in the 13th century, but converted into a Gothic hall church in the 15th. The interior features a beautiful ceiling of painted panels which dates from the early 18th century. The defensive wall around the church was built following Ottoman attacks in 1420, with storerooms for the townsfolk built on the inside. The bell tower is detached from the church and forms part of the enclosing wall. Codlea is also easily reached direct from Brașov, both by train (*from 20mins*) and frequent minibuses (*26mins*) from Autogara 1.

The final stop on the circuit is **Ghimbav** (Vidombák/Weidenbach), a small town best known today as the designated site of Brașov airport, as well as for the IAR factory, manufacturing aircraft and helicopters. It lies 7km southeast of Codlea, heading towards Brașov. The fortified church (✆ *0268 258 176;* m *0761 177 267; call in advance to arrange a visit; 4RON*) dates from the late 13th century, and is surrounded by a polygonal defensive wall with towers whose roofs resemble the points of chisels, with a single slope towards the interior of the fortress. Ghimbav is also easy to reach from Brașov, with both trains (*15mins*) and frequent minibuses from Autogara Vest (*15mins*). With your own transport, to complete the church circuit, Cristian is just 5km from Ghimbav, to the southwest.

🏠 **Where to stay** Close to the centre of the village, **Conacul Ambient** (*13 rooms; Str Griviței 5;* m *0732 200 900;* e *reservations@conaculambient.ro;* w *conaculambient. ro;* **$$$$**) is a much more upmarket place than it looks from the outside, with an indoor pool and spa, nicely decorated Romanian restaurant and a pleasant garden.

POIANA BRAȘOV At an altitude of a little over 1,000m, Poiana Brașov (w *poianabrasov. com*) is the best-equipped ski resort in Romania, with 24km of slopes, two cable cars, a gondola, two chair lifts and five ski lifts. It sits just 12km from Brașov on DN1E. The resort is located at the foot of the Postăvaru Massif, which rises to an altitude of 1,799m. Brașov municipal bus 20 brings you here conveniently and cheaply every 30 minutes from the Livada Poștei bus stop in the centre of the city. Car parking in Poiana Brașov is charged at 12RON a day. The winter season typically runs from December to April, thanks in part to the use of snow cannons.

Poiana Brașov was first discovered by skiers at the end of the 19th century, and Romania's first ski competition was held here in 1906. The resort is popular with beginners, and the Bradul (Pine Tree) slope in particular can get fiercely busy. The Stadion slope is the gentlest of all, and also popular with those making their first forays on skis or snowboard. At the other end of the difficulty scale, the Lupului

POIANA SLOPES

Piste (*pârtia*) name	Difficulty	Length	Height
Bradul	beginner	430m	71m
Drumul Roșu	beginner/intermediate	4,752m	715m
Kanzel	advanced	297m	109m
Lupului	advanced	2,605m	728m
Stadion	beginner	612m	30m
Subteleferic	advanced	2,200m	650m
Sulinar	intermediate	2,820m	635m

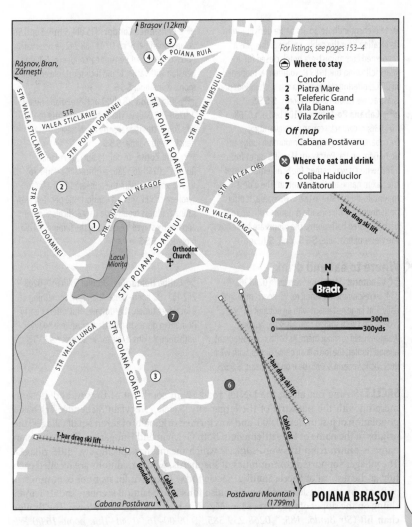

For listings, see pages 153–4

🛏 **Where to stay**

1 Condor
2 Piatra Mare
3 Teleferic Grand
4 Vila Diana
5 Vila Zorile

Off map
   Cabana Postăvaru

✖ **Where to eat and drink**

6 Coliba Haiducilor
7 Vânătorul

POIANA BRAȘOV

3

(Wolf) runs from close to the upper terminus of the gondola right back down into the resort – a height change of more than 700m.

A complex range of ski passes is available, using either a points-based system in which each ride in a cable car, chair lift or ski lift (✆ *0268 407 342;* e *office@ anateleferic.ro;* ⊕ *09.00–16.00 daily in season*) costs between 1 and 6 points, or on a time-based system. For the 2016/17 winter season examples included a full-day ski pass costing 145RON for adults and 80RON for children, or a 30-point ski pass costing 110RON for adults and 60RON for children.

🛏 Where to stay

🛏 **Hotel Piatra Mare** (186 rooms) Str Poiana Doamnei; ✆ 0268 262 021; e office@piatramare. ro; w piatramare.ro. Large 4-star hotel with a profile vaguely suggestive of a ski jump, offering a spa with large indoor pool. Its reception rooms

& conference facilities mean the place attracts wedding parties & corporate events. **$$$$**

🛏 **Teleferic Grand Hotel** (127 rooms) Str Poiana Soarelui 243; ✆ 0368 100 200; e frontoffice@telefericgrandhotel.ro;

w telefericgrandhotel.ro. Its name deriving from its location near the cable-car base, this was a renowned Communist-era hotel, closed for 20 years following the 1989 Revolution, & reopened in 2012, offering ski rentals, a spa with indoor pool & attractive wood-floored rooms. **$$$$**

🏠 **Cabana Postăvaru** (100 beds) ⚊0368 101 036; e contact@cabanapostavarul.ro; w cabanapostavaru.ro. This mountain lodge sits at 1,604m on the Postăvaru Massif & dates from 1883, when it was named the Schulerhütte after the Saxon name for the mountain. The oldest mountain shelter still in use in Romania, it offers both doubles with en suite & dorms with up to 6 beds & shared bathrooms. The rooms are basic but the views unbeatable. **$$$** (dbl), **$** (dorm)

🏠 **Pensiunea Condor** (15 dbl, 5 trpl, 2 apt) Str Poiana Doamnei 6; m 0744 688 242; e rezervari@ hotelcondor.ro; w pensiunea-condor.ro. A 3-star pension with rather bland if comfortable enough rooms & a sauna. **$$$**

🏠 **Vila Diana** (8 dbl, 1 apt) Str Poiana Ruia 3; ⚊0268 262 040; w vila-diana.com. Close to the Vila Zorile, this is a recently modernised 4-star pension with sauna. **$$$**

🏠 **Vila Zorile** (6 dbl, 11 apt) Str Poiana Ruia 6; ⚊0268 262 286; e office@vila-zorile.ro; w vila-zorile.ro. With the appearance of a large Tyrolean chalet, this is a comfortable pension with sauna & fitness room. Jude Law & Nicole Kidman apparently stayed here during the filming of *Cold Mountain*. **$$$**

✗ Where to eat and drink

✗ **Vânătorul** Str Poiana Soarelui; ⚊0268 262 354; w restaurant-vanatorul.ro; ⊕ noon–midnight daily. This large restaurant with an outdoor terrace is decorated with stuffed animals & the hunting weapons used to shoot them. As befitting a restaurant named 'Hunter', the focus is on game dishes, with wild duck, boar, venison & even bear on the menu. **$$$$**

✗ **Coliba Haiducilor** Drumul Sulinar; ⚊0268 262 137; ⊕ noon–01.00 Tue–Sun. Something of a local institution, the 'Outlaws' Hut' offers hearty Romanian dishes in a rustic atmosphere heavy with animal skins & live music some eves. **$$$**

SĂCELE Strung out along the DN1A road 12km southeast of Brașov, and close to merging with the outskirts of the larger city, Săcele (Négyfalu/Siebendörfer) has a population of just under 30,000, and was formed originally of seven small villages, the origins of the name of the settlement in both German and Hungarian. The Romanian name is drawn from the word *sătucele* which means, less specifically, 'little villages'. The villages supported communities of shepherds, whose traditions are recalled each July at the festival of **Săcele Sântilia**. Săcele today is known for its poor communities of Roma on the outskirts of town, but also for some beautiful scenery, and its winter skiing on the slopes of the Piatra Mare Massif, which rises above the town. The **Bunloc chair lift** (*Str Bunloc 185;* ⚊*0268 259 585;* ⊕ *09.00–16.00 Sat–Thu, noon–16.00 Fri; adult/child 30/16RON round trip, 20/10RON one-way*) provides an easy way of getting up into the hills. The spot has become a particularly popular one for paragliding.

SAXON FORTIFIED CHURCHES NORTHEAST OF BRAȘOV There is a collection of some of the most interesting of the Saxon fortified churches in southern Transylvania in the plains to the northeast of Brașov.

Hărman The fortified church in Hărman (Szászhermángy/Hönigberg) (*Str Pieții 2;* m *0729 745 210;* e *info@harmaninfo.com;* w *harmaninfo.com;* ⊕ *Apr–Oct 09.00–18.00 Mon–Sat, 10.00–18.00 Sun, Nov–Mar 10.00–18.00 daily; adult/child 10/5 RON*) has much in common with that in neighbouring Prejmer (pages 155–6), in being very clearly a fortress in structure, albeit one centred on the church. The latter is mentioned in a royal document of 1240 granting Hărman and several nearby churches in the Burzenland region to the Cistercian monks. Originally built as a Romanesque basilica, with a triple-nave structure, it was remodelled in the Gothic style in the 15th and 16th centuries. Note the decidedly frugal-looking wooden pews, built of a single plank of wood: these were women's pews, designed in this fashion because the female dress of the time was not easily combinable with backrests. The square bell tower, at 56m, is the tallest in the Burzenland. The four mini spires at each corner around the main one are apparently an indicator of the town's legal power to administer the death sentence.

The fortifications, which take the form of a near-circular wall around the church, were progressively built up from the mid 15th century, as a result of the increasing dangers of Ottoman attacks. As at Prejmer, the fortifications around the entrance are the most impressive, reflecting the greater vulnerability of this area. A barrel-vaulted entrance passageway runs for 20m beneath the gate tower. The arcaded walkway in front of this, again similar to one at Prejmer, is a more modern and decorative addition, dating from 1814. The whole structure was surrounded by a moat.

Inside the walls there is a small museum, with displays of Saxon interiors, costumes and a mocked-up schoolroom. There is a recording in the local dialect: as a display panel puts it in a decidedly tongue-twister fashion: 'Siebenbürgisch – Sächsisch ist die Sprache der Siebenbürger Sachsen'. And you can climb wooden staircases up into the defensive walls themselves.

Abutting the defensive wall is the chapel tower. Climb a small flight of steps to reach a vaulted room covered with late 15th-century paintings: a rare example in Transylvania of such a complete survival of medieval murals. Looking into the room from the door, you face a Crucifixion scene in the far wall; a portrayal of the Virgin Mary and child in the ceiling above, and a Last Judgement to either side; Heaven to your right and Hell to your left, the latter heavy with naked figures in boiling cauldrons.

Hărman is just 10km northeast of Braşov, lying just off the main E574 road. There are frequent **buses** (*half-hourly at peak hours; 10–20mins*) from Braşov Autogara 3. There is also a less frequent **train** service from Braşov, but Hărman railway station is located at the south end of town, just off the E574, and inconvenient for the fortified church.

Where to stay There is very basic but clean accommodation at the **Evangelical Church Guesthouse** (*4 rooms; Str Pieţii 5; contact details as for church;* **$**), in the green-walled building across the road from the church. There's no breakfast, but guests have access to the communal kitchen.

✳ Prejmer Prejmer (Prázsmár/Tartlau) lies at the easternmost edge of the area of Saxon settlement in Transylvania, and in this area, which is particularly vulnerable to external attack, it offers an example of fortified church which sits very much at the fortress end of the spectrum. It is one of the seven fortified churches of Transylvania specifically named on the UNESCO World Heritage list in 1999. The **church** (✆ *0268 362 052;* e *evkirche.tartlau@yahoo.de;* w *cetateaprejmer.ro;* ⊕ *Apr–Oct 09.00–18.00 Mon–Fri, 09.00–17.00 Sat, 11.00–17.00 Sun, Nov–Mar 09.00–16.00 Mon–Sat, 11.00–15.00 Sun; adult/child 10/5 RON*) was built by the Teutonic Knights in the early 13th century, in the form of a Greek cross. Following the banishment of the Teutonic Knights in 1240 it was one of several churches in the area to pass to the Cistercians, whose remodelling included the addition of Gothic vaulting. The altar features a mid 15th-century Gothic triptych, said to be the oldest such work in Romania painted on both sides. Note the carpets draped over the front pews, in a more modest version of the Anatolian carpet decoration found in the Black Church in Braşov.

The construction of elaborate fortress walls began in earnest after the first invasion of Turks into Transylvania in 1421. They take the form of a circular ring wall between 12m and 14m in height, and up to 5m thick at the base. The entrance to the fortress church was its most vulnerable point, and is accordingly particularly

3

elaborately defended. Entrance is through a vaulted corridor 32m in length, with a portcullis in the middle. Arranged along the inside of the fortress walls are more than 270 individually numbered rooms, on between two and four levels, connected by wooden stairs and walkways, which were used by individual families both for refuge and to store provisions in readiness for the next siege. There was even a schoolroom at which children could continue with their lessons during sieges. This is decorated with frescoes dating from the 18th century and laid out as a (rather more modern) classroom.

Basic **accommodation** is available at the Evangelical Church Guesthouse over the road (*contact details as for the church; also* m *0749 800 024*).

Prejmer is 8km from Hărman on route 10. If travelling by **train** from Braşov note that Ilieni station is closer to the church than Prejmer station itself, though neither is hugely convenient. A better bet are the frequent **minibuses** from Braşov Autogara Vest (*40mins*). There is a faster **bus** service from Braşov Autogara 1, but there are only three departures daily.

Sânpetru Just 5km north of Braşov, Sânpetru (Barcaszentpéter/Petersberg) has at its centre a 13th-century fortified church (*Str Republicii nr 642;* \ *0268 360 550;* m *0744 308 141;* w *sanpetru.sitew.org;* ⊕ *Apr–Oct 11.00–17.00 Wed–Sat, noon–17.00 Sun, Nov–Mar 11.00–16.00 Wed–Sat, noon–16.00 Sun; 5RON*). It was one of the Burzenland churches granted to the Cistercians following the expulsion of the Teutonic Knights. The church suffered various forms of damage, including its bell tower twice collapsing in the 18th century, and the building was demolished in the 1790s, with the tower erected at the other end, where the ground was found to be more stable. Around the church is an encircling inner defensive wall with more than 100 rooms arranged in two storeys in which local families would store provisions and find refuge in times of siege. Of particular note is a chapel, built around 1400 and set in the inner defensive wall, decorated with wall paintings depicting Heaven and Hell.

There are frequent **buses** from Braşov's Autogara 1 (*12mins*).

🏠 **Where to stay** Hotel Bielmann (*27 rooms; Str Republicii 133;* \ *0268 360 365;* e *office@hotel-bielmann.ro;* w *hotel-bielmann.ro;* **$$$$**) is a homely place, every inch of whose bar and restaurant area is covered in ornaments. Numerous well-fed cats seem to rule the roost. It has an outdoor pool and tennis court and a good restaurant (**$$$$**) with a mix of Romanian and pasta dishes. Its substantial prices may reflect its proximity to Braşov.

Bod Bod (Botfalu/Brenndorf) provides an example of a fortified church (*Str Tudor Vladimirescu 138; contact Manfred Copony;* m *0721 982 431*) for which earthquakes proved its undoing. Originally a Romanesque basilica dating from the 13th century, the original church was completely destroyed in a quake in 1802, and the present airy building, its pews and balconies painted in pastel green, dates from the start of the 19th century. There are just a few reminders of the old church, notably a stone font from 1491. Cracks to the side of the building are further damage wrought by the earthquake of 1977.

Keyholder Manfred Copony is the tenant of the parish house (*Str Tudor Vladimirescu 135;* **$**), in which he has set up a small exhibition on the Saxons of Bod, and also rents out four basic guest rooms.

Bod is 8km north of Hărman. There are hourly **buses** weekdays (every 2 hours at weekends) from Braşov Autogara 1, and more frequent minibuses from Braşov Autogara Vest. Both take around 25 minutes.

RUPEA Some 60km northwest of Braşov on the busy E60 highway, Rupea (Kőhalom/Reps) provides a landmark on the journey by virtue of its impressive hilltop fortress (*Cetatea Rupea;* m *0728 950 646;* ⊕ *Apr–Oct 09.00–20.00 daily, Nov–Mar 09.00–17.00 daily; adult/child 10/5RON*). It has recently been restored with the help of EU regional development funding. The restoration has, however, given the structure a decidedly new feel. Built between the 14th and 17th centuries on a strategic site at the confluence of important trading routes, it has three sets of walls, set out in the form of an ascending spiral. Some of the houses built within the fortress complex in the 16th and 17th centuries have been restored, as have a chapel and several square-based defensive towers, but there is nothing to see inside them. The views from the fortress down to the village of Rupea below and across the surrounding countryside are first rate, and give a clear feel for the importance of the site's strategic location.

HOMOROD The main E60 road bypasses Homorod (Homoród/Hamruden), but you might like to make a small detour to see the 13th-century fortified church (*contact Elisabeta Marton;* \ *0268 286 609*). Worthy of note here are the Romanesque wall paintings in the old choir beneath the bell tower. The latter can be climbed, though is a somewhat rickety experience. The church was remodelled in the late 18th century, including with the addition of a new choir. Two curtain walls surround the church, but the outer one is incomplete, having made way for the construction of a school.

Homorod is some 3km off the main road: the turning is at Rupea Gara.

VISCRI The village of Viscri (Szászfehéregyháza/Deustchweisskirch) has become something of a focus for tourists keen to get to learn more about the Saxon villages of southern Transylvania. The reason Viscri gets so much attention is to do partly with the quality of its fortified church, which is one of those inscribed on the UNESCO World Heritage list, and partly the attention the village has received from organisations and individuals dedicated to the preservation of traditional architecture and ways of life. The Mihai Eminescu Trust has restored many buildings in the village and its Romanian director, Caroline Fernolend, lives in the village. The Romanian foundation established by His Royal Highness The Prince of Wales, the **Fundaţia Prinţul de Wales România**, has a centre in the village supporting training in traditional crafts and architectural preservation. It is a picture-postcard place, though the apparently tranquil village life hides social tensions, particularly around the changing ethnic mix of the place as Roma families have moved in to properties abandoned by ethnic Saxons departing for Germany.

The **fortified church** (m *0742 077 506;* ⊕ *Mar–Oct 10.00–13.00 & 15.00–18.00 daily, Nov–Feb by appointment; 5RON*) sits on a hill above the village. The first church was built here in the 12th century by the Székelys, who lived here before the arrival of the Saxons. The latter enlarged the church in the 13th century, and it was fortified around 1500. The interior of the church is dominated by painted wooden galleries around three walls. A ceiling of panelled squares dates from 1743, when the earlier Gothic net vaulting was demolished. A defensive wall surrounds the church. The walls also house a small but interesting museum chronicling the traditions of the Saxon community of the village. There is also a bacon tower, where families kept their hams in community storage.

To get here turn left off the main E60 road between Braşov and Sighişoara at Buneşti. Viscri is 7km away, on a minor road.

🏠 Where to stay

🏠 Viscri 125 (10 dbl) House 125; **m** 0723 579 489; **e** contact@viscri125.ro; **w** viscri125.ro. Traditionally furnished rooms in an upmarket restored property. They offer a range of workshops, from cookery to photography, as well as bookable activities from truffle hunting to bread making. **$$$$**

🏠 Mihai Eminescu Trust See page 17 for booking & contact details. The Trust has 5 guesthouses in Viscri: houses 38, 39, 63, 63B & 129. 3 of these are 1-bedroom guesthouses, but House 39 has 2 bedrooms, & House 38 (*which is booked direct rather than centrally through the Trust:*

m *0748 126 616*) has 3. Local meals made by the guesthouse host are available at an additional charge. Most of the guesthouses are closed during the winter months. **$$$**

🏠 Fundaţia Prinţul de Wales România Str Principală 163; **m** 0745 575 989; **w** printuldewales.org. Located in a beautifully restored blue-walled building in the heart of the village, this facility provides B&B accommodation when it is not being used for training courses. **$$$–$$**

SAXON FORTIFIED CHURCHES NORTH OF VISCRI

Criţ The village of Criţ (Szászkeresztúr/Deutschkreuz) has by no means the most important of the Saxon fortified churches of Transylvania, but through the work of the Mihai Eminescu Trust and the presence of some good guesthouses has become something of a favoured accommodation choice for those visiting the many fortified churches in this area.

The **church** (*for the key call* **m** *0740 597 493, or ask at the Casa Kraus pension next door*) was built only in 1810–13, on the site of an earlier building which was deemed too small for the needs of the community. It has a spacious, airy interior, with a barrel-vaulted ceiling and a double gallery at the back. There is a small display of traditional local costumes at the back of the church. The defence wall around the church is much earlier, and has four of the original five towers standing. There is a display of agricultural implements in an old barn on the inside of the walls.

Criţ is just off the busy E60 highway between Braşov and Sighişoara, and visible from it.

🏠 *Where to stay*

🏠 Casa Kraus (9 rooms) House 25, Criţ; **m** 0743 255 553; **e** rezervari@casa-kraus.ro. Nicely appointed upmarket pension right next to the fortified church, with rooms elegantly furnished with traditional Saxon items, a brick-vaulted dining room & fine terrace, albeit overlooking the noisy main road. **$$$$**

🏠 Mihai Eminescu Trust See page 17 for booking & contact details. Runs 2 guesthouses in Criţ, at houses 217 & 218, each with 2 bedrooms. Meals based around local ingredients can be prepared by the guesthouse host & are charged separately. **$$$**

Meşendorf The village of Meşendorf (Mese/Meschendorf) lies 6km on from Criţ, on the same road. Its **fortified church** (*key at House 102, on the road above the church;* **m** *0740 903 744*) is an early Gothic hall church, built in the 14th century. It was strengthened for defensive purposes in 1495, including the fortification of the tower with a wooden defence level, and a defence storey over the nave. The compact interior is dominated by a wooden gallery along three walls, decorated with floral panels. The choir is barrel-vaulted, but the earlier vaulting in the nave has been replaced with a flat stucco ceiling. An inner defensive wall dates from the 15th century, with an outer wall added to the southern part of the complex in the 16th. The tower with the timber defence storey at the western end of this outer wall was used as the 'bacon tower' by villagers to store their ham and bacon. Part of this outer wall was demolished to make room for the German-language school, now derelict.

4

Covasna County

Covasna County, which rises up into the Eastern Carpathian range running along its eastern borders, is known in Romania for its spa resorts, a legacy of past volcanic activity, notably in the eponymous town of Covasna. One particularly unusual treatment here is provided by mofettes – dry 'saunas' where patients sit or stand in empty 'pools' while dense low-lying gases enter the skin, bringing various medical benefits (see box, page 171).

It is also known for the predominance of Székelys among the local population. Almost three-quarters of its inhabitants are ethnic Hungarian, mostly Székely, forming the second-highest concentration of Székelys in Romania after neighbouring Harghita County. Historically, the area formed much of the Háromszék administrative region of the Kingdom of Hungary. A *szék* in Hungarian is a seat, and Háromszék combined three Székely administrative units, Kézdiszék, Orbaiszék and Sepsiszék, its name meaning 'Three Chairs'. It is a great region in which to get to know the Székely culture better. There are many spots, for example when passing through the village of Oituz on national road 11 between Târgu Secuiesc and the neighbouring region of Moldova, at which stalls offer *kürtőskalács*, the sweet chimney-shaped cake that is a symbol of the Székely areas. And settlements are distinguished by the beautiful and elaborate wooden Székely gates (see box, page 169).

Finally, the county is distinguished by a number of interesting touristic activities developed by aristocratic Hungarian families, who were displaced from the area during the Communist period but have since returned to lay claim to their former properties. The Kálnoky guesthouses at Micloşoara and Mikes Castle in Zăbala are both excellent bases to explore the area, including its flora and fauna.

SFÂNTU GHEORGHE *Telephone code 0267*

Sfântu Gheorghe (Sepsiszentgyörgy/Sankt Georgen), pronounced 'SFUN-too-gay-OR-gay', taking its name from the famous dragon-slaying saint, is a town on the Olt River. It is known for its textiles industry, has more than its fair share of 1960s concrete blocks and is far from being the most attractive county town in Transylvania. But it merits a visit for its excellent Székely National Museum, a pleasant area around Elisabeth Park, some buildings of the distinctive architect Károly Kós, and for the opportunities offered here to learn more about Székely culture.

Some three-quarters of the local people are ethnic Hungarians, mostly Székelys, and there are many examples around the town of an ongoing cultural rift between the Székely-dominated local administration and the office of the Prefect, an appointee of Bucharest. Thus a dispute arose in 2016 over an attempt by the local authorities to extend Elisabeth Park, as this was deemed to obstruct the view of the statue of Romanian hero Mihai Viteazul: at the time of research the park extension

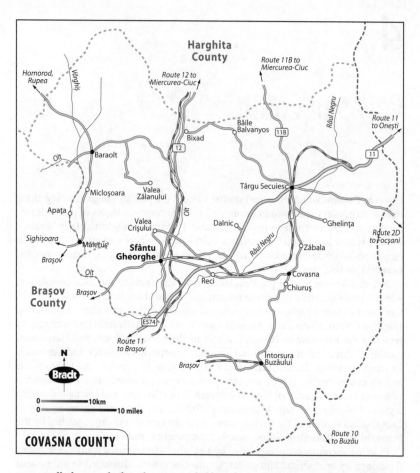

was a stalled mound of earth, surrounded by a fence. And Strada 1 Decembrie 1918, a street whose name commemorates the union of Transylvania with Romania, also features a plaque identifying it as Strada Petőfi Sándor, taking its name from the Hungarian revolutionary hero. Which is all rather confusing for the foreign visitor.

HISTORY Sfântu Gheorghe was first mentioned in 1332, though there is evidence of human settlement here from Neolithic times. It developed from the 15th century, being granted market status in 1461, and had an advantageous trading position between Transylvania and Moldavia. It was an important centre within the Kingdom of Hungary as the capital of Háromszék County, administering an area which covered present-day Covasna County and part of Brașov County. However, Tatar and Ottoman attacks in 1658 and 1661 respectively devastated the town. In the second half of the 19th century, Sfântu Gheorghe developed as a centre for textile and cigarette production. It is a major centre of Székely cultural identity, including through the work of the theatres, galleries and other cultural spaces in the town.

GETTING THERE AND AWAY The **railway station** (*Str Gării;* \0267 325 850) is 2km east of the centre along Strada 1 Decembrie 1918, across the Olt River from the town centre. There are some 15 trains daily to Brașov (*from 30mins*) and 11 to Miercurea-

Ciuc (*from 1hr*). The **bus station** (*Str Gării 2;* ☎*0267 314 630*) is 50m north of the railway station. There is also a useful separate bus service to Brașov, with departures every 30 minutes (*from 40mins*), leaving from the much more central Multitrans Bus Station (*Str Császár Bálint 6;* ☎*0267 315 368*) near the central market.

 WHERE TO STAY

🏠 Ferdinánd Panzió (7 dbl, 1 sgl, 2 apt) Str 1 Decembrie 1918 10; m 0740 180 502; e fp@zoltur. ro; w restatferdinand.ro. In an internal courtyard, accessed through an arch, this is a quiet pension in a renovated 19th-century building. There's no restaurant, but they do have a coffee shop, the Ferdinánd Presso, decorated with photos of British skier Robert Poth, a relative of the owners. **$$$**

🏠 Șugáș Hotel and Restaurant (24 dbl, 5 apt) Str 1 Decembrie 1918 12; ☎0267 312 171; e hotel@sugaskert.ro; w sugaskert.ro. A 3-star hotel right in the centre of town in a 2-storey concrete building wrapped around a courtyard. Its restaurant (**$$$**), offering some local dishes & a summer terrace, is also a good option. **$$$**

✕ WHERE TO EAT AND DRINK

✕ Bastion Str Oltului 6; ☎0367 800 801; ⏰ 11.00–23.00 daily. Located round the back of the pastel-green Arcuș Cultural Centre, this is a cosy place in winter, & has a nice terrace in summer. Pizza is the speciality here, but a wide range of other dishes are available. **$$$**

✕ Central Str 1 Decembrie 1918 8; m 0744 757 515; w centralrestaurant.ro; ⏰ 08.00–midnight Mon–Fri, 10.00–midnight Sat/Sun. Logically enough, a centrally located place, with a wide-ranging menu including some Székely dishes. Good-value lunch buffet (**$$**) Mon–Fri. **$$$**

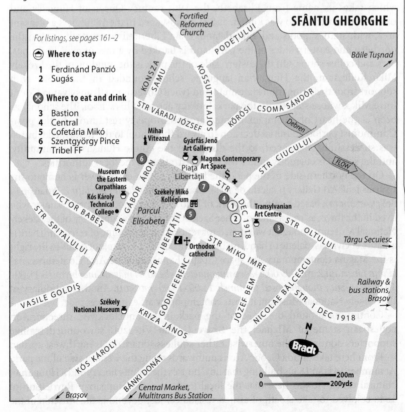

For listings, see pages 161–2

⬛ **Where to stay**
1 Ferdinánd Panzió
2 Sugás

❌ **Where to eat and drink**
3 Bastion
4 Central
5 Cofetária Mikó
6 Szentgyörgy Pince
7 Tribel FF

SFÂNTU GHEORGHE

✗ Szentgyörgy Pince Str Gabor Áron 14; ✆0267 352 666; w szentgyorgypince.ro; ⏱ 10.00–midnight daily. 'St George's Cellar' is an atmospheric place offering Hungarian & international dishes in a somewhat hard-to-find spot round the back of a building on Str Gabor Áron. $$$

✗ Cofetária Mikó Str Gröf Mikó Imre 1; m 0721 200 603; ⏱ 09.00–21.00 daily. Central café across from Elisabeth Park with a particularly fine range of sticky cakes. $

✗ Tribel FF Str 1 Decembrie 1918 2; ✆0267 352 353; ⏱ 07.00–22.00 Mon–Fri, 09.00–22.00 Sat/Sun. Good & central fast-food place serving local dishes over the counter, plus b/fast. There is also a café here. $

OTHER PRACTICALITIES

$ OTP Bank Str 1 Decembrie 1918 9; ⏱ 09.00–17.30 Mon–Fri

✚ Farmacia Dona Str Ciucului 1; ✆0372 407 231; ⏱ 08.00–21.00 Mon–Fri, 08.00–16.00 Sat

✉ Post office Str 1 Decembrie 1918 18; ⏱ 08.00–19.00 Mon–Fri, 09.00–13.00 Sat. Housed in the rather faded early 20th-century building that was once home to the Hotel Hungaria.

ℹ Tourist information office Piața Libertății 7; ✆0267 316 474; e sepsinfo@sepsi.ro; w www.saintgeorgeinfo.ro

WHAT TO SEE AND DO

Around Elisabeth Park The town centres on Elisabeth Park (Parcul Elísabeta), which takes its name from Elisabeth, the 19th-century Queen of Hungary and Empress of Austria who was known as Sisi. Landscaped in the 1880s, it is a pleasant area, with statues, pools and a bandstand. Piața Libertății wraps itself around the northern and eastern sides of the park, and is flanked by a mix of civic buildings, bars and coffee shops. On the eastern side of the park is the building of the **Székely Mikó Kollégium**, the Hungarian-language school founded in the 1850s with support from the Hungarian statesman and twice Governor of Transylvania Count Imre Mikó, whose statue is in the park, looking across at his school. The school has been at the heart of a complex dispute around property restitution: in the post-Communist period an initial decision to award the school to the Reformed Church was successfully challenged, to the dismay of the ethnic Hungarian community, and the school is currently under the administration of the local authorities.

On the northern side of the park, the building with a clock tower is home to the **Gyárfás Jenő Art Gallery** (Galeria de Artă Gyárfás Jenő) (*Piața Libertății 2;* ✆*0267 314 367;* w *sznm.ro*), based around the work of Jenő Gyárfás, a noted portrait painter who lived in the town, as well as that of other Székely artists. It is a subsidiary of the Székely National Museum, though it was closed for renovation at the time of research. There is a statue of Gyárfás, palette in hand, on the square outside. A couple of doors to the right is the **Magma Contemporary Art Space** (Spațiu Expozițional de Artă Contemporană) (*Piața Libertății 2;* m *0729 007 424;* e *magma@maybe.ro;* w *magma.maybe.ro;* ⏱ *11.00–19.00 Tue–Sun, though closed for lunch 14.00–15.00 Sat/Sun*). Another subsidiary of the Székely National Museum, it hosts contemporary art exhibitions.

Continuing around the edge of the park in an anticlockwise direction, an equestrian statue of **Michael the Brave** (Mihai Viteazul) surrounded by five supporters dominates the otherwise rather soulless square on its northwest corner.

From here take Strada Gábor Áron southwards along the western side of the park. At number 14 is an 1830s building that now houses the county library and a Hungarian cultural centre. It was here that the local leaders of the Hungarian Revolution of 1848 resolved to take a path of armed resistance. Just beyond is the **Museum of the**

Eastern Carpathians (Muzeul Național al Carpaților Răsăriteni) (*Str Gábor Áron 16;* \0267 314 139; e *secretariat@mncr.ro;* w *mncr.ro;* ⊕ *10.00–16.00 Tue–Fri; adult/child 6/1.5RON*), which emerged out of an archaeology section of the National History Museum of Transylvania, set up in Sfântu Gheorghe in 1995, and hosts temporary exhibitions. The large white building next to it was designed by architect Károly Kós in the 1920s to house a girls' school, and is now host to a technical high school named after the architect. There is a bust of Károly Kós out the front.

The Székely National Museum (Muzeul Național Secuiesc; HU: Székely Nemzeti Múzeum) (*Str Kós Károly 10;* \0267 312 442; w *sznm.ro;* ⊕ *Jun–Aug 09.00–17.00 Tue–Sun, Sep–May 09.00–16.00 Tue–Fri, 09.00–14.00 Sat/Sun; adult/child 10/5RON*) Just south of the city park, the Székely National Museum is a highlight of a visit to Sfântu Gheorghe. It is housed in an exuberant building designed in 1911 by the architect Károly Kós, with colourful tiled spires, to house a collection which had been built up from the 1870s. It covers archaeology, history and ethnography, highlighting in particular the origins, identity and heroes of the Székelys, for example with a full room devoted to Áron Gábor, the artillery officer who produced cannons for the Hungarian Revolution of 1848–49, in which he was killed.

Other sights At the northeastern corner of Piața Libertății, as it joins Strada 1 Decembrie 1918, is a classically posed statue of **St George** on horseback, despatching a supine dragon. Head eastwards from here along Strada 1 Decembrie 1918 to find, guarding a roundabout, a different take on the story. Here George is astride the back of a tubby dragon, and it is far from clear whether he is intent on killing the beast or just taking a ride. Between the two statues, the ugly modern glass-fronted building opposite the Sugás Hotel houses the **Transylvanian Art Centre** (Central Artistic Transilvănean) (⊕ *10.00–17.00 Tue–Fri, 10.00–14.00 Sat/Sun*). A subordinate unit of the Székely National Museum, it hosts temporary art exhibitions.

The **Fortified Reformed Church** (Biserica Reformată Fortificată) (*Str Cetății 1*) lies some distance northwest of the centre, suitably enough on Piața Calvin, the only surviving medieval building in the town, which has weathered damage wrought by Tatars and earthquakes. The cemetery behind the church has good examples of wooden Székely grave posts (*kopjafák*). Situated on a small hill, together with a building that once housed the German School, and another chapel, the church is part of a small complex known as the **Cetatea** ('Fortress').

AROUND SFÂNTU GHEORGHE

MICLOȘOARA Micloșoara (HU: Miklósvár) is a Székely village with a mostly ethnic Hungarian population. In an estate abutting the village, **Kálnoky Castle** (Castelul Kálnoky) is an elongated rectangular building with bastion-like structures at either end. It was constructed by István Kálnoky from 1648, though has had various later additions, including a large porch with Corinthian columns. Following the deaths of various members of the Kálnoky family without issue, the estate was eventually sold outside the family, and in the Communist period was used as a community centre for the village. It is being restored through the work of Count Tibor Kálnoky, who has taken back the family estate on a long lease, and will house a **Museum of Transylvanian Life** (Muzeul Vieții Transilvăniene), together with some accommodation.

Tibor Kálnoky has been a pioneer of a style of higher-end tourism in Transylvania which promotes traditional livelihoods and buildings, and his guesthouses here are the main reason Micloşoara is on the Transylvanian tourist map. A stay provides an excellent insight into Transylvanian village life. On warm summer evenings everyone sits outside their houses at dusk to watch the daily promenade home of the cattle along the main street. It is a wonderful rural sight and each cow knows instinctively which yard to turn into. Count Kálnoky has also renovated a small building on the main street as The Wet House, where drinks are served to guests in the summer.

In both the guesthouses and the castle you may spot various examples of the distinctive Kálnoky family crest: a bear with an arrow through its mouth, sitting on a crown. The tale behind this is that King Louis I of Hungary was surprised at close quarters by a bear while hunting. He was about to be devoured by this huge beast, when the captain of his guard, a Kálnoky family ancestor, put an arrow clean through the bear's mouth with a long-range shot. The grateful king duly rewarded him with the crest his family still, er, bears.

Count Kálnoky and his family also operate a riding centre, based in Valea Crişului (HU: Sepsikőröspatak), where there is another Kálnoky family estate, a few kilometres north of the county capital, Sfântu Gheorghe. **Kálnoky's Equestrian Centre Transylvania** specialises in one-week trail-riding holidays, including five days of trail riding between village guesthouses, and the last two nights at the Kálnoky guesthouses in Micloşoara. Guests in Micloşoara can also book day rides at the centre, including transfers. The horses are locally bred and include the Huzul, unique to this area, as well as locally bred Lipizzaners and Arabs. Riding lessons are also available (*adults €25 for a 45min lesson*).

The village of **Apaţa** 9km to the south of Micloşoara and just across the border in Braşov County holds an interesting traditional festival in April, the **Rooster Shoot** (Împuşcatul Cocoşului) (📞 *0268 284 503*). This is based on a legend that back in the 16th century, when Tatar invaders were sacking the area, the local villagers hid themselves in the fortress. The Tatars were on the point of leaving the area when they heard the crow of a rooster, which led them to the fortress, where they massacred the unfortunate villagers. The few survivors held the rooster responsible for their misfortunes. You will be relieved to hear that the event is no longer focused on the shooting of actual roosters, but rather takes the form of a children's archery competition, in which they try to hit a wooden panel with a rooster painted onto it.

Getting there and away By **car**, from Braşov drive north on the E60/route 13 towards Sighişoara and fork right after 33km just before the village of Măieruş. Turn right in the heart of the village and cross a (somewhat rickety) bridge over the Olt River. Turn left and drive north for 13km through the villages of Belin and Aita Mare before reaching Micloşoara. After the church, go down the hill and you'll see on your right a large wooden gate in front of a big white house at number 186. Turn sharp right and park in the courtyard at the back. For an additional fee the Kálnoky guesthouses will arrange a **pickup service** from Bucharest, Târgu Mureş or Cluj-Napoca airports or Braşov railway station.

⌂ Where to stay, eat and drink

✳ ⌂ **Count Kálnoky's Guesthouses** (10 rooms) Str Principală 186; m 0742 202 586; e k@transylvaniancastle.com; w transylvaniancastle.com. Housed in 2 separate complexes in the villages, 1 with 4 rooms & the restaurant building, the other with 6 rooms around an idyllic garden & yard, this place has been furnished impressively with antique Székely & Saxon furniture. Dinner is served communally, following an aperitif of *chimion*, a sweet Székely tipple with a caraway flavour. A programme of day tours to local attractions can be booked, as well as horse-&-cart rides (*€20pp for 2hrs*). **$$$–$$**

VALEA ZĂLANULUI For those visitors looking really to get away from it all in Transylvania, the hamlet of Valea Zălanului (Zalánpatak/Zalanyer Glashütte) has just 120 inhabitants and is accessed along a gravel track. The settlement originally serviced a small glass factory established here by the Kálnoky family, which has long ceased to exist. The property which formerly belonged to the senior official responsible for the administration of both the glassworks and the village has been purchased by HRH The Prince of Wales, a strong supporter of the preservation of traditional architecture and rural lifestyles in Transylvania, who has stayed here on private visits to Transylvania. When HRH is not in residence the house is available for tourists, making for a relaxing Transylvanian retreat in a beautiful rural setting.

Where to stay

✳ 🏠 The Prince of Wales's Guesthouse (7 dbl) Valea Zălanului, House 1; m 0742 202 586; e k@transylvaniancastle.com; w transylvaniancastle.com. Delightfully furnished rooms in 3 adjacent cottages, administered by Count Kálnoky's Guesthouses. They offer all-inclusive packages, with FB, based around local food & wine, & local activities include walks & visits to local craftsmen. Bicycle hire, bear watching & airport transfers are also available for an additional fee. The accent is on traditional rural living: there is no TV & motor vehicles are only used for transfers out of the village. Proceeds from the guesthouse go to HRH The Prince of Wales Foundation in Romania. **$$$$$**

BĂILE BALVANYOS Băile Balvanyos (HU: Bálványosfürdő) is a **spa resort** in the mountains on the northern border of Covasna County. It lies at an altitude of more than 800m on the southern slopes of the Bodoc Mountains, in a scenic tree-covered mountainside setting. At the heart of a former volcanic region, its attractions lie not only in the present-day spa resort but also in a range of curious features linked to the volcanic activity. Lacul Sfânta Ana, formed from an extinct volcanic crater, is just 10km away, just over the border in Harghita County. The **Pucioasa ('Sulphur') Hill** area is home to a number of small caves which form natural mofettes (page 171) through the concentrations of carbon dioxide and sulphurous gases to be found there. One bears the ominous name of Peşteră Ucigaşă ('Murderous Cave') for its particularly high concentrations of poisonous gases. This is one not to enter, though the Peşteră Puturoasă ('Stinking Cave') has been used as a mofette for more than a century. The most macabre of the local sights is the so-called **Birds' Cemetery**, an accumulation of heavy carbon dioxide gas where the gallery of an old sulphur mine collapsed. Birds flying too low drop dead as they pass through. Another nice walk is up to the ruined 13th-century **Balvanyos Fortress**. This was owned by the aristocratic Hungarian Apor family, who abandoned it in the 17th century in favour of a more comfortable manor in the nearby village of Turia (HU: Torja).

The **Alms of the Pig** (Festivalul Pomana Porcului) takes place in Băile Balvanyos in February, an event based around teams each sacrificing a pig and then preparing its meat in the traditional local way.

Băile Balvanyos is located on a winding minor mountain road between Târgu Secuiesc (20km) and Băile Tuşnad (21km), the most convenient railway station. There is no public transport.

Where to stay

🏠 Grand Hotel Balvanyos (6 sgl, 95 dbl, 11 apt) 📞0267 360 700; w balvanyosresort.ro. Large 4-star hotel at the centre of the Balvanyos Resort complex which includes the upmarket Grand Santerra Spa, an adventure park & even a petting zoo. **$$$$**

🏠 **Istvana** (9 rooms inside pension, 3 separate apts, 5 cabins) Băile Balvanyos 77; 📞 0267 365 277; e contact@complexulistvana.ro; w complexulistvana.ro. Small & rustic complex offering a range of accommodation types, including 4-bed apts, basic wooden chalets & a pension. There is a restaurant & outdoor pool. **$$** (pension), **$** (chalets)

TÂRGU SECUIESC Târgu Secuiesc (Kézdivásárhely/Szekler Neumarkt) is a quiet Székely town of some 18,000 people. Its role as a market town is central to its name in all three languages: 'marketplace' being *târg* in Romanian and *vásárhely* in Hungarian. The 'Kézdi' in the Hungarian name is a reference to the Székely Kézdi seat, one of the three that made up the Háromszék administrative unit; the Székelys in this area having first settled around present-day Saschiz, in Mureş County, which is known as Szászkézd in Hungarian. It was first mentioned in 1407 and 20 years later the Hungarian King Sigismund of Luxembourg granted it town status. Once an important trading point on routes to Moldavia, it has gradually been eclipsed by other urban centres, including Sfântu Gheorghe, and now has a decidedly out-of-the-way feel, though a pleasant one.

THE PIED PIPER RE-EMERGES

In Transylvania there's a tribe
Of alien people who ascribe
The outlandish ways and dress
On which their neighbours lay such stress,
To their fathers and mothers having risen
Out of some subterraneous prison
Into which they were trepanned
Long time ago in a mighty band
Out of Hamelin town in Brunswick land,
But how or why, they don't understand.

Robert Browning *The Pied Piper of Hamelin*

The Pied Piper is the subject of a legend from the town of Hamelin in Germany. The tale runs that, in 1284, the town was suffering from a rat infestation and a man dressed in colourful stripy clothes appeared, saying he could solve the rat problem. He used a musical pipe to lure the rats into the Weser River. When the townspeople welched on his payment, he played his pipe again and this time lured the town's children who followed him out of the town. The children disappeared into a cave and were never seen again.

The Saxons of Transylvania provided a postscript to this well-known tale, which is the denouement referred to by Browning. To explain why this population of blonde-haired, blue-eyed German-speakers lived in southern Transylvania, so far from their compatriots in Germany, a further legend developed: they were the descendants of the children taken from Hamelin by the Pied Piper, had journeyed for hundreds of miles underground, and then popped up to the surface from a Transylvanian cave. This is said to be the bat-filled cave of Mereşti, sometimes also identified as Almas, one of the numerous caves in the beautiful gorge of the Vârghiş River which straddles the boundary of Covasna and Harghita counties some 25km north of Micloşoara, beyond Baraolt. It is one of the day trips offered from Count Kálnoky's Guesthouses (page 164).

The town centres on the long and narrow Piaţa Gábor Áron, which holds a park and a statue of Áron Gábor standing in front of a cannon. This commemorates the town's role as the centre for the production of artillery for the Hungarian revolutionaries of 1848–49, under the supervision of Gábor, who was killed during the revolution. Radiating out from this square is a series of narrow alleyways, each between 2m and 4m wide and running for up to 180m. In Romanian they go by the name of *curtea*, and each is numbered.

Târgu Secuiesc is 56km northeast of Braşov on the E574/route 11. There are frequent **buses** and **minibuses** to Braşov (*from 1hr*), and several buses a day to most of the major Székely towns. **Train** connections are sparser, but include Sfântu Gheorghe (*1hr 15mins*), Braşov (*2hrs*) and Covasna (*20mins*).

Where to stay and eat

Hotel Atrium (18 dbl, 15 sgl, 4 apt) Str Abatorului 11A; ☎0367 412 223; e receptie@ atrium-hotel.ro; w atrium-hotel.ro. Modern 3-star hotel, a short walk from the centre, with its own ten-pin bowling alley (30*RON/hr*) **$$$**

Vörös Panzió (5 rooms) Piaţa Gábor Áron 19; ☎0267 360 789. Right on the central square & tastefully decorated with traditional Székely furniture, though the external wooden staircase

to the rooms can be challenging to negotiate with luggage. **$$**

Székely Vendéglő Str Şcolii 1; ☎0267 364 513; m 0744 549 859; e office@idolrestaurant.ro; w szekelyvendeglo.ro; ⊕ 09.00–midnight daily. Close to the centre, at the corner of Str Şcolii & Str Petőfi Sándor, this is a nicely furnished restaurant specialising in Székely dishes. They also have a summer courtyard. **$$$**

DALNIC Dalnic (HU: Dálnok) is a Székely village whose claim to fame is that it was the birthplace of György Dózsa, known in Romanian as Gheorghe Doja, leader of a 16th-century peasants' revolt (see box, page 167). There is a large statue of Dózsa next to the Reformed church in the centre of Dalnic, resolutely staring forward, hand on hip. It was erected in 1975 in a decidedly Communist

THE LIFE AND DEATH OF GYÖRGY DÓZSA

Born in Dalnic in 1470, Dózsa had gained a reputation for bravery in combat as a mercenary soldier fighting the Turks. His rather gruesome place in history arose out of the machinations of Hungarian Cardinal Tamás Bakócz, who had gone to Rome in 1513 to try to secure the papacy for himself, but ended up instead with a bull from the man chosen as Pope Leo X, proclaiming a crusade against the Turks. To deliver this, Bakócz turned to Dózsa, who gathered an army of peasants for the task. However, their target turned from the distant Turks to the predations of their own landed nobility. Manor houses were burnt, Hungarian landlords killed, and the papal bull revoked. Dózsa was eventually defeated at Timişoara, and was subjected to a particularly brutal execution, even by the standards of the time. To mock his pretensions to rule, he was seated on a smouldering iron throne, a red-hot crown placed on his head, a burning sceptre in his hand. A group of fellow rebels were then brought to him. Hot pliers were inserted into his skin and the other rebels were ordered to eat his flesh. Those who refused were executed on the spot; those who did so were spared. The only beneficiaries of all of this brutality from both sides were the original target, the Turks. With the land so disunited, the Ottoman invasion of 1526 was rendered much more straightforward.

style, reflecting the regime's adoption of Doja as a symbol of the struggles of the peasants against the feudal brutality of their landlords, though his Hungarianness was downplayed.

The village lies 2km off the main DN11 road (signposted) between Braşov and Târgu Secuiesc, 17km from the latter town.

GHELINŢA Ghelinţa (Gelence/Gälänz), 11km southeast of Târgu Secuiesc, is of note for the 13th-century **Catholic Church of Saint Emeric of Hungary** (Biserica Sfântul Emeric). It was built in a late Romanesque style and is celebrated in particular for its interior frescoes, which date from 1330. They depict scenes from the life of Christ as well as the legend of Saint Ladislaus. This involves Ladislaus, astride his white horse, chasing a Cuman who has kidnapped a Hungarian girl. Ladislaus catches up with the Cuman and works together with the captive girl to overcome and then despatch her kidnapper. Over the centuries the church's style was altered, incorporating many Gothic elements including an elegant fan-vaulted ceiling in the sanctuary. Above the nave is a delightful 17th-century wooden-panelled ceiling consisting of 103 painted 'cassettes' (*kazetta*) with floral motifs. No two panels are identical. You may need to ask around in the village for the key to the church.

There are four buses (weekdays only) from Târgu Secuiesc to Ghelinţa (*30mins*).

ZĂBALA The village of Zăbala (HU: Zabola) takes its name from a Hungarian word meaning 'bridle-bit', the straps of leather around a horse's head which allowed the rider to control it. The tale runs that Tatars overran villages to the north and south, but not Zăbala itself, as the locals here were able to control their opponents' horses. There are some fine Székely gates in this village.

A worthwhile sight here is the **Csángó Ethnographic Museum** (Muzeul Etnografic Ceangăiesc/Csángó Néprajzi Múzeum) (*Str Gării 789;* \0267 375 566; e *csangomuzeum@gmail.com;* w *csangomuzeum.ro;* ⊕ *09.00–17.00 Tue–Sat, 10.00–14.00 Sun*). Housed in traditional buildings around a courtyard, this is something of a curiosity, not least as Zăbala is located not in a Csángó region but a Székely one. The Csángós are a Hungarian-speaking group found mostly in nearby parts of the Moldavia region of Romania. The museum is the brainchild of Ferenc Pozsony, a professor of Hungarian Ethnography and Anthropology at the Babeş-Bolyai University, Cluj-Napoca, and is built around the ethnographic material collected by him. It includes items from local Székely, Saxon and Romanian communities, but with a particular focus on the Csángós, with the collection being particularly valuable due to the pace of cultural change in Csángó areas.

Zăbala is on the road between Covasna and Târgu Secuiesc, 8km north of the former.

Mikes Castle (Castelul Mikes)
The ancestral home of an aristocratic Székely family named Mikes, the castle gets its first mention in a diary from 1629, which recounts a wedding there. It was partially burnt down in 1704 and reworked several times; its present form is a Romantic-style redesign from 1867. Under Count Ármin Mikes in the interwar period the estate was a complex business, including wood processing, stud farming and even glass production. Like many aristocratic properties in Transylvania it suffered heavily in the Communist period, when the estate housed at different times a school and sanatorium. After a long legal process the castle has been restored to the family, and is now the home of Countess Katalin Mikes, who left Communist Romania in 1960 and, while in exile in Austria, married Shuvendu Basu Roy Chowdhury of Ulpur, part of a landowning family who ironically had also lost

estates in East Bengal when India was partitioned in 1947. Their sons Gregor and Alexander and their families are progressively converting the various buildings on the estate into high-end tourist accommodation (see below).

The estate is on the edge of Zăbala village, behind an imposing metal gateway with an intercom system, which gives way to a long beech tree-lined avenue.

Where to stay and eat

The Zabola Estate of the Count Mikes Family (9 rooms) 527190 Zăbala; m 0735 231 432; e guesthouse@zabola.com; w zabola.com. All of the bedrooms in the Machine House are beautifully furnished, with photographs of the Mikes family, log fires in winter & wooden floors. Several of the rooms feature freestanding bath tubs. There are also 2 other buildings designed to be booked as single units by larger families or groups of friends. The Old Saddlehouse is an apartment sleeping up to 8 guests in 4 bedrooms. The Garden House sleeps up to 5. The next major project in the grounds is the renovation of the 'New Castle' (actually the former administrative offices of the estate), which will provide a further 11 rooms. Meals are taken in the Old Stables & much care has been taken to recreate an interwar aristocratic feel. A range of activities are offered, including bear watching (€120 for 1–2 guests; additional guests an extra €10 to a maximum of 4), deer stalking, similarly priced, carriage rides (€30) & in winter nocturnal ice skating on one of the lakes on the estate, specially lit (€30). They also offer romantic candlelit dinners & have a sauna in the woods. It's a delightful place for a pampered break. Shuttles can be arranged to Bucharest, Sibiu or Târgu Mureș airports (€105 for up to 2 people). **$$$$$–$$$$**

COVASNA The 'spa of a thousand springs', Covasna (Kovászna/Kowasna) is a town dedicated since the 1880s to **health treatments** using natural mineral spring water and mofettes (see box, page 171), a legacy of past volcanic activity here. The town is modern in feel and dominated by concrete housing blocks.

Getting there and away To get here from Brașov, take the E574 towards Târgu Secuiesc, turning right onto road 13E (signposted) via Reci. There are at least ten buses or minibuses a day to Brașov (*around 1hr 20mins*) and several to Sfântu Gheorghe (*1hr*). There are four trains a day connecting Covasna with Sfântu Gheorghe and Târgu Secuiesc, some continuing to Brașov, but the railway station is outside the town and buses will usually be more convenient.

Where to stay and eat

Hotel Clermont (106 rooms) Str Mihai Eminescu 225A; 0267 342 123; e receptie@ clermonthotel.ro; w clermonthotel.ro. A 4-star spa hotel, close to the cardiovascular hospital east of the main centre, offering mofettes, various water treatments & massages, & a range of sports facilities. A step up in price & quality from the central spa hotels. **$$$$**

SZÉKELY GATES IN COVASNA COUNTY

A typical piece of Székely folk art is the Székely gate (*Székely kapu*), a gate with a separate entrance for pedestrians and for the horse and cart, decorated with woodcarvings featuring floral motifs, and often topped by a dovecote. They are to be found in the towns of the county, including Sfântu Gheorghe (Sepsiszentgyörgy), Covasna (Kovászna), and Târgu Secuiesc (Kézdivásárhely), as well as smaller villages across the region, among them Aita Mare (Nagyajta), Ozun (Uzon), Reci (Réty) and Zăbala (Zabola).

🏠 **Hotel Căprioara** (72 rooms) Str 1 Decembrie 1918 1–2; ☎ 0267 342 184; e receptie. caprioara@turismcovasna.ro; w hotel-caprioara.ro. Recently modernised 3-star hotel; part of the same group as the adjacent hotels Cerbul & Covasna, with which it shares a treatment centre. **$$$**

🏠 **Hotel Cerbul** (129 rooms) Str 1 Decembrie 1918 1–2; ☎ 0267 340 402; e marketing@ turismcovasna.ro; w turismcovasna.ro. An unmissable 11-storey tower with vivid polychrome walls, this 3-star hotel is a sister to the adjacent Hotel Covasna, & shares the latter's reception. **$$$**

🏠 **Hotel Covasna** (128 rooms) Str 1 Decembrie 1918 1–2; ☎ 0267 340 401; e marketing@turismcovasna.ro; w turismcovasna. ro. Built in 1972, this 5-storey hotel marked the start of mass spa tourism in the town in the Communist period. It is one of the 3 large hotels in town owned by the Turism Covasna company, all of which share a treatment centre with carbon-rich water treatments & mofettes. **$$$**

🏠 **Pensiunea Sruetti** (18 rooms) Str Brazilor 2; ☎ 0267 340 918; e sruetticovasna@gmail.com. Good-value place with simple rooms & use of the shared kitchen. **$**

🏠 **Hotel Turist** (20 dbl, 2 trpl) Str 1 Decembrie 1918 4; ☎ 0267 340 573; e office@hotel-turist-covasna.ro; w hotel-turist-covasna.ro. Basic but central 2-star hotel. B/fast not inc. Despite the connecting door & identical name, the adjacent **Restaurant Turist** (m 0762 768 829; **$$**) is under separate management, & serves Romanian dishes. **$**

What to see and do

The Spa Town The symbol of the city is the **Balta Dracului** (HU: Pokolsár), 'The Devil's Lake', a foul-looking bubbling witches' brew of muddy water and carbon dioxide. It has been tamed within a square well, covered with a grill, and topped rather unnecessarily with a metal flame. It is located within the central park, separated from the main spa hotels by a canalised stretch of the Covasna brook.

Nearby, within the central park, is a building with a green pyramidal roof. Go down the steps here to find a row of taps from which locals and tourists alike fill up plastic bottles with the mineral-rich water. Which, incidentally, smells absolutely disgusting.

Two of Covasna's celebrated mofettes are a short walk from here. Head down Strada Brazilor, which runs away from the park on the side opposite the main hotels, and take the first turning left onto Strada Petőfi Sándor. After a few metres you will see on your left the **Mofeta Bene** (w mofetabene.ro; ⊕ 14.00–17.00 Mon–Fri, 09.00–17.00 Sat/Sun; adults 4RON). The patients here head down some steps to a room with a slatted floor, where they stand still, taking care to keep their heads above the red ribbon in the centre of the room, below which the dangerous carbon dioxide gases are concentrated. Classical music plays. After their allotted stays of between 5 and 20 minutes, they leave. No-one seems to speak, giving the whole process a rather reverent feel. You are not allowed to take the mofette procedures without a medical certificate, but if you still fancy this after reading the long list of warnings about the possible dangers on the wall of the building, there is an in-house doctor here available for consultations. A few doors further along is another mofette, the **Mofeta Bardócz**.

There is a **tourist information office** at Strada Unirii 2/A (☎ 0267 340 344; e turism@primariacovasna.ro; w info-covasna.ro).

The Forest Railway and Inclined Plane There is a remarkable piece of railway engineering to be found on the edge of town, though currently in a rather derelict state. This is the **Covasna Inclined Plane**, also referred to as the Şiclău Incline. Designed in 1886 at the request of a local owner of a wood mill, it links the two sections of the forest railway between Covasna and Comandău. It was worked by gravity, with a wagon loaded with lumber descending the plane, and pulling up an empty wagon at the same time by means of a steel cable. Horses at both the top and bottom of the plane were assigned shunting duties. It ceased operations in 1999. It is located just to the east of town, in an area known as Valea Zânelor (Fairy Valley). To get here from the town centre take road 14, which runs past the Hotel Clermont and the cardiovascular hospital.

The company Calea Ferată Îngustă (CFI) has been working to restore the possibility of travel by **steam train** on the old narrow-gauge forest railway track between Covasna and Comandâu. In 2016, they ran diesel trains on this route from 30 April to 11 October, with steam trains during major holiday periods such as Orthodox Easter (m *0786 244 920*; e *office@cfi.ro*; w *cfi.ro*; *adult/child 7/5RON diesel, 10/8RON steam*). Most departures are from in front of the Hotel Clermont in Covasna.

CHIURUȘ The village of Chiuruș (HU: Csomakőrös) was originally called Kőrös in Hungarian, similar to its name in Romanian, but 'Csoma' was added to the Hungarian name in honour of its most famous son, **Sándor Kőrösi Csoma** (1784–1842), the great Székely Orientalist who walked most of the way to Tibet in a search for the origins of the Hungarian people, but who was to devote himself in Asia to writing the first Tibetan–English dictionary, and essentially founding the discipline of Tibetology.

The Hungarian Who Walked to Heaven by Edward Fox (see *Appendix 2*, pages 330–7) recounts the fascinating and unusual life of Kőrösi Csoma, who is often referred to in English sources as Alexander Csoma de Kőrös, After studying oriental languages in Göttingen, he set off in 1819, travelling largely on foot, in search of the Asian origins of the Székely people. In 1822, *en route* to Kashmir, he met the English explorer William Moorcroft, who encouraged him to journey into Tibet, learn the Tibetan language, and compose a grammar and dictionary. His efforts to do so included a 16-month stay in spartan conditions in Zanskar. His research complete, he went to Calcutta to oversee its publication. Setting out for Tibet once again from Calcutta at the age of 58, he contracted malaria and died in Darjeeling, where the Asiatic Society of Bengal erected a memorial in his honour. He was canonised as a Buddhist saint, a Bodhisattva, in Japan in 1933.

MOFETTES – A DRY BATH IN HOT AIR

Daring visitors can try a mofette or 'dry sauna' at Bâile Balvanyos, Băile Tușnad, Covasna, Borsec and Harghita-Băi. Guests stand or sit gingerly in a deep 'pool' lined with slatted benches. The vents in the sides or base of the 'pool' give out carbon dioxide-rich gases associated with past volcanic activity. Carbon dioxide-rich gas is highly poisonous, but since it is heavier than the surrounding air it can be used as a dry spa. The idea is that the gases are absorbed into the body through the skin and have a beneficial effect on the cardiovascular system, the locomotive system and some skin conditions. But treatment in a mofette is not without its risks. A medical certificate is always required before a patient is allowed to use one. A visit to a mofette must be for a specified short time. Signs warn of the importance of keeping your head above a designated point, usually marked by a ribbon, below which the dangerous gases are concentrated. And there are dark warnings about the risks associated with stirring up the gases by sharp movements – even talking. Warnings also state that small children should not go into mofettes, nor should people who are very short in height, intoxicated, ill or alone. Perhaps it's a new one for the extreme sports fans …

Next to the Reformed church in the centre of Chiuruş there is a bust of Kőrösi Csoma, with a plaque in English reading 'philologist, orientalist, founder of Tibetology'. Over the road from here is a cultural centre (*caminul cultural*) named after him, which includes a one-room exhibition dedicated to his life and works (*5RON donation expected*). This centres on a large bust of the great Tibetologist in the centre of the room, festooned with ribbons in Hungarian colours. There is also a (signposted) single-storey Kőrösi Csoma Memorial House. Neither the exhibition nor the memorial house appear to have regular opening times; ask for a key from the priest's house next to the church.

The village is just 1km south of Covasna on route 13E.

5

Harghita County

Harghita County offers some spectacular Eastern Carpathian mountain scenery, with remarkable features born of the complex geology of the area, ranging from Lake Sfânta Ana, Romania's only volcanic crater lake, to the eerie waters of Lacul Roşu; the mineral waters of Borsec to the salt mine at Praid. Two of the most important rivers in Romania, the Mureş and the Olt, start out here, and Gheorgheni has the not particularly enviable reputation as one of the coldest towns in Romania.

It has the highest percentage of ethnic Hungarians, some 85%, of any Romanian county. The large majority of these are Székelys, and Harghita, along with the neighbouring county of Covasna, is a fine place in which to learn more about the history and traditions of the Székely people. The county capital, Miercurea-Ciuc, is not a particularly attractive city, though it does house the 17th-century Mikó Castle, home to a good museum of Székely culture. And the Roman Catholic Whitsun Pilgrimage to Şumuleu, on the outskirts of the town, is a remarkable event. The second-largest town, Odorheiu Secuiesc, is a low-key but attractive place in which you may be tempted to linger for longer.

Add to the mix of attractions such diverse sights as the UNESCO-listed fortified church at Dârjiu and the pottery-makers of the village of Corund, and Harghita presents an altogether compelling travel destination. In much of the county, most of your fellow tourists will be Hungarians, but while some accommodation choices are strongly geared towards Hungarian-speaking visitors, proprietors are usually also able to communicate in Romanian and often English.

MIERCUREA-CIUC *Telephone code 0266 (or 0366)*

The county town of Harghita, Miercurea-Ciuc (Csíkszereda/Szeklerburg) is a town of a little under 40,000 people, some 80% of whom are Székelys. It is not, by any means, the most attractive town in Transylvania, with a centre dominated by windswept squares and Communist blocks, but there are some sights worth hunting down among all the concrete. The pedestrian Strada Petőfi Sándor is a pleasant place to while away an afternoon at one of its pavement cafés, and indeed for most Romanians the name Miercurea-Ciuc is associated with beer. The label on the local Ciuc beer bottles features the main sight of the town, the 17th-century Mikó Castle.

HISTORY The town lies in the Csík Basin, known in Romanian as Ciuc, on a north–south trading route along the Olt River, where this met an east–west route. Miercuri in Romanian and Szerda in Hungarian mean 'Wednesday', the town's name a reference to the Wednesday market traditionally held here. The first written record of a market town here dates from 1558. Its development was further encouraged when in 1876 it became capital of the Csík County, made up of three of the traditional Székely seats, and which largely forms the present-day Harghita

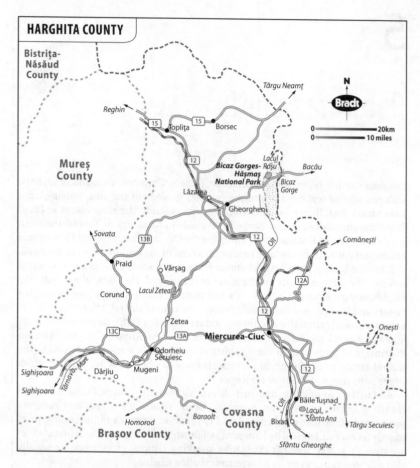

HARGHITA COUNTY

County. But by 1910 its population was still only 3,700: industrialisation during the Communist period resulted both in a rapid increase in numbers and the concrete urban landscape with which the visitor is greeted today.

GETTING THERE AND AWAY Miercurea-Ciuc is 67km north of Sfântu Gheorghe (Covasna County) on the main DN12/E578.

The **railway station** (\ 0266 315 102) is at the western end of Strada Kossuth Lajos, west of the town centre. There are two trains daily to Bucharest (*5hrs*). Other destinations include Braşov (*2hrs*), Sfântu Gheorghe (*1hr 10mins*), Gheorgheni (*1hr*) and Baia Mare (*7hrs 40mins*). The **bus station** (\ 0366 100 046) is a couple of hundred metres to the north of it, off the main Strada Braşovului. Destinations include Braşov (*2½hrs*), Odorheiu Secuiesc (*from 1hr*) and Sfântu Gheorghe (*1hr 40mins*).

City buses are operated by Csíki Trans (*Str Braşovului 3;* e *office@csiki-trans.ro;* w *csiki-trans.ro*); their website has network details and a timetable. A return ticket costs 4RON.

WHERE TO STAY *Map, opposite*
Miercurea-Ciuc is off the main tourist circuit, and the accommodation offering in town is decidedly thin.

⌂ Hotel Fenyő (100 rooms) Str N Bălcescu 11; \0266 311 493; e hotelfenyo@hunguesthotels. com; w hunguest-fenyo.ro. The 3-star Fenyő is right in the centre, in a white 8-storey block. With no AC, the place bakes in summer, & the lifts are eccentric, but there is not much competition in town. **$$$**

⌂ Három Székely Fogadó (10 rooms) Str Lunca Mare 2A Bis; m 0742 135 484; e haromszekely@yahoo.com; w haromszekely. ro. Pleasant guesthouse with basically furnished bedrooms, restaurant & a nice garden with a play area; out of the centre on the main E578 beyond the railway & bus stations. **$$**

✕ WHERE TO EAT AND DRINK *Map, below*

✳ ✕ Ristorante San Gennaro Str Petőfi Sándor 15; \0266 206 500; ⊕ 09.00–midnight daily. A really good Italian restaurant, with a menu ranging from (first-rate) pizzas to special lists of dishes featuring truffles & porcini mushrooms. There is outdoor seating on the pedestrian Str Petőfi. A plaque records that Hungarian poet & revolutionary Sándor Petőfi stayed in the building on 23 July 1849. **$$$**

✕ Bandido's Str Petőfi Sándor 25; \0266 314 749; w bandidospizza.ro; ⊕ 10.00–midnight daily. Mixing its inspirations somewhat, this is a Mexican-themed pizzeria with a good range of Mexican dishes, pizzas & Hungarian specialities. **$$**

✕ Tosca Piața Majláth Gusztáv Károly 1; m 0753 090 000; ⊕ 09.00–midnight Mon–Fri, 10.00–midnight Sat, 11.00–midnight Sun. A basic pizzeria with a nice terrace overlooking a park. **$$**

OTHER PRACTICALITIES

$ Banca Transilvania Str Kossuth Lajos 18; \0266 310 203; ⊕ 09.00–17.30 Mon–Fri
✚ Farmacia Richter Str Petőfi Sándor 13; \0266 371 515; ⊕ 08.00–20.00 Mon–Fri, 08.00–15.00 Sat

✉ Post office Str Kossuth Lajos 3; ⊕ 08.00– 19.00 Mon–Fri, 09.00–13.00 Sat

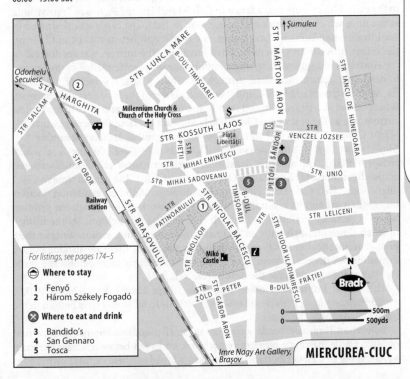

For listings, see pages 174–5

⌂ **Where to stay**
1 Fenyő
2 Három Székely Fogadó

✕ **Where to eat and drink**
3 Bandido's
4 San Gennaro
5 Tosca

MIERCUREA-CIUC

FESTIVALS By far the most important event in the town's calendar is the Roman Catholic **Whitsun Pilgrimage** to Şumuleu, known in Hungarian as Csíksomlyó. This is a Franciscan monastery church, constructed in the mid 15th century, lying some 2km to the northeast of town. The church was originally built in Gothic style, but was rebuilt in a Baroque style in the 19th century, as the smaller original church could not accommodate the increasingly popular pilgrimage. The most revered object of the church, and the centrepiece of the Whitsun Pilgrimage, is an early 16th-century 2.27m wooden statue of the Virgin Mary. The history of the pilgrimage dates to 1567, when local Székely Catholics defeated the forces of John Sigismund Zápolya, who had attempted to force them to adopt the ideas of the Reformation. Prayers were offered at Şumuleu by the whole community following the victory. Today the event can attract 200,000 flag-waving pilgrims, who gather in the meadow near the church.

Şumuleu also hosts the **Festival of 1,000 Székely Maidens** (HU: Ezer Székely Leány Napja) at the beginning of July, an event that is far less debauched than it sounds, and focuses on folk dance and costume (page 47).

The low-key but thoroughly enjoyable **Csíki Jazz** (w *jazzfestival.ro*) is usually held at the end of July, is focused on the atmospheric courtyard of Mikó Castle and attracts mostly performers from Romania and Hungary. The castle is also one of the venues for Miercurea-Ciuc's **Early Music Festival** (Festivalul de Muzică Veche), held in mid-July.

WHAT TO SEE AND DO The chief attraction of the place is the Renaissance-style **Mikó Castle** (Castelul Mikó), square in plan around a central courtyard, with four square corner towers. It is named after Ferenc Hídvégi Mikó, a captain of the county in the early 17th century and advisor to Gabriel Bethlen, the Prince of Transylvania at the time, who began work on the building in 1623. The castle was destroyed in 1661 by invading Turkish–Tatar troops, and rebuilt only between 1714 and 1716 on the orders of Austrian General Stephan Steinville. The fortress was reinforced, as the Austrians recognised its strategic importance at the eastern edge of the Empire in defending against incursions through the Ghimeş Pass. It served as a garrison for Austrian troops until 1764, and then headquartered the First Székely Regiment. It later served as a Hungarian and then Romanian garrison, and in 1970 took on its current role as the seat of the **Ciuc Székely Museum** (Muzeul Seciuesc al Ciucului) (*Piaţa Cetăţii 2;* \ *0266 372 024;* e *info@csikimuzeum.ro;* w *csikimuzeum.ro;* ⊕ *7 May–15 Oct 09.00–18.00 Tue–Sun, 16 Oct–6 May 09.00–17.00 Tue–Sun; adult/ child 10/7RON*). The museum consists of three permanent exhibitions, scattered across different parts of the castle. One of these, entitled 'The pace of time in Ciuc', offers some well-presented ethnographic displays. Another exhibition focuses on religious art and its restoration, as well as the work of the Franciscan printing house at Şumuleu, founded in the 17th century. The third chronicles the history of Mikó Castle, though with an emphasis more on getting visitors to take their photos in historical outfits than on detailed explanation. There are also temporary exhibitions. A display of local rural dwellings and Székely gates behind the castle was closed for restoration at the time of research.

The **tourist information office** Info-Ciuc (*Piaţa Cetăţii 1;* \ *0266 317 007;* e *csikinfo@szereda.ro;* w *miercureaciuc.ro;* ⊕ *08.00–16.00 Mon–Fri*) is housed in the town hall, opposite the castle.

Bulevardul Timişoarei heads north from the small roundabout immediately in front of Mikó Castle, passing a pleasant central park on its left before reaching the main square of the city, **Piaţa Libertăţii**. This is sadly a broad concrete expanse surrounded

THE AFFAIR OF THE CHEEKY SHIRT

The Communist-era brewery in Miercurea-Ciuc is now owned by Heineken. Its Ciuc Premium (w *ciucpremium.ro*) beer features the Mikó Castle on the label and serves as the town's calling card right across Romania, where it is one of the most popular brands nationally. But if you are in a Hungarian-speaking pub in Miercurea-Ciuc and ask for a 'cheeky shirt' (Csíki sört), or Ciuc beer, you might be served one of two brands. A Ciuc Premium is one possibility. The other is a brand named Igazí Csíki Sör (w *csikisor.com*), which means, in Hungarian, 'real Ciuc beer', and which appeared on the market in 2014. Heineken took the newcomers to court, arguing that Ciuc Premium was widely known as 'Ciuc beer' and thus that the new brand impinged on its intellectual property, but lost the case.

The episode serves as an example of the highly pronounced politics around language and culture in the Székely-majority counties of Romania. For many ethnic Hungarians, Ciuc Premium, though brewed locally, represents a wider Romanian identity rather than a specific Székely one. The smaller-scale production of Igazí Csíki Sör promotes the Székely community of the area through its Hungarian-language name and labelling and extensive use of Székely symbols.

The good news for the consumer is that both beers taste great.

by the rivalling uglinesses of buildings housing the County Council, the Hungarian-funded Sapientia University and Trade Unions Cultural House. The bleakness of the place is leavened by some playful fountains and a statue of Áron Márton, the revered Roman Catholic bishop in Transylvania during the Communist period.

From here head left onto the major Strada Kossuth Lajos, until you see on your right two entirely contrasting Roman Catholic churches. The **Church of the Holy Cross** (Biserica Înălțarea Sfintei Cruci) (*Str Kossuth Lajos 40*) is an 18th-century Baroque building. Behind it is the modern and extravagant **Millennium Church** (Biserica Mileniului), centred on a structure vaguely reminiscent of a central Asian yurt, with statues of angels praying around a skylight in the roof. This is flanked by two towers, each with entrances presided over by a procession of arches. Inside, the altarpiece resembles the wings of an angel. It was the work of the distinctive Hungarian architect Imre Makovecz.

One further worthwhile attraction lies a couple of kilometres south of the centre, in the neighbourhood of Jigodin Ciuc, a block east of the main E578/DN12 road at the entrance to the town. This is the **Imre Nagy Art Gallery** (Galeria de Artă Nagy Imre) (*Str Nagy Imre 175;* \ *0266 313 963;* e *nagyimregaleria@csikimuzeum.ro;* w *csikimuzeum.ro;* ⊕ *15 May–15 Oct 09.00–17.00 Tue–Sun, closed 16 Oct–14 May; adult/child 5/3RON*), which falls under the purview of the Ciuc Székely Museum and provides an extensive insight into the works of this local artist, who died in 1976. The gallery is located beside his birthplace.

HEADING SOUTH AND WEST

BĂILE TUȘNAD The peaceful **spa resort** town of Băile Tușnad (HU: Tusnádfürdő) lies in a splendid location in the beautiful wooded Olt River valley. The curative effects of the local mineral waters have been known since the 18th century, but the town dates its development as a spa resort to 1842, when news of the miraculous results

Harghita County **HEADING SOUTH AND WEST**

5

from the application of the waters to the ailing son of a local shepherd prompted the establishment of a resort company. The resort was destroyed in the 1849 Revolution, but then rebuilt, reportedly at the urging of Austrian Emperor Franz Joseph I.

The small Ciucaş Lake in the centre of the resort is an artificial construction dating from 1900. The lake is now a rather sorry and neglected sight, the pavilion restaurant in an island in the centre closed up and abandoned-looking. It has been eclipsed as the fulcrum of the resort by the adjacent new spa leisure centre called **Wellness Tuşnad** (*Str Ciucaş 9;* m *0756 118 479;* e *office@wellness-tusnad.ro;* w *wellness-tusnad. ro;* ⊕ *14.00–21.00 Mon, 10.00–21.00 Tue–Sun; adult/child 30/15RON*). Housed in the old cinema and culture house complex, it has a range of pools, jacuzzi, sauna and salt room. A flight of steps leads down to the leisure centre and lake from the DN12 highway running through the resort, immediately opposite the Romanian Orthodox church, a 20th-century building with elaborate external painting across both the church itself and the bell tower in front.

The picturesque appeal of the resort has been somewhat dented by the construction both of large Communist-era hotels and by more modern ones, but it is still an attractive spot. In recent years the town has been associated with visits by Hungarian Prime Minister Viktor Orbán to the annual Bálványos Free University summer camp, which he has tended to use as the occasion for major and sometimes controversial speeches.

Băile Tuşnad lies on the main DN12/E578, midway between Sfântu Gheorghe and Miercurea-Ciuc. There are **buses** to both Sfântu Gheorghe (*45mins*) and Miercurea-Ciuc (*55mins*), and the town is also a stop for **trains** running between these two county towns.

Where to stay and eat

Hotel Ciucaş (97 dbl, 17 apt) Aleea Sf Ana 7; 0266 335 004; e contact@hotelciucas. ro; w hotelciucas.ro. A 3-star spa hotel with an indoor pool, gym, sauna & a daunting range of therapeutic treatments. HB & FB packages also available. **$$$**

Hotel Fortuna (12 rooms) Str Kovács Miklós 68; 0266 335 216; e office@hotelfortuna.ro; w hotelfortuna.ro. Billing itself as an 'eco-boutique hotel', this is a characterful place, resembling a large chalet, with each room decorated individually, & inspired by themes ranging from sewing machines to Van Gogh. The restaurant ($$$) is pretty good. **$$$**

Hotel O3zone (117 rooms) Aleea Sf Ana 2; 0266 335 397; e rezervari@o3zone. ro; w o3zone.ro. Central 4-star hotel with a spa & conference centre, its exterior decked out in ecological shades of green & brown. **$$$**

LACUL SFÂNTA ANA This oval-shaped lake, known in Hungarian as Szent Anna-tó, has a maximum length of 620m, and is the only volcanic crater lake in Romania. It lies at a height of 950m, one of two craters of the Ciomadul volcano. In a picturesque setting surrounded by forest, the lake is a popular summer bathing and picnicking spot. It is also something of a pilgrimage centre, and there are two chapels on the lakeshore, St Anne and St Joachim. The second crater, Mohos, at an altitude of 1,050m, is larger and shallower than Sfânta Ana and is now occupied by a *Sphagnum* peat bog, known in Romanian as **Tinovul Mohoş**.

The two craters together form a nature reserve, which is administered by an environmental group called Ecos Club (m *0721 890 179;* e *ecosclub@yahoo.ro*). Car parking tickets are sold at the top of the crater, costing either 10RON a day to park at the campsite at the top and walk down, or 20RON to drive down into the crater and park close to the lake. Camping in the field here costs 5RON per tent or 10RON for a caravan. The Tinovul Mohoş peat bog, with its highly distinctive flora including several species of insectivorous plants, can be visited only as part of a guided tour. These depart from the car parking ticket-sales point above the crater every 2 hours in summer and cost 5RON per person.

To get here from Băile Tuşnad, head south on DN12, turning left at the village of Bixad, which is as close to the lake, still 17km away and uphill, as you can reach by public transport.

ODORHEIU SECUIESC

ODORHEIU SECUIESC With a population of around 34,000, some 96% of whom are ethnic Hungarians, Odorheiu Secuiesc (Székelyudvarhely/Odorhellen) is the second-largest town in Harghita County, and offers a more appealing prospect than Miercurea-Ciuc, its centre dominated by 19th-century buildings rather than concrete blocks. The first known reference to the town dates from 1334, and it became an important Székely settlement. In 1876, it became the capital of the Udvarhely County of the Kingdom of Hungary, and when Transylvania was incorporated into Romania remained the capital of the new Odorhei County. But it lost most of its administrative significance during the Communist period, and has now settled into life as a relatively prosperous provincial town, with an economy focused on the textiles industry.

Getting there and away Odorheiu Secuiesc lies off the main through roads. It is some 48km west of Miercurea-Ciuc on road DN13A, which makes for a great scenic **drive**, passing through villages with Székely gates. Route 13A then continues northwestwards from Odorheiu Secuiesc towards the spa resort of Sovata-Băi in Mureş County (pages 196–8) – another pleasant drive.

The **railway station** is about 800m northeast of the centre along Strada Bethlen Gábor, though Odorheiu Secuiesc is on a minor branch, offering three trains daily to Sighişoara (*1½hrs*). The **bus station** (*Str Târgului 10;* \0266 218 077) is close by, separated from the railway station by the Orion Mall. Destinations served include Sovata (*1hr 15mins*), Miercurea-Ciuc (*from 1hr*) and Târgu Mureş (*from 3hrs*). Note that buses operated by the Gas Tours company, who also serve Miercurea-Ciuc and Târgu Mureş, depart from a different, but nearby, bus station, **Autogara Gas Tours** (*Str Târgului 5;* \0266 218 410).

Where to stay and eat

Hotel Târnava (73 rooms) Piaţa Primăriei 16; \0266 213 963; e office@kukullo.ro; w kukullo.ro. Also known by its Hungarian-language name, Küküllő, this 3-star business hotel with restaurant & sauna is right on the central square. The cheaper doubles are without AC. **$$$$** (*superior dbl*), **$$$** (*standard dbl*)

Hotel Gondűző (22 rooms) Str Sântimbru 18; \0266 218 372; e office@gonduzo.ro; w gonduzo. ro. Sympathetically decorated 3-star hotel in a red-brick building on a cobbled street a 5 min walk from the centre. Good restaurant (**$$$**), offering some local dishes. **$$$**

Korona Panzió (9 rooms) Piaţa Primăriei 12/2; \0266 216 946; w koronapanzio.ro. Right on the main square, this guesthouse has average rooms, a restaurant (⏱ 10.00–23.00 daily; **$$$**) & a summer garden. **$$**

Petőfi Panzió (12 rooms) Str Petőfi Sándor 2; \0266 212 262; e office@petofipanzio.ro; w petofipanzio.ro. Centrally located guesthouse between the Piaţa Primăriei & the fortress. The rooms are fine if nothing special, but there is a sauna & gym & a good restaurant (**$$$**) offering Hungarian dishes. **$$**

What to see and do

What to see and do Although short on specific major attractions, Odorheiu Secuiesc is a pleasant town, and a good place in which to stroll and soak up the atmosphere of a Székely-dominated Transylvanian town. It centres on the elongated **Piața Primăriei**, named after the town hall, built at the end of the 19th century, which is the main building on the northern side of the square. Within the park at its northwestern end is a grouping of 13 statues, arranged in a boat shape, representing prominent ethnic Hungarian figures linked to Transylvania's history and culture. Those depicted range from architect Károly Kós to 19th-century politician Miklós Wesselényi. But two statues in particular have been the subject of continued controversy since they were erected in 2004. József Nyírő was a writer

THE SZÉKELYS

Spending time in Harghita, Covasna and Mureș counties is a great way to learn more about the culture of the Székely people. But the origins of the Székelys, known as Szekler in German and Secui in Romanian, is the subject of continued debate. What is clear is that the Székelys were guards of the eastern border of the Kingdom of Hungary, defending the kingdom against the threat posed by the Ottomans. They were long considered one of the three 'nations', along with the Hungarian nobility and the Saxons, ruling Transylvania, a formulation that kept the ethnic Romanians out of any semblance of power.

Some historians believe that the Székelys were Magyars, sent to guard the eastern frontier, who became different over time from other Hungarian groups because of their relative cultural isolation in the mountains of eastern Transylvania. Others have suggested that their origins lie in Turkic nomadic tribes. But if this is the case they must have switched from their original language to Hungarian at an early date.

The Székelys themselves claim to be descendants of **Attila the Hun**, and more specifically of Attila's youngest son, **Prince Csaba**. Historical fact is subsumed beneath many popular Székely legends involving Csaba. On the death of Attila, who had many sons by many wives, there was much uncertainty as to who would rule his kingdom. One version of a Székely legend which has numerous variants tells that the competition focused on two contenders: Aladár, whose mother was a German princess, and Csaba, whose mother was a princess from Greece. The Germanic tribes sided with Aladár; the Huns with Csaba. After a fierce battle Csaba was defeated, and fled to his mother's homeland of Greece. The defeated Hun warriors of Csaba's army settled in present-day Transylvania, and became the Székely people. It is said that on several subsequent occasions, when the Székely people were attacked and on the point of defeat, Prince Csaba returned to save them, riding down from the skies on a road of glittering stars as a gift from heaven.

The Székelys have brought distinctive contributions to wider Hungarian and Transylvanian culture. These include the beautiful Székely gates (see box, page 169), and the chimney-shaped cake known as *kürtőskalács*, on sale wherever people gather in festive mood in Harghita and Covasna, usually for 10RON for the whole cake. A more controversial cultural symbol is the Székely flag, with a horizontal gold bar across a blue background, and a gold sun and white moon in the top-left corner. You will see these flying in the Székely-majority counties of Transylvania, but the flag is the subject of ongoing dispute, with some Romanian politicians fearing that it supports a secessionist agenda, and there have been legal cases brought following the flying of the Székely flag from the buildings of local administrations in Harghita and Covasna.

of popular fiction, who focused on rural life in the Székely region. But he was also a Fascist and an anti-Semite who was charged after World War II with war crimes by both Romania and Hungary, dying in exile in Spain. An attempt to rebury Nyírő in Odorheiu Secuiesc in 2012 was blocked by the Romanian Government. A much bigger controversy surrounds a statue whose subject is not formally identified, but is described on the plinth as Vándor Székely Hazatalál (The Wandering Székely finds his Homeland). This has been widely interpreted as honouring Count Albert Wass, a Transylvanian aristocrat, poet and novelist who was sentenced to death *in absentia* by a Romanian tribunal in 1946 for alleged war crimes.

The wooden pavilion nearby houses a **tourist information office** in the summer months (m *0752 316 938;* ⊕ *10.00–18.00 Mon–Fri, 09.00–13.00 Sat*).

From the northern side of the square, Strada Cetăţii heads off towards the **fortress**, which dates from the 15th century but has had something of a turbulent history. It was strengthened in 1565 by John Sigismund Zápolya in order to help control the suppressed local Székelys, in which endeavour it seems to have been largely unsuccessful, as it was destroyed in 1599 by Székelys in alliance with Prince Michael the Brave. It is still popularly known as the Fortress Attacked by the Székelys. A Neoclassical building was constructed in 1891 right in the middle of the site, which today houses the József Eötvös Technological School, but the walls and corner tower of the medieval fortress are preserved around this, and you are free to walk around these.

At the eastern end of the Piaţa Primăriei is a **Reformed Church** (Biserica Reformată) built in the late 18th century, beyond which is another, smaller, square, Piaţa Márton Áron.

The town's main museum is outside the centre, just off the main DN13A heading northeast, close to the Kaufland supermarket. This is the **Haáz Rezső Museum** (Muzeul Haáz Rezső) (*Str Bethlen Gábor 2–6;* ✆*0266 218 375;* e *info@hrmuzeum.ro;* w *hrmuzeum.ro;* ⊕ *15 Mar–30 Sep 09.00–18.00 Tue–Fri, 10.00–18.00 Sat/Sun, Oct 09.00–17.00 Tue–Fri, 10.00–14.00 Sat/Sun, 1 Nov–14 Mar 09.00–16.00 Tue–Fri; adult/ child 5/2.5RON*). Named after the man whose ethnographic collections formed the basis for the museum, it is housed in the atmospheric former summer cottage of the Haberstumpf family, built in 1900, and covers the history and culture of the local area.

THE VALLEY OF THE UPPER TÂRNAVA MARE From Odorheiu Secuiesc take the DN13A eastwards towards Miercurea-Ciuc. After about 5km, at the village of Brădeşti, turn left onto minor road 138, which runs alongside the upper reaches of the Târnava Mare River. This is a really picturesque area, offering a good insight into Székely village life. You pass through the villages of **Zeta** (HU: Zetelaka) and **Sub Cetate** (Zeteváralja/Burgberg), offering some attractive Székely gates, before reaching the artificial **Lake Zeta**, formed by a dam opened in 1993, with the dual purpose of providing hydro-electric power and combating the risk of flooding. Note that, confusingly, there is another village of Subcetate (without the spacing) in the northern part of Harghita County, so be careful when setting the GPS! Taking the smaller road to the left of the lake, you snake upwards through some glorious countryside to the small village of **Vârşag** (HU: Székelyvarság), its entrance heralded by a Székely gate. The area is a popular rural holiday destination for Hungarian families; you will rarely hear any other language spoken here.

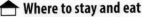 **Where to stay and eat**

Csorgókő Panzió (25 rooms) Vârşag no 524; m 0753 017 050; e csorgoko@freemail.hu; w csorgoko.panzio.ro. Wood-walled guesthouse in the beautiful village of Vârşag, with good

Hungarian meals (🕐 08.00–21.00 daily; $$) taken in warm weather on an attractive balcony. A friendly place, though catering almost entirely to a Hungarian-speaking clientele. $$

🏠 **Nap Park** (8 chalets) m 0740 821 965; e varga@naturair.eu; w nappark.eu. The Natur Air Park offers basic wooden chalets, with communal living areas & kitchens, in an attractive riverside location off the road between Lake Zetea & Vârşag, making for a good spot for group travellers looking for a rural break. Note that some of the bedrooms

have low sloping ceilings. B/fast available for an additional charge. $

🏠 **Olga Panzió** (3 houses) Zsögös utca 732, Zetea; ℡ 0266 241 221; e olga@ erdelyivendeglatas.com; w erdelyivendeglatas. com. 3 attractive houses in the village of Zetea, though with basically furnished bedrooms, with bookings available either by room or on a *kulcsosház* basis, in which guests rent the whole house, for which they are given the key, or *kulcs*. Firmly aimed at a Hungarian tourist market. $

MUGENI Located 11km southwest of Odorheiu Secuiesc on the second-class main road heading towards Cristuru Secuiesc is the village of Mugeni (HU: Bögöz). It is home to an interesting **Reformed Church** (Biserica Reformată) (*key at no 268, the parish office opposite the church with a plaque identifying it as Református Lelkészi Hivatal*) dating from the 13th century, though it owes much of its present appearance, including its vaulted sanctuary, to a 15th-century Gothic remodelling. Note the very curious narrow gap in the external wall at the base of the tower: this arose as a result of a decision in the 19th century to close the western door to the church here. But they had to leave a gap in the wall large enough to allow the bell-ringer to access the bell ropes! The nave would originally have been vaulted, but is now covered by a painted wooden-panelled ceiling dating from 1724.

The church is noted specifically for its 14th-century paintings covering the northern wall of the nave, which were uncovered at the end of the 19th century. They are laid out in three rows of scenes. The uppermost, which is the most poorly preserved, depicts tales from the life of St Ladislaus, notably his battle with the Cuman warrior who had abducted a local girl. The scenes recall those in Dârjiu (see below) and Ghelinţa (page 168), reflecting the strength of the cult of St Ladislaus in Székely areas. The middle row depicts the life of St Margaret of Antioch, focusing in rather gruesome detail on the various tortures the pious Margaret had to endure after refusing the hand of the pagan ruler Olybrius when he demanded that she renounce Christianity: flagellated, set upon with pincers and boiled in hot oil. She defeats the devil, who is depicted in the form of a dragon, but still ends up by being beheaded. The bottom row depicts the Last Judgement: Heaven to the left, Hell to the right.

DÂRJIU Dârjiu (Dârjiu Székelyderzs/Dersch) is of interest for its **fortified church** (Biserica Fortificată) (*Str Alszeg 164 or ask for the key at no 163 next door;* ℡ 0266 222 183; m 0744 557 659; e unitariusderzs@gmail.com; w 1419.ro; 🕐 *summer 10.00–19.00 Tue–Sat, 13.00–19.00 Sun, winter by appointment only; adult/child 6/3 RON*), one of the seven magnificent Transylvanian churches featuring on UNESCO's World Heritage list. It is a rare example of the typically Saxon style of fortified church in a Székely area of Romania, and is now a Unitarian church. As an early 15th-century Gothic hall church, it is rather similar in style to that at Cloaşterf (page 211), built on the site of a 13th-century Romanesque building. A rectangular defensive wall surrounds the church, which lies at an angle across the internal courtyard. There are towers at each corner of the walls, one of which, the Bacon Tower (Turnul Slăninelor), held the village's supply of ham and bacon in a form of community larder. There is an additional tower on the western wall, and a bell tower remodelled in the 18th century in Baroque style. These can all be accessed by means of rickety wooden staircases. An arcade supported by square columns runs along the inside of the walls and houses an exhibition of photographs and displays of agricultural implements.

The interior is airy, with a vaulted ceiling and pastel-painted pews. The real treasures here are the wall paintings running along the nave, which were uncovered in the course of a late 19th-century renovation. Figures and scenes depicted include St Anthony the Hermit, St Michael and the Conversion of the Apostle Paul. Best of all is a series of five scenes on the north wall of the nave depicting the popular tale of St Ladislaus on his white horse, pursuing the Cuman who has snatched a young maiden, working with the girl to overcome the Cuman, and then letting the girl wield the axe that cleaves the Cuman's head from the rest of his body.

Dârjiu is 14km south of Mugeni by road, in a somewhat remote location. From Mugeni, head towards Odorheiu Secuiesc on route 137, turning right onto road 137A after a couple of kilometres and then right at the village of Ulieș.

CORUND Corund (HU: Korond) is a village devoted to **ceramics**. Close to 200 potters are said to work here. The main road leading through the village is lined with workshops and stalls selling plates, vases, bowls and decorative objects. The pottery is often coloured green, brown and yellow, with a cobalt blue introduced by the Saxons. The motifs focus on the natural world – usually birds, animals and flowers. The quality varies considerably; it is best to focus on the workshops rather than the basic roadside stalls.

The coach operator **Csavargó Corundtrans** (*Str Piac 88;* ✆ *0266 249 000;* e *csavargo@korond.ro;* w *csavargo.ro;* ⊕ *08.00–noon & 16.00–18.00 Mon–Fri, 08.00–noon & 18.00–20.00 Sat*) has an office next door to the town hall. As well as operating a daily bus service between Odorheiu Secuiesc and Budapest, they offer a range of tourist services in Corund, including custom-made trips, from a hike linked to the history of the local aragonite industry to trout fishing.

By **car**, Corund is 24km north of Odorheiu Secuiesc on the scenic route 13A. It is served by several **buses** a day plying between Odorheiu Secuiesc and Sovata.

PRAID The small town of Praid (Parajd/Salzberg) sits at the heart of Romania's Salt Country, Ţinutul Sării, known in Hungarian as Sóvidék. Praid is known for its 'Hill of Salt', where a salt bed descending for some 2.7km also rises above the surface. Salt mining here dates back to the Roman period. The changing weight given to the rights accorded to the Székely people to exploit salt, against the sovereign's overall right to the salt mines, was an important factor in the history of the area, with local rights removed in 1714 when salt exploitation became a Habsburg privilege.

Underground salt mining in Praid dates from the opening of the bell-shaped József mine in 1762. As mining technologies changed, the first trapezoid mine was opened here in 1864, and in 1898 a horizontal tunnel was cut right into the 'Hill of Salt'. From the 1960s, changes to the geography of the mine were to permit the development of a type of medical therapy focused on patients with asthma and other respiratory ailments, involving the spending of long periods of time in salt mines. At a depth of some 120m, the temperature here is pretty constant all year round, at just under 16°C, while the air is clean and still. But with patients spending 4 hours a day down here, they needed something to do. This gave rise to the Romanian speciality of amusement centres deep underground in salt mines. Turda (page 300) offers another fine example.

At **Praid Salt Mine** (Salina Praid) (✆ *0266 240 200;* e *office@salinapraid.ro;* w *salinapraid.ro;* ⊕ *08.00–14.50 daily; adult/child 25/15RON*), an ancient bus departs from the ticket office at least every 30 minutes. It travels towards the entrance to the mine, where a sign in Romanian and Hungarian disconcertingly wishes you 'Good luck!' before heading downwards into a sloping tunnel for more than 1km. At the end of the tunnel, visitors disembark and must walk down a long flight of steps before emerging into the huge cavernous space of the trapezoidal mine chamber. Its walls are lined with picnic tables, where visitors can eat their packed lunches. The attractions have gradually become more exotic and elaborate: in addition to table-tennis tables, a playground, a shop selling salt-related souvenirs and plastic toys, and a pharmacy there is now also a 3D cinema (*10RON*), the Dinoland Felicity children's amusement park featuring bouncy castles and slides (⊕ *09.20–15.20 daily; 10RON*) and even underground rope walks at Club Aventura (w *club-aventura.ro*), which advertises itself, entirely plausibly, as Europe's first adventure park in a salt mine. The end of a gallery has been converted into an Orthodox chapel, with lines of wooden pews. In a side niche here is a salt statue of a rather wild-eyed John of Nepomuk, legendarily the confessor of the Queen of Bohemia who, refusing to divulge the secrets of the confessional, was drowned in the Vltava River at the behest of King Wenceslaus, clearly showing his bad side. He is a protector of miners, as well as bridges and sailors. There is also a small museum.

On departure, a flight of stairs takes you up one level, where there is an underground self-service restaurant (⊕ *10.00–15.00 daily; $$*) as well as an observation point looking into the bell-shaped József mine. The bus back departs from this level, though be warned that there can be quite a scrum to get it on busy days.

On the surface, Praid is a pretty scruffy place, with the area around the mine covered with small stalls offering salt-related souvenirs and generalised tat for sale. Of more interest is the large saltwater swimming pool at **Ştrand Praid** (*contact details as for Salina Praid;* ⊕ *summer months only*) in the rather ugly-looking concrete building down Strada Minei from the salt mine. Adding to Praid's list of rather unexpected attractions is a tropical **Butterfly House** (Casa Fluturilor) (*Str Küllőmező;* m *0740 557 264;* e *butterflyexhibition@gmail.com;* w *casafluturilor. ro;* ⊕ *May–Sep 09.00–19.00 daily; adult/child 7/6RON*), signposted from the salt mine. At the end of September Praid hosts a *Sarmale* **Festival** (Festival Sarmalelor), paying homage to Romania's favourite dish of minced meat wrapped in cabbage or vine leaves.

Getting there and away
By **car**, Praid is 11km north of Corund on route 13A. There are several car parks around the salt mine (*10RON/day*). **Buses** between Odorheiu Secuiesc and Sovata stop here.

🏠 Where to stay and eat

🏠 **Pensiunea Praid** (15 rooms) Str Principală 1085; ☎0266 240 471; e office@pensiuneapraid. ro; w pensiuneapraid.ro. Just off the junction of Str Principală with the turning to Gheorgheni, this is a rather institutional-looking building, with sauna, jacuzzi & fitness room. B/fast is not included, but rooms have their own kitchen facilities, & indeed the place is mainly geared to patients coming to Praid for lengthy treatment programmes in the salt mine. **$$$**

✗ **Casa Telegdy** Str Principală 1173; m 0751 010 017; ⊕ 08.00–23.00 daily. Over the road from the salt mine. Székely dishes & décor in the former house of Praid mine manager Károly Telegdy. **$$$**
✗ **Ice Italy** Str Principală 1093; m 0755 801 495; ⊕ 08.00–midnight daily. Pizzeria in the centre of town, with walls decorated with Venetian scenes. Also serves b/fast, some Hungarian dishes, pasta &, yes, ice cream. **$$**

HEADING NORTH

In the northern part of Harghita County the major attractions are natural, with some particularly dramatic scenery in and around the Bicaz Gorges-Hășmaș National Park.

GHEORGHENI The town at the gateway to this area is Gheorgheni (Gyergyószentmiklós/Niklasmarkt), with just under 20,000 people, the majority of whom are Székelys. Historically, the town is known as an important centre of Armenian settlement in Transylvania; the community arriving from Moldavia in the mid 17th century, although very few Armenians remain here today. While most tourists pass straight through Gheorgheni *en route* to the natural attractions to the east and north, it has a few worthwhile sites. The town centres on the triangular **Piața Libertății**, with a park in the middle. A few hundred metres east of here is the **Tarisznyás Márton Museum** (Muzeul Tarisznyás Márton) (*Str Rákóczi Ferenc 1;* \0266 365 229; e *muzeum@tmmuzeum.ro;* w *tmmuzeum.ro;* ⊕ *1 May–15 Oct 09.00–17.00 Tue–Fri, 10.00–17.00 Sat/Sun, 16 Oct–30 Apr 09.00–17.00 Tue–Fri, Sat/Sun by appointment; adult/child 5/3RON*), housed in an 18th-century building. It offers a range of collections of varying interest, including local history and ethnography. There is an 18th-century Baroque **Armenian Catholic church** (Biserica Armeano-Catolică) (\0266 361 517 *to arrange a visit*) a block to the north, surrounded by an encircling wall topped by tiles.

Some 6km north of Gheorgheni, along the main DN12, the village of Lăzarea (HU: Gyergyószárhegy) holds the **Lázár Castle** (Castelul Lázár) (*Str Bastionului 67*), built by the Lázár family, the oldest part of which is a tower dating from the mid 15th century, but which features a mix of Romanesque, Gothic and Renaissance styles. The future Prince of Transylvania, Gabriel Bethlen, orphaned at a young age, spent much of his childhood here under the guardianship of his uncle, András Lázár. But the fortunes of the castle deteriorated from the 18th century: it was damaged by several fires, and as the financial situation of the Lázár family became more perilous in the 19th century it could not properly be restored, and mostly became uninhabitable. It was not open to visitors at the time of research.

Getting there and away Gheorgheni lies 57km north of Miercurea-Ciuc on the main E578/DN12, and is a similar distance from Praid, on the more minor DN13B. The **railway station** is on the western edge of town, offering services to Miercurea-Ciuc (*1hr*) and Brașov (*3hrs*). The main **bus station** (*Str Gării 6;* \0266 363 999) is nearby, serving destinations including Miercurea-Ciuc (*1½hrs*) and Lacul Roșu (*from 30mins*). The DN12C east from Gheorgheni becomes increasingly spectacular towards Lacul Roșu and then the Bicaz Gorge, through which it enters the region of Moldavia. To the north, the E578/DN12 takes you to Toplița, from where the spa town of Borsec is reached along the DN15.

🏠 **Where to stay and eat** The three-star **Hotel Astoria** (*18 rooms; Str Două Poduri 2;* \0266 365 600; e *info@astoria-hotel.ro;* w *astoria-hotel.ro;* **$$$**) is central and quiet; its restaurant (⊕ *08.00–midnight daily;* **$$$**) is among the best places to eat in town, with a menu ranging from oven-fired pizza to Székely dishes. The courtyard just off the south side of Piața Libertății has cafés and an average pizzeria called **Green Café** (*Piața Libertății 15;* \0266 364 156; ⊕ *09.00–23.00 daily;* **$$**)

BICAZ GORGES-HĂŞMAŞ NATIONAL PARK Established in 1990, the Bicaz Gorges-Hăşmaş National Park (Parcul Naţional Cheile Bicazului-Hăşmaş) (*Park administration: Str Principală 664, Izvoru Mureşului;* \0266 336 540; e *pnbicaz@ mciuc.rosilva.ro;* w *cheilebicazului-hasmas.ro*) straddles Harghita County and Neamţ County in the neighbouring region of Moldavia. The park is focused on the limestone and sandstone massifs of the Hăşmaş Mountains, which are cut with many gorges, and offer good marked walking trails of varying levels of difficulty. It is noted in particular for two impressive natural features. The first is the **Bicaz Gorge**, cut by the waters of the Bicaz River, which forms a spectacular natural passage between the regions of Transylvania and Moldavia. The DN12C road through the gorge offers one of the most impressive drives in Romania. Wooden stalls dispensing cheap souvenirs irritatingly crowd the valley floor at the most scenic spots, though. The area is a popular spot for rock climbing. To get to the gorge take the DN12C road from Gheorgheni towards Bicaz: the gorge stretches for some 6km between Lacul Roşu in the west to Bicazul Ardelean in the east, the latter falling in Neamţ County. The second major sight, beautiful and eerie in equal measure, is Lacul Roşu (see below).

Lacul Roşu Lacul Roşu (Red Lake) is also popularly known as Lacul Ucigaşul (Murderer's Lake), and it is by that more sinister name that it is also known in both Hungarian (Gyilkos-tó) and in German (Mördersee). It was formed by the natural damming of the waters of the Bicaz River by a landslide following an earthquake in 1838. It lies at an altitude of 980m, and reaches a maximum depth of 10m. Compact and L-shaped in form, it offers pleasant boating (⊕ *10.00–18.30 daily in season; 10RON/30mins*), and there is a marked walk around its perimeter. The denuded trunk tips of the submerged forest still poke up above the level of the water. The reddish tinge to the water, resulting from the colour of the iron-rich alluvia deposited in the lake, and the mists that sometimes descend upon the place mean that the lake can take on a mystical, almost sinister air, although this aspect of the place can be more difficult to conjure up in the height of summer, when it can get packed with tourists. The area below the car park is a messy collection of tatty souvenir stalls and basic restaurants, but the visitor can quickly escape this for the more tranquil forested banks of the lake.

There is an **Eco-Info-Centre** (⊕ *10.00–18.00 Tue–Sun*) in the car park above the lake, offering information on local trekking routes.

Lacul Roşu is on the DN12C, 26km east of Gheorgheni, from which town there are some four buses or minibuses daily.

🏠 **Where to stay and eat** The three-star **Hotel Lacu Roşu** (*47 rooms; Lacul Roşu no 32;* \0374 473 728; e *lacurosu@gmail.com;* w *hotellacurosu.ro;* **$$$**), a short walk below the lake, has balconied rooms in a scenic location. Its restaurant (**$$$**), in a separate building, is the smartest place to eat in the resort, though hosts frequent wedding parties. Of the cluster of basic eateries below the car park, the **Panorama Restaurant** (*Lacul Roşu no 15C;* m *0743 179 400;* ⊕ *09.00–22.00 Mon–Fri, 09.00– 23.00 Sat/Sun;* **$$**) has the best views of the lake from its terraces, and trout on the menu, though it has a tendency to close early if there is little evening custom.

BORSEC For most Romanians, the name of Borsec (Borszék/Bad Borseck) is synonymous with mineral water. At an altitude of some 900m, surrounded by coniferous forests, it was known for the curative nature of its mineral water as early as the 16th century. In 1803, an Austrian named Valentin Gunther, finding

THE LEGEND OF MURDERER'S LAKE

There are many legends surrounding the formation and colour of Lacul Roşu. One tale tells of a beautiful young girl named Eszter who met a brave and handsome young man at the market in Gheorgheni. The two fell in love, but sadly it was not their destiny to find happiness, as he was called to the army. Eszter attracted the attentions of a scoundrel, who promised her bounteous riches if she would agree to be his, but she remained faithful to her true love. The scoundrel became angry and tried to kidnap her; in desperation Eszter called out to the mountains to come to her aid. The mountains responded in their own way, bringing forth a thunderous storm that caused rocks to fall, crushing both Eszter and her kidnapper and blocking the river, thus forming the lake.

A more upbeat version of the same tale has the scoundrel taking the poor girl to his hideout in a cave. The girl begs the spirit of the cave to help release her, and the spirit duly obliges, opening up an escape route through the walls of the cave. When the scoundrel finds that the girl has escaped he bangs the walls of the cave so violently that he causes the whole mountain to collapse, burying himself and forming the lake.

Another legend focuses on explaining the reddish colour of the lake waters. It is said that a fierce storm arose, causing a landslide that buried both a shepherd and his flock of sheep, who had been grazing on the fertile valley floor. Their blood oozed up into the waters of the new lake, painting them red. A variant of this story claims that the blood is that of a group of picnickers, who had been enjoying their lunch in the valley when the landslide struck.

himself cured by the local waters of whatever had ailed him, decided to develop a commercial operation here. Together with a partner named Anton Zimmethausen and an expert in glass named Eisner, they built a glass factory here, and in 1806 commenced the commercial bottling of Borsec waters. Borsec secured the title 'Queen of Mineral Waters' at the Vienna World's Fair in 1873. Nationalised during the Communist period, Borsec mineral water is now owned by the Romaqua Group and remains one of the major mineral water brands of Romania.

Borsec's development as a spa resort accompanied the commercial development of its waters. Once ranking among the most important spas in Transylvania, it decayed rapidly following the Romanian Revolution. Today the town has a population of just 2,500 people, some three-quarters of whom are ethnic Hungarian. But the place is gradually being redeveloped as a spa centre as well as a ski resort. For the time being it remains rather frayed around the edges, but the location is glorious, and there are good walking opportunities.

The lower town, which developed to house those employed in the spa resort and bottling plant, contains little of interest, and the touristic focus is on the spa up the hill. The naturally sparkling mineral waters can be tasted in five different springs, housed in latticed wooden pavilions dotted around the resort. Three of these are grouped around the pedestrianised Aleea 7 Izvoare, a verdant spot in the centre of the spa. But the most attractive spot is around an upland meadow known as **Poiana Zânelor**, 'Meadow of the Fairies', which offers a glorious carpet of wild flowers in spring and summer. It sits on an area of high ground above the southern side of the spa. The other two springs, named to honour the Hungarian heroes Kossuth and Petőfi, are encountered on the way up. The meadow is home to the Baia Poiana

Zânelor, the 'fairy bath' as an English-language sign puts it, a small open-air mineral water bath. This has seen better days, and looks far from enticing, but the English-language instructions on its use are wonderful, including the phrase: 'before using the bath take a foot bath and say the Lord's Prayer'. Nearby is another spot in which you can ease your sore feet in the waters in what is labelled 'tiny foot bath'.

Borsec is 27km from Toplița along the scenic DN15. There are **buses** to Toplița (*40mins*).

 Where to stay and eat The large, chalet-like guesthouse **Vila Riki** (*20 dbl; Str Jókai Mór 19;* ✆ *0266 337 602;* e *vilariki@yahoo.com;* w *vilariki.com;* **$$**) offers balconied rooms, a restaurant, a sauna and bicycle and ski rental.

6

Mureş County

Mureş County offers a pretty compelling package for the visitor. The county town, Târgu Mureş, is the most ethnically mixed large town in Romania, with almost equal numbers of ethnic Hungarians and Romanians, and offers beautiful Secession-style architecture and a charming provincial city feel. North of here, along the valley of the Mureş River, the once-beautiful castles of Hungarian aristocrats are emerging once more into public view after decades of Communist-era neglect housing sanatoria or psychiatric institutions. To the south of the county lies the wonderful medieval citadel of Sighişoara, and this part of the county is also home to some of the fine fortified churches established by Saxon communities in Transylvania.

Much of the county is relatively flat, dominated by the basin of the Mureş River and its tributaries, but it rises to the high Călimani and Gurghiu mountains in the north and east respectively. In the Salt Country east of Târgu Mureş is the enticing spa resort of Sovata-Băi, where you can float in the salt-rich Lacul Ursu. Add to the mix such interesting accommodation options as Valea Verde, the 'scattered hotel' concept in the village of Cund, and it is easy to see why Mureş County has an important place on many Transylvanian itineraries.

TÂRGU MUREŞ   *Telephone code 0265, sometimes 0365*

Târgu Mureş (Márosvásárhely/Neumarkt am Mieresch) is a vibrant market centre, very much a Romanian and Hungarian mix and getting the best out of both cultures. It is the most important settlement in the Székely region, but unlike the strongly Hungarian-majority towns of Covasna and Harghita, slightly less than half its population is now ethnic Hungarian. Its attractions today include some beautiful Secession-style buildings, especially the stunning Palace of Culture, and an overall pleasant ambience befitting a city centred on 'Rose Square'. It is also the home of one of the best medical schools in Romania, the University of Medicine and Pharmacy, which brings a cosmopolitan student population to the town, and was the birthplace of SMURD, Romania's well-regarded emergency response service.

HISTORY The settlement was mentioned in documents in 1332 as Novum Forum Siculorum, meaning 'new market town of the Székelys', with a population of mostly Hungarian origin. It became the main economic centre in the area, with craft guilds emerging in the 15th century. A fortress was built here in 1492, but was sacked in 1601 by Habsburg forces under General Giorgio Basta to punish the town for having sided with the Romanian leader Michael the Brave (Mihai Viteazul). It was rebuilt, with the town's guilds each charged with the construction and maintenance of one of the bastions, and the town was granted the status of a 'free royal settlement' in 1616. It became the seat of Transylvania's Supreme Court, the Royal Board, in 1754, and future revolutionaries in the events of 1848, Avram Iancu and Alexandru

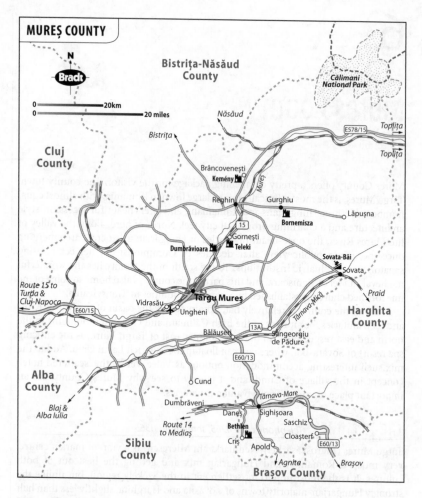

MUREȘ COUNTY

Bistrița-Năsăud County

Călimani National Park

Cluj County

Bistrița County

0 ――――― 20km
0 ――――― 20 miles

Năsăud

E578/15   Toplița

Toplița

Brâncovenești
Kemény

Reghin   Mureș

Gurghiu

Lăpușna

Bornemisza

15

Gornești
Teleki

Dumbrăvioara

Sovata-Băi

Sovata

Route 15 to
Turda &
Cluj-Napoca

E60/15

Vidrasău

Târgu Mureș

Ungheni

Praid

Târnava-Mică

Harghita County

Bălăușeri

13A

Sângeorgiu
de Pădure

Alba County

Cund

E60/13

Blaj &
Alba Iulia

Dumbrăveni

Târnava-Mare

Danes   Sighișoara

Route 14
to Mediaș

Bethlen

Saschiz

Criș

Cloașterf

Apold

E60/13

Agnita

Brașov

Sibiu County

Brașov County

Papiu Ilarian, formed their ideas here while practising as young lawyers. The town was associated with learning through the fine library of Sámuel Teleki and the mathematical studies of Farkas and János Bolyai.

The city was 89% ethnic Hungarian in 1910, but the ethnic Romanian population increased throughout the following century, further assisted in the Communist period by a policy of industrialisation, and at the time of the 2011 census Romanians formed 52% of the city's population, Hungarians 45%, making this one of the most ethnically mixed cities in Romania. Târgu Mureș witnessed ethnic clashes in 1990, resulting in five deaths. The Hungarian playwright András Sütő (1927–2006) was blinded in one eye when the offices of the Democratic Union of Hungarians (UDMR) were attacked. While political differences remain between the communities, the city is now a peaceful, relaxed place, where you will hear both Hungarian and Romanian widely spoken.

GETTING THERE, AWAY AND AROUND

By air Târgu Mureș Transilvania Airport (Aeroportul Transilvania Târgu Mureș; TGM) (*Târgu Mureș–Ludus road, Vidrasău, 547612 Mureș County;* ⟍ *0265 328 259;*

e *office@aeroportultransilvania.ro*; **w** *aeroportultransilvania.ro*) is situated 15km southwest of central Târgu Mureş on route 15/E60 near the village of Vidrasău. The airport is used only by the Hungarian carrier **Wizz Air** (**w** *wizzair.com*), which has direct flights from Târgu Mureş to London Luton (*5 times per week*), and also serves a range of other European cities, including Paris, Madrid and Frankfurt. At the time of writing Târgu Mureş airport was, however, closed, following concerns about the condition of the runway. The local authorities had committed to making the necessary improvements, so hopefully the airport will reopen soon. The previous connection options between the airport and the city had included a P-Airbus shared **transfer service** to the main hotels, bookable through Wizz Air, **taxis** (*approx 30RON*) and a range of car-hire offices.

By rail and bus The main railway station and bus station are to the southwest of the centre. The **railway station** is at Piaţa Gării, off Bulevardul Gheorghe Doja (✆*0265 236 284*), though Târgu Mureş is something of a backwater in the Romanian railway network, and the train will rarely be your fastest option. For example, there is one train daily to Sibiu (*7hrs*), one train to Cluj (*3hrs*) and one to Bucharest (*9hrs*).

There is a much wider range of options by **bus**. The **Autogara Voiajor** (*Str Gheorghe Doja 143;* ✆*0265 237 774*) is beyond the train station, further south along Bulevardul Gheorghe Doja. It serves many destinations in Romania, as well as some international ones. The nearby **Autogara Siletina** (*Str Bega 2*) is mostly focused on local routes of little interest, but some buses to Turda, Cluj and Oradea depart from here. Many microbuses leave for Sighişoara (*every hour, 1hr 10mins*). Other bus and microbus connections include Cluj (*at least 13 daily, 3hrs*), six to Sibiu (*3hrs*), five to Miercurea-Ciuc (*4 hrs*) and three to Bistriţa (*from 2½hrs*). If you're arriving by bus, try to get dropped off in town rather than having to walk back from the bus station – minibuses from Sighişoara, for example, will drop off near the top of Bulevardul 1 Decembrie 1918, by Piaţa Victoriei.

Taxi companies

🚗 **Cornisa** ✆0265 204 943, 0265 211 111
🚗 **Cristitaxi** ✆0265 204 949

🚗 **Transaldea** ✆0265 204 941

Car hire

🚗 **Avis** Târgu Mureş airport; **m** 0733 104 321; **e** targumures@avis.ro; **w** avis.ro; ⏰ 09.30–18.00 daily

🚗 **Oltea** B-dul 1 Decembrie 1918 291D; ✆0265 255 350; **w** rentacar.targu-mures.ro; ⏰ 08.00– 18.00 daily. Also has an office in the airport.

WHERE TO STAY

🏠 **Hotel Privo** (40 rooms in new hotel building, plus 6 in Villa Csonka) B-dul Gheorghe Doja 27; ✆0365 424 442; **e** rezervari@hotelprivo. ro; **w** privo.ro; Upscale modern hotel which has as its core the 1910 Art Nouveau Villa Csonka, the one-time home of local photographer Geza Csonka. It is perched on a hill off B-dul Gheorghe Doja to the southwest of the centre, but accessed from Str Urcuşului. The Villa Csonka rooms have a higher tariff than the main hotel rooms. Impressive but expensive international restaurant ($$$$$). **$$$$$**

🏠 **Hotel Plaza V** (66 rooms) Piaţa Trandafirilor 46–47; ✆0365 730 000; **e** office@plazahotel.ro; **w** plazahotel.ro. A centrally located business hotel, with both 4- & 5-star rooms, & a decidedly off-putting glittering black lobby. Has a spa & fitness centre. **$$$$$** (5-star rooms), **$$$$** (4-star)

🏠 **Hotel Concordia** (30 dbl, 4 suites) Piaţa Trandafirilor 45; ✆0265 260 602; **e** rezervari@ hotelconcordia.ro; **w** hotelconcordia.ro. A central 4-star hotel with pool, fitness centre, zebra-print sofas in the lobby, tacky artwork in the rooms & a restaurant ($$$) in a

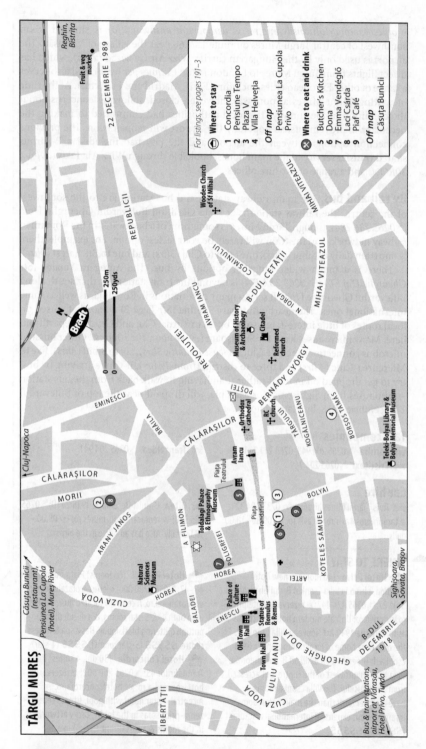

TÂRGU MUREȘ

For listings, see pages 191–3

Where to stay
1 Concordia
2 Pensiune Tempo
3 Plaza V
4 Villa Helveția

Off map
Pensiunea La Cupola
Privo

Where to eat and drink
5 Butcher's Kitchen
6 Dona
7 Emma Vendéglő
8 Laci Csárda
9 Piaf Café

Off map
Căsuța Bunicii

250m
250yds

Reghin,
Bistrița

Fruit & veg
market

22 DECEMBRIE 1989

REPUBLICII

Wooden Church
of Sf Mihail

COSMINULUI

AVRAM IANCU

B-DUL CETĂȚII

N IORGA

MIHAI VITEAZUL

MIHAI VITEAZUL

Museum of History
& Archaeology

Citadel

Reformed
church

REVOLUȚIEI

EMINESCU

BRĂILA

POȘTEI

Orthodox
cathedral

CĂLĂRAȘILOR

BERNADY GYÖRGY

RC
church

TÂRGULUI

KOGĂLNICEANU

BORSOS TAMÁS

Teleki-Bolyai Library &
Bolyai Memorial Museum

CĂLĂRAȘILOR

MORII

ARANY JÁNOS

A FILIMON

Toldalagi Palace
& Ethnography
Museum

Piața
Teatrului

Avram
Iancu

Piața
Trandafirilor

BOLYAI

KÖTELES SÁMUEL

CUZA VODĂ

HOREA

POLIGRAFIEI

Natural
Sciences
Museum

HOREA

BALADEI

ENESCU

Palace of
Culture

Statue of
Romulus
& Remus

Old Town
Hall

Town Hall

ARTEI

IULIU MANIU

CUZA VODĂ

GHEORGHE DOJA

B-DUL
DECEMBRIE
1918

LIBERTĂȚII

Căsuța Bunicii
(restaurant),
Pensiunea La Cupola
(hotel), Mureș River

Cluj-Napoca

Sighișoara,
Sovata, Brașov

Bus & train stations,
airport at Vidrasău,
Hotel Privo, Turda

N

Bradt

converted turn-of-the-last-century building. **$$$$**

🏠 **Pensiune Tempo** (27 rooms) Str Morii 27; 📞 0265 213 552; e office@tempo.ro; w tempo.ro. Offering rooms in both 3- & 4-star categories, it is in the same complex as the popular Laci Csárda restaurant (see below). **$$$**

🏠 **Villa Helveția** (11 rooms) Str Borsos Tamás 13; 📞 0265 216 954; e office@villahelvetia.ro. Central 3-star pension close to the Teleki-Bolyai Library with a restaurant, wine cellar & terrace. **$$$**

✖ WHERE TO EAT AND DRINK

✖ **Căsuța Bunicii** Piața Matei Corvin 2; 📞 0265 307 011; w lacupola.ro; ⏰ 10.00–23.45 daily. Some 1km north of the town centre, this is a rustic place serving local dishes. You can stay here too, at the Pensiunea La Cupola (*10 rooms*; **$$$**). **$$$**

✖ **Dona** Piața Trandafirilor 43; 📞 0265 250 256; w restaurantuldona.ro; ⏰ 07.00–midnight daily. With a terrace on the central square, this is a good place for a coffee or ice cream, as well as offering an extensive if unremarkable menu with mainly Italian & Romanian dishes. **$$$**

✖ **Laci Csárda** Str Morii 27; 📞 0265 213 552; w tempo.ro; ⏰ 10.00–midnight daily. Capacious wooden-panelled restaurant with a large courtyard, serving Transylvanian Hungarian specialities & offering live Roma music. **$$$**

✖ **Butcher's Kitchen** Piața Trandafirilor 13; m 0771 462 591; ⏰ 09.00–22.00 Mon–Fri, 11.00–23.00 Sat. A funky street food place, offering burgers & their speciality beef sandwich. Székely Igazí Csíki Sör beer on draught. **$$**

✖ **Piaf Café** Str Bolyai 10; m 0771 525 526; w piafcafe.ro; ⏰ 08.00–01.00 Mon–Thu, 08.00–03.00 Fri, 10.00–03.00 Sat, 10.00–midnight Sun. An extensive cocktail list serves to reinforce the mesmerising effect of the illuminated red & white bottles behind the bar. Also an exhibition space for upcoming artists. **$$**

✳ ✖ **Emma Vendéglő** Str Horea 6; 📞 0265 263 021; ⏰ 08.00–20.00 Mon–Sat, 08.00–18.00 Sun. Hungarian Transylvanian basement restaurant. Everyone has the excellent-value menu of the day, served at the counter. **$**

OTHER PRACTICALITIES

$ **Unicredit Bank** Piața Trandafirilor 44; 📞 0265 261 790; w unicredit.ro; ⏰ 09.00–17.00 Mon–Fri

✚ **Ropharma** Piața Trandafirilor 36–38; 📞 0265 266 649; ⏰ 08.00–20.00 Mon–Fri, 09.00–14.00 Sat

✉ **Post office** Str Revoluției 2A; m 0725 902 393; ⏰ 08.00–19.00 Mon–Fri, 09.00–13.00 Sat

WHAT TO SEE AND DO

Around Piața Trandafirilor The colourful main square, the Square of Roses (Piața Trandafirilor) stretches for a long way in a northeasterly direction towards the black-and-white neo-Byzantine **Romanian Orthodox Cathedral** (Catedrala Ortodoxă-Română) (1925–34), built right opposite and dwarfing the 18th-century Baroque **Roman Catholic Church** (Biserica Romano-Catolică). The church and the equestrian statue of **Avram Iancu** in front provide an ethnic Romanian counterpoise to the Hungarian Secessionist buildings towards the southern end of the square.

Another worthwhile sight at the northern end of Piața Trandafirilor is the **Toldalagi Palace** (Palatul Toldalagi), a Baroque building dating from 1772 which now houses the **Museum of Ethnography and Folk Art** (Muzeul de Etnografie și Artă Populară) (*Piața Trandafirilor 11*; 📞 *0265 250 169*; w *muzeumures.ro*; ⏰ *09.00–16.00 Tue–Fri, 09.00–14.00 Sat, 09.00–13.00 Sun; adult/child 6/3RON*). With good collections of local dress, textiles and ceramics, it is more interestingly presented than many equivalent collections in Romania.

At the beginning of the 20th century, the influential Hungarian mayor Dr György Bernády (1864–1938) shaped the cityscape, his name being associated with the modernisation of the city and in particular with the construction of the Art

Nouveau Secessionist-style buildings which are today its principal tourist attraction. The jewel in the crown is the **Palace of Culture** (Palatul Culturii/Kultúrpalota) (*Piaţa Trandafirilor;* ⊕ *09.00–18.00 Tue–Fri, 09.00–16.00 Sat/Sun; adult/child 12/6RON*), built between 1911 and 1913, and one of the most important and beautiful buildings of the Transylvanian Secessionist movement. Externally, the building features polychrome roof tiles and mosaics made by **Miksa Róth**, the Budapest genius of colour and glass, but the external decoration does little to prepare you for the riotousness of the interior. The mirrored entrance hall is exuberant enough, and leads on to gilt and floral wallpaper everywhere, but the most striking room in the building is the **Hall of Mirrors**; not a fairground novelty but a stunning hall filled with fantastic stained-glass windows from the artist's workshop. The windows illustrate ancient Székely legends and folklore. The building centres on a **concert hall** with great Art Nouveau chandeliers and a pipe organ. Concerts of the State Philharmonic are held here, but it also has a range of exhibitions and museums in the rooms around the concert hall.

One interesting display contrasts the mayoralties of Dr György Bernády at the start of the 20th century, with its promotion of Hungarian cultural identity, and that of the interwar mayor Emil Dandea, governing the town when Transylvania had been incorporated into Romania, and who promoted Romanian cultural identity through works such as the Orthodox cathedral, the statue of Avram Iancu and a statue of **Romulus and Remus** feeding from the she-wolf, which stands in a patch of garden next door and emphasises the Latin origins of the town. The Palace of Culture also contains a **Romanian modern art gallery**, with a range of 19th- and 20th-century pieces including the inevitable painting of an ox cart by Nicolae Grigorescu. Another gallery is devoted to the folksy Communist-era sculptures and paintings of **Ion Vlasiu**, and there is a **Hungarian Classical Art Gallery**, comprising mostly 19th-century works.

The **ticket office** for the Palace of Culture, including for concerts of the State Philharmonic, is separate from the main entrance, and to be found at the corner of the building (*Str George Enescu 1;* ☏ *0365 451 034*). The main **tourist information office** (*Str Enescu 2;* ☏ *0365 404 934;* e *turism@cjmures.ro;* w *cjmures.ro;* ⊕ *Jun–Aug 08.00–16.00 Mon & Sat, 08.00–18.00 Tue–Fri, Sep–May 08.00–16.00 Mon–Thu, 08.00–15.00 Fri*) is just next door.

There is another fine Secessionist-style building over the road, the **Old Town Hall** (completed in 1907), which now houses the office of the Prefect of Mureş County as well as the County Council administration. Like the Palace of Culture, the building is the work of Budapest architects Dezső Jakab and Marcell Komor, and is dominated by a square clock tower standing to one side. Visits are in theory possible, covering the clock tower and internal courtyard (*adult/child 6/2RON; tickets sold from the Palace of Culture tricket office*), but at the time of research the tower was closed for renovation.

The **town hall** next door, built in the late 1930s, is another of the buildings promoted by mayor Emil Dandea in a Romanian, neo-Brancovean style with a columned loggia, in sharp contrast to its Hungarian-inspired neighbour.

There are a couple of sights on or around Strada Horea just to the northwest of Piaţa Trandafirilor. The **Natural Sciences Museum** (Muzel de Ştinţele Naturii) (*Str Horea 24;* ☏ *0365 430 390;* w *muzeumures.ro;* ⊕ *09.00–16.00 Tue–Fri, 09.00–14.00 Sat, 09.00–13.00 Sun; adult/child 6/3RON*) is one to save for rainy days. If you do come this way, make the short detour along Strada Aurel Filimon to see the elegant domed beige-and-white **synagogue** (*Str Aurel Filimon 21;* ☏ *0265 261 810;* ⊕ *09.00–12.30 Mon–Fri, though they ask you to ring at least 1 day beforehand*), dating from 1899.

The Teleki-Bolyai Library and the Citadel From Piața Trandafirilor head along Strada Bolyai, southeastwards and up the hill to reach the Baroque **Teleki-Bolyai Library** (Biblioteca Teleki-Bolyai) (*Str Bolyai 17;* \0265 261 857; w *telekiteka. ro;* ⊕ *10.00–18.00 Tue–Fri, 10.00–13.00 Sat/Sun; free admission*). It was founded by Hungarian aristocrat Count Sámuel Teleki, who served as Chancellor of Transylvania from 1791 until his death in 1822. An avid book collector, he amassed some 40,000 volumes and opened the library in 1802, since when it has been in continuous use. The collection was expanded in the 1950s when the library of the local Protestant College was moved here, and the enlarged collection was given the name Teleki-Bolyai Library. Portraits of Sámuel Teleki look down upon his collection, as if to check that all is in good order. Among the items on display is an engraved copy of the US Declaration of Independence dating from 1819.

The same building houses the **Bolyai Memorial Museum** (Museul Bolyai) (*contact details & opening hours as above*), with displays on the lives of a father and son, Farkas and János Bolyai, two outstanding mathematicians who spent most of their lives here. It was in this city that Farkas Bolyai published his greatest work, the *Tentamen,* in 1832, a farsighted treatise on the foundations of mathematics. A renaissance man, he wrote plays, penned a book on forestry and designed fuel-efficient stoves. His son János was a pioneer of non-Euclidean geometry and gives his name to the 'Bolyai' in Romania's largest university, Babeș-Bolyai in Cluj. Outside the museum, statues of Farkas and János Bolyai rest under a tree.

Head in a northeasterly direction along tree-lined suburban streets and family houses up to the citadel (Cetate) (⊕ *09.30–21.00 Tue–Sun; free admission*), whose main entrance is on Bulevardul Cetății. The fortress dates from 1492, though was rebuilt in the 17th century after it was destroyed in 1601. It has a pentagonal form with seven bastions, each maintained by one of the town guilds. It has recently been somewhat excessively restored, creating an attractive and green environment, marred by jarring features such as an ugly and discordant glass-domed **tourist information office** (not yet opened at the time of writing).

The **Reformed Church** (Biserica Reformată din Cetate) within the citadel is the oldest building in Târgu Mureș, originally built in a Gothic style in the 14th century as part of a Franciscan Monastery, and converted to a Reformed church in the 16th century.

The two-storey yellow-walled building within the citadel houses a **Museum of History and Archaeology** (Muzeul de Istorie și Arheologie) (\ *0365 400 414;* ⊕ *09.00–16.00 Tue–Fri, 10.00–14.00 Sat/Sun; adult/child 6/3RON*), which is still under development: at the time of research there were just two open rooms, one devoted to Dacian art, the other featuring a display on the human skeleton.

Further north, along Strada Avram Iancu, the second right heading east for 100m is the **Wooden Church of Sf Mihail** (Biserica de Lemn Sfântul Arhanghel Mihai) (1793–94) sitting in a large churchyard with an onion dome and a beautiful interior. Romanians seek out this church because it is said that national poet Mihai Eminescu slept in the porch in 1866 while passing through Târgu Mureș on the way to Blaj, as there was no room at any of the taverns. Further north towards the railway line, the **fruit and vegetable market** (*Piața 22 Decembrie 1989*) is a good place to buy local fruit and vegetables, as well as homemade Romanian cheeses.

HEADING EAST

SÂNGEORGIU DE PĂDURE If you are taking road 13A towards the spa resort of Sovata-Băi from either Târgu Mureș or Sighișoara, there is a worthwhile stop to be made in the small town of Sângeorgiu de Pădure (Erdőszentgyörgy/Sankt

Georgen auf der Heide), which has an unexpected connection with the British royal family.

This predominantly ethnic Hungarian settlement has at its heart the elegant two-storey **Rhédey Castle** (Castelul Rhédey) (*Piaţa Rhédey 1;* \ *0265 578 707;* ⊕ *10.00–17.00 daily; 5RON*). This dates from the 17th century, but was comprehensively rebuilt at the start of the 19th. The home of the Rhédey family until 1885, it was purchased that year by a merchant named Rudolf Schuller, and later passed to the Romanian state, serving as local government offices and then a school until 2009. It has been comprehensively restored with the help of EU regional development funding, and now houses a tourist information office and museum space, with a series of exhibitions. The most interesting chronicles the life and death of the nearby village of Bezidu Nou, lost beneath the waters of an artificial lake created by a dam construction in the 1980s. The castle's British royal connection is that it was the childhood home of Claudia Rhédey, the grandmother of Queen Mary of Teck, wife of King George V. A statue of Claudia stands in the grounds outside.

Claudia was born here in 1812, and in 1835 married Duke Alexander of Württemberg. Their son, Francis of Teck, was to marry into the British royal family; his eldest daughter, Mary of Teck, moved to the very heart of the family on marrying the future King George V. Sadly, Claudia was already long dead: killed at the age of 29 following a carriage accident while visiting her husband at a military training camp in Austria.

There are more connections to Claudia Rhédey to be seen in the **Reformed Church** (Biserica Reformată) immediately opposite the castle. It was initially a Catholic church, and is mentioned in a document from 1333. It has served as a Reformed church since 1640. It was of course supported by the local aristocrats, the Rhédey family, and it is here that Claudia's remains lie. Two plaques in the church emphasise the connections with the British royal family. The first, in memory of Claudine Countess Rhédey, was erected in 1904 by 'her granddaughter Victoria Mary Princess of Wales'. The second, immediately underneath, records the gift in 1935 from Her Majesty Queen Mary through which 'the church in which some of her ancestors lie buried was improved and restored'. The church interior today is welcoming, with colourful benches painted in typical blue and red Székely designs.

Entrance to the church is included in the admission fee for the castle: staff will also show you the guest book signed by His Royal Highness The Prince of Wales during a visit here in 2008 to see the place where his great-great-great-grandmother is buried.

There are reasonably frequent **buses** or **minibuses** from Sângeorgiu de Pădure to Târgu Mureş (*50mins*) and Sovata (*40mins*).

SOVATA-BĂI The town of Sovata (HU: Szováta) and adjacent resort of Sovata-Băi (HU: Szovátafürdő) are located in a beautiful wooded valley in a salt-rich region known as the **Ţara Sarelui/Sóvidék (Salt Country)** (see also *Praid*, pages 183–4). Sovata-Băi was a popular spa resort in the late 19th and early 20th centuries and, unlike some other Romanian spas, has seen considerable investment following the collapse of the Communist regime, even if some of its places to stay are rather spartan. Today the resort is a mix of attractive wooden-walled villas with little spires and large Communist-era hotel complexes that have undergone various degrees of refurbishment.

The resort centres on the salty waters of **Lacul Ursu** (Bear Lake) (⊕ *10.00–13.00 & 15.00–18.00 daily; adult/child 25/20RON*), which gets packed out at the height of summer, mostly with Hungarian and domestic tourists. The lake was formed in 1875, when following a downpour a sinkhole was produced in a hay-meadow that became full of water and collapsed. Its saltiness makes a relaxed float easy, and the water is said to offer all manner of health benefits, particularly in the treatment of rheumatic illnesses.

Lacul Ursu is apparently the largest heliothermal salt lake in Europe; its particularly strong heliothermal properties arising because of a rain-fed less salty stratum overlying the saltier waters below, which helps to trap solar energy in the latter. Indeed, the 2-hour pause in the middle of the day when swimming is not allowed is not an example of poor tourism planning but is scheduled in order to preserve the heliothermal properties of the water.

It sits within the 79ha Bear Lake Nature Reserve (Rezervaţia Naturală Lacul Ursu), a forested area with a distinctive ecology arising from its underpinning by a salt massif covered by a thin layer of particularly rich soil. The reserve houses several smaller salt lakes: Aluniş (Hazelwood), Mierlei (Blackbird), Roşu (Red) and Verde (Green). There is also the freshwater Lacul Paraschiva, and the rock salt mound just beyond Red Lake known as Muntele de Sare. There are many footpaths and marked trails around the lakes, which make for pleasant walks.

Another saltwater lake just outside the nature reserve is **Lacul Negru** (Black Lake), alongside Strada Bradului within the resort, which has also been developed as a swimming and treatment centre.

A nice way to get a quick overview of the resort is by taking the **mini train** (m *0744 628 086; 6RON*) which departs from the roundabout on Strada Trandafirilor in front of Bear Lake for a 20- to 25-minute tour of the resort whenever a critical number of passengers has arrived.

Getting there and away Sovata is situated 45km due east of Târgu Mureş. It is best reached by first heading south on the E60 towards Sighişoara. After 20km, turn left at Bălăuseri onto route 13A and drive for 40km through small villages and beautiful farming land to reach Sovata. From there look for signs to Sovata-Băi, the lake resort and hotels. By **bus**, frequent microbuses leave Târgu Mureş bus station for Sovata every day (*1½hrs*). There are also several buses from Odorheiu Secuiesc (*just over 1hr*) and Miercurea-Ciuc (*2½hrs*).

Tourist information The **tourist information office** (*Str Trandafirilor;* ☏ *0365 082 197;* ⊕ *10.00–17.00 Mon–Sat*) is located in the pavilion below the Danubius Hotel Sovata, near Lacul Ursu, but its staff are unhelpful and take pains to point out that they can't assist with accommodation bookings. **Salt Lake Travel** (*Str Bradului 2/A;* ☏ *0265 577 421;* e *cazare@sovatatravel.ro;* w *sovatatravel.ro;* ⊕ *Sep–Jun 09.00–17.00 Mon–Fri, 09.00–16.00 Sat, Jul & Aug 10.00–21.00 Mon–Sat, 10.00–14.00 Sun*) is a private travel agency, but in many ways more helpful than the official tourist information office.

 Where to stay

Danubius Hotel Brădet (88 dbl, 5 apt) Str Vulturului 68; ☏ 0265 570 506; e sovatahotel@ szovata.ro; w danubiushotels.ro. The Hungarian Danubius Hotel Group occupies centre-stage in the Sovata-Băi accommodation scene, running the 3 main large hotels in the resort. Directly up the hill from its sister hotel, the Sovata, the Brădet offers a broadly similar deal, but with slightly higher prices due to more recent modernisation. **$$$$$**

Danubius Hotel Sovata (168 rooms) Str Trandafirilor 111; ☏ 0265 570 151; e sovatahotel@ szovata.ro; w sovatahotel.ro. The 6-storey white concrete Sovata is mainly geared towards all-inclusive package arrangements. The upside is access included to the excellent spa (the warm salt pool is particularly relaxing) & to Lacul Ursu; the downside is a restaurant based around a buffet which prizes quantity over quality. They have some rooms equipped for disabled guests, & a wide range of medical treatments for those referred by doctors. $$$$$

🏠 **Hotel Pacsirta** (16 rooms) Str Trandafirilor 85/A; ☎0365 082 480; e iroda@hotelpacsirta.ro; w hotelpacsirta.ro. A stylish small hotel, built in 2010 but in the style of the traditional wooden villas of Sovata-Băi. The most expensive rooms have wooden balconies. Lack of AC is a possible drawback in summer. $$$$$ ($$$$ without balcony)

🏠 **Hotel Făget** (134 rooms, 2 apt) Str Vulturului 39; ☎0265 570 651; e sovatahotel@ szovata.ro; w danubiushotels.ro. The ugly sister of the Danubius hotels in the resort, the Făget is connected to the Brădet by a pedestrian overpass: walking across it is like stepping back 30 years. The

group will at some point get round to modernising the Făget & hiking up prices to its sisters' levels; until it does expect décor & service reminiscent of Communist times. $$$

🏠 **Pensiunea Speranța** (8 rooms, 2 apt) Str Trandafirilor 63; ☎0265 570 540; e pensiuneasperanta@yahoo.com; w pensiuneasperanta.ro. At the upper end of the guesthouse bracket: rooms have AC & b/fast is included. There is off-road parking & a nice garden. $$$

🏠 **Pensiunea Szeles** (4 rooms) Str Trandafirilor 77A; m 0745 815 630. Sovata-Băi is full of small guesthouses with rooms to rent signs. The Szeles is typical of this category: no frills, no b/fast (though access to the kitchen is included), but clean & central. $$

✗ Where to eat and drink

✗ **Boema** Str Bradului 36; ☎0265 571 102; ⊕ noon–midnight daily. Wide-ranging menu, including traditional Romanian & Székely dishes, with a pleasant terrace. $$$

✗ **Ciuperca Mică** Str Bradului 42; ☎0265 570 298; w ciupercamica.ro; ⊕ 09.00–23.00 daily. Also

known by its Hungarian name, Kicsi Gomba, the 'little mushroom' is housed in a hexagonal building next to the Gate 2 entrance to Lacul Ursu. The menu includes international & local dishes, but with some enticing touches & ingredients, as in their gnocchi with a wild garlic sauce. $$$

Other practicalities The nearest post office and banks are in the adjacent town of Sovata, but there is an **ATM** on Strada Trandafirilor opposite a small **supermarket** gloriously named Kevin (*Str Trandafirilor 84*). The latter is also a good place to stock up on your souvenir rainbow-coloured bath salts. The resort also has a pharmacy, **Farmacia Montana** (*Str Trandafirilor 82*; ☎*0374 930 747*; ⊕ *09.00–21.00 daily*).

HEADING NORTH

CASTLES ALONG THE MUREȘ RIVER VALLEY The Mureș River valley leads north out of Târgu Mureș to Reghin. The main DN15 follows the course of the river through a series of villages with manor houses and castles built by some of the leading aristocratic families of Transylvania. These castles have had tough histories. Nationalised by the Communists, they were mostly used as hospitals, sanatoria or to house local administrations, and their condition deteriorated sharply. They have gradually been restored to the heirs of their former owners; also the return of properties seized by the Communists is a slow-moving and complex legal process. Their new owners are now trying to bring the castles back to their former glory. This is a fascinating time to visit the area, as you witness the transition of once fine stately homes from derelict shells towards something closer to their previous splendour.

The town at the heart of this area, **Reghin** (Szászrégen/Regen), lying at the confluence of the Mureș and Gurghiu rivers, has a population of some 33,000 and is known throughout Romania as a centre of violin production. The Hora factory, founded in 1951, claims the title of the largest factory for bowed instruments and guitars in Europe. Reghin was long based around two adjacent communities, German and Hungarian, but most of the ethnic Germans have now left, and ethnic Romanians form the majority of the population.

Reghin is 30km north of Târgu Mures on the DN15. There are frequent buses and minibuses (*50mins*).

Dumbrăvioara Some 15km north of Târgu Mureș, the village of Dumbrăvioara merits a brief stop to visit the mausoleum of the Teleki family, located in a low whitewashed building outside the village. Among the members of the family buried in the **Teleki Mausoleum** are Count Sámuel Teleki (1739–1822), one-time Chancellor of Transylvania and founder of Târgu Mureș's Teleki Library (page 195). Sámuel Teleki also built the Baroque Teleki Castle in Dumbrăvioara, which now houses a school. Also buried here is his grandson, another Sámuel Teleki (1845–1916), a noted explorer of Africa who named Lake Rudolf (now Lake Turkana) after Crown Prince Rudolf of Austria.

To reach the mausoleum, turn right at the village off route 15 onto a more minor road marked for Sângeru de Pădure. Then turn right again beside a Romanian Orthodox church onto an unpaved road. The mausoleum is visible on your left, at the top of a slope. There are both **buses** and **trains** from Târgu Mureș to Dumbrăvioara, taking about 30 minutes, from where you will have to walk to the mausoleum itself.

Gornești Another couple of kilometres on is the village of Gornești (HU: Gernyeszeg), which has at its centre a rather grander palace linked to the Teleki family. The estate at Gornești came into the possession of Mihály Teleki in 1674. One of his grandsons, László Teleki, inherited the estate and constructed **Teleki Castle** (Castelul Teleki) (☏ *0265 214 977;* m *0749 356 134;* ⊕ *10.00–18.30 daily, but call ahead; donation expected*), a fine Baroque palace in the place of the old fortress. László was the elder brother of Sámuel, who was building the Dumbrăvioara Castle down the road. In 1874, István Bethlen, who was to be Prime Minister of Hungary in the 1920s, was born here. In common with so many of the aristocratic estates in Romania, the castle suffered deeply during the Communist period, when it was used as a sanatorium for children with tuberculosis. It was restored to the descendants of the Teleki family in 2011, and they have embarked on the painstaking process of restoring it. A few rooms have been furnished to give a sense of their original grandeur, and as a venue for functions. The gardens are overgrown, but hint at their former glory when, at the start of the 19th century, József Teleki, grandson of László, converted the park from a French to an English style.

The castle is situated 17km north of Târgu Mureș on route 15 towards Reghin. Gornești is served by a few **trains** daily from Târgu Mureș (*30mins*).

Brâncovenești The village of Brâncovenești (Marosvécs/Wetsch) is of note for the 16th-century **Kemény Castle** (Castelul Kemény) (m *0741 225 141;* ⊕ *10.00– 17.00 Tue–Sun, but call in advance; suggested donation adult/child 15/7RON*), built in Renaissance style. It was given in 1648 by Prince George II Rákóczi to Prince János Kemény, who served as Rákóczi's chief adviser and later became Prince of Transylvania. It remained in the Kemény family for the next 300 years. Confiscated by the Communists, it was used as a psychiatric hospital, but was restored to the heirs of the Kemény family in 2014. A monument containing some of the ashes of controversial ethnic Hungarian writer Albert Wass, condemned as a war criminal in Romania, lies in the grounds of the castle.

Brâncovenești is also known for its **Cherry Festival** (Târgul Cireșelor), held on the first Sunday in July.

Brâncovenești lies 10km north of Reghin on the main DN15 towards Topliţa.

THE GURGHIU RIVER VALLEY Some 13km east of Reghin, along the valley of the Gurghiu River, the village of **Gurghiu** (Görgényszentimre/Görgen) is home to **Bornemisza Castle** (Castelul Bornemisza) (🕐 *08.00–17.00 daily; free admission*), located in the centre of the village. The first palace to be built here was the work of Prince György Rákóczi I in the mid 17th century, but in 1734 the estate was leased by the Bornemisza family. They built the current castle, together with a renowned dendrological park in the grounds. They had to surrender the estate in the mid 19th century on the expiry of the lease, though not until the conclusion of a trial lasting 27 years. Back in state ownership, the place was later used as a hunting lodge by Prince Rudolf Josef, the Crown Prince of Austria, who is best remembered for his death in a suicide pact with his mistress, Mary Vetsera. It later hosted a forestry school.

Today the castle is in very poor condition: the county museum reportedly has the challenging task of attempting to transform it into a centre for culture. The two-storey castle, topped by an onion-domed tower, runs along one side of an interior courtyard which is decorated with stone sphinxes. Other buildings around the courtyard include a Greco-Catholic church. The dendrological park is behind the castle, and still makes for a pleasant if rather overgrown place to stroll.

One of the better known of Transylvania's **Girls' Fairs** (Târgul Fetelor); (*contact the village administration on* ☏ *0265 536 003*) is held each year on the Mociar Plateau outside Gurghiu, usually at the end of June. These were traditionally events where girls and boys from the surrounding area looking to wed could meet potential partners, though they have lost their original purpose and are now more generic celebrations of local folk traditions.

The drive further eastwards along the Gurghiu River valley is an increasingly scenic one, the road lined with cherry and walnut trees, deep red roses, purple clematis and vines heavy with grapes, though the quality of the road becomes gradually poorer too. Some 45km east of Reghin the road terminates in the Gurghiului Mountains at **Lăpușna**, a forest settlement at an altitude of 815m, known for its **Royal Hunting Lodge** (Castelul Regal de Vânătoare). King Ferdinand acquired 4ha of forest and meadow land here in 1923, and construction began of the impressive wooden lodge, which was finalised in 1933. It hosted aristocratic hunting parties during the reign of King Carol II, and later those of the Communist elite under Ceaușescu. Soviet leader Khrushchev was a guest here. A few hundred metres away is the **wooden Church of St Nicholas** (Biserica de Lemn Sfântul Nicolae), built in 1779 and purchased in 1939 by King Carol II from the village of Comori to serve as a place of prayer for the royal family. A monastery was established here in 1997, with the role, *inter alia*, of taking care of the church.

It is difficult to explore the Gurghiu River valley without your own transport. There are **buses** from Târgu Mureș only as far as Reghin (*about 50mins*).

CĂLIMANI NATIONAL PARK In the far northeast of Transylvania, on the border of Mureș and Suceava counties, and including also parts of Harghita and Bistrița-Năsăud, the Călimani Mountains (Munţii Călimani) are a large volcanic massif, with the 2,102m Pietrosul Călimani as their highest point. The mountains centre on a large volcanic crater, with a diameter of 10km, around which the highest peaks are situated. The lower slopes are covered with forests of beech, spruce, juniper and Arolla pine (*Pinus cembra*), with dwarf pine and alpine rose characteristic of higher altitudes. The Călimani National Park (*Sat Saru Dornei no 54C, Suceava County;* \0230 371 104; e *calimanipark@gmail.com;* w *calimani.ro*) was established in 1990, and is one of the largest in Romania.

The park is easier to access from the Suceava side, where the park administration is based, than from the Transylvania one, although there are hiking possibilities northwards into the massif from both Răstoliţa and Stânceni in Mureş County, on the DN15 between Reghin and Topliţa.

SIGHIŞOARA *Telephone code 0265, sometimes 0365*

Situated 55km southwest of Târgu Mureş, Sighişoara (Segesvár/Schassburg) is the archetypal Transylvanian town, just how we imagine it. The 12th-century Saxon citadel town does not disappoint and everything looks like a Dracula film set, from the dusty lower town to the steep climb up to the citadel itself, adorned by a fairytale clock tower, the covered wooden steps up to the Gothic church on the hill and the ancient medieval houses lurching into narrow cobble-stoned streets.

Sighişoara has a great atmosphere that even the cheesy Dracula souvenir shops cannot diminish. The historic centre of the town is a UNESCO World Heritage Site and a miss-at-your-peril item on the Transylvanian tour agenda.

Walking through the ancient cobbled streets, sloping to the middle where ancient shallow drains ran, you can admire the crumbling **burghers' houses** in the walled citadel district, each one a little shabby with pastel green, custard or plum paint peeling from beneath the shuttered windows, but still evocative of a more magical time. The walls of the citadel include nine surviving towers, the most impressive being the **Clock Tower** (Turnul cu Ceas), once home to the city hall and whose spire dominates the Sighişoara skyline. Visitors reach the citadel's inner treasures through an arch in the tower, climbing up a steep, cobbled path.

HISTORY Founded by Transylvanian Saxons, Sighişoara is one of the most beautiful and best-preserved medieval towns in Europe. Its citadel was built in the 12th century, when it was known as Castrum Sex, in reference to the six-sided Roman fort on whose site the place was built. In 1298, the town was mentioned as Schespurch, and in 1367 it was awarded urban status under the name Civitas de Segusvar.

In the 14th and 15th centuries, Sighişoara's industrious burghers, craftsmen and tradesmen provided the funds for the construction of a strong defence system guarded by 14 towers and several bastions. Each tower was built, maintained and defended by a craft guild. The most striking is the 14th-century Clock Tower, which controlled the main gate of the defensive wall.

GETTING THERE, AWAY AND AROUND
By air The closest airports are at **Târgu Mureş** (TGM; 48km), **Cluj-Napoca** (CLJ; 145km) and **Sibiu** (SBZ; 87km), although Târgu Mureş was closed for repairs at the time of writing.

By rail and bus The railway and bus stations are situated north of the centre over the Târnava Mare River. The **railway station** (Gară Sighişoara) is at Strada Libertăţii 52 (\0265 771 886). Trains connect Sighişoara to Bucharest (*5hrs by fastest train*), Braşov (*2–3hrs*) and Cluj-Napoca (*3hrs*). For Sibiu a change of trains is needed at either Mediaş or Copşa Mică, which makes the bus a better option between these towns. There are also international connections, including Budapest (*13hrs*).

The **bus station** is close by, at Strada Libertății 53 (☏*0265 771 260;* ⊕ *04.30–18.00 daily*). There are numerous buses to Târgu Mureş (*1½hrs*), and a few buses a day to other Transylvanian destinations, including to Mediaş (*1hr*) and Sibiu (*2hrs*). There's even one bus a week making a 29-hour journey to Paris.

Parking
There is car parking in various places in the lower town, notably Piaţa Octavian Goga, conveniently at the base of the citadel. Tickets cost 1.5RON an hour or 5RON per day. Access by car to the citadel itself is allowed only if you are staying there.

TOURIST INFORMATION
The tourist information centre is in the central Piaţa Octavian Goga (*no 8;* ☏ *0265 770 415;* e *office@sighisoara-infotourism.com;* w *infosighisoara.ro;* ⊕ *10.00–18.00 Mon–Sat*).

 WHERE TO STAY *Map, see opposite*
Sighişoara's charm as a well-preserved UNESCO-listed medieval citadel has an inevitable consequence in terms of both tourist numbers and hotel prices, which are closer to those of the Transylvanian cities than other towns of Sighişoara's size. But prices drop considerably out of the main summer season, when there are some real bargains to be had.

✳ 🏠**Fronius Residence** (11 rooms) Str Şcolii 13; ☏0265 779 173; e contact@fronius-residence. ro; w froniusresidence.ro. Smart boutique hotel at the heart of the citadel, with individually designed rooms. **$$$$$**

🏠 **Doubletree by Hilton Sighişoara – Cavaler** (74 rooms) Str Consiliul Europei 6; ☏0365 085 555; w doubletree3.hilton.com. Between the citadel & the Târnava Mare River, this offers all you would expect from the brand. **$$$$**

🏠 **Pensiunea şi Pivniţa lui Teo** (3 dbl, 1 apt) Str Şcolii 14; ☏0265 771 677; e office@delateo. ro; w delateo.ro. This small pension in the heart of the citadel offers an intriguing combination of bed & booze, with tasting of the local wine & *palincă* included in the room rate. There is an atmospheric vaulted wine cellar, with a shop & a quiet inside courtyard. **$$$$**

🏠 **Casa Cu Cerb** (2 sgl, 8 dbl) Str Şcolii 1; ☏0265 774 625; e info@casacucerb.ro; w casacucerb.ro. The Stag House is in a historic building on Piaţa Cetăţii, named after the mural, stag skull & antlers on the corner. The restaurant (**$$$**) is one of the better places to eat in the citadel, & yes, there is deer on the menu. **$$$**

🏠 **Casa Legenda** (4 dbl, 1 quad) Str Bastionului 8B; m 0748 649 368; e contact@legenda.ro; w legenda.ro. A pretty basic but clean pension just north of the citadel's main square. B/fast not included, but guests have access to the kitchen. **$$$**

🏠 **Casa Wagner** (5 sgl, 24 dbl, 5 suites) Piaţa Cetăţii 7; ☏0265 506 014; e office@casa-wagner.com; w casa-wagner.eu. In the citadel, this 400-year-old building painted bright orange houses a stylish pension with antique furnishings & an inner courtyard. There's a good restaurant (**$$$**) & a wine cellar. **$$$**

🏠 **Hotel Bulevard** (15 rooms) Str 1 Decembrie 1918 5; ☏0265 770 700; e info@hotelbulevardsighisoara.ro; w hotelbulevardsighisoara.ro. New hotel in the lower town which tries to capture the spirit of bygone days. The interwar theme is developed further in the restaurant (**$$$**), though purists will lament the fact that the 'English breakfast' includes a croissant. **$$$**

🏠 **Pensiune Casa Saseasca** (8 rooms) Piaţa Cetăţii 12; ☏0265 772 400; e office@ casasaseasca.com; w casasaseasca.com. Small pension in the heart of the citadel, looking out onto Piaţa Cetăţii, although the entrance is on the other side of the building opposite the Church of the Dominican Monastery. Hand-painted furniture & an inner courtyard. **$$$**

🏠 **Pensiune Lelila Inn** (5 dbl, 1 trpl) Str Tâmplarilor 14; ☏0265 779 332; e contact@lelilainn-sighisoara.ro; w lelilainn-sighisoara.ro. Small, rustic-feeling pension between the Shoemakers' Tower & the Tailors' Tower. **$$$**

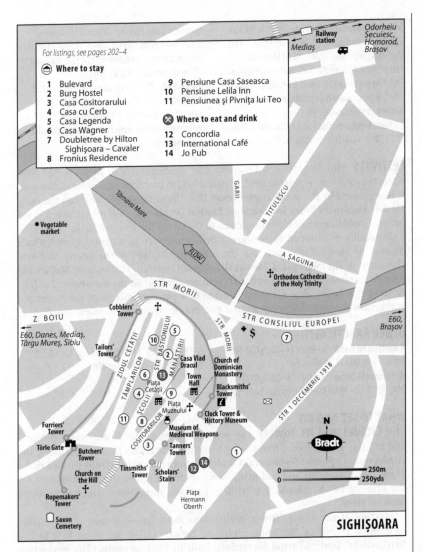

For listings, see pages 202–4

🏠 **Where to stay**

1 Bulevard
2 Burg Hostel
3 Casa Cositorarului
4 Casa cu Cerb
5 Casa Legenda
6 Casa Wagner
7 Doubletree by Hilton
   Sighişoara – Cavaler
8 Fronius Residence

9   Pensiune Casa Saseasca
10 Pensiune Lelila Inn
11 Pensiunea şi Pivniţa lui Teo

❌ **Where to eat and drink**

12 Concordia
13 International Café
14 Jo Pub

SIGHIŞOARA

🏠 **Burg Hostel** (7 dbl, 1 sgl, 2 trpl plus dorms) Str Bastionului 4–6; ☎ 0265 778 489; e burghostel@ibz.ro; w burghostel.ro. Doubles as well as dorms in a renovated medieval building between the main square & the Cobblers' Tower. **$$ ($ for dorm beds)**

❌ **WHERE TO EAT AND DRINK** *Map, see above*

Dining options in Sighişoara are less enticing than in many larger Transylvanian towns. The best places in the citadel are mostly restaurants linked to pensions and boutique hotels, like the Casa cu Cerb and Casa Wagner (see opposite). The lower town offers more variety with Piaţa Hermann Oberth the centre of activity.

❌ **Concordia** Piaţa Hermann Oberth 1; ☎ 0265 774 029; ⊕ 10.00–01.00 daily. Popular Italian restaurant with a terrace on Piaţa Hermann Oberth offering a long list of pizzas & pasta dishes. They also do take-away. **$$**

✕ **International Café** Piața Cetății 8; ☏ 0365 730 334; w veritas.ro; ⏱ Jun–Aug 09.00–19.00 Mon–Sat, Sep–May 10.00–18.00 Mon–Sat. Part of the House on the Rock, run by the Veritas Christian organisation, this is a wholesome place offering pies, salads & toasted sandwiches & great homemade lemonade. **$$**

🍴 **Casa Cositorarului** Str Cositorarilor 9; ☏ 0265 771 550; w casa-cositorarului.ro; ⏱ 09.00–midnight daily. Pleasant café near the Covered Stairs, with good cakes & salads, though rude service can mar the experience. It is also a small (3-room) pension (**$$$**). **$$**

🍴 **Jo Pub** Piața Hermann Oberth 7; ☏ 0265 777 970; ⏱ 10.00–midnight daily. On a large terrace just beneath the Concordia, & like its neighbour pizzas seem to be its most popular offering. **$$**

FESTIVALS Mid-August sees **Proetnica** (*Str Bastionului 4-6;* m *0724 925 398;* e *proetnica@ibz.ro;* w *proetnica.ro*), a festival held to promote intercultural dialogue. It is organised by the youth organization IBZ, the same people who run the Burg Hostel. **Sighişoara Blues International Festival** (w *blues-festival.ro*) attracts a good international line-up of blues musicians to the city at the end of March.

Especially in summer, visitors are quite often treated to a photo-op with locals dressed up in medieval garb, but the fullest celebration of the town's medieval character is the **Sighişoara Medieval Festival** (Festivalul Sighişoara Medievală) (w *sighisoaramedievala.ro*), an annual event usually held on the last weekend of July. At least, that is the idea: the event failed to take place in 2016, with the municipal authorities blaming challenges around new public procurement rules.

OTHER PRACTICALITIES

$ **Raiffeisen Bank** Str Morii 14–18; ☏ 021 306 3002; ⏱ 09.00–17.30 Mon–Fri

✚ **Farmacia Dona** Str Morii 14–18; ☏ 0372 401 354; ⏱ 08.00–20.00 Mon–Fri, 09.00–14.00 Sat

✉ **Post office** Str Octavian Goga 12; ☏ 0265 772 055; ⏱ 09.00–17.00 Mon–Fri

WHAT TO SEE AND DO

The Citadel and its Towers For several centuries, Sighişoara was a political and military stronghold. From the 14th century, the guilds built towers along the citadel walls to protect **Sighişoara's Citadel** (Cetatea Sighişoara) from Turkish raids. These stored supplies and had firing windows for cannons, shells and arrows. Of the original 14 towers and five artillery bastions, nine towers and two bastions have survived.

Starting at the Clock Tower, Sighişoara's most iconic image, it is possible to make a circuit of the walls. Doing so anticlockwise, we come first to the **Blacksmiths' Tower** (Turnul Fierarilor), built in 1631 to protect the monastery church. Next, the **Cobblers' Tower** (Turnul Cizmarilor), first mentioned in 1521, stood above the road along the Târnava Mare River. Today it houses a local radio station. The **Tailors' Tower** (Turnul Croitorilor) has a double gateway and guarded a subsidiary entrance to the citadel opposite the Clock Tower. It was destroyed in a fire in 1676, and later rebuilt. The **Furriers' Tower** (Turnul Cojocarilor) forms the **Törle Gate** with the octagonal **Butchers' Tower** (Turnul Măcelarilor). The **Ropemakers' Tower** (Turnul Frânghierilor), home to the cemetery guard, is the only inhabited tower. Then we need to go back down Strada Scării in order then to head east towards the **Tinsmiths' Tower** (Turnul Cositorarilor), a complex structure that is variously rectangular, pentagonal, octagonal and hexagonal at different levels. Next to it the **Tanners' Tower** (Turnul Tăbăcarilor) is a simple square tower. The ninth tower, the Clock Tower, is the most impressive of all.

Around Piața Muzeului Sighișoara's Museum Square (Piața Muzeului) is dominated by the stunning **Clock Tower** (Turnul cu Ceas), the symbol of the city, built in the 14th century and enlarged in the 16th. There was a fire in 1676 when gunpowder deposits located in the Tailors' Tower exploded, following which Austrian architects rebuilt the roof of the Clock Tower in its present Baroque style, somewhat reminiscent of the tower of St Vitus Cathedral in Prague, and colourful tiles were added in 1894. Unlike the other towers, it was not owned by one specific guild but by the town as a whole, and served as the seat of the municipal authority.

The 17th-century Swiss-built clock gives the building its name and a key part of its character, with a range of figurines carved from linden wood moved by the clock's mechanism. On the citadel side, Peace holds an olive branch, accompanied by a drummer. Above them are Justice, a blindfolded figure raising a sword, and Righteousness with a set of scales, accompanied by angels representing Day and Night. At 06.00, the day angel makes an appearance, replaced at 18.00 by the night angel, carrying two burning candles. On warm summer evenings, a large crowd gathers in Museum Square to watch the latter event, selfie sticks at the ready, though it is inevitably followed by a collective murmur of disappointment at the relatively undramatic manner in which the exchange of angels is accomplished. The side overlooking the Lower Town features seven figures, representing pagan gods personifying different days of the week. The spire on top of the tower ends in a small golden sphere topped by a meteorological mast featuring a cockerel; rain is predicted if the cockerel faces west.

The Clock Tower now houses the **History Museum** (Muzeul de Istorie) (*Piața Muzeului 1;* \ *0265 771 108;* e *info@muzeusighisoara.com;* w *muzeusighisoara.ro;* ⊕ *15 May–15 Sep 09.00–18.30 Tue–Fri, 10.00–17.30 Sat/Sun, 16 Sep–14 May 09.00–15.30 Tue–Fri, 10.00–15.30 Sat/Sun; adult/child 14/3.5RON*). It offers a somewhat miscellaneous collection, ranging from displays relating to the influential town guilds to an account of the life of rocket pioneer Hermann Oberth, who carried out some of his early experiments in Sighișoara. But for many visitors, the reason for paying the admission fee is to be found in the excellent view from the balcony on the top of the tower.

There are two other small (and eminently skippable) museums around Museum Square, both of which fall under the purview of the History Museum, and have the same contact details and opening times. The **Torture Chamber** (Camera de Tortură) (*adult/child 4/1RON*) lies at the entrance to the square approached along Strada Turnului, in the former military prison beneath the Clock Tower. The museum comprises a single windowless room, with displays describing various methods of torture. The **Museum of Medieval Weapons** (Muzeul de Arme Medievale) (*adult/child 6/1.5RON*) sits on the south side of the square, a stone's throw from the Clock Tower, and is one for aficionados only. If you want to visit all three museums, a composite ticket is available, offering a small discount on the individual prices (*adults 20RON*).

Just along the square from here is the **Casa Vlad Dracul** (*Str Cositorarilor 5*), the birthplace of the future Vlad Țepeș, the Impaler, and one of the inspirations for the figure of Count Dracula (see box, pages 208–9). The Vlad Dracul in the name of the building is actually a reference to his father, who lived in the place with his young family before his ascent to the throne of Voievode of Wallachia. A plaque on the wall reads:

În această casă a locuit   In this house lived
între anii 1431–1435   between 1431–1435

domnitorul Ţării Româneşti	governor of the 'Romanian Land'
VLAD DRACUL	VLAD DRACUL
fiul lui Mircea cel Bătrîn	son of Mircea the Elder

The building now houses an uninspiring tourist-trap restaurant, but if you're in a kitschy frame of mind, head up to a small room on the first floor where, for 5RON, you can visit the room that they claim to be **'Dracula's birthplace'**. You are greeted not by a crib but by a coffin, and by the brief attentions of a man whose job title must read as something like 'tourist frightener'. The opposite side of Piaţa Muzeului is dominated by the **Gothic Church of the Dominican Monastery** (Biserica Mănăstirii Dominicane) (*Str Cositorarilor 13;* ✆ *0265 771 195;* ⊕ *Jun–Sep 10.00–18.00 daily, Oct–May 10.00–17.00 daily; admission 5RON*), which served as the church of the 13th-century Dominican monastery demolished at the end of the 19th century. The current church dates from 1677. It is now an Evangelical Church of the Augsburg Confession, the church of the Lutheran Saxons of Romania. As in Braşov's Black Church, a collection of 16th- and 17th-century oriental carpets decorate the interior. Classical-music concerts are often held here, and the church retains a working Baroque organ. In the square next to the church is a **bust of Vlad III Ţepeş** looking pretty sinister. Just beyond is the **Town Hall** (Primăria), a surprisingly large building dating from the 1880s.

To the Church on the Hill Just a few metres from Museum Square, **Citadel Square** (Piaţa Cetăţii) is the very heart of the upper town, a picture-postcard spot of pastel-coloured medieval buildings, now mostly offering food, drink and lodging. From here Strada Şcolii heads up towards the hill at the very top of the citadel. At the top end of the street you reach the **Covered Stairs** (Scara Acoperită), also known as the Scholars' Stairs, which lead up towards the school and church on the hill above. Built in 1642, the covered wooden passage offered winter protection for schoolchildren and parishioners heading up the hill. There are now 175 steps. At the top, the **Church on the Hill** (Biserica din Deal) (*Str Scării 10;* ⊕ *10.00–18.00 daily*) was built between the 14th and 16th centuries. It is one of the largest Gothic churches in Transylvania, with a 42m bell tower. Initially a Catholic church, it became a Lutheran building following the conversion of the Saxons of Sighişoara to that faith in the 1540s. As a Lutheran church, the fine interior frescoes of its earlier incarnation were not valued, and they were painted over in the 18th century, but they were recovered in 20th-century renovations, and now rank among the finest murals of the 14th to 16th centuries to be found in Transylvania. The building also features the only church crypt in Transylvania, with coffin niches in which leading citizens of the town were buried. The exterior of the church is relatively plain, in part reflecting the dual role of Saxon churches in Transylvania as places of fortification. The **Saxon Cemetery** (⊕ *08.00–20.00 daily*) behind the church is an atmospheric spot.

AROUND SIGHIŞOARA

DANEŞ Situated 8km west of Sighişoara on route DN14 to Mediaş, the village of Daneş is particularly smartly turned out, with flowers in pots and baskets everywhere. The main point of interest is the swanky country club Domeniul Dracula Daneş, which offers a good base for seeing the area, especially for visitors interested in equestrian pursuits.

Where to stay and eat

Centru Ecvestru (equestrian centre) Dracula Daneş (17 rooms) Same contact details as Domeniul Dracula Daneş (see below) & part of the same complex. Offers horseriding & carriage rides. **$$$**

Domeniul Dracula Daneş (16 rooms) Str Principală 804; \0265 772 211; e info@dracul.ro; w dracul.ro. Centred around a restaurant offering an extensive menu of Romanian & international dishes (**$$$$**), in a 5ha site with gardens, an outdoor swimming pool & place for barbecues. It is on the eastern side of Daneş village, just off the main road down a signposted turning to the south. **$$$**

Hanul Dracula Daneş (21 dbl) Same contact details as Domeniul Dracula Daneş (see left). 5km away from the main complex, in a more secluded site with its own restaurant (**$$**). **$$$**

CRIŞ From the village of Daneş, a turning to the south off the main Sighişoara to Mediaş road is signposted for Criş (Keresd/Kreisch), 10km away. Criş is an attractive village whose main sight is the Renaissance-style **Bethlen Castle** (Castelul Bethlen) (\ *0265 713 355;* ⊕ *summer 10.00–17.00 Tue–Sun, winter call ahead or ring the bell on arrival; adult/child 10/5RON*), which overlooks the place on a small hill.

The castle was one of the many residences across Transylvania of the influential Bethlen family, this one belonging to the Bethlen of Beclean branch of the family. The nucleus of the complex is the manor house on its western side, which dates from the Middle Ages. Its most striking feature is a large circular tower, built in the late 16th century by Mihály Bethlen. The tower was extended in the 1680s by Elek Bethlen, who added the rather primitive relief figures of watchmen that run around the top of the tower. Elek Bethlen was also responsible for the Renaissance-style loggia on the manor house and the extension to the eastern wing of the castle, across the courtyard from the manor house. Note the small loggias at either end of the wing and the Renaissance-style stone window- and doorframes. Elek Bethlen included this wing as part of the walls of a rectangular defensive structure surrounding the complex, with four corner towers. A particularly fine octagonal tower was transformed into one of these, becoming the northeastern tower of the castle.

The castle suffered greatly during the Communist period, and is now being restored slowly through the work of the St Francis Foundation, to whom the castle is currently leased. The interiors are mostly bare, though there are some display panels in the manor house behind the loggia, and the restored chapel building on the ground floor of the Elek Bethlen Wing displays some fine vaulting. Note also at various places around the castle the family crest of a crowned snake.

CUND The small village of Cund (Kund/Reussdorf) sits in an isolated and scenic spot some 10km north of Dumbrăveni, off the road between Sighişoara and Mediaş. The quality of the road beyond Dumbrăveni is very poor, however, and in wet weather or without a 4x4 it is better accessed by turning west off the E60 at Bălăuseri, between Sighişoara and Târgu Mureş, and then approaching the village from the north, via Bahnea. Formerly a Saxon village, it now houses a mix of ethnic Hungarians and Romanians, following the departure of most of the Saxons to Germany.

The village centres on the **Evangelical church** (*key at Valea Verde; page 209*), built in the 15th century in the Gothic hall church style. Today it is in a very sorry state, though a renovation project is planned. There is a Gothic vaulted ceiling in the choir, but the wooden-panelled ceiling that once covered the nave is gone, and the organ is falling to pieces. The altar is currently being housed for safekeeping in the

Church on the Hill in Sighişoara. The derelict building in front of the church is the former German-language school.

At the one junction in the village, the enterprising István Varga has set up a small but innovative cheese-making business, **Manufactura de Brânză** (*Cund 137*; m *0749 968 944*; e *info@manufacturadebranza.ro*). This is one of a range of similar enterprises being set up across rural Romania, in part a response to the very low milk prices obtainable by dairy farmers.

However, the main reason Cund is now on the Transylvania tourism map is through the work of Jonas and Ulrike Schäfer, who have set up the Valea Verde resort

VLAD DRĂCULEA – THE MAN BEHIND THE MYTH

Bram Stoker and Hollywood have given us more than 150 versions of Dracula. Christopher Lee and Béla Lugosi, an ethnic Hungarian from Lugoj, Timiş County, have played the vampire count perhaps most memorably.

The real-life figure whose life was woven into Stoker's fictional count was born in or around 1431 in Sighişoara, the son of the future Vlad II, whose title 'Dracul' was applied following his induction into the Order of the Dragon (*draco*) of King Sigismund of Luxembourg. The boy, the future Vlad III, acquired the sobriquet Drăculea, often rendered abroad as Dracula, meaning 'son of Dracul'. The family moved to Târgovişte in 1436, to take up residence in the palace when Vlad senior became Voivode of Wallachia.

In 1442, ordered to come to the Ottoman sultan as a demonstration of loyalty, Vlad Dracul did so and was promptly imprisoned. On his release he had to leave his sons Vlad and Radu with the sultan to guarantee his continued obedience. Vlad was held there until 1448. This Turkish captivity played an important role in his upbringing, and he was reportedly particularly interested in the Turkish method of impaling prisoners on stakes.

John Hunyadi, the Regent-Governor of Hungary, arranged the assassination of Vlad senior and Drăculea's elder brother, Mircea, who was tortured and buried alive. Vlad Drăculea, breaking into Wallachia with an Ottoman army, became its ruler in 1448, although this first term lasted only two months. He was to rule Wallachia again between 1456 and 1462, after he had invaded with Hungarian support, and finally in 1476.

During his reigns he committed many cruelties and thus established his reputation, earning him the posthumous moniker of 'Ţepeş' ('Impaler'). Victims were bound spread-eagled, then a stake was hammered up through the rectum as far as the shoulder, whereupon they were left to die in agony, raised up for the crowd to watch.

Vlad's first major act of revenge was aimed at the boyars of Târgovişte for not being loyal to his father. Legend has it that he arrested all the boyar families who had participated at a princely Easter Sunday feast. The older ones were impaled on stakes while the others were forced to make the gruelling 80km trek from the capital Târgovişte to Poenari in the Argeş River valley. Vlad then ordered the boyars to build him a fortress on the ruins of an older outpost. Legend has it that since so many died in the process, he was able to refresh the noble stock and at the same time create an impregnable fortress, whose ruins can be visited today at the southern tip of Lacul Vidraru (page 241).

Vlad feuded with just about everybody. In 1457, he accused the Saxons of supporting rival claimants to his Wallachian throne and burnt many of their in the village, a scattered hotel complex involving a central restaurant and reception and a series of guesthouses around the village owned or managed by the resort.

 ## Where to stay and eat

⚹ 🏠 Valea Verde Str Principală 119; 📞0265 714 399; e reservations@valeaverde.com; w discover-transilvania.com. Former manager of German boy band Echt (their gold discs hang in reception), Jonas Schäfer has now turned restaurateur & owner of this high-end 'scattered' hotel. Choose between 4 rustic apartments on the main site, 6 apartments around a large courtyard in the village, & 4 holiday homes in the village. There is a restaurant offering high-

villages in southern Transylvania. In 1460, he wiped out the forces of one rival for his throne, Dan III, and then attacked the Bârsa Land around Braşov and Făgăraş, again resorting to impalement to punish those who had supported Dan's claims.

Despite his reputation for cruelty, Vlad III is a popular figure for many Romanians; the source of that popularity lies in his successes against the Ottomans. After failing to pay tribute to the sultan, he declared war on the Turks in 1462, attacking their camps and inflicting heavy casualties. It was said that when, during the course of the fighting, the Turks entered the (then deserted) town of Târgovişte, they were appalled to discover a field of some 20,000 men, women and children impaled on stakes. The sultan was reported to have concluded that such a diabolical leader could not be deprived of his country. The main Ottoman army left Wallachia, but they left behind a smaller contingent of troops under the command of none other than Vlad's brother Radu, who had acquired the sobriquet 'the Handsome' and had remained loyal to Turkey. Vlad sought the help of the Hungarian leader Matthias Corvinus against the Ottomans, but Corvinus did not trust Vlad and instead had him taken prisoner in 1462. He was held at Visegrád, near Budapest until 1475. He seems to have been released at the request of the Moldovan leader Stephen the Great, who wanted a Wallachian ruler who would be a stout enemy of the Ottomans. During much of Vlad's imprisonment the Wallachian throne had been held by his pro-Ottoman brother Radu, but the latter's sudden death in 1475 set the stage for Vlad's return. Vlad indeed regained the throne of Wallachia in 1476, but held it for only two months.

There are several versions of his death. Some sources say he was killed in battle against the Ottomans near Bucharest in December 1476. Others say he was assassinated by disloyal Wallachian boyars while out hunting. Still other reports claim that Vlad was accidentally killed by one of his own men. According to some accounts, Vlad's body was decapitated by the Turks and his head sent to Istanbul, where the sultan displayed it on a stake as proof that the Impaler was finally dead. Vlad's headless body was reportedly buried at a monastery on an island in Lacul Snagov (pages 136–7), although some doubt that he is actually still resting there (see also box, pages 208–9).

Romanians are keen to point out to visitors that Vlad Ţepeş was in no sense associated with vampirism. While Stoker's character of Count Dracula took some features from the Wallachian leader, the stories of vampires were drawn from quite separate writings on the superstitions of Transylvania by Emily Gerard. And so Romanians are decidedly ambivalent about the way their country is so closely associated with the fictional count; while recognising the tourist potential they see him as a foreign creation, not a Romanian one.

end meals & wines (**$$$$$**), with local truffles a speciality (they organise periodic truffle- hunting weekends & even the cat is called Truffle). **$$$$**

SASCHIZ Heading west out of Sighişoara, on the hectic E60 highway, after 21km you will reach Saschiz (Szászkézd/Keisd), which is one of the seven Transylvanian villages with fortified churches inscribed on the UNESCO World Heritage list. Its **fortified church** (*contact Dorothea Batea-Ziegler on* m *0748 831 360;* ⊕ *Apr–Oct 10.00–17.00 Wed–Mon, Nov–Mar 14.00–16.00 Wed–Mon, or ring a day in advance to ask to visit outside these hours; adult/child 6/3RON*) is right in the heart of the village. It is a late Gothic hall church, built between 1493 and 1525 on the site of an earlier Romanesque church. Unusually, the place of shelter for the villagers of Saschiz in times of attack was not in fortified structures around the church but above the nave itself: from the exterior, a line of square windows high up shows where the villagers would have sheltered. Next to the church is a separate bell tower which was remodelled at the end of the 17th century to resemble the clock tower in Sighişoara, with a roof covered with multi-coloured enamel tiles, four corner turrets and a pointed spire. This aping of the tower in Sighişoara is a reminder of the long rivalry between the two settlements, a feud in which Saschiz lost out.

On the hillside overlooking the village are the remains of a 14th-century **fortress**, which has six towers. It originally had the function of place of refuge for the villagers during attacks, but the church took over this function as the castle was felt to be too far from the village. It makes for a pleasant walk of about 1.2km from the village.

Saschiz is also the headquarters of some interesting ventures dedicated to preserving rural livelihoods. The **ADEPT Foundation** (Fundaţia ADEPT) (*Str Principală 166;* ✆ *0265 711 635;* e *saschiz@fundatia-adept.org;* w *fundatia-adept. org;* ⊕ *08.00–17.00 Mon–Fri*) runs a wide range of rural development projects. One of their most interesting ventures, a **pottery workshop** (Atelierul de Ceramică Saschiz), is in the village. Cross the main road next to the church and head up the cobbled lane opposite. The workshop is housed in a modern-looking white-walled building. It is focused on reviving the old local tradition of cobalt blue-coloured engraved ceramic pieces, through a partnership with the UK-based Camelia Botnar Foundation. The ADEPT Foundation also runs the **tourist information office** next door to the church (⊕ *May–Oct 08.00–17.00 Mon–Fri*), with helpful staff and interesting display panels about Saschiz and the surrounding area. They also sell the (very reasonably priced) cobalt-blue pottery, as well as a range of jams and preserves – another ADEPT initiative. In winter, when the tourist office is closed, you can go instead to the main ADEPT Foundation office (see above), which is just below the church, across the small square. Somewhat pointlessly, given the quality of the service offered by the ADEPT-run office, there is also an official tourist information office (✆ *0265 711 808,* e *turism@saschiz.ro;* w *turism.saschiz. ro;* ⊕ *10.00–18.00 daily*) in the courtyard of the town hall a couple of doors away.

Another interesting local initiative offering a great means of buying good-quality local produce is the UK-run **Pivniţa Bunicii** (*Str Principală 354;* ✆ *0265 711 788;* e *info@pivnitabunicii.ro;* w *pivnitabunicii.ro*), signposted from the main road through the village. 'Grandmother's cellar' offers an enticing range of cordials, jams and preserves, and even a Dracula's Delight tomato chutney.

APOLD Apold (Apold/Trappold) is home to an impressively sited **fortified church** (*contact Asociaţia casApold; Str Principală 244;* m *0722 208 495;* e *casapold@gmail.com;* w *facebook.com/casapold;* ⊕ *Jun–Sep 11.00–15.00 Mon– Fri, Oct–May by appointment only; donation expected*) in the centre of the village on a hilltop. Originally a Romanesque basilica dating from the 13th century, like many Transylvanian fortified churches it was remodelled in the 15th century into a Gothic hall church. The fortress aspects of the church were considerably strengthened in the 16th century, and are quite imposing, including two encircling walls, with towers, and the fortified western bell tower of the church.

Apold is 15km south of Sighişoara, on the road to Agnita. There are six buses a day from Sighişoara during weekdays, two at weekends.

CLOAŞTERF Cloaşterf (Miklóstelke/Klosdorf) has a well-preserved 16th-century **fortified church** (*key at House 99;* \0265 711 674), which sits within a rectangular defensive wall. The present-day church was built on the site of an older one between 1521 and 1524. The name of the architect, Stefan Ungar of Sighişoara, is still commemorated in an inscription behind the altar. It retains many late Gothic features, including an elegant net-vaulted ceiling. A later painted wooden gallery running along three sides of the interior is decorated with floral motifs and paintings of different fortified churches. The Baroque altar dates from the 18th century with, unusually, the organ above it, rather than at the back of the church.

The defensive wall has four corner towers, though that in the southwest corner was replaced in 1819 with a tall bell tower. The house of the castle keeper next to this dates from the same period.

Cloaşterf is just 2km off the main E60 highway (signposted), though lies on a very minor road.

SEND US YOUR SNAPS!

We'd love to follow your adventures using our *Transylvania* guide – why not send us your photos and stories via Twitter (@*BradtGuides*) and Instagram (@*bradtguides*) using the hashtag #Transylvania. Alternatively, you can upload your photos directly to the gallery on the Transylvania destination page via our website (w *bradtguides.com/transylvania*).

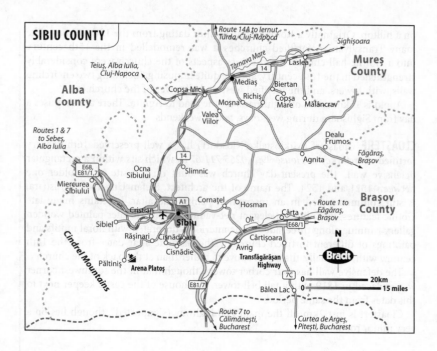

7

Sibiu County

Sibiu County rivals Braşov as the centre of tourism in Transylvania. Its principal city, Sibiu, is one of the most alluring in all of Transylvania, with a beautifully preserved medieval core of interlocking squares, some great museums and a busy cultural calendar including one of the best theatre festivals in Europe. The large majority of the population of Sibiu County today is ethnically Romanian, but the Transylvanian Saxon community has played an important role in its development, and the county is home to some of the most beautiful of the Saxon fortified churches of southern Transylvania. Those at Biertan and Valea Viilor are inscribed on the UNESCO World Heritage list.

While much of Sibiu County comprises undulating terrain, with fields in the valleys separated by forested hills, to the south the land rises sharply to the mountains of the Southern Carpathians, marking the border with Wallachia. The mighty Făgăraş range rises to more than 2,500m and offers fine hiking, as do the Lotru and Cindrel ranges further east. The Mărginimea Sibiului region on the northern slopes of the latter has preserved a distinctive culture based around the ethnic Romanian population of its pastoral villages. The museum at Sibiel dedicated to the technique of painting icons on glass highlights one of the traditions of the area. The Cindrel Mountains are also home to Romania's highest ski resort, at Păltiniş.

The main road southwards into Wallachia between these peaks is the E81, which scenically follows the Olt River as it runs southwards from Sibiu to Râmnicu Vâlcea. But a more adventurous option is to drive right over the Făgăraş range by means of the Transfăgărăşan Highway, one of the most spectacular drives in Romania. Bâlea Lake, near the top of the highway, is home in winter to Romania's Ice Hotel, when the tourist looking for something different can eat dinner from an ice plate before retiring to their ice bed.

With other attractions in the county ranging from saltwater lakes to Baroque gardens, a Cistercian monastery to a great open-air museum, this is a part of Transylvania where you will want to linger.

SIBIU *Telephone code 0269, sometimes 0369*

Sibiu (Nagyszeben/Hermannstadt) is one of the most visitor-friendly cities in Transylvania, and a great place to explore on foot. The old part of the city has two levels. The 'Upper Town' contains most of Sibiu's historic sites, which are handily located around three charming adjacent squares, Piaţa Mare (Great Square), Piaţa Mică (Little Square) and Piaţa Huet (Huet Square). The 'Lower Town' is an appealing tangle of old houses and cobbled streets. Connecting the Upper and Lower towns are dozens of tunnels, stairways and hidden passages, emerging suddenly into sun-drenched, pastel-painted squares, which are fun to explore. The city offers stretches of medieval walls, a Gothic cathedral and Baroque palaces, and has two important museum complexes: one a group of museums under the Brukenthal label, with the remarkable collections of an 18th-century Governor of Transylvania at its heart, and the second the ASTRA complex, the best open-air museum in Transylvania. Add to this a busy cultural calendar, including a theatre festival of European importance, an extensive range of accommodation options and some impressive restaurants, and it is easy to see why Sibiu is many people's favourite Transylvanian city, and a place that rewards an extended stay.

HISTORY Sibiu was founded by German settlers in the 12th century. Its first known documented reference comes from 1191, when it is referred to as Cibinium, a name deriving from the Cibin River, on which the city is sited. The German name for the city, Hermannstadt, is said by some to derive from the presence of one Hermann of Nuremberg among the original settlers. Sibiu rapidly developed as one of the leading cities of Transylvania, with hard-working Saxon merchants making the most of the trade route along the Olt River gorge between Transylvania and Wallachia. Its craft guilds were at the heart of urban life, their numbers progressively growing from 19 in 1376 to 29 by the late 16th century and 40 by 1780. One of the Siebenbürgen (pages 17–19), Sibiu was protected by sturdy city walls, and saw centuries of conflict with Mongol and then Turkish forces.

When in the late 17th century Transylvania fell under the protection of the Habsburgs rather than the Ottomans, Sibiu became its capital. For most of the 18th century and again for a short period in the 19th, it was the residence of the governors of Transylvania. In the late 18th century, Governor Samuel von Brukenthal built a grand Baroque palace in the city to conserve his art collection, which remains to this day one of the treasures of Sibiu. In 1861, the Transylvanian Association for Romanian Literature and the Culture of the Romanian People, more pithily known as ASTRA, was established in the city. It played an important role in the promotion of the cultural identity of the Romanians in Transylvania, and ASTRA remains important to the city, in the management of a complex of museums and other cultural facilities. They also run a great souvenir shop.

Although most of the ethnic German community had left Sibiu by the Romanian Revolution of 1989, in common with Saxon communities elsewhere in Transylvania, the city has been led since 2000 by the Democratic Forum of Germans in Romania. From 2000 its mayor was Klaus Iohannis, until his election as the President of Romania in 2014, on a platform which emphasised his record in the effective management of the city. In 2007, Sibiu was Romania's first ever European Capital of Culture, and the city is known throughout Romania for its particularly busy programme of high-quality cultural events. As Capital of Culture it focused on its multi-cultural history and the role of its German, Romanian, Hungarian and Roma communities in shaping it, together with its self-styled image as an 'old young city', combining impressive historic attractions with decidedly contemporary cultural ones. The city's economy has changed markedly since the revolution, with the closure of much Communist-era heavy industry and its replacement by new investment, particularly from Germany.

GETTING THERE, AWAY AND AROUND
By air Sibiu International Airport (SBZ) (*Şosea Alba Iulia 73*; \ *0269 253 135*; w *sibiuairport.ro*) is situated 5km west of Sibiu city centre on the confusingly multi-denominated highway 1/7/E68/E81. The airport offers flights to a range of European cities, with Germany particularly well served. **Tarom** (w *tarom.ro*) flies from Sibiu to Munich, **Blue Air** (w *blueairweb.com*) to Stuttgart, **Austrian Airlines**

(w *austrian.com*) to Vienna, **Wizz Air** (w *wizzair.com*) to London Luton, Madrid, Milan and several German airports, and **Lufthansa** (w *lufthansa.com*) twice daily to Munich. **Bus 11** runs between Strada Andrei Șaguna in the city centre and the airport roughly every 20 minutes on weekdays, but much less frequently at weekends; tickets cost 1.5RON. Given the closeness of the airport to the city centre, **taxis** are an affordable option, at around 25RON.

By rail and bus Sibiu's railway and bus stations are situated to the northeast of the centre, on Piața 1 Decembrie 1918, at the eastern end of Strada General Gheorghe Magheru, a 15-minute walk from Piața Mare in the heart of the historic centre. Bus 5 runs from the railway station to Piața Unirii.

The **railway station** [217 G1] (*Gara Sibiu; Piața 1 Decembrie 1918 6;* \0269 211 *139*) offers services to Bucharest (*6hrs*), Brașov (*3hrs*), Deva (*from 2hrs 20mins*) and Timișoara (*from 5hrs 20mins*), among others. The **bus station** [217 G1] (*Autogara Transmixt; Piața 1 Decembrie 1918 6;* \0269 217 757) is right next door. Note that although most inter-urban buses depart from here, or close to it, a few private operators, notably the DACOS company, use the Autogara Q7 (*Strada Școala de Înot 1;* \0269 232 826), which is south of the centre near the municipal stadium. Daily buses and maxi-taxis run to Alba Iulia (*around 20 daily, 1½hrs*), Brașov (*15 daily, 2½hrs*), Cluj-Napoca (*18 daily, 3½hrs*), Deva (*8 daily, 2½hrs*) and Târgu Mureș (*6 daily, around 3hrs*).

Public transport There is a comprehensive and cheap local bus system (*full network information is at* w *tursib.ro*). Tickets cost 1.5RON and need to be purchased (from machines or ticket kiosks) before you board. There is also a one-day ticket option for 5RON, but since most of the main attractions lie within the pedestrianised streets of the Old Town, you are only likely to need to use buses to get to the more far-flung sights like the ASTRA Museum of Traditional Folk Civilisation (bus 13), as well as the airport (bus 11) and railway and bus stations (bus 5 from Piața Unirii).

Taxis Taxis are relatively inexpensive and widely available. The price per kilometre is marked on the outside of the car.

🚕 **Star** \0269 953
🚕 **Taxi 924** \0269 924

🚕 **Taxi 942** \0269 942

Car hire
🚕 **Avis** Sibiu airport; m 0729 800 393; e sibiu@avis.ro; w avis.ro
🚕 **Europcar** Sibiu airport; m 0730 801 060; w europcar.ro

🚕 **Thrifty** Sibiu airport; m 0742 219 193; w thriftyrentals.ro

TOURIST INFORMATION The tourist information centre is centrally located in Piața Mare [216 C4] (*Str Samuel Brukenthal 2, Piața Mare;* \0269 208 913; e *turism@ sibiu.ro;* w *turism.sibiu.ro;* ⊕ *May–Sep 09.00–20.00 Mon–Fri, 09.00–18.00 Sat/Sun, Oct–Apr 09.00–17.00 Mon–Fri, 09.00–13.00 Sat/Sun*).

🏠 **WHERE TO STAY** *Map, pages 216–7*
There is a good range of accommodation available in all price categories, with rates generally higher in the peak summer season, as elsewhere in Transylvania. Some

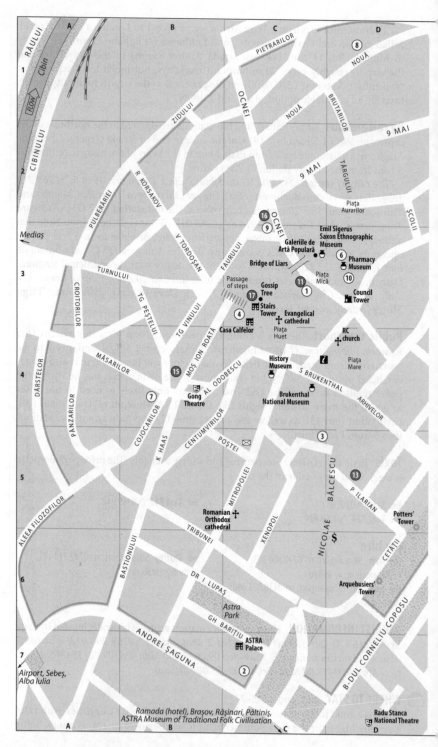

RAULUI

Cibin

FLOW

CIBINULUI

Mediaş →

PULBERARIEI

R KORSAKOV

ZIDULUI

V TORDOŞAN

OCNEI

PIETRARILOR

NOUA

NOUA

BRUTARILOR

9 MAI

TARGULUI

ŞCOLII

8

FAURULUI

OCNEI

9 MAI

Piaţa
Aurarilor

Emil Sigerus
Saxon Ethnographic
Museum

16

9

Galeriile de
Artă Populară

6 Pharmacy
Museum

TURNULUI

TG PEŞTELUI

Bridge of Liars

Piaţa
Mică

10

CROITORILOR

Passage
of steps

Gossip
Tree

11

1

Council
Tower

TG VINULUI

MOŞ ION ROATĂ

17 Stairs
Tower

Evangelical
cathedral

RC
church

MĂSARILOR

4

Casa Calfelor

Piaţa
Huet

DARSTELOR

PÂNZARILOR

COJOCARILOR

15

AL ODOBESCU

History
Museum

Piaţa
Mare

S BRUKENTHAL

7

Gong
Theatre

Brukenthal
National Museum

ARHIVELOR

K HAAS

CENTUMVIRILOR

POŞTEI

3

BĂLCESCU

13

P ILARIAN

ALEEA FILOZOFILOR

BASTIONULUI

MITROPOLIEI

TRIBUNEI

Romanian
Orthodox
cathedral

XENOPOL

NICOLAE

$

Potters'
Tower

CETATII

DR I LUPAŞ

Arquebusiers'
Tower

Astra
Park

GH BARITIU

ANDREI ŞAGUNA

ASTRA
Palace

2

B-DUL CORNELIU COPOSU

Airport, Sebeş,
Alba Iulia

Ramada (hotel), Braşov, Răşinari, Păltiniş,
ASTRA Museum of Traditional Folk Civilisation

Radu Stanca
National Theatre

A   B   C   D

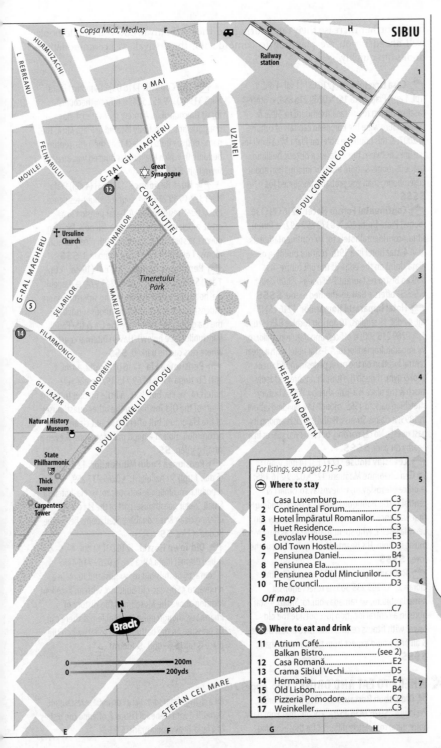

SIBIU

Copşa Mică, Mediaş

Railway station

HURMUZACHI

L. REBEANU

9 MAI

FELINARULUI

MOVILEI

G-RAL GH MAGHERU

UZINEI

Great Synagogue

CONSTITUŢIEI

B-DUL CORNELIU COPOSU

Ursuline Church

FUNARILOR

G-RAL MAGHERU

Tineretului Park

SELARILOR

MANEJULUI

FILARMONICII

P ONOFREIU

GH LAZĂR

B-DUL CORNELIU COPOSU

HERMANN OBERTH

Natural History Museum

State Philharmonic

Thick Tower

Carpenters' Tower

N

Bradt

| 0 | 200m |
| 0 | 200yds |

ŞTEFAN CEL MARE

For listings, see pages 215–9

Where to stay

1	Casa Luxemburg	C3
2	Continental Forum	C7
3	Hotel Împăratul Romanilor	C5
4	Huet Residence	C3
5	Levoslav House	E3
6	Old Town Hostel	D3
7	Pensiunea Daniel	B4
8	Pensiunea Ela	D1
9	Pensiunea Podul Minciunilor	C3
10	The Council	D3

Off map

| | Ramada | C7 |

Where to eat and drink

11	Atrium Café	C3
	Balkan Bistro	(see 2)
12	Casa Romană	E2
13	Crama Sibiul Vechi	D5
14	Hermania	E4
15	Old Lisbon	B4
16	Pizzeria Pomodore	C2
17	Weinkeller	C3

7

hotels further increase their rates during the Theatre Festival, and you should book well ahead if you are planning to come during the festival, as accommodation books out quickly.

🏠 **Casa Luxemburg** [216 C3] (1 sgl, 4 dbl, 1 trpl, 1 apt) Piaţa Mică 16; 🝪0269 216 854; e office@casaluxemburg.ro; w casaluxemburg.ro. Sibiu & Luxembourg were the European capitals of culture in 2007, & this boutique hotel on Piaţa Mică explores the links between the 2 places: a historic building, spacious rooms & more touristic information about Luxembourg than you probably bargained for. **$$$$**

🏠 **Continental Forum Hotel** [216 C7] (136 rooms) Piaţa Unirii 10; 🝪0372 692 692; e forum.sibiu@continentalhotels.ro; w continentalhotels.ro. A 4-star hotel in a 19th-century building on Piaţa Unirii on the edge of the old centre. Its Balkan Bistro restaurant (⌚ noon–23.00 daily; **$$$$**) offers a Balkan-themed menu. **$$$$**

🏠 **Hotel Împăratul Romanilor** [216 C5] (8 sgl, 44 dbl, 19 studios, 10 apt) Str Nicolae Bălcescu 4; 🝪0269 216 500; e office@imparatulromanilor.ro; w imparatulromanilor.ro. A 3-star hotel with a great central location on the main pedestrianised street, pool & gym, though the furnishings are decidedly kitsch & the place is a little shabby. With a history stretching back to 1555, though in a building rebuilt in 1895, it claims Strauss, Brahms & Liszt among its past guests. No car parking, but reserved spaces in a nearby car park. **$$$$**

🏠 **Levoslav House** [217 E3] (4 dbl, 7 apt) Str Gen Gheorghe Magheru 12; 🝪0269 216 185; e office@levoslav.ro; w levoslav.ro. Smart & central 4-star boutique hotel in a 1840 building that was once the home of Slovak composer Ján Levoslav Bella, who spent many years as director of music in Sibiu. His bearded bust greets you in the foyer. **$$$$**

🏠 **Ramada** [216 C7] (127 rooms) Str Emil Cioran 2; 🝪0269 235 505; e reservations@ramadasibiu.ro; w ramadasibiu.ro. Smart 4-star hotel in a central location just outside the old town, with fitness centre, extensive b/fast buffet, & all one would expect from the Ramada chain. **$$$$**

✳ 🏠 **The Council** [216 D3] (14 rooms) Piaţa Mică 31; 🝪0369 452 524; e office@thecouncil.ro; w thecouncil.ro. A nicely renovated 4-star boutique hotel, centrally located in Piaţa Mică. The name derives from the fact that the 14th-century building in which the hotel is housed was an early town hall. **$$$$**

✳ 🏠 **Huet Residence** [216 C3] (4 dbl) Piaţa Huet 3; 🝪0269 216 854; e office@huet-residence.ro; w huet-residence.ro. A 3-star pension in a great, albeit not heavy-luggage-friendly, location down the steps off Piaţa Huet, with nicely furnished rooms, 1 of which even has a piano in it. **$$$**

🏠 **Pensiunea Daniel** [216 B4] (10 dbl, 1 trpl, 1 apt) Str Măsarilor 1; 🝪0269 243 924; e daniel@ela-hotels.ro; w ela-hotels.ro. The smarter & more expensive of the 3 central guesthouses run by the Ela group: the others are the Ela & the Podul Minciunilor (see below). Has an internal court where cars can be parked. **$$$**

🏠 **Pensiunea Ela** [216 D1] (3 dbl, 4 trpl, 1 apt) Str Nouă 43; 🝪0269 215 197; e ela@ela-hotels.ro; w ela-hotels.ro. A little further from the heart of the Old Town than the other guesthouses of the Ela group, but offers basic but clean accommodation at a good price for Sibiu, & even a small garden. **$$**

🏠 **Pensiunea Podul Minciunilor** [216 C3] (5 dbl, 1 trpl) Str Azilului 1; 🝪0269 217 259; e podul.minciunilor@ela-hotels.ro; w ela-hotels.ro. Small, 2-star guesthouse, part of the Ela group, offering clean & reasonably priced rooms below the Bridge of Lies. **$$**

🏠 **Old Town Hostel** [216 D3] (2 dbl, 4-, 6- & 8-bed dorms) Piaţa Mică 26; 🝪0269 216 445; e contact@hostelsibiu.ro; w hostelsibiu.ro. In a renovated 450-year-old building, with an excellent location above the Museum of the History of Pharmacy, though noise is a problem & there can be pressure on the bathrooms & toilets when the place is full. **$$** (dbl), **$** (dorm)

✘ **WHERE TO EAT AND DRINK** *Map, pages 216–7*

✘ **Old Lisbon Restaurant** [216 B4] Str Târgul Peştelui 4; 🝪0269 436 467; ⌚ noon–midnight daily. Something completely different for those looking

for a change from *sarmale*: a Portuguese restaurant, decorated with scenes of Lisbon & offering cod dishes to a fado-heavy soundtrack. **$$$$**

✗ Atrium Café [216 C3] Piața Mică 16; m 0723 287 486; w atriumcafe.ro; ⊕ 10.00–03.00 daily. Sympathetic décor, central location, pizzas cooked in a wood-fired oven & a good range of vegetarian dishes in an international menu, though service can be slow. Under the same management as Casa Luxemburg. **$$$**

✗ Casa Romană [217 E2] Str General Magheru 40; ☎0369 442 966; w casaromanasibiu.ro; ⊕ 07.00–midnight daily. Pizzeria also serving pasta & salad dishes, between Piața Mare & the railway station. There is also a 9-room guesthouse here, Casa Romana 1 (**$$$**). **$$$**

✗ Crama Sibiul Vechi [216 D5] Str A Papiu Ilarian 3; ☎0269 210 461; ⊕ noon–midnight daily. This atmospheric place in a vaulted brick cellar serves Transylvanian dishes, including some less commonly encountered specialities like *balmoș*. **$$$**

✱✗ Hermania [217 E4] Str Filarmonicii 2; m 0755 055 999; w hermania.sobis.ro; ⊕ 11.00–midnight daily. Housed in the remodelled concert hall which accommodated the Hermania Choir from 1887 to 1949, and then the Sibiu Philharmonic until 2004, this is an atmospheric Saxon-themed restaurant offering dishes like *Hanklich*, Saxon butter cake. The owners also run a trout hatchery, so trout dishes are particularly prominent. A 'they visited us' list at the back of the menu tells you that you are following in the footsteps of Nicolas Cage & the Ramón Valle Trio. **$$$**

✗ Weinkeller [216 C3] Str Turnului 2; ☎0269 210 319; w weinkeller.ro; ⊕ noon–midnight daily. Interesting Transylvanian menu served in an atmospheric location either in a small internal courtyard or a brick-vaulted cellar. **$$$**

✗ Pizzeria Pomodore [216 C2] Str Ocnei 10; ☎0369 440 541; w pomodore.ro; ⊕ 11.00–midnight daily. Untouristy pizza place close to the Podul Minciunilor. Also offers the Transylvanian speciality *balmoș*, made from cornflour & whey cream. **$$**

ENTERTAINMENT

Festivals The local authorities in Sibiu devote a particularly large portion of the municipal budget to culture, and this is reflected in a stream of cultural events through the year filling Piața Mare, especially during the summer season. Among the most interesting are the **Sibiu Jazz Festival** (Festivalul de Jazz Sibiu) (☎*0269 219 810; w sibiujazz.ro*) in late May, the **Medieval Festival of Transylvanian Fortresses** (Festivalul Medieval Cetăți Transilvane) (☎*0369 405 253; e contact@fmct.ro; w fmct.ro*) in late August, a **Pottery Fair** (Târgul Olarilor) (w *traditiisibiene.ro*) over the first weekend of September, and Sibiu's version of the Munich Oktoberfest, the **CibinFEST** (☎*0269 224 246; w cibinfest.ro*) at the end of September, the last focused on a giant beer tent in Piața Mare. **MaiFest** is a celebration of springtime and of the traditions of the local Saxon community. In 2016, it was delayed a month because of bad weather, and local newspapers joked that it had become JuniFest. But the largest and most important event of all is the **Sibiu International Theatre Festival** (Festivalul Internațional de Teatru Sibiu) (☎*0269 210 092; w sibfest.ro*), developed in the early 1990s by Romanian actor Constantin Chiriac, which has grown into the largest festival of performing arts in Romania and one of the major theatre festivals of Europe. Held in mid-June, it features a large menu of Romanian and international productions in theatres across the city, as well as free open-air performances and concerts in both Piața Mare and Piața Mică.

The ASTRA National Museum Complex also organises a range of events, including the **National Festival of Folk Traditions** (Festivalul Național al Tradițiilor Populare) (w *muzeulastra.ro*) in mid-August and the **ASTRA Film Festival** (☎*0269 202 430; w astrafilm.ro*), which is focused on documentary films, in October.

Theatres and concert halls Outside of the festivals, there are some excellent permanent venues in Sibiu. The **State Philharmonic of Sibiu** (Filarmonica de Stat Sibiu) [217 E5]; (*Str Cetatii 3–5;* ☎*0371 112 559; e filarmo@filarmonicasibiu.ro; w filarmonicasibiu.ro*), offering a good programme of classical music, was once housed in the building which is now home to the Hermania Restaurant, but moved in 2004 to the historic Thalia Hall, which dates from 1787. The **Radu Stanca National Theatre** (Teatrul Naţional Radu Stanca) [216 D7] (*B-dul C Coposu 2;* \0269 210 092; w *tnrs.ro*), as well as lying at the heart of the International Theatre Festival, is an important theatre in its own right, centrally located on the side of Piaţa Unirii. The ticket agency for the theatre is on the pedestrianised Strada Nicolae Bălcescu in the Old Town [216 D5] (*Str Nicolae Bălcescu 7;* \0369 101 578; e *ticketing@sibfest.ro;* ⊕ *11.00–18.00 Tue–Sat, 10.00–14.00 Sun*). The **Gong Theatre** (Teatrul Gong) [216 B4] (*Str Alexandru Odobescu 4;* \0269 211 349; e *ticketing@teatrulgong.ro;* w *teatrulgong. ro*) is a children's theatre, particularly noted for puppetry.

OTHER PRACTICALITIES

$ **Raiffeisen Bank** [216 D6] Str Nicolae Bălcescu 29; ⊕ 09.00–17.30 Mon–Fri

✉ **Sibiu 1 Post Office** [216 C5] Str Mitropoliei 14; \0269 323 179; ⊕ 08.00–19.00 Mon–Fri, 09.00–13.00 Sat

✚ **Farmacia Sibiu Polisano Pharma** [217 F2] Str Constituţiei 24 (though entrance is on Str Gen Gheorghe Magheru); \0269 433 924; ⊕ 08.00– 21.00 Mon–Fri, 08.00–14.00 Sat

SHOPPING A great shop for souvenirs, **Galeriile de Artă Populară** [216 C3] (*Piaţa Mică 21;* \0269 432 250; e *gap@muzeulastra.ro;* ⊕ *May–Sep 10.00–18.00 Tue–Sun, Oct–Apr 09.00–17.00 Tue–Sun*) on Piaţa Mică is run by the ASTRA National Museum Complex and offers authentic Romanian handicrafts, from traditional embroidered blouses to pottery. **Gossip Tree** [216 C3] is a small shop at the top of the Passage of Steps selling imaginative clothing and jewellery by local designers (*Str Turnului 2;* m *0742 985 489;* ⊕ *10.00–20.00 Mon–Fri, 11.00– 19.00 Sat*).

WHAT TO SEE AND DO

Around Piaţa Mare [216 D4] The largest of the three interlocking squares which form the heart of the Old Town of Sibiu, the spacious Piaţa Mare is fringed by some of the finest buildings of the city. Among them is the 18th-century **Brukenthal Palace**. It is a Baroque building, modelled on the palaces of Imperial Vienna, and was the home of Baron Samuel von Brukenthal, a figure who has exerted an enormous influence on both the history of Sibiu and on the current artistic richness of the city. Brukenthal was appointed first Chancellor of Transylvania and later its Governor, and during his years of high office gradually amassed a valuable collection of artworks. The building now displays this collection, as the **Brukenthal National Museum** (Muzeul Naţional Brukenthal) [216 C4] (*Piaţa Mare 4–5;* \0269 217 691; e *info@brukenthalmuseum.ro;* w *brukenthalmuseum.ro;* ⊕ *21 Mar–21 Oct 10.00–18.00 Tue–Sun, also closed 1st Tue of each month, 22 Oct–20 Mar 10.00– 18.00 Wed–Sun; European art gallery 20RON, Romanian art gallery 12RON, other sections 6RON, courtyard only 1RON*). The core of the collection, displayed in three rooms, is known as the 'masterpieces of the Brukenthal collection', comprising 23 paintings, most of which were transferred by the Communists to the National Art Museum in Bucharest in 1948 and returned to Sibiu in time for the city's year as European Capital of Culture. Among the best of these are Jan van Eyck's *Man in a Blue Turban* and Pieter Bruegel the Elder's *The Massacre of the Innocents*, which moves the Biblical story into the setting of a Dutch village in winter, as a comment on the behaviour of the occupying Spanish troops ahead of what was to become known as the Eighty Years' War. At the time of research, the gallery was closed for reorganisation. The rest of the museum contains an extensive collection of

European and Romanian art, Anatolian rugs, a gypsotheque and lapidarium, and an interesting and rather spooky basement exhibition on the Gothic revival. There is a good deal to see, but some of the displays are more engaging than others.

If you are planning to visit several museums in Sibiu, it may be worth investing in a six-museum ticket (*45RON*), which covers all the museums under the administration of the Brukenthal National Museum, including the museums of history, pharmacy and natural history as well as the main one.

The north side of Piaţa Mare is graced by the **Roman Catholic Church** (Biserica Romano-Catolică Sfânta Treime) [216 D4] (*Piaţa Mare 2;* \0269 211 508; ⊕ 06.00–19.00 Mon–Sat, 08.30–19.00 Sun). Following the Reformation, Sibiu lacked a Roman Catholic church for some 150 years. Austrian troops stationed here demanded one and following long negotiations with the (Protestant) town council, the Jesuit monks who had accompanied the Austrians were allowed to build a church, which was consecrated in 1733. The Baroque-style building has an exuberantly decorated interior.

Strada General Gheorghe Magheru heads northeastwards from Piaţa Mare towards the railway station. Although something of a detour from the major sites of the centre, there are a couple of interesting religious buildings along this route. The **Ursuline Church** (Biserica Ursulinelor) [217 E3] (*Str Gen Magheru 38;* \0269 430 754) started out life in the 15th century as a Dominican monastery, was abandoned following the Reformation, but reoccupied in the 18th century by Ursuline nuns, who restored the Gothic building in a Baroque style. A painted statue of St Ursula stands in a niche above the entrance.

A little further on, turn right onto the busy Strada Constituţiei to reach the **Great Synagogue** (Sinagoga Mare) [217 F2] (*Str Constituţiei 11;* ⊕ 09.00–noon daily; adult *4RON*), built by architect Ferenc Szalay in 1899 with a red brick and concrete exterior in an eclectic style, with funds collected by Sibiu's Jewish community.

Heading away from the main square in the other direction, **Strada Nicolae Bălcescu** [216 D4], Sibiu's busiest pedestrian street, leads south from Piaţa Mare towards the modern Piaţa Unirii, and is lined with cafés and bars that spread out their terraces in spring and summer to create an almost Mediterranean atmosphere.

Around Piaţa Mică [216 D3] After the pedestrianised calm of Piaţa Mare, Piaţa Mică, the 'Little Square' immediately to its north, can appear somewhat chaotic, its centre a car park, fringed with numerous (mostly indifferent) bars and restaurants. It is connected to Piaţa Mare beneath the **Council Tower** (Turnul Sfatului) [216 D3] (*Piaţa Mică 1;* ⊕ 10.00–20.00 daily; *2RON*) a square-based clock tower which served as an entry gate to the town at the end of the 13th century. It has had something of a turbulent history: the upper stories collapsed in 1585. The Council Tower has variously served as a grain storehouse, a fire watchtower, a temporary prison and a museum of natural science. It currently houses temporary exhibitions, but most visitors come for the view from the top.

The road arrives from the Lower Town up into Piaţa Mică beneath the pedestrian **Bridge of Liars** (Podul Minciunilor) [216 C3], the first cast-iron bridge in Romania, built in 1859 on the site of an earlier wooden bridge. There are various different stories as to how the bridge earned its name, most of them involving liars of various kinds, whether in affairs of business or of the heart, being thrown off it. It is a highly photogenic spot, especially as it looks across a distinctive Lower Town scene, with houses having narrow horizontal windows in their roofs, giving them the air of faces with suspicious half-closed eyes.

The square is home to the **Museum of the History of Pharmacy** (Muzeul de Istoriei a Farmaciei) [216 D3] (*Piaţa Mică 26;* \ *0269 218 191;* w *brukenthalmuseum.ro;* ⊙ *same as Brukenthal National Museum; adult/child 10/2.5RON*), located in a historic building dating from the 1560s, which housed a pharmacy from around 1600. The exhibition is laid out like a classical pharmacy. At the front, a reconstructed shop is decked out with wooden counters and stacks of jars recreating the atmosphere of a traditional apothecary. The laboratory behind features a display of objects used in the making of medicines. There is also a display on homeopathy, reflecting the fact that Samuel Hahnemann, its founder, worked for a couple of years in Sibiu as physician to Baron Samuel von Brukenthal: his research during this period, including into traditional Transylvanian folk remedies, and his study of the books in Brukenthal's vast library were an important element in the development of his theories.

Another museum housed in the square is the small **Emil Sigerus Saxon Ethnographic Museum** (Muzeul de Etnografie Săsească Emil Sigerus) [216 C3] (*Piaţa Mică 21;* \ *0269 202 422;* e *sigerus@muzeulastra.ro;* w *muzeulastra.ro;* ⊙ *10.00–18.00 Wed–Sun; adult/child 5/1RON*), part of the ASTRA museum complex, and located above the Galeriile de Artă Populară. Its nucleus is the ethnographic collection of the eponymous Emil Sigerus.

To the north of Piaţa Mică down a flight of steps is the peaceful and intimate Piaţa Aurarilor (Goldsmiths' Square), surrounded by charming old houses. For many years it was a key passage between Piaţa Mică and the Lower Town, the two connected by a stairway.

Around Piaţa Huet

[216 C3] Lying immediately to the southwest of Piaţa Mică, Piaţa Huet is dominated by the **Evangelical Cathedral** (Biserica Evanghelică) [216 C3] (\ *0269 213 141;* ⊙ *summer 09.00–20.00 daily, winter 09.00–17.00 daily; adult/ child 5/2RON to visit the church, 5/2RON for the tower, 8/3RON both church & tower*). This Gothic building has a tall spire atop its square-based tower, with four little spires flanking it, an architectural feature which looks attractive today but would have been an ominous sign for medieval visitors, as it was an indication that the town had the right to impose the death sentence. It was built from the 14th century on the site of a 12th-century Romanesque church. The simple, stark interior is in total contrast to that of the Catholic church. A large fresco, painted in 1445 by Johannes of Rosenau, covers much of the chancel's north wall. The mural shows the Crucifixion and marks a transition in painting from late Gothic style to Renaissance. On the west side is an organ designed by a German master in 1672, remodelled in 1915 with 6,000 pipes, making it the largest organ in Transylvania. Organ concerts are held at 18.00 on Tuesday evenings in summer (*adult/child 10/5RON, including a visit of the tower*). There is another, smaller, Baroque organ in the gallery on the south side, which also boasts a beautiful fan-vaulted ceiling.

Behind the main organ on the west side of the church is a room whose walls are lined with the decorated tombstones of prominent local leaders, with a distinct emphasis on former mayors of Sibiu. The first tombstone next to the door on the south wall is that of Mihnea the Bad, the son of Vlad the Impaler. A ruler of Wallachia who had made too many enemies, Mihnea was forced to take refuge in Transylvania and was murdered in 1510 as he was leaving a service in the church.

The statue in front of the church is that of **Georg Daniel Teutsch**, a 19th-century bishop of the church and historian of the Transylvanian Saxons. He is depicted clutching a Bible.

In the northwest corner of the square, the **Stairs Tower** (Turnul Scărilor) [216 C3] stands at the top of a flight of steps leading down to the Lower Town.

Immediately next to this is the **Casa Calfelor** [216 C3] (*Piaţa Huet 3;* ☏*0269 211 988;* e *office@heritas.ro;* w *heritas.ro;* ⊕ *09.00–13.00 & 14.00–17.00 Mon–Fri*), an interesting project by an organisation called Heritas who have renovated the building, the Journeyman's Guildhouse, as offices and a lodging house for young visiting craft workers, an echo of the medieval tradition of wandering from town to town to gain experience of different workshops through which young craft workers learnt their trade. Notice the wooden post outside: by tradition, journeymen on leaving the lodgings bang a nail or other metal object into it to ensure that their onward journey will be successful. Just down the steps and on your left is what claims to be the oldest restaurant in Romania, the **Golden Barrel** (Butoiul de Aur) [216 B3].

From the southern end of Piaţa Huet, Strada Mitropoliei heads southwestwards. The first building on your right is the **Casa Altemberger**, one of the most important secular Gothic buildings in Transylvania, with an attractive courtyard. Its present form dates from the late 15th century, when it was owned by a mayor of Sibiu named Thomas Altemberger. The building was purchased by the municipal authorities in 1545 as the new site of the town hall, and it retained this function until 1948. It now hosts the **History Museum** (Muzeul de Istorie) [216 C4] (*Str Mitropoliei 2;* ☏*0269 218 143;* w *brukenthalmuseum.ro;* ⊕ *same as Brukenthal National Museum; adult 20RON, additional 6RON to visit Treasury, 1RON to access courtyard only*).

The attractively presented displays are focused on the first floor of the building and include a series of dioramas chronicling the emergence of human settlements in the region, a section devoted to the Transylvanian glass industry, and the work of the guilds of Sibiu, with some particularly elaborate creations from the locksmiths. An exhibition on the work of the Magistrate of Sibiu is set in the room in which the City Council met, its members seated around the large table in the centre of the room. The Magistrate brought together the most important officials of the town, including the mayor and senior judges.

There is weaponry downstairs, including an interesting collection of oriental weapons, and a Roman lapidarium in the basement, which is based around the archaeological collection of Baron Samuel von Brukenthal, including many items from Apulum (present-day Alba Iulia). A medieval lapidarium next to this includes stonework retrieved from buildings which had been demolished and a row of tombstones. The final room across the courtyard is devoted to the Romanian independence movement.

Continuing along Strada Mitropoliei you reach on your left the **Romanian Orthodox Cathedral** (Catedrala Ortodoxă Mitropolitană Sf Treime) [216 C5] (*Str Mitropoliei 33–35;* ⊕ *06.00–20.00 daily*) with two imposing square towers and a low dome behind, its external decoration comprising bands of orange and beige brickwork. Constructed from 1902 to 1906, it has a lavishly painted, spacious interior. The faithful kiss the relics of Andrei Şaguna to the right of the entrance. Şaguna was a 19th-century bishop of the Orthodox Church in Transylvania who played an important role in the advocacy of the rights of Romanians in Transylvania at the time of the Hungarian Revolution of 1848–49.

Strada Mitropoliei ends at the western edge of the **Astra Park** (Parcul Astra) [216 C6], a small city park laid out in the late 19th century following the demolition of part of the city walls. It honours the ASTRA association, founded in 1861 to promote the literature and culture of the Romanians of Transylvania, and the park is full of statues of noted figures linked to the movement. The **ASTRA Palace** (Palatul ASTRA) [216 C7] (*Str Gheorghe Bariţiu 5–7;* ☏*0269 210 551*), on the side of the park, was the centre of the movement's activity, and still houses an important library.

Along the city walls A stretch of the medieval walls running along the southeastern edge of the Old Town makes for a nice stroll. Strada Cetății, which follows the line of the walls, modestly labels itself as 'the most beautiful street in Sibiu'. It runs past the 15th-century **Arquebusiers' Tower** (Turnul Archebuzierilor) [216 D6], which was later rebaptised the Drapers' Tower, and is then pedestrianised for a stretch from the square-based **Potters' Tower** (Turnul Olarilor) [216 D5] going eastwards beyond the octagonal **Carpenters' Tower** (Turnul Dulgherilor) [217 E5]. On the other side of the walls here, in the paved trench between two grassy slopes, is the Sibiu Theatre Festival 'Walk of Fame', honouring the stars, like US actor Tim Robbins in 2016, who have graced the festival. Immediately beyond the Carpenters' Tower is the Thalia Hall of the **State Philharmonic** of Sibiu [217 E5], a theatre since 1788, though rebuilt on several occasions. The building has a Neoclassical appearance when viewed from the front and a medieval one from the rear, where it incorporates the Thick Tower (Turnul Gros) [217 E5] of the city walls.

Continuing along Strada Cetății, you reach on the right the **Natural History Museum** (Muzeul de Istorie Naturală) [217 E5] (*Str Cetății 1; \0269 436 545; w brukenthalmuseum.ro; ⊕ same as Brukenthal National Museum; adult/child 13/3.25RON*). It is housed in a building specifically designed at the end of the 19th century to house the collection of the Transylvanian Society for Natural Sciences, and offers fossils, minerals and dioramas packed with stuffed animals. Model dinosaurs prowl the gardens outside.

Outside the city There is a major attraction some 6km out of the centre within the Dumbrava Sibiului Nature Reserve. This is the **ASTRA Museum of Traditional Folk Civilisation** (Muzeul Civilizației Populare Tradiționale ASTRA) (✳ *Str Pădurea Dumbrava 16–20; \0269 202 447; e centruldeinformare@muzeulastra. ro; w muzeulastra.ro; ⊕ May–Sep 10.00–20.00 daily, Oct–Apr 09.00–17.00 daily; adult/child 17/3.5RON*). Spread out over some 96ha, of which 40ha are occupied by the exhibits, this lays claim to the title of the largest open-air ethnographic museum in Europe. It is part of the ASTRA National Museum Complex, which has its origins in the efforts in 19th-century Transylvania to promote a Romanian cultural identity, culminating in the opening of the ASTRA Museum in Sibiu in 1905. The open-air museum is the most important of the many ongoing ASTRA initiatives in and around Sibiu today. Many traditional rural dwellings, churches, workshops and mills are scattered attractively in parkland around a lake, exhibits ranging from a mine entrance from the Apuseni to windmills from Dobrudja. This is a great place just to walk around, but the display materials are informative too, making it a great opportunity to learn about traditional life in Romania. Visits are particularly productive in summer, when the park hosts frequent cultural events and more of the buildings are open to visitors. You need to allow a day if you want to take in most of the exhibits, and there is a restaurant within the grounds. Bus 13 takes you here from the train station and central Sibiu, with a roughly hourly service.

HEADING SOUTH AND WEST

The area to the south and west of Sibiu offers a wide range of attractions, including some fine Saxon fortified churches, for example those of Cisnădie and Cristian, the mountain resort of Păltiniş and the saline lakes of Ocna Sibiului. The communities in the hillier parts of this region, clustered in the valleys of rivers flowing off the Cindrel

Mountains, form a culturally unique area known as the **Mărginimea Sibiului**, which was long a stronghold of ethnic Romanian traditions and cultures. The influence of the Romanian Orthodox Church is reflected in the local tradition of icon painting on glass. Shepherding was a central part of the economy of what was for centuries a border area between Transylvania in the north and Wallachia in the south, and the frequent migrations of shepherds over the mountains between the two areas was an important avenue of continued cultural communication. The traditional local costumes of the area, dominated by black and white, are distinctive too, especially the black felt hats of the traditional male dress. Among the villages which best offer an insight into the culture of the Mărginimea Sibiului are Răşinari and Sibiel.

CISNĂDIE Some 10km south of Sibiu, Cisnădie (Nagydisznód/Heltau) is a small town of some 13,000 people, settled by Saxon colonists in the 12th century. It developed into a noted centre for the weaving of wool. The main sight is its **fortified church** (*Str Cetății 1–3;* \ *0269 564 597;* e *office@ekh.ro;* w *ekh.ro;* ⊕ *10.00–13.00 & 14.00–18.00 Mon–Sat, 11.00–13.00 & 14.00–18.00 Sun; adult/ child 7/4RON*) right in the town centre. This dates from the 12th century and originally had the form of a Romanesque basilica. The church was fortified in the late 15th century, with the addition of four storeys above the choir. The large square-based west tower, which can be climbed, adds further to the particularly substantial feel of the main church building. The church is surrounded by a double set of oval defensive walls, which once had a moat between them. There are various exhibitions dotted around the buildings of the complex, including one on the history of Communism.

There is a **tourist information office** (*Str Cetății 1;* \ *0269 561 236;* e *info_cisnadie@ sibiu-turism.ro;* w *www.cisnadie.ro;* ⊕ *09.00–17.00 Mon–Fri, 09.00–13.00 Sat*) next to the church.

Some 4km west of Cisnădie is the village of **Cisnădioara** (Kisdisznód/ Michelsberg), which has an atmospheric **fortified church** (m *0726 877 782;* ⊕ *Mar–Oct 10.00–18.00 Tue–Sun, Nov–Feb 10.00–15.00 Tue–Sun; adult/child 7/4RON*) on a hill above the village. It is a three-aisled Romanesque basilica, probably dating from the 13th century. Unusually among the Saxon fortified churches of southern Transylvania, this was modified relatively little in later centuries. It is surrounded by a defensive wall with three towers. There was apparently a local tradition in which young men of the village wishing to prove their worth to the family of their prospective bride had to cart heavy rocks from the riverbed up to the fortifications, which could then be thrown down at the enemy below in times of siege.

There are frequent **buses** from Sibiu to Cisnădie (*25mins*).

Where to stay

✱ 🏠 **Secret Transylvania** (4 dbl) Str Bisericii, Cisnădioara; \ 0269 562 119; m 0742 247 664; e admin@secrettransylvania.co.uk; w secrettransylvania.co.uk. Rooms in 2 restored village houses in Cisnădioara, though in high season these are generally only available as part of (recommended) all-inclusive packages, including Sibiu airport transfers, FB & daily excursions. They also offer winter packages featuring a night at the Ice Hotel at Bâlea Lake (pages 240–1). **$$$$$**

RĂŞINARI Răşinari (Resinár/Städterdorf) is a village within the Mărginimea Sibiului on the 106A road between Sibiu and Păltiniş, about 12km south of Sibiu. The village has an **ethnographic museum** (*Str Octavian Goga 1527;* m *0733 490 642;* ⊕ *09.00–16.00 Tue–Sat, 09.00–14.00 Sun; adult/child 4/2RON*), which, as well as offering displays of traditional village interiors, describes the techniques of resin-tapping which gave the village its name: *răşină* is the Romanian word for resin. Răşinari was the birthplace of Octavian Goga, a Romanian politician active in the interwar years, whose brief spell as prime minister in early 1938 is mainly recalled for the introduction of anti-Semitic legislation. One of the main roads in the village is named after him. Răşinari used to be connected to Sibiu by a **tramline**, constructed in 1947, which ran scenically through the Dumbrava Forest, but this closed in 2011, although there is periodic talk of re-establishing a tramway aimed at tourists.

There is a **tourist information office** (*Str Sibiului;* ✆*0269 558 022;* e *info_rasinari@ sibiu-turism.ro;* ⏰ *09.00–18.00 Tue–Fri, 10.00–17.00 Sat, 10.00–15.00 Sun*) in the village.

🏠 Where to stay and eat

🏠 **Pensiunea Curmatura Stezii** (23 rooms, 7 wooden huts) DJ 106A, Km 16 Sibiu–Păltiniş; ✆0269 557 310; e info@curmaturastezii.ro; w curmaturastezii.ro. Located some 5km west of Răşinari on the road towards Păltiniş, in an attractive spot among woodland, this large pension has a restaurant with terrace, basic rooms rated as '2 daisies', nicer ones as '5 daisies' &, in summer only, very basic wooden huts. **$$$** (5-daisy rooms), **$$** (2-daisy rooms), **$** (wooden huts)

🏠 **Badiu's Guest House** (6 dbl, 1 suite) Str Octavian Goga 786; m 0745 308 276; e info@ badiuguesthouse.ro; w badiuguesthouse.ro. Nicely decorated rooms & a set dinner available (*€15*) featuring local dishes & wine. **$$**

PĂLTINIŞ Some 35km southwest of Sibiu, Păltiniş (Szebenjuharos/Hohe Rinne), at an altitude of 1,440m in the Cindrel Mountains, is the highest resort in Romania. It is a popular **ski resort** in winter, but is also a draw in summer, by virtue of its fine mountain location within an area of conifer forest and the accessibility of its hiking trails.

It was established in 1894 by the Siebenbürgischer Karpatenverein (SKV), the initial lure being the mountain air for the treatment of lung diseases. The German name for the resort, Hohe Rinne, was taken from that of a local spring, but the resort later adopted the Romanian name Păltiniş. Some of the original resort buildings, whose designs ape Tyrolean chalets, survive today. In the grounds of a small wooden hermitage church (Schitul Păltiniş) in the resort, built in the 1920s, is the grave of Romanian philosopher Constantin Noica, who died in 1987.

A **chair lift** (*telescaun*) (✆ *0269 574 067;* e *office@telescaunpaltinis.ro;* w *telescaunpaltinis.ro;* ⏰ *09.00–17.00 Mon–Fri, 09.00–18.00 Sat/Sun; 13RON return, 10RON one-way*) serves the **Onceşti** ski run at the heart of the resort, which is equipped with snow cannons and floodlights. Ski and snowboard equipment can be hired. Onceşti has a newer rival, the ski complex of **Arena Platoş** (w *arenaplatos. ro*), equipped with a chair lift and four ski lifts, which also has snow cannons and floodlighting. Arena Platoş is around 3km from the centre of Păltiniş itself, on the DJ106A road back towards Răşinari. Hiking possibilities around Păltiniş in summer range from circuits of around 3 hours, one marked with blue circles, the other blue triangles, to a strenuous full-day hike to the top of Mount Cindrel, at 2,244m, taking in the Bătrâna and Rozdeşti peaks on the way, marked with red triangles.

Bus 22 leaves Sibiu railway station three times daily and stops at Răşinari.

🏠 Where to stay

🏠 **Hohe Rinne Păltiniş** (75 dbl, 13 apt) Str Principală 1; ✆0269 215 000; e hoherinne@ hoherinne.com; w hoherinne.com. Close to the Onceşti slope, this smart hotel with the feel of an oversized chalet is the modernised Casa Turiştilor, dating back to the 1960s. It offers a choice of superior rooms (with balcony) & standard rooms (without), a spa with indoor pool, saunas & even a salt therapy cave, & has mountain bikes for rent. **$$$$**

🏠 **Hotel Cindrel** (43 dbl, 4 apt) Păltiniş; ☎0269 574 056; e contact@hotelcindrel.ro; w hotelcindrel.ro. A 3-star hotel with indoor pool & sauna, restaurant with terrace, balconied rooms & mountain bikes for rent, but looking rather tired around the edges. **$$$**

CRISTIAN Situated 10km west of Sibiu on route E68/81 heading towards Sebeş, Cristian (Kereszténysziget/Grossau) is a Saxon settlement dating from the 12th century, though its first known documentary mention dates from 1223. Its **fortified church** (biserica fortificată) (*Str X 40; contact Maria Marasescu on* m *0751 146 061;* w *www.cristian.sobis.ro;* ⊕ *08.00–13.00 & 14.00–17.00 daily by appointment; adult 7RON*) is located on a flat site in the heart of the village. It was constructed in the 13th century as a Romanesque basilica dedicated to St Servatius, a saint who was popular in the regions of origin of the colonists. Only a few parts of the church, including the base of the bell tower, have survived from this period. It was rebuilt in the late 14th century, and then at the end of the 15th century was converted into a vaulted late Gothic hall church by a master builder from Sibiu called Andreas Lapicida. There are a number of 18th-century Baroque features inside, notably the pulpit, and a wooden altar from 1719.

Cristian was one of the Transylvanian villages to receive members of the Landler group: these were Austrian Protestants deported to Transylvania under the orders of the (Catholic) rulers Charles VI and later Empress Maria Theresa between 1734 and 1776. Relations between the Landler and the longer-established Saxon community were not always warm, and though both groups prayed at the same church, they used different doors to come in.

The defensive wall around the church is an irregular polygon in form. Its towers include an octagonal bacon tower (Turnul Slăninii), which still has some hams hanging from the rafters to demonstrate to visitors the functioning of this community larder. Local jams, preserves and spirits are sold here. There is a two-room museum within the church grounds, with displays of the largely black-and-white Landler costumes and the more colourful Saxon ones, together with a Saxon interior.

One other feature not to miss within the church complex is to be found on the walls of the vicarage: this is a 'plague pulpit', comprising an overhanging wall of the building with two small windows. This was to allow sermons to be given during times of plague while allowing the priest to avoid physical contact with his flock.

Cristian is also noted for its large **stork** population: the locals tell you that more storks nest here than in any other community of equivalent size in Romania. The large stork nests are certainly much in evidence at the tops of telegraph poles. The storks are considered good luck, and there is a local NGO called Prietenii Berzelor (Friends of the Storks) (*Str XVI 10;* ☎*0269 579 497;* w *prieteniiberzelor.ro*) which allows you to view one of the stork nests via a webcam.

There are frequent **buses** to Cristian from Sibiu (*30mins*), operated by the Transmixt company.

🏠 **Where to stay**

🏠 **Casa Pandora** (8 rooms) Str XXIV 12; ☎0269 579 717; e info@casapandora.ro; w casapandora.ro. A quiet guesthouse in spacious grounds, with an orchard, on the edge of the village. The pleasantly furnished rooms are on 2 levels. **$$**

🏠 **Casa Parohială** (10 rooms) Contact details as for the fortified church (see above). Very basic accommodation is available in the vicarage, with shared bathrooms. No meals served, but there is access to the kitchen. There are even straw-covered bunks in a converted wooden outbuilding which once accommodated beehives. **$**

SIBIEL Sibiel (Szibiel/Budenbach), 24km west of Sibiu, is within the Mărginimea Sibiului and one of the group of Romanian villages to be formally declared a 'tourist village' in the Communist era. Its main lure for visitors is the remarkable **Father Zosim Oancea Museum of Icons on Glass** (Muzeul de Icoane pe Sticlă Preot Zosim Oancea) (*Str Bisericii 329*; \ *0269 552 536*; w *sibiel.net*; ⊕ *winter 07.00–13.30 & 14.00–19.00 daily, summer 08.00–13.30 & 14.00–20.00 daily; adult/child 5/3RON*), a collection put together by a priest, Zosim Oancea, who endured years of detention in the Communist era. On his release in the early 1960s, he was appointed to a parish in Sibiel, where he developed the idea of establishing a museum to showcase the beautiful work of icons painted on glass, and persuaded local people to donate their icons in order to set it up. The painting of icons on glass developed in the 18th century has long been a particularly strong tradition of the Mărginimea Sibiului area, which is well represented in the museum. But it also contains good collections from other parts of Transylvania where this form of religious art was also prominent, including the area around Nicula in northern Transylvania and the Şchei neighbourhood of Braşov. The museum also has a collection of religious texts and other examples of local craftwork. It is located in the centre of the village, in the grounds of the **Church of the Holy Trinity** (Biserica Sfânta Treime). If the latter is locked, ask the staff at the museum to open it up for you; it contains 18th-century frescoes by brothers Stan and Iacob of Răşinari, which had been covered over by whitewash, to be brought to light in the 1960s through the efforts of Father Zosim Oancea.

To get here from Sibiu, head west on the E68/81 towards Sebeş, turning off to the left at Săcel. Slower local **trains** heading westwards from Sibiu stop at Sibiel (*30mins*).

🏠 **Where to stay** On the edge of the village is **Pensiunea Mioriţică** (*8 dbl, 1 apt; Str Râului 197A*; m *0740 175 287*; e *coldeasv@yahoo.com*; **$$**), a friendly and unusual guesthouse with a delightful garden focused on a stream running right through the property. There are displays of local craft items and Communist relics collected by the owner.

MIERCUREA SIBIULUI Miercurea Sibiului (Szerdahely/Reussmarkt), with a population just below 4,000, is one of the smallest communities with the formal status of a town in Romania, and has something of a village feel, although the expansive central square hints at grander aspirations. At the back of the square sits the **fortified church** (*Str Pompierilor 27; ask at no 25 for a key if it is locked*). Its square-based tower, with wooden defensive features, stands guard over the square. The church was built in the 13th century as a Romanesque basilica, but extensively altered in the 15th century, when the oval defensive wall was also heightened. The interior is Transylvanian Baroque in feel, including the elaborate altar, centred on a sculpture of the Crucifixion, with a small painting of the Last Supper beneath. Large wooden store chests sit under the pitched roof around the inside of the defensive wall.

Miercurea Sibiului is on the E68/E81 highway to Sebeş, 35km west of Sibiu, and can also be accessed from the A1 motorway running parallel to this. There is one **bus** a day to Sebeş (*30mins*) and a couple to Sibiu (*from 45mins*). It is also served by **trains** running between Sibiu and the junction at Vânţu de Jos.

🏠 **Where to stay** About 3km west of Miercurea Sibiului, close to the border with Alba County, on the main E68 highway is the **Comfort Hotel** (*33 dbl, 1 suite; Băile Miercurea 1*; \ *0269 533 033*; e *mail@comfort-hotel.ro*; w *comfort-hotel.ro*; **$**), a motel-like place with plenty of car parking and functional accommodation in an ugly building on the edge of the run-down spa resort of Băile Miercurea Sibiului.

OCNA SIBIULUI Some 15km northwest of Sibiu, the small town of Ocna Sibiului (Vízakna/Salzburg) has an economy based around the presence of one of the largest salt reserves in Romania. Salt was collected here from Dacian times. The bell-shaped workings characteristic of mines constructed before the end of the 18th century have resulted in a series of deep saltwater lakes formed in these mines after they were abandoned, and Ocna Sibiului has developed as a tourist resort around them. Studies of the curative effects of the saline lakes here were made back in 1820, and the place was formally inaugurated as a therapeutic resort in 1858.

The **Ocna Sibiului Lakes** (*Str Salinelor 7;* m *0735 301 901;* e *info@lacuriocnasibiului. ro;* w *lacuriocnasibiului.ro;* ⊕ *1 May–15 Sep daily; adult/child 15/10RON, sunbed rental 10RON*) comprise a large group of saltwater lakes strung out east of Strada Salinelor. One of these is called the Lacul Fără Fund (Bottomless Lake), a legacy of the Francisc Grube Salt Mine, abandoned in the late 18th century. But at a maximum depth of 34m it rather pales beside Lacul Avram Iancu, formed from the Fodina Maior salt mine, abandoned in 1817. Reaching a depth of 128m, the latter is the deepest manmade lake in Romania. Lacul Brâncoveanu, formed on the site of a salt mine abandoned in 1699, has the highest salt concentration of all the lakes at Ocna Sibiului. Lacul Negru is a focus for those looking to take mud baths. These lakes offer swimming facilities of varying degrees of sophistication, and can get very crowded at the height of summer.

On the opposite side of Strada Salinelor are the more developed attractions of the **Ştrand** (*Str Băilor 26;* ℩ *0269 541 473;* e *infoocnasibstrand@sibiu.astral.ro;* w *ocnasibiului.eu*), which has a further three saltwater lakes known as Horea, Cloşca and Crişan after the leaders of the peasant uprising of 1784, with depths between 34m and 45m, as well as a hotel and sun terrace.

There is a railway station in the resort, Băile Ocna Sibiului, conveniently located for the lakes. There are **train** connections to Sibiu (*20mins*) and Mediaş (*1hr*). By **car**, turn right at the first junction of the new A1 motorway to the west of Sibiu, which takes you straight to Ocna Sibiului by way of the village of Şura Mică. Most of the main **accommodation** options in the resort are rather rundown, and this might best be visited as a day trip from Sibiu.

HEADING NORTH

SLIMNIC The village of Slimnic (Szelindek/Stolzenburg) is of note for its impressive ruined 'Peasant fortress' (Cetatea ţărănească) (m *0748 547 143;* ⊕ *summer 10.00– 19.00 daily, winter 10.00–dusk daily, but call in advance; 3RON*), which sits atop a hill above the village. The location was strategically important on the main route between Sibiu and Mediaş, and a castle was built here in the 14th century. It is a good example of the fortresses of refuge of the Saxon area of Transylvania, a type of defensive structure that generally preceded the fortified churches more typical of the region. There is a Gothic chapel with a bell tower above. Construction of a Gothic hall church was started to the south of this, but never completed. The fortress was conquered in 1529 by the forces of John Zápolya, and again in 1706, during the uprising of Francis II Rákóczi, when it was partially destroyed. Slimnic is 17km north of Sibiu, on the DN14 towards Mediaş. The fortress, to the right of the road in the village, is a local landmark.

COPŞA MICĂ Copşa Mică (Kiskapus/Kleinkopisch) is a small town of some 5,000 people which became known internationally for all the wrong reasons, when it was identified in the 1990s as one of the most polluted towns in Europe. Two local factories were at the root of much of the pollution. The Carbosin factory, built in the 1930s to produce carbon black, used for dyes, was responsible for a black soot that permeated the town and everything in it. The factory was closed in 1993. The second factory, Sometra, was a producer of non-ferrous metals. The citizens of Copșa Mică were found to have a life expectancy some nine years below the national average. The streets of the town are no longer blackened with soot, but the soil in the area is still contaminated, and much remains to be done.

Copșa Mică is 42km north of Sibiu, on the DN14 towards Mediaș. It has **train** connections to Mediaș (*20mins*) and Blaj (*50mins*), though there is little reason to stop here.

VALEA VIILOR Valea Viilor (Nagybaromlak/Wurmloch) is noted for its **fortified church** (biserica fortificată) (*Valea Viilor no 341;* m *0745 519 173;* ☉ *Apr–Oct 09.00– noon & 14.00–17.00 Mon–Fri, Nov–Mar call to arrange a visit; 5RON*), one of the seven specifically listed as a UNESCO World Heritage Site. The church, which is right in the centre of the village, makes a fine sight, with a large tower over the choir at the eastern end providing a counterpoise to the west tower. Both towers are topped by defensive galleries. Buttresses on the external walls of the church create a series of tall niches crowned with semicircular arches. And the building is encircled by an oval-shaped defensive wall, with a wooden wall-walk. The current church dates from the 15th century, nothing surviving of an earlier church on the site, and was fortified around 1500. The striking heightening of the building above the choir dates from this period. There is impressive net vaulting above the choir. The altar dates from 1779.

Valea Viilor is 47km north of Sibiu. Take the DN14 to Copșa Mică then turn right, signposted for Valea Viilor.

MEDIAȘ The town of Mediaș (Medgyes/Mediasch) was settled by Saxons in the 13th century, its first known documentary mention dating from 1267, though the site had been inhabited since the Neolithic period. It received city status in the mid 14th century, and its defensive walls were built between the 15th and 16th centuries, initially at the instigation of Matthias Corvinus. One of the seven Transylvanian towns comprising the Siebenbürgen, Mediaș was an important centre, and hosted the Diet of Transylvania on several occasions. More recently, its economy has been focused on the production of methane gas, as the town sits in Romania's largest natural gas field. The local football team rejoices in the name Methane Gas Mediaș, and the headquarters of the state-owned natural gas company Romgaz are here.

The heart of the town is the quiet Piața Regele Ferdinand I, a verdant spot with a fountain in the centre. The **Casa Schuller** (*Piața Regele Ferdinand I 25;* \0269 831 347) on the square is a 16th-century building in Transylvanian Renaissance style, with an arched entrance guarded by statues of two mythical creatures holding balls in their mouths. It was refurbished with German Government support and now hosts various cultural activities.

From the square head up Strada Honterus to reach the **citadel**. This is centred on the **Evangelical Church of St Margaret** (Biserica Evanghelică Sfânta Margareta) (*Piața Castelului 1;* \0269 841 962; e *kastellmediasch@yahoo.de;* ☉ *summer 10.00–19.00 daily, winter 10.00–15.00 daily; adult/child 5/3RON*). Built on the site of earlier churches, the present building dates mostly from the 15th century, with a net-vaulted nave and choir. Some 40 Anatolian rugs, dating from the 16th to 19th centuries, decorate the interior; the second-largest collection in Romania. Also of note is a fine altarpiece dating from the 1480s. The church currently hosts three other pre-Reformation altars, which were brought here from other churches in the area for security reasons. The baptismal font, which dates from around 1380, is said to be the oldest in Transylvania. The square-based Trumpeters' Tower, topped by a tall green spire, stands in the northwestern corner of the church. More than 68m high, it has a decided lean. On Monday evenings in summer the church holds organ concerts at 19.00.

The original oval defensive wall around the church has been modified by a range of later buildings, whose functions ranged from town hall to German school. There are some interesting buildings in this castle complex. Next to the square-based Ropemakers' Tower is the house in which Stephan Ludwig Roth was born in 1796. Roth was a reform-minded priest who opposed attempts by the authorities to make Hungarian the official language of Transylvania, and supported more rights for the Romanians of Transylvania. He was executed in 1849 during the turbulent Hungarian Revolution, an event which did much to align Saxon sympathies towards Vienna and away from the Hungarian revolutionaries. The Tower of St Mary beyond the south side of the church contains some impressive frescoes from the 1450s, and, less serenely, later also apparently served as a place of torture.

Taking Strada Nicolae Iorga from Piaţa Regele Ferdinand I you reach the restored **Goldsmiths' Tower** (Turnul Aurarilor), one of the remaining structures of the old city walls. The **tourist information office** (*Str Nicolae Iorga;* \0369 455 444; e *info_medias@sibiu-turism.ro;* ⊕ *08.00–noon & 12.30–16.00 Mon–Fri*) is on the same street. Near the entrance to the citadel, the **Kastell Bookshop** (*Piaţa George Enescu 8;* ⊕ *10.00–18.00 Mon–Sat, 11.30–18.00 Sun*) has local maps and guides.

Mediaş lies on route 14, some 55km north of Sibiu and 35km west of Sighişoara. The **railway station** (\0269 846 101) is at the southern edge of the town centre on Strada Unirii. Mediaş is on a main railway line, and connections include Sighişoara (*1hr*), Braşov (*3½hrs*) and Cluj-Napoca (*3hrs 20mins*). The **bus station** (*Autogara Mediaş; Str Unirii 11;* \0369 108 768) is nearby. There are five buses and minibuses daily to Sibiu (*1hr*).

🏠 Where to stay and eat

🏠 **Hotel Traube** (15 rooms) Piaţa Regele Ferdinand I 16; \0269 844 898; e receptie@ hoteltraube.ro; w hoteltraube.ro. Centrally located on the main square, this is a 3-star hotel in a historic building. It also has a restaurant with a terrace, combining local & international dishes (**$$$**). It is looking a little frayed around the edges, but is comfortable & sympathetically furnished. **$$$**

🏠 **Fabini Apartments** (5 rooms) Piaţa Regele Ferdinand I 5; m 0728 714 340; e contact@ fabiniapartments.eu; w fabiniapartments.eu. Across the main square from the Traube, this offers simply furnished rooms with a kitchenette. The reception is in the Tio Tom Bistro next door. **$$**

MOŞNA Moşna (Szász-Muzsna/Meschen) has an impressive **fortified church** (biserica fortificată) (\ *0269 862 141;* m *0744 624 776;* ⊕ *09.00–18.00 Mon–Sat, noon–18.00 Sun, but call in advance; 8RON*), which originated as a 14th-century Gothic building but was reconstructed in 1485 by the noted stonemason Andreas Lapicida of Sibiu. The interior is particularly striking, with ribbed net vaulting above the choir, nave and aisles, and eight paired columns, each pair sculpted in a different manner. Lapicida's talent is also seen in the sculpture of the pulpit and the arch over the sacristy. The reconstruction work involved the fortification of the church; it is surrounded by an 8m-high outer wall. The interior aspect of this features a line of brick arches, above which is a wall walk. A small museum has been installed here, focusing on the costumes and tools of the Saxon community. The wall walk ends at the **Bacon Tower** (Turnul Slăninilor), where there is a display of hams hanging from the rafters, harking back to the days when it was used as a community storage facility. A plaque on the wall inside the complex recalls the visit to the church of HRH The Prince of Wales in 1998, during his first official visit to Romania. On the eastern side of the complex a large square-based gate tower stands just outside the defensive wall. The size of the church complex is a reflection of Moşna's former importance: it once competed with Mediaş and Biertan in a bid to become the local administrative capital, a battle it was to lose to the former, gradually sinking into the status of a simple village. The school next to the church is named in honour of Stephan Ludwig Roth, who was the priest here at the time of the 1849 Hungarian Revolution, the year of his execution as a staunch advocate of the rights of the Romanians of Transylvania.

Recently Moşna has also developed something of a reputation for ecological farming. **Bio-Moşna** (*Str Cetăţii 543;* \ *0269 862 206;* e *willyschuster@yahoo. com*), an ecological farm set up by Willy and Lavinia Schuster, is a great place to buy fresh homemade cheese and jam. It sits in the street running behind the fortified church. Moşna is also noted for its **cabbage festival** (Festivalul Verzei), a relatively recent tradition, usually held over the second weekend in October and highlighting the impressive local quality of this vegetable. Folk music, dancing and, of course, cabbage-related cuisine all feature.

Moşna is 10km south of Mediaş along a good minor road.

BIERTAN Biertan (Berethalom/Birthälm) is a prosperous-looking large village whose central square is dominated by the large and impressive **fortified church** (\ *0269 868 262;* ⊕ *Apr–Oct 10.00–13.00 & 14.00–17.00 daily; admission 10RON*), which features defensive structures running down the hill towards the square. The church is one of those inscribed on the UNESCO World Heritage list in 1999, and among the largest and most visited of all the Saxon fortified churches of Transylvania. The first church was built here in the 14th century, but the present building dates from the start of the 16th, its size an indication of Biertan's wealth, which was at least partly down to the local wine industry. When Lucas Unglerus, who was born here, was made Lutheran Bishop of Transylvania in 1572, Biertan became the Episcopal see, a role it held until 1867.

The ticket office for the church sells a range of guides (albeit mostly in German) and some postcards. From the ticket office, a restored covered wooden staircase heads up the hill. The staircase brings you out inside the inner of the two circles of defensive walls. There is also a third partial wall, all adding up to an impressive and complex array of defensive structures. The towers in the inner wall include the Catholic chapel, a place for prayer for those who did not convert to Protestantism, which features some late-Gothic frescoes. The building in the walls to the left of this, which currently houses a two-room museum, is apparently a place in which quarrelling couples were locked together, with just a single bed, plate, knife, fork and spoon, as a last-ditch attempt to see whether they could get on. Another tower houses tombstones of priests and bishops of the church, including Lucas Unglerus.

As regards the church itself, its structure is that of a hall church, with three aisles. An inscription in Latin over the chancel arch records that the building of the church was completed in 1522. The folding altar, dating from the late 15th to the early 16th centuries, is remarkable, with a carved Crucifixion scene surrounded by painted panels, many showing scenes from the life of the Virgin and the life of Christ. Another unmissable feature of the interior of the church is the sacristy door, with its hugely elaborate lock. It dates from 1515, though was restored in 1889 in order to be shown at the Paris Exposition.

Outside the inner wall, accessible from the first exit from the covered stairway, halfway up, is a former roadway up to the church, with flying buttresses forming delightful arches above it.

An **annual meeting of Transylvanian Saxons** is held in Biertan on the first Saturday after 15 September, featuring a parade in folk costume, a fair and music.

Biertan lies some 9km south of route 14 between Mediaş and Sighişoara: **drive** for 17km east from Mediaş and turn right (signposted) near Dumbrăveni. There are between four and six **buses** and **minibuses** daily to Mediaş (*50mins*)

🏠 Where to stay and eat

🏠 **Mihai Eminescu Trust** Str Nicolae Bălcescu 2; see page 17 for booking & contact details. The MET have a 2-bedroom guesthouse in the village decorated in a traditional Transylvanian style. Homemade meals can be prepared by arrangement. **$$$**

🏠 **Pensiunea Oppidum** (5 rooms) Str George Coşbuc 24; m 0740 679 119; e pensiunea. oppidum@yahoo.it; w cazare-biertan.tk. Immediately over the road from the Dornröschen, this is a friendly guesthouse in an 18th-century building with garden, & comfortable rooms, though shared bathrooms. Good b/fast inc. **$$$**

🏠 **Unglerus Medieval Resort** Str 1 Decembrie 1918 1; m 0742 024 065; e office@ biertan.ro; w biertan.ro. The big player in the Biertan tourism industry, centred on the Unglerus Medieval Restaurant (⊕ *10.00–22.00* daily; **$$$**) just next to the entrance of the church. A large place, scattered over various rooms & terraces, with heavy wooden chairs, medieval-themed paintings & a hit-&-miss menu ('Mediterranean salad' mostly comprised cabbage & cheese). It is a favoured lunch stop for coach parties. The Unglerus Tourist Agency is also housed in the same building as the restaurant, & they run 3 guesthouses in the village: the Thomas is right opposite the restaurant; the Unglerus & Michael are each a short walk away. The reception for all is at the restaurant. **$$$**

🏠 **Casa Dornröschen** (10 rooms) Str George Coşbuc 25; ☎0269 244 165. A guesthouse mostly geared towards German visitors, around the back of the fortified church (along an alleyway signposted from the church ticket office) & even located within the outer walls. **$$**

COPŞA MARE Copşa Mare (Nagykapus/Grosskopisch) lies some 3km away from Biertan in the valley to the east, making for either a good walk or a straightforward short drive. As with most of the Saxon villages in the area, the main sight is the **fortified church** (biserica fortificată) (*donation expected*), which is located on the village's eastern hillside. The key is obtained from the family living within the church walls. It was initially built in the early 14th century, but heavily modified during the process of fortification in the 16th. The main entrance to the church is at the base of the tower. The interior is in a pretty poor state, with the flooring a mix of bricks, concrete and gravel and the organ, dating from 1800, in sore need of repair. The altar, with its Corinthian columns, is mid 19th century. A rectangular wall surrounds the church.

The real attraction of the place, however, lies in the charm and picturesque setting of the village.

🏠 **Where to stay** Four guesthouses collectively known as the **Copşa Mare Guesthouses** (*9 rooms; Copşa Mare 146;* m *0746 046 200;* e *copsamare@gmail.com;* w *copsamare. ro;* **$$$$$**) have been sensitively restored by Paolo and Giovanna Bassetti, from the four-bedroom White House to the duplex apartment of the Green House. Breakfast is included; other meals can be provided if requested 24 hours in advance, and are served centrally at the Yellow House. Rates are high for Transylvania, but the quality is good.

RICHIŞ Richiş (Riomfalva/Reichesdorf) lies some 6km south of Biertan on a minor but good road. It is an attractive village, several of whose houses have been renovated by western European expatriates. Settled by Saxons in the 13th century, it is noted for its vines. The overall feel is much quieter and less touristy than Biertan.

The **church** (*contact Johann Schaas; Richiş no 87;* ☏ *0269 258 429;* ⊕ *visiting by appointment; donations welcome*) is a three-aisled towerless building dating from the 14th century, which is believed to have originally been part of a monastery. The church grounds are entered through a bell tower which is mostly of 19th-century vintage. The former external defensive wall was mostly demolished in the early part of the 20th century, its stone used for other public buildings in the village, so it is not immediately obvious that the church in Richiş is indeed part of the family of Saxon fortified churches in Transylvania. Inside the church itself, note the interesting stone carving of the capitals, including several examples of pagan 'green men', a highly unusual feature in a Transylvanian church. The vaulting in the nave features some impressive carved bosses. Note also the complex lock on the sacristy door, like that at Biertan: the church authorities were clearly taking no chances.

There is an **information point** (*Richiş no 290;* ☏ *0269 258 585;* e *prorichis@gmail. com;* w *prorichis.ro;* ⊕ *10.00–14.00 Tue–Sun*) in the building next to the church, run by the Pro Richiş non-governmental organisation, an initiative by the Dutch family that runs the Curtea Richvini guesthouse. Richiş also plays host to the small-scale but delightful **Transylvanian Book Festival** (w *transylvanianbookfestival.co.uk*), organised by Lucy Abel-Smith, a Briton living in the village, though to no fixed calendar.

⌂ **Where to stay** Run by a Dutch family, **La Curtea Richvini** (*6 rooms;* ☏ *0269 258 475;* e *info@lacurtearichis.ro;* w *lacurtearichis.ro;* **$$$**) is a guesthouse offering peaceful accommodation in the restored parish house, having been sympathetically decorated, though bathrooms are not en suite. There is also a walled campsite.

MĂLÂNCRAV Mălâncrav (Almakerék/Malmkrog) has the highest proportion of remaining Saxons in any village in Transylvania, in part a consequence of the relatively isolated location of the village, in part the retention here of an Evangelical priest. It is an attractive village, which has benefited from the restoration work of the Mihai Eminescu Trust (MET; page 17). Among the MET's projects in the village has been the replanting of a derelict apple orchard and the establishment of a new fruit-processing plant, producing excellent apple juice. Unusually for a Saxon village, Mălâncrav was the property of the Hungarian Apáfi family from 1340 until the 18th century. The **Apáfi Mansion** above the village has been lovingly restored by the MET, its Ionic-columned façade looking out across a fine garden. When the Apáfi line ran out in the 18th century the mansion fell into the hands of the influential Bethlen family and then a family named Haller, who rebuilt the manor in the 1830s.

The major attraction of the village is an impressively sited **fortified church** (*biserica fortificată*) (*keys at House 307 & at the Casa Parohială; 5RON donation requested*) on a small hill overlooking the village, right next to the Apáfi Mansion. It was built in the late 14th century by the Apáfi family. Its exterior, of unplastered stone, is unusual for Transylvanian churches. In the 15th century, the church was surrounded by a defensive wall.

The most significant feature of the church lies inside: some of the most important Gothic mural paintings in Romania, dating from the 14th century. The finest of these are in the choir. The many scenes depicted here include a Crucifixion, the Last Supper, Judas committing suicide and Jesus washing the feet of the Disciples. There are other paintings on the north wall of the nave: these are in a poorer condition as they were painted over after the Reformation. Another notable feature is the 15th-century Gothic folding altar, which is centred on a portrayal of the Virgin Mary and Child, but opens up to reveal paintings of St George and the Archangel Michael, each slaying dragons.

Each July the Saxon community still holds the traditional **Kronenfest** (Sărbătoarea Coroanei), the focus of which is a tall wooden pole topped by oak branches, from which dangles a basket full of sweets. The worthiest young man of the village has to climb the trunk and throw the sweets down to the children waiting below. The day also involves local costumes, dancing and the return on holiday of Saxons who emigrated to Germany.

To get to Mălâncrav, turn south off the main road between Sighişoara and Mediaş at a turning 3km west of the village of Daneş, marked for Laslea. You reach the latter after 1 km: Mălâncrav is another 12km further on.

🏠 **Where to stay** The restored **Apáfi Mansion** (*5 rooms;* **m** *0724 000 350;* **w** *experiencetransylvania.ro;* **$$$$$**) is the showcase accommodation offering of the MET, elegantly furnished throughout and including a fine library. Prices exclude meals, which should be booked separately. The MET also offers cheaper accommodation in one of three nicely restored houses in the village (*nos 276, 297 & 335;* **$$$**). All their offerings are priced per person rather than per room, so they're better value for the single traveller.

HEADING EAST

AGNITA AND THE HÂRTIBACIU VALLEY
Agnita (Szentágota/Agnetheln) is a small town of some 8,000 people on the Hârtibaciu River, and the market centre for the villages of this part of Sibiu County. It has an impressive **fortified church** just across the canalised river from the town centre (there is a footbridge, as well as road bridges further away from the centre). This was originally a Romanesque basilica, and was transformed in the early 16th century into a Gothic hall church. The western tower was raised in this period and given a defensive level with wooden parapets. The Baroque altar dates from 1650, though harks back in its design to the Gothic triptych altars. The external defensive wall was demolished in the 19th century, though four defensive towers are still standing, two of them in the grounds of a neighbouring school. The square in front of the church is named in honour of Georg Daniel Teutsch, the Lutheran bishop and historian, who was a preacher at the church in the 1860s.

Agnita is the northern terminus of a fascinating project to restore the narrow-gauge **Sibiu–Agnita Railway** (**e** *mihai@sibiuagnitarailway.com;* **w** *sibiuagnitarailway. com,* **w** *spurfilm.eu*) along the quietly undulating Hârtibaciu Valley. The railway started out life as a narrow-gauge line from Sighişoara to Sibiu, completed in 1910 and with a total length of 123km. The section from Sighişoara to Agnita was closed in the mid 1960s, replaced by a new road between the two towns. The line from Sibiu to Agnita continued to operate until 2001, and was essentially abandoned. A group of Romanian volunteers, supported by the British charity SAR UK Supporters' Group, is painstakingly restoring the line and buildings, and hopes to run steam trains again on the line between Sibiu and Agnita. They currently rent a steam train for occasional open days covering a restored stretch of track around the village of Cornăţel. You will hear the steam locomotive being affectionately referred to in Romanian as a *mocăniţă,* or 'coffee machine', which its steam and noise is said to evoke.

There are several attractive villages in the Hârtibaciu Valley. Of particular interest is **Hosman** (Holcmány/Holzmengen), on the left bank of the Hârtibaciu River, and one of the stops along the Sibiu–Agnita Railway. Its **fortified church** (m *0742 153 005*; ⊕ *by appointment; donation expected*) was originally built in the 13th century in the Romanesque style, and the most important feature of the church today is the west door, one of the most significant surviving Romanesque sculptural compositions in Transylvania. Ottoman predations in the 15th century were so bad that Hosman was temporarily deserted. The church was fortified at the end of the 15th century, when the aisles were demolished and the tower was raised and given additional military features. It is surrounded by two defensive walls, the innermost of which is oval in plan.

Also worth a visit in the village is the **Moara Veche** (*Str Crucii 211; contact Gabriela Cotaru on* m *0740 959 389 or 0748 800 049;* e *info@moara-veche.ro;* w *moara-veche.ro;* ⊕ *May–Sep noon–16.00 Mon–Sat, but call at least a day in advance; donation expected*), an old mill that has been carefully restored by a local non-governmental organisation, the Asociaţia Hosman Durabil, with support from the Mihai Eminescu Trust. A minor but good and attractive road runs along the Hârtibaciu Valley from Sibiu to Agnita. The Transmixt bus company runs three to five **minibuses** daily between the two towns (*1hr 40mins*). Hosman (*1hr from Agnita*) is a stop on this route.

🏠 **Where to stay** In the small village of Nucet, around 20km from Sibiu, the **Bio Haus Cioran** (*8 rooms; Nucet no 198;* m *0744 642 025;* e *office@bio-haus.ro;* w *bio-haus.ro;* **$$**) is an eco-friendly wooden guesthouse in spacious grounds with attractive views. Breakfast is included; other meals are organised on request, with a focus on the use of home-grown ingredients. It makes a good base for exploring the Hârtibaciu Valley.

DEALU FRUMOS Dealu Frumos (Lesses/Schönberg) is a picturesque small village centred on a particularly attractive **fortified church** (biserica fortificată) (✆ *0269 517 585;* ⊕ *visiting by appointment; donation expected*). First built as a Romanesque basilica in the 13th century, it was remodelled around 1500 into a hall church, and is elaborately fortified, with two square-based towers with parapeted defensive storeys. The church is surrounded by a square outer wall dating from the early 16th century, with corner towers at an oblique angle to the walls.

Dealu Frumos is 8km east of Agnita on the picturesque minor road 105 which runs south to join the main E68 highway at the triumphantly named village of Voila in Braşov County.

🏠 **Where to stay** Making much of its physical location at the geographical centre of Romania, **Pensiunea Elisabeta** (*10 rooms; Dealu Frumos no 350;* m *0740 908 254;* e *info@centrultarii.ro;* w *centrultarii.ro;* **$$**) trades on Dealu Frumos's other claim to fame. It is a functional but attractively sited pension on some high ground outside the village.

AVRIG Avrig (Felek/Freck) is a small town of some 12,000 people just off the busy E68 Sibiu–Braşov highway, of interest for **Brukenthal Palace** (Palatul Brukenthal) (*Str Gheorghe Lazar 39;* ✆ *0269 523 111;* e *office@palatulbrukenthalavrig.ro;* w *palatulbrukenthalavrig.ro;* ⊕ *gardens 08.00–22.00 daily, exhibition 10.00–18.00 daily; gardens adult/child 5RON/free, exhibition adult/child 10/5RON*), the Baroque summer residence of Samuel von Brukenthal, Governor of Transylvania in the late

18th century. The Baroque palace abuts the street, but is more impressive from the garden side to the rear, where it fans out towards the gardens with a U-shaped floor plan. The estate remained with the Brukenthal family until 1872, and after a succession of further owners was acquired by the Evangelical church in Sibiu. It served as a sanatorium for most of the 20th century, and has now been restored to the Evangelical church, under the administration of the Samuel von Brukenthal Foundation (w brukenthal.org), who are trying to refurbish the buildings. The palace itself is particularly degraded, and currently houses an exhibition of Transylvanian Saxon ethnography, but the real treasure here is the gardens, the only late Baroque park in southern Transylvania, and inspired by the Imperial palaces and gardens of Vienna. From the palace you descend a flight of steps into the garden, which includes English and Dutch gardens as well as an orangery dating from the 1770s and now converted into a restaurant and accommodation. Indeed, the gardens suffer somewhat from an evident lack of clarity as to whether the goal here is the restoration of an 18th-century garden or the development of a modern events facility, exemplified by the large tent, evidently intended for weddings, which fills one lawn.

The palace is signposted from the main E68, 1.4km from the junction. Avrig is 26km east of Sibiu. There are up to eight **buses** and **minibuses** a day from Sibiu (*40mins*). Avrig lies on the railway line between Sibiu (*1hr*) and Brașov (*3hrs*).

Where to stay and eat Visitors can stay at the **Palatul Brukenthal Avrig** (*15 rooms; address & contact information opposite;* **$$$**), which has accommodation in the converted orangery in the grounds of the palace. The rooms are more basic than you might expect from the aristocratic setting, and the cheapest ones have a shared bathroom, but there is no arguing with the charm of the surroundings. There is also a restaurant (**$$$**) with a nice terrace serving Romanian dishes, salads and pasta.

TRANSFĂGĂRĂȘAN HIGHWAY Route DN7C runs north–south for some 90km, from a junction with the E68 Sibiu–Brașov highway in Transylvania, southwards to a village named Bascov near the city of Pitești in Wallachia. Climbing to a height of some 2,042m, it is the second-highest paved road in Romania after the Transalpina, and makes for a spectacular drive. Its international fame was boosted by a 2009 episode of the BBC TV series *Top Gear,* when the host Jeremy Clarkson enthusiastically pronounced it 'the best road in the world'.

The Transfăgărășan owes its existence to the obsessions of Romanian dictator Nicolae Ceaușescu, and in particular his determination, following the Soviet invasion of Czechoslovakia in 1968, to construct a new military access route between Wallachia and Transylvania which, unlike the existing routes, would not run along one of the river valleys, which he perceived as too easy for Soviet troops to attack. The highway was built between 1970 and 1974, mainly by military personnel, and was delivered at a huge cost in lost lives: officially 40 died, but the true figure was probably much higher.

Note that the highway is only open during late summer. The most mountainous central section between Bâlea Cascadă in Sibiu County and Piscu Negru in Argeș County, Wallachia, is typically shut between 1 November and 30 June, but these dates are subject to modification based on the weather conditions, and if you are intending to drive the route close to its usual closure times, you should check before you set out that the road is open with the Dispeceratul Drumuri Naționale (\ *021 264 3333 or* \ *0800 800 301*). Bâlea Lake remains open throughout the year, but when the road is closed is reachable only by the cable car from Bâlea Cascadă.

Both because of the spectacular nature of the scenery and the challenging features of the road, with its numerous hairpin turns and steep ascents, conquering the Transfăgărăşan has become a target not just for drivers and motorcyclists, but is also a frequent component of charitable cycling challenges, and you may even see people attempting the climb using even more difficult means of transport, like roller skis.

From Sibiu County, the route starts at a roundabout some 3.5km east of the village of Scoreiu on the E68 Sibiu–Braşov main road, with a turning to the right signposted for Cârtişoara and Bâlea Lac. After around 12km of driving through

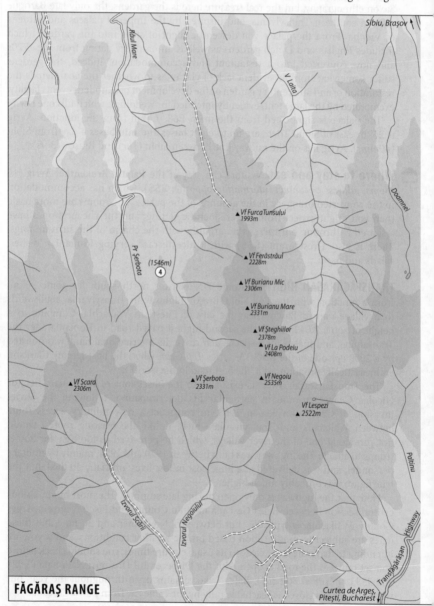

FĂGĂRAŞ RANGE

flat meadows, the road suddenly begins to climb into forest, and up towards the mountain station of Bâlea Cascadă.

Bâlea Cascadă Located at the mathematically pleasing altitude of 1,234m, this place serves as the departure point for the cable car heading up to Bâlea Lake and also has a decidedly ugly concrete mountain lodge, initially built in the early 1970s to accommodate officers of the Romanian army who were constructing the highway. The usual range of tatty souvenir shops in little wooden huts is also to be

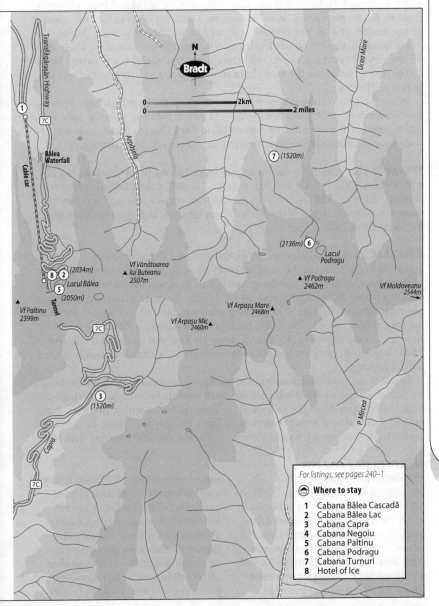

For listings, see pages 240–1

🛏 **Where to stay**

1 Cabana Bâlea Cascadă
2 Cabana Bâlea Lac
3 Cabana Capra
4 Cabana Negoiu
5 Cabana Paltinu
6 Cabana Podragu
7 Cabana Turnuri
8 Hotel of Ice

found here. But there are some good summer walks from here, particularly to the Bâlea Waterfall up the valley, a walk of some 40 minutes from the Cabana on a route marked by red circles. A more challenging route of 2–3 hours up to Bâlea Lake is marked by blue triangles. This route also continues down the mountainside in the other direction back to Cârtişoara, a walk of at least 3 hours.

The **cable car** (*telecabina;* m *0745 072 602;* ◷ *Nov–Mar 09.00–17.00 daily, Apr–Oct 09.00–18.00 daily; adult/child 30/15RON one-way*) runs for 3.7km from here up to Bâlea Lake. Note that it only runs regularly a few times a day (in 2016 at 09.30, noon, 15.00 and 17.45 from Bâlea Cascadă), making additional trips whenever there are ten people waiting. This can make for a considerable wait for small groups in low season. It does not operate at all in bad weather. If you are driving the Transfăgărăşan, there is no particular reason to use the cable car at all, other than for the views it provides, as you will arrive at its terminus by road anyway. But it comes into its own after the road closes from this point upwards, as the only way to reach Bâlea Lake.

While there is no conventional public transport up the Transfăgărăşan, a private tour company runs the **Bâlea Bus** (✆ *0269 211 344;* w *baleabus.ro*) twice daily from Sibiu (departing from outside the Thalia Hall) to Bâlea Cascadă. Tickets cost 60RON one-way, and advance online reservation through their website is compulsory.

⌂ ***Where to stay*** The three-star mountain lodge **Cabana Bâlea Cascadă** (*26 dbl, 2 trpl, 1 quad, 2 apt;* ✆ *0269 211 703;* m *0724 244 463;* e *cascada@balea-turism.ro;* w *balea-turism.ro;* **$$$**) is in a grim Communist-era building with a rather run-down restaurant. It is part of the Bâlea Turism Group, which also runs the Cabana Paltinu at Bâlea Lake.

Bâlea Lac
As the road climbs further, the sight of a dense sequence of hairpins across the high mountain grassland is a really arresting one. The signs warn not just of 'dangerous bends' but 'really dangerous bends'. At almost the highest point of the road is a deeply picturesque glacial lake at 2,034m, around which are congregated several lodges, a collection of huts selling souvenirs, and the terminus of the cable car from Bâlea Cascadă. This is also the location in winter for Romania's famed ice hotel and an accompanying ice church, some 4m high and modelled on the one at Mălâncrav, which can even be booked for weddings. The church is usually opened in mid-January.

In one of the more blatant attempts to put a price tag on something which should be free, an ugly glass-sided **belvedere** has been constructed on a hillock above the lake, looking back down the valley and the Transfăgărăşan, with a 2RON entrance fee and a stuffed bear as your companion. There are very few takers; most visitors preferring to gaze upon the same view for free to the side of this jarring structure.

⌂ ***Where to stay and eat***
⌂ **Hotel of Ice** (variable, but in 2016 13 dbl, plus additional 4 dbl in separate igloos) ✆ 0269 523 111; e bookings@hotelofice.ro; w balealac. ro. Romania's only ice hotel, it is remodelled each year, with rooms individually sculptured around an overall theme. The ice is cut directly from the frozen Bâlea Lake. The room temperature is around 0°C: blankets, furs & a sleeping bag are provided. The rooms in separate igloos are around 50% more expensive. Its ice bar (◷ *09.00–21.00 daily*) specialises in cocktails served in glasses carved from ice. The food at its restaurant is served on plates of ice (though prepared at the Cabana Bâlea Lac next door, run by the same company). The Cabana is also where your luggage is stored (& the source of the loos). The ice hotel is open from late Dec until the end of winter. Various winter pursuits are offered, from ice sculpting to sledding.

Note that if you are driving you have to leave your car at the cable-car base at Bâlea Cascadă for the duration of your stay. **$$$$$**

🏠 **Cabana Bâlea Lac** (6 dbl, 4 trpl, 3apt) 📞0269 523 517; e cabana_balealac@yahoo.com; w balealac.ro. Idyllically located wooden 3-star lodge, right on a promontory jutting into Bâlea Lake. Its restaurant (**$$$**) includes game dishes & trout, served on an attractive lakeside terrace. A second lodge nearby, **Cabana Bâlea Lac II**

(*3 sgl, 15 dbl, 3 apt*) is similarly priced but less strikingly situated, & essentially serves as overspill when the main lodge is full. Poor customer service can let the place down. **$$$**

🏠 **Cabana Paltinu** (15 dbl, 2 apt) 📞0269 211 703; m 0724 244 464; e paltinu@balea-turism. ro; w balea-turism.ro. A 3-star mountain lodge situated above Bâlea Lake, with a restaurant & sauna (*30RON for 30mins*). **$$$**

Onwards to Bucharest Immediately after leaving Bâlea Lac the road enters the 884m Bâlea Tunnel, which has the distinction of being the longest road tunnel in Romania. When you emerge from it you have left Transylvania and entered Argeş County in the southern Romanian region of Wallachia. Since many tourists drive the Transfăgărăşan Highway on their way either into or out of Transylvania from Otopeni airport in Bucharest, it may be useful to describe the route. The DN7C descends into the valley of the Argeş River, and forest reappears, until the road joins the bank of **Lacul Vidraru**, an artificial lake some 10km long, formed by the construction of the 166m-high Vidraru Dam in the mid 1960s to generate hydro-electric power. The road passes right across the top of the dam. Note the decidedly Communist-era statue of Prometheus on the hill above, holding an electricity bolt in the manner of a weightlifter raising his bar.

Some 5km to the south of the dam, high on a rocky outcrop overlooking the road, is the ruined **Poenari Castle** (Cetatea Poenari), first built in the 13th century, but best known for its connections with Vlad the Impaler, who recognised the potential of its impressive location above a strategic pass and remodelled the place in the 15th century. By the 17th century it was already in ruins, and a landslide in 1888 wrought further damage. The castle can be visited (📞021 313 1947; ☉ *summer 09.00–18.00 daily; adult/child 5/2RON*), but note that this involves a walk up some 1,480 steps.

Route 7C continues southwards to the historic town of Curtea de Argeş, a one-time capital of Wallachia whose monastery is the resting place for the kings and queens of Romania. It then continues a further 30km south, joining the main E81 highway at the village of Bascov, just outside Piteşti. From here, one of Romania's few motorways, the A1, leads in a southeasterly direction for 107km to Bucharest. If your goal is Otopeni airport, however, there is a disadvantage to taking this motorway, as it brings you to western Bucharest, while the airport is to the north, and the ringroad connecting the two gets badly congested. A more scenic option, but which does require more time, is to take smaller roads from Curtea de Argeş via Târgovişte, another historic town with connections to Vlad the Impaler and of more recent renown as the place of Ceauşescu's execution, and then Ploieşti, and then taking the E60m highway south to Otopeni.

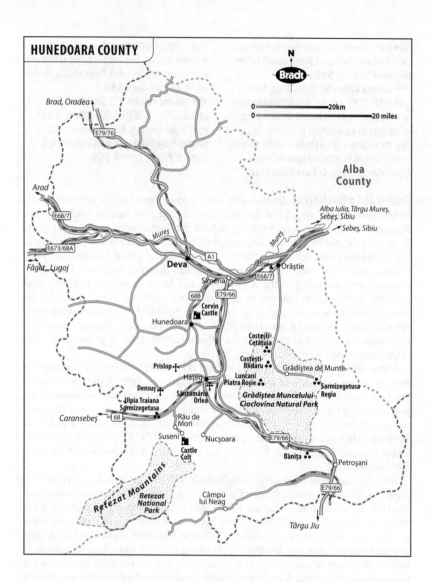

HUNEDOARA COUNTY

N

Bradt

0 ——————— 20km
0 ——————— 20 miles

Brad, Oradea

E79/76

Arad

E68/7

E673/68A

Făget, Lugoj

Mureş

A1

Deva

Alba
County

Alba Iulia, Târgu Mureş,
Sebeş, Sibiu

Sebeş, Sibiu

Mureş

Uroi

Orăştie

Simeria

E68/7

68B

E79/66

Corvin
Castle

Hunedoara

Costeşti-
Cetăţuia

Costeşti-
Blidaru

Grădiştea de Munte

Prislop

Luncani
Piatra Roşie

Sarmizegetusa
Regia

Haţeg

Grădiştea Muncelului-
Cioclovina Natural Park

Densuş

Sântămăria
Orlea

Ulpia Traiana
Sarmizegetusa

Caransebeş

68

Râu de
Mori

Suseni

Castle
Colţ

Nucşoara

Băniţa

Petroşani

Retezat Mountains

Retezat
National
Park

Câmpu
lui Neag

E79/66

Târgu Jiu

8

Hunedoara County

Hunedoara County, in the southwest corner of Transylvania, is a mountainous area divided by the Mureș River, which cuts straight across its rectangular form from east to west. To the north of the Mureș, the land rises up into the Apuseni Mountains, while to the south it climbs into the Southern Carpathians. The area has an association with declining heavy industry, particularly the steel manufacturing centre of Hunedoara and the coal mining towns around Petroșani in the south of the county, which appear to suggest that this might be unpromising terrain for the tourist. But this could not be further from the truth. For this is not just a county particularly rich in history, but one which to many Romanians seems to represent the very birthplace of the Romanian people, which in the popular imagination was forged as a mix of the Dacian peoples and of the Romans who conquered them. Hunedoara County includes most of the Dacian fortresses of the Orăştie Mountains inscribed on UNESCO's World Heritage list, including the Dacian capital of Sarmizegetusa Regia. And here too lie the remains of the capital of the Roman province of Dacia, Ulpia Traiana Sarmizegetusa. The statues in the main squares of the county capital, Deva, portray both the Roman Emperor Trajan and the Dacian King Decebal.

Hunedoara County is also home to the oldest national park in Romania in the glorious Retezat Mountains, a land of numerous 2,000m peaks and glacier lakes, as well as one of the most beautiful castles in all Romania, Corvin Castle, owned by the remarkable John Hunyadi. Add to the mix Romania's oldest continually functioning church and a geological park based around the dwarf dinosaur fossils characteristic of the area, and it is clear that Hunedoara is actually one of the most distinctive and beguiling of the counties of Transylvania.

DEVA *Telephone code 0254*

Deva (Déva/Diemrich), the capital of the county, is dominated by a fortress atop a steep-sided volcanic hill. It is relatively low-key as Transylvanian provincial capitals go, and in truth much of the urban architecture comprises ugly Communist-era blocks, but exploring its fortress, some attractive buildings, notably the 16th-century Magna Curia, and a laidback pedestrianised strip along Strada 1 Decembrie 1918 add up to a pleasant day of sightseeing. Deva also serves as a good base for exploring the wider attractions of Hunedoara County.

HISTORY The history of Deva is linked closely to that of the volcanic hill, known as the Hill of the Djinn, because of a legend telling of a mighty battle between the spirits (*djinns*) of the Retezat Mountains and those of the plain. The hill offered a superb strategic location, controlling the route into Transylvania through the Mureș Valley, and it was perhaps inevitable that the hill would have been chosen as the site of a fortress. There is documentary evidence of a castle here from the rule of Béla IV

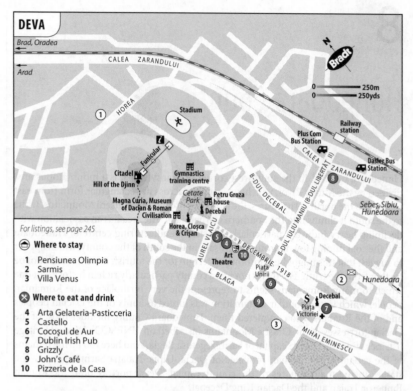

DEVA

Brad, Oradea

Arad

CALEA ZARANDULUI

HOREA

Stadium

0 ——— 250m
0 ——— 250yds

Railway station

Plus Com Bus Station

CALEA ZARANDULUI

Dasler Bus Station

Funicular

Citadel
Hill of the Djinn

Gymnastics training centre

B-DUL DECEBAL

B-DUL IULIU MANIU (B-DUL LIBERTĂȚII)

Sebeș, Sibiu, Hunedoara

Magna Curia, Museum of Dacian & Roman Civilisation

Cetate Park

Petru Groza house

Decebal

AUREL VLAICU

Horea, Cloșca & Crișan

For listings, see page 245

Where to stay

1 Pensiunea Olimpia
2 Sarmis
3 Villa Venus

Where to eat and drink

4 Arta Gelateria-Pasticceria
5 Castello
6 Cocoșul de Aur
7 Dublin Irish Pub
8 Grizzly
9 John's Café
10 Pizzeria de la Casa

Art Theatre

1 DECEMBRIE 1918

L BLAGA

Piața Unirii

Hunedoara

Decebal

Piața Victoriei

MIHAI EMINESCU

of Hungary in 1269. A gloomy Hungarian folk ballad tells of how 12 stonemasons agreed to build the fortress of Deva for a fee of half a bushel of gold and half a bushel of silver. But whatever they built by day collapsed overnight, and whatever they built during the night had fallen down by the next day. For some reason they determined that in order to strengthen the walls they needed to burn at the stake whichever stonemason's wife arrived first at the castle and mix her ashes in with the building materials; a misfortune which befell the wife of the head stonemason, Kelemen Kőműves. When informed of her fate, she accepted it, asking only that she be allowed to return home to say goodbye to her little son. This was allowed, and on returning back to the castle she was duly burnt to death. Interestingly, there is a very similar tale in Romanian folklore: the legend of Master Manole, relating to the chief architect of the monastery of Curtea de Argeș in Wallachia, who has to wall his wife into the building to allow it to stand.

It became one of the most important fortresses in Transylvania. In the 15th century, King Ladislaus V of Hungary presented John Hunyadi (see box, pages 250–1) with Deva and 56 surrounding villages. The founder of the Unitarian Church of Transylvania, Dávid Ferenc, was imprisoned in the castle, having fallen foul of the authorities for a range of religious views, in particular his denial of the need to invoke Jesus Christ in prayer, and died here in 1579.

The fortress saw action in the defence against Ottoman raids, in the uprising of Francis II Rákóczi in 1704, in the peasants' revolt led by Horia, Cloșca and Crișan in 1784, and in the Hungarian Revolution of 1848–49, when Hungarian revolutionaries managed to occupy the citadel. On 13 August 1849, a powder store in the fortress exploded, causing major damage and signalling the end of its military role.

In the Communist period Deva was linked in Romania with a very different matter: gymnastics. It has been home to the national training centre since the late 1970s, other than a five-year break from 2011 when the senior team was moved closer to Bucharest. It is associated in particular with the Romanian golden era of female gymnastics, when Nadia Comăneci and her successors were a major force in world gymnastics.

GETTING THERE AND AWAY Deva is located 123km west of Sibiu. The new A1 motorway connects the two cities. A northern route along the E81 highway to Alba Iulia and Cluj-Napoca joins the motorway close to Sebeş. The **railway station** (`0254 212 725`) sits at the eastern end of Bulevardul Iuliu Maniu, at the edge of town but walkable from the centre. There are several trains daily to Cluj-Napoca (*4hrs*) and Sibiu (*3½hrs*). The **Dasler Bus Station** (`0254 231 030`), just to the east of the railway station, has frequent buses to Hunedoara (*40mins*). The nearby **Plus Com Bus Station** (`0254 211 411`), on the other side of the railway station, has buses to destinations further afield. Note though that some places, like Orăştie (*30–45mins*), are rather unhelpfully served by buses from both stations. Two local **taxi companies** are **Astral Taxi** (`0254 221 111`) and **Euro Taxi** (`0254 223 344`).

WHERE TO STAY *Map, see opposite*

Villa Venus (9 dbl, 2 suites, 1 family room) Str Mihai Eminescu 16; `0254 212 243`; **e** office@ villavenus.ro; **w** villavenus.ro. Boutique 5-star with a central location & well-furnished rooms, though with an odd focus on selling beauty products, & priced rather expensively for provincial Deva. **$$$$**

Hotel Sarmis (118 rooms) Str Mareşal Averescu 7; `0254 214 731`; **e** sarmis.deva@unita- turism.ro. A 3-star offering from the Unita Turism group in a pale-green block. Central, but could do with some modernisation. **$$$**

Pensiunea Olimpia (9 rooms) Str Horea 100A; `0254 219 030`; **m** 0721 902 098; **e** pensiuneaolimpia76@yahoo.com; **w** pensiunedeva.ro. A 2-star guesthouse on the northwestern edge of town, opposite a petrol station, & a shortish walk to the funicular to the citadel. **$$**

WHERE TO EAT AND DRINK *Map, see opposite*

Cocoşul de Aur B-dul Iuliu Maniu 9; **m** 0767 651 253; ◷ 09.00–22.00 daily. The 'Golden Rooster' offers traditional Romanian food, & an upstairs terrace. **$$$**

Dublin Irish Pub Piaţa Victoriei 8; **m** 0734 880 033; ◷ noon–midnight daily. Offers steaks, pizza & pasta on a 1st-floor terrace overlooking Piaţa Victoriei, & a menu offering lengthy treatises on 'the history of soup' & suchlike. There is also a pub here (◷ *until 06.00 Fri/Sat*). **$$$**

Grizzly Calea Zarandului 43; **m** 0786 713 911; **w** grizzlyfood.ro; ◷ 09.00–23.00 Mon–Fri, 10.00–23.00 Sat/Sun. Despite a rather unpromising location opposite the railway station, this is Deva's most innovative restaurant, with international & fusion dishes. They also run a fast-food joint next door. **$$$** (restaurant), **$$** (fast food)

Castello Str Aurel Vlaicu 1; `0254 213 883`; ◷ 08.00–22.00 Mon–Fri, 13.00–22.00 Sat, 10.00–22.00 Sun. Offers a wide-ranging menu of Italian & Romanian dishes, & outdoor seating along Str 1 Decembrie 1918. **$$**

Pizzeria de la Casa Str 1 Decembrie 1918 11; **m** 0736 631 777; ◷ 09.00–23.00 Mon– Thu, 09.00–midnight Fri, 10.00–midnight Sat, 10.00–23.00 Sun. Simply furnished place on the pedestrianised stretch of Str 1 Decembrie 1918. It offers exactly what it promises: good-value pizzas in a range of sizes from personal to huge. **$**

Arta Gelateria-Pasticceria Str 1 Decembrie 1918 21; **m** 0724 305 663; **w** cofetariaarta.ro; ◷ 08.00–22.00 Mon–Fri, 10.00–22.00 Sat/Sun. A nice place for a break between sightseeing, with chairs on the pedestrianised street outside, good cakes & ice cream. **$**

John's Café Str Mihai Eminescu 2; `0254 233 511`; ◷ 19.00–05.30 Thu–Sat, 19.00–02.00 Sun– Wed. Not a café, but a somewhat grungy pub & club on the corner of Eminescu & Bariţiu streets. **$**

OTHER PRACTICALITIES

$ **Unicredit Bank** B-dul 1 Decembrie 1918; ⊕ 09.00–17.00 Mon–Fri

➕ **Farmacia Remedia** Piaţa Victoriei; ✎0254 224 488; ⊕ 24hrs

✉ **Post office** B-dul Decebal 16; ⊕ 08.00– 19.00 Mon–Fri, 09.00–13.00 Sat

WHAT TO SEE AND DO

The Fortress Deva's tourist literature describes the place as 'The Town of the Fortress', and indeed the citadel atop the Hill of the Djinn at the northern end of the centre is the town's dominant feature. You can climb up to the citadel from behind Cetate Park, but there is also a **funicular** (*telecabina*; ⊕ *May–Sep 09.00–21.00 daily, Oct–Apr 08.00–20.00 daily; adult/child 10/5RON return; 6/3RON one-way*), though its downside is that the starting point is not on the town-centre side of the hill, but rather on the eastern side. It runs for 278m and is apparently the only funicular in Romania with a kink in the middle. At the entrance to the funicular a plaque in Romanian describes the attractions of the fortress in a rather overwrought fashion, starting: 'if the stones of the fortress could speak, they would tell us things which would make us laugh and cry.'

On the side of the car park at the entrance to the funicular is a line of statues of female Romanian gymnasts. Nadia Comăneci is third from the left. Beyond the fence behind this, the white-painted building with the five Olympic rings on the outside wall is the national **gymnastics training centre**. The **tourist information office** (⊕ *09.00–17.00 daily*) is also here, in the circular cabin to the right of the entrance to the funicular.

Entrance to the fortress itself is free. The views are great from the ramparts, and you get something of a sense of the three encirclements of walls, but there is very little in the way of explanation on offer, and large sections of the walls have been rather jarringly over-restored.

The town Much of central Deva comprises ugly concrete blocks, but there is a pleasant district between Piaţa Unirii and Cetate Park at the base of the fortress hill. The leafy Piaţa Unirii has a statue of **Trajan**, and indeed Deva's municipal statuary is rather focused on the twin figures of the Roman emperor and of Dacian leader Decebal, as representing the two peoples from whom Romanians claim their descent.

Running north of Piaţa Unirii, Strada 1 Decembrie 1918 is pedestrianised, populated with open-air cafés, and makes for a good place to gravitate in the evenings. Halfway down, the **Art Theatre** (Teatrul de Artă) (*Str 1 Decembrie 1918 15;* ✎*0354 738 703;* e *contact@teatruldeartdeva.ro*) is housed in a fine Art Nouveau building dating from 1911, the work of Dezső Jakab and Marcell Komor who also designed the Palace of Culture in Târgu Mureş (page 194). At the street's northern end, a path continues towards Deva's most attractive building, the two-storey pink-walled **Magna Curia**, which is also known as Bethlen Castle. It was originally built in the 16th century by the Hungarian commander of the Deva Fortress garrison, but was remodelled in 1621 in a Renaissance style by Gabriel Bethlen, the then Prince of Transylvania. The present form of the building also reflects further later modifications, in a Baroque style. It currently houses a **Museum of Dacian and Roman Civilisation** (Muzeul Civilizaţiei Dacice şi Romane Deva) (*Str 1 Decembrie 1918 39;* ✎ *0254 216 750;* e *muzeucdr.deva@gmail.com;* w *mcdr.ro;* ⊕ *summer 10.00–18.00 Tue–Sun, winter 09.00–17.00 Tue–Sun; adult/child 10/2 RON*), with displays focused on finds from important Dacian and Roman archaeological sites in Hunedoara County. There is a lapidarium around the back of the building with some Roman sculptures as well as a line of stone Dacian blocks from Sarmizegetusa Regia. In front of the building are three busts on high pillars of the leaders of the 1784 peasants' revolt, **Horea, Cloşca and Crişan**.

Beside the museum is the pleasant **Cetate Park**, which is home to a statue of Dacian leader **Decebal**. On the southern side of the park, alongside Strada Avram Iancu, the Cubist-style 1920s building is the former home of **Petru Groza**, who as prime minister in the aftermath of World War II helped to preside over the consolidation of Communist power in Romania, and the abdication of the king.

Piaţa Victoriei at the southern end of Bulevardul 1 Decembrie 1918 is centred on another statue of Decebal, this time an equestrian one, behind which is a fountain, whose playful water displays set to music are the focus of warm summer evenings' strolling for the citizens of the town. Behind this in turn is an ugly Communist-era block housing the House of Culture.

OTHER SIGHTS IN HUNEDOARA COUNTY

ORĂŞTIE Orăştie (Szászváros/Broos), 25km east of Deva, is a small town, colonised by Saxons, which serves as the entry point for exploration of the Dacian fortresses located in the mountains to the south. It lies on the main E68/DN7 road between Deva and Sebeş, close to the new A1 motorway, which follows a similar route. The rocky outcrop at **Uroi**, halfway between Orăştie and Deva, at Simeria, is a landmark clearly visible from the road and a popular jump-off point for hang-gliders. The rock also serves as the battleground for **Dac Fest**, held across one weekend in mid-September, a historical re-enactment event where Dacians do battle with their Roman adversaries.

Orăştie offers one highly distinctive accommodation option, just off the E68 heading west out of town towards Deva: the Arsenal Park military-themed holiday centre. There are frequent **buses** between Orăştie and both Deva (*30–45mins*) and Alba Iulia (*from 40mins*). **Trains** also serve both Deva (*30mins*) and Alba Iulia (*40mins*).

🏠 **Where to stay** Based on the site of a former ammunition factory, **Arsenal Park** (*capacity for 230 guests in rooms of varying degrees of eccentricity; Str Codrului 25;* ✆ *0354 501 001;* e *office@arsenalpark.ro;* w *arsenalpark.com;* **$$$**) has been transformed into a military-themed amusement park (⊕ *08.00–20.00 daily; 10RON for non-guests*), with all manner of military hardware dotted around the 88ha site in the midst of a forest. Activities on offer range from a water park to paintball, and even a military training session in which participants get to go on a route march and crawl under camouflage nets. You can choose to sleep like an ordinary soldier in six-bed dormitory rooms, or in the 'General's villa' with two bedrooms, dining room and a jacuzzi. Other options are a room in which the bed is placed on the carriage of an artillery piece or an 'officer room', which is basically a standard double.

DACIAN FORTRESSES OF THE ORĂŞTIE MOUNTAINS In 1999, six Dacian fortresses were listed as UNESCO World Heritage Sites. One, Căpâlna, is in Alba County (page 269); the other five are in Hunedoara County. These fortresses were built between 100BC and AD100. They are centred on the Dacian capital of Sarmizegetusa Regia, which is both the most impressive and the easiest to visit. The other fortresses defended access routes to the capital.

8

Two of the fortresses, Costeşti-Cetăţuia and Costeşti-Blidaru, are close together near the modern village of Costeşti, and like Sarmizegetusa Regia itself are accessed from the road running south from Orăştie. The other two fortresses, Piatra Roşie and Băniţa, are accessed from the main E79 highway further west. This is a beautiful area, much of which falls within the **Grădiştea Muncelului-Cioclovina Natural Park** (*Aleea Parcului 21, Deva;* \0254 211 569; e *pngm_c@yahoo.co.uk;* w *gradiste.ro*), an area of mountains, forests and karst landscapes.

Costeşti The village of Costeşti is located 17km south of Orăştie, conveniently on the road that heads further south to the major site of Sarmizegetusa Regia (see below). You pass beneath a modern gate over the road, decorated with reliefs of the Dacian kings Decebal and Burebista. There is a small **tourist information centre** (m *0729 112 372;* ⊕ *08.00–16.00 daily*) just beyond the gate. Two of the UNESCO-listed Dacian sites are accessed from here.

A turning to the right immediately after the gate is marked to the fortress of **Costeşti-Cetăţuia**, which is some 2km up a very rough track, accessible by 4x4. Alternatively, it is a 40-minute walk on foot, with the path marked by yellow crosses. From the last point accessible by car the path heads further uphill for another 100m to reach the site, which is at the top of the 561m Cetăţuia Hill. With a mix of earth and stone defensive walls, this is a quiet site, offering good views across the surrounding countryside. The highest plateau features two square structures made up of three rows of stone blocks, which represent the sites of towers with associated living quarters. Both are protected beneath corrugated roofs.

The second fortress at Costeşti is **Costeşti-Blidaru**. From the same departure point, this is accessed by a footpath marked with vertical blue stripes. It is a steep 2km walk, taking around 50 minutes. There is no vehicle access to the site. It is on a hill, at a height of around 705m, offering good views across the valley below. The Dacians flattened the top of the hill to obtain a relatively level surface, and built a fortress with stone walls, comprising two linked precincts which were built at different times. Six rectangular towers are believed to have been both military in nature and to have served as living quarters, with a tower inside the fortification probably serving as the residence of the chief.

✳Sarmizegetusa Regia (⊕ *May–Aug 09.00–20.00 daily, Mar/Apr & Oct/Nov 09.00–18.00 daily, closed Dec–Feb; adult/child 5/2RON*) The most important and by far the most visited of the Dacian fortresses is Sarmizegetusa Regia, some 23km south of Coştesti along a road which runs through the attractive Oraştie River valley. It was the capital of the Dacians before their defeat at the hands of the Romans. The capital was moved here by Burebista, who ruled in the 1st century BC, from the town of Argedava in present-day southern Romania, and reached its height under King Decebal a century and a half later. It was partially dismantled in AD102 by the Romans, following their victory in the First Dacian War, and definitively destroyed in the Second Dacian War in AD106. The Romans established a garrison here and later, when setting up the capital of Roman Dacia some 40km away, named it after the Dacian site, as Ulpia Traiana Sarmizegetusa.

As you drive towards the site there is a small building on the left-hand side of the road at the site entrance, offering a missable exhibition on Dacian gold (*2RON*). The car park is another 3km further on. And from the car park you walk up an easy cobbled path for a further 1.5km to the site itself. This brings you into the west gate of the city, and the fortress area, where the walls are constructed of large stone blocks. From here, the marked Visitor Route 1 heads down the hill beside an ancient road paved with limestone slabs, and probably originally used for processions, to the sacred area. This is laid out on impressive artificial terraces. On the upper terrace the Large Andesite Temple displays the andesite column bases of a building which had six rows of ten columns each. A lower terrace includes a mix of rectangular and circular temple bases, including the Large Circular Temple, the focus of most of the photographs of the site, where some wooden columns have been rather speculatively placed in response to archaeological evidence of wooden posts plastered with clay. This temple dominated the sacred area, but was destroyed by the Romans. Another, smaller, circular temple lies nearby. Also on this terrace are the remains of two quadrilateral temples and the remarkable circular andesite altar, comprising a central disc surrounded by ten 'rays' made of andesite slabs. It is believed that sacrifices would have been performed here. On the lowest terrace, in the southern part of the sacred area, is a limestone temple, rectangular in form, with 60 circular column bases on which wooden columns once stood.

Back up in the fortress, Visitor Route 2 takes you around the fortress walls, past the south gate, returning to the main entrance.

The other Dacian fortresses The remaining two UNESCO-listed Dacian fortresses in Hunedoara County form a separate small group that is accessed most easily from the E79 highway which runs southwards from Simeria. The fortress of **Luncani Piatra Roşie** was built to guard the entrance to the Strei River valley and the access route to the Dacian capital, Sarmizegetusa Regia. The hill known as Piatra Roşie (Red Rock), reaching a height of more than 800m, is a little isolated at the end of the Luncani Valley. The easiest access road is to turn off the main E79 at Călan, towards and through the village of Boşorod. The fortress was built of stone in a rectangular shape with four towers at the corners and a fifth in the middle of the east wall. The remains of a sanctuary have been identified outside the fortress walls.

Băniţa lies just off the E79 between Haţeg and Petroşani. The road brings you close to the base of the hill known as Piatra Cetăţii on which the fortress is sited, but the route is very steep and not advisable without a guide. Three artificial terraces were laid out beyond a monumental gate, but the site was damaged in the 1860s with the construction of the nearby railway, and the difficulties of getting to the site have also limited the extent of archaeological research done here.

HUNEDOARA It is a sad irony that one of Transylvania's most impressive and beautiful castles should be found in one of its least attractive towns. Hunedoara (Vajdahunyad/Eisenmarkt) is a dreary sprawl of concrete housing estates linked to its once-important iron and steel industry.

Iron production in the local area dates from the 17th century. The main Hunedoara ironworks were opened in 1884, and were linked with an intensification of iron-ore extraction in the nearby mountains. Steel production here commenced in 1892 and was expanded in the late 1930s, with machinery brought in from Nazi Germany. In the Communist period the plant was known as the Combinatul Siderurgic Hunedoara, and the steelworks here were expanded further, with the population of the town increasing to 87,000. The local football team, Corvinul Hunedoara, was for a time one of the top teams in the country. Following the 1989 Revolution, the steel industry lost its former markets and struggled to remain competitive. Many parts of the complex were shut down, and what was left was privatised in 2003 and is now owned by the ArcelorMittal group. The town's population has fallen back to 60,000, and the collapse of the steel industry has left a legacy of unemployment and abandoned factory buildings.

Hunedoara is 18km south of Deva. Take the E68 heading east out of Deva and turn right after 6km, signposted for Hunedoara. There are numerous **buses** and **minibuses** between Hunedoara and Deva (*40mins*). A rather scruffy car park near the castle (*7.5RON*) is fringed by souvenir stalls.

Where to stay and eat

Hotel Ciuperca (32 rooms) Str Carol Davila 1; m 0724 572 743; w hotelciuperca.ro. A 3-star place on a hillside on the edge of town, with a restaurant & outdoor pool. **$$**

Hotel Rusca (106 rooms) B-dul Dacia 10, Hunedoara; 0254 717 575; e mail@hotelrusca. ro; w hotelrusca.ro. Modernised 3-star concrete block in the centre of town. There is a small additional charge for rooms with AC. **$$**

Restaurantul Rustic Str Libertății 4; 0254 713 424; w restaurantulrustic.ro; ⏰ 08.00–23.45 daily. Mix of Romanian & international dishes; in town some 700m from the castle. **$$$**

What to see and do

Corvin Castle (Castelul Corvinilor) (*Str Castelului 1–3*; m *0786 048 718*; e *contact@castelulcorvinilor.ro*; w *castelulcorvinilor.ro*; ⏰ *09.00–20.30 Tue–Sun*,

JÁNOS HUNYADI – THE WHITE KNIGHT

Known as Ioan de Hunedoara in Romanian and Hunyadi János in Hungarian, János Hunyadi was a Voivode (ruler) of Transylvania from 1441 to 1456, and an important figure in the political history of southeastern Europe in the 15th century. He is remembered today as the father of Matthias Corvinus, the celebrated King of Hungary from 1458 to 1490 and by his admirers as the White Knight, a central figure in the defence of Christendom against the Ottomans.

The ethnicity of János's father, Voyk or Voicu, is the subject of continuing academic debate, though son János in his youth was often referred to by a nickname meaning 'Vlach', strengthening arguments that the family's origins were Romanian. Academics disagree about the origins of János's mother too, suggesting variously that she may have been Romanian or Greek. The intensity of debate around the issue is all part of wider characterisations of both János Hunyadi and Matthias Corvinus, which tend to emphasise their links with Romania when coming from Romanian sources, and with Hungary when coming from Hungarian ones. Voyk served as a knight in the royal court of King Sigismund of Hungary, and he and his family were granted Hunyad Castle and its estate by the king in 1409.

János's very rapid rise was explained away by detractors through tales suggesting that he was in fact the illegitimate son of King Sigismund and a beautiful local woman named Elisabeta. A variant of this tale is used to explain the origins of the coat of arms of the Corvins, by which Hunyadi's family is also known, of a raven with a ring in its beak. This runs that King Sigismund, not wanting to see his lover Elisabeta considered unworthy, arranged for her to marry Voicu from his court, and bestowed upon them the Hunyad Castle. He also gave Elisabeta a golden ring, such that his unborn son would later be able to recognise them. Years later, when János was a child, the ring was left for a moment on a dinner table, and a raven stole off with the ring in its beak. Young János saw the incident, took a bow and shot the raven, thus saving the precious ring. The crest can be seen in many places in Hunedoara Castle.

In the manner of young noblemen of the time, János spent his youth serving at the courts of powerful benefactors. He married a high-ranking Hungarian noblewoman named Erzsébet Szilágyi, a member of a Hungarian family close to

10.30–20.30 Mon; adult/child May–Aug 30/5RON, Mar-Apr & Sep-Oct 25/5RON, Nov–Feb 20/5RON) A truly magnificent sight and a highlight of any trip to southwest Transylvania, first impressions of the Corvin Castle are magical, or perhaps more accurately fairytale, in character, from its dramatic approach over a wooden bridge across a deep gorge to the riot of square and circular towers, battlements and precipitous walls it offers. The great travel writer Patrick Leigh Fermor called it 'fantastic and theatrical' and 'at first glance, totally unreal'. It is outside the centre of town, but signposted.

The castle was given in 1409 by the Hungarian King Sigismund of Luxembourg to a loyal knight of his court named Voyk. Voyk's much more famous son, John Hunyadi (see box, below), carried out a major expansion of the castle, in a Renaissance-Gothic style, drawing upon his experience of military strategy. Further expansions were ordered by John's son, Matthias Corvinus. The castle left the possession of the Corvin family in the early 16th century; of more than 20 owners until the castle became Habsburg property in 1725, the most significant was Gabriel Bethlen, Prince of Transylvania from 1613 to 1629, who carried out some significant additions. A major fire in 1854 caused considerable damage, and the castle was neglected for

King Sigismund, and then himself entered Sigismund's retinue, becoming a 'court knight' and applying himself to the study of military tactics. During this period the Ottomans were making increasingly menacing incursions into Serbia and Transylvania. János Hunyadi distinguished himself in fighting against them, and advanced further through his support for Vladislaus, King of Poland, in the civil war of 1440–41 over the crown of Hungary, after which he was appointed joint Voivode of Transylvania. He repelled an Ottoman invasion of Transylvania in 1442, and gained a reputation across the Christian world for his defence of Christian territories against Ottoman attacks. He was known for an aggressive, decisive military style, and for the use of mercenaries to enhance the professionalism of his forces. In 1443, he joined King Vladislaus in the 'long campaign' against the Ottoman Empire, which, however, ended in defeat and the death of the king at the Battle of Varna.

With the child Ladislaus V now King of Hungary, although under the guardianship of Frederick III of Germany, Hunyadi was proclaimed in 1446 as 'governor', and exercised many royal prerogatives. The next few years for Hunyadi were marked by a complex series of conflicts, alliances, advances and setbacks, his opponents reconciling with him as a new Ottoman threat loomed.

After capturing Constantinople in 1453, Sultan Mehmed II, better known as Mehmed the Conqueror, moved next towards Serbia, long an Ottoman vassal, but which was now in alliance with the Hungarians and paid the tribute only irregularly. Mehmed planned to move against Hungary itself thereafter. Mehmed's forces arrived at Belgrade and besieged the city. Hunyadi assembled a flotilla of some 200 vessels on the Danube, destroyed the Ottoman flotilla, and relieved the fortress. The defeated sultan retreated, ushering in a period of relative peace in that part of the region for more than 60 years. Pope Callixtus III had ordered that the bells of every church in Europe ring out at noon to pray for the defenders of Belgrade, an event which turned into a celebration following the victory, and is still maintained in Catholic churches today. The aftermath of the victory was a bitter one for the Hungarians, however: a plague broke out in the crusaders' camp and Hunyadi was one of its victims. He is buried in the Roman Catholic cathedral in Alba Iulia.

decades thereafter until more recent renovation work restored it to its rightful place as one of Transylvania's most important tourist attractions.

The numerous rooms and towers of the castle are accessed from a central courtyard. Entering the castle on the wooden footbridge resting on a series of stone piers, you first reach the square-based New Gate Tower. There is the inevitable exhibition of instruments of torture here; a sign, entirely ignored, above the door declares that children below the age of 12 may not enter. Immediately to the south of this is the Palace of Festivities, which contains two large halls. That on the ground floor is known as the Knights Hall, with a row of octagonal columns through the centre. It was the assembly place of the military officers, and today holds an exhibition of arms and armour. Immediately above this, and similarly divided by a line of columns, is the vaulted Council Hall. In the Capistrano Tower nearby is a room with an impressive Gothic fireplace, said to have been the home of the Franciscan friar St John of Capistrano, a papal legate, who became known as 'the soldier saint' for his work alongside John Hunyadi in the defence of Belgrade, where, like Hunyadi, he succumbed to the plague.

Separated from the rest of the castle is the imposing square-based Neboisa Tower, the name deriving from the Serbian for 'do not be afraid'. It was one of the defensive structures constructed by John Hunyadi and is connected to the rest of the castle by an atmospheric gallery, some 33m long. The massive semicircular White Tower on the east side of the castle is much later, and dates from the modifications to the castle carried out under Gabriel Bethlen. The next tower to the north of this is the circular Drummers' Tower. Nearby is a well, surrounded by a circular railing, around which a legend circulates remarkably similar to that of the fortress of Râşnov (page 142). It is said that John Hunyadi promised freedom to a group of Ottoman prisoners in the castle if they found water. They dug the well for many years, and did eventually reach water, but unfortunately for them Hunyadi had by then already died. His widow, Erzsébet Szilágyi, was of a less compassionate nature and had them executed anyway. An inscription in Arabic, which was apparently found on the wall of the well, has been placed on a buttress of the nearby chapel: it records that the inscription was written by a slave named Hasan.

On the northern side of the courtyard, the Matia Wing was an addition under Hunyadi's widow Erzsébet Szilágyi in Renaissance style, and includes an attractive loggia, with a rare example from this period of frescoes of a non-religious character. The souvenir shop is also here.

HAŢEG

HAŢEG Haţeg (Hátszeg/Wallenthal) is a small town of some 9,000 people on the main E79 road between Deva (41km north) and Petroşani (47km southeast). It serves as a good base for exploring a cluster of interesting sights in the surrounding area, including the Prislop Monastery, the intriguing church at Densuş and the Roman city of Ulpia Traiana Sarmizegetusa, as well as a gateway to the Retezat National Park to the south. And it is of interest in its own right as the site of discovery of a number of species of dwarf dinosaurs (see box, page 253).

The promotion of the remarkable palaeontological interest of the area is the mission of the **Haţeg Country Dinosaurs Geopark** (Geoparcul Dinozaurilor – Ţara Haţegului) (*Str Libertăţii 9A;* \ *0254 777 853;* e *hateggeoparc@yahoo.com;* w *hateggeoparc.ro;* ⊕ *15 May–15 Sep 10.00–18.00 Wed & Fri, 10.00–16.00 Sat, 16 Sep–14 May by prior appointment only*), an interesting initiative of the University of Bucharest. The main visitor centre in Haţeg includes exhibits on local legends linked to dragons, as well as a full-scale reconstruction of the bird-like *Balaur bondoc*. Other exhibitions within the geopark are scattered across several sites in neighbouring villages. Thus in the village of **General Berthelot** there is a **Science and Art Centre**, open on the same timetable, which is difficult to miss, as there is a full-scale model of the long-necked sauropod *Magyarosaurus dacus* out the front. Inside is a display of dinosaur eggs and a model of another local dinosaur, *Zalmoxes robustus*, a bipedal herbivore named after a Dacian deity. In Baron Nopcsa's birth village of **Sânpetru** are two small adjacent museums. The **House of Dwarf Dinosaurs** (⊕ *15 May–15 Sep 10.00–17.00 Tue–Sat, 10.00–14.00 Sun, 16 Sep–14 May by appointment; other contact details as for Geopark*) contains exhibits on Nopcsa's work and on the dwarf dinosaurs he discovered, while the House of Traditions next door has displays on local ethnography.

There are only one or two **buses** a day from Hațeg to Deva (*1hr*), and with many of the surrounding places of interest not accessible by public transport, this is an area which can be challenging without your own vehicle.

Where to stay and eat Right in the centre of town, the **Art Motel** (*2 sgl, 5 dbl, 1 apt; Str Tudor Vladimirescu 2, Bl 15;* m *0746 022 447;* e *artmotel@geraico.ro;* w *geraico.ro;* **$$**) offers comfortable rooms, if small and somewhat fussily decorated

LITTLE DINOSAURS

Baron Franz Nopcsa, a local ethnic Hungarian aristocrat from the village of Sânpetru, near Hațeg, became interested in the dinosaur bones dug up by his younger sister on their estate in 1895. Upon enrolling at the University of Vienna, Nopcsa rapidly established himself as an expert in the emerging science of palaeontology. He discovered that many of the dinosaur skeletons he was unearthing around his estate were significantly smaller than their cousins elsewhere. These included a dwarf sauropod dinosaur growing to a length of around 6m which he named *Titanosaurus dacus*, but which was later rebaptised *Magyarosaurus*. Sauropods elsewhere typically grow to several times this length. To explain this oddity, Nopcsa argued that in the late Cretaceous period the area around the present-day town of Hațeg was a large offshore island in the Sea of Tethys, and promoted a theory of 'insular dwarfism', arguing that the limited resources available in islands would have the effect over a succession of generations of reducing the size of animals. His theory has since been widely accepted.

Other curious dinosaurs to have been discovered in the region include the fearsome-looking *Balaur bondoc*, or 'stocky dragon', discovered as recently as 1997, a bird-like dinosaur with double sickle claws. This shows no effect of insular dwarfism, but rather characteristics of insular gigantism, arising from the rule developed by evolutionary biologist J Bristol Foster that while larger creatures on islands will gradually evolve into smaller ones, because of the limited food resources, smaller ones tend to get larger, because of reduced predator numbers.

The versatile Baron Nopcsa also became one of the leading experts on the language, history and culture of Albania, and was a strong supporter of the independence of the country, which was then a province of the Ottoman Empire. He lost his estates in Transylvania following World War I, when the region became part of Romania, and moved to Vienna where he met a tragic end in 1933 when, suffering from depression, he murdered first his secretary and close companion Bajazid Elmaz Doda, and then committed suicide.

8

with hanging drapes, above an unexpectedly good restaurant, the Bistro Art Grill (⊕ *08.00–22.30 daily; $$*), with local dishes and a menu written in the local dialect – glossary provided.

PRISLOP Situated around 12km northwest of Hațeg, the **Prislop Monastery** (Mănăstirea Prislop) is one of the most important Romanian Orthodox monasteries in Transylvania. Situated in an attractive location in the Parâng range, it was originally founded around 1399, but had fallen into ruin by the mid 16th century. The current church dates from its re-foundation in that period by Zamfira, daughter of the then ruler of Wallachia, who reportedly rebuilt the monastery in gratitude for having been healed by the waters of a nearby spring. It became a Greco-Catholic monastery before passing back to the Romanian Orthodox Church during the Communist period.

Today Prislop Monastery is one of the major places of Romanian Orthodox pilgrimage in Romania, a fact closely linked to the figure of Arsenie Boca, who became Father Superior of the monastery on its passing to the Romanian Orthodox Church in 1948 and remained here as a father confessor after the community was changed from one of monks to nuns. Boca carried out extensive restoration and rebuilding works at the monastery, where he is today regarded as its third founder. Boca was a charismatic priest as well as talented artist, and was regarded as a figure of great suspicion by the Communist authorities, who arrested him several times and forced him out of the Prislop Monastery in 1959, after which he was transferred to Bucharest. The monastery complex itself was converted by the authorities to use as an old people's home, though it was again restored as a monastery in 1976. Arsenie Boca died in 1989 and is buried at the monastery. His grave is beside the path on the hillside above the main monastery complex; visitors queue patiently to pray at the grave and to lay flowers. A path continues beyond the grave to a hermit's cave in the forest, which serves as an additional stop on the pilgrims' trail. The sheer numbers of devout visitors pose some unusual problems for the nuns: signs on the path to the cave urge visitors not to throw coins into the forest.

To get here, drive north from Hațeg for 6km along road 687A, then turn left at Silvașu de Jos and continue for another 6km via the village of Silvașu de Sus. There are numerous flower sellers on the way, for pilgrims looking for a bouquet to lay at Arsenie Boca's graveside. There is no public transport.

SÂNTĂMĂRIA ORLEA On the main E79, some 3km south of Hațeg, the village of Sântămăria Orlea (HU: Őraljaboldogfalva) is worth a stop to see the **Reformed Church** (Biserica Reformată), built in the 13th century in a style mixing Romanesque with early Gothic. The oldest of the frescoes inside dates back to the 14th century. Historians are divided over whether the church was initially established as a Romanian Orthodox place of worship or as a Catholic one, probably by ethnic Hungarian settlers. In the mid 15th century, the village, including the church, was granted by John Hunyadi to the local Cândea family, also known by the Hungarian name of Kendeffy, and the church was certainly Catholic following that family's conversion to Catholicism. It became a Reformed church a century later. The **Kendeffy Castle** nearby was built in the late 18th century, nationalised by the Communists and later used as a hotel. It is now closed up and in a sad state.

DENSUȘ The village of Densuș (HU: Demsus) contains a fascinating church with an ancient and yet somewhat mysterious history, and which claims the title of the oldest church in Romania at which religious services are still held. **Densuș Church** (Biserica

Densuş) incorporates a considerable amount of building material from the Roman site of Ulpia Traiana Sarmizegetusa, some stones containing Roman inscriptions, and various columns and statues, giving the place a highly unusual feel. Some historians have gone further, suggesting that the building has pagan origins, proposing that there may have been a Dacian temple to the god Zalmoxis on the site, and that it was then occupied by a Roman temple dedicated to Mars, or possibly that it was the mausoleum of one General Longinus Maximus, killed by the Dacians. Evidence used to support the proposal that the building's origins are that of a pagan temple include the fact that the altar is to the south rather than to the east, as would be usual for buildings constructed as Christian places of worship. The current structure of the church owes much to a remodelling in the 13th century. There are murals inside the church, including a painting of Jesus wearing traditional Romanian clothing, dating from the 15th century. The altar is formed of a tombstone from which the lettering has been removed. Above it are two stone lions, standing back to back. From the mid 16th century it was a Reformed church, during which time the interior paintings were covered over, later served a Greco-Catholic congregation, and returned to Romanian Orthodoxy in the late 19th century.

Densuş lies 14km southwest of Haţeg. Take the DN68 towards Băuţar and turn right in the centre of Toteşti village. If the church is closed, ask at House 15 on the main road for the key.

ULPIA TRAIANA SARMIZEGETUSA Colonia Ulpia Traiana Augusta Dacica Sarmizegetusa (to give it its full title) was the capital city of Roman Dacia, taking its name from the former Dacian capital of Sarmizegetusa Regia (pages 248–9), which is some 40km away in the mountains south of Orăştie, providing a naming confusion which, two millennia on, sends visitors to the wrong place even today. It was founded by the first governor of the province, Decimus Terentius Scaurianus, around AD109. Covering an area of around 30ha and well fortified, it was the political and administrative centre of the province of Dacia in the 2nd and 3rd centuries. The imperial road from the Danube up to the northern outpost of Porolissum passed through the city.

The **Roman site** (⚲ *0254 776 418;* w *cetateasarmizegetusa.ro;* ⊕ *08.00–20.00 daily, museum 09.00–17.00 daily; adult/child 10/2RON*) is interesting to visit and includes a quadrilateral forum, a palace of the Augustales, an order of priests responsible for maintaining the cult of Augustus, several temples and most impressively an amphitheatre which had a capacity of around 5,000. The seating around the latter originally comprised stone benches lower down, individually reserved for local dignitaries, while the poorer classes would sit on wooden benches above. Close to the amphitheatre are the remains of a Temple of Nemesis, to whom the gladiators would pray before braving the arena. The **museum** in the attractive-looking villa next to the site displays objects found at it.

Sarmizegetusa is 18km southwest of Haţeg on the main DN68. This continues on to the 700m pass known as the **Iron Gate of Transylvania** (Poarta de Fier a Transilvaniei) which marks the boundaries of Hunedoara and Caraş-Severin counties and thus the southwest boundary of Transylvania. There were no fewer than three battles in this area during the wars between the Romans and Dacians. It was supposedly the site of another battle in 1442, when John Hunyadi's forces defeated an Ottoman army, though some historians argue that the battle actually took place at an entirely different pass which also bore the name Iron Gate at the time. A monument in the form of a giant mace was erected near the village of Zeicani in 1896 to mark the presumed spot of the conflict, but this was destroyed in

1992, apparently because the monument was associated in the minds of some with Hungarian rule in Transylvania.

🏠 **Where to stay** Run by one of the staff at the archaeological museum, **Pensiunea Ulpia Traiana** (*2 sgl, 3 dbl; Sarmizegetusa no 153;* m *0744 984 613;* e *office@ ulpiatraiana.webpro.ro;* w *ulpiatraiana.webpro.ro;* **$$**) is a nice guesthouse offering good local cooking. Bathrooms are shared.

SUSENI The small village of Suseni lies just south of the larger settlement of Râu de Mori, the community of origin of the influential local Cândea or Kendeffy family. Suseni is home to the attractive stone-walled **Colţ Church** (Biserica Colţ), built in the early 14th century with frescoes on the interior walls, some of which are in a poor state, and a pyramidal roof on its square-based tower.

Another worthwhile sight here is **Castle Colţ** (Cetatea Colţ), a walk of some 45 minutes from Suseni. A romantic ruined fortress on an imposing crag, the building dates from the 14th century and was built by the Cândea family. Many believe that the place was the inspiration for the castle of Jules Verne's 1893 novel *The Carpathian Castle*, though some authorities prefer the theory that Verne's fictional castle was modelled on Devín Castle in present-day Slovakia. Verne's novel in turn may have been one of the sources of inspiration for Bram Stoker's *Dracula*, published four years later.

Local road 686 from Sântămăria Orlea brings you to Suseni, via the villages of Sânpetru and Râu de Mori.

RETEZAT NATIONAL PARK Established in 1935, Retezat is the oldest national park in Romania. The highest mountain range here is granite, with high peaks and glacial lakes. A more southerly range, known as the Little Retezat (Retezatul Mic), is limestone, its peaks slightly lower than those to the north, and its surface drier, with caves and deep valleys. The French geographer Emmanuel de Martonne studied the range in the early 20th century and discovered that the horizontal platforms found at similar elevations throughout the Carpathians, particularly pronounced at Retezat, were the result of erosion by the sea.

The highest point of the Retezat range, Peleaga Peak, rises to 2,509m, just 35m lower than Moldoveanu Peak in the Făgăraş Mountains, the highest point in Romania. The Retezat Mountains contain more than 20 peaks above 2,000m, more than any other range in Romania. The main range of the Retezat Mountains is also known for its chain of glacial cirque lakes. **Lacul Bucura**, at an altitude of 2,040m below Peleaga Peak, is the largest glacier lake in Romania, with a length of some 550m. And **Lacul Zănoaga** further west takes the title of Romania's deepest glacial lake, reaching a maximum depth of 29m.

There is a particularly rich flora in the natural park, with colourful plants to be found here including the glacier pink, yellow gentian, red vanilla orchid, edelweiss and globeflower. Animals found in the park include bears, wild boar, lynx, wolves and chamois. Farming communities on the edge of the park have land-use rights in the alpine pastures for their livestock. The area of the Gemenele Scientific Reserve within the park has a particularly high degree of protection: visitor access is controlled here and camping or the lighting of fires is not allowed within the scientific reserve.

The **Retezat National Park Administration** (*Nucşoara no 284;* \ *0254 779 969;* e *office@retezat.ro;* w *retezat.ro*) is based near the village of **Nucşoara**, to the north of the park. There is a **visitor centre** here (⏰ *Jul–Sep 09.00–19.00 daily, Oct–Jun*

09.00–16.30 Mon–Thu, 09.00–14.00 Fri), and another one further to the west at **Ostrovel**, close to the village of Râu de Mori.

Accessing the park from the **north**, the villages of Râu de Mori and Sălaşu de Sus are the main routes of entry. There are some accommodation options along the scenic road running south from Râu de Mori in the Râul Mare River valley along the western edge of the park. There is also accommodation available at the Complexul Alpin Râuşor, at the end of a minor road which heads southeast from Râu de Mori through Suseni and then south. This was originally developed as a workers' retreat in the Communist era by the steelworks in Hunedoara, fell into disrepair after the Romanian Revolution, but has gradually been redeveloped by private tourism concerns into a winter skiing and summer hiking base. There are further accommodation options in mountain lodges at Cârnic, which lies immediately to the north of the park boundary at the end of a minor road running southwards from Sălaşu de Sus, through Nucşoara. The closest railway station is at Ohaba de Sub Piatră, from where there are trains north to Deva (*70mins*) and east to Petroşani (*1½hrs*). However, this still leaves you far to the north of the park. Subcetate station to the north is even further, but potentially more useful, as fast trains from Bucharest stop here (*from 7hrs*).

An alternative access route is from the **east**, along the initially deeply unpromising DN66A, which heads westwards just south of Petroşani along the Jiul de Vest River, via the declining coal-mining towns of Vulcan, Lupeni and Uricani, before approaching the park to the west of Câmpu lui Neag. The Cheile Buţii Tourist Complex (page 260) lies just off this road, almost at the park boundary. The closest railway station to the park from this direction doesn't even get as close as Uricani.

The massif is crossed by marked trails, and offers fine panoramas of mountain peaks and glacier lakes, frequently enjoyed in solitude.

Where to stay Within the national park itself, accommodation is limited to basic mountain lodges (*cabanas*) and to designated camping areas, usually next to the

ROMANIAN HIKING VOCABULARY

peşteră	cave	vârf, pisc	peak
colţ	cliff	câmpie	plain
mor	cloud	ploaie	rain
stâncă	crag	râpă	ravine
câmp	field	creastă, coamă	ridge
ceaţă	fog	râu	river
pădure or codru	forest	piatră, stâncă	rock
cheie	gorge	stână	sheepfold
deal, măgură	hill	zapada	snow
cabană	hut	izvor	spring
gheaţă	ice	pârâu	stream
lac	lake	culme	summit
mlaştină	marsh	vale	valley
poiană	meadow	sat	village
pas	pass	vreme, timp	weather
păşune	pasture	padure	wood
potecă, traseu	path		

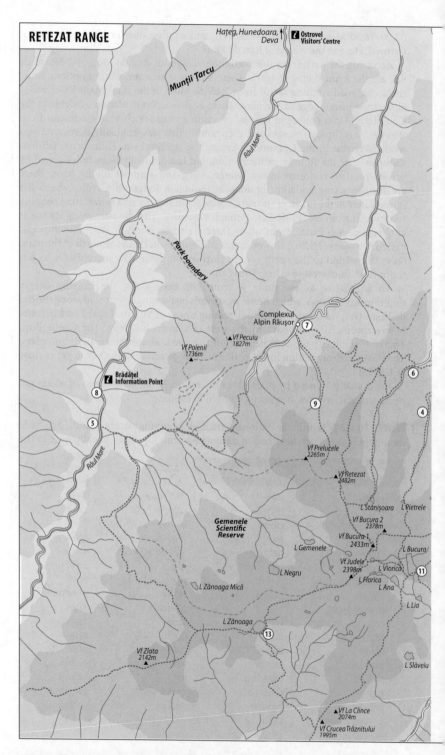

RETEZAT RANGE

Munții Țarcu

Hațeg, Hunedoara, Deva

Ostrovel Visitors' Centre

Râul Mare

Park boundary

Complexul Alpin Râușor 7

6

Vf Pecuiu 1827m

Vf Poienii 1736m

Brădățel Information Point

8

9

4

5

Râul Mare

Vf Prelucele 2265m

Vf Retezat 2482m

L Stânișoara   L Pietrele

Gemenele Scientific Reserve

Vf Bucura 2 2378m

L Gemenele

Vf Bucura 1 2433m

L Bucura

L Negru

Vf Judele 2398m

L Viorica

11

L Florica

L Zânoaga Mică

L Ana

L Lia

L Zânoaga

13

L Slăveiu

Vf Zlata 2142m

Vf La Clince 2074m

Vf Crucea Trăznitului 1995m

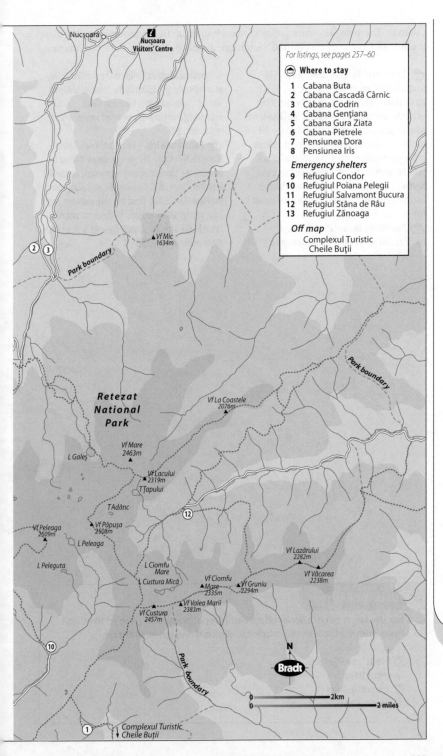

Nucșoara

i Nucșoara
Visitors' Centre

For listings, see pages 257–60

⌂ **Where to stay**

1 Cabana Buta
2 Cabana Cascadă Cârnic
3 Cabana Codrin
4 Cabana Genţiana
5 Cabana Gura Ziata
6 Cabana Pietrele
7 Pensiunea Dora
8 Pensiunea Iris

Emergency shelters
9 Refugiul Condor
10 Refugiul Poiana Pelegii
11 Refugiul Salvamont Bucura
12 Refugiul Stâna de Râu
13 Refugiul Zănoaga

Off map
    Complexul Turistic
    Cheile Buţii

Park boundary

(2)(3)

▲ Vf Mic
1634m

*Retezat
National
Park*

▲ Vf La Coastele
2076m

Park boundary

L Galeş

▲ Vf Mare
2463m

▲ Vf Lacului
2319m
T Ţapului

(12)

T Adânc

▲ Vf Păpuşa
2508m

Vf Peleaga
2509m

L Peleaga

▲ Vf Lazărului
2282m

L Peleguţa

L Ciomfu
Mare
L Custura Mică

▲ Vf Ciomfu
Mare
2335m

▲ Vf Gruniu
2294m

Vf Văcarea
2238m

▲ Vf Valea Marii
2383m

▲ Vf Custura
2457m

(10)

Park boundary

N

Bradt

0   2km
0   2 miles

(1) Complexul Turistic
     ↓ Cheile Buţii

8

cabanas. There are also emergency shelters higher up in the mountains. But there is a broader range of accommodation immediately outside the park boundaries.

Complexul Turistic Cheile Buţii (39 rooms, 5 apt) Câmpu lui Neag; ☎0253 210 279; m 0741 063 365; e cheile_butii@yahoo.com; w cheile-butii.ro. In a glorious setting close to the national park boundary, & accessed via the DN66A road from Petroşani, this offers accommodation in 3 adjacent lodges: the 3-star Cabana Poiana Soarelui, slightly cheaper Cabana Cuibul cu Dor, & smaller wooden Vila Prietenilor, which has 5 apartments with balconies. There is a restaurant & tennis court. **$$$–$$**

Pensiunea Dora (25 beds) Râuşor; m 0722 566 929; e info@pensiuneadora.ro; w pensiuneadora.ro. Right on the park boundary, at an altitude of 1,350m at the Complexul Alpin Râuşor, this place offers basic but clean accommodation in 2-, 3- or 4-bed rooms, with a restaurant. **$$**

Pensiunea Iris (13 rooms) Valea Râului Mare; m 0744 605 262; w geraico.ro. Owned by Geraico, the same company responsible for the Art Motel in Haţeg, this is a nicely located place along the Râul Mare, 500m from the park entrance, with basic rooms & a restaurant. Of the room options, those in the attic are slightly cheaper & older than those in the annexe. **$$–$**

9

Alba County

Alba County has a significant place in the establishment of Romanian national identity. Its capital, Alba Iulia, centred on a remarkable 18th-century citadel, is associated with Michael the Brave, who in 1600 first, and very briefly, united the three regions of Wallachia, Moldavia and Transylvania which make up modern Romania. And this was the city in which, on 1 December 1918, delegates representing Romanians in Transylvania voted unanimously for unification with Romania. The eastern part of the county is dominated by the Apuseni Mountains, also closely associated with the fight for the rights of ethnic Romanians in Transylvania, especially through the 1784 peasants' revolt of Horea, Cloşca and Crişan and the leading role of Avram Iancu in the struggles around the revolution of 1848–49.

The Apuseni also provide some glorious natural attractions, from ice caves to karst scenery, and manmade ones such as the gold-mining galleries cut by the Romans at Roşia Montană. And the Apuseni provide the opportunity to learn something about the culture of the Moţi people, who have a strong reputation across Romania for both hardiness and patriotism. There is perhaps no better occasion to do so than the celebrated Mount Găina Girls' Fair in July near the village of Avram Iancu, traditionally an occasion for rural matchmaking, but now much more about music and drinking.

ALBA IULIA   *Telephone code 0258*

Alba Iulia (Gyulafehérvár/Karlsburg) is a thoroughly worthwhile destination in a Transylvanian tour for its impressive 18th-century star-shaped citadel, and for the many historic buildings within it, with links to important historic figures like John Hunyadi and Michael the Brave and more recently with Alba Iulia's central role in the unification of Transylvania with Romania following World War I.

The citadel is largely pedestrianised, and a great place to wander, but there are very few restaurants or places to stay within it, so visitors will need to spend some time in the mostly undistinguished Lower Town outside its walls.

HISTORY Alba Iulia has a long and distinguished history. The present city is located close to a Dacian fortress named Apulon. After Dacia was incorporated into the Roman Empire, the important settlement of Apulum, taking its name from the Dacian one, was located on the site of the modern city. It was the capital of the Roman province of Dacia Apulensis, covering southern Transylvania and the Banat, and the 13th Twin Legion (Legio XIII Gemina) was based here. This was a particularly celebrated unit of the Imperial Roman army – the one with which Julius Caesar had famously crossed the Rubicon many years earlier.

The Hungarian chronicle *Gesta Hungarorum* mentions that a ruler named Jula, grandfather of King Stephen I of Hungary, established the capital of his dukedom there in the 10th century. It was the seat of the Catholic Transylvanian bishopric from at least

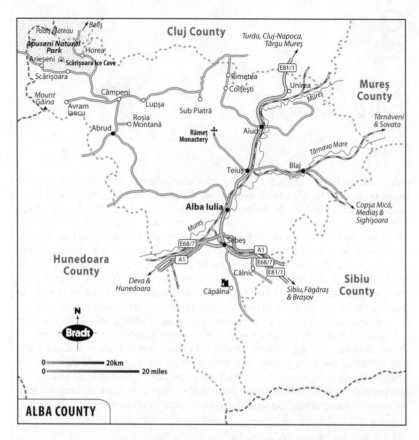

the 11th century and was an important centre during the 15th-century rule of John Hunyadi, who is buried in the Catholic cathedral. It served as the capital of the Eastern Hungarian Kingdom and thereafter the Principality of Transylvania from 1541 to 1690.

Alba Iulia's association with the development of the Romanian nation stems originally from the campaigns of Michael the Brave, who in 1599 entered the city following his victory at the Battle of Şelimbăr against the Hungarian Transylvanian forces of Andrew Báthory, to claim the title of Voivode of Transylvania. When the following year Michael also gained control of the province of Moldavia, the three major constituent units of the future state of Romania were briefly united. It would be more than 300 years before they were brought back together.

Alba Iulia was to play a central role in that process too. Following the end of World War I, with Romania on the winning side, 1,228 representatives of Romanians in Transylvania, the Banat, Crişana and Maramureş gathered in the city on 1 December 1918 for the National Assembly of the Romanians of Transylvania and Hungary, at which they voted unanimously for unification with Romania. Ten days later King Ferdinand signed the unification into law. The incorporation of Transylvania into Romania was agreed by the international powers at the Treaty of Trianon in June 1920, the peace treaty between the Allied Powers and Hungary.

Alba Iulia's status as the city representing Romanian unification was further cemented in 1922, when it was the site of the symbolic coronation of King Ferdinand and Queen Marie as the sovereigns of Greater Romania.

GETTING THERE, AWAY AND AROUND

By air The closest airports are at **Cluj-Napoca** (CLJ), 94km away, and **Sibiu** (SBZ), 73km.

By rail and bus The bus (*Str Iaşilor 94;* ☎*0258 812 967;* w *stpalba.ro*) and **railway** (☎*0258 811 100*) stations are both located 2km southeast of the citadel on the main road Bulevardul Ferdinand. Numerous city buses serve the bus stops for both the railway station (*gara*) and bus station (*autogara STP*). There are frequent buses to Cluj-Napoca (*2hrs*), Deva (*1½hrs*) and Sibiu (*1½hrs*). In most cases, train frequencies are lower than those for bus services, and travel times a little higher, including Cluj-Napoca (*2½hrs*), Sibiu (*2½hrs*) and Deva (*1½hrs*).

Parking There are several car parks around the citadel: at the time of research parking was free, but a 2RON per-hour charge was being planned.

Taxi companies
- 🚗 **AS Taxi** ☎0258 946
- 🚗 **Florea Taxi** ☎0258 945
- 🚗 **FM Taxi** ☎0258 944
- 🚗 **Gicu Trans** ☎0258 920

TOURIST INFORMATION The **tourist information office** (*Aleea Sfântul Capistranu 28;* ☎*0371 337 148;* e *turism@apulum.ro;* w *visitalbaiulia.com;* ⊕ *May–Sep 09.00–21.00 daily, Oct–Apr 10.00–17.00 daily*) is located below street level amid a maze of fortress walls near the Parcul Unirii.

🏠 WHERE TO STAY   *Map, page 264*

🏠**Hotel Medieval** (28 rooms) Str Militari 13; ☎0374 079 990; e office@hotel-medieval. ro; w hotel-medieval.ro. A new hotel in a historic building around a secluded courtyard within the citadel, offering both the highest-end & most central option in Alba Iulia. The staff sport medieval outfits, & guests have free entry to the Route of the Three Fortifications (page 265), which was set up by the hotel's developers, the Corint Group. **$$$$**

🏠**Hotel Transilvania** (76 dbl, 4 apt) Piaţa Iuliu Maniu 11; ☎0258 812 052; e office@ hoteltransilvania.eu; w hoteltransilvania.eu. A nice modernisation hides the Transilvania's Communist-era origins. It offers both smartly furnished 4- & still-comfortable 3-star-rated rooms. It is located in the Lower Town. Has bicycles for hire (*10RON/hr*). **$$$$** (4-star), **$$$** (3-star)

🏠**Hotel Cetate** (5 sgl, 91 dbl, 4 apt) Str Unirii 3; ☎0258 811 780; e alba@imparatulromanilor.ro; w alba.imparatulromanilor.ro. An ugly-looking 12-storey concrete block in a good central location close to the western entrance to the citadel. In some need of renovation. **$$$**

🏠**Hotel Parc** (72 rooms) Str Primăverii 4; ☎0258 811 723; e office@hotelparc.ro; w hotelparc.ro. Down in the Lower Town, though only a short walk from the citadel, this place offers 4-star & 3-star rooms & has an indoor pool. Comfortable enough, but has a slightly tired feel. **$$$**

🏠**La Maison de Caroline** (14 rooms) Str Primăverii 11; ☎0358 101 227; e contact@lmdc.ro; w lamaisondecaroline.ro. Caroline's house in Alba Carolina is a comfortable small hotel in a historic building with spacious rooms. **$$$**

🏠**Pensiunea Obelisc Caffe** (1 sgl, 2 dbl, 2 trpl) Str Mihai Viteazul 6; m 0767 465 142; e office@obeliscalba.ro. In a great location almost at the eastern gate of the citadel, the Obelisc offers basic but clean rooms, together with a café that also serves pizza & light meals (**$$**) between overpowering floral-wallpapered walls. The place has changed its name frequently, & you may also hear it described as the Flamingo & the Bliss. **$**

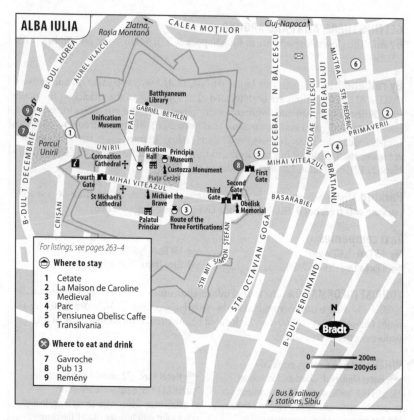

ALBA IULIA

Zlatna, Roşia Montană
CALEA MOTILOR
Cluj-Napoca

B-DUL HOREA
AUREL VLAICU

Batthyaneum
Library

GABRIEL BETHLEN

Unification
Museum

PACII

DECEBAL
N BĂLCESCU

MISTRAL
STR FREDERIC

NICOLAE TITULESCU
ARDEALULUI

PRIMĂVERII
STR FREDERIC

Parcul
Unirii

B-DUL 1 DECEMBRIE 1918

UNIRII
Coronation
Cathedral ✝

Unification
Hall

Principia
Museum

Custozza Monument

Piaţa Cetăţii

First
Gate

MIHAI VITEAZUL

I C BRĂTIANU

Fourth
Gate

MIHAI VITEAZUL

St Michael's
Cathedral ✝

Michael the
Brave

Third
Gate

Second
Gate

Obelisk
Memorial

BASARABIEI

CRIŞAN

Palatul
Princiar

Route of the
Three Fortifications

STR OCTAVIAN GOGA

STR MIT SIMON ŞTEFAN

B-DUL FERDINAND I

N

Bradt

0 ————— 200m
0 ————— 200yds

For listings, see pages 263–4

🛏 Where to stay
1 Cetate
2 La Maison de Caroline
3 Medieval
4 Parc
5 Pensiunea Obelisc Caffe
6 Transilvania

✖ Where to eat and drink
7 Gavroche
8 Pub 13
9 Remény

Bus & railway
stations, Sibiu

✖ WHERE TO EAT AND DRINK *Map, see above*

✖ **Gavroche** B-dul 1 Decembrie 1918
105–7; ☎ 0358 401 203; ⏰ 08.00–midnight
Mon–Thu, 08.00–01.00 Fri, 09.00–01.00 Sat,
09.00–midnight Sun. Not a Michelin-starred
French restaurant but a self-styled brasserie with
a couple of French dishes, like *coq au vin*, amid an
international menu of burgers, quesadillas & lots
of pasta, served against a backdrop of loud music &
TV sports. $$$

✖ **Pub 13** Str Aleea Sf Capistrano 1; m 0728
444 415; e contact@pub13.ro; w pub13. ro;
⏰ noon–23.00 Sun–Fri, noon–midnight Sat.
This place is also known as the Restaurant
Medieval, which gives a much better feel

for what it actually is: a medieval-themed
restaurant in an atmospheric circular brick
powder house within the citadel walls. The long
menu even includes frogs' legs, along with many
dishes with 'medieval' in the title–including a
medieval pizza. $$$

✖ **Remény** B-dul 1 Decembrie 1918 20, Bl
M11–12; m 0742 790 066; ⏰ 10.00–22.30
daily. Across Parcul Unirii from the western
gate of the citadel, this place offers
Hungarian & Transylvanian dishes within a
menu featuring lots of international standards.
$$$

FESTIVALS AND EVENTS Between May and September there is a **Changing of the
Guard** (Schimbarea Gărzii) ceremony in the centre of the citadel daily at noon: it is
entirely a confection for tourists, but no less enjoyable for that, and involves 'troops'
dressed in Austrian Imperial garb. There is a further ceremony at 21.00 on Friday
and Saturday evenings in summer, with the Friday show preceded by a mock battle
between Romans and Dacians.

The **Dilema Veche Festival** in late August takes its name from a weekly cultural magazine, and makes for a good low-key festival offering a mix of debates and discussions on political and cultural themes, and music.

The **Ziua de Mâine Folk Festival** (Festivalul de Folk 'Zina de Mâine') (\0258 812 076; w *folkalba.ro*) takes place in November.

OTHER PRACTICALITIES

$ BRD B-dul 1 Decembrie 1918 Bl M12; \0258 833 168; ⏰ 09.00–17.00 Mon–Fri

✚ Farmacia Sic Volo B-dul 1 Decembrie 1918 Bl M11; \0258 830 395; ⏰ 07.00–midnight daily

✉️ **Post office** Str Nicolae Titulescu 10A; ⏰ 08.00–19.00 Mon–Fri, 09.00–13.00 Sat

WHAT TO SEE AND DO

Entering the Citadel The defining structure in Alba Iulia, inside which all the main tourist attractions are concentrated, is its citadel, the largest in Romania. Its highly distinctive form, in the shape of a star with seven points topped with bastions, was created between 1716 and 1735 by the architect Giovanni Morando Visconti. Officially named the Alba Carolina Citadel, its form owes much to the system of military architectural engineering developed in 17th-century France by the Marquis de Vauban, with its characteristic use of geometric shapes such as pentagons and stars.

Entering the citadel from the east, along Strada Mihai Viteazul, you pass through the triple-arched First Gate of the fortress, also named the **Poarta Carol de Jos**, in Baroque style with reliefs of mythological scenes. The road bears left up a long ramp, to what remains of the Second Gate, partly demolished in the 19th century. You arrive at a large open space looking out over the Lower Town below, which is dominated by the stone **Obelisk of Horea, Cloşca and Crişan**, built in the 1930s to commemorate the 150th anniversary of the execution in the city of the leaders of the Romanian peasant uprising of 1784–85. Some 22.5m high, it was sculpted by Iosif Fekete in an Art Deco style. A winged representation of the goddess of victory looks out over the town, while a rather battered relief of the three leaders, in a frame whose outline represents the map of Greater Romania, faces the centre of the citadel. From here you walk into the central area of the citadel through the Third Gate, the **Poarta Carol**, approached across a bridge over the moat. This Baroque gate, with three entrances, is the most impressive of all of those of the citadel, and is topped with an equestrian statue of Holy Roman Emperor Charles VI.

The interior of the citadel is largely pedestrianised, full of interesting religious and administrative buildings, supplemented by modern statues of Austrian troops, ladies in their finery and the like, and a great place to stroll. From the Third Gate, you find yourself on Strada Mihai Viteazul, which runs in a straight line through the centre of the citadel and along which most of the major sights are to be found. On your left beyond the Third Gate is the entrance to the **Route of the Three Fortifications** (Traseul Celor Trei Fortificaţii) (m *0722 665 833*; ⏰ *10.00–19.00 Tue–Sun; adult/child 15/5RON*), which offers a tour around the buildings, bastions and walls of the southwestern part of the citadel, including elements of the Roman, medieval and Vauban fortresses (hence 'three fortifications').

Around Piaţa Cetăţii Strada Mihai Viteazul brings you to Piaţa Cetăţii, a large square in the centre of the citadel. Within the square, and guarded by statues of Roman soldiers, the **Principia Museum** (Muzeul Principia) (⏰ *10.00–21.00 Tue–Sun; adult/child 10/5RON*) encloses part of the Roman *castrum* of Apulum, headquarters of the 13th Twin Legion. You are beckoned into the museum, through

9

a modern Corinthian-columned arch, by a statue of Septimius Severus. There are some pieces of Roman statuary on the cobbled square just outside the museum. Also on the square is the **Custozza Monument**, an obelisk crowned with a pair of wings, which commemorates those members of the local infantry regiment killed at the Battle of Custozza in 1866, in which the Imperial Austrian army decisively defeated that of Italy; a battle which did not, however, alter the overall course of the Seven Weeks' War, of which this was a part. Austria was eventually forced to concede to Italy's Prussian allies, and to cede Venetia to Italy.

The Ionic-columned façade of the 1 December 1918 University occupies the northern side of the square. On the western side, but entered from Strada Muzeului further on, is the **Unification Hall** (Sala Unirii) (⊕ *10.00–19.00 Tue–Sun; free admission*), built in 1900 as an officers' casino. Its great moment in history came on 1 December 1918 when delegates to the Great National Assembly met here, it being the largest hall in town, to approve unanimously the unification of Transylvania, the Banat, Crişana and Maramureş with Romania. It was further embellished in 1922 for the coronation ceremony of King Ferdinand and Queen Marie as the sovereigns of the new Greater Romania. Some 21 bronze busts of political figures who contributed to the 'Great Unification' were placed around the building in 1993. You are welcomed into the building by busts of the king and queen, and somewhat unexpectedly find yourself walking through some ethnographic displays before reaching the vaulted Union Hall itself. Portraits of Romanian cultural heroes decorate the arch over one end of the room, with portraits of Romanian rulers, ending with King Ferdinand, the other. The texts of various key resolutions and proclamations along the road to the Great Unification are set out on the walls.

Across Strada Muzeului, one block to the west of Piaţa Cetăţii, is the **Unification Museum** (Muzeul Naţional al Unirii) (*Str Mihai Viteazul 12–14;* \0258 813 300; e *contact@mnuai.ro;* w *mnuai.ro;* ⊕ *Jun–Sep 10.00–19.00 Tue–Sun, Oct–May 10.00–17.00 Tue–Sun; adult/child 8/4RON*). This is an interesting museum, whose displays were clearly laid out with the purpose of providing historical support for the Great Unification. There are good displays of Dacian and Roman artefacts, the latter focused on the Roman city of Apulum. Impressive statuary includes Hercules making short work of a snake. There is much focus on historical episodes that brought the people of Greater Romania together, from common resistance, strengthened by Christianity, against migrant peoples from the east, to the brief uniting of Wallachia, Moldavia and Transylvania by Michael the Brave in 1600, with Alba Iulia as his capital. There is much on the development of Romanian resistance in Transylvania to the inequalities faced under Habsburg rule, including the 1784 peasant revolt led by Horea, Cloşca and Crişan, and the Great National Assembly of May 1848 in Blaj. Reaching a crescendo with the Great National Assembly of 1 December 1918 in Alba Iulia, the historical narrative then stops.

Back on Strada Mihai Viteazul, there is an equestrian **Statue of Michael the Brave**. Behind this is the **Palatul Princiar**, once the residence of Transylvanian princes, including Michael the Brave, but now in bad shape and not open to the public. A black relief on its northern wall, in need of some repair, commemorates the 1600 union of Transylvania, Wallachia and Moldavia.

The Catholic and Romanian Orthodox cathedrals
Continuing west along Strada Mihai Viteazul you immediately reach on your left **St Michael's Cathedral** (Catedrala Sfântul Mihail) (*Str Mihai Viteazul 21;* \0258 811 602; ⊕ *07.00–19.00 daily*). A Catholic cathedral, it dates originally from the 11th century, but this

building was largely replaced in the 13th century with the Romanesque three-nave basilica that forms the basis of the present-day church. It was a Protestant place of worship between 1565 and 1715, but was taken back by the Catholic Church and now serves as the cathedral of the Roman Catholic Archdiocese of Alba Iulia. It is a beautiful building. The Lászai Chapel on the northern side of the church, a 1512 addition to the renovation of the cathedral's northern entrance, is considered the oldest example of Renaissance architecture in Transylvania, and features some delightful stone bas-reliefs.

The cathedral is also known as the resting place of some of the ethnic Hungarian figures who have been most influential in Transylvania's history. Chief amongst these is the 15th-century statesman John Hunyadi, who is buried in the first chapel on the right when looking towards the altar, alongside his brother and son Ladislaus, the elder brother of Matthias Corvinus. The Várday Chapel houses the elaborate carved tombs of the Polish-born Queen Isabella Jagiellon, the widow of Hungarian King John Zápolya in the 16th century, and her son John Sigismund Zápolya. Others buried in the cathedral include Gabriel Bethlen, the influential Prince of Transylvania from 1613 to 1629. There is also a plaque here to Áron Márton, the bishop of the Catholic Church in Transylvania during the Communist regime, who was imprisoned for several years for his outspokenness on religious freedom and human rights, a marble bas relief showing a caring face. There are many wreaths beneath the plaque, decorated with ribbons in the Hungarian colours of red, white and green.

Across Strada Mihai Viteazul stands the Romanian Orthodox **Coronation Cathedral** (Catedrala Încoronării) (*Str Mihai Viteazul 16;* ☉ *06.30–21.30 Mon– Sat, 07.30–21.30 Sun*), built in a neo-Romanian style between 1921 and 1922 for the coronation of Ferdinand and Marie as King and Queen of Greater Romania on 15 October 1922. A 58m-high bell tower stands above the entrance, flanked by busts of King Ferdinand and Queen Marie. There are further portraits of Ferdinand and Marie on the rear wall of the nave of the cathedral, which is in the form of an inscribed Greek cross. The cathedral is surrounded by a cloister, giving the place a vaguely monastic feel.

A short walk north of here, at the top of Strada Păcii, is the **Batthyaneum Library** (Biblioteca Batthyaneum) (*Str Gabriel Bethlen 1*), founded at the end of the 18th century by the Roman Catholic Bishop of Transylvania, Ignác Batthyány. He transformed the Baroque former Trinitarian church into a library and amassed a collection of some 18,000 books and manuscripts, the oldest dating from the 9th century. He also established an astronomical observatory here. It is not generally open to the public. A restitution claim for the property made by the Roman Catholic Church was before the courts at the time of research.

The main western exit to the citadel is through the **Fourth Gate** between the Catholic and Roman Orthodox cathedrals decorated with the double-headed eagle of Austria.

HEADING SOUTH

SEBEŞ The German name for Transylvania, Siebenbürgen, referred to the seven cities of the Saxons of the region. Six are better known today, and among the major touristic destinations of Transylvania. They are Bistriţa, Braşov, Cluj, Mediaş, Sighişoara and Sibiu. The last of this seven is Sebeş (Szászsebes/Mühlbach). If it were one of the actors in John Sturges's 1960 western it would be Brad Dexter – the member of the Magnificent Seven whom nobody can quite remember, but who was a fine actor nonetheless.

It was established in the 12th century by Transylvanian Saxons, brought to the area to defend the southern frontier of the Hungarian Kingdom. It developed into an important medieval town, surrounded by fortress walls with towers that were each defended by one of the town guilds. The fortifications were, however, insufficient to withstand a devastating Ottoman attack in 1438. Sebeş played a significant role in Transylvania's history: the Diet of Transylvania met here on several occasions, and John Zápolya, King of Hungary from 1526, died in the town in 1540. There were further setbacks too, including the effects of another fierce Ottoman attack in 1661. Sebeş suffered further in 1707 at the hands of the troops of Francis II Rákóczi, during his failed insurrection against Habsburg rule, in which the Transylvanian Saxons sided with the Habsburgs. The city's first mayor elected following unification with Romania was a lawyer named Lionel Blaga, whose much better-known brother, Lucian Blaga (see box, pages 78–9), born in the nearby village of Lancrăm, was a towering figure of interwar Romanian cultural life.

The town centres on the Piaţa Primăriei, which accommodates a well-tended patch of greenery. The western side of this square is dominated by the **Evangelical Church** (Biserica Evanghelică) (*Piaţa Primăriei 5;* \0258 731 693; ⊕ *10.00–13.00 & 15.00–17.00 Tue–Sat, 15.00–17.00 Sun*), with its square tower topped with a polychrome tiled spire. First built by Saxon colonists at the start of the 13th century as a Romanesque basilica, it was later rebuilt in an early Gothic style following the partial destruction of the earlier building during a Mongol attack in 1241. Inside, the impressive altar is 13m high and 6m wide, said to be the largest in all Transylvania.

The northern side of the square centres on the spired confection of the town hall. A couple of doors down is the **Ioan Raica Municipal Museum** (Muzeul Municipal Ioan Raica) (*Str Mihai Viteazul 4;* \0258 735 240; ⊕ *08.00–16.00 Tue–Fri, 10.00– 16.00 Sat/Sun; adult/child 2/1RON*), housed in the former Princely Palace. It is the building in which John Zápolya died, and it hosted a number of Diets of Transylvania. The collection focuses on the archaeology and history of the area.

From the central square, walk eastwards along the main Bulevardul Lucian Blaga, turning right onto Strada Traian when you reach the Lucian Blaga Cultural Centre, just before you get to a small park. You will soon see on your right the 15th-century square-based **Student's Tower** (Turnul Studentului), one of the few remaining towers of the original city walls, together with an adjacent stretch of wall. It is more correctly known as the **Tailors' Tower** (Turnul Croitorilor), due to the guild responsible for it. The popular name derives from a local legend. It is said that during the devastating Ottoman attack, a group of townsfolk opposed the decision of the town authorities to surrender, and barricaded themselves into the tower. All were either killed or captured by the Turks, the latter group including a boy known as the 'Student of Romoş'. He appears to have been one Christian Cloos, whose life continued in a no less eventful fashion. He was sold on from one master to another, before finally being released from captivity after 20 years. He wrote a book about his experiences, published in Rome in 1475, which became a bestseller of its time. Martin Luther even wrote a preface to one of its editions. The Student's Tower is regarded as a symbol of resistance. It is not open to visitors.

Sebeş is on the main E81 highway, just 16km south of Alba Iulia. It also lies just off the new AI motorway running eastwards from Sibiu. The train and bus stations are close to each other, a 20-minute walk east of the centre, though some buses to Sibiu, Alba Iulia and Cluj, notably those operated by the FANY group, more conveniently depart from the town centre. There are frequent **buses** to Sibiu (*1hr*), Alba Iulia (*20–30mins*) and Cluj-Napoca (*2½hrs*). Train connections include Sibiu

(1hr 40mins) and Deva *(1½hrs)*. Alba Iulia is better reached by bus, as trains go via Vânţu de Jos, where a change is often needed.

CÂLNIC The little village of Câlnic (Kelnek/Kelling) is of interest for the well-preserved **Câlnic Citadel** (Cetatea Câlnic) (**m** *0740 234 297;* ⊕ *1 Apr–15 Sep 09.00–19.00 daily, 16 Sep–31 Mar call in advance; adult/child 6/3RON*), one of the seven inscribed on UNESCO's list of Transylvanian villages with their fortified churches. The history of the citadel at Câlnic is, however, very different from that of most of the fortified churches in the region, as it started out as the fortified residence of a local nobleman, built in the 13th century. In an area subject to frequent Ottoman attacks, the keep, which served as the residence, and is known as the Siegfried Tower, was protected by a high stone defensive wall with a moat on the outside. In 1430, the then owner of the citadel sold the place to the local community before moving away. The new owners, the local Saxon community, extended the fortifications further, building a second defensive wall and adding further height to the keep, not least to enable defenders posted there to fire over the enlarged walls. They also constructed a chapel within the courtyard. The keep now houses a well-presented ethnographic display, while the chapel is used as a venue for temporary art exhibitions. The well-maintained gardens in the interior of the citadel add to the restful feel of the place.

Câlnic lies 13km southeast of Sebeş: take the E81 towards Sibiu and turn right after 9km, signed for Câlnic. There are several **buses** a day from Sebeş *(20mins)*, though note that these only run on weekdays.

CĂPÂLNA Five of the UNESCO World Heritage-listed Dacian fortresses of the Orăştie Mountains lie in Hunedoara County (pages 247–8), but the sixth, Căpâlna, is in Alba. Built in the 1st century BC, the role of the fortress was to guard the Dacian capital, Sarmizegetusa Regia, from possible attack along the Sebeş Valley. It suffered the fate of most of the Dacian citadels: destruction by the Romans in or around AD106.

The fortress was built on a 610m hill on the left bank of the Sebeş River. Characteristically, the Dacians levelled the top of the hill to create the fortress, surrounding this with a limestone wall. Two towers were built close to the main access road up into the fortress, one of which probably served as the chieftain's home. Their bases, of limestone blocks, are still to be seen. Căpâlna seems to have combined the roles of military garrison and chieftain's residence: archaeologists have found no evidence of any civilian settlement outside the fortress walls.

To get here take road DN67C southwards from Sebeş, reaching the village of Căpâlna after 17km. After the road crosses a bridge over the Sebeş River you will need to complete the last couple of kilometres on foot, up a forest path.

THE APUSENI MOUNTAINS

One of the glories of the Romanian natural environment, the Apuseni Mountains form part of the Western Romanian Carpathians, comprising the western line of the rough triangle of ranges around the Transylvanian Plateau. 'Apus' in Romanian is 'sunset', signifying the western location of the mountains. The Apuseni comprise a number of distinct ranges. Some of the most spectacular areas have been incorporated into the **Apuseni Natural Park** (Parcul Natural Apuseni) (**e** *office@parcapuseni.ro;* **w** *parcapuseni.ro*). The distinguished speleologist Emil Racoviţă pushed for the creation of a protected area in the Apuseni Mountains in the 1920s,

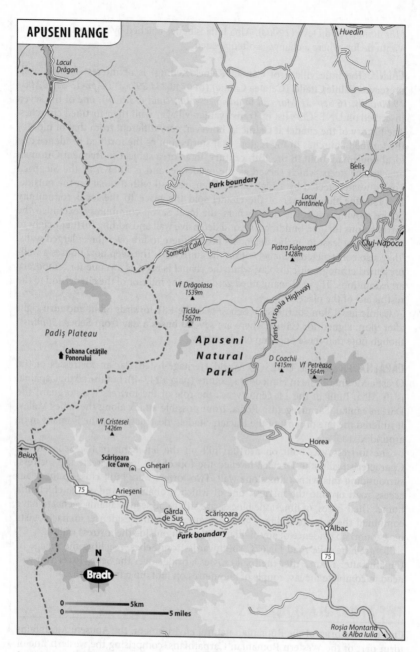

Huedin

Lacul
Drăgan

Park boundary

Beliş

Lacul
Fântânele

Someşul Cald

Piatra Fulgerată
1428m

Cluj-Napoca

Vf Drăgoiasa
1539m

Ticlău
1567m

Apuseni
Natural
Park

Padiş Plateau

Cabana Cetăţile
Ponorului

D Coachii
1415m

Vf Petreasa
1564m

Trans-Ursoaia Highway

Vf Cristesei
1426m

Horea

Beiuş

Scărişoara
Ice Cave

Gheţari

75

Arieşeni

Gârda
de Sus

Scărişoara

Albac

Park boundary

75

N

Bradt

0   5km
0   5 miles

Roşia Montană
& Alba Iulia

but the establishment of the park had to await the fall of Communism. The park
falls into the territory of three counties: Alba, Cluj and Bihor, the last outside
Transylvania, and the main park administrative office is in Bihor County. But there
are many attractive natural features in the portion of the park within Alba County,
particularly ones associated with limestone geology, including karst relief, deep
gorges and numerous cave systems.

One of the most beautiful areas is the **Padiş Plateau** (Platoul Padiş), a classic karst landscape on the Bihor side of the border with Alba County, with streams disappearing underground and unexpectedly springing up and a distinctive flora, including plants such as the bright yellow globeflower. Accommodation is available on the plateau at the **Cabana Cetăţile Ponorului** (*19 rooms;* m *0740 007 814;* e *cazare@padis.ro;* w *padis.ro;* **$$**), in rooms for either two or four people, most with their own bathroom, which is located on a forest road accessible from the Bihor side of the mountains, via Pietroasa. From the Alba side, however, a hike is required to the *cabana*, with cars able to go no further than the hamlet of Cobleş in Arieşeni Comune. The *cabana* is close to the impressive Cetăţile Ponorului limestone outcrop and cave system.

In an emergency requiring mountain or cave rescue call Salvamont on 0725 826 668, or the standard Romanian emergency number, 112. The main office of the Salvamont organisation covering the Apuseni Mountains is based in Oradea in Bihor County (*Str Sovata 34/A, Oradea;* 0359 436 022; e *salvamontbihor@yahoo. com*; w *salvamontbihor.ro*).

Companies offering hiking holidays in the Apuseni Mountains include **Apuseni Experience** (page 61) and **Johan's Green Mountain** (page 61).

ARIEŞENI The village of Arieşeni (Lepus/Leppusch), scenically located on the Arieşul Mare River in the far western corner of Alba County, is known as a ski resort in winter but also makes a good base for exploring the sights around the Alba side of the Apuseni, with a range of comfortable pensions on offer, strewn out for several kilometres along road DN75. Coming here from Albac to the east, the road passes through the **Albac Gorge** (Cheile Albacului), a striking steep-sided limestone gorge. There are eight **buses** a day eastwards to Câmpeni; three westwards to Oradea.

Where to stay

Pensiunea Casa Motului (13 rooms)
Galbena 468; 0258 779 089; w casamotului.ro.
Located 3km west of Arieşeni on the DN75, this is a well-appointed pension in nice grounds with a brook running through them. A good restaurant, & bicycles available to hire. **$$$**

Pensiunea Vraja Muntelui (14 rooms)
Bubeşti 76A; m 0766 633 300;
e pensiuneavrajamuntelui@yahoo.com. The 'charm of the mountains' is a large modern chalet on the main DN75 through the hamlet of Bubeşti, west of Arieşeni. The restaurant (**$$$**) serves regional dishes like *balmoş*, a purée of cornflour & whey cream. **$$$**

ROŞIA MONTANĂ Roşia Montană (Verespatak/Goldbach) has been a centre of the gold-mining industry since pre-Roman times. The Romans called the area Alburnus Maior; its gold was an important source of wealth for the Roman Empire, with elegant trapezoidal galleries carefully cut with picks and chisels. It was also a major gold-mining centre for the Austro-Hungarian Empire, when explosives were used for the opening of galleries, allowing penetration deeper into the massifs. The artificial ponds which were used in this period to provide the water used to drive the stamp mills, which pounded the rock to extract the ore, are still a feature of the local landscape. The many private companies operating small mines in the area in the early 20th century were abruptly terminated when the industry was nationalised by the Communists in 1948. The workings of the Communist period, comprising both underground galleries and open-cast mining, further altered the landscape. The town is best known in Romania today for an ongoing acrimonious debate about the future of its mining industry.

A great place to get a feel for the history of gold mining in the area is the **Roşia Montană Gold Mining Museum** (Muzeul Mineritului Aurifer de la Roşia Montană) (✳ *Str Minei 1;* ✆ *0258 783 165;* ⊕ *summer 08.00–14.00 daily, winter 08.00–14.00 Mon–Fri; adult/child 8/4RON*). It is situated in the lower part of the village, on the left-hand side of the road as you drive in towards the village centre, and offers no indication that a museum is to be found here. It is instead hidden behind a rather forbidding gate presenting itself as the headquarters of the Roşiamin subsidiary of the Romanian state-owned mining organisation Minvest Deva. But don't let the absence of advertising put you off: thanks in part to a really enthusiastic and knowledgeable guide, this is a first-rate and highly unusual museum.

The highlight here is an escorted visit to the Roman mine galleries below ground here. The gate to enter the Roman mine has 'Alburnus Maior' written above the door. On either side of the door, a plaque in Latin and Romanian sets out the text of tablet XVIII, one of a number of wax tablets on wood which were discovered in the Roman galleries, where they were probably hidden at the time of the Marcomannic invasion of AD167. The original tablets are now found in several European museums; those in Bucharest unfortunately not on public display. The tablets record various details about the mining operations, including labour contracts and the sale of slaves, demonstrating that both forced labour and free waged labour was used. The particular significance of tablet XVIII lies both in a reference to Alburnus Maior and the inclusion of a specific date, 6 February AD131.

THERE'S GOLD IN THEM THAR HILLS

The Roşia Montană Gold Corporation (RMGC) was established in the late 1990s, bringing together a Canadian investor, Gabriel Resources, and the Romanian state-owned mining company Minvest Deva. They proposed a project which would run for some 25 years and develop the gold and silver reserves of Roşia Montană with open-cast mining, and the use of cyanide leach technology to extract the gold from the ground rock. The sludge would be deposited in a tailings pond, requiring the building of a dam in the Corna River valley. The RMGC said that the project would bring jobs to a depressed region and money to the Romanian economy, and that environmental concerns would be mitigated by the use of the latest technology.

The project split both the local community and national opinion. Some saw it as the natural continuation of a tradition of gold mining in the valley that has stretched back for two millennia. Others strongly opposed the project, on a range of grounds. At the forefront of these were environmental concerns. The proposed use of cyanide leaching was particularly controversial, against the backdrop of the Baia Mare cyanide spill in 2000, when a dam holding contaminated waters burst, resulting in considerable damage to downstream ecosystems. There were concerns, too, over the likely impact of the project on sites of cultural significance, and on communities in the valley, and over the level of transparency around the project.

The RMGC began to purchase properties in the area to allow for the commencement of the project. But the opposition was mobilising. A non-governmental organisation, Alburnus Maior (w *rosiamontana.org*), was established in 2000 by a local farmer named Eugen David, bringing together members of the community who had refused to sell their properties to the corporation. This was joined by campaigners such as the Franco-Swiss environmentalist Stephanie Roth. Other local NGOs formed later included the Fundaţia Culturală Roşia Montană,

Entering the mine, you descend 157 steps, and then walk along 40m of vaulted modern gallery to reach the Roman galleries. The latter are truly remarkable. They have been painstakingly dug using picks or hammers and chisel: in places it is possible to make out the chisel marks on the walls. Niches in the walls were used to place ceramic lanterns. And the galleries have a distinctive trapezoidal shape, between 1.8m and 2.5m at the base, narrowing to 1–1.4m at the top. More than 6km of Roman galleries have been identified at Roşia Montană, of which the museum tour gives you just a taste. The tour also takes in part of a modern gallery, cut in the 20th century, with an arched ceiling.

Above ground, there is a collection of equipment showing the development of techniques for extracting the gold. These include stone mortars of the Roman period, as well as two wooden stamp mills, in which a waterwheel turned an axle which dropped heavy wooden beams down onto the rocks; a technique still in use in the area until the mines were nationalised by the Communists in 1948. More modern technologies displayed include a steel stamp mill made in the early 20th century by Fraser and Chalmers of Erith, and a Hungarian ball mill from the 1930s. There is also a lapidarium with Roman votive altars, and inside a fascinating display of photographs of the mining industry in the interwar period, when it was characterised by many small private enterprises, including panning for river gold and rocks being loaded onto panniers carried by horses.

The galleries visited in the museum tour are some of those of the Orlea massif, which is not actually the most important by the scale and duration of mine working.

which has focused on the cultural importance of the area, and Made in Roşia Montană (w *madeinrosiamontana.ro*), which distributes and sells woollen items made by local women in an effort to develop alternative sources of income for this poor community. International NGOs such as the Open Society Institute added their support to the opposition, which mobilised through events such as FânFest, a summer multi-art festival held in the valley. Much was written and filmed about the project, including the documentary film *New Eldorado* by Hungarian director Tibor Kocsis.

The political frictions around the project came to a head in 2013, when the government of then Prime Minister Victor Ponta put draft legislation before parliament which would have allowed the long-delayed project to start by allowing the company the right to use compulsory purchase orders in respect of those local residents who had refused to sell, as well as establishing time limits for the granting of all necessary permits. A series of street protests followed, in Bucharest and across the country, in what was the largest civic movement in Romania since the fall of Communism. The draft legislation proposed by the government was rejected by the Senate on 19 November 2013.

Following this decision, RMGC has taken the case to international arbitration, seeking compensation for the blocking of the project. In January 2017, as one of the last acts of the Culture Minister under the technocratic government of Dacian Cioloş, the Romanian Government submitted to UNESCO a proposal for the listing of Roşia Montană as a World Heritage Site in recognition of its remarkable gold-mining patrimony. But visiting Roşia Montană gives a clear sense that an important challenge for the future will be to rebuild the cohesion of a community that has become bitterly divided by the different positions of its members on the project.

As you drive up into the village, the Cetate massif on your right has been extensively altered by a large Communist-era open-cast mine, developed in the 1970s but now closed. Behind the village the Cârnic massif offers the most comprehensive series of mine workings through an era of two millennia, particularly in the Roman, Austro-Hungarian and Communist periods.

In the main village square, a former pharmacy houses the **Apuseni Gold Exhibition** (Aurul Apusenilor) (*Str Piața 325*), funded by the Roșia Montană Gold Corporation (RMGC). It includes a room of archaeological finds, and another on the history of the mining industry in Roșia Montană, and has a replica of a Roman gallery entrance around the back. It is, however, no longer regularly open. Immediately across the square a very different perspective is offered at the **Fundația Culturală Roșia Montană** (*Str Piața 321;* m *0728 444 941;* w *fundatia-culturala-rosia-montana.com*), one of the NGOs established in opposition to the RMGC project. And a walk round the centre of Roșia Montană gives a very clear sense of a community divided, with many abandoned buildings, sold to the RMGC, and posters and placards both in support of and against the project (see box, pages 272–3).

To reach Roșia Montana by **car**, turn right (signposted) off the Abrud–Câmpeni road (route 74A) at Coasta Henții onto route 742. There is no regular public transport.

AVRAM IANCU The village formerly known as Vidra de Sus (HU: Felsővidra) now bears the name of its most famous citizen, Avram Iancu, who rallied the peasants of the Apuseni Mountains to the Romanian cause in the Revolution of 1848–49 (see box, opposite).

His birthplace, the **Avram Iancu Memorial House** (Casa Memorială Avram Iancu) (m *0755 870 654;* ⊕ *10.00–18.00 Sun & Tue–Fri, 10.00–16.00 Sat; adult/child 6/4RON*), is an early 19th-century building with white walls and a particularly tall, steeply pitched wooden roof typical of the local style. It was opened as a memorial museum back in 1924, on the 100th anniversary of Iancu's birth. King Ferdinand attended the opening. Alongside the two-room house in which he lived, there is a museum with a couple of rooms telling the story of Iancu's life, in Romanian only, in a hagiographic style. It includes a room devoted to local Moț costumes and a large ethnographic display in the basement. There is also a library and a small chapel.

The village of Avram Iancu is also renowned for the annual **Mount Găina Girls' Fair**, one of the most important folk festivals in Romania, which takes place in July, in part in Avram Iancu village itself but mainly on the nearby peak of Muntele Găina ('Hen Mountain'), at an altitude of over 1,400m. The fair developed as an opportunity for girls and boys looking to marry to find potential partners drawn from a pool much larger than their local village. It was well known by the 19th century, and Austrian Emperor Franz Joseph I attended the 1852 event, but it has now lost all traces of its original purpose. The events in the village of Avram Iancu itself are focused around folk music and costume, while up on the mountain proceedings are more like a Romanian version of the Glastonbury Festival, albeit focused on folk music, with visitors camping out, bands performing late into the night and, if it has rained, loads of mud.

To get here, turn westwards off the main DN75 at the small village of Mihoești, just to the west of Câmpeni, crossing immediately over the barrage of a dam, and then following the scenic road for 14km.

SCĂRIȘOARA ICE CAVE Situated right up in the northwest corner of Alba County, deep in the Apuseni mountain forests, the Scărișoara Ice Cave (Peștera Scărișoara)

The reputation of the Moți people of the Apuseni Mountains for determined fighting for the rights of the marginalised ethnic Romanian people when Transylvania lay under Habsburg control is linked in part to the revolt led by Horea, Cloșca and Crișan in 1784, but most firmly to the career and personality of Avram Iancu, born in 1824 in the village which now bears his name.

A lawyer who was working in Târgu Mureș when the Hungarian Revolution broke out in 1848, Iancu was appalled that the Hungarian revolutionaries were opposed to the abolition of the serfdom in which most of the Romanians of Transylvania lived. He began to mobilise the peasants of the Apuseni Mountains against Transylvania becoming part of Hungary, and participated in the Great National Assembly of Romanians in Blaj in May 1848. As Hungary declared its independence, Iancu was in Câmpeni, beginning to organise an army of Moți peasants. At another National Assembly in Blaj in September 1848, the delegates reiterated their opposition to the incorporation of Transylvania into Hungary, and pledged their support for the Austrian emperor. The Austrian military commander in Transylvania, General Anton von Puchner, organised the territory into prefectures and, using terminology drawn from ancient Rome, named Iancu as Prefect of the Auraria Gemina Legion, made up of Moți recruits and based at Câmpeni.

The Austrians were initially no match for the Hungarian forces under Józef Bem, with Iancu and his Moți forces, in their fastness in the Apuseni Mountains, forming the most effective resistance to the Hungarians. Iancu's popular nickname, Crăișorul Munților ('the little king of the mountains'), originates from this period. Russia then joined the fray on the side of the Austrians in April 1849. As the tide gradually turned against the Hungarians, they tried, too late and too half-heartedly, to reach an alliance with the Romanians, with Nicolae Bălcescu as an intermediary. Communist historians, never happy with the idea of Romanian peasant revolutionaries fighting against Hungarian leader Kossuth, who was much praised by Marxists, tended to make much of Bălcescu's meeting in May 1849 with Kossuth, but in truth there was never a real deal struck. When the Hungarian Revolution was defeated, Iancu and his men surrendered their weapons to the Habsburgs. But the Austrians were fearful of Romanian nationalism, and considered Iancu dangerous. He was kept under surveillance and even briefly arrested in 1849 and 1852. Disillusioned in his later years, he died in 1872 and was buried, according to his own wishes, near the tree in Țebea, Hunedoara County, which is said to be the place where in 1784 the revolt of Horea, Cloșca and Crișan started.

(m *0753 470 285*; ⊕ *10.00–18.00 Mon–Sat, 10.00–17.00 Sun; adult/child 11/8RON*) is perhaps the major specific natural attraction within that part of the Apuseni Mountains falling within Transylvania. The cave was already known to travellers in the 19th century: German geographer Adolf Schmidl made a map of it in 1863. It was studied by noted Romanian speleologist Emil Racoviță in the 1920s, and was the first Romanian cave to be designated a national nature monument, in the 1930s. The deposit of ice is believed to be a relic from the late Holocene period. Its preservation since the ice age is a function of the specific topography and ventilation of the cave, though it is gradually melting, having lost about 2m since Racoviță first studied it.

Visitors are taken down in groups. Access is by means of a large swallow hole some 48m deep and 60m wide. You descend a steep staircase, and then enter the cave proper on a wooden boardwalk. In summer be prepared for the marked drop in temperature as you enter the Sala Mare, or Great Room, of the cave, which has at its centre a large block of ice. The temperature here rarely rises much above 0°C. With a volume of more than 70,000m³, this is one of the largest subterranean ice blocks in the world. On the northwestern side of the Sala Mare visitors are able to look out across a second chamber, known as 'The Church', as the impressive ice stalagmites are said to resemble an altar.

The ice cave sits in an impressive location near the hamlet of Ghețari at an altitude of some 1,165m. To get here from the main DN75 road, turn to the north (signposted) at the village of Gârda de Sus. Ghețari is 10km on: the road is good quality, but steep in places and narrow throughout, which can lead to some excitement if you encounter a tour bus coming the other way. Note that the village of Scărișoara, which sits on the DN75 some 4km east of Gârda de Sus, is nowhere near the cave. Car parking in Ghețari is charged at 5RON. There is also a hiking trail to Ghețari from Arieșeni marked with red triangles, which takes at least 4 hours.

From the car park a path leads 600m to the cave entrance, punctuated by little wooden chalets at which Moț-style thick bilberry or cheese pancakes are sold. Other vendors in summer sell plastic cups filled with forest fruits, plastic bottles of pine syrup, and small versions of the *tulnic* horn of the Apuseni Mountains, which look and sound like the local equivalent of a *vuvuzela*.

HOREA Formerly named Arada, the village of Horea (Arada/Arroden), was given a Communist-era rebranding in 1968 to honour its most famous son, Vasile Ursu Nicola, better known as Horea, one of the leaders of the 1784 Transylvanian revolt, along with Cloșca and Crișan. Horea became the voice of the exploited and politically marginalised ethnic Romanian peasantry in a Transylvania ruled by the Habsburgs: the peasants' uprising he led was quickly put down, and Horea executed, the revolt serving as an early indication of a European revolutionary sentiment that was to erupt in France just five years later.

Horea's birthplace actually lies in the hamlet of Fericet, in a remote but beautiful setting above the village. A signposted 3km track takes you there (navigable with a 4x4 in dry weather), and there is also a footpath from Horea village. The house in which Horea was born no longer exists, but a stone cross was erected on the spot in the 1930s. Nearby is the small wooden **Horea Memorial House** (Casa Memorială Horea) with two rooms, one holding ethnographic items, the other a display in Romanian about Horea and his legacy. Ask at the house below the museum for the key. Across the track is a distinguished-looking ash tree said to have been planted by Horea himself.

Horea lies on the DN1R road which connects Albac in Alba County with Huedin in Cluj County to the north. It is an attractive, winding road through forests, which is being marketed as the **Transursoaia Highway**, punctuated by small villages focused on wood processing and a dozen small springs *en route*, with little wooden shrines at each and glasses provided for travellers wishing to try the water.

Where to stay Under construction at the time of research, **Căsuța din Povești** (*3 rooms; Horea no 23;* m *0765 060 525;* $) is a fairytale house with a tall thatched roof and should offer the intriguing prospect of a restaurant offering local dishes and traditional basic accommodation on straw mattresses.

LUPȘA The village of Lupșa (Nagylupsa/Wolfsdorf) lies 16km east of Câmpeni on the main DN75 road towards Turda. It is worth stopping at the **Pamfil Albu**

Ethnography Museum (Muzeul Etnografic Pamfil Albu) (*Str Principală 7*; m *0743 041 939;* ◔ *09.00–13.00 & 14.00–18.00 Tue–Sun; adult 4RON*) on the main road, housing the extensive ethnographic collection of local teacher Pamfil Albu, and now run by his daughter, whose knowledgeable commentaries about the items in the collection provide much of the charm of the place. Displays of tools are organised by task, from beekeeping to hunting, and there is a display upstairs related to the local mining industry. A second building houses material related to local folk traditions, from weddings to carol singing, and there is a copy of a flag taken by local delegates to the Great National Assembly meeting in Alba Iulia on 1 December 1918 (the original was apparently purloined by the Securitate in the Communist period).

SUB PIATRĂ The small village of Sub Piatră ('Under the Rock') sits under the limestone heights of the Piatra Bedeleului. In those mountains, south of the village, is the newly developed resort complex of Raven's Nest, one of the most remote tourism offerings in Transylvania in a spectacularly beautiful setting.

To get to Raven's Nest, take the turning off the DN75 signposted for Sub Piatră at the village of Sălciua de Jos. Head south, past Sub Piatră village, as the road narrows and becomes unpaved and increasingly difficult, until you pass a sign which rather worryingly tells you that no motor vehicles are permitted. Raven's Nest is 500m further on.

⌂ **Where to stay and eat** Located 950m up in the Trascău range within the Apuseni, **Raven's Nest** (✱ *10 dbl, 1 apt;* ☏ *0374 050 255;* e *contact@ravensnest.eu;* w *ravensnest.eu;* **$$$**) is an attractive new complex surrounded by a latticed hazel fence. Its rooms are in three delightfully restored traditional houses, with *prix-fixe* meals based on good local cooking served in the adjacent Dragon's Tavern. There are two belvederes laid out with relaxing seating offering great Apuseni panoramas. Actually getting to the place is not for the faint-hearted, and it is closed in winter.

HEADING NORTH FROM ALBA IULIA

BLAJ Blaj (Balázsfalva/Blasendorf), a small city of some 20,000 people, now feels decidedly off the beaten track, but it has two related claims to importance, as a key centre of the Greco-Catholic Church and a centre for the development of a Romanian national consciousness in the 18th and 19th centuries.

Blaj owes its importance to Inocenţiu Micu-Klein, Bishop of the Greco-Catholic Church, who in 1737 moved the seat of the bishopric from Făgăraş to Blaj, which was until that time a small aristocratic estate. Micu-Klein laid out the foundations of a new city, including a Greco-Catholic cathedral, whose foundation stone was laid in 1741. The **Holy Trinity Cathedral** (Catedrala Sfânta Treime) sits in Piaţa 1848, the park-filled square which marks the centre of town. With its façade flanked by two square-based towers, its external appearance is that of a Catholic church, but the Baroque interior includes a glorious iconostasis, considered one of the loveliest in Romania. There is also a pulpit, from where on 14 May 1848 the Vice-President of the Blaj Assembly, Simion Bărnuţiu, delivered the speech which essentially set out the manifesto of the revolutionary movement of Transylvanian Romanians. To the right-hand side of the iconostasis, the simple marble tomb is that of Micu-Klein, his remains having been returned in 1997 from Rome, where he had spent his final years in exile, following conflict with the Habsburgs over his calls for greater rights for the Romanians of Transylvania. The opposite tomb is that of Cardinal Alexandru Todea, a Greco-Catholic bishop who was imprisoned during the Communist regime and died in 2002.

In the two-storey building immediately to the right of the cathedral, the first public school in the country to teach in the Romanian language was established in 1754. The parallel building to the left of the cathedral is the Greco-Catholic Theology Faculty of the Babeş-Bolyai University. A plaque records that poet Mihai Eminescu stayed here during his visit to Blaj in 1866, when he came to learn more about the town so closely associated with Romanian nationalism. In the **Piaţa 1848 Park** immediately in front is a statue of Eminescu recalling his visit and the 'Little Rome' epithet given to the town by the poet. Other statues in the park include a particularly wild-eyed rendering of Bărnuţiu.

Just beyond the southwest corner of the square, down Strada Petru Pavel Aron, is the **Archbishop's Castle**. Also known as the Apafi Castle, this is the oldest building in the town and is now the residence of the Cardinal of the Greco-Catholic Church of Romania.

One block to the north of Piaţa 1848 is the town's main street, Bulevardul Republicii, along which banks, shops and services are congregated. Just off this is the **Avram Iancu Park**, whose main sight is a 600-year-old oak tree surrounded by a small fence. This is known as *Avram Iancu's Oak*, as it seems that the Romanian revolutionary leader was a friend of the then Metropolitan of the Greco-Catholic Church, Alexandru Sterca-Şuluţiu, and the two would sit for hours under the shade of the tree, talking politics. There is a new **tourist information office** (*0358 100 356;* e *blajcnipt@yahoo.com;* w *viziteazablajul.ro;* ⊕ *08.00–16.00 Mon–Fri*) in a pavilion in the park.

The **History Museum** (Muzeul de Istorie) (*Str Dr Vasile Suciu 28;* m *0756 089 207;* ⊕ *08.00–16.00 Mon–Fri admission free*), named after ethnic Romanian historian Augustin Bunea, lies a couple of blocks to the north. It covers archaeology, history, ethnography and modern art, and includes material (in Romanian only) on the important role played by Blaj in the development of the movement known as the Transylvanian School (Şcoala Ardeleană) in promoting the culture and history of the Romanians of Transylvania, emphasising their Latin origins and promoting a Latin-based alphabet.

Another worthwhile place to visit lies just to the east of the town centre, adjacent to the main market (Piaţa Mare). The **Liberty Plain** (Câmpia Libertăţii) is the site of the Blaj Assembly of May 1848, a major gathering of the Romanians of Transylvania. A second assembly was held here in September of the same year. The place is today marked by a large park, centred on a decidedly Communist-era monument named *Gloria*, in which three abstract female figures holding up laurel branches stand in front of a large gate. Around the monument are 26 bronze busts depicting the major figures of the Romanian movement. Of these, 24 are original, but those of the Orthodox and Greco-Catholic bishops Andrei Şaguna and Ioan Lemeni were added after the fall of Communism, which had sought to downplay the role of the Church in the campaigns of the Romanians of Transylvania to secure their rights.

Blaj is 40km northeast of Alba Iulia. By **car**, head north out of Alba Iulia on route DN1 (E81) towards Teiuş and Turda, turning right onto the DN14B for Blaj at Teiuş. There are several **buses** daily from Alba Iulia to Blaj (*1hr 10mins*). **Train** connections from Blaj include Sighişoara (*2hrs*), Cluj-Napoca (*2½hrs*) and Alba Iulia (*50mins*).

🏠 **Where to stay** The best place to stay amid a decidedly short list of options in Blaj is probably **Pensiune Montana Popa** (*17 rooms; B-dul Republicii 4;* ☎ *0258 710 489;*

e *pensiune@montanapopa.ro;* **w** *montanapopa.ro;* **$$**), which is functional, clean and central.

AIUD Aiud (Nagyenyed/Strassburg am Mieresch) is a town of some 20,000 people, centred on an attractive citadel. It is known, *inter alia*, for the 'Wedge of Aiud', an aluminium wedge found next to some mastodon bones during construction work outside the town in 1974. UFO enthusiasts have speculated that the wedge may be part of an alien spaceship; others argue that it is just a tooth from a modern excavator bucket. It is not on display to the public, and even its location is not publicised. Aiud was also the birthplace, in 1841, of the remarkable Florence Baker, a Székely girl, most of whose family was killed in the Hungarian Revolution of 1848–49, and who was destined to be sold as a slave to the local *pasha* in Vidin in the then Ottoman Empire, but was instead abducted by the British explorer Samuel Baker, a middle-aged widower. He took her with him to Africa, where he was attempting to find the source of the Nile, and ended up marrying her.

In Romanian, the name of Aiud is more often associated with its prison, which held many political detainees both during the Antonescu regime in World War II and the subsequent Communist one.

Aiud Citadel (Cetatea Aiudului) is located in the centre of town. It dates from the 14th century, though was extended in the 16th and 17th, and is an irregular pentagon in form with nine towers, each of which was the responsibility of a different guild of the town. The citadel houses two churches: the taller of the two, with a square tower topped with a spire, is the **Reformed Church** (Biserica Reformată), built in a late Gothic style at the end of the 15th century. The squatter church next to it is the **Lutheran Church** (Biserica Luterană), which dates from the 19th century.

The grand-looking pale-yellow three-storey building over the road from the fortress is **Bethlen Gábor College** (Colegiul Naţional Bethlen Gábor) (*Str Bethlen Gábor 1;* ****0258 861 947; **w** *bethlengabor.ro*), which was established in Alba Iulia in 1622 by Gabriel Bethlen (Bethlen Gábor in Hungarian), the then Prince of Transylvania. It moved to Aiud in 1662. Badly damaged by Austrian troops in 1704, it was rebuilt with the help of £11,000 raised by Christians in the United Kingdom. It is still a school today. There is a small Museum of Natural Sciences on the first floor (⊕ *08.00–16.00 Tue–Fri, 09.00–13.00 Sat/Sun*), which claims to be the oldest in Romania, dating from 1720.

Aiud lies on the main route 1 (E81) between Alba Iulia and Turda, about 32km north of the former. There are frequent **buses** to Alba Iulia (*45mins*), Turda (*30mins*) and Cluj-Napoca (*1hr 20mins*). The **railway** station is east of the town centre. Aiud is on a main line and is well connected, including to Cluj-Napoca (*around 2hrs*), Alba Iulia (*from 30mins*), Sighişoara (*2hrs*) and Deva (*1hr 40mins*).

RÂMEŢ The **Romanian Orthodox Râmeţ Monastery** (Mănăstirea Râmeţ) (****0258 880 111; **e** *manastirearimet@gmail.com*) is one of the largest in Transylvania, as home to a community of more than 90 nuns. It has an impressive location at the base of a steep mountain range. Unusually among the historic monasteries of Romania, it was not established by a grand princely benefactor but by a group of hermitic monks: indeed, the name Râmeţ has its origins in the Romanian word for 'hermit'. The **old church** here, with a square-based tower and vaulted ceiling, contains some wall paintings of considerable age. An inscription on one of these, covering part of the arch in the centre of the church and protected by a sheet of glass, identifies the artist as one Mihu from Crişul Alb, the year as 1377, and refers to the founder of the monastery as Archbishop Ghelasie. Other paintings are of a later date, including some sponsored by Michael the Brave in 1600.

The monastery was one of the targets of the Austrian campaigns against the Romanian Orthodox Church in the late 18th century, and was damaged in 1762 by the forces of General Adolf von Buccow. Following suspicions that the monastery had favoured the peasants' revolt of Horea, Cloșca and Crișan in 1784, it was dissolved at the order of the Austrians. The church continued to function, but as an ordinary parish church, and a school was set up here. It became a monastery again only in 1940. Fifteen years later its community of monks was replaced by one of nuns. The monastery was dissolved again in 1959, this time by the Communist authorities, the nuns moving to the nearby town of Aiud where they turned their activities to carpet making. Ten years later they were allowed to return. In 1982, work begun on the construction of a **new church** close to the old one, built in a style that combines elements of the traditional church architecture of the three main Romanian regions of Wallachia, Moldavia and Transylvania. A silver box here contains relics of Archbishop Ghelasie, who was canonised in 1992.

Next to the old church, in the former school building, is a small **museum** (*1RON*), with a collection of icons on both wood and glass and some ethnographic exhibits.

The monastery is accessed from the village of Teiuș, which lies on the E81 highway between Alba Iulia and Aiud. It lies 18km from Teiuș (signposted to the monastery) on a road running along the attractive Geoagiu River valley. Don't follow the road signposted simply to 'Râmeț' from Aiud, which takes you to the village of that name on a hilltop far above the monastery.

UNIREA Unirea (Felvinc/Oberwinz) is a village of a little under 4,000 people, today mostly ethnic Romanian, though with an appreciable Hungarian minority, which historically was the capital of a community of Székelys living in the Arieş River valley (Aranyos in Hungarian), in an administrative area known as the Aranyosszék (Scaunul Arieşului in Romanian). Székelys were granted land in this area, which lies far to the west of the main Székely communities in Harghita, Covasna and Mureş counties, as a reward for their bravery in battles against the Tatars, and settled here around 1270, much later than the Székely settlements further east.

Unirea lies directly on the main E81 between Aiud (16km to the south) and Turda (20km to the north). Unirea is a stop for **buses** running between Aiud (*20mins from Unirea*) and Turda (*15mins*).

RIMETEA Rimetea (Torockó/Eisenmarkt) is a spiffy village of white-painted houses with green shutters, standing at the foot of the dramatic mountain known as the Piatra Secului (HU: Székelykő), or Székely Stone. They say the sun rises twice in Rimetea because it appears briefly at dawn before disappearing behind the Székely Stone and reappearing later over the village. A blue cross footpath runs from the village to the peak, at 1,129m. Also signposted from the centre of the village is a watermill (*moară de apă*) which dates from 1752.

The harmony of the buildings in the historic village, most of whose inhabitants are ethnic Hungarians, owes much to the Rimetea Heritage Conservation Project, supported by the Transylvania Trust Foundation, in which house owners receive a conservation grant provided that work on their properties is carried out according to sound conservation practices. The village originally developed as an iron-mining centre, but is now focused on tourism, especially from Hungary.

There is a four-room **Ethnographic Museum** (Muzeul Etnografic) (✆ *0258 768 001*; ⊕ *09.00–17.00 Tue–Sun; adult/child 4/2RON*), housed in the large two-storey white-painted building in the centre of town, which is also home to the mayor's office. The museum is located at the back of the building, up the stairs and along the balcony. Exhibits include the distinctive local dress, which includes Saxon, Székely and Magyar influences.

Four kilometres to the south, on the Aiud road, the neighbouring village of Colţeşti has a ruined **fortress**, known both as Cetatea Colţeşti and Cetatea Trascăului, on a rocky outcrop above the settlement. It was built at the end of the 13th century by the head of the Thorotzskay family, and largely destroyed by Austrian forces at the start of the 18th. It offers good views across to the Piatra Secului.

Rimetea is also known for the traditional **Înmormântarea Fărşangului** festival (HU: Farsangtemetés Torockón) held at the beginning of March. It is a festival dedicated to the symbolic burial of winter, and looking forward to the spring ahead, and involves a procession around the village of young people in traditional costume, carrying a white coffin. By tradition, all the usual rules of the village are suspended on festival day, so it can turn quite raucous.

Getting to Rimetea from Turda, take the DN75 eastwards towards Câmpeni, turning left after 20km at Buru onto a more minor road signposted for Aiud. Rimetea is 8km on. The road continues on to Aiud 26km further on, through the impressive gorge known as the **Cheile Vălişoarei**. There are several **buses** a day to Aiud (*1hr*) on weekdays, but only one on Sundays.

🏠 **Where to stay and eat** There are numerous guesthouses in the village, though most are firmly targeted at the Hungarian market. The agency **Alpin Tour** (*House*

39; \0258 861 902; **m** *0724 522 343*) offers accommodation with local families, either on a room-only basis (**$**) or including home-cooked meals.

🏠 **Casa Demeter** (3 rooms) House 123; **m** 0723 873 877; **w** demeterpanzio.ro. Sympathetically furnished guesthouse, though bathrooms are not en suite. Good home-cooked food is served at their sister guesthouse, the Pensiunea Dr Demeter Bela, 250m away. **$$$** (HB)

✳🏠 **Conacul Secuiesc** (23 rooms) House 77, Colțești; \0258 768 277; **m** 0730 210 768; **e** office@conaculsecuiesc.ro; **w** conaculsecuiesc.ro. Located in the neighbouring village of Colțești, this is a modern building in the style of a traditional manor house, in a landscaped garden looking towards the Piatra Secului. Rooms have Székely-style hand-painted furniture, & the good restaurant (**$$$**) serves both Hungarian & Romanian dishes. Bicycles are available for rent. **$$**

☕ **László's Coffee Shop** House 36; **m** 0748 421 346; **w** facebook.com/LaszlosCoffeeShop; 🕐 09.00–21.00 daily, closed during winter. An unexpectedly funky café in the heart of the village, helping to address the paucity of places to eat & drink in Rimetea, with coffee, shakes & ice cream. **$**

10

Cluj County

Cluj-Napoca is the largest city in Transylvania, but one whose considerable attractions are all too often rather overlooked by tourists to the region in favour of the beautiful medieval cores of Sibiu, Braşov and Sighişoara. Yet the city boasts some of the finest museums in the region, a rich history dating to Dacian times, important buildings such as the Gothic St Michael's Church, and the largest student population in the region, fuelling a lively cultural scene whose highlights include Romania's most important film festival and the Untold music festival in summer. With a rapidly developing IT industry, Cluj-Napoca has a prosperous feel and provides a great base for exploring the surrounding countryside. With the largest airport in Transylvania, the city is also an important point of entry for the wider region.

The surrounding Cluj County is geographically varied, with the land rising in the south and west into the Apuseni Mountains, while to the east is the undulating terrain of the Transylvanian Plain, known in Romanian as the Câmpia Transilvaniei and in Hungarian as the Mezőség. More undulating terrain to the west of Cluj-Napoca marks the region known in Romanian as Ţara Călate and in Hungarian as Kalotaszeg.

The county is a relatively ethnically mixed one: the majority of the population is ethnic Romanian, but ethnic Hungarians make up around 20% of the inhabitants. Both the Câmpia Transilvaniei and Ţara Călate areas are known in particular for their strong folk traditions, with villages like Sic famous for their retention of ethnic Hungarian folk cultures, while Pălatca is renowned for the fine quality of its mainly Roma musicians.

Many of the county's attractions, like the Baroque palace at Bonţida, are easy day trips from Cluj-Napoca, but other parts of the area, such as the section of the Apuseni Mountains falling within Cluj County, reward longer stays.

CLUJ-NAPOCA   *Telephone code 0264, sometimes 0364*

'There is an air of pride about Cluj', wrote Walter Starkie in 1929. Cluj-Napoca (Kolozsvár/Klausenburg) is the largest city in the region, attracting tourists with the slogan 'the heart of Transylvania'. At first glance, Cluj-Napoca is not as attractive as the two main southern Transylvanian cities of Braşov and Sibiu, but it was the Hungarian provincial capital, known to the Magyars as Kolozsvár during the Austro-Hungarian Empire, and is the second-largest city in all Romania after Bucharest. It does not have an intact medieval Old Town heart like those in Sibiu, Sighişoara or Mediaş, but its Baroque and Art Nouveau façades are fine, it has a good range of places to eat and stay, offers an increasingly lively cultural programme, is one of the main centres in Romania for modern art and design, and its large university population, centred on the Babeş-Bolyai University, gives the place a youthful buzz. The city could easily entertain you for several days. Driving in Cluj-Napoca is not fun, but hiring a car there is easy and there are many small villages, lakes and mountains in the vicinity that are best explored with your own wheels.

HISTORY Cluj-Napoca can trace its origins back to at least the 2nd century AD, when the Dacian settlement 'Napuca' was first mentioned. After the Romans conquered Dacia, they renamed the place 'Napoca' and gave it the title of 'municipium' in AD124. The place was evacuated by the Romans in AD274, and then disappeared from the history books for close to a millennium.

It returned as part of the Kingdom of Hungary, when in the 12th century the Hungarian kings encouraged German settlers to come and develop a town here, which the Germans called 'Klausenburg', on the site of the old Roman municipium. In 12th-century documents the place was being referred to as 'Castrum Clus', meaning 'closed citadel', and from this the name Cluj seems to have developed.

In the 16th century, Cluj was an important centre of the Reformation in Transylvania. It was a major centre for Hungarian cultural life in the region before World War I, and the city's ethnic Hungarian minority still puts on a lively programme of cultural events.

In 1974, Ceaușescu added 'Napoca' to Cluj's name to remind everyone of the city's Daco-Roman origins, though everyone simply refers to the place as Cluj. Gheorghe Funar, a politician of the now-defunct Romanian National Unity Party (PUNR), was mayor of the city from 1992 to 2004, pursuing a controversially nationalistic agenda that fuelled frictions with the Hungarian minority. The current mayor, former prime minister Emil Boc, has pursued a more inclusive policy, though there is continued cultural haggling between Romanian and Hungarian historians over Cluj's most famous son, Matthias Corvinus, known as Matei Corvin in Romanian and Hunyadi Mátyás in Hungarian. As with his father Ioan de Hunedoara/Hunyadi János (see box, pages 250–1), both countries are eager to claim him as their own.

GETTING THERE, AWAY AND AROUND

By air Avram Iancu International Airport Cluj (CLJ) (*Str Traian Vuia 149*; \0264 307 500; e *office@airportcluj.ro*; w *airportcluj.ro*) is 8km east of the city centre on the E576 towards Bistrița. **Bus** routes 5 and 8 run from the airport to Piața Mihai Viteazul in the centre at 10-minute intervals on weekdays and every 20 minutes at weekends (and note that the last bus on the weekend leaves the airport shortly before 21.00). Bus tickets (*4RON*) are sold at the kiosk next to the bus stop. Don't forget to validate your ticket on the bus. There are also plenty of waiting **taxis** outside. As the airport is so close to the city, it should not cost more than around 20–25RON to get to the centre, but some taxi drivers will try to persuade obviously foreign visitors to pre-agree an inflated price for the journey. Your best course is to insist that they use their meter. There is also a range of **car-rental** offices in the Arrivals hall. There are ATMs at both the Arrivals and Departures halls, and a Banca Transilvania exchange office at the Departures terminal (⊕ *08.00–19.00 daily*).

There are frequent flights between Cluj and Bucharest with **Tarom** (w *tarom.ro*). The Hungarian low-cost carrier **Wizz Air** (w *wizzair.com*) also operates this route, as well as to a wide range of destinations across Europe, including London Luton and Doncaster Sheffield in the UK. **Blue Air** (w *blueairweb.com*) has domestic services to Bucharest, Constanța, Iași and Timișoara, as well as flights to London Luton, Birmingham, Liverpool and Dublin. **Lufthansa** (w *lufthansa.com*) runs several flights a day between Cluj and Munich, and there are flights a few times a week to Warsaw with **LOT** (w *lot.com*) and Istanbul with **Turkish Airlines** (w *turkishairlines. com*). It is well worth looking at flight options direct to Cluj before assuming that your Transylvanian holiday needs to involve a transit through Bucharest.

By rail The **railway station** [289 C1] (*Str Garii 1–3*; \0264 433 647; m 0731 990 518) is 20 minutes' walk north of the centre, over the Someș River and along Strada Horea.

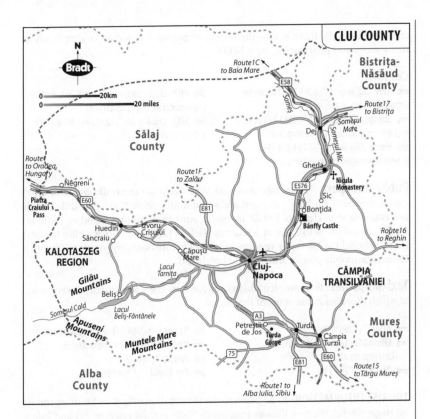

The fastest inter-city **trains** connect Cluj-Napoca with Bucharest (*9hrs*), Brașov (*5½hrs*), Mediaș (*3hrs*), Sighișoara (*3½hrs*), Oradea (*2½hrs*), Arad (*4½hrs*) and Timișoara (*5hrs*). A wide range of other domestic destinations are served too, albeit mostly on slower trains. There are also several international trains to and from Budapest (*at least 7hrs*).

By bus The main **bus station** [289 C1] (*Str Giordano Bruno 1–3;* \0264 455 249; w *autogarabeta-cluj.ro*) is 5 minutes' walk further northwest from the railway station. Destinations include Alba Iulia (*2hrs*), Brașov (*5hrs, but there are also faster minibuses, 4hrs, departing from outside the railway station, which also stop in Târgu Mureș & Sighișoara*), Bistrița (*2½hrs*), Bucharest (*8½hrs*), Reghin (*3hrs*), Sibiu (*from 3½hrs*) and Târgu Mureș (*2½hrs*). There are also frequent services to Budapest.

The **Eurolines bus station** [289 C1], for Eurolines international services, is at Cluj Autogara Sens Vest (*Str Fabricii 105;* \0364 730 238; e *cluj.autogara@eurolines.ro*; w *eurolines.ro*).

By car European highways E60, E81 and E576 all meet in Cluj-Napoca, and the city will also be served by the A3 motorway, currently under construction but long delayed, which will eventually link Bucharest with Transylvania and connect onwards to the M4 motorway in Hungary.

In the city centre **parking** spaces are metred (*1RON for 30mins; cheaper outside the centre*), but the credit card facility on the meters often does not work. Since meters don't take notes, this often requires an infuriatingly large number of 50 bani coins. Fortunately, there is also the option of buying a one-day parking ticket at many shops and pharmacies, for 9.5RON.

Car hire

🚗 **Avis** Cluj airport; ☎0264 274 113; e cluj.
airport@avis.ro; w avis.ro
🚗 **Europcar** Cluj airport; ☎0264 274 278;
e cluj@europcar.com.ro; w europcar.ro
🚗 **Hertz** Cluj airport; ☎0264 274 165;
e reservations@hertz.ro; w hertz.ro

🚗 **PHP** Cluj airport; m 0747 288 200; e office@
phprentacar.ro; w phprentacar.ro
🚗 **SIXT** Cluj airport; ☎0264 274 046; e cluj@
sixt.ro; w sixt.ro

Public transport

Several **bus** (*autobuz*), **tram** (*tramvai*) and **trolleybus** (*troleibuz*) routes connect Cluj-Napoca's main areas and tourist attractions. Schedule details are available at w ctpcj.ro. Public transport runs from around 05.00 to 23.00 on weekdays and 06.00 to 22.00 at weekends. Tickets (*2RON for 1 trip within the city*) must be bought at kiosks or vending machines before boarding, or via SMS with a Romanian mobile phone, and validated on board.

Taxi companies

Taxis are plentiful in Cluj-Napoca. There are numerous companies, of which those below are some of the largest.

🚕 **Atlas** ☎0264 969
🚕 **Clima&Confort** ☎0264 943;
w climasiconfortcluj.ro
🚕 **Diesel** ☎0264 946

🚕 **Napoca** ☎0264 953; w taxipronapoca.ro
🚕 **Nova** ☎0264 949; w nova-taxi.ro
🚕 **Pritax** ☎0264 942
🚕 **Pro Rapid** ☎0264 948

TOURIST INFORMATION

In addition to the information offices and tour operators on pages 58–62, the free listings magazines Şapte Seri (w sapteseri.ro) and Zile şi Nopţi (w zilesinopti.ro) have details of forthcoming events and activities. They can be picked up in many hotels and bars.

🛈 **Tourist information office** [289 D3]
Bulevardul Eroilor 6–8; ☎0264 452 244;
w visitclujnapoca.ro; ⏰ 08.30–20.00 Mon–Fri,
10.00–18.00 Sat/Sun. Helpful central office run by
the city council.
🛈 **Cluj National Tourism Information
Centre** [289 C3] Str Memorandumului 21; ☎0264
450 410; e contact@cniptcluj.ro; w clujtourism.ro;
⏰ May–Sep 09.00–19.00 Mon–Fri, 09.00–17.00

Sat/Sun, Oct–Apr 09.00–17.00 daily. Based in the Ethnographic Museum, this is an office run by the Cluj County administration, & includes information about the wider county as well as the city.
Cluj Guided Tours m 0745 043 025;
e contact@clujguidedtours.ro. Offers a free tour in English nightly at 18.00, departing from the Matthias Corvinus statue. Donation expected.

🏠 WHERE TO STAY *Map, pages 288–9*

Cluj-Napoca offers a reasonably good range of accommodation covering all price categories, but book well in advance if you are coming during one of the city's flagship events, such as the Untold Festival, in order to get your first choice.

🏠 **City Plaza** [289 C3] (42 dbl) Str
Sindicatelor 9–13; ☎0264 450 101; e contact@
cityhotels.ro; w cityhotels.ro. Upmarket
(if somewhat bland) 5-star business hotel
with the good Marco Polo Restaurant

(⏰ *07.00–10.30 & noon–23.00 daily*;
$$$), bar & lounge & conference facilities.
$$$$$
🏠 **Hotel Beyfin** [289 E2] (28 dbl, 3 suites)
Piaţa Avram Iancu 3; ☎0264 403 804; e info@

hotelbeyfin.com; w hotelbeyfin.com. Centrally located business hotel with a rooftop terrace looking across to the Orthodox cathedral. **$$$$**

🏠 **Hotel Capitolina City Chic** [289 C5] (24 rooms) Str Victor Babes 35; ☎ 0264 450 490; e office@hotel-capitolina.ro; w hotel-capitolina. ro. Up quite a steep hill on the edge of the city centre, but the rooms are designed with a creative touch. It's part of the same group as the Lol et Lola & Apartamente Hotel Gutinului. The Capitolina City Chic also serves as the reception & point of contact for the latter, a 10min walk away at Str Gutinului 5, an apartment block in a quiet location that is a good option for longer stays. **$$$$**

🏠 **Hotel Fullton** [289 D2] (17 dbl, 2 suites) Str Sextil Pușcariu 10; m 0729 999 444; e office@ hotelfullton.ro; w hotelfullton.ro. The rooms are nothing special, but the location is great, in the old part of the centre. Offers both 3-star & cheaper 2-star-graded rooms. **$$$**

🏠 **Hotel Lol et Lola** [289 C5] (20 rooms) Str Neagră 9; ☎ 0264 450 498; e office@loletlolahotel. ro; w loletlolahotel.ro. Self-consciously funky, with décor verging at times on the psychedelic, but in a quiet spot with its own parking. Formerly the Hotel Capitol. **$$$**

🏠 **Hotel Melody Central** [289 D2] (25 rooms) Piața Unirii 29; ☎ 0264 597 465; e rezervari@centralmelody.com; w centralmelody. com. Great central location, with some rooms (for which a small supplement is payable) looking straight across to St Michael's Church. The downsides are that it can be noisy & the rooms are rather shabby. **$$$**

🏠 **Retro Hostel** [289 D4] (4 dbl, 3 sgl, 2 trpl, dorms) Str Potaissa 11–13; ☎ 0264 450 452; e retro@retro.ro; w retro.ro. Clean, friendly, popular budget accommodation just 500m from Babeș-Bolyai University on a quiet street. **$**

✗ WHERE TO EAT AND DRINK   *Map, pages 288–9*

Cluj-Napoca has one of the best ranges of restaurants in Romania. The large student population has nurtured some clusters of bars and restaurants specifically geared to student tastes and budgets, notably Strada Piezișă to the east of the centre. Overall there's a much larger range of cuisines on offer than in most Transylvanian towns and cities. Cluj's own contribution to international cuisine is the meat and cabbage dish *varză a la Cluj*, widely available in the more traditional places around town.

✗ **Boema** [289 E2] Str Iuliu Maniu 34; m 0734 414 414; ⊕ 11.00–02.00 daily. Entered through a cobbled arched gateway, you eat either on a shaded summer terrace or in the restaurant upstairs. Good international menu. **$$$$**

✗ **Chios Restaurant** [288 A3] Parcul Central; m 0753 059 359; w chios.ro; ⊕ noon–midnight daily. Right in the middle of the boating lake in the central park, this is a self-consciously trendy spot with a lounge bar on one side of the building & the Carrousel by Chios Restaurant on the other. International menu. There is also a (cheaper) snack bar, wittily called Chioșc. **$$$$**

✗ **Casa Ardeleană** [289 D2] Sora Shopping Centre, B-dul 21 Decembrie 1989 5; ☎ 0264 439 451; ⊕ noon–midnight daily. In the unpromising setting of the basement of an ugly shopping centre, opposite a slot-machine arcade, this restaurant is decked out in rustic style & offers hearty, traditional Romanian cuisine. Varză a la Cluj is among the offerings on the menu.

✗ **Casa Vikingilor** [288 A5] Str Hașdeu 70; ☎ 0264 236 306; w casavikingilor.ro; ⊕ 24hrs. Pub & student-oriented restaurant, serving such delights as a metre-long sausage. **$$$**

✗ **Indigo** [288 A5] Str Piezișă 10; ☎ 0364 142 306; w indigorestaurant.ro; ⊕ noon–midnight daily. Good Indian restaurant with some fine vegetarian curries, in a place with purplish décor. **$$$**

✗ **Livada** [288 B4] Str Clinicilor 14; m 0722 111 115; w restaurantlivada.ro; ⊕ 09.00–23.30 Mon–Sat, noon–23.30 Sun. Eclectic international & Romanian menu at a restaurant noted for a large, shady terrace befitting a restaurant named 'Orchard'. Just west of the city centre. **$$$**

✗ **Roata** [289 C2] Str Al Ciurea 6; ☎ 0264 592 022; e rezervari@restaurant-roata.ro; ⊕ noon–23.00 daily. Hearty traditional Romanian & Transylvanian dishes, with a terrace. **$$$**

CLUJ-NAPOCA

For listings, see pages 286–8

⊖ Where to stay

1	Apartamente Hotel	
	Gutinului	D5
2	Beyfin	E2
3	Capitolina City Chic	C5
4	City Plaza	C3
5	Fullton	D2
6	Lol et Lola	C5
7	Melody Central	D2
8	Retro Hostel	D4

❌ Where to eat and drink

9	Boema	E2
10	Casa Ardeleană	D2
11	Casa Vikingilor	A5
12	Chios	A3
13	Demmers Teehaus	D3
14	Dolce Vita	A5
15	Francesca	C2
16	Fresh Healthy Drink Bar	E2
17	Indigo	A5
18	Livada	B4
19	Păstăioase	E3
20	Pergola Terasa	B1
21	Roata	C2

NOTE For key to accommodation and eating and drinking, see left

✕ Dolce Vita [288 A5] Str Piezişă 24; ✆ 0264 590 141; ⏰ 11.00–01.00 daily. Str Piezişă is a lively student area during term time & can be pretty quiet outside it. This is a reasonable pizzeria at its heart. $$

✱ ✕ Păstăioase [289 E3] B-dul Eroilor 37; ⏰ 10.00–22.00 daily. This is a *vărzărie*, a restaurant specialised in cabbage dishes, particularly *varză a la Cluj*. Simply furnished & cheap, it recalls earlier times. $

⊟ Demmers Teehaus [289 D3] Piaţa Unirii 9; m 0731 307 897; w demmer.ro; ⏰ 10.00–20.00 daily. Nicely sited for a sightseeing break, this shop-cum-café offers an enormous range of teas. $

⊟ Francesca [289 C2] Piaţa Muzeului 6; m 0756 632 444; e cafeneauafrancesca@gmail. com; ⏰ 08.00–20.00 Mon–Fri, 09.00–20.00 Sat/Sun. Tiny café, appropriately opposite the Franciscan church, serving great coffee (including Turkish coffee) & homemade cakes. $

⊟ Fresh Healthy Drink Bar [289 E2] Sora Shopping Centre; ⏰ 09.00–21.00 Mon–Fri, 10.00–18.00 Sat. Wonderful freshly squeezed juices & smoothies from this stand near the entrance to the Sora Shopping Centre. $

☆ Pergola Terasa [288 B1] Dealul Cetatuia; m 0745 154 013; ⏰ 10.00–23.00 daily. A terrace with a great view overlooking the city from this bar just below the Freedom Monument. Doesn't serve food. $

ENTERTAINMENT

Festivals As befits Transylvania's most cosmopolitan city, Cluj hosts a wide range of sporting and cultural events. Romania's largest international film festival, the **Transylvanian International Film Festival (TIFF)** (w *tiff.ro*) began in 2002, and screens films at a range of locations around the city. It takes

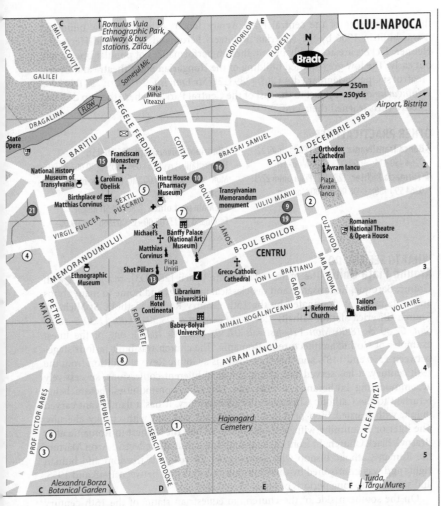

CLUJ-NAPOCA

N

Bradt

0 ——————— 250m
0 ——————— 250yds

Airport, Bistrița

Romulus Vuia
Ethnographic Park,
railway & bus
stations, Zalău

EMIL RACOVIȚA

GALILEI

DRAGALINA FLOW

Someșul Mic

Piața
Mihai
Viteazul

State
Opera

REGELE FERDINAND

G BARIȚIU

Franciscan
Monastery (15)

COTIȚA

CROITORILOR

PLOIEȘTI

B-DUL 21 DECEMBRIE 1989

BRASSAI SAMUEL

Orthodox
Cathedral

Avram Iancu

National History
Museum of
Transylvania

Carolina
Obelisk

Birthplace of
Matthias Corvinus

SEXTIL
PUȘCARIU (5)

(21)

Hintz House
(Pharmacy
Museum) (10)

(16)

BOLYAI

Transylvanian
Memorandum
monument

IULIU MANIU

(9)

(2)

Piața
Avram
Iancu

(19)

VIRGIL FULICEA

(4)

MEMORANDUMULUI

St
Michael's

Matthias
Corvinus

Bánffy Palace
(National Art
Museum)

Piața
Unirii

B-DUL EROILOR

JÁNOS

CENTRU

CUZA VODA

Romanian
National Theatre
& Opera House

Shot Pillars (13)

Ethnographic
Museum

PETRU
MAIOR

FORTĂREȚEI

Hotel
Continental

Librarium
Universității

Babeș-Bolyai
University

Greco-Catholic
Cathedral

ION IC BRĂTIANU

MIHAIL KOGĂLNICEANU

G
GABOR

BABA NOVAC

Reformed
Church

Tailors'
Bastion

VOLTAIRE

(8)

AVRAM IANCU

CALEA TURZII

PROF VICTOR BABEȘ

REPUBLICII

BISERICII ORTODOXE

(6)

(3)

(1)

Hajongard
Cemetery

Turda,
Târgu Mureș

Alexandru Borza
Botanical Garden

place annually during the first week of June, before moving to Sibiu later in the month.

A more recent addition to the city's calendar is the **Untold Festival** (w *untold. com*) in early August. The first event was held in 2015, coinciding with Cluj's stint as European Youth Capital, and it immediately established itself as Romania's largest electronic music festival, attracting some 240,000 spectators.

Theatres and concert halls The main venues for Untold and other big sporting events and rock and pop concerts are the **Cluj Arena** [288 A3] (*Aleea Stadionului 2*), a stadium which is home to the FC Universitatea Cluj football club and seats 30,000, and the neighbouring **Sala Polivalentă** [288 A3] (*Aleea Stadionului 4;* ✆ *0264 483 160;* e *secretariat@polivalentacluj.ro;* w *polivalentacluj.ro*), an indoor arena with a capacity of 10,000. The **Romanian National Theatre and Opera House** (Teatrul și Opera Națională Cluj-Napoca) [289 F3] (*Piața Ștefan cel Mare 2–4; opera details:* ✆ *0264 592 466;* e *pr@operacluj.ro;* w *operacluj.ro; theatre details:* ✆ *0264 592 826;* e *contact@teatrulnationalcluj.ro;* w *teatrulnationalcluj.ro*) decorates the southern side of the central Piața Avram Iancu. A bright-yellow building, it was built in 1906 by the Austrian architects Ferdinand Fellner and Hermann Helmer. Tickets are accessibly priced, though performances of popular operas sell out early. The low grey-domed building of the **Hungarian State Theatre and Opera** (Teatrul și Opera Maghiară din Cluj) [289 C2] (*Str Emil Isac 26–28*; m *754 050 150*; w *hungarianopera.ro*), just to the east of the Central Park, is where the pop duo the Cheeky Girls learned their 'craft'.

OTHER PRACTICALITIES
$ **Banca Transilvania** [289 D3] Piața Unirii 22; \0264 450 414; ⏱ 09.00–17.00 Mon–Fri
✚ **Farmacia Richter** [289 D2] Piața Unirii 27/1; \0264 590 488; ⏱ 08.00–20.00 Mon–Fri

Librarium Universității [289 D3] Str Universității 1; m 0754 096 260; ⏱ 10.00–21.00 Mon–Sat, 10.00–20.00 Sun. Has some books in English.
✉ **Main post office** [289 D2] Str Regele Ferdinand 33; ⏱ 08.00–19.00 Mon–Fri, 09.00–13.00 Sat

WHAT TO SEE AND DO
Around Piața Unirii The main square, Piața Unirii [289 D3], resplendent with Gothic, Baroque, Renaissance and neoclassical buildings and home to many shops and restaurants, is dominated by the 15th-century Roman Catholic **St Michael's Church** (Biserica Sfântul Mihail) [289 D3] (⏱ *Mass at 08.30, 10.00, 11.30 & 18.00 Sun, 07.30 & 18.00 Mon–Fri, festivals 07.30, 10.00 & 18.00*), one of the finest examples of Gothic architecture in Romania. The church was built in four stages between 1350 and 1487, and the clock tower is a Gothic Revival addition from the 19th century. It has served as a church of four different confessions, successively accommodating Lutheran, Calvinist and Unitarian communities, before being returned to the Catholic Church in the 18th century. It has a flamboyant carved pulpit, with learned men of religion jostling for position with cheeky cherubs. The interior is stunning with soaring Gothic arches, the highest in Romania after Brașov's Black Church. In front of the church is a statue of a reflective Áron Márton, the Roman Catholic bishop who campaigned for religious freedom and human rights and was imprisoned by the Communist authorities between 1948 and 1955, and subjected to long periods of house arrest after that.

On the southern side of the church, an equestrian statue of the 15th-century ruler **Matthias Corvinus** [289 C2] has been a controversial figure ever since it was created by János Fadrusz in 1902, and the centre of a long dispute between ethnic Romanians and Hungarians over the wording on the plinth, which was initially 'Mathias, King of Hungary', but which now reads 'Mathias Rex'. Nearby, in the centre of the cobbled square, a perspex roof covers some remains of the Roman settlement of Napoca, but the perspex is so worn that it is difficult to make anything out. The square often plays host to fairs and concerts.

The eastern side of Piața Unirii houses the 18th-century Baroque **Bánffy Palace** [289 D3], where the **Art Museum** (Muzeul Național de Artă) (*Piața Unirii 30*; \0264 596 952; w *macluj.ro*; ⏱ *10.00–17.00 Wed–Sun; adult/child 8.80/2.02RON*) offers an excellent collection of 19th- and 20th-century Romanian art, including a good range of works by Romania's most famous painter, Nicolae Grigorescu. Of other key Romanian artists of this period, Theodor Aman, Ștefan Luchian, Theodor Pallady and Nicolae Tonitza are all well represented. The museum also hosts temporary exhibitions and holds various cultural events in its attractive arcaded courtyard.

Nearby, at the corner of Piața Unirii and Strada Regele Ferdinand, sits the **Hintz House** (Casa Hintz) [289 D2], which served as Cluj's first and longest-running pharmacy (1573–1949) and is now home to the **Pharmacy Museum** (Muzeul Farmaciei) (✳ *Piața Unirii 28*; ⏱ *10.00–16.00 Mon–Wed & Fri, noon–18.00 Thu; adult/child 6/3RON*). This has a fascinating, atmospheric collection, including bottles of 'Elixir of Love', sold in the 18th century and decorated with courting couples. The elixir was apparently mostly spiced red wine. There is also 'mummy powder', which could sell for the same price as gold for its weight, and was partly responsible for an upsurge in the looting of ancient Egyptian tombs. The museum is one of the gems of Cluj, but note that there is a very steep staircase down to the basement laboratory.

Across the square, in the southwest corner, stands the **Hotel Continental** [289 D3], once known with geographical imprecision as the Hotel New York, built in the 1890s in an eclectic style with Baroque tones dominating. It is currently closed for restoration. Nearby, the **'Shot Pillars' Monument** [289 D3], by sculptor Liviu Mocan, comprising seven bulbous bronze columns, stands on the pavement in memory of those killed on that spot during a violent confrontation with the authorities in the 1989 Romanian Revolution. The columns have symbolic bullet holes.

North and west of Piața Unirii The cobbled Strada Matei Corvin takes you from the northwest corner of Piața Unirii to the house where Matthias Corvinus was reportedly born in 1443 (*Str Matei Corvin 6*), a low 15th-century building, now part of the local University of Art and Design. A plaque in Romanian and English tells us: 'The Romanian Matthias Corvinus is considered the greatest of all Hungarian kings.' I suspect that the adjacent plaque in Hungarian phrases it slightly differently.

A short walk further north along the pedestrianised street brings you to the cobbled and shaded Piața Muzeului [289 C2], centred on the **Carolina Obelisk**, which celebrates the visit to the city in 1817 of Emperor Francis I of Austria and his wife Carolina Augusta. On the eastern side of the square, the **Franciscan Monastery and Church** (Mănăstirea și Biserica Franciscană) [289 D2] (*Str Victor Deleu 4*; ⏱ *07.00–19.00 daily; free admission*) is one of the city's oldest buildings, built in the 13th century on the site of an older church destroyed by Tatar attacks and enlarged by the Dominican order in the 15th century with the support of Ioan de Hunedoara. With the banishing of the Catholic orders in 1556, it had various uses, including a school, before being taken back by the Franciscans on their return to the city in 1728.

Immediately to the west of Piața Muzeului is the **National History Museum of Transylvania** (Muzeul Național de Istorie a Transilvaniei) [289 C2] (*Str C Daicoviciu 2*; ☎ *0264 595 677*; ⌨ *mnit.ro*; ⏱ *10.00–16.00 Tue & Thu–Sun, noon–18.00 Wed; adult/child 6/3RON*), whose permanent collection has been closed for years for renovation. At the time of writing, all that was on offer was a series of lacklustre temporary exhibitions, such as a rather poor attempt to bring Dacian times to life through virtual reality (the admission fee fluctuates according to the number of these on show at the time).

A couple of blocks northwest of here is the pleasant **Central Park** [288 A3], which includes within its grounds the nicely restored casino building (⏱ *10.00–20.00 daily; free admission*), now housing events and temporary exhibitions as part of the Cluj Centre for Urban Culture, as well as a **boating lake** [288 A3] that offers rides on pedalos decked out as swans, flamingos, dragons and motor cars (⏱ *10.00–20.30 daily; adult/child 12/6RON/half hour*).

Close to the Hungarian Theatre is a footbridge, the **Podul Elisabeta** [288 B2], across the Someşul Mic River. It is one of the increasingly large number of bridges around the world being colonised by locks – apparently a symbol of eternal love. From the northern bank, paths wind up the **Citadel Hill** (Dealul Cetatuia) [288 B1], something of a hangout for Cluj's student romantics, to the **Freedom Monument** [288 B1], a large cross erected in memory of those who died in World War I. An Austrian fortress was built here in the 18th century to ensure control of the city by keeping an eye on the residents' behaviour, rather than ensuring its defence. Graffiti-covered remnants of the fortress languish behind the monument, close to the hulking white Hotel Belvedere.

Strada Memorandumului, running westwards from Piaţa Unirii, contains the **Ethnographic Museum of Transylvania** (Muzeul Etnografic al Transilvaniei) [289 C3] (*Str Memorandumului 21*; \ *0264 592 344*; e *contact@muzeul-etnografic.ro*; w *muzeul-etnografic.ro*; ⊕ *10.00–18.00 Wed–Sun; adult/child 4/2RON*) with a collection of more than 65,000 folk items. Founded in 1922, the museum offers an excellent introduction to Transylvanian folk art and traditions, with sections devoted to trades, lodging, pottery, food, textiles, costumes and customs. It is housed in the La Redoute Palace, which in the 18th and 19th centuries was the home of the White Horse Inn, hosting Transylvanian Diets and concerts. A plaque records that Liszt performed here twice. It was also the site of the 1894 trial of the signatories of the Transylvania Memorandum. The museum has an open-air counterpart, the **Romulus Vuia Ethnographic Park** [289 C1] (*Str Tăietura Turcului, located north of town on Hoia Hill, bus 30 from Piaţa Unirii*; e *contact@muzeul-etnografic.ro*; w *muzeul-etnografic. ro*; ⊕ *summer 10.00–18.00 Wed–Sun, last admission 17.00, winter hours 09.00–16.00 Wed–Sun, last admission 15.00; adult/child 4/2RON*), founded in 1929 with three gorgeous 18th-century wooden churches, peasant houses and outbuildings for grinding gold ore, sheep rearing and tanning.

Further west from the Ethnographic Museum, Strada Memorandumului becomes Calea Moţilor, and you eventually reach the **Calvinist Church** (Biserica Reformată) [288 A4] at number 84. It was built in 1913 by the renowned architect Károly Kós, who designed the entire building and its fixtures and fittings. It is known as the Cockerel Church because of the motifs all over the building symbolising St Peter's threefold denial of Christ before the cock crowed. There are some beautiful features, including the stonework in the form of a large triangle around the entrance.

The Boulevard of Heroes to the University District The Boulevard of Heroes (Bulevardul Eroilor) runs eastwards from Piaţa Unirii to **Piaţa Avram Iancu** [289 F2]. At the Piaţa Unirii end is a curious monument consisting of two tall grey columns linked at the top by a bell. It commemorates the 100th anniversary of the 1894 trial of the signatories of the Transylvanian Memorandum, which demanded equality of rights for the Romanian community – its signatories securing prison sentences for their efforts. Heading down Bulevardul Eroilor, you pass on your right the Baroque confection of the **Greco-Catholic Cathedral of the Transfiguration** (Catedrala Greco-Catolică Schimbarea la Faţă) [289 E3] at number 10. This provides a good example of the way in which many churches in Transylvania have provided a home for different faiths according to the changing political and religious climate. It was built in the 1770s by a Roman Catholic order, and Queen Maria Theresa donated 7,000 florins to rebuild the tower after the first effort collapsed. It was later ceded by the Vatican to the Greek Catholic Church; the Romanian Orthodox Church took over with the suppression of the Greco-

Catholic Church in the Communist period, and following a court case the Greco-Catholic Church took it back in 1998.

If Piața Unirii is full of reminders of Cluj's links with Hungarian history, Piața Avram Iancu offers important reminders of its Romanian heritage. The square centres on a tall **statue of Avram Iancu** [289 F2] teetering on a high pillar, erected in 1993 on the initiative of Mayor Gheorghe Funar. Iancu is flanked by three stylised *moți* figures, each blowing on a long horn known as a *tulnic*. On the northern side of the square is the imposing **Orthodox cathedral** (Catedrala Ortodoxă) [289 E2] (⊕ *06.00–13.00 & 17.00–20.00 Mon–Sat*), built between 1923 and 1933.

Heading south, some of the old city walls can be seen at Piața Ștefan cel Mare and the square **Tailors' Bastion** (Bastionul Croitorilor) [289 F3], at Piața Baba Novac, dates from the 15th century. The bastion is part of the Centru de Cultura Urbana, and hosts temporary exhibitions (⊕ *10.00–18.00 daily; free admission*).

Heading west from here along Strada Mihail Kogălniceanu, you reach the **Reformed Church** (Biserica Reformată) [289 E3], looking very sprightly following restoration, the largest single-nave Gothic church in Transylvania. Originally a Franciscan church whose construction was supported by Matthias Corvinus, it has held a Reformed Church congregation since the 17th century. It has a light, airy feel – look out for summer evening concerts. The statue of St George out the front is a copy of one made by sculptors of Cluj for Prague Castle in the 14th century. Continuing your walk westwards you reach the three-storey brick bulk of the central building of the **Babeș-Bolyai University** (Universitatea Babeș-Bolyai) [289 D3] (*Str Mihail Kogălniceanu 1*), whose faculties are spread out around the adjacent streets. The largest university in Romania, it teaches in both Romanian and Hungarian (and indeed German), symbolically taking its name from both a renowned Romanian scholar, bacteriologist Victor Babeș and a Hungarian one, mathematician János Bolyai.

A block to the south of here, with its entrance on Strada Avram Iancu, is the **Hajongard Cemetery** (Cimitirul Hajongard) [289 E4] (*Str Avram Iancu 24–26*; ⊕ *08.00–21.00 daily*), running up the hill from the road. Its tombs offer a roll-call of municipal history. Around the back of the administration block on your right is a map showing the notable graves, though this focuses almost exclusively on burials of ethnic Hungarians and omits prominent ethnic Romanians like speleologist Emil Racoviță, whose grave is a few metres up on the left-hand side of the path to the right. The grave of the ethnic Hungarian architect Károly Kós is further up the same path on the right, his family tombstone based around two Doric columns.

Up the hill to the south is the **Alexandru Borza Botanical Garden** (Grădina Botanică Alexandru Borza) [289 D5] (*Str Republicii 42*; \0264 592 152; ⊕ *08.00–20.00 daily, greenhouses ⊕ 09.00–18.00*; *adult/child 10/5RON*), belonging to the Babeș-Bolyai University and stretching over hills and valleys with several greenhouses, a Japanese garden and a huge collection of cacti. Describing itself as the 'garden of the five continents', with different areas devoted to different geographical regions, it also has a large area laid out by species type, and a more ornamental section close to the entrance. There is also a **Botanical Museum** (Muzeul Botanic) (⊕ *08.00–15.00 Mon–Fri*) on the ground floor of the Botanical Institute.

HEADING WEST

From Cluj-Napoca it's a 42km drive to Huedin and the scenery along route 1 (E60) towards Oradea and the border with Hungary is lovely, with little grass-covered hills almost like waves rolling past, dotted with bushes. This is a region known as the **Ţara Călate** (HU: Kalotaszeg), a culturally distinctive area with a large Hungarian population. The local embroidery is particularly famous: known as *írásos*, meaning 'drawn' or 'written', as the designs are drawn onto the cloth before being stitched, it consists of stylised leaves and flowers, in bold colours, usually red on a white background. The Hungarian Reformed churches in this area are famous for their coffered ceilings made of beautifully painted square panels or 'cassettes' (*kazeta*) and also painted pews and galleries. The cemeteries deserve attention, too, for their carved wooden headstones, originating from pre-Christian Hungarian traditions. The Hungarian composers Béla Bartók and Zoltán Kodály travelled around Kalotaszeg in the early 20th century collecting thousands of old melodies, which served as a rich vein of inspiration for their own compositions as well as preserving the local folk music.

HUEDIN Huedin (Bánffyhunyad/Heynod), a town of around 9,000 people, is the largest settlement in the area. It was founded in the Middle Ages, though the centre is quite modern. The Bánffy family were the town's landlords for more than five centuries until 1848, which explains the town's Hungarian name. The road leading west out of Huedin has a cluster of **Roma palaces** (see box, page 307), with shining tin roofs, turrets, balconies and towers; quite a sight in the sunshine, although many are unfinished.

Trains running from Cluj-Napoca, Braşov and Bucharest to Budapest all stop in Huedin. There are several **buses** a day from Cluj-Napoca (*1hr*). By **car**, it is on the main route 1 (E60) towards Oradea and Hungary. On the road to Huedin, you'll pass through **Căpuşu Mare** (Nagykapus/Grossthoren), where there are many stalls alongside the road offering baskets and ceramic objects, and **Izvoru Crişului** (Körösfő/Krieschwej), with more roadside craftwork on offer: baskets, straw hats, jugs, brown bowls, embroidered tablecloths and sheep fleeces. The 18th-century Reformed church on the hill above this village is one of the prettiest in the Kalotaszeg region. The E60 is not the most restful of roads, however, as there is a good deal of lorry traffic heading to Hungary.

NEGRENI On the second weekend of every October, the village of Negreni (which is known throughout the region as Fekete-tó, Hungarian for 'Black Lake') turns into a vast **open-air market and fair** when all the hotels and pensions are booked up long in advance as people arrive from all over Romania – and many from Hungary – to meet up with their mates, buy farming equipment, catch up on gossip, eat *mici* (spicy skinless sausages) and toast everyone's good health with endless shots of *ţuică*. Many traders turn up on the Thursday and Friday, and there is an animal market on the following Monday; however, the best day is Saturday, especially if you're looking for folk crafts, antiques or unusual, ancient musical instruments.

Negreni is 25km west of Huedin on route 1/E60. **Buses** and **trains** from Cluj-Napoca are packed for the fair.

PIATRA CRAIULUI Not to be confused with the Piatra Craiului National Park in Braşov County, this is a mountain pass that marks the border between Cluj County in Transylvania and Bihor County in the Crişana region. Habsburg emperor-in-waiting Joseph II apparently travelled this way before his coronation and the new road was linked to his name: Királyhágó or 'King's Pass'. From the top of the mountain there is a great view towards Bihor County and Hungary to the west and back east over the rolling hills of Transylvania. The pass itself is not very photogenic, having something of a truck-stop feel. The Vegas Restaurant (**m** *0744*

143 944) claims to be open non-stop. On the right, a forest road leads to the **Piatra Craiului Monastery** (Mănăstirea Sfântul Ioan Iacob Hozevitul) (❭*0259 315 668*), hidden in the heart of the woods, 3km off the main road. There is an attractive small wooden Orthodox church here, in the process of being dwarfed by the construction of a large modern concrete one.

SÂNCRAIU Sâncraiu (HU: Kalotaszentkirály) has a Reformed church dating from the 13th century with a particularly fine wooden ceiling decorated with some 220 'cassette' panels. The village is also home to the **Davincze Tours Travel Agency** (*Sâncraiu no 291*; ❭*0264 257 580*; m *0745 637 352*; e *davincze54@gmail.com*; w *kalotaszeg-davincze.ro*), specialising in tourism in the Kalotaszeg region, and can help arrange accommodation in family-run guesthouses in Sâncraiu and across the area (**$**). For groups larger than 15 they can offer events such as traditional Kalotaszeg music and even folk-dancing classes. The village lies 5km southwest of Huedin.

LACUL BELIȘ-FÂNTÂNELE This two-in-one lake was created artificially in the 1970s with the damming of the Someșul Cald River. During the construction of the Fântânele Dam, the old village of Beliș (Jósikafalva/Seedorf) was moved away from its original location in the valley to the nearby hills, but occasionally, in drought-ravaged summers, the spire of the village's Roman Catholic church, built in the village in 1913 by Count Ioan Urmanczy and usually lying well below the lake's surface, can be seen rising from the depths.

Reached through attractive winding roads through the forest, the main touristic centre on the lake is the **Statiunea Beliș-Fântânele**, situated close to the Fântânele Dam. The scenery is great, though the small resort does have something of a slightly down-at-heel Communist feel. There is also a tourist information office (❭*0374 676 729*; ⊕ *opening hours erratic*) up the hill in the centre of the new village of Beliș. It is difficult to get around here without your own transport.

 Where to stay and eat

🏠 **Hotel Bianca** (25 dbl, 5 apt) 407075 Fântânele, Comuna Râșca; ❭*0264 334 163*. Great views across the lake amid the pine forest, but the place is decidedly run down & rather redolent of the Communist period. The restaurant (**$$**) is just across the road below the hotel. **$$$**

🏠 **Pensiunea Fântânele** (10 rooms) Beliș-Fântânele; m *0745 471 344*; e pietrelealbe@

gmail.com; w pensiuneafantanele.ro. A basic guesthouse in a secluded forested location. Most rooms have shared bathrooms, & there's a shared kitchen & dining room. To get here, head off the road onto a rough track immediately on the Betiș side of the Fântânele Dam: the guesthouse is an orange-painted building about 600m up. **$**

HEADING NORTH

BONȚIDA Bonțida (Bonchida/Bonisbruck) is a settlement of under 5,000 people within the Câmpia Transilvaniei (HU Mezőség – 'fieldness'), a landscape of rolling hills between Cluj-Napoca and Târgu Mureș. The population of this area is a mix of Romanians, Hungarians and Roma, and the Transylvanian folk culture is particularly rich. Bonțida's touristic draw is **Bánffy Castle** (Castelul Bánffy) (*Bonțida no 246*; ❭*0264 439 858*; e *office@transylvaniatrust.ro*; w *transylvaniatrust. ro* or w *heritagetraining-banffycastle.org*; ⊕ *10.00–20.00 daily*; *3RON*), whose sumptuous park once gave the place the title of 'Versailles of Transylvania'. The Bánffy family came into possession of the estate in the 14th century, and the castle was built, rebuilt and remodelled over successive centuries.

The castle is entered through a gate that forms part of the 18th-century Baroque restoration initiated by Dénes Bánffy, who inherited the castle when he was 12. He spent his youth in Vienna at the court of Empress Maria Theresa, who sent him to Transylvania as a high dignitary in charge of the imperial stud farms. His new structures were designed in the spirit of the Viennese Imperial Baroque style, focused on a U-shaped courtyard with riding hall, stables and servants' quarters, and decorated with 37 Baroque statues, representing characters from Ovid's *Metamorphoses*. The only statue still in place on the parapet depicts Helios driving the chariot of the sun. The last member of the Bánffy family to live at Bonțida was Miklós, a multi-talented politician, stage designer and author of *The Transylvania Trilogy* (page 50). Bánffy had been involved in a failed attempt in 1943 to persuade both Hungary and Romania to abandon their alliance with Germany and seek peace with the Allies, and in revenge for this activity, the estate was devastated in 1944 when the retreating German troops plundered the castle, then set it on fire. The Communist period was no kinder: the castle was used as a set for Romanian director Liviu Ciulei's 1964 film *Forest of the Hanged*, which won him the Directors' Award at Cannes. A scene in the film involving a fire was realised by actually setting fire to one of the buildings. In 2000, the castle was included in the World Monuments Fund's (w *wmf.org*) list of the 100 Most Endangered Sites in the World.

The Transylvania Trust (w *transylvaniatrust.ro*) is working to restore the castle. The initiative is thoroughly worthwhile, though it does essentially mean that visitors to the place are coming to a building site. The first part of the complex to be restored was the kitchen building, which incorporates a round 17th-century bastion, once part of the castle defences. The **Art Café** within the bastion offers drinks and ice cream. A square-based tower, which now has a pronounced lean, was added in the 1850s to offer views across the parkland. Nearby, the Miklós Building, named after Miklós Bánffy, dates mostly from the 1820s, though with another 17th-century bastion incorporated into it, and serves as the office building of the International Built Heritage Conservation Training Centre.

The grounds of the castle provide the venue for the annual **Electric Castle** music festival (w *electriccastle.ro*), which first took place in 2013. Held in June or July, it attracts an audience of more than 100,000 to watch international acts across a range of genres. The festival supports the restoration of the castle.

Bonțida has a **tourist information office** (*Str Mihai Eminescu 164B;* \0264 262 022; ⊕ *08.00–16.00 Mon–Thu, 08.00–13.00 Fri*), though the staff there seem unable to do more than dole out a leaflet about the place.

Travelling by **car**, Bonțida is 33km from Cluj-Napoca on the E576 towards Dej. Frequent **buses** leave Cluj-Napoca bus station daily for Bonțida (*30mins*). Special buses are laid on from the Cluj Arena during the Electric Castle festival. There are also **trains** to Cluj, though these are less frequent and a few minutes slower.

GHERLA Gherla (Szamosújvár/Neuschloss, Armenierstadt) was once an important centre for the Armenian minority. Modern Gherla dates from around 1700, when the Transylvanian Armenians were granted the right by the Austrian emperor to build their own town, and a group of 70 Armenian families came here from Bistrița to settle it. The town, which took the name Armenopolis, was the first grid-planned town in the whole Austrian Empire. Many Armenians became successful cattle traders and the settlement was a wealthy urban centre. Armenians were accorded considerable autonomy in Transylvania: strangers needed the written approval of the municipal authorities even to enter the place.

Very few Armenians still remain in Gherla, a town of around 20,000 people, and those that do now speak Hungarian rather than Armenian. But there are some pleasant late Baroque-style houses built by the Armenian trading families, typically with a niche on their front wall where a statue of a protecting saint would have been placed – very few of which, however, survived the Communist period.

The town's centre of gravity is Piața Libertații, occupied by a small park populated by swinging benches. On one side of the park stands the town's main sight, the **Baroque Armenian-Catholic Cathedral** (Catedrala Armeano-Catolică) (*contact Mr Estegar;* m *0762 658 571*), built between 1748 and 1804. To the left of the main altar is the 'Rubens Chapel', which contains the main treasure of the cathedral, a large *descent from the Cross,* attributed to Rubens. Originally a gift from the Austrian emperor, for whom the Armenians had an important role as money-lenders, the painting has a decidedly complex history, having been in a range of hands before reaching Gherla, stolen from the church by Hungarian troops in 1944, and finally returning to it in 1999 via a museum in Cluj. Gherla is also famous for its prison, sited in the 16th-century bastioned **Martinuzzi Castle**. A jail from the 18th century, it had a dark reputation in the Communist period, and today remains a maximum-security prison.

There is a centrally located **tourist information office** (*Piața Libertații 3;* \0264 241 925; ☉ 07.30–15.30 Mon–Wed, 07.30–17.00 Thu, 07.30–14.00 Fri).

Gherla is 45km northeast of Cluj-Napoca. Frequent **buses** travel along the E576 highway to Dej. The journey from Cluj to Gherla is around 50 minutes.

SIC Sic (Szék/Secken) is a former salt-mining town, which gradually declined to village status following the closure of the mines. It plays an important role in Transylvanian Hungarian culture as a place where folk traditions and music are lovingly preserved. On special occasions the women in the predominantly Magyar village still wear red and black costumes, colours reportedly originating from the Tatar invasion of 1717: red for blood and black for mourning. The invasion is commemorated on 24 August each year, St Bartholomew's Day, with concerts and fireworks. Sic is equally famous for its enthusiasm for folk music, though folk dance nowadays is mostly in evidence at weddings and special events.

There are occasional **buses** from Cluj to Sic (*1½hrs*), but these do not run every day. By **car**, the quickest route from Cluj-Napoca follows a high loop heading north to Gherla on the E576 and turning right onto the road signed for Țaga and then right again after 2km and heading south through the countryside to Sic.

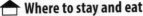 **Where to stay and eat**

Sóvirág Panzió (3 dbl, 7 twin, 2 apt) Str 1 no 504, Sic/Szék; m 0745 208 426; e sallai_ janos@yahoo.com; w soviragpanzio.ro. Located at the beginning of the village when approaching from Gherla, the Sóvirág has clean rooms with furniture painted with folk motifs such as red tulips on black & a large, rustic restaurant (**$$**). **$$**

NICULA In 2002, **Nicula Monastery** (Mănăstirea Nicula) (\ *0264 241 835;* e *manastireanicula@yahoo.com*) celebrated 450 years since its first written mention in 1552. The village and surrounding forest get their name from the 14th-century hermit Nicolae. The fortunes of the monastery were to change dramatically in 1699, when an icon of the Virgin Mary, painted by one Luca of Iclod 18 years earlier, was observed to shed tears for 26 days in a row, a forewarning of tough times ahead for Transylvania. Nicula (HU: Füzesmikola) was turned into a place of pilgrimage, and on 15 August, the Assumption of the Virgin Mary, around

100,000 people cram into the little village, down from a figure of 300,000 annually in the wake of the Romanian Revolution.

There are three churches at the site, which is attractively positioned on the side of a hill above the village of Nicula. The quaintest, around which pilgrims circulate on their knees on 15 August, is a small wooden church, its interior decorated with icons painted on glass, a Nicula speciality. The original wooden church was destroyed by a fire in 1973, and the one seen today is actually an 18th-century church that was moved here from the village of Năsal after the fire.

The second church was built at the end of the 19th century, at which point the monastery was administrated by the Greco-Catholic Church, and it combines an exterior that looks distinctly Catholic in style with a sumptuous iconostasis centred on the weeping icon of the Virgin Mary, the latter subject to a controversial restoration in the early 1990s courtesy of the Cluj National History Museum, and looking distinctly different in many ways from the same icon portrayed in a fresco immediately behind the pulpit.

Under Communist Romania, in 1948, the Greco-Catholic Church was repressed and the monastery again fell under Romanian Orthodox administration. It has remained so to date, and a third church is now under construction, much larger than either of the other two, in a grand style combining Byzantine and neo-Romanian elements favoured by the modern Orthodox Church.

Travelling by **car**, head off the E576 at Gherla, onto the road signed for Ţaga and then right after 2km towards Sic. Nicula is the first village you pass through. Turn left in the village for the monastery.

DEJ A town of some 30,000 people at the confluence of the Someşul Mare and Someşul Mic rivers, Dej (Dés/Desch) owes its development to the salt-mining industry. Once a county seat, the fortunes of Dej declined during the Ceauşescu period, when it was incorporated into Cluj County, and made to host some particularly noxious industries (which closed following the 1989 Revolution). Locals believe that Ceauşescu deliberately penalised the place because of its associations with his predecessor, Gheorghe Gheorghiu-Dej, who was a railway union activist in the town for a time, and acquired the suffix to his name here as a means of distinguishing him from other activists with the same surname.

The main sight in town is the Gothic-style **Reformed Church** (Biserica Reformată) (*Str Traian*), which was constructed as a Catholic church in the 15th century, and subject to numerous modifications over the centuries. The ceiling today is a flat wooden construction: truncated bases of arches at the top of the stone columns on either side of the nave are evidence that it would once have been more soaring. The stone pulpit, later painted to look like wood, was built in 1752, the work of renowned carver Dávid Sipos. The slim tower reaches a height of more than 70m, providing a local landmark. As is the case with so many Transylvanian churches, it has served a wide range of confessions during its lifetime.

The Reformed church sits on the side of Piaţa Bobâlna, the town's main square, which has a small park in the middle centred on a **Monument of the Great Union**, a statue honouring three local politicians who promoted the union of Transylvania with Romania. The **Municipal Museum** long stood on this square, but was closed in 2016 awaiting relocation to a new site. A block to the south, the **synagogue** (*Str Înfrăţirii 1;* \0264 215 179; ⊕ 08.00–13.00 Mon–Fri) was built in 1907. In the small square in front of it, a sombre statue of a family group staggering forward commemorates those Jews of Dej who were gathered into a wretched ghetto in the Bungur Forest outside the town in 1944 before being sent to the Auschwitz concentration camp.

Dej is 60km northeast of Cluj-Napoca, on the E576 highway. Frequent **buses** (*1hr from Cluj*) travel along the E576.

🏠 Where to stay and eat

🏠 **Hotel SunGarden Therme** (53 rooms) Str Libertăţii 1; `\`0264 222 622; e office@ sungardentherme.ro; w sungardentherme.ro. Formerly known as the Black Tulip, & lying just outside the town centre over the river, this is the best of the town's hotels. **$$$**

🏠 **Hotel Someş** (30 rooms) Str Mărăşeşti 1–3; `\`0264 213 330. At the other end of the scale, this is a crumbling 1970s Communist-era throwback in sore need of renovation & without a functioning restaurant. It is, however, central & cheap. **$**

✖ **Red Wine Bistro** Piaţa Bobâlna 4; m 0722 784 000; w red-wine.ro; ⊕ 07.00–midnight Mon–Thu, 07.00–01.00 Fri, 10.00–01.00 Sat, 10.00–midnight Sun. With red leather chairs to mask the wine stains & musical instruments on the walls, this is a good central place with a wide-ranging menu. Good-value set lunch Mon–Fri. **$$$**

HEADING SOUTHEAST

TURDA Turda (Torda/Thorenburg) is a major draw for tourists thanks to its remarkable salt mine, which is one of the most visited paying attractions in the country, but while many tourists simply visit the mine and then leave, the town itself has a significant history and a low-key charm. Established by the Dacians, it became a significant Roman settlement, then named Potaissa, and was the basecamp of the Fifth Macedonian legion until Aurelian's withdrawal from Dacia in AD274. The fortress of the legion lies on a hilltop in suburban Turda, though it is likely to be of interest only to Roman history buffs. In the medieval period Turda often played residence to the Diet of Transylvania, and in 1568 the **Diet of Turda** granted freedom of worship and equal rights for Transylvania's four 'accepted' faiths: Roman Catholic, Lutheran, Calvinist and Unitarian.

Turda today is centred on the long and partially pedestrianised Piaţa Republicii, fringed by the elegant mansions constructed by prominent Hungarian families. The dominant building here is the **Turda Veche Reformed Church** (Biserica Reformată Turda Veche) (*Str B P Haşdeu 1*), dating from the late 14th century. The tower is an early 20th-century reconstruction after the old one fell down. Across the gravelled square next to the church lies the **Turda History Museum** (Muzeul de Istorie Turda) (*Str B P Haşdeu 2*; `\`0264 311 826; e muzeulturda@yahoo.com; ⊕ Sep–Apr 10.00– 17.00 Tue–Sun, May–Aug 10.00–17.00 Tue–Fri, 11.00–19.00 Sat/Sun; adult/child 6/3RON*). It is housed in an elegant stone 15th-century building known as the Palatul Voievodal, though whose actual function for most of its history was, more prosaically, the tax office of the salt mine. The museum is attractively laid out and informative: highlights include finds from the Roman camp at Potaissa; the grave of a late 5th-century Gepid princess nicknamed 'Franziska', who appears to have died from an infected tooth and was buried with an impressive range of jewellery; and items related to the Raţiu family, an important political force in Romania over several generations.

The northern end of Piaţa Republicii is sealed by the **Roman Catholic Church** (Biserica Romano-Catolică) (*Piaţa Republicii 54*), built in a late Gothic style and then given a Baroque makeover. Just beyond, at Piaţa Republicii 52, the exuberant secessionist-influenced building of the former Turda Casino now houses the **Municipal Theatre**, whose name was changed in 2014 to honour the theatre director and actor Aureliu Manea, who died in that year.

The highlight of Turda is, however, on the northern edge of town, some 3km from the centre; the **Turda Salt Mine** (Salina Turda) (✳ *Aleea Durgăului 7;* ↘*0364 260 940;* e *office@salinaturda.eu;* w *salinaturda.eu;* ⊕ *09.00–17.00 daily, until 19.00 in peak summer season; adult/child 30/15RON).* The signs at the entrance tell you that two million tourists visited the place between 1992 and 2013, and from the chaos in the car park on summer weekends (*5RON/day*) you can believe it. There is a second entrance, known as the *intrarea veche,* or 'old entrance', slightly closer to the centre of town at the end of Strada Tunel in the suburb of Turda Nouă. There is very little parking here, and it is more likely to suit visitors staying overnight in Turda.

Salt has been extracted in Turda since ancient times, and the mines were worked here until 1932, when competition rendered them unprofitable. After World War II the cool interior of the mine was used for storing cheese. Following the Romanian Revolution, a plan was hatched to turn the mine into a tourist attraction, and this has been amply realised, although the emphasis is placed more on amusement than education.

The visitor first reaches the 917m-long Franz Jozef gallery, dug in the late 19th century, which runs between the two entrances. From here, descend the stairs or make the long wait for the lift down into the Rudolf Mine, 42m deep, and the last of the mines to be constructed. Its sharply angled trapezoidal structure contrasts with the rougher-hewn Josef and Terezia mines, built in a bell-shape according to earlier mining technologies. The ceiling is spiked with salt stalactites: the area directly below these carefully roped off to visitors. But the most unexpected feature of the Rudolf Mine is what now fills it: a funfair complete with big wheel (*5RON/ride*), table tennis and pool tables – there's even crazy golf. From the Rudolf Mine another lift descends to the base of the Terezia Mine, which holds, even more eccentrically but quite beautifully, a boating lake. A cascade of salt crystals flows from above like a frozen waterfall. Romanian doctors frequently prescribe time in a salt mine for those with various respiratory ailments, and the Gizela Mine is now a treatment centre, though it can also be visited, for an additional 10RON, on one of two guided tours daily (⊕ *11.00 & 14.00*); its main attractions being its particularly beautiful salt crystal formations. Note that food and drink are not allowed in the mine.

For those passionate about Romanian history, there is another worthwhile site at the very southern edge of Turda, the **Monument to Michael the Brave** (Monumentul lui Mihai Viteazul). Past a rather grim industrial area, the signposted spot is on a wooded hillside. Here is the tomb of Michael the Brave, the ruler revered by Romanians as the first to unite, albeit briefly, the principalities of Moldavia, Wallachia and Transylvania. An inscription next to the tomb describes in rather hagiographic fashion Michael's life and achievements, and his assassination in 1601 at the hands of General Giorgio Basta, his betrayer, concluding that this 'is a holy place, a place of patriotic pilgrimage'. Next to the tomb is an obelisk put up in 1977, at the height of the adulation of Michael the Brave within Ceaușescu's Romania, its three sides symbolising the three principalities he ruled. It is 1,601cm high, evoking the year of his death. The modern Mihai Voda Monastery, still unfinished, stands next to the monument.

There is a **tourist information centre** in the centre of town at Piața Republicii 45 (w *turismturda.ro;* ⊕ *09.00–17.00 daily*). The Anglo-Romanian travel agency **Transylvania Live** has its head office in Turda (*Str Razboieni 31A;* ↘*0364 411 666;* e *office@visit-transylvania.eu;* w *visit-transylvania.eu; office* ⊕ *09.00–16.00 Mon–Fri*).

Turda is 32km southeast of Cluj-Napoca on the hectic E60/E81 highway. It is not on a railway line, but **buses** and **maxi-taxis** run regularly to Cluj-Napoca (*30mins*), Târgu Mureș (*1hr*) and Alba Iulia (*35mins*).

Transylvania has a deep-rooted shepherding culture. A selection of the types of cheese to look out for includes the following.

Brânză afumată	Smoked cheese
Brânză de vaci	Cottage cheese
Brânză topită	Processed cheese
Caş	Unsalted semi-soft fresh cheese, usually made from sheep's milk, a bit like feta
Caşcaval	A medium or hard yellow cheese, like Cheddar
Şvaiţer	A yellow cheese, like *caşcaval,* but with large holes like a Swiss Emmental (hence the name: 'Swiss')
Telemea	*Caş* that has been stored in brine
Urdă	A soft unfermented cheese, made from whey after making *caş,* somewhat similar to ricotta.
Brânză de burduf	A speciality of southeastern Transylvania that is well worth seeking out. *Caş* is salted and then kept in a sheep's stomach or skin.
Brânza în coajă de brad	Salted *caş* kept in a cylindrical shape and covered with pine bark, whose flavour it takes on

Where to stay and eat

Hotel Salis (24 rooms) Str Basarabiei 44; 0364 140 333; e receptie@salisspahotel.ro; w salisspahotel.ro. A modern 5-storey hotel & spa, located north of the centre in the suburb of Turda Nouă, a 10min walk from the *intrarea veche* entrance to the salt mine. **$$$$**

❋ Hotel Castelul Prinţul Vânător (8 sgl, 2 dbl, 1 trpl, 4 junior suites, 2 suites) Str Şuluţiu 4–6; 0264 316 850; e contact@huntercastle.ro; w huntercastle.ro. An exuberantly decorated place, which also has an eye on the Dracula-themed tourism market by adding '& Dracula' to some of the publicity materials about the hotel. The showers are like caves with stone walls, & there are hunting trophies all over. The restaurant (⏰ 07.00–midnight daily; **$$$**) apes a medieval banqueting hall, complete with a huge, gory battle mural, & there is a mosaic-strewn terrace garden. They also have a sauna (*€15/hr*). **$$$**

Hotel Potaissa (24 rooms) Piaţa Republicii 6; 0364 103 238; e office@potaissahotel.ro; w potaissahotel.ro. Almost the polar opposite of the Prinţul Vânător, this is a subdued place decorated in pale colours in the town centre. They also have a spa. **$$$**

❋ Raţiu Family Guesthouse (7 rooms) Piaţa 1 Decembrie 1918 1; 0264 312 543; m 0728 989 091; e casadeoaspetiratiu@gmail.com. This characterful & comfortable place in the town centre is part of the Raţiu Democracy Centre, an initiative set up by the family of the late Ion Raţiu, a political exile in the UK during the Communist era who ran unsuccessfully for president in 1990 following its fall. Images of Ratiu's trademark bow tie are found everywhere here. In the same complex, La Papion (⏰ 09.00–21.00 Mon–Thu, 09.00–23.00 Fri/Sat; **$**) is a fine café that hosts frequent cultural events organised by the centre. They are hoping to restart the annual food & culture festival known initially as Turda Fest, later Transilvania Fest (w transilvaniafest.com), which has suffered a hiatus because of problems over the venue. Expect a thoroughly worthwhile event showcasing small-scale producers if they do get it going. **$$**

✗ Taittu Bistro Bar Piaţa Republicii 6; 0264 309 370; w taittu.ro; ⏰ 08.00–23.00 Sun–Fri, 08.00–03.00 Sat. Next to the Potaissa Hotel, this place is a mix of bar & self-service restaurant. **$$**

Other practicalities

$ **Banca Transilvania** Piaţa Republicii 14;
🕐 09.00–17.00 Mon–Fri

✚ **Farmacia Ducfarm** Piaţa Republicii 13;
📞 0264 314 484; 🕐 08.00–20.00 Mon–Fri,
09.00–18.00 Sat, 09.00–15.00 Sun

TURDA GORGE Turda Gorge (Cheile Turzii) is a drive of some 15km northeast of Turda. Head for the village of Petreştii de Jos, where you turn left onto a rough track, reaching a place to park the car after 1km. It offers a fascinating (if far from level) walk along the side of a stream at the base of 300m limestone cliffs, which are also a major destination for rock climbing. The karst environment is home to some unusual plants like the twisted-leaf onion (*Allium obliquum*), otherwise mostly associated with central Asia. The 3km-long gorge has a large variety of morphological features: caves, fossils, towers and arcades formed by the river's repeated attempts to penetrate the limestone walls. Over the wooden bridge next to the car park is a small **campsite** (*10RON/day to pitch your tent*). There is, in theory, an admission fee for the gorge (*adult/child 4/2RON*), but the booth is usually shut.

SEND US YOUR SNAPS!

We'd love to follow your adventures using our *Transylvania* guide – why not send us your photos and stories via Twitter (🐦 *@BradtGuides*) and Instagram (📷 *@bradtguides*) using the hashtag #Transylvania. Alternatively, you can upload your photos directly to the gallery on the Transylvania destination page via our website (w *bradtguides.com/transylvania*).

11

Bistriţa-Năsăud County

Spare a thought for poor Bistriţa. Dracula-seeking foreign tourists flock to such places as Bran Castle and Sighişoara, birthplace of Vlad the Impaler, but only a small fraction of them make it to Bistriţa-Năsăud County, yet it is here that the Transylvania section of Bram Stoker's novel is actually set. What Dracula sites there are here are either low-key or kitsch, the Hotel Castel Dracula at Piatra Fântânele falling into the latter category.

Bram Stoker set his novel here with good reason, describing the count's home region as 'in the midst of the Carpathian Mountains; one of the wildest and least-known portions of Europe'. Much of the north and east of the county is mountainous and forms part of the Eastern Carpathian range. The Someşul Mare River crosses the county, and another river, the Bistriţa, was dammed in the Communist period, creating the attractive recreation area of Lacul Colibiţa.

Bistriţa-Năsăud is a much more solidly ethnic Romanian county than Mureş County to the south, with Romanians making up some 90% of the population. Historically, the colonisation of Germans, who were invited to settle the frontier areas of the Kingdom of Hungary, was important here as well as in southern Transylvania, and the region became known as Nösnerland. Very few ethnic Germans remain today.

Bistriţa-Năsăud County is one of the least touristy areas of Transylvania, but its county town, Bistriţa, has a certain low-key charm, and this is a good region in which to explore rural communities, forests and high peaks.

BISTRIŢA *Telephone code 0263, sometimes 0363*

Bistriţa (Beszterce/Bistritz) is a charming if rather isolated city of around 70,000 people on the Bistriţa River, which only gets attention because of the Dracula link. Bram Stoker chose the area as the setting for Dracula's castle, and Stoker's lead character Jonathan Harker stops in Bistriţa on his way to stay with the count. It serves as a worthwhile base for exploring the county, with a clutch of interesting sights, especially its beautiful main square dominated by an elegant Saxon Evangelical church.

The city centre consists of two distinct parts: to the southwest is the medieval district surrounding the Piaţa Centrală; the pedestrianised Strada Liviu Rebreanu provides the link up in a northeasterly direction to the Orthodox 'Coroana' church and a more modern district with some of the most popular hotels.

HISTORY Archaeological findings show that the area has been inhabited since the Neolithic Age. German colonists founded the town in the 12th century, then calling the place Nosa, or Nösen. It was sacked by the Tatars in 1241. In the 13th century, the town acquired its present name, which derives from the Bistriţa River flowing through

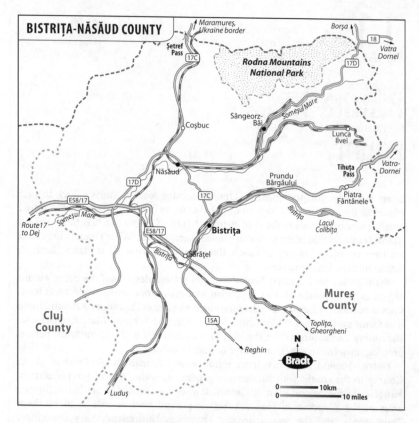

| BISTRIȚA-NĂSĂUD COUNTY |

Maramureș, Ukraine border
Borșa
Șetref Pass
17C
18
Vatra Dornei
Rodna Mountains National Park
17D
Someșul Mare
Sângeorz-Băi
Coșbuc
Lunca Ilvei
Tihuța Pass
Vatra-Dornei
Năsăud
17D
Prundu Bârgăului
Piatra Fântânele
17C
Bistrița
E58/17
Lacul Colibița
Someșul Mare
Route17 to Dej
E58/17
Bistrița
Bistrița
Sărățel

Mureș County

Cluj County
15A
Toplița, Gheorgheni
Reghin
N
Bradt
0 — 10km
0 — 10 miles
Luduș

the centre. The name comes from the Slavic word *bystrica* meaning 'fast-flowing water'. Ethnic Germans still, however, refer to the area as Nösnerland. It comprised one of the seven fortress towns or Siebenbürgen, the German name for Transylvania.

In the Middle Ages the town flourished economically, being well sited for trade between Transylvania and Moldavia. It became a free royal town in the 14th century, with a large degree of autonomy. Matthias Corvinus gave the city the right to fortify itself in 1465, and the local guilds embarked on building some 6km of defensive walls. The city's defences were damaged in 1602 by the troops of Austrian General Giorgio Basta, and further damage was wrought by a fire in 1758. In 1862, on the order of the Austrian Court, the city walls were demolished, and the city gradually extended beyond its former perimeter.

If you are wondering why the centre of town is full of variously coloured fibreglass ostriches with crowns on their heads, this is the symbol of Bistrița. It dates back to the rule of Louis I of Hungary in the 14th century, who was a member of the House of Anjou. Bistrița, as a free town under royal protection, was able to adopt one of the symbols of that house: a crowned ostrich with a horseshoe around its neck.

GETTING THERE, AWAY AND AROUND The railway and bus stations are situated next to each other to the northwest of the centre off the northern end of Strada Gării. From the **bus station** (*Str Rodnei 1A;* 0263 233 655) at least 12 buses and minibuses leave daily for Cluj-Napoca (*2hrs*), three to Târgu Mureș (*from 2½hrs*) and at least hourly buses to Năsăud (*from 40mins*). From the **railway station**, Bistrița

Nord (☎ *0264 592 321*), there are four daily connections to Cluj-Napoca (*3hrs*) but with Bistriţa sited on a branch line, there is often a need to change at the nearby station of Sărăţel for other major destinations.

Local **taxi companies** are **Unitaxi** (☎ *0263 949, 0263 206 666*) and **Total** (☎ *0263 211 999*).

WHERE TO STAY *Map, page 306*

Hotel Metropolis (57 rooms) Str Parcului 19; ☎ 0263 205 020; e reservations@ hotelmetropolis.ro; w hotelmetropolis.ro. The plushest hotel in town, across the Municipal Park from the town centre, with business facilities, spa & smart, modern rooms. **$$$$$**

Coroana de Aur (98 rooms) Piaţa Petru Rareş 4; ☎ 0263 232 470; e hotel@hcda.ro; w hotelcoroanadeaur.ro. Offering both 4- & 3-star rooms (the bathrooms are unrenovated in the latter), this is a yellowish-hued central hotel of Communist vintage, but much modernised since then, which casts itself, without very clear justification, as the direct descendant of the Golden Krone Hotel in which Jonathan Harker

stayed in Bistriţa. **$$$$** (4-star), **$$$** (3-star)

Hotel Bistriţa (44 dbl, 1 apt) Piaţa Petru Rareş 2; ☎ 0263 231 154; e hotel@hotel-bistrita. ro; w hotel-bistrita.ro. A terracotta-painted 3-storey hotel tucked behind the Prefecture & County Council building on Piaţa Petru Rareş. Has both 3-star & better-appointed 'business class' rooms. **$$$**

Hotel Codrişor (27 dbl, 2 apt) Str Codrişor 28; ☎ 0263 233 814; e hotel@hotelcodrisor.ro; w hotelcodrisor.ro. Part of the same group as the Coroana de Aur, this is a cheaper alternative beyond the municipal park, over a footbridge across the Bistriţa River. **$$**

WHERE TO EAT AND DRINK *Map, page 306.*

Casa Doamnelor Str Liviu Rebreanu 16; ☎ 0263 235 863; ⊕ 08.00–02.00 Mon–Sat, 09.00–02.00 Sun. Central, traditional-style Romanian restaurant offering a quiet terrace through an archway from the street & tables out on the pedestrianised Str Rebreanu. **$$$**

Crama Veche Str Albert Berger 10; ☎ 0263 218 047; m 0730 011 812; w crama-veche.ro; ⊕ 10.00–midnight daily. Within the building of the Palatul Culturii, entered from the back & down some stairs, this is an atmospheric cellar restaurant decorated in rustic Romanian style & with an interesting Transylvanian menu. Has a large outside terrace, the Corrida en Sol. **$$$**

Old House Pub & More Str Dornei 25; m 0785 243 262; w oldhouse-pub.ro; ⊕ (restaurant) 08.00–midnight Mon–Fri, noon–midnight Sat/Sun. Combines a pub on several levels with the Old House Garden restaurant, the latter offering a terrace & a wide-ranging menu

from burgers to some speciality Romanian dishes, including wild boar. **$$$**

Rapsodia Piaţa Petru Rareş 1; m 0737 377 328; ⊕ 09.00–midnight Mon–Fri, 11.00–midnight Sat/Sun. Smartly decorated restaurant in a 1930s neo-Romanian style building, with an outside terrace wrapped around the building & soothing music. International menu. The artworks on the walls are for sale. **$$$**

Patiseria Petermann Piaţa Centrală 15; m 0749 229 482; ⊕ 08.00–22.00 Mon–Fri, 09.00–20.00 Sat. An old-fashioned patisserie right on the Piaţa Centrală, with great pies & cakes, though just 2 tables to sit at. **$**

Popeye Str Liviu Rebreanu 36; ☎ 0263 230 582; ⊕ 08.30–23.00 daily. A fast-food place with the usual range of burgers & hot dogs, but also good cheap Romanian specialities like *mititei* & tripe soup. They have seating on pedestrianised Str Rebreanu. **$**

OTHER PRACTICALITIES

$ BCR Piaţa Petru Rareş 1A; ⊕ 09.00–17.30 Mon–Fri, 09.00–13.00 Sat

✚ **Farmacia Salvia** Str Ştefan cel Mare 1; ☎ 0263 219 773; ⊕ 08.00–20.00 Mon–Fri, 08.00–14.00 Sat

✉ **Post office** Str Ştefan cel Mare 9; ⊕ 08.00–19.00 Mon–Fri, 09.00–13.00 Sat. Situated quite a long way out of the centre, to the northeast of town.

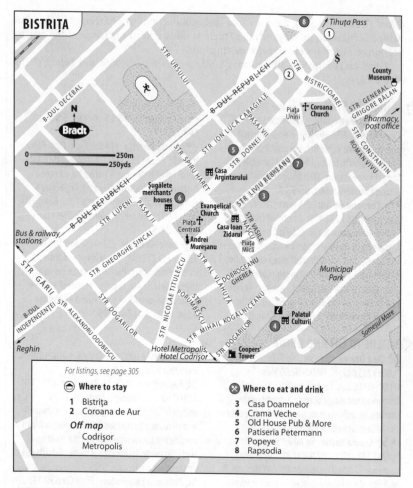

BISTRIȚA

↑ Tihuţa Pass

🚶 Str Ursului

B-dul Decebal

B-dul Republicii

N

Bradt

0 ——— 250m
0 ——— 250yds

Str Spiru Haret

Str Ion Luca Caragiale

Str Casai VII

Str Dornei

🏛 Casa
Argintarului

Șugălete
merchants'
houses 🏛 **6**

Evangelical
Church

Piaţa
Centrală ✝

♦ Andrei
Mureşanu

Str Lupeni

B-dul Republicii

Str Gheorghe Şincai

Pasaj II

Casa Ioan
Zidarul

Piaţa
Mică

Str Vasile Naşcu

Str Liviu Rebreanu

3

7

5

Piaţa
Unirii

✝ Coroana
Church

Str Bistricioarei

Str General
Grigore Balan

County
Museum 🏛

Pharmacy,
post office

Str Constantin Roman Vivu

Bus & railway
stations

Str Gării

B-dul Independenţei

Str Alexandru Odobescu

Str Dogarilor

Str Nicolae Titulescu

Str C. Porumbescu

Str Al. Vlăhuţă

Str Dobrogeanu
Gherea

Str Mihail Kogălniceanu

Str Dogarilor

Municipal
Park

Someşul Mare

📷 🏛 Palatul
Culturii

4

Reghin

Hotel Metropolis,
Hotel Codrişor

🏛 Coopers'
Tower

For listings, see page 305

🛏 **Where to stay**

1 Bistriţa
2 Coroana de Aur

Off map
   Codrişor
   Metropolis

🍴 **Where to eat and drink**

3 Casa Doamnelor
4 Crama Veche
5 Old House Pub & More
6 Patiseria Petermann
7 Popeye
8 Rapsodia

WHAT TO SEE AND DO

It was on the dark side of twilight when we got to Bistritz, which is a very interesting old
place. Being practically on the frontier – for the Borgo Pass leads from it into Bukovina
– it has had a very stormy existence, and it certainly shows marks of it. Fifty years ago a
series of great fires took place, which made terrible havoc on five separate occasions. At
the very beginning of the seventeenth century it underwent a siege of three weeks and
lost 13,000 people, the casualties of war proper being assisted by famine and disease.

Count Dracula had directed me to go to the Golden Krone Hotel, which I found,
to my great delight, to be thoroughly old-fashioned, for of course I wanted to see all I
could of the ways of the country.'

From Jonathan Harker's journal, Chapter 1, Dracula, *by Bram Stoker*

Around the Piaţa Centrală The Piaţa Centrală is the delightful focus of the Old Town.
Its northern side is flanked by a lovely 15th- and 16th-century arched arcade of merchants'
houses known as the Șugălete. This was the commercial centre of the medieval town.
Another echo of medieval Bistriţa is the series of narrow pedestrian streets (or 'passages')
which originally connected the main streets with the castle walls.

The Piaţa Centrală is dominated by the imposing **Saxon Evangelical Church** (Biserica Evanghelică) (⊕ *tower visits: 09.00–17.00 Tue–Fri, 10.00–18.00 Sat, noon–18.00 Sun; adult/child 10/5RON*), dating from the 14th and 15th centuries. The church was constructed originally in a Romanesque style but later rebuilt in a Gothic design. In 1560, the municipal authorities signed a contract worth 3,000 florins with a noted Swiss architect named Petrus Italus da Lugano to remodel it again, this time into a Renaissance style. The tall nave, with circular pink columns, is decorated with flags representing the guilds of the town. At 75m, the church tower is one of the tallest in Romania, and offers a great view from the top. A lift takes you there.

A statue in Piaţa Centrală close to the church depicts **Andrei Mureşanu,** a Romanian poet and 1848 revolutionary born in the town whose poem *Deşteaptă-te române!* (*Wake Up Romanians!*) provides the lyrics of the Romanian national anthem. He is depicted raising his arm aloft, in revolutionary fashion.

Just northeast of the square, the **Silversmith's House** (Casa Argintarului) (*Str Dornei 5; ⊕ 10.00–18.00; free admission*), built in the early 16th century in a Gothic style, was also given a Renaissance makeover by Petrus Italus da Lugano during his stay in the town, at the request of the wealthy jeweller who occupied it, including the addition of stone columns flanking the entrance. The building survived a fire in 1758 and a proposal in the 1930s to demolish it, seen off by historian Nicolae Iorga. It now houses the German cultural centre and has exhibitions on the German community of Bistriţa and the manufacture of silver.

Along Strada Liviu Rebreanu The café-lined pedestrianised **Strada Liviu Rebreanu** marks the heart of the city. The most impressive of the buildings lining it is the **Casa Ioan Zidarul**, dating from the 15th century, which features a stone balcony and elegant stonework around the windows and arches. It recently housed the Restaurant Central and was up for sale at the time of research. Heading northeast along Strada Liviu Rebreanu, a plaque at number 27 reports that this is the site of the Golden Crown Hotel, where Jonathan Harker stopped overnight on his way to the Borgo Pass. At the end of the street you come to Piaţa Unirii, with a statue of Alexander Ioan Cuza, who secured the unification of Moldavia and Wallachia by being elected separately to rule each of them in 1859. The square is surveyed by the 13th-century **'Coroana' Church** (Biserica 'Intrarea în Biserică a Maicii Domnului') (*Piaţa Unirii 8*), which advertises itself as the oldest building in Bistriţa. It is a white-painted building with a rose window above the entrance and buttressed sides. Originally a Franciscan monastery, it features both Gothic and Baroque elements from later remodellings, and became a Romanian Orthodox church in 1948. The popular name of 'Coroana' simply derives from its proximity to the Coroana de Aur Hotel. It is also referred to, somewhat cumbersomely, as the Church of the Holy Mother's Entrance into the Church.

Northeast of here is the **County Museum** (Muzeul Judeţean) (*Str G-ral Grigore Bălan 19*; \ *0263 211 063*; w *complexulmuzealbn.ro*; ⊕ *Oct–Mar 09.00–17.00 Tue–Sun, Apr–Sep 10.00–18.00 Tue–Sun; adult/child 5/2RON*) offering a mix of archaeology, history, ethnography, natural science and art.

The Municipal Park Further worthwhile sights lie southeast of the Piaţa Centrală, towards the Bistriţa River. The lovely, shaded Municipal Park hosts the **Palatul Culturii**, named in honour of George Coşbuc, a poet born in the county in 1866, who is best known for his writings on rural life. It has been recently renovated to show off its Neoclassical finery. A seated statue of Coşbuc surveys it from the park, apparently approvingly. At the end of July Bistriţa hosts an international folklore festival called **Nunta Zamfirei** (Zamfira's Wedding), named after one of Coşbuc's best-known works. In the southwest part of the park is the **Coopers' Tower** (Turnul Dogarilor), the only one of the original 18 towers of the city wall to have survived, thanks to a colourful set of uses, including as a psychiatric hospital and a detention centre for prostitutes. A preserved stretch of the wall alongside makes this a pleasant ensemble. The tower has a gallery with a collection of folklore masks and puppets.

OTHER SIGHTS IN BISTRIŢA-NĂSĂUD COUNTY

LACUL COLIBIŢA This lake is a favoured summer resort of Bistriţa-Năsăud County, lying at an altitude of more than 800m in the Căliman Mountains. It is an artificial creation, established as part of a late Communist-era project to generate hydro-electric power by damming the Bistriţa River. The inhabitants of Colibiţa village were moved to accommodate the lake. Some 13km in length, it offers plenty of watersports and a range of accommodation options, though unrestricted access to the lakeshore can be difficult to find.

To get here head northeast out of Bistriţa along the E58/route 17, an important highway in the direction of Bucovina and Moldova. At the railway level crossing at **Livezile**, opportunistic mushroom or berry sellers, depending on the season, thrust huge buckets at their captive audience. After 23km, turn right at Prundu Bârgăului. The next settlement you pass through, Bistriţa Bârgăului, is as far as conventional public transport options from Bistriţa will take you (*approx 4 trains & 4 buses per day; 50mins*). But you still have 7km uphill to get to the lake. The road quality is poor for the last couple of kilometres before the dam.

There is a **tourist information centre** (✆*0363 401 331;* ⏰ *09.30–16.20 Mon–Fri*) in a wooden hut on the right-hand side of the road coming up from Prundu Bârgăului, about 3km before you reach the dam.

All of the accommodation options below are located on the north side of the lake. If arriving from Prundu Bârgăului turn left when you reach the dam rather than crossing over it.

🏠 Where to stay and eat

🏠 **Caliman Club Outdoor Centre** (3 rooms) Colibița 229A; ✆0363 401 510; e calimanclub@ gmail.com; w calimanclub.com. 3 nicely furnished rooms in an attractive traditional house, part of the activity centre of Caliman Club (page 61), which is focused on adventure holidays including white-water rafting, lake kayaking, mountain biking, skiing & rock climbing. Note that in high season they are reluctant to take guests who haven't booked activity packages. The centre is poorly signposted, but is located just up the hill from the Fisherman's Resort. **$$$**

🏠 **Fisherman's Resort** (26 rooms, 3 apt, 4 bungalows) Colibița 229B; ✆0363 401 630; w fishermans.eu. Laid out on a peninsula, this is the swankiest place to stay on the lake. The room rate includes access to their curious artificial beach, replete with straw umbrellas, use of a sun lounger & outdoor pool. Non-guests can use these too, for 25RON. There are stacks of sporting options, including hire of canoes (*25RON/hr*), rowing boats (*40RON/hr*) & bicycles (*25RON/hr*). The large lake-view restaurant (**$$$**) serves mainly Romanian dishes, with a particular focus on trout. **$$$**

🏠 **Pensiune Lumina Lacului** (8 rooms) Colibița 275; ✆0263 265 570; e info@ missionswerkosteuropa.de; w pension-lumina-lacului.eu. A friendly guesthouse running down the side of a steep slope above the lake. They offer a range of canoe & boat rentals & can organise guided tours by boat. Profits from the guesthouse support a German missionary organisation in Botoșani, Moldavia. As well as standard guest rooms they have some cheaper 4-bed cabins. **$$**

PIATRA FÂNTÂNELE AND THE TIHUȚA PASS At an elevation of 1,200m, the Tihuța Pass (Pasul Tihuța), in the Bârgău Mountains, connects Bistrița-Năsăud County with the neighbouring region of Bucovina. The views and scenery are superb but, other than as a route towards the famous painted monasteries of Bucovina, the place is basically visited today because of its connections with Bram Stoker's novel *Dracula*. In Hungarian, the Tihuța Pass is called Borgó, and it was to the 'Borgo Pass' that Count Dracula despatched a carriage to collect Jonathan Harker, who made his way there from Bistrița.

Dracula hunters make for the small village of **Piatra Fântânele**, home to the **Hotel Castel Dracula** (page 310), an ugly concrete block with some faux-Gothic features, which essentially represents a Communist-era vision of how to use the Dracula legend to prise hard currency from foreign tourists. In the car park at the front is a bust of Bram Stoker (1847–1912) holding a copy of the novel, acknowledging the Romanian tourist industry's debt to the Irish author. The stuffed animals in reception and medieval touches in the restaurant pile on the effect. On the hill overlooking the hotel a large cross appears to offer a Christian riposte to all the pagan nonsense below.

Ask at the reception to visit **Dracula's Tomb** (3RON), which is every bit as kitsch as you would expect and features a couple of touches that are not for the faint-hearted.

Piatra Fântânele also offers skiing in winter, and there is a **chair lift** (m *0743 344 586;* ⏰ *10.00–20.00 daily; 10RON return*) just below the Hotel Castel Dracula, which runs to a 1,180m viewpoint across the valley. And you have more opportunities than anyone would wish to buy your Dracula T-shirt, vampire mask and, er, garden gnomes from the wooden stalls along the main road below the hotel.

To get here, take the main E58/route 17 highway from Bistrița. Piatra Fântânele is right on the main road, about 22km beyond Prundu Bârgăului. It is an attractive

11

drive; haystacks shaped like ripe pears dot the grassy slopes between the pine forests. Check the weather forecast in winter for the state of the pass. There are two buses a day from Bistriţa to Piatra Fântânele (*1hr*).

🏠 **Where to stay and eat** Beneath the layers of Dracula-related kitsch, the **Hotel Castel Dracula** (*62 dbl, 2 trpl, 3 apt; 427363 Piatra Fântânele;* ✆ *0263 264 010;* e *rezervari@hotelcasteldracula.ro;* w *hotelcasteldracula.ro; $$$*) is a somewhat tired but clean three-star hotel. The restaurant (*$$$$*) features the heaviest menu I've ever seen, replete with quotes from 'the book' and the inevitable Dracula-themed dishes; though one that isn't, sautéed rooster testicles, sounds far scarier than a 'Dracula skewer'.

NĂSĂUD A small town of some 10,000 people, Năsăud (Naszód/Nussdorf) lives in the shadow of a history more illustrious than its rather sleepy present, in particular as the headquarters of the Romanian Second Border Regiment, established by the Austrian Court in 1762. The Năsăud Border Guards fought with distinction within the Austrian forces against the French in the Napoleonic Wars, notably at the Battle of Arcole. The regiment stayed loyal to the Austrian Empire in the revolution of 1848–49, but in 1851 the Austrian Imperial Government disbanded the border regiments in Transylvania, including Năsăud. An Autonomous Romanian District of Năsăud was established in 1861, but with its demise in 1876, the town fell under the sway of its larger brother, Bistriţa, and has remained there ever since.

The **Museum of the Năsăud Border Guards** (Muzeul Grănicleresc Năsăudean) (*B-dul Grănicerilor 19;* ✆ *0263 361 363;* ⊕ *08.00–17.00 Mon–Fri, 10.00–17.00 Sat & Sun; adult 4RON*) in the centre of town offers a comprehensive history of the Romanian Second Border Regiment, as well as an ethnographic section featuring some of the distinctive peacock-plumed hats traditionally worn by young men, and now a symbol of the Năsăud area. Around the back is a wooden peasant's house dating from 1870, which was moved here from the village of Ilva Mare.

Năsăud is north of Bistriţa on national road 17C: there are buses at least every hour (*from 40mins*).

COŞBUC Some 13km north of Năsăud, the village of Coşbuc is of interest for an attractive wooden bridge across the Sălăuţa River and the house in which Romanian poet George Coşbuc was born in 1866. He is known for centring his poetry on the lives of ordinary, especially rural, people. The village, previously known as Hordou (HU: Hordó), was renamed in his honour.

His birthplace, by the side of the main road through the village, is now a **memorial museum** (Muzeul Memorial George Coşbuc) (⊕ *Oct–Mar 09.00–17.00 Wed–Sun, Apr–Sep 10.00–18.00 Wed–Sun; adult/child 4/2RON*). The single-storey building, with a plaque and bust outside honouring the poet, is divided between an exhibition of his life and work (in Romanian only) and a two-room recreation of how the house would have looked at the time of his birth.

The village is located on national road 17C between Năsăud and the Maramureş region to the north.

LUNCA ILVEI Lunca Ilvei (HU: Ilvatelek) is a village nestling up against the mountains separating Transylvania from the neighbouring region of Bucovina. It offers a good place for a rural break, in a picturesque area. To get here take the DN17D eastwards from Năsăud, turning off onto a more minor road at Ilva Mică. Lunca Ilvei is another 32km further on. Note that there is no direct road connection northwards from the Tihuţa Pass to Lunca Ilvei. It is a stop on the railway line between Cluj-Napoca and Suceava. There is also one bus, on weekdays only, from Bistriţa to Lunca Ilvei (*2hrs 45mins*), which passes through Năsăud.

🏠 **Where to stay** The **Casa Alexandra** (*7 dbl; Str Grănicerilor 93, Lunca Ilvei;* \ *0264 525 513;* m *0722 218 295;* e *cornelia_ureche@yahoo.com;* w *ecolunca.ro;* \$) is a delightful wooden holiday home, built in a rustic style. The living room is dominated by a large ceramic stove, guests have use of the kitchen and there is a traditional bread oven and barbecue in the garden. If you have a large party, it is possible to rent the whole house (*600RON/night or 999RON for the weekend*), sleeping a maximum of 22 people. Breakfast is not included, although this and other meals can be provided for an additional charge for a minimum of four guests.

SÂNGEORZ-BĂI Sângeorz-Băi (Oláhszentgyörgy/Sankt Georgen) is a decidedly run-down spa resort in an attractive upland setting on the Someşul Mare River. The spa became popular in the late 19th century, when it was known as the 'Baths of Hebe', taking its name rather optimistically from that of the Greek goddess of youth and cup-bearer to the gods. A rather less plausible alternative version of the origin of the name comes from the urgings to travellers from hospitable locals to *Hai bei!* ('Come on, drink!'), with the two words then shortened to *hebe*. In the Communist period the town became a spa centre for the masses with the construction of two monolithic hotels, the Hebe and the Someş. The former had the largest capacity of any hotel in Romania when it was built.

The feel of the resort today is much closer to its Communist past than its imperial one. There are clusters of springs in the centre of the resort housed in grotty concrete pavilions, with each tap accompanied by a plaque setting out a detailed chemical composition of the water. The calcium-rich waters particularly attract patients with a range of digestive problems.

Sângeorz-Băi is around 20km east of Năsăud on road 17D. There are no convenient public transport options beyond Năsăud.

🏠 **Where to stay and eat**

☀🏠 **Popasul Verde** (3 rooms) Str Valea Borcutului 4D; \ 0263 371 713; e info@ popasulverde.ro; w popasulverde.ro. An ecologically friendly clay-built home with a grass-covered roof looking like something straight out of a fairytale, this is by far the most attractive place to stay in Sângeorz-Băi. Note that they prefer to rent out the place as a whole, so may be reluctant to take single-room bookings in high season. It is on the edge of town: to get here continue up Str Trandafirilor beyond the Hebe & take the 2nd road on the right beyond the pavilion housing the springs. \$\$\$

🏠 **Hotel Hebe** (215 dbl, 5 apt) Str Trandafirilor 10; \ 0263 370 521; e receptie@hotel-hebe.com; w hotel-hebe.com. Still offering an approximation of the Communist spa experience, the hulking concrete Hebe has 2-star & 3-star rooms, &

a mostly elderly clientele taking medically prescribed courses of treatment. \$\$

🏠 **Hotel Someşul** (110 rooms) Str Trandafirilor 15; \ 0263 370 500. The other big Communist-era block, just over the road from the Hebe, the Someşul also offers a mix of 2- and 3-star rooms, though is if anything shabbier than its neighbour. \$\$

🏠 **Via Sindi** (10 rooms) Str Izvoarelor 95; \ 0263 370 163. Sângeorz-Băi is full of basic but cheap pensions. This one is typical, in a house rather resembling a church in style. Room only. \$

✗ **Restaurant Megapark** Str Trandafirilor 7A; \ 0263 370 445; ⊕ 10.00–midnight daily. Logically enough sited by the side of the central park across from the Hebe, this place is mainly focused on wedding parties, has wildly tasteless interior decoration & an international menu. \$\$\$

11

RODNA MOUNTAINS The Rodna Mountains (Munții Rodnei) form some of the highest peaks of the Eastern Carpathians, with a long continuous ridge stretching for more than 50km from west to east. Its two highest points are Pietrosul Rodnei (2,303m) and Ineu (2,279m). The mountains straddle three administrative areas in Romania: Bistrița-Năsăud County in Transylvania, Maramureș County to the north, and Suceava County in Bucovina, and indeed the ridge constitutes a natural northern border between Transylvania and Maramureș. Since 1932 the range has been included in the **Rodna Mountains National Park** (Parcul Național Munții Rodnei) (*Str Principală 1445, Rodna;* ℰ *0263 377 715;* e *apnmr@bistrita.rosilva.ro;* w *parcrodna.ro*). The park administration can provide information about guided hikes.

The main access resort for the Rodna Mountains is the small ski resort of Borșa, which lies on the Maramureș side, and from which there is a chair lift up into the mountains. The **Prislop Pass** (Pasul Prislop) on the DN18, which rises to 1,416m, is an impressive mountain pass connecting the Maramureș and Bucovina regions across the eastern end of the Rodna Mountains. The **Hora la Prislop** festival is held here in mid-August, as a celebration of the links between the Romanian regions of Transylvania, Maramureș and Moldavia, and featuring folk dance in traditional costume. To the west the **Șetref Pass** on the DN17C is also impressive, linking Transylvania with Maramureș, though reaching only the relatively modest altitude of 817m.

12

Sălaj County

Sălaj is the Cinderella county of Transylvania: in the northwest corner of the region, it lies off most tourist itineraries. Indeed, not all of Sălaj is considered to lie in Transylvania proper: the county also partly falls into the historical region of Crişana. It takes its name from the Sălaj River, known in Hungarian as Szilágy, and occupies the Someş Plateau between the Apuseni Mountains and the Eastern Carpathians.

Sălaj is renowned in Romania as the birthplace of many influential political figures, including the 19th-century Hungarian Reformist politician Miklós Wesselényi; Simion Bărnuţiu, one of the leaders of the Romanian revolutionary movement of 1848; influential interwar prime minister and Peasants' Party founder Iuliu Maniu; and another key figure in the Peasants' Party and political prisoner in the Communist era, Corneliu Coposu. Dacian Cioloş, the technocratic Prime Minister of Romania from 2015 until 2017, was also born here.

It offers one of the most important Roman archaeological sites in Romania at Porolissum, the capital of the Roman administrative unit of Dacia Porolissensis, as well as one of the best botanical gardens in the country at Jibou, and an attractive and untouristy landscape of forested rolling hills, wooden churches and shadoof-style counterpoise lift wells.

ZALĂU   *Telephone code 0260, sometimes 0360*

Zalău (Zilah/Zillenmarkt), with a population under 60,000, is the least tourist-oriented of the Transylvanian county capitals. It possesses no unmissable sights, but combining a visit to the archaeological site of Porolissum just outside the town with one to the good County Museum provides the basis for a worthwhile stay of a couple of nights. And Zalău is centrally located within Sălaj County, making it a potentially helpful base for wider exploration of one of the least-known Romanian counties.

HISTORY The area that is present-day Zalău lay a few kilometres to the west of the Roman camp of Porolissum, which guarded the border of the Roman Empire along the Meseş Mountains. This tract of land was inhabited by free Dacian tribes. Zalău town seems to have been established as early as AD900, its trading importance based on its position between central Europe and Transylvania. The town was destroyed by Mongols in 1241, but soon recovered, and was granted market town status by Matthias Corvinus in 1473. Control of the town switched over the centuries between Hungary, the Principality of Transylvania and the Ottomans, with occasional boosts for municipal fortunes, such as the increased autonomy granted to Zalău following the victory of Michael the Brave in the nearby Battle of Guruslău in 1601.

It became the capital of the Szilágy County, broadly corresponding to present-day Sălaj, in 1876, and became part of Romania under the Treaty of Trianon

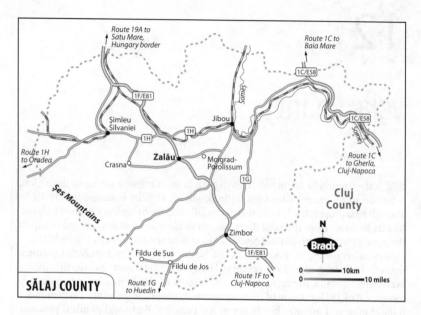

SĂLAJ COUNTY

Route 19A to Satu Mare, Hungary border

Route 1C to Baia Mare

1F/E81

Someş

Şimleu Silvaniei

Jibou

1C/E58

1C/E58

Someş

1H

1H

Route 1H to Oradea

Crasna

Zalău

Moigrad-Porolissum

Route 1C to Gherla, Cluj-Napoca

Şes Mountains

1G

Cluj County

N

Bradt

Zimbor

0 ──── 10km
0 ──── 10 miles

Fildu de Sus

Fildu de Jos

1F/E81

Route 1G to Huedin

Route 1F to Cluj-Napoca

settlement in 1920. It was one of the Transylvanian towns subjected to an intensive programme of industrialisation under Ceauşescu, which was in part an attempt to alter the ethnic balance of this once-ethnic Hungarian-majority town through the influx of large numbers of ethnic Romanian workers from further south. Ethnic Romanians now comprise more than 80% of the population. The presence of many ugly concrete apartment blocks is another side effect of the town's Communist-era industrialisation.

The name of the town was also changed in the Communist era, from Zălau to Zalău, reportedly on the grounds that the former had an overly 'rustic' feel to it for a developing industrial centre.

GETTING THERE, AWAY AND AROUND The **bus station** (*Str Tudor Vladimirescu 54A;* \0260 606 143; e *autogaracento@yahoo.com;* w *cento.ro*) is north of the town centre at the intersection of Strada Vladimirescu and Bulevardul Mihai Viteazul. There are frequent buses to Cluj-Napoca (*1hr 30mins*). Other destinations served include Huedin (*2hrs*) and Oradea (*4hrs*).

The **railway station**, Zalău Nord (*B-dul Mihai Viteazul 100;* \0260 662 131) is even less central – much further up Bulevardul Mihai Viteazul in the industrial area north of the town, and closer to the village of Crişeni than to central Zalău. There are connections to Jibou (*40mins*), one train a day to Cluj-Napoca (*3hrs*) and two to Satu Mare (*2hrs*).

Town buses 1 and 2 run along Bulevardul Mihai Viteazul between the railway station and the centre.

Two local **taxi companies** are **Pro Taxi** (\0260 611 111) and **Euro VIP** (\0260 606 060).

WHERE TO STAY *Map, see opposite*
As might be expected from a town off the tourist map, Zalău offers no really enticing accommodation options, though there are several reasonably priced mid-range hotels which are fine for a night or two.

🏠 **Griff Hotel** (23 dbl, 2 apt) Str Crişan 21; ☎0260 619 125; e office@griffhotel.ro; w griffhotel.ro. A few hundred metres north of the main central sights; rooms are spacious & reasonably appointed, if bland. **$$$**

🏠 **Hotel Brilliant Plaza** (5 dbl, 5 sgl) Str Maxim D Constantin 8; ☎0260 615 066; e office@hotelbrilliantplaza.ro; w hotelbrilliantplaza.ro. Good location near the Reformed church, & smarter rooms than the other central options. Blessed with AC &, curiously, fitness equipment. **$$$**

🏠 **Hotel Meseş** (30 dbl, 4 apt) Piaţa 1 Decembrie 1918 11A; ☎0260 661 050. Renovated Communist-era hotel with uninspiring rooms, but in a quiet central location with plenty of car parking. **$$$**

🏠 **Hotel Porolissum** (72 dbl, 4 suites) Str Unirii 1; ☎0260 613 301; w hotelporolissum.ro. Renovations can't hide the 1970s Communist-era origins of this red & beige concrete block, & its bedrooms are decorated in depressing shades of brown, but the central location is great. **$$$**

✕ WHERE TO EAT AND DRINK *Map, see below*

✕ **Casa Boierului** Str Gheorghe Lazăr 22; m 0744 380 645; ⏲ 09.00–midnight Sun–Thu, 09.00–04.00 Fri/Sat. North of the centre, a restaurant decorated in traditional Romanian style, with a long menu featuring some unusual dishes (turkey testicles, anyone?), though service can be slow. Live Roma music some evenings. **$$$**

✕ **Saladina** Str Unirii (in passage); ☎0260 616 845; ⏲ 07.30–22.30 daily. Central place with a wide-ranging menu, including Romanian &

Hungarian dishes &, logically, plenty of salads. **$$$**

✕ **Pizza King** B-dul Mihai Viteazul 1/B (in passage); ☎0360 106 080; ⏲ 08.30–midnight Mon–Thu, 08.30–01.00 Fri, 09.30–01.00 Sat, 11.30–midnight Sun. Decent pizzeria in a pub-like setting with movie memorabilia, flock wallpaper & wooden booths. Menu also ranges across pasta dishes & salads. **$$**

OTHER PRACTICALITIES

$ Raiffeissen Bank Str Unirii 19; ⏲ 09.00–17.30 Mon–Fri

✚ Prima Farm Str Unirii Bl 2; ⏲ 08.00–20.00 Mon–Fri, 08.00–18.00 Sat

✉ Post office Str Parcului 2; ☎0260 616 409; ⏲ 08.00–19.00 Mon–Fri, 09.00–13.00 Sat

WHAT TO SEE AND DO The heart of town is **Piaţa Iuliu Maniu**, and all the sights of Zalău are within easy walking distance from here. The square features a statue of the Hungarian politician **Baron Miklós Wesselényi**, born nearby in Jibou. The 1902 work of Hungarian sculptor János Fadrusz, who also sculpted the equestrian statue of Matthias Corvinus in Cluj (page 290), the statue depicts a peasant expressing his gratitude to Wesselényi for his support for the abolition of serfdom. There is an unusually helpful **tourist information office** (*Piaţa Iuliu Maniu 4–6; ☎0360 566 100; e contact@turismzalau.ro; w turismzalau.ro; ⏲ 09.00–17.00 Mon–Fri*) in the Clădirea

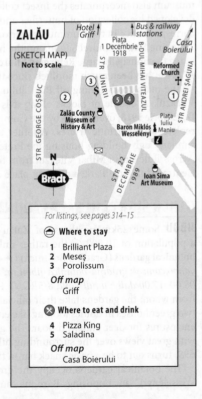

For listings, see pages 314–15

🏠 **Where to stay**
1 Brilliant Plaza
2 Meseş
3 Porolissum
Off map
Griff

✕ **Where to eat and drink**
4 Pizza King
5 Saladina
Off map
Casa Boierului

Sălaj County ZALĂU

12

Transilvania, the large building dating from 1895 which runs along the southern part of the square, though the entrance is on Strada Gheorghe Doja. The Vasile Lucăcel History Section of the **Zalău County Museum of History and Art** (Muzeul Judeţean de Istorie şi Artă) (*Str Unirii 9;* \0260 612 223; *e muzeul. zalau@gmail.com;* w *muzeulzalau.ro;* ⊕ *09.00–17.00 Tue–Sun; adult/child 8/2RON*), a block to the northwest on Strada Unirii, offers a well laid-out canter through the history of the area with a series of reconstructed interiors: Neolithic, Dacian and Roman. There is a large mock-up of a market day at Zalău, an interesting room focusing on Romania under Ceauşescu that includes a domestic interior of the time, with a carpet hanging on the wall portraying the *Abduction from the Seraglio* (*Răpirea din Serai*) which was found in numerous Romanian households and has become a kitsch symbol of the era, and a display of warriors through the ages, from Neolithic to World War II. There are displays on some of the many prominent Romanian political figures to have hailed from Sălaj County, and an unusual exhibition of burial techniques down the years. The courtyard outside is filled with Roman and medieval statuary.

Another branch of the County Museum is to be found a couple of blocks away up Strada Gheorghe Doja. The **Ioan Sima Art Museum** (Muzeul de Artă Ioan Sima) (*Str Gheorghe Doja 6;* \0260 633 200; ⊕ *09.00–17.00 Mon–Fri; adult/child 4/1RON*) is based around the paintings of local artist Ioan Sima, born in the village of Pericei in 1898. Most of the pieces in the collection date from the 1950s and 1960s when Sima was based in Cluj, and include many portraits of female students in the city, as well as paintings of vases of flowers. Somewhat incongruously, the museum also incorporates the insect collection of local man Adalbert Takács, who developed his collection of butterflies and beetles from around the world mostly by correspondence in the Communist period.

Taking Strada Andrei Şaguna up the hill to the north of Piaţa Iuliu Maniu, you reach the unusually large **Reformed Church** (Biserica Reformată), which dates from 1712 but has been much modified since then.

The main road leading off Piaţa Iuliu Maniu to the north is Bulevardul Mihai Viteazul. A couple of blocks along it is the barren concrete expanse of **Piaţa 1 Decembrie 1918**, overlooked by the Communist-era Trade Unions Cultural House, replete with patriotic friezes. Another side of the square is taken up with the similarly ugly building housing the Prefecture and offices of the County Council. Across Bulevardul Mihai Viteazul from the square, a flight of steps leads up to the Central Municipal Park; a pleasant place on a hot day.

OTHER SIGHTS IN SĂLAJ COUNTY

JIBOU Some 25km northeast of Zalău the town of Jibou (Zsibó/Siben), with a population of 10,000, is the rather unlikely location for one of Romania's best **botanical gardens** (Grădina Botanică) (✳ *Str Parcului 14;* \0260 641 617; *e ccb_jb@ yahoo.com;* w *gradina-botanica-jibou.ro;* ⊕ *Apr–Oct 07.00–19.00 daily, Nov–Mar 08.00–17.00 daily; adult/child 8/5RON*). Founded in 1968 by Professor Vasile Fati, from whom the gardens take their official name, it covers some 35ha, and includes two greenhouses in domes looking like enormous golf balls, a small aquarium, and enclosures for deer and wild boar. The gardens are set out on an undulating site with great views over the surrounding hills. Andreea's Secret Garden (m *0758 063 698*) turns out to be a basic snack bar in the park.

The botanical gardens occupy the grounds of the **Wesselényi Castle** (Castelul Wesselényi), an imposing Baroque building whose side facing the gardens includes an impressive arcaded loggia. Square bastions stand at its four corners. Construction began in 1778 by Miklós Wesselényi Senior, and was completed in 1810. The style of the building has much in common with that of the Bánffy Castle at Bonţida. Its period of greatest glory came under Wesselényi's son, also a Miklós Wesselényi, an important Reformist Hungarian politician. It suffered greatly during the Communist era, when it was used variously as a school, museum and children's centre, but has now been restored to the heirs of the Wesselényi family. It stands mostly empty and forlorn, a rather sorry backdrop to the botanical gardens.

There are several **trains** daily from Zalău to Jibou (*40mins*). By **car**, head north towards Bocşa on the E81 and turn right after 5km onto the 1H road, signposted for Jibou.

MOIGRAD-POROLISSUM Some 10km east of Zalău on a scenic road in the direction of Creaca sits the important archaeological site of the Roman settlement of Porolissum. On reaching the modern village of Moigrad-Porolissum from Zalău, turn left at the small war memorial; the site is 2km beyond and above the village.

The Roman military camp of **Porolissum** (\0260 612 223; ⊕ Apr–Oct 10.00–19.00 daily; adult/child 4/1RON) was set up in AD106. It seems to have taken its name from an earlier Dacian settlement nearby. It was established at the time of Trajan's Second Dacian War, at a key location for the defence of the Roman northwest frontier: the most accessible crossing point of the Meseş Mountains overlooking the plains of the Tisza River to the west. A civilian centre developed around the military camp, bringing together both Roman colonists and the local Dacian population, and during the reign of Septimius Severus it was granted the status of municipium. The Romans abandoned the place with Aurelian's withdrawal from Dacia in AD271, but it seems to have remained inhabited for several hundred years thereafter.

The ticket office is located at the Roman customs post, this having been a frontier town. From there you walk up a stretch of the cobbled imperial road that linked Porolissum with Napoca (present-day Cluj-Napoca) and points south. This brings you to the rectangular **castrum**, the Roman military fort. The dual-arched Praetorian Gate, the main entrance to the castrum, and an adjacent stretch of wall have been reconstructed, somewhat over-exuberantly. The cobbled Via Praetoria then takes you into the castrum, whose two main streets intersect in the centre, where the headquarters building (*principia*) was located. The installation of jarring electric lighting here is a real shame. Crossing over the intersection, walk out of the castrum through the Porta Decumana, from which a modern stone path curves round to the **amphitheatre**, believed to be the greatest public building of Roman Dacia, seating 5,000 spectators. A section of seating has been reconstructed. On the side of the amphitheatre low walls mark the site of a Temple of Nemesis, a place of last-minute entreaties by gladiators about to enter their field of combat.

Excavations here are ongoing. This is a tranquil hilltop site teeming with wild flowers, which gets far fewer visitors than its size and importance merit.

🏠 **Where to stay and eat** A basic modern pension just 400m away from the site, **Pensiune Casa Romana** (*7 rooms; no 228/A Moigrad-Porolissum;* m *0763 395 266;* e *casaromana2007@yahoo.com;* **$$**) has been designed with some architectural nods to ancient Rome. They also have a restaurant (⊕ 11.00–22.00 daily; **$$$**) where you can dine on 'Porolissum steak' (with truffle oil, since you ask) after a site visit.

CRASNA Crasna (Kraszna/Krassmarkt) is a majority ethnic Hungarian community, worth a visit for its 14th-century **Reformed Church** (Biserica Reformată) (*Str Cserey*

Farkas 2; \0260 636 072) in the centre of the village. This has an impressive square tower, with a defensive level and mini turrets at each corner of the spire, dating from 1708. The interior features a beautiful ceiling, installed in 1736, of painted wooden panels decorated with scenes of flowers and animals.

Crasna lies 20km west of Zalău on road 191C through Meseşenii de Jos. There are several **buses** a day from Zalău (*30mins*).

ŞIMLEU SILVANIEI Şimleu Silvaniei (Szilágysomlyó/Schomlenmarkt) is a small town of some 16,000 people, whose history is closely linked to the aristocratic Báthory family, which played an important role in Transylvania. Şimleu Silvaniei entered into the family's possession with the marriage in 1351 of Lászlo Báthory to Anna Medgyesaljai, becoming the family's main residence in Transylvania. In the 16th century, the family constructed a **fortress residence** (Cetatea Medievală Báthory) (*Str Stephan Báthory*) in the centre of town, which was, however, damaged by repeated Turkish and Tatar attacks and fell into decline, becoming the property of the town in 1774. It is now a ruin.

A couple of blocks to the east of here, beyond the town hall, is a very sobering site, based at the **synagogue**, built in 1876, which by the early 2000s had been abandoned and fallen into disrepair. With support from the US-based Jewish Architectural Heritage Foundation it has been restored, and transformed into a North Transylvania Holocaust Memorial Museum (Muzeu Memorial al Holocaustului din Transilvania de Nord) (*Piaţa 1 Mai;* m *0744 630 536;* e *sinagoga@ gmail.com;* w *mmhtn.org;* ④ *10.00–17.00 Tue–Fri, 11.00–15.00 Sat/Sun; free admission*). During the months of May and June 1944, in the period in which northern Transylvania was administered by Hungary, the Jewish population of the town was forcibly moved to the Cehei Ghetto, based around the buildings of the Klein brick factory 5km out of the town. Working-age male Jews had already been despatched to the Eastern Front as forced labourers, so those sent to the ghetto were mainly the elderly, women and children. After a few weeks in the ghetto, living in appalling conditions, the Jews here were transported to the Auschwitz concentration camp. Many arrived there in such poor condition that they were selected immediately for the gas chambers.

Overlooking the town and lying just to the north of the Báthory Fortress is a **Roman Catholic Church** (Biserica Romano-Catolică) (*Str 1 Mai 1A*) which dates from the 1530s. At the time of the Reformation, the influence of the Báthory family kept the church in the Roman Catholic fold. A bust in front of the church depicts István (Stephen) Báthory, Voivode and then Prince of Transylvania from 1571 to 1586, and later King of Poland by virtue of his marriage to Queen Anna Jagiellon, in honour of whose birth in 1533 the church was built by his father, István VIII Báthory. The younger István Báthory's niece, incidentally, was the notorious Elizabeth Báthory, accused of torturing and killing hundreds of girls, giving rise to legends that she bathed in the blood of virgins as a means of retaining her youth. The place of these alleged crimes, however, was a castle in present-day Slovakia.

From Zalău, **drive** north along the E81 and turn left after about 10km onto the 1H road signposted for Vârşolţ and Şimleu Silvaniei. There are frequent **buses** from Zalău (*40mins*).

🏠 **Where to stay** Rather prosaically located on the main DN1H road as it bypasses the town centre, the **Pensiunea Castle Inn** (*15 dbl, 3 apt; Str Partizanilor 43;* \0260 676 811; w *castle.ro;* **$$$**), as the name suggests, is a guesthouse built to resemble a castle, with circular spired towers and battlements. It has a restaurant, pool and fitness centre, plus a garden teetering between romantic and kitsch, with a footbridge over a little stream. The main drawback is that it is heavily geared to wedding parties, which can be noisy, all-night affairs. It might be good to check that none is booked for your preferred night.

FILDU DE SUS The wooden churches of the region of Maramureș, north of Transylvania, were included in the list of UNESCO World Heritage Sites in 1999, characterised by tall, slim towers and charming, folksy, interior paintings of Biblical scenes. The construction of churches in wood was a response by local communities to a prohibition by their Catholic Austro-Hungarian rulers against building Orthodox churches in stone. There are wooden Orthodox churches in the Sălaj region to the south too, and while these don't reach quite the mastery of the best of the Maramureș churches, some are fine, notably that at the village of Fildu de Sus (HU: Felsőfüld), close to the southern county border with Cluj County. The **wooden church** (biserica de lemn) (\0260 667 569; ⊕ Apr–Sep 08.00–20.00 Mon–Sat, noon–20.00 Sun, Oct–Mar 08.00–16.00 Mon–Sat, noon–16.00 Sun, but it is recommended to call in advance; donation expected) dates from 1727, though it was enlarged in the mid 19th century. It features both well-preserved interior frescoes dating from 1856 and a tall needle-like wooden spire reaching a height of 40m.

Travelling by **car**, drive south from Zalău on route 1F for 30km to Zimbor, then fork right onto route 1G to Fildu de Jos (HU: Alsófüld). Turn right onto a minor road and drive for 8km to Fildu de Sus.

Appendix 1

LANGUAGE

Romanian is a Romance language that evolved from the Vulgar Latin spoken by the Roman conquerors of the region, though it has since added many words from the languages of neighbouring peoples, including German, Turkish, Hungarian and Slavic. In the 19th century, many loan-words were introduced from French, often in a bid to be westernising and modern, usually at the expense of Slavic words. And in the later 20th and early 21st centuries, most of the imports have been from English: thus the Romanian word for 'computer' is *computer*. But these English loan-words are treated grammatically just like any other Romanian words, so 'the computer' is *computerul*. It is an official language in both Romania and the Republic of Moldova, and is also widely spoken in parts of Serbia and Ukraine with significant ethnic Romanian populations. Because of its Latin roots, a knowledge of French, Italian, Spanish, Portuguese or Latin will all aid in understanding Romanian. The alphabet is close to English, although the letters K, Q, W and Y are found only in foreign loan-words.

Romanian **grammar** is somewhat complex. There are three genders: masculine, feminine and neuter. Neuter nouns behave like masculine ones in the singular and feminine ones in the plural. It has five cases: nominative, accusative, genitive, dative and vocative, but the last is used only in a small range of situations, and the forms in both the nominative and accusative and the genitive and dative are mostly identical, so it is not quite as hard to learn as all that. Unlike most other Romance languages, the definite article is attached to the end of the noun, thus 'the bus' is *autobuzul*. Adjectives change in respect of both number and gender. But the good news is that Romanians are very enthusiastic at any attempts by foreigners to speak even a modest amount of Romanian, and forgiving of grammatical mistakes.

In those parts of Transylvania with a majority ethnic Hungarian population, especially in Harghita and Covasna counties, you will hear more Hungarian than Romanian spoken, and some basic Hungarian phrases are included here. A knowledge of German can also be helpful, even if Transylvania's remaining Saxon communities are now very small. But Romanians have embraced English-language learning with enthusiasm, and you will find it widely understood.

THE ROMANIAN ALPHABET

A, a   /a/ like the 'a' in 'father'
Ă, ă   /ǎ/ like the 'a' in 'alone', a bit like 'er'
Â, â   /â/ no equivalent in English, like 'uh'
B, b   /be/ like the 'b' in 'bed'
C, c   /ce/ pronounced 'ch' before 'i' or 'e', but 'k' before other letters. The letter
         'c' before an i or e can be hardened by adding an 'h' as in '*cheile*' (gorge),
         pronounced 'key-ley'. This can be challenging for English-speakers, as it seems
         counterintuitive (since in English the 'h' has a softening effect, as in 'church')

D, d	/de/ like the 'd' in 'dot'
E, e	/e/ tends to be pronounced 'ye' at the beginning of a word, otherwise like the 'e' in 'ten'
F, f	/ef/ like the 'f' in 'foot'
G, g	/ge/ rather like the letter c, it is pronounced in a soft way before 'i' or 'e', like the 'g' in 'gym', but before other letters, or when an 'h' is added in front of the i or e, it is pronounced 'g' as in 'garden', such as the name Gheorghe (pronounced 'gay-OR-gay')
H, h	/haş/ like 'h' in 'help'; it is not pronounced when following c or g and in front of the letters e or i
I, i	/i/ usually like the 'ee' in 'week', but when it is placed at the end of a word the 'i' is almost silent, see Bucureşti (pronounced 'Boo-KOO-resht', though the i has the effect of softening the 't' at the end)
Î, î	/î/ pronounced like â, but more slack-jawed 'uh'
J, j	/zhe/ like the 's' in 'pleasure'
K, k	/ca/ like the 'k' in 'kilo
L, l	/le/ like the 'l' in 'light'
M, m	/em/ like the 'm' in 'moth'
N, n	/en/ like the 'n' in 'night'
O, o	/o/ like the 'o' in 'port'
P, p	/pe/ like the 'p' in 'pink'
Q, q	/kü/ like the 'k' in 'king'
R, r	/er/ a rolled 'r' sound
S, s	/es/ like the 's' in 'sit'
Ş, ş	/she/ like the 'sh' in 'shop'
T, t	/te/ like the 't' in 'cat'
Ţ, ţ	/tse/ like the 'ts' in 'cats'
U, u	/u/ like the 'oo' sound in 'group'
V, v	/ve/ like the 'v' in 'vast'
W, w	/dublu ve/ usually pronounced similarly to 'v'
X, x	/ics/ sometimes pronounced as the 'cks' in 'licks', on other occasions as the 'gs' in 'sprigs'
Y, y	/igrec/ like the 'i' in 'ship'
Z, z	/zed/ like the 'z' in 'zip'

ROMANIAN VOCABULARY
Essentials

Good morning	*Bună dimineaţa*
Good day	*Bună ziua*
Good evening	*Bună seara*
Good night	*Noapte bună*
Goodbye	*La revedere*
See you soon	*Pe curând*
Bon voyage!	*Drum bun!* (literally 'good road')
Welcome	*Bine aţi venit*
I am happy to be here	*Bine v-am găsit!* (literally 'good to have found you')
What is your name?	*Cum vă numiţi?* or *Cum vă cheamă?*
My name is …	*Mă numesc …*
How are you?	*Ce mai faceţi?* (formal)/*Ce mai faci?* (informal)

Pleased to meet you/the same here	Încântat de cunoştinţă (pronounced 'uhn-kun-tat de koo-nosh-tint-ser')/Şi eu
I/we thank you	Mulţumesc/Mulţumim
You're welcome (after thanks)	Cu plăcere or pentru puţin
Where are you from?	De unde sunteţi?
I am from Great Britain/England	Sunt din Marea Britanie/Anglia
Cheers!	Noroc!
Yes	Da
No	Nu
Please	Vă rog ('Ver rog')
Do you speak English?	Vorbiţi englezeşte? ('Vor-beetsi ing-lez-esh-teh')
I don't understand	Nu înţeleg ('Noo uhnts-ell-egg')
I don't speak Romanian	Nu vorbesc româneşte
I am sorry	Îmi pare rău
Excuse me	Scuzaţi-mă
Please go ahead!/Come in!	Poftim!/Poftiţi!
I beg your pardon?	Poftim?/Poftiţi?
Please could you speak more slowly?	Puteţi să vorbiţi mai rar, vă rog?
Do you understand?	Înţelegeţi? ('unts-ele-jhets')

Questions

How?	Cum?	When?	Când?
What?	Ce? ('cheh')	Why?	De ce? ('deh cheh')
Where?	Unde?	Who?	Cine? ('chinay')
Which?	Care?		
How much/many?		Câţi/câte? ('kuhts'/'kuhteh')	
How much does this cost?		Cât costă? ('kuht koster')	
When does ... open/close?		Când se deschide/închide ...? ('kuhnd seh des-key-deh /uhn-key-deh ...?')	

Numbers

1	unu/una	6	şase ('shaseh')
2	doi/două	7	şapte ('shapteh')
3	trei	8	opt
4	patru	9	nouă ('no-wer')
5	cinci ('cheench')	10	zece ('zecheh')
11	unsprezece ('OON-spreh-zeh-cheh')		
12	doisprezece ('DOY-spreh-zeh-cheh') or douăsprezece		
13	treisprezece ('TRAY-spreh-zeh-cheh')		
14	paisprezece ('PIE-spreh-zeh-cheh')		
15	cincisprezece ('CHEEN-chi-spreh-zeh-cheh')		
16	şaisprezece ('SHY-spreh-zeh-cheh')		
17	şaptesprezece ('SHAPte-spreh-zeh-cheh')		
18	optsprezece ('OPT-spreh-zeh-cheh')		
19	nouăsprezece ('NO-wer-spreh-zeh-cheh')		
20	douăzeci ('do-wer-ZECH')		
21	douăzeci şi unu/una ('do-wer-ZECH shee oonoo')		

30	*treizeci* ('tray-ZECH')
40	*patruzeci* ('patroo-ZECH')
50	*cincizeci* ('cheench-ZECH')
60	*şaizeci* ('shy-ZECH')
70	*şaptezeci* ('shap-te-ZECH')
80	*optzeci* ('opt-ZECH')
90	*nouăzeci* ('no-wer-ZECH')
100	*o sută* ('o SOO-ter')
200	*două sute* ('do-WER SOO-tay')
1,000	*o mie* ('o MEE-eh')
2,000	*două mii* ('do-WER mee')

Note that in spoken Romanian the cumbersome '*–sprezece*' ending is typically shortened to '*-şpe*', so that 11 becomes *unşpe*, and so on.

Time

What time is it?	*Cât este ceasul?* ('kuht yesht-eh chas-ool')
It is ...	*Este ...*
half past three	*trei şi jumătate* or more colloquially *trei jumate*
quarter to/past two	*două fără un sfert/şi un sfert*
six o'clock sharp	*şase fix*
today	*azi* or *astăzi*
tomorrow	*mâine* ('MUY-neh')
yesterday	*ieri* ('yehr')
in the morning	*dimineaţa*
in the afternoon	*după amiaza* ('doo-per am-yazer')
in the evening	*seara* ('say-ara')
this week	*săptămâna acesta* ('suhp-tuh-MOOHN-ah-ah-che-stah')
last week	*săptămâna trecută*
next week	*săptămâna următoare* or *săptămâna viitoare*
daily	*zilnic* or *în fiecare zi*

Days of the week

Monday	*luni* ('loon')
Tuesday	*marţi* ('marts')
Wednesday	*miercuri* ('mee-HER-coor')
Thursday	*joi* ('zhoy')
Friday	*vineri* ('vee-NEHR')
Saturday	*sâmbătă* ('sam-bar-tah')
Sunday	*duminică* ('doo-me-nee-ker')

Months

January	*ianuarie* ('yan-WAH-ree-eh')
February	*februarie* ('feb-RWAH-ree-eh')
March	*martie* ('MAR-tee-eh')
April	*aprilie* ('ah-PREEL-ee-eh')
May	*mai* ('my')
June	*iunie* ('YOO-nee-eh')

July	*iulie* ('YOO-lee-eh')
August	*august* ('ow-GOOST')
September	*septembrie* ('sep-TEHM-bree-eh')
October	*octombrie* ('ok-TOHM-bree-eh')
November	*noiembrie* ('noy-EHM-bree-eh')
December	*decembrie* ('deh-CHEHM-bree-eh')

Getting around and public transport

I'd like ...	*Aş dori ...*
... a one-way ticket to Braşov	*... un bilet dus la Braşov*
... a return ticket	*... un bilet dus-întors*
How much is the fare to ...?	*Cât costă până la ...?* ('Kuht koster puhner la')
How do I get there ...	*Cum ajung acolo ...*
... by bus/train/car/plane?	*... cu autobuzul/trenul/maşina/avionul?*
What time does the train for Mediaş leave?	*La ce oră pleacă trenul la Mediaş?* ('La cheh orer plak-er trenul la Mehdeh-ASH')
Is this place free?	*E liber acest loc?*
Yes, it is. Take a seat!	*Da, poftiţi. Luaţi loc!*
first class	*clasa întâi* ('klass-er uhn-tuy')
second class	*clasa a doua* ('klass-er a dower')
berth in the sleeping car	*cuşetă la vagonul de dormit*
platform	*peron*
ticket office	*casă de bilete*
timetable	*orar*
bus station	*autogară*
railway station	*gară*
airport	*aeroport*
bus	*autobuz*
tram	*tramvai*
train	*tren*
plane	*avion*
car	*maşină* ('mash-een-er')
taxi	*taxi*
minibus	*microbuz/maxi-taxi*
motorbike/moped	*motocicletă/motoretă*
bicycle	*bicicletă*
boat	*barcă*
cruise ship	*vas de croazieră*
port	*port*
arrival/departure	*sosiri/plecări*
hand/checked luggage	*bagaj de mână/pentru cală*
here	*aici*
there	*acolo*
Bon voyage!	*drum bun!* or *călătorie plăcută!*
border	*graniţă*
passport	*paşaport*

Private transport

Is this the road to ...? — *Care este drumul spre ...?*
Where is the nearest service station? — *Unde este cea mai apropiată benzinărie?*
Please fill it up — *Plinul, vă rog*
I'd like ... litres of ... — *Puneți ... litri de ...*
... diesel — *... motorină*
... unleaded petrol — *... benzină fără plumb*
My car has broken down — *Mașina mea are o pană de motor*
car document (ID) — *talon*
insurance — *asigurare*

Road signs

Danger	*pericol*	Keep right	*tineți dreapta*
Detour	*ocolire*	Caution	*atenție*
One-way	*sens unic*	Slow down	*reduceți viteza*
No entry	*intrarea interzisă*	Icy road	*polei*
Speed limit	*limită de viteză*		

Directions

Where is ...?	*Unde este ...?*	north/south	*nord/sud*
Go straight ahead	*Mergeți drept înainte*	east/west	*est/vest*
To the left/right	*la stânga/la dreapta*	near	*aproape*
... at the traffic lights	*... la semafor*	opposite	*vis-a-vis*
toward	*spre*		

Street signs

entrance/exit	*intrare/ieșire*	toilets –	*toalete –*
open/closed	*deschis/închis*	men/women	*bărbați/femei*
push/pull (on doors)	*împingeți/trageți*	information	*informație*

Accommodation

Could you recommend a cheap/good hotel? — *Puteți să-mi recomandați un hotel ieftin/ bun?*

Do you have any rooms available? — *Aveți camere libere?*
I'd like ... — *Aș vrea ...*
... a single room — *... o cameră cu un pat*
... a double room — *... o cameră cu pat dublu*
... a room with two beds — *... o cameră cu două paturi*
... a room with a bathroom — *... o cameră cu baie*
How much is it per day/week? — *Cât costă pe zi/pe săptămână?*
Is there hot water? — *Este apă caldă?*
Are dogs allowed? — *Sunt permise câini?*
Is breakfast included? — *Micul dejun e inclus?*
I am leaving early in the morning — *Plec mâine dimineață devreme*

Food

A table for ... people please — *O masă pentru ... persoane, vă rog?*
Waiter! (getting attention) — *Ospătar! ('os-puh-TAHR')*
I am a vegetarian — *Sunt vegetarian(ă)*
I don't eat pork — *Nu mănânc carne de porc*
Do you have any vegetarian dishes? — *Aveți mâcăruri vegetariene?*

Could you please bring me a …		*Puteţi să-mi aduceţi … ,vă rog*	
… one fork/knife/spoon/glass		*… o furculiţă/un cuţit/o lingură/un pahar*	
Bon appetit!		*Poftă bună!*	
The bill, please		*Nota de plată, vă rog*	
bread	*pâine*	fruit	*fruct*
butter	*unt*	apples	*mere*
cheese	*brânză*	bananas	*banane*
jam	*gem*	grapes	*struguri*
oil	*ulei*	pears	*pere*
eggs	*ouă*	plums	*prune*
vinegar	*oţet*	tomatoes	*roşii*
pepper	*piper*	vegetables	*legume*
salt	*sare*	boiled/mashed/	*cartofi natur/piure/*
sugar	*zahăr*	fried potatoes	*prăjiţi*
rice	*orez*	lamb	*miel*
beans	*fasole*	ham	*şuncă*
onion	*ceapă*	sausages	*cârnaţi*
Garlic	*usturoi*	meatballs	*chiftele*
skinless sausages	*mititei ('mici')*	soup/sour soup	*supă/ciorbă*
peppers	*ardei*	stew	*tocană*
carrots	*morcovi*	beer	*bere*
aubergine/eggplant	*vinete*	red/white wine	*vin roşu/alb*
cucumbers	*castraveţi*		('veen-ROH-shoo'/'ahlb')
cabbage	*varză*	local brandy	*ţuică, palincă*
mushrooms	*ciuperci*	fruit juice	*suc*
salad	*salată*	coffee	*o cafea*
fish	*peşte*	tea	*un ceai*
trout	*păstrăv*	herbal tea	*ceai de plante*
pike	*ştiucă*	with milk	*cu lapte*
perch	*biban*	with lemon	*cu lămâie*
meat	*carne*	water (mineral)	*apă minerală*
beef	*vită*	water (still)	*apă plată ('AH-*
chicken	*pui*		*puh PLAH-tah')*
pork	*porc*	ice cream	*îngheţată*

Shopping

Do you have any …?	*Aveţi …?*
I would like …	*Aş vrea* or *aş dori …*
I/we have …	*Am/avem …*
How much is it?	*Cât costă?*
It costs too much	*Costă prea mult*
Yes, I'd like …	*Da, aş vrea …*
Do you accept credit cards?	*Acceptaţi carduri de credit?*
Do you have anything …?	*Nu aveţi ceva …?*
… cheaper/better	*… mai ieftin/mai bun*
… smaller/bigger	*… mai mic/mai mare*
bookshop	*librărie*
stationers	*papetărie*
souvenir shop	*artizanat*
tobacconists	*tutungerie*

Colours Note that names of colours, like all adjectives, change form according to the gender and number (singular or plural) of the noun they are referring to. The examples given here are the masculine singular forms.

black/white/grey	*negru/alb/gri*
red/blue/yellow	*roşu/albastru/galben*
green/orange	*verde/portocaliu*
purple/brown	*mov/maro*

Communications

Where is …?	*Unde se află …?*
… the nearest bank?	*… cea mai apropiată bancă?*
… the nearest post office?	*… cea mai apropiată poşta?*
… the church?	*… biserica?*
… the embassy?	*… ambasada?*
… an exchange office?	*… un birou de schimb valutar?*
… the tourist office?	*… biroul de turism?*
… a travel agency?	*… o agenţie de turism or de voiaj?*
… an ATM?	*… un bancomat?*

Emergencies

Emergency!	*Urgenţă!*
Help!	*Ajutor!*
Call a doctor	*Chemaţi un doctor*
There's been an accident	*A avut loc un accident*
I've been injured	*Am fostrănit(ă)*
I'm lost	*M-am rătăcit*
Go away!	*Pleacă de aici!*
Police	*poliţia*
Fire/fire brigade	*foc/pompieri*
Ambulance	*ambulanţa*
Thieves!	*Hoţii!* ('hohtzy!')
hospital	*spital*
I've got diarrhoea	*Am diaree*
I've been vomiting	*Am vomitat*
Doctor	*doctor*
prescription	*reţetă*
pharmacy	*farmacie*
painkiller/antibiotic	*analgezic/antibiotic*
tampons	*tampoane* ('tum-POAH-neh')
condom	*prezervativ*
sunblock	*cremă de plajă*
soap/shampoo	*săpun* ('suh-POON')/*şampon* ('sham-pon')
toothbrush/toothpaste	*periuţă de dinţi/pastă de dinţi*
I am …	*Sunt …*
… diabetic	*… diabetic(ă)*
I've got asthma	*Am astm*
I'm allergic to …	*Sunt alergic(ă) la …*
… penicillin/peanuts/bee stings	*… penicilină/arahide/înţepături de albine*

Children

Is there a …?	Aveţi …?
… baby changing room?	… o cameră de schimbat scutecele?
… a children's bed?	… un pătuţ de copii?
Do you have …?	Aveţi …?
… infant milk formula?	… lapte pentru sugari?
… nappies/potty/high chair?	… scutece/oliţă/scaun special pentru bebeluşi?
… children's menu?	… meniu pentru copii?
… babysitter?	… bonă or baby-sitter
Are children allowed?	Este permis accesul copiilor? or Copiii au voie?

Other

my/our	meu/nostru (Note that possessive adjectives, like all adjectives, change form according to gender and number. The examples given are masculine singular forms; the feminine singular equivalents are mea and noastră.)
he/his/she/her	el/lui/ea/ei
and/some/but	şi/nişte/dar
this/that	acesta/acela
expensive/cheap	scump/ieftin
good/bad	bun/rău
beautiful/ugly	frumos/urât
old/new (things)	vechi/nou
old/young (people)	bătrân/tânar
early/late	devreme/târziu
hot/cold	fierbinte/rece
easy/difficult	uşor/greu
light/heavy	uşor/greu (same as above)
fast/slow	repede/încet
a little/a lot	puţin/mult
good/very good	bun/foarte bun
OK/fine	bine
OK	în regulă
perhaps	poate

SOME BASIC HUNGARIAN PHRASES

English	Hungarian
Good day	Jó napot ('YAW NOP-ot')
Hello/bye (informal)	Szia ('SEE-ya')
Good evening	Jó estét ('YAW ESH-tate')
Goodbye	Viszontlátásra ('VEE-sont-lah-tah-shro')
Bon voyage!	Jó utat! ('YAW OOT-ot')
My name is	A nevem ('ah NEV-em')
What is your name?	Hogy hivják? ('hodge HEAVE-yak?')

I am English/American/Australian	*angol/amerikai/austrál vagyok* ('ONG-ol'/'OM-eri-koi'/'OW-stral VODGE-ok')
How are you?	*Hogy van?* ('HODGE von?')
Thank you	*Köszönöm* ('CUR-sir-nuhm')
You're welcome (after thanks)	*Kérem* ('KIR-em')
Cheers!	*Egészségére!* ('EGG-ace-sheg-ir-reh')
Yes/no	*Igen/nem* ('IG-en'/'nem')
Please	*Kérem* ('KIR-em')
Do you speak English?	*Beszél angolul?* ('BEH-sail ONG-ol-ool?')
I don't understand	*Nem értem* ('nem IR-tem')
I don't speak Hungarian	*Nem beszélek magyarul* ('nem BEH-sail-eck modge-ah-rool')
Excuse me	*Elnézest* ('EL-nay-zesht')
Sorry	*Bocsánat* ('BOTCH-ah-not')
A beer please	*Egy sört kérek* ('Edge shirt KIR-eck')
Where is the ...?	*Hol van a ...?* ('HOL von a ...?')
... bus station/railway station?	*... busz állomás/pályaudvar?* ('boose AH-lo-mash/PIE-ya-ood-vah')
... post office/bank/pharmacy?	*... posta/bank/gyógyszertár?* ('POSH-tah/bonk/GEORGE-sair-tah')
... tourist information centre?	*... turisztikai információs központ?* ('TUR-ist-ik-oi IN-for-mats-iosh KUZ-pont')
Two tickets, please	*Kettő jegyet, kérek* ('KET-tuh YEDGE-et KIR-ek')
Do you have a room available?	*Van kiadó szobája?* ('VON KEE-ah-doh SOB-ai-yah?')
WC (gents'/ladies')	*WC férfi/női* ('vay-tsay FER-fee'/'NUH-ee')
one/two/three/ten	*egy/kettő/három/tíz* ('edge'/'KET-tuh'/'HAH-rom'/'teaze')

Appendix 2

FURTHER INFORMATION

BOOKS
Fiction and biography

Bánffy, Miklós *The Phoenix Land* Arcadia Books, 2011. A fascinating memoir of life in the region following World War I by Miklós Bánffy, a Hungarian politician and author of the *Transylvanian Trilogy* of novels.

Bánffy, Miklós *They Were Counted* Arcadia Books, 2016; *They Were Divided* Arcadia Books, 2016; *They Were Found Wanting* Arcadia Books, 2016. First published in the 1930s, Bánffy's *Transylvanian Trilogy* is a fascinating insight into the milieu of aristocratic Hungarian estate owners in Transylvania in the early 20th century.

Bugan, Carmen *Burying the Typewriter* Picador, 2012. Moving and sobering account of a childhood in Communist Romania as the daughter of a dissident.

Dragomán, György *The White King* Black Swan, 2015. A story of the life of 11-year-old Djata in Ceauşescu's Romania; her father is absent, having been taken by the Securitate.

Eminescu, Mihai *Poems and Prose* Center for Romanian Studies, 2000. Published to mark the 150th anniversary of the birth of Romania's greatest poet, this offers a good selection of English translations of his poetry and prose.

Fox, Edward *The Hungarian Who Walked to Heaven: Alexander Csoma de Kőrös 1784–1842* Short Lives Series, Faber and Faber, 2006. The decidedly unusual life of the Transylvanian linguist who set off eastwards in search of the origins of the Magyar people and ending up by becoming an expert in Tibetan culture and the compiler of the first Tibetan–English dictionary.

Manning, Olivia *The Balkan Trilogy* Arrow Books, 1992. The adventures of Guy and Harriet Pringle in Bucharest and then Greece at the dawn of World War II, based on Manning's own experiences. The novels were adapted by the BBC as the 1987 TV series *Fortunes of War,* starring Kenneth Branagh and Emma Thompson.

Marie, Queen of Romania *The Lost Princess* S W Partridge, 1924. The lovely Princess Dorinda enlists the help of the witch Carabaracola and two little imps, Jenky and Jonky, to help her find her lost sister. Six charming tipped-in colour plates plus numerous black-and-white text drawings by Mabel Lucie Attwell.

Marie, Queen of Romania *Peeping Pansy* Hodder & Stoughton, 1919. Another children's story by the British-born Romanian queen with illustrations by Mabel Lucie Attwell.

Marie, Queen of Romania *Story of my Life* Charles Scribner's Sons, 1934. Long autobiographical account by Queen Marie.

Pakula, Hannah *The Last Romantic: A Biography of Queen Marie of Roumania* Simon & Schuster, 1985. Excellent and detailed biography of Queen Marie, which also gives a clear account of the development of Romania during the early 20th century.

Verne, Jules *The Castle of the Carpathians* Fredonia Books, 2001. First published in 1893, there is much debate as to which castle inspired Verne's novel. Many believe this to be Colț Castle in Hunedoara County, though others have suggested that the model may be Devin Castle in present-day Slovakia.

Travel and photography For all Bradt's guides, see w bradtguides.com/shop.

Bailey, Chris *The Railways of Romania* Locomotives International, 2002. A well-illustrated description of the Romanian railways.

✳ Blacker, William *Along the Enchanted Way. A Story of Love and Life in Romania* John Murray, 2010. Fascinating account of the author's life in Romania from 1996, with a peasant family in Maramureş and falling in love, twice, with Roma girls in Transylvania.

Călinescu, Petruț and Hodoiu, Ioana *Pride and Concrete* Igloo Media, 2013. A fascinating photo-led study of the extravagant and often only partly inhabited rural houses built through the remittances of Romanian migrant workers to western Europe.

Crane, Nicholas *Clear Waters Rising* Penguin, 1997. Account of a 17-month walk across Europe's mountains, from northwest Spain to Istanbul, taking in the Romanian Carpathians.

Douglas-Home, Jessica *Once Upon Another Time* Michael Russell Publishing, 2000. Remarkable account by the founder of the Mihai Eminescu Trust about bringing reading material to support dissidents in the Eastern Bloc in the 1980s.

Dunlop, Tessa *To Romania With Love* Quartet, 2012. Account of an unconventional love affair which arose from volunteering in a Romanian orphanage.

Evans, Andrew *Ukraine: the Bradt Travel Guide (4th edition)* Bradt Travel Guides, 2013

✳ Fermor, Patrick Leigh *Between The Woods and the Water* John Murray, 2004. His sequel to *A Time of Gifts*, this is a wonderful account by one of the greatest travel writers of the Hungarian and Romanian legs of his pre-war walk from the Hook of Holland to Istanbul, much of it spent as the guest of Hungarian aristocrats in Transylvania.

Fonseca, Isabel *Bury Me Standing: The Gypsies and their Journey* Vintage, 1996. Well-researched study of the Roma communities of eastern Europe by a writer who learned Romani and lived with them.

Gerard, Emily *The Land Beyond the Forest* 1888, reprinted by Cambridge University Press, 2011. An account of two years in Transylvania by novelist Emily Gerard, who was there accompanying her husband, an Austrian army officer. Bram Stoker used her account in his research for *Dracula*.

Goodwin, Jason *On Foot to the Golden Horn* Picador, 2003. Account of a journey on foot from Poland's Baltic coast to Istanbul, first published in 1993.

Hall, Donald *Romanian Furrow: Colourful Experiences of Village Life* Bene Factum Publishing Ltd, 2007. Details the journey made in 1933, looking for the rural life which was disappearing back home.

Harding, Georgina *In Another Europe: A Journey to Romania* Hodder & Stoughton, 1990. Account of a 1988 bike ride from Vienna to Istanbul, reaching Romania at a difficult time at the end of the Communist era.

Hoffman, Eva *Exit into History: A Journey through the new Eastern Europe* Penguin, 1994. An account by a Polish-born writer of travels through eastern Europe, including Romania, soon after the fall of Communism.

Kurti, László *The Remote Borderland: Transylvania in the Hungarian Imagination* State University of New York Press, 2001. A perspective on the role of Transylvania in the Hungarian imagination.

Lizard, Thomas and Gheorghiu, Oana *How to Survive Romania* Lizard and Partners, 2014. Light-hearted guide to some of the more curious Romanian customs. Makes a nice souvenir.

Mitchell, Laurence *Serbia: the Bradt Travel Guide (5th edition)* Bradt Travel Guides, 2017
Murphy, Dervla *Transylvania and Beyond* Arrow, 1993. Journey by bicycle and foot immediately after the fall of Ceaușescu, overcoming both a robbery and a car accident at the start of her travels.
Ogden, Alan *Fortresses of Faith: A Pictorial History of the Fortified Saxon Churches of Romania* Center for Romanian Studies, 2000. Well illustrated with black-and-white photographs.
Ogden, Alan *Moons & Aurochs: A Romanian Journey* Orchid Press, 2007. An unusual journey through Romania focusing on some of the quirkier and less widely known peoples and historical episodes.
Ogden, Alan *Romania Revisited: On the Trail of English Travellers, 1602–1941* Center for Romanian Studies, 2000. Intertwines an account of Ogden's own travels around Romania in 1998 with the writings of earlier English travellers.
Ogden, Alan *Winds of Sorrow: Travels in and Around Transylvania* Orchid Press, 2007. Tales from Ogden's travels in Transylvania between 1998 and 2004.
Palin, Michael *New Europe* Weidenfeld & Nicolson, 2008. Companion to the BBC TV series exploring the countries of eastern Europe which once lay beyond the Iron Curtain.
Phillips, Adrian and Scotchmer, Jo *Hungary: the Bradt Travel Guide (2nd edition)* Bradt Travel Guides, 2010
Riley, Bronwen *Transylvania* Frances Lincoln, 2008. Attractive coffee-table book, beautifully photographed by Dan Dinescu.
Ross, Julian *Travels in an Unknown Country: A Mounted View of Transylvania* Long Riders' Guild Press, 2004. Equestrian journeys across the Transylvanian countryside described by a former resident of the region, who established a horseriding centre in Bistrița-Năsăud County.
Simon, Ted *The Gypsy in Me: From Germany to Romania in Search of Youth, Truth, and Dad* Random House, 1997. An account of Simon's 2,400km journey (mostly on foot), between his mother's Germany and his father's Romania.
Sitwell, Sacheverell *Roumanian Journey* Bloomsbury Reader, 2012. Account of a four-week trip to Romania made by Sir Sacheverell Sitwell in the 1930s.
Spinder, Stephen *Ten Years in Transylvania* Stephen Spinder Fine Art Photography, 2004. A photo-led book in English and Hungarian focusing on the folk culture of ethnic Hungarian communities in Transylvania.
Starkie, Walter *Raggle-Taggle: Adventures with a Fiddle in Hungary and Roumania* John Murray, 1933. Account of a journey made by Walter Starkie in 1929, living amongst Roma people by using his violin as a form of introduction. He repeated the model in northern Spain in a follow-up book entitled *Spanish Raggle-Taggle*.

Nature

Akeroyd, John *The Historic Countryside of the Saxon Villages of Southern Transylvania* ADEPT Foundation, 2006. Fine study of the old-growth woodland and high nature-value meadows around the Saxon villages.
Gorman, Gerard *Birding in Eastern Europe* Wildsounds, 2006. Authoritative guide by the founder of Probirder, with illustrations by Szabolcs Kokay.
Gorman, Gerard *Central and Eastern European Wildlife* Bradt Travel Guides, 2008. Engaging and fully illustrated guide to the wildlife of the entire region.
Gorman, Gerard *Woodpeckers of Europe: A Study of the European Picidae* Bruce Coleman Books, 2004. Gerard Gorman is above all an authority on woodpeckers, and this is a comprehensive survey, well illustrated by Szabolcs Kokay.
Roberts, James *Romania: A Birdwatching and Wildlife Guide* Burton Expeditions, 2000. Informative guide by an experienced mountain expert, married to a Romanian, who tragically died in 2002.

Roberts, James *The Mountains of Romania* Cicerone Mountain Walking Guide, 2004. Published posthumously, this is somewhat out of date but still contains much of interest on walking in the Carpathians.

Language

Deletant, Dennis and Alexandrescu, Yvonne *Complete Romanian* Teach Yourself, 2016. A good introductory course, with accompanying CD.

Gönczöl-Davies, Ramona *Romanian: An Essential Grammar* Routledge, 2007. Good concise survey of Romanian grammar, though best suited to more advanced learners.

Gönczöl, Ramona and Deletant, Dennis *Colloquial Romanian: The Complete Course for Beginners* Routledge, 2012. With an accompanying CD, this offers a good practical introduction to Romanian grammar and vocabulary.

Leviţchi, Leon *Dicţionar Român Englez* Teora, 2005. Available in bookshops in Romania, this is a comprehensive Romanian–English dictionary with 60,000 words.

Leviţchi, Leon and Bantaş, Andrei *Dicţionar Englez Român* Teora, 1999. The companion volume to the above, this is a good English–Romanian dictionary. At the time of research there is no really good dictionary combining Romanian–English and English–Romanian in a single volume.

History Many histories have been written of Transylvania, but few are impartial. Accounts from Romanian and Hungarian historians are frequently sharply different in perspective, and often seem to be crafted in order to present a particular point of view.

Boia, Lucian *History and Myth in Romanian Consciousness* Central European University Press, 2001. Fascinating account of the way in which ideological imperatives have frequently influenced the prevailing view of Romanian history.

Boia, Lucian *Romania: Borderland of Europe (Topographics)* Reaktion Books, 2001. Entertaining and thought-provoking introduction to Romanian history from an eminent historian and commentator.

Djuvara, Neagu *A Brief Illustrated History of Romanians* Humanitas, 2014. Well-illustrated and ambitious study from scholar and diplomat Djuvara.

Fabini, Hermann *The Church-Fortresses of the Transylvanian Saxons* Monumenta, 2010. With a foreword by HRH The Prince of Wales, this has particularly useful floor plans of all of the fortresses.

Gallagher, Tom *Theft of a Nation: Romania Since Communism* C Hurst & Co Publishing, 2005. Critical study of Romania in the 1990s by a British political scientist.

Kinross, Lord *The Ottoman Centuries: The Rise and Fall of the Turkish Empire* William Morrow, 1979. A fine history of the Ottoman Empire from an eminent historian.

Klepper, Nicolae *Romania: An Illustrated History* Hippocrene Books, 2002. Interesting historical overview from a Romania-born US writer.

Lehrer, Milton G *Transylvania: History and Reality* Bartleby Press, 1986. First published in 1944, and written strongly from the Romanian viewpoint.

Mackenzie, Andrew *Journey into the Past of Transylvania* Robert Hale Ltd, 1990. Historical account by a polymath, parapsychologist and writer of detective stories.

Makkai, László *History of Transylvania V1 From the Beginnings to 1606 (East European Monographs)* Columbia University Press, 2002. The first of a mammoth three-volume history of Transylvania, and translated from Hungarian. Comprehensive, though written from a Hungarian viewpoint. Makkai also wrote the second volume, with Zoltán Szász contributing the third.

Makkai, László, *History of Transylvania V2 From 1606 to 1830 (East European Monographs)* Columbia University Press, 2002

Pascu, Ştefan *A History of Transylvania* Wayne State University Press, USA, 1983. Transylvanian history from a Romanian viewpoint during the Communist era.

Péter, László (ed) *Historians and the History of Transylvania (East European Monographs)* Columbia University Press, 1993. Essays on the relationship between different historical interpretations and social and political conflict in Transylvania.

Szász, Zoltán *History of Transylvania V3 From 1830 to 1919 (East European Monographs)* Columbia University Press, 2002

Tökes, László *The Fall of Tyrants: The Incredible Story of One Pastor's Witness, the People of Romania and the Overthrow of Ceauşescu* Good News Publishing, 1991. Autobiographical account by the Timişoara pastor whose attempted eviction was the spark for the events of 1989, though he is not one to hide his light under a bushel.

Cuisine

Klepper, Nicolae *Taste of Romania: Its Cookery and Glimpses of Its History, Folklore, Art, Literature and Poetry* Hippocrene Books Inc, 2011. An interesting exploration of Romanian culture via its food, incorporating more than 150 recipes.

Muresan, Florin *Transylvanian Cookbook* Master Print Bucharest, 2016. Beautifully illustrated collection of 100 Transylvanian recipes.

Dracula, vampires and superstitions

Augustyn, Michael *Vlad Dracula: The Dragon Prince* iUniverse, 2014. A biography of Vlad the Impaler.

Belford, Barbara *Bram Stoker: A Biography of the Author of Dracula* Alfred Knopf, 1997. The author's life among Victorian literary and theatrical society.

Bibeau, Paul *Sundays with Vlad: From Pennsylvania to Transylvania, One Man's Quest to live in the World of the Undead* Broadway Books, 2007. Humorous account of the travels of journalist Paul Bibeau in a quest to understand the *Dracula* myth.

Bunson, Matthew *The Vampire Encyclopaedia* Gramercy Books, 2001. An A–Z of everything to do with vampires, with a focus on literary and film portrayals.

Florescu, Radu R and McNally, Raymond T *Dracula, Prince of Many Faces: His Life and Times* Little, Brown, 2005. A biography of Vlad the Impaler, exploring his similarities and differences to the fictional count.

Florescu, Radu R and McNally, Raymond T *In Search of Dracula* Robson Books, 1998. A scholarly account of Vlad the Impaler, which first appeared some years earlier. The 1998 edition includes, *inter alia*, an account of Ceauşescu's attempts to elevate Vlad to Romanian national hero status.

Kligman, Gail *The Wedding of the Dead: Ritual, Poetics and Popular Culture in Transylvania* University of California Press, 1992. Interesting study on peasant rituals in Transylvania.

Kostova, Elizabeth *The Historian* Sphere, 2006. Somewhere between a Gothic novel and detective thriller, weaving in the stories of Vlad the Impaler and Count Dracula.

Leatherdale, Clive *Dracula: The Novel and the Legend* Aquarian Press, 1985. Well-written study which combines analysis of Stoker's novel with an account of the vampire in folklore and literature.

Miller, Elizabeth *A Dracula Handbook* Xlibris, 2005. Well-researched question-and-answer factbook covering all angles on Stoker's work and the fictional count.

Murray, Paul *From the Shadow of 'Dracula': A Life of Bram Stoker* Jonathan Cape, 2004. Biography of Bram Stoker, covering his literary and theatrical connections and the relationship of his most famous novel to other works of Irish horror.

Newman, Kim *Anno Dracula* Titan Books, 2011. With its starting point the remarriage of Queen Victoria to Count Dracula, this is the first novel in Kim Newman's *Anno*

Dracula fantasy series in which the count was not defeated by the heroic figures of Stoker's novel, and vampires are taking over Britain.

Stoker, Bram *Dracula* Wordsworth Editions, 1993. The classic that created both a legend and an entire film and publishing industry. First published in 1897.

Summers, Montague *The Vampire in Lore and Legend* Dover Publications, 2001. Looking region by region at vampire myths, by a specialist on witchcraft and the occult.

Treptow, Kurt W *Vlad III Dracula: The Life and Times of the Historical Dracula* Center for Romanian Studies, 2000. Interesting study of Vlad the Impaler, and of the conflicting interpretations of him, from evil tyrant to hero of Christian Europe.

Wright, Dudley *Vampires and Vampirism: Legends from Around the World* Lethe Press, 2001. Vampire tales from around the globe.

CDs of Transylvanian music

Báré – Magyarpalatka Fono, Hungary. Good energetic recording from the Mácsingó family, from the village of Báré.

Blues for Transylvania Hannibal, UK. One of many fine recordings of Transylvanian folk music by the Hungarian band Muzsikás.

Hungarian Music from Transylvania: Sándor 'Neti' Fodor Hungaroton, Hungary. A great recording of the virtuosity of the late fiddle player Sándor 'Neti' Fodor, accompanied by Budapest dance house musicians.

Magyarpalatka – Hungarian Folk Music from the Transylvanian Heath Hungaroton, Hungary. Fine mix of Hungarian and Roma dances from the Magyarpalatka Band of the Cluj County village of Pălatca.

Maramoros: The Lost Jewish Music of Transylvania Hannibal, UK. The Hungarian band Muzsikás turns its attention to the Jewish traditional music of Transylvania.

Musiques de Transylvanie Fonti Musicali, France. Focusing on the music of ethnic Hungarian communities across Romania, though with some Romanian tunes too, it is performed by Hungarian musicians on Budapest's dance house scene.

Muzică Țigănească din Transilvania Ethnophonie, Romania. Album of Roma music from Transylvania recorded in part at the Peasant Museum in Bucharest.

Romania: Wild Sounds from Transylvania, Wallachia & Moldavia World Network, Germany. A lively collection, including Taraf de Haidouks from Wallachia and the Moldavian Fanfare Ciocărlia.

Roumanie: La Vraie Tradition de Transylvanie Ocora, France. Dating from the Communist period, a good selection of Romanian folk music from Transylvania.

The Blues at Dawn in Kalotaszeg ABT, Hungary. A fine recording of folk music from the Kalotaszeg region featuring the Budapest-based Ökrös Ensemble, accompanied by renowned guest musicians including the late fiddle player Sándor 'Neti' Fodor and Hungarian vocalists Márta Sebestyén and András Berecz.

The Edge of the Forest: Romanian Music from Transylvania Music of the World, US. A mix of songs and instrumental tracks, including some from the Maramureş region north of Transylvania.

Transylvanian Folk Music: Szászcsávás Band Thermal Comfort, Hungary. Great recording of this Roma band from Mureş County.

Transylvanian Portraits Koch, Austria. Great album from Budapest-based vocalist Márta Sebestyén supporting the Ökrös Ensemble, focusing on ethnic Hungarian music from the region.

Village Music from Romania AIMP, Switzerland. Archive recordings by the Romanian musicologist Constantin Brăiloiu in 1933–43 on his travels around the country, which then formed part of his Archives Internationales de Musique Populaire at the Geneva Ethnographic Museum, who have released this three-CD box.

WEBSITES

w aboutromania.com Contains links to a huge range of Romania-themed websites

w acceptromania.ro Romania's main organisation promoting the rights of the LGBT community, including organising the annual Bucharest Pride march in May

w alpinet.org Information on visiting Romania's mountain areas

w asociatiaaer.ro Website of the Romanian Ecotourism Association

w autogari.ro Useful source of information on inter-city bus routes and timetables

w beyondtheforest.com Travel company website with a good deal of background information on Transylvania

w blueairweb.com Low-cost Romanian airline

w carpathianparks.org Information about protected areas throughout the Carpathians

w castelintransilvania.ro Project focused around the restoration of historic castles and manor houses in the region

w cfr.ro The Romanian state railway company

w eco-romania.ro Information on ecotourism and related activities

w fundatia-adept.org Website of the ADEPT NGO, supporting high nature-value farmland landscapes in Transylvania

w gov.ro Official website of the Romanian Government

w infofer.ro Information about Romanian railways, including an online timetable

w infomontan.ro Information about accommodation options in the Prahova Valley

w kalnoky.org Website of the Kálnoky Foundation, supporting sustainable development initiatives in Transylvania

w meniulzilei.info Restaurants in Târgu Mureş with patchy coverage of Cluj-Napoca

w milvus.ro Website of a Târgu Mureş-based environmental NGO

w outinmures.ro Useful online guide to places to go and eat in Târgu Mureş

w romania-insider.com English-language website focused on news about Romania and stories of interest to expats

w romaniatourism.com Website of the Romanian National Tourist Office

w roving-romania.co.uk Braşov-based travel agency offering plenty of useful advice

w sapteseri.ro Online version of the listings magazine covering the major cities across Romania, including Transylvania

w sibiu.ro Website of the Sibiu municipality

w sor.ro Website of the Romanian Ornithological Society

w tarom.ro Website of the Romanian national airline

w tiff.ro Transylvania International Film Festival

w transporturban.ro Public transport in Cluj-Napoca

w transylvaniancastle.com Website of Count Kálnoky's Guesthouses at Micloşoara

w turism.ro Rather general website about tourism in Romania

w visitclujnapoca.ro Good site covering what to do and where to stay in Cluj-Napoca

w www.mihaieminescutrust.org Website of the Mihai Eminescu Trust (MET), supporting village conservation projects

w www.wildtransylvania.com Interesting website produced by Paul White, a British conservationist living in Transylvania

w wizzair.com Hungarian low-cost airline

w zabola.com Website of the Mikes family and the accommodation at their estate in Zăbala

w zilesinopti.ro Online version of the listings magazine, with pages for Braşov, Cluj-Napoca, Sibiu, Bistriţa and Târgu Mureş

Index

Page numbers in **bold** indicate major entries; those in *italics* indicate maps.

DISCARD

INDEX OF ADVERTISERS